D1029376

Turin and the British in the Age of the Grand Tour

The Duchy of Savoy first claimed royal status in the seventeenth century, but only in 1713 was Victor Amadeus II, Duke of Savoy (1666–1732), crowned King of Sicily. The events of the Peace of Utrecht (1713) sanctioned the decades-long project the Duchy had pursued through the convoluted maze of political relationships between foreign powers. Of these, the British Kingdom was one of their most assiduous advocates, because of complementary dynastic, political, cultural and commercial interests. A notable stream of British diplomats and visitors to the Sabaudian capital engaged in an extraordinary and reciprocal exchange with the Turinese during this fertile period. The flow of travellers, a number of whom were British emissaries and envoys posted to the court, coincided, in part, with the itineraries of the international Grand Tour which transformed the capital into a gateway to Italy, resulting in a conflagration of cultural cosmopolitanism in early modern Europe.

PAOLA BIANCHI teaches Early Modern History at the Università della Valle d'Aosta. She has researched and written on the journeys of various English travellers who came to Italy in the eighteenth century to be presented at the Savoy court and to be part of Piedmont society. Her publications include *Onore e mestiere. Le riforme militari nel Piemonte del Settecento* (2002); *Cuneo in età moderna. Città e stato nel Piemonte d'antico regime* (with A. Merlotti) (2002); *Sotto diverse bandiere. L'internazionale militare nello stato sabaudo d'antico regime* (2012); *L'affermarsi della corte sabauda. Dinastie, poteri, élites in Piemonte e Savoia fra tardo Medioevo e prima età moderna* (with L.C. Gentile) (2006); *Le strategie dell'apparenza. Cerimoniali, politica e società alla corte dei Savoia in età moderna* (with A. Merlotti) (2010); and *Storia degli Stati sabaudi. 1416–1848* (with A. Merlotti) (2017).

KARIN WOLFE is a Research Fellow at the British School at Rome. Her research focuses on topics in seventeenth- and eighteenth-century Italian history, including art, architecture, patronage and collecting, as well as the history of cardinals and the Grand Tour. Her publications include *Roma Britannica: Art Patronage and Cultural Exchange in Eighteenth-Century Rome* (edited with D.R. Marshall and S. Russell, British School at Rome, 2011). She is presently completing a monograph on Francesco Trevisani: *Francesco Trevisani (1656–1746): A Universal Painter, Catalogue Raisonné*.

British School at Rome Studies

Series editors
Christopher J. Smith
Director of the British School at Rome

Susan Walker
Chair of Publications and member of the Council of the British School at Rome

Rosamond McKitterick
Chair of the British School at Rome's Faculty of Archaeology, History and Letters and member of the Council of the British School at Rome

Gill Clark
Registrar and Publications Manager of the British School at Rome (to 2017)

British School at Rome Studies builds on the prestigious and longstanding *Monographs* series of the British School at Rome. It published both definitive reports on the BSR's own fieldwork in Rome, Italy and the Mediterranean, and volumes (usually originating from conferences held at the BSR) on topics that cover the full range of the history, archaeology and art history of the western Mediterranean.

Rome, Pollution and Propriety. Dirt, Disease and Hygiene in the Eternal City from Antiquity to Modernity
Edited by Mark Bradley, with Kenneth Stow

Old Saint Peter's, Rome
Edited by Rosamond McKitterick, John Osborne, Carol M. Richardson and Joanna Story

The Punic Mediterranean. Identities and Identification from Phoenician Settlement to Roman Rule
Edited by Josephine Crawley Quinn and Nicholas C. Vella

The present volume has been published in collaboration with and with a financial contribution from the Consorzio di Valorizzazione Culturale La Venaria Reale.

Turin and the British in the Age of the Grand Tour

Edited by

PAOLA BIANCHI
Università della Valle d'Aosta

KARIN WOLFE
British School at Rome

CAMBRIDGE
UNIVERSITY PRESS

CAMBRIDGE
UNIVERSITY PRESS

University Printing House, Cambridge CB2 8BS, United Kingdom

One Liberty Plaza, 20th Floor, New York, NY 10006, USA

477 Williamstown Road, Port Melbourne, VIC 3207, Australia

4843/24, 2nd Floor, Ansari Road, Daryaganj, Delhi – 110002, India

79 Anson Road, #06-04/06, Singapore 079906

Cambridge University Press is part of the University of Cambridge.

It furthers the University's mission by disseminating knowledge in the pursuit of education, learning, and research at the highest international levels of excellence.

www.cambridge.org
Information on this title: www.cambridge.org/9781107147706
DOI: 10.1017/9781316556276

First published 2017

Printed in the United Kingdom by T.J. International Ltd. Padstow Cornwall

A catalogue record for this publication is available from the British Library.

ISBN 978-1-107-14770-6 Hardback

Cambridge University Press has no responsibility for the persistence or accuracy of URLs for external or third-party internet websites referred to in this publication and does not guarantee that any content on such websites is, or will remain, accurate or appropriate.

The publisher and the British School at Rome gratefully acknowledge the collaborative and financial support provided by the Centro studi della Reggia di Venaria.

La Venaria Reale

Contents

v

Figures

Contributors

Paola Bianchi holds an undergraduate and a graduate degree (PhD) from the Università di Torino and trained at the Università di Padova. She now teaches at the Università della Valle d'Aosta. She has worked to reconstruct the journeys of various English travellers who came to Italy in the eighteenth century to be present at court and to be part of society. She has written essays dealing with these issues, focusing on the role played by the Royal Academy of Turin as a cosmopolitan institution. Among her publications are the books: *Onore e mestiere. Le riforme militari nel Piemonte del Settecento* (Turin, 2002); *Cuneo in età moderna. Città e Stato nel Piemonte d'antico regime* (with A. Merlotti) (Milan, 2002); *Sotto diverse bandiere. L'internazionale militare nello Stato sabaudo d'antico regime* (Milan, 2012); *L'affermarsi della corte sabauda. Dinastie, poteri, élites in Piemonte e Savoia fra tardo Medioevo e prima età moderna* (with L.C. Gentile) (Turin, 2006); *Le strategie dell'apparenza. Cerimoniali, politica e società alla corte dei Savoia in età moderna* (with A. Merlotti) (Turin, 2010); and *Storia degli Stati sabaudi. 1416–1848* (with A. Merlotti) (Brescia, 2017).

Cristina Bracchi holds a PhD in the history of languages and Italian literature, and studies textual theory and criticism, cultural history, reception theory and women's literature. She is a member of the Società Italiana delle Letterate, of the Archivi delle Donne in Piemonte, and of the Centro Interdisciplinare di Ricerche e Studi delle Donne dell'Università di Torino. Among her publications are: *Prospettiva di una nazione di nazioni. An Account of the Manners and Customs of Italy di Giuseppe Baretti* (Alessandria, 1998); *Le carte socratiche della poesia. L'otium critico settecentesco e il canone oraziano* (Turin, 2001); and (as editor) *Poetiche politiche. Narrative, storie e studi delle donne* (Padua, 2011).

Annarita Colturato teaches musical bibliography at the Università di Torino in the Department of Humanities. She is a member of the Scientific Board of *Fonti musicali italiane* (periodical of the *Società Italiana di Musicologia*) and *Gli spazi della musica*, Università di Torino, is on the governing board of the Istituto per i Beni Musicali in Piemonte and is a member of the scientific committee of the Academia Montis Regalis orchestra, and responsible for various research projects, as well as a participant in exhibitions and conferences. She has edited catalogues of music collections of international importance, collaborated on several of the most authoritative collected works in the field of music and has conducted extensive research concentrating especially on eighteenth-century Italian music. Her most recent monograph is *Mettere in scena la regalità. Le feste teatrali di Gaetano Pugnani al Regio di Torino* (Lucca, 2012).

Paolo Cornaglia is an architect who holds a PhD in history and criticism of architectural and environmental heritage. He graduated from the *École des Hautes Études en Sciences Sociales* in Paris, and is an Associate Professor of History in the Department of Architecture and Design at the Politecnico di Torino. His research encompasses aristocratic residences and courts from the seventeenth to the nineteenth centuries, focusing on architectural spaces, architectural layout and decoration, as well as gardens. He is a member of the Scientific Committee of the Centro Studi del Consorzio La Venaria Reale. Among his recent publications are: *Giuseppe Battista Piacenza and Carlo Randoni. The Royal Palaces of Turin and Genoa (1773–1831)* (Turin, 2012); *Filippo Juvarra 1678–1736, architetto dei Savoia* (ed. with A. Merlotti and C. Roggero) (Rome, 2014); and *Il risveglio del giardino* (ed. with M.A. Giusti) (Lucca, 2015).

Edward Corp is Emeritus Professor of British History at the Université de Toulouse. His publications include *The King over the Water: Portraits of the Stuarts in Exile after 1689* (Edinburgh, 2001) and a three-volume history of the Jacobite courts: *A Court in Exile: The Stuarts in France, 1689–1718* (Cambridge, 2004); *The Jacobites at Urbino* (Basingstoke, 2009); and *The Stuarts in Italy, 1719–1766* (Cambridge, 2011).

Paolo Cozzo is Professor of the History of Christianity and the Church in the Historical Studies Department of the Università di Torino. He is principally interested in the history of ecclesiastical institutions, in religious life in the modern and contemporary periods, concentrating especially on the relationships among politics, religion and devotion in the states of the *Ancien Regime*. Among his publications are *La geografia celeste dei duchi di Savoia. Religione, devozioni e sacralità in uno Stato di età moderna. Secoli XVI–XVIII* (Bologna, 2006) and *Andate in pace. Parroci e parrocchie in Italia dal Concilio di Trento a papa Francesco* (Roma, 2014).

Francesca Fedi is a Professor of Italian Literature at the Università di Pisa. Her special research interests are the prose of Machiavelli, literature and drama of the eighteenth century, the relationship between Masonic culture and literary genres in the Age of Enlightenment, Neoclassic poetry and the work of Giacomo Leopardi. She has dedicated various contributions to the subject of Vittorio Alfieri, including: 'Fra Corinto e il Nuovo Mondo: il paradigma di Timoleone' in *La Rassegna della Letteratura Italiana* (2003); the entry on 'Alfieri, Vittorio' in the *Enciclopedia Machiavelliana* (Rome, 2014); 'Una foresta tra storia e politica: osservazioni su Alfieri traduttore di Pope' in *Lo spazio tra prosa e lirica nella letteratura italiana* (Bergamo, 2015); and 'Una triste cometa. Dislocazioni del mito nella Maria Stuarda alfieriana' in *Viaggi per scene in movimento* (Pisa conference, February 2016, publication of the proceedings forthcoming).

Christopher M.S. Johns is Norman and Roselea Goldberg Professor of History of Art at Vanderbilt University. His research interests include art, architecture and visual culture of the eighteenth century. Johns is the author of four books: *Papal Art and Cultural Politics: Rome in the Age of Clement X* (Cambridge, 1993); *Antonio Canova and the Politics of Patronage in Revolutionary and Napoleonic Europe* (Oakland, 1998); *The Visual Culture of Catholic Enlightenment* (Pennsylvania, 2014); and *China and the Church: Chinoiserie in Global Context* (Oakland, 2016). He is a fellow of the Center for Advanced Study in Visual Art and the American Academy in Rome, where he was Resident in History of Art in 2004.

Alastair Laing began by studying South German Rococo architecture and stucco, but since being one of the curators of the François Boucher exhibition at the Metropolitan Museum of Art in New York, the Detroit Institute of Arts, and the Grand Palais in Paris in 1986–7 and editor and main author of the catalogue, he has devoted himself to that artist. Between 1986 and 2013 he was Adviser/Curator of Pictures and Sculpture for the National Trust, mounting its centenary exhibition, *In Trust for the Nation*, at the National Gallery in 1995–6, and overseeing the publication of the 13,500-odd oil paintings in its houses for six of the volumes published in 2013 by the Public Catalogue Foundation, and now available online through ArtUK. In 2015 he was a senior fellow at the Morgan Library, and gave the inaugural Eugene Thaw lecture, on Boucher's drawings, of which he is compiling a *catalogue raisonné*.

Tommaso Manfredi is an architect who teaches at the Università Mediterranea in Reggio Calabria in the Department of Architecture, Architectural Heritage and Urban Planning. He researches the history of architecture and city planning in the modern and contemporary periods with a particular interest in Francesco Borromini, Carlo Fontana, Filippo

Juvarra, Ferdinando Fuga, Luigi Vanvitelli, Francesco Milizia and Giacomo Quarenghi; the education of European architects in the eighteenth and nineteenth centuries; the urban history of Rome; and seventeenth- and eighteenth-century treatises on which he has published extensively. He is the author of the monographs: *I Virtuosi al Pantheon. 1700–1758* (with G. Bonaccorso) (Rome, 1998); *La costruzione dell'architetto. Maderno, Borromini, i Fontana e la formazione degli architetti ticinesi a Roma* (Rome, 2008); and *Filippo Juvarra. Gli anni giovanili* (Rome, 2010).

Andrea Merlotti holds an undergraduate and a graduate degree (PhD) from the Università di Torino. He is now the Director of the Centro Studi at La Venaria Reale. He is the author of several studies into the noble class under the Savoyard State, and continues to research the court of Turin and its aristocratic society. Among his publications is *L'enigma delle nobiltà. Stato e ceti dirigenti nel Piemonte del Settecento* (Florence, 2000). He has edited several volumes, including *Le strategie dell'apparenza. Cerimoniali, politica e società alla corte dei Savoia in età moderna* (with P. Bianchi) (Turin, 2010); *Stato sabaudo e Sacro Romano Impero* (with M. Bellabarba) (Bononia, 2014); *Casa Savoia e Curia romana* (with J.F. Chauvard and M.A. Visceglia) (Rome, 2015); and *Le cacce reali nell'Europa dei principi* (Florence, 2016). For the Centro Studi at La Venaria Reale he organizes and takes part in conferences in collaboration with other cultural institutions. He contributes to regular exhibitions at the Venaria Reale and acted as a curator for some exhibitions, including *La Reggia di Venaria e i Savoia. Arte, magnificenza e storia di una corte europea* (2007–8); with A. Barbero, *Cavalieri. Dai Templari a Napoleone* (2009–10); *Carrozze regali. Cortei di gala di papi, principi e re* (2013–14); *Dalle regge d'Italia. Tesori e simboli della regalità sabauda* (Genova, 2017); and *Storia degli Stati sabaudi. 1416–1848* (with P. Bianchi) (Brescia, 2017). Since 2015 he has been a member of the Scientific committee of the Centre de recherche du Château de Versailles.

Andrew Moore, formerly Keeper of Art at Norwich Castle Museum and Art Gallery, now works for the Attingham Trust for the study of historic houses and collections. He was Co-Director of the Attingham Summer School (2011–16) and is now a Study Programme Director. He has curated or co-curated a number of exhibitions, accompanied by publications including regional assessments of the Grand Tour (1985); the influence of Dutch and Flemish painting (1988); and Portraiture (1992). In partnership with the State Hermitage Museum, St Petersburg, he published the collection of Sir Robert Walpole, *A Capital Collection* (with L. Dukelskaya) (New Haven,

CT, 2002). He is currently Guest Curator for the exhibition *The Paston Treasure* (Yale Center for British Art and Norwich Castle 2018) and he is researching the Grand Tour of Thomas Coke. In 2007 he was Paul Mellon Senior Fellow at the British School at Rome.

Cristina Mossetti (BA in History of Art from Università di Torino, diploma in archival studies and paleography PhD in the History and Criticism of Cultural Heritage from the Università di Milano) worked from 1980 to 2013 for the Soprintendenza per i Beni Storici Artistici del Piemonte, Ministero Beni Culturali, including overseeing the territories of Novara, Asti, Casale and the city of Turin. She was the Director of the Villa della Regina, Turin from 1994 to 2013, where she coordinated a project of research, restoration and its reopening to the public. She was a member of the Commissione Scientifica Residenze Reali del Piemonte and was Adjunct Professor of History and Restoration Techniques at the Università di Torino. She has published research on seventeenth- and eighteenth-century patronage, the Piedmontese patrimony and on restoration methodologies. With L. Caterina (Università l'Orientale di Napoli) she has worked to promote a project on the *Gabinetti 'alla China'*, and the culture of Chinoiserie and oriental furnishings in eighteenth-century Piedmont. Since 2014 she has served as Scientific Advisor to the Castello di Masino, FAI – Fondo Ambiente Italiano.

Toby Osborne (Balliol College, Oxford, BA, 1990, DPhil, 1996), taught at Warwick and Oxford before taking up his current position at the University of Durham in 1996. He is interested in the House of Savoy in an international context, early modern diplomatic culture and the papal court. He is currently completing a general book on the papal court, and is running a research network on cross-cultural diplomacy in the early modern period. In a third strand of research, he is working on a research monograph on royalty in Italy, with a focus on the House of Savoy, the Medici and Venice.

Andrea Pennini graduated from the *Università di Torino* in 2008 and earned his doctorate in historical sciences from the Università del Piemonte Orientale in 2012. He now collaborates with the Department of Jurisprudence at the *Università di Torino*. His principal areas of interest are political and diplomatic institutions of the Savoy States in the early modern period. His publications include *Con la massima diligentia possibile. Diplomazia e politica estera sabauda nel primo Seicento* (Rome, 2015) and 'Attraversare le Alpi per volere del duca. Percorsi e relazioni dei diplomatici sabaudi nel primo Seicento' in *La Maison de Savoie et les Alpes: emprise, innovation, identification Xve–XIXe siècle* (*Collection Sociétés, Religions, Politiques*, edited by S. Gal and L. Perrillat) (Chambéry, 2015).

Edoardo Piccoli is Associate Professor in Architectural History at the Politecnico di Torino. He graduated with a degree in Architecture from the Politecnico di Torino, where he also received his PhD. He has received a Diplôme d'Etudes Approfondies in Civilisation de la Renaissance from the Centre d'Etudes Supérieures de la Renaissance at Tours. His research focuses primarily on eighteenth-century architecture. He has edited books and contributed essays to reviews, collective works and exhibition catalogues.

James Rothwell is a Senior Curator with the National Trust and also acts as the Trust's National Adviser on Silver. He has undertaken extensive research on the subject of silver and was the joint author of the catalogue of the renowned collection of plate at Dunham Massey, published in 2006. He is now concentrating on the silver at Ickworth, which constitutes one of the Trust's most significant collections, and has recently published a catalogue of that collection.

Cristina Ruggero has a degree in the History of Art from the University of Freiburg in Breisgau and Münich, with additional specialization in German language. She was a research assistant at the Biblioteca Hertziana in Rome (2000–14). In recent years she has published the results of her research on Filippo Juvarra, concentrating on his work as a draftsman. In 2010 she was awarded the Hanno-und-Ilse-Hahn Prize for her research into the art of drawing and into sculpture of the seventeenth and eighteenth centuries. Her current project, *Microcosm Hadrian's Villa: An Artistic Interaction Space in 18th- and 19th-Century Europe*, is supported by a DFG Research Grant.

Christopher Storrs graduated with Honours in Modern History from the University of Oxford (St Catherine's College), and obtained his PhD from the University of London (London School of Economics). His research interests centre on early modern Europe, and in particular on Spain and Italy (where he is especially interested in the Savoyard state). In terms of themes, he is particularly interested in international relations (war and diplomacy), state formation and empire and the nobility – or nobilities – of Europe in the same period. His publications include *War, Diplomacy and the Rise of Savoy 1690–1720* (Cambridge, 1999); *The Resilience of the Spanish Monarchy 1665–1700* (Oxford, 2006); (as editor) *The Fiscal-Military State in Eighteenth Century Europe* (Farnham, 2009); and *The Spanish Resurgence*

1713–1748 (New Haven, CT, 2016). Dr Storrs is Reader in History in the School of Humanities at the University of Dundee.

Karin Wolfe (MA, PhD Courtauld Institute) is a Research Fellow at the British School at Rome. She has published on Roman seventeenth- and eighteenth-century cardinals, patronage, art, architecture and the Grand Tour. She is co-author (with M. Jacobs) of the chapter of Italian drawings in *Drawings for Architecture, Design and Ornament, the James A. Rothschild Bequest at Waddesdon Manor* (Waddesdon Manor, 2006); co-editor (with D.R. Marshall and S. Russell) of *Roma Britannica: Art Patronage and Cultural Exchange in Eighteenth-Century Rome* (London, 2011); and is currently editing *American Latium: American Artists and Travellers In and Around Rome in the Age of the Grand Tour* (with C.M.S. Johns and T. Manfredi). She is completing writing a monograph on the painter Francesco Trevisani (1656–1746).

Jonathan Yarker recently completed a PhD at Trinity College, Cambridge. He has contributed to a number of publications on the Grand Tour including: *Digging and Dealing in Eighteenth Century Rome* (New Haven, CT, 2010); *The English Prize, the Capture of the Westmorland, an Incident of the Grand Tour* (New Haven, CT, 2012); and *Richard Wilson (1713–82): A European Master* (New Haven, CT, 2014). He has held fellowships at the Lewis Walpole Library, Farmington, NM; Yale Center for British Art, New Haven, CT; Huntington Library, California; and most recently as a Paul Mellon Rome Fellow at the British School at Rome. He is currently working on an account of the life and activities of the banker and dealer Thomas Jenkins entitled 'The Business of the Grand Tour'. He is a director of Lowell Libson in London.

Olga Zoller is an independent art historian who earned her PhD from the University of Bonn (Rheinische-Friedrich-Wilhelms-Universität), in 1994. After working extensively in the field of cultural policy, she resumed art historical research in 2007, focusing on the Piedmontese architect and engineer, Giovanni Battista Borra (1713–70). Thanks to a fellowship awarded in 2011 by the Yale Center for British Art, New Haven, CT, she carried out research at the Paul Mellon Collection. In the Mellon Collection her focus was on the group of almost 100 watercolour drawings by Borra intended to be reproduced as engravings. She is concurrently working on a monograph about these important drawings, together with Borra's extensive collaboration with British archaeologists.

Foreword

I was delighted to have had the opportunity to attend the conference *Torino Britannica: Political and Cultural Crossroads in the Age of the Grand Tour* (19–22 June 2013), co-organized by the British School at Rome and the Centro Studi della Reggia di Venaria, Turin, hosted jointly by the two institutes in Rome and in Turin, and which was supported by the Paul Mellon Centre for Studies in British Art. The conference proceedings have been reworked and now appear as an impressive volume of 22 chapters, *Turin and the British in the Age of the Grand Tour*, representing an important scholarly addition to European cross-cultural studies in the early modern period, covering a host of subjects that will be unfamiliar and at the same time highly illuminating.

The premise for *Torino Britannica* developed from a conference organized in 2006 at the British School at Rome entitled *Roma Britannica: Art Patronage and Cultural Exchange in Eighteenth-Century Rome* (16–17 February 2006; publication of the same name, edited by David Marshall, Susan Russell and Karin Wolfe, 2011, the British School at Rome). *Roma Britannica*, supported by the Paul Mellon Centre, was intended to celebrate art and cultural exchange between Britain and Rome, and, significantly, first proposed taking into account the experiences of the Italians who interacted with British travellers, as well as the contributions of the Italians who travelled to Britain in search of cultural acclaim, subjects undervalued in previous Grand Tour studies. *Turin and the British in the Age of the Grand Tour* develops further the essential themes of cultural exchange in a series of case studies; politically, diplomatically, socially, artistically and religiously, while also raising the crucial questions initiated by the *Roma Britannica* project, of examining the reverse side of the equation of Grand Tour travel, comprising the Turinese reaction to British political, social and cultural developments and considering Turinese diplomats, writers, artists and musicians who migrated to Britain. This lively exchange characterizes the great cultural cosmopolitanism that defined Grand Tour Europe, leading to extensive and far-reaching interactions and transpositions of individuals and ideas, notwithstanding national rivalries, religious intolerances and politically and geographically hazardous travel conditions.

Turin and the British in the Age of the Grand Tour also extensively explores the underpinning of what constituted a Grand Tour city, including diplomatic and political expediency, tourist, educational and travel exigencies, architectural and artistic beauty and modernity and cultural distinction. The volume further focuses on the unique and fundamental role that the Turin Royal Academy (founded in 1678) played in the education and cultural formation and preparation for over a century of British and European youths, equipping them for the international positions they would pursue as modern statesmen.

The Paul Mellon Centre for Studies in British Art is proud to have contributed to the realization of this joint British–Italian project, which examines intellectual cross-currents between Britain and Turin: a cultural exchange which contributed directly to the Enlightenment; ideas and social processes which it is hoped will continue as primary goals to construct political, ethical and cultural exchanges for future generations.

Martin Postle
Paul Mellon Centre for Studies in British Art

Preface and Acknowledgements

Turin and the British in the Age of the Grand Tour explores previously neglected aspects of the relationship between Turin and Britain in the period 1600–1800, a period when Savoy-Piedmont was one of the principle political powers of modern Europe. The chapters collected here, by an international group of scholars, in a range of disciplines, offer fresh perspectives on this important subject, and are the result of two separate cultural initiatives, which both pursue ideas of intellectual and artistic exchange between Italy and Europe in the early modern period.

The first was a groundbreaking conference sponsored in 2006 by the British School at Rome – 'Roma Britannica: Art Patronage and Cultural Exchange in Eighteenth-Century Rome' – which resulted in the publication of the same name in 2011, that sought to redefine the cultural relationship between Britain and Rome in the eighteenth century, focusing not only on the Grand Tour, but also taking into account the frames of reference of the Italians, who increasingly valued the economic and cultural power of the largely Protestant island that lay beyond their traditional objects of attention, France and Spain.[1] The second was a cultural initiative recently undertaken by the Centro Studi della Reggia di Venaria, to examine the State of Savoy's international relationships. Thus far, this project has given rise to two publications: *Stato sabaudo e Sacro Romano Impero* (2014), the result of a collaboration with the Italo-Germanic Historical Institute in Trento,[2] and the *Casa Savoia e Curia romana dal Cinquecento al Risorgimento* (2015) with the École Française in Rome and La Sapienza University of Rome.[3]

The premise for *Turin and the British in the Age of the Grand Tour* was first mooted between the editors of this book, Paola Bianchi and Karin Wolfe, and two of the contributors, Andrea Merlotti and Tommaso

---

[1] The conference, *Roma Britannica: Art Patronage and Cultural Exchange in Eighteenth-Century Rome*, took place at The British School in Rome, 16–17 February 2006. The conference proceedings of the same title, edited by David Marshall, Susan Russell and Karin Wolfe, were published in 2011 by The British School at Rome at the British Academy.

[2] Marco Bellabarba and Andrea Merlotti (eds) 2014, published by il Mulino, Bologna.

[3] Jean-François Chauvard, Andrea Merlotti and Maria Antonietta Visceglia (eds) 2015, published by the École Française de Rome.

Manfredi, during a conference dedicated to the architect Filippo Juvarra (who worked in Savoy and visited Britain), held in Turin and at the Reggia di Venaria in 2011.[4] Originally proposed as *Torino Britannica: Political and Cultural Crossroads in the Age of the Grand Tour*, the project was endorsed by the cultural institutions of the British School at Rome and the Reggia di Venaria, resulting in a conference held jointly by the two, in Rome and in Turin, in 2013.[5] The present volume includes and elaborates upon the multitude of ideas that were presented and discussed. The 22 chapters and four appendices contained in this volume foreground new avenues of research perspectives emphasizing the cross-cultural exchange between Britain and Savoy in the early modern period. As a result, this volume will add greatly to the existing Anglo-Italian bibliography and renew and revitalize interest in the topics under examination. *Turin and the British in the Age of the Grand Tour* marks an important advance in the interdisciplinary study of Britain and the Italian peninsula at a key moment, when the politics of dynasticism was giving way to the modern nation state.

We wish to thank for their support the Paul Mellon Centre for Studies in British Art, and especially Martin Postle, Deputy Director for Collections and Publications, who attended the conference in Rome and in Turin. We gratefully acknowledge the efforts of Valerie Scott and her colleagues in the British School Library and Archive for curating the exceptional exhibition of travel books and guides and original drawings which were displayed at the conference. Thanks are also due to Gill Clark, Registrar and Publications Manager at the British School at Rome for the progress from conference to book. Finally, many thanks go to Paola Bianchi and Karin Wolfe, representing the Centro Studi della Reggia di Venaria and the British School at Rome, for their commitment to this project. Much gratitude is also due to the many individual members of both institutes who worked so hard in planning the conference, especially Lara Macaluso (Reggia di Venaria) and Christine Martin (the British School at Rome). Thanks for help with the editing of the publication also goes to Lisa Beaven, and, for translations, to Davina Thackera and especially Alison Kurke, and for exceptional editorial

---

[4] The conference proceedings were published in two volumes, *Filippo Juvarra (1678–1736), architetto dei Savoia, architetto in Europa. Atti del Convegno internazionale*, vol. I edited by Paolo Cornaglia, Andrea Merlotti and Costanza Roggero and volume II edited by Elisabeth Kieven and Cristina Ruggero, Campisano Editore Roma, 2014.

[5] *Torino Britannica: Political and Cultural Crossroads in the Age of the Grand Tour*, 19–21 June 2013. The conference was organized by the scholarly committee of Joanna Kostylo (The British School at Rome), Karin Wolfe (The British School at Rome), Paola Bianchi (Università della Valle d'Aosta), Andrea Merlotti (Reggia di Venaria) and Tommaso Manfredi (Università Mediterranea di Reggio Calabria).

assistance in the preparation of the index for this volume, to Anselmo Nuvolari Duodo.

Andrea Merlotti
Centro Studi della Reggia di Venaria
Christopher J. Smith
The British School at Rome

Introduction

PAOLA BIANCHI AND KARIN WOLFE

Although the Duchy of Savoy had claimed royal status since 1632,[1] it was only in 1713, elevated by the Treaties of Utrecht, that Victor Amadeus II, Duke of Savoy (1666–1732), was crowned King of Sicily (Fig. 0.1).[2] This signalled the moment that the Savoy, projecting their dominion over the Mediterranean, rightfully entered into play on the European strategic chessboard that, in the following century, would lead to the unification of the entire Italian Peninsula under their rule. The momentous events of 1713 sanctioned a decades-long project that the Duchy had pursued with cunning and perseverance through the convoluted maze of political relationships between foreign powers. Of these, the British Kingdom was one of their most persistent advocates, because of complementary dynastic, political and commercial interests.[3] The Savoy–British relationship would intensify over the course of the eighteenth century, against the background of the pressing threat of the neighbouring Kingdom of France and the Holy Roman Empire: a threat that ultimately led to the Napoleonic Wars, which fundamentally changed the landscape of Europe and altered the nature of this relationship. In the two centuries leading up to this point, however, a notable stream of British diplomats and visitors to the Savoy capital engaged in an extraordinary and reciprocal exchange with the Turinese. This flow of travellers, a number of whom were British emissaries and envoys posted to the Savoy court, coincided only in part with the itineraries of the international Grand Tour that transformed the Savoy capital into a gateway to Italy along the land routes to and from France.

A desire to explore this fertile period of cultural exchange in the long relationship between Turin and Britain led to the 2013 conference *Torino*

---

[1] See: Oresko 1999; Osborne 2002; Bianchi and Gentile 2006; Barberis 2007; Bellabarba and Merlotti 2014.

[2] On the Treaties of Utrecht, see, in the first instance: Kamen 2001. On the role of the Savoyard State, see: Symcox 1983a; Symcox 1983b; Storrs 1999; Bély 2013. On Savoyard representatives in Utrecht, see Bianchi, with additional bibliography, in Crespo Solana and Schmidt-Voges (in press).

[3] For British political and diplomatic relations with Turin before and after 1713, see in particular Parts I–III of this volume. See also: Bianchi and Merlotti (2017).

Figure 0.1 Francesco Cichè, *Allegory of the Coronation of Duke Victor Amadeus II crowned King of Sicily*, in D. Pietro Vitale, *La felicità in trono...* Palermo, Regia stamperia, 1714, Private collection.

Britannica: Political and Cultural Crossroads in the Age of the Grand Tour, from which this book originates.[4] The premise of the conference was to recover the less celebrated and previously underappreciated pathways along which intellectual and artistic trends were spread across Europe in the early modern period, including those relating to politics, diplomacy, society, education, religion, literature, music, architecture and the arts. More than this, however, the aim was to draw attention to the unique aspects of this connection, understudied in comparison to more established historiographic models of British relations with celebrated capitals of the grand tour, such as Rome and Venice. These aspects included the 'modernity' of the culture and of the city-state of Turin. In addition, the conference addressed a previously overlooked, and yet critical feature of the international movement of the grand tour – the grand tour 'all'inverso' – or, the reverse phenomenon

---

[4] *Torino Britannica: Political and Cultural Crossroads in the Age of the Grand Tour*, a conference co-organized by the British School at Rome and the Centro Studi della Reggia di Venaria, Turin, was held on 19–22 June 2013, with two days (19–20 June) at the British School at Rome and two days (21–22 June) at the Reggia di Venaria, Turin.

represented by the Turinese protagonists who travelled to Britain, including Anglophile poets and playwrights such as Giuseppe Baretti and Vittorio Alfieri; architects such as Filippo Juvarra (Sicilian by birth, but court architect to the Savoy) and Giovanni Battista Borra; sculptors, including three generations of the Plura family; and musicians such as Gaetano Pugnani and Felice Giardini.[5]

The resulting publication, *Turin and the British in the Age of the Grand Tour*, considers Turin as not only the capital of an ancient and enduring state, but as a border territory, intimately tied to the rest of Europe by a complex network of relationships, typified by the way in which British historiography translates the phrase 'Stati sabaudi' interchangeably, and not unambiguously, to signify, on the one hand, the geographical region 'Savoy Piedmont', and on the other, the political expression of 'the Savoyard State'. The city of Turin is the hinge of these two meanings of the term. Indeed, it is difficult to separate the history of the city from the events of the state, just as it is impossible to discuss the urban history of Turin without considering the role of the capital as the seat of a court and a government.

Home to the Savoy court since 1563 (although already in the sixteenth century the principal administrative centre of the state),[6] by the end of the seventeenth century Turin proved a unique stopping-point for visitors in the larger Italian context of the grand tour. With its rational, orthogonal grid of streets deriving from the city's ancient Roman origins, Turin appeared 'modern' to travellers, as well as uniform and clean (Fig. 0.2).[7] Piazza San Carlo, with its regularly faced porticoes, was not only built in emulation of the great royal squares of Paris from which it was directly inspired, but was reminiscent generally of the grand urban spaces that characterized the capitals of Europe. The area around the Palazzo Reale (Fig. 0.3), where all the government buildings were located, functioned as a concentrated locus of political administration for the Savoy rulers, demonstrating their determination to wield power outwardly through urban organization as much as through a tightly controlled political apparatus. Successive Savoy rulers redeveloped existing buildings in this area, but also patronized large *ex novo* building projects, such as that undertaken for the realization of the

---

[5] For the theme of the Grand Tour 'all'inverso' see, in this volume, Parts IV–VI. See also, in particular, Marshall and Wolfe in Marshall *et al.* 2011: 3–6.

[6] Barbero 2002. On the various locations of the court in the Royal residences, see Merlotti in Piccoli and De Pieri 2012: 59–83.

[7] On urbanism and military fortifications in Turin, see: Pollak 1991; for seventeenth- and eighteenth-century urban studies, see: Griseri and Romano 1989; Cornaglia 2012a; Kieven and Ruggero 2014.

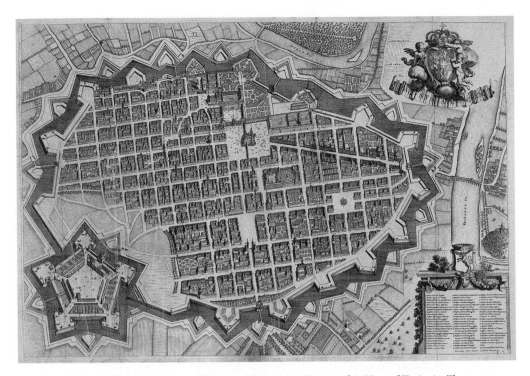

Figure 0.2 Giovanni Tommaso Borgonio, *Topographic View of Turin*, in *Theatrum Statuum Regiae Celsitudinis Sabaudiae Ducis*, Amsterdam, Blaeu, 1682, vol. I, plate 8, Reggia di Venaria.

great diagonal axis of the Via Po that extends from Piazza Castello, across the Borgo Nuovo, to the Piazza d'Armi, known today as Piazza Vittorio Veneto (Fig. 0.4). In the face of the overriding image of orderliness that the city presented to visitors, individual buildings and *palazzi*, incorporated into the long, straight street facades, receded into the background. Royal residences were the exception to this: the royal palaces and administrative offices, and especially the magnificent royal suburban villas, arranged in a configuration resembling a crown around the city, were singled out for commentary, especially by British travellers (see below, Figs 6.3, 6.8–6.9).[8]

This same élite group of visitors also commented on the world of polite society in which the Savoy family, following strict protocol, dictated the rules of etiquette of the Turin court – as John Boyle, 5th Earl of Cork and 5th Earl of Orrery (1707–62), observed with much curiosity in 1754:

No clock-work ever moved with greater exactness, than this court. Every minute fulfils its destiny, and turns round its own axis with the royal inhabitants of

---

[8] See Andrew Moore in this volume, Chapter 6. See also: Merlotti 2014.

Figure 0.3 Giovanni Tommaso Borgonio, *View of the Piazza of Palazzo Reale*, engraved by Romyn de Hooge, in *Theatrum Statuum Regiae Celsitudinis Sabaudiae Ducis*, Amsterdam, Blaeu, 1682, vol. I, plate 11, Reggia di Veneria.

Turin. Already we have beheld over and over again, the same royal scenes; the same princes, and the same princesses in the same coaches, taking the air, at the same hour, to the same place. They seem all married to time, and I presume that it is a kind of adultery to vary half a dozen minutes from the sun.[9]

Part I of the volume, dedicated to *Britain in Turin: Politics and Culture at the Savoy Court*, examines the dynastic relationships between the Savoy Duchy and the Stuarts from the beginning of the modern period, the backdrop against which a dense web of associations with British visitors and British politics is set. Toby Osborne's paper (Chapter 1) reveals what he has described as the nature of the 'special relationship' that arose from 'a virtuous circle of travel and diplomacy, due to shared political interests and dynastic ties'. He charts Stuart relations with the Savoy court, originally through

---

[9] His *Letters from Italy* (1754–5) were published posthumously, 'printed for B. White' in 1773: 52–3.

REGIÆ BIBLIOTHECÆ, EQVESTRIS ACADEMIÆ, VETERIS CASTRI CVM SVO VTRINQVE FORO, AD SEPTENTRIONEM INSPECTIO.

Figure 0.4 Giovanni Tommaso Borgonio, *View of the Piazza of the Palazzo Reale, showing the Quadrant of the Turin Royal Academy in the lower left-hand foreground,* in *Theatrum Statuum Regiae Celsitudinis Sabaudiae Ducis*, Amsterdam, Blaeu, 1682, vol. I, plate 13, Reggia di Veneria.

the Stuarts' ambassadorial representatives, important cultural agents and mediators, travellers as much as diplomats, posted continuously to Turin from 1612 to 1640. But Osborne also discusses the wider implications of travel between Britain and Catholic Europe during this period, including the ongoing complications related to Protestantism (and the related British search for a historical legitimacy for Anglicanism), which were highlighted in the Savoy region, by the presence of the Waldensian population sited in the Alpine valleys, 'one of Europe's most unstable confessional frontlines'.

Andrea Pennini (Chapter 2) continues the theme of Stuart–Savoy relations, focusing on the several matrimonial negotiations to join the Stuarts and Savoys during the first decade of the seventeenth century, particularly the crucial question for the Savoy of marriage prospects with King James's heir, Prince Henry Frederick Stuart (1594–1612). While the repeated

attempts by the Savoy court through the strenuous efforts of their ambassadors abroad to secure alliances with the Stuarts were not realized for many
years, this study reveals the intensity of the political and diplomatic relations
between the two, and especially the determination of the Duchy of Savoy to
enter into dynastic ties with Britain above all other countries, an argument
supported by extensive new archival documentation and correspondence.

Edward Corp (Chapter 3) takes up this narrative at the point of its successful conclusion for the Savoy in the later seventeenth century with the 1684
marriage of Duke Victor Amadeus to James II's niece, his sister's daughter, Anne-Marie de Bourbon Orléans (1669–1728) (Fig. 0.5; Fig. 3.2). As a
result of this union, the Jacobite claim to the British thrones, following the
Glorious Revolution of 1688, could have devolved upon the death of Queen
Anne to the Duchess of Savoy and her two sons, Prince Victor Amadeus
of Savoy (1699–1715) and Prince Charles Emmanuel III (1701–73),
a situation keenly followed on the European political stage (see Fig. 3.1, for
the Jacobite succession in 1712). Corp analyses the wide-ranging ramifications of this political possibility, and the diplomatic bargaining power that
it provided for a period to the Savoy dynasty. A passage from a letter written
from Turin in March 1709 by Lord Charles Somerset (1689–1710) to his
aunt, Lady Anne Somerset, Countess of Coventry (1673–1763), reveals that
both sides were acutely aware of this situation. He recounts:

I went to wait upon the present Duchess, who is not one of the most beautiful but
I believe indeed one of the best Women in the World. She was extremely affable to
me and told me what particular Esteem she had for the English Nation, being her
self, as she expressed it, the better half an English Woman, for as your Ladyship
knows, she is the next heir to the Crown of England if the Roman Catholicks were
not debarred from succeeding.[10]

The increase in British diplomats and travellers to Turin over the ensuing
century, from 1688 until the catastrophic involvement of the State of Savoy in
the French revolutionary wars, is charted by Christopher Storrs (Chapter 4).
Alongside the evolving protocol of British diplomacy at the Savoy court and
the impact of British residents in Turin, Storrs notes a marked Anglophilia
taking hold after the successive wars with France: 'another respect in which
Turin was British in the eighteenth century'. Storrs has also compiled a

---

[10] See Lord Charles Somerset's diary of 1709, photographic reproduction of Badminton MSS,
FMR 3/1 and 2, and FMT/B1/2/14 in RBF/9/34, State Foreign Papers, Archive, Paul Mellon
Centre for Studies in British Art. Somerset died unmarried in Rome in 1710. For the life of
Anne-Marie de Bourbon Orléans, later Duchess of Savoy, then Queen of Sicily and Queen of
Sardinia, see: Nobili Vitelleschi 1905; Reineri 2006.

Turin

Rivoli

Le Pont Riviere

Anne Marie D'Orleans Duchesse de SAVOYE
Fille de Monsieur Philipe de France, Duc DOrleans, Frere Vnique
du Roy, et, d'Henriette Stuart D'Angletere, nacquit le 27 Aoust 1669.
Son merite la fit Epouser son Altesse Royale le Duc de Sauoye le
10 Auril 1684. Se Vend A Paris chez F.Iollain, a la ville de Cologne.

Figure 0.5 Unknown artist, *Anne Marie d'Orléans, Duchesse de Savoye, with the Town of Turin and the Castle of Rivoli*, engraved by François Jollian, Paris, Bibliothèque Nationale de France.

highly useful appendix of the diplomats and visitors to Turin during the eighteenth century, an important contribution to a more integrated research approach to British foreign policy in Piedmont (Appendix I).

The second part of the volume, Part II, *Turin: Gateway to Grand Tour Society*, foregrounds the most important draw for British visitors, the Turin Royal Academy (Accademia Reale).[11] Opened in 1678, the Academy offered up-to-date and prestigious instruction in military and diplomatic culture to a wide range of young Europeans who frequented this élite institution over the course of a period of months or even years, nurturing a cosmopolitan exchange between future statesmen, diplomats and military officers. Far from a simple *Ritterakademie*, it was a fulcrum between the court and the various secretaries of state (the Academy was housed in an extension of

---

[11]   See Paola Bianchi in this volume, Chapter 5 and Appendix III.

the Palazzo Reale), as well as a pivotal focus of activity among the nobles of Piedmont. Becoming an important rite of educational passage, the Academy taught not only martial arts and equitation, but also mathematics, geography, history and languages (Italian and French). In addition to these traditional subjects, it also taught social skills and gentlemanly virtues necessary for diplomacy and salon conversations, for the fashionable society of the continent: in short, it offered a modern education for gentlemen destined for public life. To gain a true sense of the Academy's European reputation, it is worth repeating the lengthy report compiled about the institution by the Anglo-Irish priest, John Chetwode Eustace (1762–1815):

Its [Turin's] academy enjoyed a considerable degree of reputation, and was crowded with foreigners, attracted in part by the attention which the king condescended to show to the young members, and partly by the cheapness of masters, and by the facility of instruction in every branch and language. This academy was indeed a most useful establishment, and extremely well calculated to usher young men into the world in the most respectable manner, and to fashion them to courts and to public life. A year passed in it, with the least application, enabled them to prosecute their travels with advantage, not only by supplying them with the information necessary, but by procuring them such connections with the first families in all the great cities as might preclude the formalities of presentation, and admit them at once into the intimacy of Italian society. Without this confidential admission (which few travellers have enjoyed for many years past) the domestic intercourse of Italians, and consequently the character of the nation, which is never fully and undisguisedly unfolded unless in such intercourse, must continue a mystery. Now, the academy of *Turin*, where the young students were considered as part of the court, and admitted to all its balls and amusements, placed this advantage completely within their reach, and was in this respect, and indeed in most others, far superior to Geneva, where the British youth of rank were too often sent to learn French and scepticism.[12]

Paola Bianchi (Chapter 5) outlines the precise structure and educational aims of the various strata of the Academy, and explains its political relation to the Savoy court. In addition she explores the surprising religious 'promiscuity' of the Savoy polity, comprising Catholics, Protestants ('religionari') and Jews, and how this controversial religious heterogeneity, which brought the Savoyard State into conflict with the papacy, was also reflected in the student body of the Academy, which went so far as to cater for it. Bianchi also provides a separate appendix of British students who attended the Turin Royal Academy during the eighteenth century, an invaluable reference for scholars of Grand Tour studies, and British historiography (Appendix II).

---

[12] Eustace 1815: 370.

Andrew Moore (Chapter 6) follows the specific trail of one young British aristocrat at the Academy, Thomas Coke, later 1st Earl Leicester (1697–1759). Coke's period in Turin is contextualized in his lengthy Grand Tour, which lasted from 1712 to 1718, and which, as Moore demonstrates, provided the basis for the inspiration for Coke's building of Holkham Hall, 'giving rise to a new interpretation of British Classicism' and inspiring also his collecting of pictures and sculptures. Significantly, Coke's social contacts at the Academy and at the Savoy court, and his admiration for Prince Eugene of Savoy (1663–1736), are brought to light, providing a personal case study of relations between Britain and Turin.

Alongside the importance of the Academy for exchanges with Britain, other contributors target the spaces of sociability shared by the various British presences in Turin in the eighteenth century, such as salons and masonic circles. Edoardo Piccoli (Chapter 7) follows the social forays of the British into the private salons of the Pallavicini, and their relations with the Protestants, the Torras, in a chapter dedicated to the residency and residential quarters of the British in Turin, mainly centred around the Protestant community in the area of San Federico. Andrea Merlotti (Chapter 8) continues the theme of the social interaction of the British at the court of the Princes of Savoy Carignano and the court of Anne-Marie d'Orléans, exploring the connection between the British in Turin and Freemasonry as a sphere of contact, especially that surrounding the Turin masonic lodge, 'Saint Jean de la Mysterieuse'. The chapters in Part II share a common dialogue, criss-crossing the intersections of international experience in the eighteenth-century Savoy capital. Moreover, British itineraries in Turin and in the Piedmont region are unravelled, thanks also to the painstaking research into housing and banking, undertaken by Piccoli and also discussed by James Rothwell (Chapter 10).

British travellers to Piedmont have, until now, only been sporadically investigated by scholars, among whom Jeremy Black must be singled out, for drawing attention to the exception represented by the Savoy court within the canons of a tour of Italy.[13] Anecdotes about Turin as a stopping-place for visitors are also recorded in a fundamental essay by Michael Wynne,[14] as well as in countless entries of the *Dictionary of British and Irish Travellers*

---

[13] 'British tourists in Italy were presented often to the Pope, the Kings of Naples and Sardinia, the Grand Duke of Tuscany, the Dukes of Parma and Modena and the Governor of Milan, but their courts did not dominate the pastimes of British tourists to the Peninsula, with the exception of the King of Sardinia's court at Turin'; see: Black 1999: 216. See also: Black 1984; 1989.

[14] Wynne 1995; 1996.

in Italy, compiled from the Brinsley Ford Archive by John Ingamells.[15] But it is high time that these separate and scattered sources were contextualized and, above all, verified in a prosopographic reconstruction. Moreover, from a strictly biographical point of view, it is necessary to see the visit to and into contemporary Turin as a predetermined choice for many, a destination selected specifically for its particular cultural benefit. This is the case for several well-known British public figures, who spent formative periods of their lives in the Savoy capital. An important example in this respect is John Montagu, 4th Earl of Sandwich (1718–92), whose youthful travels around major Italian cities had been documented, but whose sojourn in Turin had long been forgotten.[16] A letter sent by Philip Stanhope, 4th Earl of Chesterfield, in 1749, before his son set out for Piedmont, reveals the hidden history of these important educational sojourns at the Savoy court and Academy:

The months that you are to pass there will be very decisive ones for you. The exercises of the Academy, and the manners of courts must be attended to and acquired; and, at the same time, your other studies continued. I am sure you will not pass, nor desire, one single idle hour there: for I do not foresee that you can, in any part of your life, put out six months to greater interest, than those next six at Turin.

   We will talk hereafter about your stay at Rome and in other parts of Italy. This only I will now recommend to you; which is, to extract the spirit of every place you go to. In those places which are only distinguished by classical fame, and valuable remains of antiquity, have your classics in your hand and in your head; compare the ancient geography and descriptions with the modern, and never fail to take notes. Rome will furnish you with business enough of that sort; but then it furnishes you with many other objects well deserving your attention, such as deep ecclesiastical craft and policy.[17]

'To extract the spirit of every place you go to' was an aim shared not only by Grand Tourists, but by many categories of travellers, including diplomats, soldiers, businessmen, artists, writers and musicians: all of whom appear in the pages of this volume as part of the fundamental background network of international relationships established in the eighteenth century. A complex network that was woven together, not only by the practice of travel and leisure, but also because of specific institutional aims: educational, political and professional.

[15]   Ingamells 1997.
[16]   For the biography of Sandwich see: Rodger 1993.
[17]   Lord Chesterfield, *Letters to his Son*, letter LXVIII, London, 19 April 1749.

But the question remains: why did the British demonstrate a cohesion and continuity almost certainly superior to other nationalities present in the cultural and social fabric of Turin? Why, even today, do well-recognized traces (even if their relationships to one another are still to be identified) remain in the fabric of the contacts between Piedmont and Britain? The authors of the chapters in this volume offer a variety of answers, which have a clear common denominator, the *fil-rouge* of *Torino Britannica*: modernity. For unlike other Italian cities that were traditionally seen as foci for the past, Turin was singled out by foreign visitors as an exception to this rule. The capital's appeal lay in its contemporary qualities, appreciated above all by British visitors, who were undoubtedly more receptive to the city's social, economic and cultural distinctiveness, but also to the pompous court ceremonies that were often recorded in the pages of the *London Gazette*.[18]

For aristocratic travellers, whose presence increased notably after the institution of the Kingdom of Sicily in 1713, the court represented the only opportunity in Turin to socialize, until the mid-eighteenth century when access to *salotti* and *conversazioni* was allowed. By the second half of the eighteenth century, foreign criticism of the Savoy court began to emerge. On his arrival in Turin in 1764, Edward Gibbon (1737–94) wrote to his father describing one of the most sophisticated courts in Europe, but one that had fallen prey to bigotry. During the same period, his near contemporary James Boswell (1740–95) complained of the licentiousness and libertinism he experienced first hand in the salon of the Countess of Saint Gilles, and while this ambit was outside the official remit of the court, it was none the less frequented by the same set of courtiers, and in particular, by British travellers and delegates. Reading between the lines of Boswell's attack, it is apparent he adopted Protestant Britain's view of Catholic customs. However, notwithstanding literary topoi, Turin retained its reputation as a centre for fashionable aristocratic society well into the late eighteenth century, while its architecture and art collections continued to be admired.[19]

The opinions of foreigners, and of British travellers and diplomats in particular, regarding the magnificence of the court and the state of the arts and architecture in Turin, had played an important role in Savoy diplomacy, beginning in the early seventeenth century. Osborne evidences the reports of the lavish hospitality extended by Charles Emmanuel I (1562–1630) to Sir Henry Wotton (1568–1639) in 1616, when he visited Turin.[20] A fundamental

[18] On the history of *London Gazette* (1665–1965) see: Handover 1965.
[19] See Merlotti 2004. See also in this volume: Paola Bianchi, Chapter 5; Andrea Merlotti, Chapter 8; and James Rothwell, Chapter 10.
[20] On Wotton, see Toby Osborne, Chapter 1, p. 37, note 32.

feature of this hospitality included a tour of the Duke's grandiose ancestral portrait gallery, demonstrating the early interest of the Savoy rulers in the iconographical implications of dynastic portraiture, a theme which dominated their artistic patronage throughout the later seventeenth and eighteenth centuries.[21] Indeed, the Savoy based a significant part of their dynastic staging in the grand arena of Europe upon excellence in the decorative and architectural arts, which they perceived as intrinsic to the diplomatic success of their court and symbolic of their inordinate ambitions. A celebrated example of this is the magnificent atlas printed in two volumes, the *Theatrum Sabaudiae* (*Teatro degli Stati del Duca di Savoia*), commissioned by Charles Emmanuel II (1634–75) and completed during the reign of Victor Amadeus II, by Johan Blaeu's workshop in Amsterdam as a propagandistic tool. As Moore describes: 'The volumes successfully acted as a political statement that challenged the court of Versailles, demonstrating the extent of the wealth and territories of the Alpine principality, helping to overturn the notion of the Alps as geographically isolated.' In 145 views, the *Theatrum Sabaudiae* presents the city of Turin rationally developed beyond its ancient Roman nucleus, with its surrounding crown of ducal residences and the entire State of Piedmont as a vital and essential part of the Europe of the nation states.

The thrust of this publication, with its expansive and forward-looking perspective, was embraced in the following century by Victor Amadeus II, who envisioned monumental architecture and urbanism as a strategy to glorify his sovereignty (Fig. 0.6). The key figure in the artistic and architectural renewal of Turin during Victor Amadeus II's reign was the versatile architect from Messina, Filippo Juvarra (1678–1736), who the King called to his court in 1714, and whom he employed as the inspired director of the arts for the next twenty years (see Fig. 13.3).[22] Juvarra's responsibility was not only for building churches, palaces, squares and monuments, but also for providing designs and decorative schemes for interiors to other artists he recruited, including painters and Chinoiserie specialists. He was also put in charge of ephemeral decorations for court rituals and celebrations. Juvarra's coordination of commissions during the reign of Victor Amadeus II brought about a highly organized system for the arts that has been described as a 'bureaucratization of the court arts at Turin',[23] which finally led to the 'regi studi' of painting, sculpture and applied arts, established as state schools, intended to

---

[21] For Charles Emmanuel I's collection, see: Romano 1995.
[22] For Juvarra's role as impresario of the arts, see: Wolfe 2014a, 2014b. For more on Juvarra and for architecture and urbanism as a strategy to glorify sovereignty, see Tommaso Manfredi, Cristina Ruggero and Jonathan Yarker in this volume.
[23] Oresko 1999: 251.

Figure 0.6 Unknown artist, *The Duke of Savoy* (Victor Amadeus II wearing the Order of the Annunciation), engraved by John Simon, London, Cooper, c. 1710, British Museum, London, © The Trustees of the British Museum.

give a uniform and updated style, not only to royal commissions, but also to all of those generated by the noble circuit gravitating around it.[24] It was precisely this style that was unanimously recognized by foreign visitors.

---

[24]   On the state schools and particularly on the important role of architects and engineers, see: Binaghi 1999; 2003; 2010; 2012.

The presence of Juvarra at this juncture ushers in the cultural contributions of the next three parts of this volume. These contributions cover aspects of reciprocal patronage, collecting, architectural history, the aesthetic of Chinoiserie and gardens. Toby Osborne describes the whole process of this cultural exchange as 'cultural brokerage': 'the buying, commissioning and exporting of works of art, artists and musicians, along with the standard political requirements of diplomatic business'. Part III, *Torino Britannica: Diplomacy and Cultural Brokerage*, borrows Osborne's term to follow and investigate these key themes.

One of the first diplomats to Turin to recognize the importance of Juvarra's cultural mandate was the erudite Anglo-Irish diplomat and art collector, John Molesworth (1679–1726), British Envoy Extraordinary and Plenipotentiary to the Court of Victor Amadeus II, the protagonist of Karin Wolfe's contribution (Chapter 9). Molesworth was a privileged observer of political and artistic life in Turin from 1720–5, a decisive period during which court art in Turin was raised to the level of an *instrumentum regni* by Juvarra in his role as 'architect of the King'. In his letters to his Florentine protégé, the architect Alessandro Galilei (1691–1737), Molesworth conveyed an unprecedented intimacy with the famous 'Don Philippo', but also, based on his previous experience of the artistic scene in Florence, set out to develop a new architectural aesthetic for Britain – which he described as, at that time, plunged in a 'dreadfull Abyss' (for Molesworth's correspondence, see Appendix IV). The cultural connections woven by Molesworth among Florence, London, Dublin and Turin reflect the vital and enterprising period subsequent to George I's ascension to the throne, in which the influence of the writings of Lord Shaftesbury and Jonathan Richardson expanded the artistic and architectural culture of Britain in the direction of a new, autonomous identity based upon an abstract and ancestral idea of Greek and Roman classicism.

If Molesworth attempted, unsuccessfully, to expose the Savoy court to the tastes of Florence filtered through their Greek canons, his later successor, the wealthy George William Hervey, Lord Bristol (extraordinary envoy in Turin from 1755 to 1758), was able to tap into and benefit from the latest Turinese fashions in silver, his principal avenue of patronage. As explored here for the first time by James Rothwell (Chapter 10), Hervey employed Andrea Boucheron (c. 1692–1761) and Paolo Antonio Paroletto (1736–95), master silversmiths active at the Savoy court, to modernize and enhance his already rich collection of French and English silver with about 70 new pieces, an extraordinary group of objects still found today at Ickworth House in Suffolk. These objects of art represent not only the excellent quality of Savoy craftsmanship, but the public and private grandeur (fully concomitant with that of the Savoy court) that the British envoy identified with as a diplomat, which as Rothwell writes, 'was as important a part of effective diplomacy as charming the king and his ministers, and spying'. Lord Bristol's skill as spymaster may be implicit in the outstanding suite of Turinese mid-century furniture and fittings still surviving at Ickworth, which probably were gifted to him by Charles Emmanuel III (1701–73) (Figs 0.7 and 0.8).[25]

Alongside the works of art which were exported from Turin, artists also left the city to improve their abilities, and to update their provincial style. Among the group of artists 'exported' was the portrait painter, Domenico Duprà (1689–1770), long ignored by scholars, and now the subject of an important chapter by Jonathan Yarker (Chapter 11). Duprà was sent to Rome by Juvarra to refine his skills in the studio of the painter, Francesco Trevisani, Juvarra's friend and former courtier at the court of Cardinal Pietro Ottoboni, thereafter travelling to Portugal, to work in the service of King John V (1689–1750). Returning again to Rome, Duprà was occupied for a decade as portraitist to the exiled Stuarts and their court, all the while carrying out commissions for notable Italians. He finally returned to Turin in 1750 to take up the official role of 'royal portrait painter', a particularly significant position, in light of the extraordinary value conferred by the Savoy on dynastic portraiture. As Yarker demonstrates, Duprà was instrumental in creating the image of a new iconography for the court nobility, in part adapting the methods he had developed in Rome for portraits of British travellers. Duprà portrayed James George Hamilton, 6th Duke of Hamilton (1724–58), who spent most of 1752 in Turin, in this novel, royal style (see Fig. 11.5).

The painter John Francis Rigaud (1742–1810) was also a compelling artistic figure for cultural relations between Turin and Britain. Born in Turin to French parents, Rigaud trained with the Savoy court painter, Claudio Francesco Beaumont (1694–1766), before embarking on his own extensive Grand Tour around Italy. He travelled to Paris before settling in London in 1771, effectively importing his Turinese style of painting to the British capital. His success was evident in his admission as an associate to the Royal Academy in 1772, and expressed by his famous 1782 painting, depicting the founding members of the Academy: Sir William Chambers, Joseph Wilton and Sir Joshua Reynolds (Fig. 0.9).

---

[25] See James Rothwell, Chapter 10 in this volume; see also Jonathan Yarker, Chapter 11, on the practice of the Savoy kings presenting gifts to British diplomats.

Figure 0.7 Unknown artist, *Charles Emmanuel III, King of Sardinia*, engraved by John Brooks, London 1746, British Museum, London © The Trustees of the British Museum.

Paolo Cozzo's contribution (Chapter 12) returns to the diplomatic sphere of 'cultural brokerage' in a discussion of the Chapel of the Savoy Embassy in London, registered as belonging to the Embassy of the Kingdom of Sicily in 1715, two years after Victor Amadeus II's ascension to the throne. Via

Figure 0.8 Mid-Eighteenth-Century Furniture from Turin, Drawing Room, National Trust (Bristol Collection), Ickworth, © National Trust Images, Photograph: Andreas von Einsiedel.

archival sources and inventories, Cozzo demonstrates that the establishment of the Chapel was intended to serve the propaganda for the newly created Kingdom, and it quickly became a crucial reference point not only for Savoyards abroad, but also for British and foreign Catholics alike, and even for many non-Catholics who were attracted by the exceptional quality of the music performed there. Cozzo reveals the ways in which the Chapel functioned as an alternative space for diplomacy in the form of religious ritual, music performance and artistic display. It housed several fine liturgical

Figure 0.9 John Francis Rigaud, *Sir William Chambers, Joseph Wilton and Sir Joshua Reynolds*, oil on canvas, © National Portrait Gallery, London.

objects bearing the hallmarks of the noted Turin silversmith Andrea Boucheron (see Figs 12.3–12.4).

Among the many worshippers frequenting the Savoy Chapel in London at different times were certainly Filippo Juvarra and Giovanni Battista Borra (1713–70), each the subject of chapters in Part IV, *Turin and Britain: Architectural Crossroads*. Juvarra's own personal Grand Tour to London and Paris in the summer of 1719, on a roundabout return to Turin from a long stay in Lisbon (a harbinger of Duprà's), made him a particularly important cultural catalyst in the relationship between the architectural cultures of Britain, Italy and Europe in general. Tommaso Manfredi (Chapter 13) examines Juvarra's sojourn abroad, analysing the contacts he cultivated, to reflect more broadly on the role of 'royal architect' in the Europe of the Grand Tour, and on the characterization of this role within the British and Turinese contexts, bearing in mind the varying national attitudes toward the representation of political power through architecture. These attitudes were to profoundly affect the stylistic implications of architecture, ranging from classicism to neo-classicism.

Manfredi draws attention to the coincidence that Juvarra was present in London precisely when Richard Boyle, 3rd Earl of Burlington (1694–1754), was preparing to leave for his second trip to Italy, to focus on the work of the great Renaissance architect, Andrea Palladio. This artistic enthusiasm on the part of Lord Burlington would subsequently be of great consequence for architectural history and the history of revivalism. A probable meeting in London between these two cultural pioneers, resulted in Juvarra later presenting a gift of an album of evocative drawings of architectural *capricci* to Burlington. This 'homage' is examined and reinterpreted by Cristina Ruggero (Chapter 14), who dissects the symbolic content of the individual drawings and who also explains the context of the contemporaneous British cultural ambit – consumed with an interest in antiquarianism – in which this highly personal, and yet avant-garde aesthetic presentation was conceived.

Giovanni Battista Borra, the Piedmontese-trained architect, engineer and draftsman, took part in a scientific-archaeological expedition to the Levant in 1750–1, together with a group of English travellers and an Irish scholar, Robert Wood, to draw and accurately reconstruct ancient architecture and its decoration, that would be published in two volumes which proved to be highly influential, *The Ruins of Palmyra* (1753) and *The Ruins of Balbec* (1757). Disembarking from his travels in London in 1752, Borra arrived at, and contributed to, the key moment when British architectural culture was shifting toward the study of the antique. Olga Zoller (Chapter 15) traces Borra's assimilation of this new classicizing sensibility as it was reflected in his subsequent international career. Borra designed the first neo-classical garden structures to be realized in Britain at Stowe in 1752, for Richard Grenville, 1st Lord Temple (1711–79), and upon his return to Piedmont in 1756, he transformed the Baroque castle of Racconigi into a neo-classical summer residence for Prince Luigi Vittorio of Savoy Carignano (1721–78). At Racconigi, Borra also had a hand in designing several interiors, in various styles ranging from decorations derived from antique examples, to 'exotic' typologies, such as Chinoiserie, influenced by Chinese models.

The Savoy court was the pacesetter in Italy for Chinoiserie furnishings and decorations, a theme taken up in Part V, *Britain and Turin: Chinoiserie as an International Aesthetic*. In Christopher Johns' words (Chapter 16): 'As an international artistic style that was both chic and fashionable, Chinoiserie was also perceived to be cosmopolitan and progressive. Moreover, it was widely considered authoritative, not in and of itself but in relation to its deployment in the residences and public buildings of Europe's ruling classes.' Johns argues that the Chinoiserie decorations and furnishings commissioned by the Savoy royals were directly related to elite European sociability during the age of the grand tour in terms of the etiquette of *politesse* required, and that this 'exotic' taste served to promote Savoy splendour, and thus promote the dynasty's political ambitions. Providing an in-depth study of the exoticist interiors at the Castle of Racconigi, Cristina Mossetti (Chapter 17) definitively attributes much of this eclectic decoration to Borra, including the furnishings described in the contemporaneous documents as 'alla china'. Like Johns, she also examines the internationalism of Chinoiserie and its dependence on diplomacy, evidencing that much 'alla china' decoration imported to Piedmont actually came from Britain, explaining that it was the Savoy envoys and diplomats to London, directed by the Savoy rulers, who acquired the latest fashionable furnishings, including 'Chinese papers' (Chinese wallpaper). It was in the hands of the designers in Piedmont, however, including Juvarra, Borra and Pietro Massa, the leading Chinoiserie decorator in Turin during the middle decades of the eighteenth century, that the style took on new connotations and was revisited in innovative models for interior furnishings and decorations, unique to this region.

Paolo Cornaglia (Chapter 18) demonstrates that Piedmont was similarly receptive to British styles and evolving fashions for garden and landscape designs, alongside other European models, and he charts how these new ideas filtered into the Savoyard State, throughout the late eighteenth and into the beginning of the nineteenth centuries, by the specific formal developments of the principal gardens. His chapter investigates the social and diplomatic pathways through which information about garden and landscape design travelled, including via official Savoy emissaries, aristocratic interactions like marriages and freemasonry networks. Beginning with the 'English' Garden at Venaria Reale, which Cornaglia demonstrates was in no way a reflection of a contemporaneous English garden, but which nonetheless reflected the fascination with the cultural context of English garden design at an early stage, he progresses through such overlapping stylistic variations as the picturesque, including the Racconigi gardens designed from 1787 by Giacomo Pregliasco (1757–1825) and the Palazzo Grosso di Riva gardens from 1796–7 by Leopoldo Pollack (1751–1806); the Anglo-Chinese, including the unexecuted garden design for Villastellone designed in 1784 by the gardener, Guglielmo Gullini; and the 'Capability' Brown style, rural English landscape garden at Villastellone, ongoing from 1784 to

1804 and attributed to various members of the Wallace family of gardeners from Scotland. His chapter concludes with the work of the Franco-German landscape gardener, Xavier Kurten (1769–1840), who designed Piedmont's largest landscape park at Racconigi in the English style of Brown, beginning in 1821, destroying the earlier work of Pregliasco, and thus prefiguring the arrival of a new era, artistically, socially and politically.

The final section of the book, Part VI, is dedicated to *Turin in Britain: Cultural Exchange in Grand Tour Europe*, an exploration of the grand tour in reverse following the emigration, as well as the temporary sojourns of the Piedmontese artists, musicians and writers who transposed their cultural activities to Britain. The Plura family of Torinese sculptors, the subject of Alastair Laing's contribution (Chapter 19), began their migration with Carlo Giuseppe Plura (1663–1737), who transplanted the first seeds of Piedmontese Baroque culture to north Yorkshire, where he is documented as the author of various stucco interior decorations at Castle Howard. His son, Giuseppe Antonio (1724–56), was born and trained in Turin but emigrated to Bath, establishing himself there as a sculptor of note and marrying a local woman, before moving to London. One of his sons, Joseph Plura (1753–?) trained at the Royal Academy schools, before setting out in 1777 on a Grand Tour of Italy (introduced by a letter written by Giuseppe Baretti, who had known his parents in Bath), where he carved several busts of British travellers, bringing the family talent full circle in Britain.

Felice Giardini (1716–96), Gaetano Pugnani (1731–98), Carlo Chiabrano (1723–before 1776) and Giovanni Battista Viotti (1755–1824) are some of the cast of musicians and composers charted by Annarita Colturato (Chapter 20) who were drawn to Britain for their careers. As she explains:

London was a modern musical *eldorado*: clubs, Masonic lodges and other social gatherings featured music prominently; theatres and concert societies craved talented composers and instrumentalists; aristocratic families lured virtuosos for private academies and lessons; music publishers raced against Parisian and Dutch colleagues to print the latest musical compositions; newspapers were eager to crown new celebrities and spur artistic rivalries.

Yet Colturato also reveals the downside of this outwardly flourishing scene, as once, in Britain, the Turinese musicians and composers often struggled to make ends meet, with some reduced to penury and others resorting to teaching, selling instruments or becoming impresarios.

Unlike the artists and musicians who travelled to Britain to secure the international fame and financial gain that eluded them in Turin, Cristina Bracchi (Chapter 21) discusses how the literary critic and author, Giuseppe

Baretti (1719–89), while admiring Britain and the British language from an idealistic viewpoint, sought equally to present Italy accurately to the English nation in the interest of improving cultural exchange. She details that Baretti's *An Account of the Manners and Customs of Italy; with Observations on the Mistakes of some Travellers with regard to that Country*, published in London in 1768, is as much a literary response to eighteenth-century cultural relations between Italy and Britain, as it is a description of Italy. Indeed, the work was specifically written in response to Samuel Sharp's *Letters from Italy, describing the Customs and Manners of that Country, In the Years 1765, and 1766. To which is Annexed, An Admonition to Gentlemen who pass the Alps, in their Tour through Italy*, published in 1766. Bracchi cites a letter from Baretti to Boswell that explains the motives for his spirited critical defense of the reputation of Italy:

I am likewise printing an account of Italy in two small volumes, and am handling pretty roughly some of your British travellers and their Italian Itineraries. The impertinence of these people has of late exceeded all bounds, and I will endeavour to put a stop to it for the future, by vindicating my Country, and proving that they are but silly liars when they say, that there is nothing in Italy but ignorance and folly, vice and poverty.

If Baretti integrated himself fully into the cultural and artistic elite in London, even to the point of assuming the role of 'Secretary for Foreign Correspondence to the Royal Academy', in which he was immortalized in a portrait by Reynolds (Fig. 0.10), Vittorio Alfieri (1749–1803), as Francesca Fedi explains (Chapter 22), idealized Britain, as 'a paradigm of the best form of society and government in the Europe of his time'. Despite his misgivings regarding British politics during the writing of *Maria Stuarda* (1788), a period that coincided with the last phase of the Anglo-American conflict, he nonetheless retained his admiration for British culture. It is significant that *Turin and the British in the Age of the Grand Tour* closes with Alfieri's myth of Britain 'cultivated over his lifetime through study and through an attempt to acquire a detached and objective view of Italian anomalies'.

The 'Alferian' conclusion to this volume coincides with the 1799 closure of the Turin Royal Academy by the Napoleonic regime. This marked an institutional turning point for the Savoy State that also bore heavy repercussions on the influx of foreigners into Turin. The Academy, the authentic breeding ground for the vital cosmopolitan, aristocratic community present in Turin in the eighteenth century, closed its apartments to make way for a Napoleonic Lyceum (1804–14), an inferior version of the military institutes

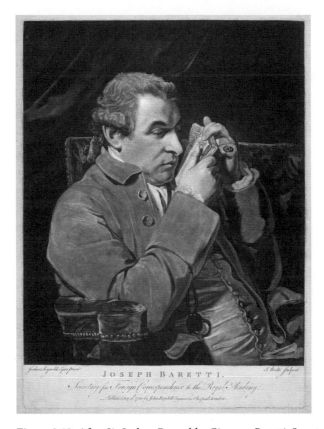

Figure 0.10 After Sir Joshua Reynolds, *Giuseppe Baretti, Secretary for Foreign Correspondence to the Royal Academy, 1773*, engraved by John Watts, London, Boydell, 1780, © National Portrait Gallery, London.

of Fontainebleau and the École Polytecnique.[26] Opened to 'French youth of the XXVII division', the Lyceum ended the international atmosphere that had matured over the course of more than a century. With the fall of the French government and the restoration of the government of Savoy, the newly constituted and renamed *Accademia Militare di Torino* assumed national connotations, entirely at odds with the Royal Academy's standing in the seventeenth and eighteenth centuries. With the attention of the Savoy kings now focused on the Italian Peninsula, and British statesmen increasingly involved in running the British Empire, never again would Savoy and Britain have so much in common, sharing a cosmopolitan culture in the elegant social spaces of one of Europe's most fashionable cities.

[26] *Etat de situation du Lycée de Turin au 1er janvier 1808*, Archives Nationales de France, Paris, F 17, doc. 1611.2 (microfilm, in Archivio di Stato di Torino).

PART I

Britain in Turin: Politics and Culture at the Savoy Court

1 | England and Savoy: Dynastic Intimacy and Cultural Relations Under the Early Stuarts

TOBY OSBORNE

To understand the origins of a *Torino Britannica*, we need to examine the context of early Stuart contact with Europe, most particularly the intersections between diplomacy and the cultures of collecting and patronage that emerged during the first decades of the seventeenth century. The year 1604 is invariably taken as a watershed in accounts of Anglo-European relations. James VI of Scotland's accession to the English throne in March 1603 paved the way for the signing of the Treaty of London, 28 August 1604, ending decades of cold and hot war between England and Spain.[1] Peace, in turn, heralded the beginning of a new period of cultural openness. English and Scottish collectors in the orbit of the Stuarts looked with much greater interest, and greater ease, to the practices of patronage and collecting in continental (and specifically Catholic) Europe, even if Elizabethan England was not as hermetically sealed as this narrative might imply.[2]

As this strongly suggests, while discussions of early seventeenth-century collecting primarily address the importance of courtiers as collectors, the framework within which travel and collecting occurred was largely the construction of more regular and formal diplomatic contact between the Stuarts and Catholic Europe after 1604; we cannot discuss Anglo-European social and cultural relations without examining the emergence of a distinctive style of diplomacy that characterized Stuart England before the civil war. This diplomacy was itself largely the product of the Stuarts' dynastic politics: of James's marriage in 1589 to Anne of Denmark; the negotiations with various continental dynasties for Prince Henry's hand prior to his death in 1612; the failed Spanish Match of 1623 between James' younger son, Prince Charles, and the Infanta Maria Ana; and Charles' eventual marriage in 1625 to the Bourbon princess, Henrietta Maria. It is worth making the obvious, but important, point that from 1603 until Mary Stuart's accession in 1688, England had an unbroken succession of Catholic queens (the republican experiment aside). Despite troubled relations between some of these consorts and

[1] All dates are given in the New Style unless otherwise stated.
[2] For discussion of this, see: Chaney 1998: esp. chapter 3; Woolfson 1998.

their husbands, they undoubtedly made contact on various political and cultural levels with Catholic Europe both more necessary and easier. In turn, the Stuarts' ambassadorial representatives were, as we know, important cultural agents and mediators, and often significant collectors in their own rights. Figures such as Henry Wotton, Dudley Carleton, James Hay, Walter Montagu, Balthasar Gerbier, and the Duke of Buckingham, combined diplomatic service with collecting, cultural brokerage and self-education (and all had contact in one way or another with the Savoys during our period). The dividing line between diplomat and traveller was fine, as John Stoye observed in his classic study of seventeenth-century English travellers.[3]

Interest in Catholic Europe was not, however, trouble-free. True, the Madrid court profoundly shaped Prince Charles' cultural preferences, not least as his trip there was to be his only experience of travel abroad, and the Spanish Netherlands furnished England with the two living artists who probably did more than any other to add a dash of modern glamour to the court – Peter-Paul Rubens and Anthony van Dyck.[4] Yet beyond the court's rarefied air, popular hostility to the Spanish Habsburgs remained profoundly ingrained in the mental world of many English Protestants. The failure of the Spanish Match witnessed not just national relief but euphoria, as Charles returned a bachelor from Madrid and set England on a path to war against Spain, with the support of Buckingham, his mentor and future favourite.[5] Relations with other parts of Catholic Europe were more equivocal, though still not straightforward. There was ambivalence towards France as a Catholic kingdom that during the 1620s oppressed its Huguenot community – itself a contributory factor in the outbreak of war with England in the late 1620s – but which under Richelieu was also an enemy of the enemy, Spain.[6] Venice too occupied an ambiguous place, for despite the Serene Republic's formally Catholic alignment, it had a deeply uncertain relationship with Rome, as the Interdict crisis of 1606–7 demonstrated. Nor was the republic's relationship with Spain any warmer. When the Duke of Savoy appealed for military support against Spain during the 1610s, his rhetoric targeted Venice as a fellow independent Italian power, and Venice was repeatedly seen as a potential ally by the Stuarts for wider

---

[3] See: Stoye 1952: introduction. For a fine recent account, see: Chaney and Wilks 2013.

[4] On the cultural impact of the 1623 trip, see, for example: Brown and Elliott 2002: esp. 156–91; Brotton 2006.

[5] The fullest account of this period remains: Cogswell 1989.

[6] For instance: Smuts 2008; Hibbard 1983. On Anglo-French cultural contact, consult: Chaney and Wilks 2013: chapters 3–6.

anti-Habsburg alliances during the 1610s and the early phases of the Thirty Years War.[7]

Here, then, are three interwoven elements that need to be considered together, and which collectively form a narrative of contact between England and Catholic Europe: of a growth in travel against a backdrop of relative peace; of travel facilitated by increased dynastic and diplomatic contact; and finally of a lingering confessional unease amongst some hotter Protestants that had the potential still to complicate Anglo-European relations. As previously suggested, these accounts have tended to focus on relations with Spain and the Spanish Netherlands, France and Venice. One state, though, has often been absent from these discussions: the Duchy of Savoy.[8] This relative historiographical lacuna is surprising because Savoy was to become pivotal to England from the 1610s, even though early seventeenth-century Turin lacked the pull of other court-capitals as a centre for collecting. While this volume is concerned primarily with the first theme, of the undoubted cultural importance of Savoy to English and Scottish travellers from the later 1600s, the groundwork was put in place in the first half of the century by the growth of diplomatic contact. It is with this second theme – the construction of a dynastic and diplomatic framework that fundamentally informed Anglo-Savoyard cultural interchange – that this chapter is principally concerned.

But what of the third issue: of Protestant enmity towards Catholic Europe? Can we detect confessional concerns amongst Englishmen towards Savoy during our period, and could they have made Savoy a problematic destination? It would come as no surprise if that were the case. The Savoyard states were on one of Europe's most unstable confessional frontlines, often exacerbated by the dukes of Savoy themselves. Geneva, the beacon of Reformed religion during the sixteenth century, had, as we know, established its independence from its Savoyard-controlled bishopric in 1536, though Savoy's dukes were evidently reluctant to relinquish their claims to the territory. Geneva's independence was both literal and metaphorical: the city was largely bounded by Catholic powers and assailed by the forces of the antichrist. In October 1582, the Genevan Syndics and Council had written to Elizabeth I begging for assistance for their defence against the threats of the Savoyard duke.[9] A number of leading Tudor aristocrats were

---

[7]   On Savoy's rhetorical appeals to Venice against Spain see, most famously: Tassoni 1855. On the possibilities of England allying with Venice and Savoy, read: Larminie 2006.

[8]   Though see: Osborne 2007a; and more generally: Osborne 2002.

[9]   The National Archives, Kew, State Papers (TNA SP) 96/1/3-v, 7 October 1582. A second letter of 7 October to the same effect was addressed to Francis Walsingham: SP 96/1/5-v, and a

Figure 1.1 After Sir Anthony van Dyck, *Charles Emmanuel I, Duke of Savoy*, engraved by Pieter Rucholle, Antwerp, Meyssens, c. 1630, British Museum, London, © The Trustees of the British Museum.

moved to contribute to the Genevan cause in 1583, and a similar collection was organized amongst clergymen.[10] Subsequent pleas were made in 1586, 1589 and 1590, and a voluntary collection was licensed by the queen in 1590.[11] The fate of Geneva seemed frequently at risk from Savoy. As recently as December 1602 Duke Charles Emmanuel I (Fig. 1.1) had tried unsuccessfully to regain the city, in the famously botched *Escalade*, when his forces were thwarted in their efforts to scale the city's defensive walls

further petition on the same date was sent to Lord Burghley. British Library [BL] Landsdowne MS 35, fols 184-v.

[10] For example, TNA SP 12/159/138, 'The names of noblemen that are moved to contribute to the relief of Geneva', c. March 1583; SP 12/161/49–56v, 'The contribution of the clergy and laity within the Diocese of Canterbury towards the relief of the town of Geneva', c. June 1583.

[11] For example, BL Landsdowne 50, fols 35-v, Syndics and Council of Geneva to Walsingham, 20 December 1586; Landsdowne 60, fols 171–2, to Burghley, 14 September, 1589: TNA SP 96/1/ 42-v, Elizabeth I to Geneva, 19 July 1590 (o.s.?).

by ladder – what the Jacobean courtier and ambassador Dudley Carleton described as 'a ridiculous practice, yet likely enough to have bin effected'.[12]

The sufferings of the Waldensian community, part of which inhabited Piedmont's Alpine valleys, were also known in Tudor and Stuart England. John Foxe had written of them in his monumental *Book of Martyrs*, the key text other than the Bible for English Protestants. This fixed in the Protestant mind a shared identity with their Piedmontese brethren who suffered for the true religion, even though, as Foxe himself realized in his marginal corrections to the 1570 edition, the claim of a massacre of Waldensians in the Val d'Angrogna in Piedmont was in fact a mistake in geography (the specific incident occurred in Provence).[13] Just as importantly, Foxe and other prominent Protestant scholars and divines identified the pre-Reformation Waldensians as proto-Protestants. The Waldensians' views, so they argued, paralleled their own, and provided Anglicanism with the legitimacy of a backstory that belied Catholic claims of Protestantism as an illegitimate novelty.[14]

There were powerful reasons, then, as to why Savoy might have been viewed as a threat to the Protestant International. Surprisingly, though, in the early 1600s Savoy appears not to have attracted the same levels of hostility reserved for other parts of Catholic Europe. For much of this period, the duchy appears to have remained almost entirely under the radar of popular English Protestant religious sensitivities. Strikingly there seems to have been a near-complete absence of responses to the *Escalade*, in contrast to the aid offered to Geneva under Elizabeth I. To my knowledge, the city's providential salvation simply did not register as a matter of celebration in polemics or sermons, and nor did Geneva's sufferings, aside from a voluntary contribution for the city which James I requested his Anglican bishops to organize in 1603. Even that, it should be added, was only of limited success as James had to reissue the appeal some months later – the collection's initial failure in the kingdom's northern counties was certainly noted.[15] On the contrary, we know that during the 1610s Duke Charles Emmanuel I flirted with an alliance involving various Protestant powers, including Bern, which had been instrumental in securing Geneva's separation from Savoyard control in the first place. From the perspective of

[12] TNA SP 14/6/55v, Carleton to Chamberlain, 15 January 1604.

[13] Evenden and Freedman 2011: 177–8.

[14] Cameron 1993: 185–207; Facey 1987: 165–6.

[15] TNA SP 14/4/14–15, James I to the Archbishops of Canterbury and York, 9 October 1603 (o.s.?); SP 15/36/40–2, James I to the Archbishop of Canterbury and the Bishops in convocation, 26 April 1604 (o.s.?); Hatfield House Cecil Papers [Hatfield CP], 106/57, Archbishop of York to Cranborne, 8 October 1604 (o.s.?).

committed English Protestants, a narrative could be constructed that James I's alignment with his Savoyard counterpart, through a potential marriage or by alliance, in fact served Protestantism's wider interests by moderating Charles Emmanuel I's policies towards Geneva.[16]

The Waldensians also seemingly failed to excite widespread attention during the early seventeenth century. True enough, as mentioned earlier, some Protestant scholars such as James Ussher, author in 1613 of *Gravissimae quaestionis, de Christianarum ecclesiarum in Occidentis praesertim partibus*, continued to frame the Waldensians as the natural predecessors of English Protestants. But intense and focused feeling only began to crystallize in the middle years of the century. On 24 April 1655 Savoyard troops, under instruction from Duke Charles Emmanuel II, carried out a notorious and bloody suppression of Waldensians, women and children amongst them. Most famously, John Milton penned his sonnet, *On the Late Massacre in Piedmont*, as a polemical response to these events, and he was not alone. In 1658, for instance, Samuel Morland (an ambassador to Turin during the Protectorate) published his *History of the Evangelical Churches of the Valleys of Piemont*, directed, as its introduction claimed, 'principally to all the faithful and compassionate Souls of the *English* Nation, who have been grieved for the Afflictions of *Joseph*'. The work recorded the national collection of 1655 for the Waldensians, and Oliver Cromwell's diplomatic interventions, and his call for a national day of prayer and humiliation.[17] Support for the Waldensians continued after the Restoration. Parliamentary journals record the passage of a private bill, initially passed in 1660 and revised in 1662, for the resolution of a dispute over the moneys collected during the Protectorate for Piedmont, under the guidance of a committee of the House of Lords.[18] Nor was this to be the last occasion on which the sufferings of the Waldensians provoked outrage and a sense of confessional solidarity. When they faced renewed persecutions from 1686, a series of polemics appeared in England reiterating the narratives of Protestantism under threat from tyrannical Catholicism and of the Waldensians as the historical antecedents of Protestants. These works became inscribed into the broader ideological backdrop to the Glorious Revolution.[19]

---

[16] Larminie 2006: 1309–10; Smith 1907a: I, 115. See also TNA SP 14/71/17, Biondi to Carleton, 9 October 1612. Some confessional concerns were expressed about a potential Anglo-Savoyard marriage. For example, TNA SP 14/67/109–10, 'Opinions in reference to suitable alliances for the Prince of Wales and Princess Elizabeth', circa December 1611.

[17] TNA SP 96/6/121-v, Cromwell to the Magistrates of Geneva, 7 June 1655 (o.s.?); Moreland 1658: esp. Book Four. See also Whitelock 1732: 629, 665; Mears *et al.* 2013: 602–5.

[18] See: Lords 1771: 166–7, 169, 183, 185, 192, 210–11, 212, 235, 367, 377, 400, 405, 412, 413, 453, 473.

[19] Marshall 2006: chapter 2. The Waldensians were also of importance to William III's European strategies. Storrs 1999: 293–311.

Nevertheless, we should reiterate that expressions of empathy and indignation – however potent and genuine – were of the mid- and later seventeenth century. Confessional sentiments seemingly did little to hinder the warming of relations at the princely level between the early Stuarts and Savoys. It might well be argued that Savoy emerged during the early 1600s as one of the Stuarts' most consistent and important allies on the stage of European power politics. Between 1612, when Sir Henry Wotton arrived in Turin to serve as an extraordinary ambassador as part of the negotiations for an Anglo-Savoyard marriage, until Secretary Peter Morton's departure from Savoy in 1642 there was almost continuous presence in Turin of a variety of official diplomatic representatives of differing categories: extraordinary and ordinary ambassadors, *chargés d'affaires*, agents and secretaries.[20] This is revealing. Sovereigns in our period chose where they had regular ambassadorial missions with care, and certainly there was no culture as yet of permanent European diplomacy. Princes and states had to account for a combination of political sensitivities – of where it was expedient to send representatives – and the sheer costs of doing diplomacy. It was neither desirable nor feasible to maintain diplomatic presences in all states, and the choices sovereigns made of where they sent representatives accordingly reflected their priorities and preferences. In this same period, there was a similarly continuous Stuart diplomatic presence only in France and Spain, and to a degree in Denmark, connected to the Stuarts through James's consort. Tellingly, there was more contact than with the Stuarts' co-religionists, including the Dutch Republic. That alone serves as a measure of Savoy's importance to England under the first two Stuart kings.

Why, then, did England and Savoy matter to each other? As noted earlier, James I might have considered the warming of relations with Savoy as a means of tempering the threat to Geneva, though there may well have been other attractions too. For some, it seemed as if they were in fact natural allies. At a princely level, James I and Charles Emmanuel I shared important qualities, both conceiving themselves as senior figures on the international diplomatic stage. By the seventeenth century, James I was Europe's longest reigning monarch, having come to his throne as a thirteen-month-old baby in 1567; Charles Emmanuel – four years older than his Stuart counterpart – succeeded to his ducal throne in 1580. Both princes also ruled states that were of the second rank but which enjoyed important geo-strategic

---

[20] Bell 1990a: 228–32. The Venetians reported in August 1613 that James I 'has decided to maintain an agent perpetually at Turin, recalling the secretary who is now there'. Venice 1907: 44.

resources: England as a power that was generally believed to have a powerful maritime presence, and Savoy as a gatekeeper to the Alps.[21]

These factors provided the backdrop to the dynastic politics of the 1610s, which in turn reinforced the connections between English and Savoyard interests. Just as the marriage strategies of the Stuarts set the tone for the burgeoning relationships with the Habsburgs and Bourbons, the same was true of Anglo-Savoyard relations. As Andrea Pennini discusses elsewhere in this volume, negotiations for a union joining the Stuarts and Savoys was a dominant feature of relations in the critical years of 1611–12, involving principally James' heir, Prince Henry Stuart.[22] There was indeed intense speculation around Europe as to whom Henry, one of Europe's most eligible princely bachelors, might marry, as vividly seen in the letters sent by Venice's ambassador in Turin at the time, Vicenzo Gussoni, which analysed the various permutations and consequences of an English marriage with Spain, France, Tuscany and Savoy.[23] This was a uniquely powerful moment reflecting not just the variety of potential marriage options available at that juncture, but more importantly just how enmeshed the Protestant Stuarts were with the dynasties of Catholic Europe, Savoy included.

Although the Anglo-Savoyard marriage projects of the 1610s failed, the two ruling dynasties joined indirectly through the Bourbons, following the marriages between the Savoyard prince Victor Amadeus and Christine de France in 1619, and Charles Stuart and Henrietta Maria in 1625. This locked England and Savoy into a particular dynamic of international relations, predicated on an understanding that their interests were bound to France and also Spain by the weaving together of their ruling families. On this point, it is worth stressing that the royal Stuarts appear not to have looked on the ducal Savoys as a lesser dynasty, even though Charles I was to remain cautious about formally recognizing Savoy's self-proclaimed royalty following the *trattamento reale* of 1632.[24] In the first phase of the Anglo-Savoyard marriage negotiations, James had indeed gone out of his way to stress the quality of the House of Savoy's lineage, as if he knew that this was a matter of sensitivity to Duke Charles Emmanuel I. And we know of the Savoys' sense of self-worth, utterly convinced as they were of their intrinsic royalty underscored by centuries of marriages into Europe's imperial and royal families. So far as they were concerned, their status was in their blood, if

---

[21] Osborne 2002: 5–7.

[22] See: Pennini 2012; and also pp. 41–55 in this volume.

[23] For example, Archivio di Stato, Venice, Dispacci degli ambasciatori al Senato, Savoia, filza 35, 23, Gussoni to the Senate, 20 May 1612.

[24] Osborne 2014.

not by common acceptance of other sovereign dynasties. When in October 1610, shortly before lasting diplomatic contact was established between the Stuarts and Savoys, Viscount Cranborne (the son of the earl of Salisbury, one of James I's leading ministers) was in Turin on his tour of Europe, Charles Emmanuel I warmly welcomed him to court. On visiting the ducal gallery and library (probably Charles Emmanuel's principal cultural assets), what struck Cranborne, as he recounted in his record of his journey, were the portraits of family members covering eight centuries. Savoy's dynastic pedigree was of central importance to a process of royal self-fashioning and outward promotion, as Cranborne's tour clearly suggests.[25]

That is not to say that the burgeoning Anglo-Savoyard relationship was trouble-free, or that travel suddenly boomed. True, the duchy controlled key routes into the peninsula, which facilitated the importance of Turin as a transit point to other places in north Italy; the emergence of a *Torino Britannica* was partly the product of travel to or from other Italian destinations, especially Venice, as well as a product of deepening dynastic intimacy. But the Alpine weather could equally hamper free movement, as the delays faced by visitors to Turin testify. The very considerable body of diplomatic correspondence sent back to London from Savoy suggests another factor that might have affected freedom of movement. Official ambassadorial letters were dominated – perhaps unsurprisingly given the usual remit of an ambassador – by the politics of war. While James I cultivated his image of the *rex pacificus* (it was Dudley Carleton and Isaac Wake who partly can be credited with brokering the treaty of Asti in 1615, ending Savoy's war with Spain), the bellicose Charles Emmanuel I had a less enviable reputation for inconstancy and incessant restlessness.[26] The first war for Mantua and Monferrato (1613–15) and Savoy's confrontations with Spain dominated Wake's correspondence during the 1610s, a decade when other parts of Europe enjoyed relative peace. And with war, certainly in the late 1620s during the second war for Mantua and Monferrato (1628–31), came plague, a factor that further hampered ambassadorial movement in north Italy.

Ironically, war also strengthened Anglo-Savoyard political relations, as mutual need, borne out of the international power politics of the 1610s and especially the 1620s, entwined them. Both grounded international policies, like their dynastic politics, during the first decades of the seventeenth century principally on their relations with France and Spain. It seems that some in London and Turin, like Buckingham and Scaglia, came to believe

---

[25] Hatfield CP, 317/1, 'The earl of Salisbury's Journall.' See also: Chaney and Wilks 2013: 158–9.
[26] On Carleton and Wake's mediation, see: Larminie 2006: 1308–9.

that English and Savoyard interests were best served by acting together as a lever against those Catholic superpowers, most evidently during the 1620s when the Caroline regime found itself at war with both.[27] In short, England and Savoy converged within a powerful nexus of dynasticism, war and self-interest. A clear measure of the growing strength of relations can be seen in the remarkably warm ways diplomats and travellers were treated at both courts, and of the growing importance of English missions to Turin for training aspiring courtiers. For the remainder of this chapter we will see this through the experiences of a sample of English visitors to Turin.[28]

Perhaps the most significant visitor was not in fact on an official diplomatic mission. Thomas Howard, the 2nd Earl of Arundel, probably the greatest collector of early Stuart England, was in Italy in 1612, returning between 1613 and late 1614 with his wife, Alethea Talbot, and then accompanied by Inigo Jones, for whom Italy was to prove a revelation in his formation as an architect. Savoy was on their itinerary during this second tour. The Arundels arrived in Turin in September 1614, and received a lavish welcome from Duke Charles Emmanuel, along with a gift of two horses, possibly reflecting the particular importance of hunting to the Torinese court. The timing of the visit to Turin, in 1614, and the fact that he appears to have been invited there directly by Charles Emmanuel, should be placed in the context of the projects for the Anglo-Savoyard marriages of the previous three years. Even though Arundel was not on a formal ambassadorial mission, the warmth of his reception may well have served as a very public assertion of growing Anglo-Savoyard affinity.

Alethea was to return with her sons and entourage to Turin on a subsequent tour of Italy, over the winter of 1622–3, possibly, it has been suggested, with Anthony van Dyck in her company, marking the artist's first contact with the Savoyard ruling House (and, it is worth adding, possibly serving in the longer term as another point of cultural contact between the Stuarts and Savoys). She was lavishly received and entertained over the course of her stay, recalling the reception she and her husband had earlier enjoyed, and reiterating the wider benefits her presence conferred on the Savoys.[29] The duke, we might suppose, was again keen to impress on his illustrious visitors a sense of princely magnificence and of Turin as a cosmopolitan court, even if the city at that time could not match the status of Venice or

---

[27] Osborne 2002: part II.

[28] The clearest example of favour shown to a Savoyard diplomat can been seen in the experiences of Alessandro Scaglia in London during the 1620s. Osborne 2002: 97–100, 133–4.

[29] For example, TNA SP 92/9/301, Wake to Carleton, 5 December 1622. On Van Dyck's importance to Savoy, consult: Vaes; Osborne.

Rome. This is an important point. Turin was not necessarily a destination for English visitors under the early Stuarts because of the opportunities for collecting it presented. Yet the energy expended by the Savoys in putting on magnificent displays for visitors, and the fact that a succession of high-profile Stuart courtiers like the Arundels experienced the Savoyard court, surely had an impact on Anglo-Savoyard cultural relations, and possibly laid the markers for Turin to emerge as one of Europe's more important cultural capitals by the eighteenth century.

The example of the Arundels in Turin was far from unique, as we see when we examine the experiences of other visitors, most notably Sir Henry Wotton. Certainly, Wotton needs no introduction, as a polymath courtier whose importance to the cultural identity of the early Stuarts ranks with Thomas Howard. His diplomatic mission in 1612 to Turin, as part of the Anglo-Savoyard marriage negotiations, was marked by a level of appropriate grandeur that also matched Arundel's welcome two years later (Wotton had also been warmly received on his first informal visit to Turin in 1611). In return for gifts sent to London by Charles Emmanuel I, Wotton took a return gift from James I of '10 ambling horses, sumptuously caparisoned in severall kinds, and jewelled sword', reportedly valued at the enormous sum of 16,000 pounds.[30] In the Savoyard states, he was lavishly received, his lodgings reportedly hung with Charles Emmanuel I's own tapestries, some wrought with gold and silver thread. In fact, at Rivoli, so overbearing were the receptions that it was said that he 'lets everyone see he has had enough of them'.[31] Wotton returned in May 1616, and was again at the receiving end of exceptional favour. As Isaac Wake acerbically commented, Wotton was 'entertained here with that excess of courtesy with which this prince [Charles Emmanuel I] doth use to oppress all such as come in the name of his majesty'.[32]

Wotton's 1612 mission is also significant because of the size and quality of his entourage. It is worth stressing that ambassadors dispatched abroad typically travelled with followers, comprising not just functionaries but often family relatives and gentlemen who might themselves add lustre to missions. A large entourage communicated the standing of the ambassador and by extension the prestige of his prince, and it also flattered the hosts: magnificent diplomacy was a symbolic language of mutual appreciation between

---

[30] See: Smith 1907a: I, chapter VI; II, 1; Venice 1905: 472. For Wotton's instructions, see Hatfield CP, 196/71, fols 125–6, March 1612.

[31] Venice 1905: 522. The Venetians recorded further feasts, hunts and entertainments put on for Wotton, albeit with less spectacle. Venice 1905: 537.

[32] TNA SP 92/4/152, Wake to Carleton, 31 May 1616.

princes. There was often a practical aspect to the entourage too, for ambassadorial missions provided training for younger or aspiring courtiers, the means for completing a cosmopolitan education. Amongst those who travelled with Wotton to Turin were the future Earl of Warwick, and the future Duke of Newcastle; in total, Wotton's entourage counted 50 horses.[33]

A similar number followed Dudley Carleton for his mission to Turin in the autumn of 1614 despite the difficult weather, among them Isaac Wake, mentioned previously.[34] The value to Wake of his exposure to Turin soon became apparent as he was to emerge as the most significant English ambassador to Savoy in our period, serving on missions there between 1614 and 1624, 1625 to 1626, and 1628 to 1631. We might go so far as to describe him as a Savoyard 'expert', if only for the sheer length of his service in Turin, cemented by his formative experiences under Carleton. As suggested earlier, his extensive correspondence was dominated by questions of war and politics. His letters also provide insights into the Savoyard court's cultural life, with, for instance, the various invitations he received to ducal hunts, reflecting the particular cultural importance of hunting at the court of Charles Emmanuel I, and references to lavish court tilts and entertainments, especially in 1620.[35] And as with Wotton and Carleton's missions before, Wake's extensive periods of service in Savoy facilitated travel for others. To take one notable example, sometime in 1617 it seems that John Pory was with Wake in Turin, possibly serving as his secretary. Born in 1572, the colourful Pory, an associate of the traveller and writer Richard Hakluyt, was himself a significant traveller, translator, cultural broker and adventurer: he would later journey to Virginia in North America.[36] It was not in fact his first visit to Turin. In July 1613, while William Parkhurst was serving as James I's agent in Turin, John Pory passed through the city on his four-year journey around Europe and the Mediterranean.

Another Stuart courtier in effect educated through Wake's mission was Peter Morton, who was later secretary in Turin, 1635–42. Morton indeed demonstrates a sense of continuity from one Englishman in Turin to another, not least as he also served Basil Feilding, a nephew of the former favourite the Duke of Buckingham, and the future 2nd Earl of Denbigh, and this chapter's last example of a diplomat-traveller at the Savoyard court. We can infer from a letter written by another secretary, John Hales, to Feilding

[33] Smith 1907a: I, 120–1.
[34] Stoye 1952: 163–4.
[35] For example, TNA SP 92/4/11v, Wake to Carleton, 16 October 1615; 92/7/17, Wake to Carleton, 18 February 1620.
[36] Powell 1977.

in November 1634, that Feilding had visited Turin before his formal mission of late 1634, repeating a pattern set by earlier diplomats like Wotton and Wake who had their first experience of Turin as travellers. Hales was probably referring to a visit Feilding made in 1631 when he had been in Geneva, though travel then had been severely hampered by the plague. As Hales' letter suggests, Feilding had made some impact on the Torinese court:

Your lordship will bee infinitely welcome unto this Court and princes, as well for the glory and splendour of your quality and character as for your owne particular honors and virtues. Madame [Duchess Christine?] is impatient to see you and there is no question but hir Highnesse will renue hir dancing quarrel. Wee have still brave ladies in this Court, but those that were fayrest in your lordship's time, as the fatt Busca, the dainety Chalais and the wanton Princesse of Masseran are married and gon awaye.[37]

Feilding went on to serve as Charles I's representative in Turin, between 1637 and 1639, the last ranking ambassador before the English civil war disrupted formal diplomatic relations. We might add that Feilding was in his own right a significant collector and artistic broker, even though it was Venice rather than the Savoyard capital that was to prove his cultural touchstone.[38] We should not lose sight, though, of the more important point. As the succession of visitors mentioned in this chapter suggests, Turin was gradually marking its place on the map of European courtly centres for the English. This was a virtuous circle: the framework was set by formal ambassadorial relations, which provided opportunities for more informal travel and education, in turn facilitating more diplomatic contact.

If, in conclusion, we return to the threefold narrative that began this chapter, we see how Savoy fits into a typology of English travel to Catholic Europe in ways that have generally been neglected in existing studies. There was, it is true, some confessional unease about Savoy, and there were occasional difficulties in reaching Turin because of war, weather and the plague. These factors, however, did little to hamper the warming of relations at the highest social and political levels before the mid-1600s. Rather, a distinctive style of relations was constructed under James I and Charles Emmanuel I during the 1610s, and then cemented by Charles I during the 1620s. These relations were grounded on shared political interests and enmeshed within a web of marital negotiations and dynastic affiliations that bound them on various levels to the Bourbons and Habsburgs. This political and dynastic

---

[37] Historical Manuscripts Commissions 1911: 9. More generally consult: Denbigh 1915: esp. chapter V.

[38] For example: Shakeshaft 1986.

framework facilitated travel to Turin as a succession of Stuart courtiers made the crossover from travel to diplomatic service, in several instances moving between Venice and Turin. The Savoyard court capital evidently occupied an important place in strategies of the first Stuart monarchs, as the sheer frequency of diplomatic relations attests. Correspondingly, we should add, the cloyingly enthusiastic welcomes accorded to English visitors indicate just how important they were to validating the Savoyard dukes' aspiration to rank their dynasty and court capital in Europe's premier league. A special relationship was put into place between England and Savoy under the first two Stuart kings that served both dynasties and which in turn encouraged travel. As we will see vividly through this volume, that relationship was to blossom over the course of the seventeenth century and beyond.

2 | Marriage Proposals: Seventeenth-Century Stuart–Savoy Matrimonial Prospects and Politics

ANDREA PENNINI

In the Europe of the dynastic states, matrimonial politics took on particular importance, in both the foreign and domestic arena of politics. It was through marriage that alliances of varying durations were formed, intersecting and changing lines of succession to the throne and, particularly for the princes of intermediate ranking, producing instruments of affirmation and ascent on the world stage. It is no surprise, therefore, that Charles Emmanuel I, with his nine children, tried constantly to interject himself into continental diplomacy to secure matrimonial alliances with major European and Italian courts and royal houses in order to achieve both territorial expansion and, above all, to secure a royal title.[1]

In the context of constant searches by the court of Turin for the best possible (and feasible) solutions, these 'dynastic affinities', already extensively analysed by Toby Osborne, made a matrimonial union between the houses of Stuart and Savoy more than hypothetical and breathed new life into the centuries-old Anglo-Savoy relationship.[2]

It is no mere coincidence, therefore, that just six months after the ascent to the English throne of James I, on 22 September 1603, Filiberto Gherardo Scaglia di Verrua, ambassador of the Duke of Savoy at Rome, wrote in the margins of a memo about the progress of the Anglo-Spanish negotiations:

To renew the friendship between the King of Spain and England, with the strongest and most secure lineage that nature and the law of God have left to us, one could propose a marriage between a Savoy princess and the Prince of England.[3]

The diplomat's proposal was very tempting for Charles Emmanuel I, who sought marriages with kings or emperors for his daughters.[4] Two years later,

---

[1] Merlotti 2009.
[2] See Toby Osborne's chapter in this volume.
[3] 'Per rinnovare dunque l'amicitia fra i Re de Spagna e Inghilterra del più forte e più sicuro legname che ci habbi lasciato la natura, e la lege di Dio, si potrebbe proporre matrimonio d'una delle Principesse di Savoia col Principe d'Inghilterra.' *Relazione trasmessa da Roma dello Stato de' negoziati di Pace, che si maneggiavano tra le Corone d'Inghilterra e di Spagna* (1603), Turin National Archives (hereafter AST), Corte, Materie Politiche per il Rapporto all'Estero, Negoziazioni con Inghilterra e Olanda, Inghilterra, mz. 1, n. 3.
[4] Merlin 1991: 16–23.

the duke returned to the English hypothesis in the instruction 'circa il modo di regolarsi con altri principi' at the end of his last will and testament.[5] In this document, Princess Margherita was destined to marry the emperor, but if that marriage failed to take place, she might instead marry the Prince of Wales.

The Prince of Mantua could only be considered as a last-resort spouse. Isabella followed the fortunes of her elder sister. If she were to marry a prince of the Empire, then Isabella would have to marry the heir to the throne of England. However, in observance of the new course of Savoy foreign policy, three years later the two elder princesses married the Dukes of Mantua and Modena, respectively, thwarting the true aims of both of the princesses.[6]

For the whole of the first decade of the seventeenth century, the preoccupation of Charles Emmanuel I with England was real but aleatory,[7] and indeed, throughout this period there was no significant Savoy presence in Britain. It comes as no surprise that, in 1609, Nicolò Molin, Venetian ambassador to London, stated

For the Duke of Savoy, likewise due to distance and in order not to be indebted to the states of one prince or the other, there could be little occasion for disgust or for love.[8]

Although a Savoy legation was still a long way off, the Grand Duchy of Tuscany was working in England to engineer an Anglo-Tuscan marriage,[9] and the presence of the Medici family there was carefully monitored from Turin. The diplomatic war for primacy was underway among the Italian states: it began with the granting of the grand ducal title in 1569 by Pius V to Cosimo I de' Medici, and would end in favour of the Savoy dynasty only with the acquisition of a royal title.[10]

Despite Tuscan plans, the perception of England at the Savoy court changed radically only in the spring of 1610, when the Duke of Savoy

---

[5] Pennini (in press). The memo, dated 1605, is in the Turin archives; for the text, see: Ricotti 1865: II, 425–40.

[6] Spagnoletti 2003: 161–2.

[7] In 1604, the Venetian ambassador, Francesco Priuli, commenting on the international relations of Charles Emmanuel I, stated that, aside from the Spanish and French sovereigns, 'Dei altri re d'Europa non si cura il signor Duca, fuor che di quello d'Inghilterra' ('The Duke does not concern himself with other European kings, aside from the English sovereign'): Priuli 2006: 59.

[8] 'Del signor Duca di Savoja, medesimamente e per la lontananza e per non correre alcun interesse tra gli Stati dell'uno e dell'altro principe, poca occasion vi può esser di disgusto o di amore.' Firpo 1965: I, 543.

[9] Bazzoni 1871: 3–32; Crinò 1957: 7–40; Sodini 2001.

[10] Gribaudi 1904; Stumpo 1984; Panicucci 1996; Angiolini 2006; Osborne 2007a.

and Henri IV, King of France, signed an offensive and defensive alliance against the Habsburgs. This pact sealed the marriage between the Prince of Piedmont and Élisabeth of Bourbon and provided for an expansion of the coalition with England.[11] However, just a few days after the alliance was signed, the French king was assassinated and his widow, Maria de' Medici, who then ascended to the throne, decided against ratifying the treaty, thereby exposing the Duchy of Savoy to the reprisals of Felipe III. Caught in the embrace of Spain without the support of the French, the Turin court was forced to evaluate the alternatives, among which was the English crown.

The opportunity to begin negotiations leading to an Anglo-Savoy marital alliance came early in 1611, when Henry Wotton passed through Turin on his way back to London after a stint at the embassy in Venice. In the Savoy capital, the English diplomat was received by Charles Emmanuel I, who granted him at least three audiences, during which a possible matrimonial alliance between the English and Savoy crowns was discussed.[12] During his years in Venice, Wotton had already had an opportunity to discuss the Duke's vague matrimonial plans with the Savoy legates. Such plans coincided well with his proposals to establish Protestantism in Italy. It was no mere coincidence, therefore, that the English diplomat soon become London's point of contact for all ducal envoys.

Following the meeting in Turin, Charles Emmanuel I sent Claudio Cambiano di Ruffia, Count of Cartignano,[13] to London to negotiate a double wedding between the houses of Savoy and Stuart. This was the first time that explicit reference was made to a marriage between Elizabeth Stuart and Prince Victor Amadeus of Piedmont in the court circles of Turin.[14]

The count left Turin on 12 February 1611, and arrived in London after a stop in Paris on 22 March. He was welcomed to London by Wotton, who reaffirmed his complete support of the mission, although he urged the diplomat to refrain from immediately launching double marriage negotiations, suggesting that he concentrate instead on the more important union of the

---

[11] Marconcini 1965; Merlin 2010: 13–19.

[12] Smith 1907b: I, 114.

[13] Cambiano di Ruffia, son of Emmanuel Philibert's chamberlain, served as soldier and butler under Charles Emmanuel, who rewarded him for his service with the office of Count of Cartignano in 1609. Merlin 1991: 133.

[14] *Minuta d'Istruzione del Duca di Savoia Carlo Emanuele I al Conte di Cartignano per il di lui viaggio in Inghilterra a fare proposizione di matrimonio del figlio di suddetto duca con la Principessa figlia del Re della Gran Bretagna* (1611), AST, Corte, Materie Politiche per il Rapporto all'Interno, Matrimoni, mz. 25, n. 6.

Prince of Piedmont.[15] The arrival of Cartignano hardly went unnoticed and indeed the Piedmontese Count wrote to Turin the day after his arrival:

Many judgments were made about my coming and the French were doubtful, others wished that I had come to ask his Majesty not to help the Genevans, others made the most outrageous judgments that could possibly be made.[16]

An ignorance of and interest in this mission is also evidenced by the words of the ambassador to the Medici family, Ottaviano Lotto:

The gestures made toward him [Cartignano] are most favourable; and in this matter I believe it certain and very true that the aforementioned house [of Savoy] should be decorated and that the Ambassador should provide money from the king's purse; he should, as is usual, have returned to London next Saturday, the 26th; but out of respect for the ambassador he will return tomorrow, the 25th, and will grant him an audience tomorrow. Her Majesty the Queen has also returned. These extraordinary gestures make me believe that he brings something of taste.[17]

It would seem, therefore, that there was a discreet willingness to go ahead with these matrimonial negotiations. The only concession was that princess Elizabeth Stuart would not be required to convert to Catholicism before marrying.[18] The Count of Cartignano made no comment on the matter and the negotiations moved on to more practical matters. On 14 April 1611, the Count met with four of the king's closest advisors: Robert Cecil, Count of Salisbury, who strongly opposed the negotiations; Henry Howard, Count of Northampton; Thomas Howard, Count of Arundel; and Ludovic Stewart, Duke of Lennox. These gentlemen formed the 'commission' appointed by the King of England to draw up the marriage contract.

At this point, however, Ruffia was forced to leave the court of James I to return to the Duke of Savoy to report on what progress had been made, and also to obtain a mandate granting him full power of attorney in these matters. When he reached Turin, Ruffia presented Charles Emmanuel I

---

[15] Smith 1907b: I, 119.

[16] 'Si fanno molti giudicii sopra questa mia venuta et li francesi dubitano, altri vogliono sia venuto a richieder questa Maestà a non dar soccorso ai Ginevrini, altri fanno li più stravaganti giudicii che dir si possa.' *London, March 23rd 1611*, AST, Corte, Lettere Ministri, Inghilterra, mz. 1, n. 10.

[17] 'Le dimostrazioni che si fanno verso di lui [il Cartignano] sono favoritissime; et in questo punto credo cosa certa, et verissima che la sopraddetta casa [di Savoia] sia addobbata e l'ambasciatore spesato d'ordine et con borsa del re; il quale per ordinario doveva tornare a Londra il sabato futuro, alli 26; ma per rispetto di detto ambasciatore torna oggi S.M. alli 25, et domani gli dà udienza. Et è tornata anche la Maestà della regina. Queste straordinarie carezze fanno credere che egli porti qua cosa di gusto.' Guasti 1857: 57.

[18] Passamonti 1934–5: 287–8.

with an interesting report about England and the state of the negotiations. After explaining matters in England, Cartignano reflected at length in the document on reconquering Geneva and neighbouring territories. Indeed, an alliance with the pre-eminent Protestant power would make it possible to discourage the people of Geneva from pursuing what Turin referred to as 'usurpation'. Moreover, the diplomat claimed that, since France and Spain did not oppose an Anglo-Savoy union, the conditions were ideal for quickly signing the marriage contract. Another interesting issue was the succession to the throne. According to Cartignano, given the fact that the two male heirs were physically weak and therefore very unlikely to outlive their father, the marriage between the Prince of Piedmont and Elizabeth would likely lead the house of Savoy to take the English crown. The legate ended his report with the most convincing reason for pursuing the union: England was a strongly ascendant country, feared by the two powers bordering the Duchy. Consequently, an alliance would be a veritable 'life insurance policy' for the Savoy states.[19]

The report omitted mention of the relationship with the Vatican, which in no way approved of the arrival of a Protestant princess in Turin. Indeed the messenger of Savoy, Pietro Francesco Costa, reported to Rome that:

Count Ruffia told me that he had discussions in England about the marriage of this princess with that prince, but that they were difficult; with that proposal I made him understand that a marriage was not possible between Catholics and heretics, without a dispensation from the Pope.[20]

The marriage between the Prince of Piedmont and the daughter of James I could only proceed with the permission of Paul V, who, at the end of the summer of 1611, sent the monk, Paolo da Cesena,[21] to Charles Emmanuel I 'to state clearly to him the wish of His Beatitude that the proposal of marriage between his son and the heretic princess of England be withdrawn'.[22] The private meeting between the Duke and the papal legate took place

---

[19] *Relazione Cartignano*, AST, Corte, Materie Politiche per il Rapporto all'Interno, Matrimoni, mz. 25, n. 6.

[20] 'Il conte di Ruffia mi ha detto di haver tenuto ragionamento in Inghilterra del maritaggio di questa principessa con quel Prencipe; ma di havervi trovato difficultà; col qual proposito mi son lasciato intender seco non potersi contra dire matrimonio fra Cattolici et heretici, senza dispensa della sede Apostolica.' *Lettere di Monsignor Nunzio in Savoia al Signor Cardinal Borghese 1609–1612*, Archivio Segreto Vaticano (hereafter, ASV), Segreteria di Stato, Nunziatura di Savoia, b. 161.

[21] Paolo da Cesena was general of the Capuchin Order from 1613 to 1618. Marraccini 1748: III, 151, XLVII.

[22] To 'specificargli il desiderio di Sua Beatitudine che receda dal proposito di sposare suo figlio con la eretica principessa d'Inghilterra.' Siri 1677: II, 559.

on 18 September at the Monte dei Cappuccini above the capital. Charles Emmanuel, supported by three theologians,[23] concentrated on turning the situation around to his advantage. Indeed, while Rome was worried that the marriage might breathe new life into reform in Italy – as Wotton hoped – creating a dangerous precedent, he intended to instead maintain the view that an Anglo-Savoy union would in fact be the first step towards full reconversion of the British Isles to Catholicism. In any case, the Duke reaffirmed his fidelity to the Vatican and asked Paul V to find an alternative solution. On the other hand, the monk affirmed that, while the hope of converting the Princess was sufficient to begin negotiations, the wedding could not possibly proceed unless this conversion had taken place.[24]

The proposals from Savoy, however, were at odds with those of the real pretender to Elizabeth's hand: the Prince-elector of the Palatinate, Frederick V.[25] As the head of the Protestant Union, he needed to guarantee himself an heir and wanted to enter into an alliance with England, a country that he considered to be the greatest Protestant power in the world. James I and the Count of Salisbury considered this marriage to be an opportunity to play a major role among the German Protestant princes.[26]

Meanwhile, Cartignano's absence from London began to be felt. On 13 July, Ottaviano Lotto wrote:

Of the ambassador of the Duke of Savoy, who is awaited here, one no longer discusses; and there are many different judgments about his negotiations; indeed, it is believed that many things militate against them, and that, in the end, it will be the Count Palatine of the Rhine who will win the very noble and beautiful princess.[27]

Indeed, his second mission began only in October of 1611, and ended at the beginning of the following year, but the inertia in this game of matchmaking became clear in the autumn. Despite the fact that Cartignano tried to leverage the English Catholic community that would have preferred a

---

[23] The three theologians were Camillo Balbiani, theologian of the inquisition in Turin; Orazio Scozia, known for a report he compiled on Pope Gregory XIII (Pastor 1930: XIX, 50); and Father Isidoro Pentorio, Barnabite, legate to the Savoy dynasty, for whom he carried out several diplomatic missions, including that in Milan during the first Monferrato crisis (Ricotti 1865: IV, 45). *Pareri di diversi teologi sopra il quesito fattogli se un Principe Cattolico possa accasarsi con una principessa eretica* (1611), AST, Corte, Materie Politiche per il Rapporto all'Interno, Matrimoni, mz. 25, n. 6.

[24] Passamonti 1934: 293–305.

[25] Pursell 2003.

[26] Strong 1986a: 79–80.

[27] 'Dell'ambasciator del signor duca di Savoia, che si aspetta qua, non se ne ragiona più; et per conto dei suoi negozii i giudizi sono molto differenti; anzi si crede, che tante cose militino in contrario, che alla fine il conte palatino del Reno sia per ottener egli la vittoria nobilissima e bellissima principessa.' Guasti 1857: 60.

marriage between Elizabeth and Felipe III (who had recently been wid-owed), the lack of consent from Rome and the vague attitude of Spain elim-inated any remaining hopes of sealing the marriage deal. The messenger confirmed, with no small degree of malice, the failure of the Savoy mission to England:

The Secretary of Count Ruffia came here in the diligence [stage coach] of England and it is unknown precisely how much he brought, however it means that His Highness did not have the satisfaction that he had sought in that negotiation.[28]

Following the failure of these first matrimonial negotiations with England, plans for Victor Amadeus were put on hold until 1617 (also partly due to war-related events). Subsequently negotiations were begun in the hopes of securing a marital alliance with the young Christine of France.

While negotiations involving the Prince of Piedmont were put on hold, for reasons relating to age, gender and political opportunity, the court of Turin was now forced to focus its attention on the marriages of the Princesses Maria Apollonia and Francesca Caterina. Between 1611 and 1612, the Duke, after evaluating various possibilities, opted for the two solutions that he presumed would contribute most to the dynasty's greater prestige. The younger of the sisters, Caterina, was destined to marry Henri, Duke of Nemours, a member of a lesser branch of the Savoy family and head of the party opposing the monarchy in France. The Duke hoped to marry Maria off, on the other hand, to the Prince of Wales, and to continue negotiations with the English court.[29]

At the end of 1611, after Cartignano's English negotiations for an alli-ance for Victor Amadeus had failed, discussions about the marriage between the Duke of Nemours and Caterina, so strongly desired by Turin but opposed by Madrid,[30] also collapsed.[31] At this point, all the efforts of

---

[28] 'È venuto qua in diligenza d'Inghilterra il Secretario del Signor Conte di Ruffia, et non si sa precisamente quanto habbia portato, si intende nondimeno che Sua Altezza non ha avuto in quella negotiatione la soddisfattione che desiderava.' *Lettere di Monsignor Nunzio in Savoia al Signor Cardinal Borghese 1609–1612*, ASV, Segreteria di Stato, Nunziatura di Savoia, b. 161.

[29] Bianchi 1936: 21–34.

[30] The marriage would have led to the reincorporation of the territories overlooking Geneva (which were owned by the Duke of Nemours), into the Duchy of Savoy, strengthening the Savoy presence at the French court.

[31] On 26 September 1611 armed French soldiers, led by the secretary of the Duke of Nemours, entered the home of the secretary of the Spanish agent in Turin to frighten him. The Spanish agent immediately reported this event to the Duke of Savoy, who, however, did not give him the diplomatic apology ('soddisfatione') requested by the court of Madrid. Infuriated, the Spanish rejected any initiatives of the Savoy legates. This diplomatic fracas ended with a stalling of the planned nuptials and the departure of the Duke of Nemours from the Savoy capital. Ricotti 1865: IV, 20–7; Bianchi 1936: 31–8.

Savoy converged, not without some difficulty,[32] on the proposed marriage of Maria in England. Once again, the great opponent of the Savoy was the Count of Salisbury, who thought it appropriate to marry the heir to the throne of England to a princess of a major power, even a Catholic. However, the failures of the weddings planned by three English courts in German territory and the death of the influential minister, breathed new life into the Savoy schemes.[33]

Two obstacles remained in the way of Savoy diplomacy: Maria de' Medici, who supported the Tuscan legates who had been negotiating between the Prince of Wales and a princess of the Medici family, but did not rule out the idea of a marriage to one of her own daughters; and Paul V, who was unlikely to grant his *placet*.

The problems of the negotiating table did not end there, however. Indeed, while negotiations carried out by the Count of Cartignano never got to the point of discussing money matters, the potential dowry became a pivotal issue because England found itself in a phase of considerable financial and social difficulty and needed both money and stability. The Anglo-Savoy marriage would not resolve either matter satisfactorily especially since the Savoy treasury was not particularly healthy either, and a princess from a devoutly Catholic family like Maria's would be unlikely to quell unrest within England's Protestant community. The absence of important rivals to the marriage, however, worked in favour of Charles Emmanuel I. Indeed, despite the fact that James I still had hopes of a marriage alliance with Spain, the only direct rival for the marriage to the Prince of Wales remained the Grand Duchy of Tuscany.

The Franco-Tuscan 'syndicate' came out in full force in the double mission of July 1612, when the French ambassador to London tried to prevent an acceleration of the Savoy negotiations while Tuscan legates headed to Rome to consider the *affaires religieuses*.[34] The worries of the court of Turin centred mainly on this second aspect of the mission. While the transalpine mission could be addressed with careful diplomatic policy in England, if the Pope approved the Tuscan marriage to the detriment of the Piedmontese union the Savoy delegation was undoubtedly destined to fail.

---

[32] 'In Inghilterra non bisogna pensarci havendo così assicurato il Conte di Cartignano essendo i pensieri di quel Re già volti e stabiliti altrove' ('In England there is no need to worry, the Count of Cartignano assured, as the thoughts of that King have already turned to other options'). *Matrimonio di Caterina con il duca di Nemours*, AST, Corte, Materie Politiche per il Rapporto all'Interno, Matrimoni, mz. 25, n. 7.

[33] Passamonti 1934: 496.

[34] Villani 2009: 217–33.

It was no coincidence that, in July of 1612, the relationship between Charles Emmanuel I and Luigi Lorenzo Birago, Count of Vische and ducal ambassador to the Papacy, became closer.[35] Turin's worries were well founded: on 7 July, the agent of Savoy in Rome wrote to the Duke that, despite the church being somewhat surprised by his proposals, the Florentines were negotiating the wedding with the Pope. Despite a certain amount of scepticism on the part of Vische, negotiations for permission continued all summer long, and in the middle of August the Piedmontese diplomat informed Charles Emmanuel I of the rumours that were circulating in Rome: in order to be allowed to take place, the marriage would have to be celebrated according to Catholic rites. At this point – and for the first time – Charles Emmanuel I feared seriously that he would lose out to Cosimo II.[36] This fear was evident in the instructions given by the Duke to Giovanni Battista Gabaleone, banker, diplomatic statesman and one of the leading protagonists of the London negotiations between 1612 and 1613.[37]

If it is told to you, and it is true, that the Florentines are pursuing the negotiation actively, with many offers of money, and that it is feared that the King might find himself in poverty, do not be influenced by that, you can suggest to them that it is unbelievable that such a great king would not still want to make a difference in the circumstances of one house to another: in any event he knows, and has always said to him, that he would not remain for money, and you who went with him to reassure him of this that there is no further need for concern about the amount of the dowry, unless His Majesty commands, that is that she likes him, however much we beg her, I do not want to put my daughter into competition [as part of a deal] against the Florentine [daughter], because there are so many differences in status we would feel that this way of dealing is wrong, more than anything else, and we would assure His Majesty that we would never act in this unworthy way.[38]

---

[35] Merlotti 2006: 251–2.

[36] Strong 1986b: 63–75.

[37] Merlotti 1998: 817–19.

[38] 'Se vi dicesse, che è vero, che i fiorentini cacciano il negozio vivamente, con molte offerte di danari e che teme che, per trovarsi il Re in strettezza, non inclini da quella parte, potrete soggiungerli, che non credibile, che un così gran Re non volesse far ancora differenza dalla conditione di una Casa all'altra: tuttavia egli sa, che sempre se gli è detto, che per il denaro, non restarebbe, ed che voi siete andato colà per assicurarlo di quello stesso ed che non occorre altro in materia della somma della dote, salvo Sua Maestà comandi ciò che le piace, ma che ben la supplichiamo, a non voler mettere in bilancia, né in concorrenza, mia figlia, con quella di Fiorenza, perché, come vi è tanta differenza di conditione, sentiressimo questa forma di trattare più di ogni altra cosa et l'assicuriamo che Sua Maestà non ci farà mai questo torto.' *Istruttione al conte Gabaleone per il suo viaggio in Inghilterra in ordine alla trattazione del matrimonio della Principessa Maria con il Principe di Galles primogenito di S.M.* (1612), AST, Corte, Materie Politiche per il Rapporto all'Interno, Matrimoni, mz. 25, n. 7.

The Duke of Savoy used the lever of prestige, reminding his legate and, consequently, the King of England that an Anglo-Tuscan wedding would be a *mésalliance* for Henry. However, the pitfalls to the ambitions of Savoy were not restricted to the manoeuvres of the Grand Duchy. At the end of the summer, the Parisian court, while continuing to support Cosimo II, began to think of an English marriage for a *fille de France*, while the Catholic church, seeking to make peace with James I, looked into the possibility of an Anglo-Spanish marriage.

On 16 July, Fulvio Pergamo – another Savoy agent in Whitehall – sent Turin a report recounting the audience that the Spanish delegation had held with the King of England. Not wishing to instigate a diplomatic crisis, he accepted the apology of the Catholic crown for its negotiations in France. However, Pergamo emphasized that, as a result of this meeting, James I was no longer convinced of the honesty of Spain's intentions.[39] Having ruled out a wedding to one of his daughters, Felipe III gave his direct support to the Savoy mission.[40]

During the summer of 1612, Giovanni Battista Gabaleone and Fulvio Pergamo worked hard to dispel the mistrust of the English crown, while the Tuscan delegation had encountered a different attitude. Indeed, while the Grand Duchy had no difficulty in finding economic resources, it was hard pressed to affirm its dynastic prestige. Charles Emmanuel I had no problems about the rank of his family, but he definitely had a limited 'budget' at his disposal. At the end of August, Gabaleone sent a declaration given to him by Wotton, stating that:

Florence offered seven hundred thousand scudi, and they would doubtless offer as much as one million, and France produced a million in cash and another hundred toward the education of the daughter according to their ways, with a hundred other situations by a very astute man.[41]

Parallel to the negotiations conducted by Gabaleone, Maria de' Medici proposed a marriage between the Prince of Wales and her daughter, Christine. Anglo-French negotiations, while informal, were much swifter than those conducted with Savoy, and within the space of a month, the two parties had succeeded in finding an agreement for the dowry (a million escudos) and on the Princess' religion (compliant with that of the groom).

---

[39] *London, July 26th 1612*, AST, Corte, Lettere Ministri, Inghilterra, mz. 1, n. 12.

[40] Claretta 1872: 98–9.

[41] 'Firenze haveva offerto settecento millia scudi che ne darà senz'altro sino a un millione, et che Francia essibisce un millione de contanti, et la figlia da educarla a modo loro con altre cento circostanze da huomo molto astuto.' *London, August 23rd 1612*, AST, Corte, Lettere Ministri, Inghilterra, mz. 1, n. 13.

The only unsolved problem regarded Christine's age, as she was too young to be married immediately.[42]

Despite the increasing fierceness of the Franco-Medicean competition, on 22 September Gabaleone wrote to Turin that James I, in a private audience, had stated that:

only Carlo Emanuele had honored me more than all of the princes of Christianity put together, by having asked me at that time, for the daughter and now, for the son; marriages are chosen in heaven and concluded on earth, should that which you wish to see come about, I shall always be in your debt.[43]

It is not entirely clear whether the Savoy legate's optimism reflected the reality of his personal convictions or whether it indicated a choice made to reassure the Duke. What is certain, however, is that things were not exactly the way Gabaleone had represented them to the court of Turin. At the beginning of the autumn, two facts caused the Savoy diplomatic world to tremble. The first was that, on 25 September, after the dramatic failure of the Tuscan legations and a first meeting, matrimonial negotiations between the English and French courts for the marriage between Henry Stuart and Christine of Bourbon officially began. The second was the triumphal arrival in London of the Elector Palatine for his engagement to Elizabeth Stuart, confirming the lack of intention by the English court to return to the Catholic Church. Having acknowledged this news, while the merchant from Chieri remained confident that the much desired result would be achieved, on 16 October Charles Emmanuel I requested that the negotiations be completed as quickly as possible.[44] On 28 October, in an encrypted letter, Gabaleone admitted that he faced obstacles, reporting that the Archbishop of Canterbury and the whole Anglican Church were fiercely opposed to the wedding between the heir to the throne and a Catholic princess. Furthermore, the legate was forced to admit that English support for – or perhaps it would be better to say, absence of opposition to – a new enterprise in Geneva was impossible.[45]

---

[42] Passamonti 1934: 509.

[43] 'Che Carlo Emanuele solo mi ha più honorato nel farmi richiedere all'hora la figlia et hora il figlio che tutti i Principi della Cristianità insieme; i matrimoni si eleggono in Cielo e si concludono in terra, avvenga ciò che si voglia sarò sempre obbligato a Sua Altezza.' *London, September 22nd 1612*, AST, Corte, Lettere Ministri, Inghilterra, mz. 1, n. 13.

[44] *Diverse lettere del Duca di Savoia Carlo Emanuele primo, del Cardinale Maurizio e del Principe Tomaso suoi figlioli al Cavalier Gabaleone ambasciatore del Duca in Londra per negoziare il matrimonio della Principessa Maria di lui figlia col Principe di Galles, che non ebbe effetto per la morte immatura di questo* (1612), AST, Corte, Materie Politiche per il Rapporto all'Interno, Matrimoni, mz. 25, n. 7.

[45] *London, August 23rd 1612*, AST, Corte, Lettere Ministri, Inghilterra, mz. 1, n. 13; Guasti 1857: 277–8.

At the end of October, despite considerable efforts by the agents and the good relationship between the King of England and Charles Emmanuel I, the Savoy delegation encountered the unfavourable opinion of the marriage held by the Church of England and shared by much of the court. This firm opposition, together with the absence of an agreement between Savoy and the Pope, and the need of James I to calm unrest within the realm, made it increasingly difficult to find a positive solution. The Anglo-French negotiations, which had replaced those with Tuscany, seemed much more agile. Unlike the Duke of Savoy, Maria de' Medici had more money and greater political independence from the Pope, which made it easier for her to comply with requests from London.[46]

Study of the archival documents demonstrates that the success of the Anglo-Savoy marriage was very unlikely indeed, yet in one of his essays, the English historian, Roy Strong, claims with certainty that this marriage was essentially a foregone conclusion.[47] Nevertheless, an imponderable event occurred that ruined every diplomatic effort, namely, the death of Prince Henry (Fig. 2.1).[48] Henry's death and the consequent passage of the title of Prince of Wales to his younger brother, Charles, completely changed the English scenario and forced all stakeholders to reevaluate their plans and positions.

In the spring of 1613, Marquis Francesco Villa[49] travelled from Turin to express his condolences. He also had to observe the new balance of powers at Whitehall and request English support in the first crisis of the Monferrato. Meanwhile, in the English capital, the dogged work of Gabaleone continued unabated (along with that of his whole entourage) to recommence negotiations for the marriage of Princess Maria of Savoy to the new heir to the English throne.

The Savoy position in relation to the previous negotiations had deteriorated considerably, because the greatest advantage of Savoy diplomacy had over that of France – Christine's age in relation to that of the prince – had ceased to be important. Indeed, while the third daughter of the Queen of France was too young to marry Prince Henry, Maria and her sister Caterina were – most probably – too old to marry Charles Stuart.[50]

---

[46] Villani 2009: 229.

[47] 'If Henry had not died on 6 November 1612, he would have married a daughter of Charles Emmanuel, Duke of Savoy'; see: Strong 1986b: 60.

[48] *London, November 12th 1612*, AST, Corte, Lettere Ministri, Inghilterra, mz. 1, n. 13.

[49] Because of his close relationship with Cardinal Aldobrandini, Francesco Villa, descended from a noble Ferrarese family, entered the service of Charles Emmanuel. At the beginning of the seventeenth century, he became state advisor and chamberlain, and in 1602 was honoured with the title of Knight of the Order of the Annunziata. AST, Corte, Materie Politiche per il Rapporto all'Interno, Ordini Militari, Ordine della SS. Annunziata, mz. 4, n. 3.

[50] Maria was born in 1594, Caterina in 1595, while Christine of France was born in 1606. Henry was also born in 1594, while Charles was born in 1600.

Figure 2.1 Robert Peake, the Elder, *Henry Frederick Stuart, Prince of Wales*, oil on canvas, c. 1604–10, Palazzo Reale, Ministero dei Beni e delle Attività Culturali e del Turismo, Polo Reale di Torino.

The issue of age was further complicated by the difficult contingencies for the House of Savoy after the attack on Monferrato, as well as by the mistrust and diplomatic isolation of the Kingdom of Spain, which, as mentioned earlier, following the collapse of the marriage to one of the Spanish *infantas*, had always supported an Anglo-Savoy wedding for dynastic and family reasons.[51] There were three reasons for the Spanish impasse in London: the succession to the Imperial throne after the death of Rodolfo II; the continuing growth of the English Catholic movement sustained by Madrid; and – last but not least – the American matter of Virginia, over the possession of which there was considerable friction between the two crowns.

French agents in London were aware of the weakness of the Spanish party and, consequently, of that of Savoy, and they were counting on signing

[51] *Gabaleone to Asti* (25 February 1613), The National Archives, State Foreign Papers, SP 92/ 1, f. 90.

a rough agreement quickly. In the overall framework of rearming in view of a new religious battle, France's hybrid position in relation to the Protestants made an alliance with England possible, without too many consequences for fragile internal balances on the other side of the Channel.

The differences between the Kingdom of France and the Duchy of Savoy were related to economy and prestige, but what tipped the scales in favour of Paris was also the amount of time available. Indeed, while the French were perfectly able to sit and wait while the English court took its time, the Savoy delegation needed to reach an agreement quickly, since it faced political difficulties elsewhere and, above all, it had no diplomatic support. The King of England, for his part, was assessing every possible solution. France was offering plenty of money, which was appealing in view of the empty English coffers, meaning there was little Protestant objection to an Anglo-French marriage. However, French projects for expansion in North America and the influence of the French state in Europe slowed down the court's initial enthusiasm in London. Spain, on the other hand, offered the prestige of a family – the Hapsburgs – who ruled half of Europe and almost the entire American continent, where James intended to recover the money he needed to settle his debts. At the same time, however, the Spanish power did not guarantee sufficient liquidity to help England, and its army was spread across too many fronts to be able to do more than maintain the status quo. Moreover, Protestant circles looked with mistrust at the support the Spanish crown in Madrid continued to provide to Catholic dissidents in England.

Despite the Savoy diplomats' incessant pleading for a marriage, the small Savoy duchy, compared to the two main rivals of the 'century of iron', had very little to offer James I. At the beginning of August 1613, the Spanish ambassador to London informed the Duke of Savoy through his legate that

Truly Your Highness is a worthy prince, but in terms of a marriage it seems that there are two major difficulties that block the plans you had: the first is the significant age difference, the second is the dowry that for Your Majesty was a considerable burden, especially due to the recent wars, which meant you could not do great things, one had hoped that Your Majesty might have obtained six hundred thousand scudi in cash from a certain private individual that would have been very useful, a hundred thousand could have been given to the country.[52]

---

[52] 'Veramente Vostra Altezza è principe che merita, ma al matrimonio li parea ci siano due difficoltà assai potenti per impedir li suoi disegni quando l'havesse: la prima l'età molto differente, la seconda la dote che havendo havuto Vostra Altezza molte gravezze et particolarmente in queste ultime guerre non poteva far grandi cose, sì bene sperava da un certo privato che Vostra Altezza haveva havuto da un privato da seicento mila scuti contanti che potevano servire, cento milla potrebbe dare il paese.' London August 8th 1613, AST, Corte, Lettere Ministri, Inghilterra, mz. 1, n. 13.

At the end of the summer of 1613, despite a succession of other half-hearted attempts,[53] and until 1622, all hopes of marriage between Maria of Savoy and Charles Stuart faded further. The English prince indeed eventually married a French princess (Henrietta Maria of Bourbon, youngest child of Henri IV), but not Christine, who, ironically, went on to become the Duchess of Savoy. Maria, on the other hand, along with her sister Caterina, became a nun.

---

[53] *Discorsi sopra altri matrimoni progettati della suddette* (1611–22), AST, Corte, Materie Politiche per il Rapporto all'Interno, Matrimoni, mz. 25, n. 7.

3 | The Court of Turin and the English Succession, 1712–20

EDWARD CORP

By the year 1708 the War of the Spanish Succession had already lasted for more than six years and the French had been defeated at Blenheim, Ramillies and Turin. The Franco-Jacobite attempt to turn the tide by invading Scotland had failed, and the French army, in which the Stuart King James III was serving as a volunteer, was about to be defeated at Oudenarde. It was at this time that the under-secretary of state at the Stuart court at Saint-Germain-en-Laye discovered that six junior Jacobite officers were planning to assassinate Victor Amadeus II, Duke of Savoy.

The Duke was the father-in-law of two of Louis XIV's grandsons, the duc de Bourgogne and King Philip V of Spain, and was thereby closely linked to the Bourbons. But he had changed sides in the war in 1703, considerably weakening the French by obliging Louis to deploy an entire army to protect Provence against an attack from Piedmont. Anything which weakened France also reduced the prospects of a Stuart restoration, so the group of six Jacobites determined to assassinate the Duke of Savoy hoped significantly to influence the future course of the war. The Duke, they said, was 'the author of all of France's misfortunes and consequently those of their own king'.[1]

To obtain this information the under-secretary had sworn a solemn oath not to give away the plan to anyone in France. He therefore wrote to a friend serving in the Prussian army outside France and asked him to thwart the assassination plot by alerting King Frederick I.[2] As a result the King of Prussia wrote to the Duke of Savoy shortly before the assassins planned to strike, and the plot came to nothing.[3]

This incident raises the obvious question: why did the under-secretary at Saint-Germain betray the plan to assassinate the Duke, if the latter's death would have strengthened France and thus increased the prospects of a Stuart restoration? One answer, of course, is that most people were instinctively opposed to political assassination. But there is another answer: the

---

[1] British Library (hereafter BL.) Add MSS 61254, fol. 88, Nairne to Aikenhead, 23 June 1708.
[2] BL. Add MSS 61254, fol. 89, Nairne to Aikenhead, 23 June 1708.
[3] BL. Add MSS 61254, fol. 87, Frederick I to Victor Amadeus II, from Golize, 22 September 1708.

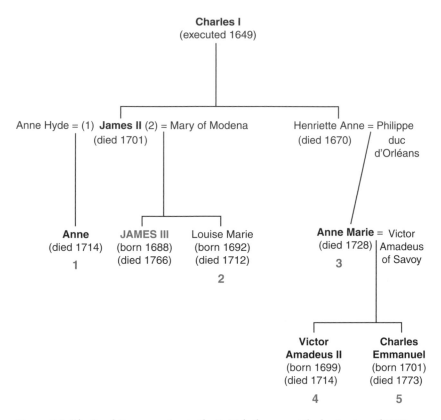

Figure 3.1 The Jacobite succession to the British thrones at the beginning of 1712. Diagram by author.

Duke of Savoy's wife and elder son were third and fourth in the legitimist or Jacobite line of succession to the British thrones.

The House of Savoy had been dynastically linked to the Stuarts since two sisters of Louis XIII of France had married Duke Victor Amadeus I of Savoy and King Charles I of England. James II, who succeeded as King of England in 1685, was therefore the first cousin of Charles Emmanuel II of Savoy, and first cousin once removed of the latter's son Victor Amadeus II who succeeded as duke in 1675. The link had been greatly strengthened in 1684 when James II's niece, his sister's daughter Anne-Marie de Bourbon Orléans, had married Victor Amadeus II.

In the winter of 1688–9 James II had been deposed in the Glorious Revolution and replaced on the thrones of England, Scotland and Ireland by William and Mary. The change had then been given statutory sanction in the Bill of Rights, which excluded all Catholics from the succession. Yet many people – the Jacobites – remained loyal to James II and to his son, who succeeded him in exile as James III, and refused to recognize the legitimacy of Catholic exclusion. As the years went by, these people turned their attention increasingly to the Duchess of Savoy.

From 1702, when the War of the Spanish Succession started and William and Mary were both dead, until 1712, the line of succession to the British thrones was as follows (Fig. 3.1). James III, the only legitimate son of James II, was the Jacobite king. In the event of his death the Jacobite throne would pass *first* to his elder half-sister Anne (the de facto queen in England) who had no surviving children, and then, *second*, to James's younger sister, Princess Louise-Marie, born in exile in 1692; *third*, to his first cousin Anne-Marie, daughter of James II's sister Henriette-Anne, who was the wife of Victor Amadeus II, Duke of Savoy and now known as Anne Marie; *fourth*, to Anne Marie's elder son, the Prince of Piedmont, also called Victor Amadeus, born in 1699; and *fifth*, to Anne Marie's second son, Charles Emmanuel, born in 1701.

At the time of the assassination plot, in 1708, James III was only twenty years old and unmarried. His sister Louise-Marie was only sixteen. Had they both died without children, then the Jacobite claim to the British thrones would have passed after the death of Queen Anne to the Duchess of Savoy and her two sons. And such an eventuality was by no means unlikely. In 1711 and 1712 the courts of Versailles and Saint-Germain were hit by deadly illness. The Dauphin died of smallpox in 1711, and both the duc and duchesse de Bourgogne died of measles in 1712. As it happened, both James III and Louise-Marie contracted smallpox in 1712. The princess died, but James recovered.[4] By 1712, therefore, the Duchess of Savoy was one step closer to the British thrones. And when Queen Anne died in 1714 Anne Marie became the immediate heiress-presumptive in the Jacobite succession. It was obvious to all Jacobites, and of course to Duke Victor Amadeus, that the House of Savoy had a very real prospect of inheriting the legitimist or Jacobite claim to the British thrones. In the event James III did not marry until 1719, and did not have a son and heir until December 1720.[5] Throughout that period, therefore, the prospects of the Jacobite movement were linked to the ambitions of the family of the Duke of Savoy. Therefore it must be considered what the attitude of Victor Amadeus II was to the prospect of his wife and son inheriting a kingdom.

Obtaining royal status had in fact been a fundamental Sabaudian diplomatic goal for most of the seventeenth century. The Dukes of Savoy had

[4] Corp 2004a: 280.
[5] For the exiled Stuart court during these years, see: Corp 2009; 2013.

claimed to be the *de jure* Kings of Cyprus since 1485, though the claim had been allowed to lapse during the sixteenth century. In 1632 it had been formally re-asserted by Victor Amadeus's grandfather, and since then the Dukes of Savoy had done all they could to obtain the 'trattamento reale', that is to be treated as a sovereign 'royal highness' rather than a 'serene highness'. By the 1690s Victor Amadeus had succeeded in his aim. Partly as a result of dynastic marriages, particularly by joining the Habsburgs in the League of Augsburg in 1690, and finally by making it a condition of the marriage of his daughter to Louis XIV's grandson the duc de Bourgogne in 1696, Victor Amadeus had obtained what he wanted: he was entitled to use the closed crown of a king, he dined with a 'nef' on his table and his ambassadors were treated as equal to the ambassadors of the other European kings.[6]

Being a sovereign 'royal highness' was not, however, the same as being a sovereign 'royal king', and this distinction was emphasized in 1701 when the Elector of Brandenburg was formally recognized as being King in Prussia. Exercising the 'trattamento reale' therefore took on a new dimension. Victor Amadeus determined to exploit his strategic position straddling the Alps and northern Italy to obtain a kingdom.[7]

This might have made him an active Jacobite, and indeed his French wife and French mother could be described as such.[8] When the English Parliament passed the Act of Settlement in 1701, excluding all non-Anglicans from the royal succession, and establishing the Dowager Electress of Hanover as heiress to Queen Anne, the Duke of Savoy authorized his wife to issue a formal protestation against this violation of her hereditary

---

[6] Oresko 1997: 272–3, 316, 343, 345–6. The Duke of Savoy had been accorded the 'trattamento reale' by the King of England since 1682, but Victor Amadeus II took advantage of the War of the League of Augsburg to obtain it from France. After waiting to see who would win the war in Ireland, he formally broke with James II in 1690 and recognized William III and Mary II as joint monarchs of England, Scotland and Ireland. He then joined the League of Augsburg against France. In 1696 he made a separate peace with Louis XIV to obtain the 'trattamento reale' and once again recognized James II as king. In writing to say how pleased she was, Mary of Modena told him that 'j'ay vû pour quelque temps avec grand regret un eloignement apparent entre les plus proches que le sang et l'amitié avoient si fortement liez ensemble' (Historical Manuscripts Commission (1902–23) (hereafter HMC), I, 120, 3 November 1696). Despite this, Victor Amadeus again recognized William III in 1697 (Oresko 1991: 371; Storrs 1999: 152).

[7] Oresko 1997: 348.

[8] Oresko 2004: 34, 39. See, for example, HMC *Stuart* IV, 143, Dowager Duchess of Savoy (Madama Reale) to Mary of Modena, 27 March 1718: 'j'ay toujours conservé dans mon coeur les anciens sentimens pleins d'estime et de respect dans lesquels V.M. m'aura de tout temps connue à son égard et dont les expressions n'ont cessé que par les temps malheureux qui avoient à mon grand regret interrompu tout commerce.'

rights to the English throne.[9] But in fact this seems to have been no more than a negotiating position. Victor Amadeus' sights were set elsewhere.

The death of Charles II of Spain in 1700 had not, as expected by many, resulted in the partition of the Spanish Empire. Instead Louis XIV's second grandson, the duc d'Anjou, had inherited both Spain and her entire Empire – in the New World, but also in Italy. The result was the War of the Spanish Succession, in which the Austrian Habsburgs challenged the right of Philip V to be King of Spain, demanding a partition of the Spanish Empire which would at least give the Kingdoms of Naples and Sicily and the Duchy of Milan to the Archduke Charles (later Emperor Charles VI). Savoy entered the war on the side of the two Bourbons, Louis XIV and Philip V, but it soon became clear that there was nothing to be gained from them. Changing sides and supporting the Habsburgs, however, offered the prospect of obtaining the Kingdom of Sicily in any future partition of the Spanish Empire. That is exactly what Victor Amadeus did in 1703. Yet the Austrian Habsburgs were allied to the Dutch and to the Whig government of Queen Anne, both of them committed to maintaining the Act of Settlement and the Hanoverian Succession. This meant, of course, that the Duke of Savoy had thrown in his lot with the anti-Jacobites, and that his own ambition to become a king came into direct conflict with the pretensions of his wife to succeed to the British thrones. Victor Amadeus was prepared to take advantage of his wife's claim to strengthen his own negotiating position, and no doubt he genuinely regretted that he could not support her claim. But the practical result was that James III could not expect any support from the court of Turin. Both the Duchess and the Dowager Duchess of Savoy remained extremely well disposed,[10] but the Duke himself would do nothing to alienate either the Habsburgs or the ministers of Queen Anne, because that would undermine his hopes of becoming King of Sicily in any peace settlement at the end of the war.

When the peace treaties were signed at Utrecht and Rastadt in 1713 and 1714, Philip V remained King of Spain, but the Spanish Empire in Italy was partitioned between the Austrian Habsburgs and the Duke of Savoy. Victor Amadeus and his wife Anne Marie travelled to Palermo for their coronation as King and Queen of Sicily in 1713 and remained there until September 1714 (Fig. 0.1).[11] It was while they were there that Queen Anne died and the Hanoverian Succession came into effect. Princess Louise-Marie had

---

[9]   Storrs 1999: 152. The protestation was dated 6 April 1701, and there is a copy in Paris, Archives Diplomatiques, CP Angleterre 211.

[10] Oresko 2004: 39.

[11] Oresko 2004: 40–1.

died in 1712, Queen Anne was now dead, and James III was still unmarried. The Duchess of Savoy, now Queen of Sicily, was therefore the Jacobite heiress (Fig. 3.2).[12]

The partition of the Spanish Empire was never accepted by Philip V as a permanent solution, so Victor Amadeus's possession of Sicily depended in large part on the support of Great Britain, the United Provinces and Austria as guarantors of the peace settlement of Utrecht-Rastadt. The new King of Sicily could not afford to lose the support of the Mediterranean fleets of the two maritime powers, or of the Habsburg army stationed in the Kingdom of Naples, so all attempts by James III to stimulate his backing for the Jacobite cause were bound to fail. As King Victor Amadeus put it to James in January 1715, 'he did protest he wished him all happyness imaginable, and would even be ready to contribute to it, whenever it lay in his power, provided' – and this of course was what mattered – 'provided it was not directly contrary to the good of his country and family'.[13]

By the Treaty of Utrecht James III was obliged to leave Saint-Germain and move his court to the Duchy of Lorraine. It was from there that he made his way secretly through France to join the Jacobite rising in Scotland led by the Earl of Mar in the winter of 1715–16. The failure of that rising coincided with the death of Louis XIV, and left James III dependent on the support of Spain and the hospitality of the Pope. Philip V and James III both wanted to revise the peace settlement by recovering the Spanish possessions in Italy and overthrowing the Hanoverian Succession. Victor Amadeus II, George I, the Habsburg Emperor Charles VI and the Dutch, now supported by the duc d'Orléans as Regent of France, were committed to *maintaining* the settlement. No longer welcome in either France or Lorraine, James moved his court to Avignon. It was there, in the autumn of 1716, that he developed a fistula necessitating an operation that might have killed him. If he had died at that time, still unmarried and with no direct heir, then Queen Anne Marie of Sicily would have become the new Jacobite monarch of Great Britain and Ireland, and Victor Amadeus would have been placed in the embarrassing and even dishonourable position of not supporting his wife's legitimate claims. There was obvious relief in Turin

---

[12]　See: Storrs 1999: 153. 'Victor Amadeus' relations with the Jacobite court in exile, especially after 1713, have hardly been dealt with in the secondary literature.'

[13]　HMC *Stuart*, I, 342, Berwick to James III, 11 January 1715. See also HMC *Stuart* II, 44, F. Oglethorpe to Mar, 28 March 1715: 'the King of Sicily … desired … to inform our master of his zeal for his interest … he [Victor Amadeus] desired … to assure our master that, if ever he [James] attempted anything again he should always find him ready to serve him, and that their own affairs must be very bad if they did not assist him.'

when the news was received in November 1716 that James III had recovered.[14] As the Jacobite representative in Turin put it, 'this King's politics are more inclined to present preservation than to future hopes'.[15]

Despite this, while James III was at Avignon in 1716 he did all he could to obtain the support of the King of Sicily, though he must have realized that he had no real prospect of success. His overtures to Victor Amadeus had two aims. The first was to persuade him to employ Scottish soldiers who had been forced into exile after the failure of the recent Jacobite rising. Both France and Spain had recruited regiments of Irish troops after the defeat of James II in Ireland in 1691, and the colonels of those regiments wielded influence at Paris and Madrid. James III hoped that Victor Amadeus would be tempted to recruit some of the new Scottish exiles, and thereby accept Jacobite influence at Turin.[16] It soon became clear that Victor Amadeus was not prepared to do this,[17] and the reason was not hard to find, as the Jacobite representative at Turin explained:

George has just now begun to pay him [Victor Amadeus] what was due by the late Queen, which was ordered by Parliament a year ago. Part of the money he has received, the rest is coming from England so that he dares not do anything to disoblige George.[18]

The idea of recruiting Scottish soldiers was therefore dropped.

James III's second aim in his negotiations with the King of Sicily was more important, but equally unsuccessful. As he put it in June 1716: 'we have but too good ground to apprehend that we shall be very soon forced to leave our present residence and that we should be obliged to reside somewhere in Italy'. Not wanting to enter the Papal States, he therefore sent one of his courtiers to entreat the Queen of Sicily to persuade her husband to 'allow us to reside somewhere in his territories'.[19] The envoy reported back in July that:

The Queen made great professions of her readiness to serve you, but said the necessity the King was under of keeping fair with the Elector [namely George I] on account of Sicily, would not, she feared, permit him to comply with what was desired, [but] that she would speak to him notwithstanding.

---

[14] HMC *Stuart* III, 186, Murray to Mar, 6 November 1716.

[15] HMC *Stuart* II, 272, T. Oglethorpe to Mar, 10 July 1716.

[16] HMC *Stuart* II, 155, Dillon to Mar, 15 May 1716; 184, Mar to Dillon, 26 May 1716; 244, James III to Bagnall, June 1716.

[17] HMC *Stuart* II, 265, Bagnall to Mar, 8 July 1716; 266, Bagnall to James III, 8 July 1716.

[18] HMC *Stuart* II, 271, T. Oglethorpe to Mar, 10 July 1716.

[19] HMC *Stuart* II, 244, James III to Bagnall, June 1716.

Figure 3.2 Unknown artist, *Anne Marie d'Orléans, Queen of Sardinia*, oil on canvas, c. 1725, Reggia di Venaria.

She did speak to him, but it was no good. James III was informed:

she desired I would not mention the business I cam[e] upon to the King, because it would only embarrass him, and he would be sorry to be obliged to give me a refusal.[20]

This meant that when James had to leave Avignon in February 1717 he had no option but to seek refuge in the Papal States.

James III and his courtiers travelled via the Duchy of Savoy and over the Col du Mont Cenis into the Principality of Piedmont, where they arrived on 21 February.[21] Victor Amadeus had agreed to allow James to pass through his territories, and he even sent the Marchese di Cavaglià and other servants to greet and wait on him, but he would not allow him to make an official visit to Turin.[22] After travelling via Susa and Rivoli, James entered Turin incognito on 24 February and saw the King and Queen of Sicily and also the Dowager Duchess of Savoy. He then spent the night at Victor Amadeus's summer palace at Moncalieri,[23] before travelling on via Alessandria to Tortona, and thence into the Duchy of Parma.[24] The Queen and Dowager Duchess were both delighted with James, and sent enthusiastic letters of support to Mary of Modena at Saint-Germain,[25] but their opinions carried no political weight. In a letter written at Villanuova d'Asti, one day after his visit to Turin, James III admitted that 'I could get no good out of the King

20 HMC *Stuart* II, 266, Bagnall to James III, 8 July 1716. See also 243, Bagnall to Mar, 31 June [sic] 1716. For Bagnall's accounts of his mission from Avignon to Turin, see Bodleian Library, Carte MSS 211, f. 321.

21 BL. Add MSS 31260, f. 20, Nairne to Gualterio, 23 February 1717; HMC *Stuart* III, 535, Paterson to Mar, 24 February 1717. King Victor Amadeus had ordered that the road over the mountain pass should be cleared of snow. According to the Duke of Ormonde, who accompanied James III, 'il y a mille hommes de commandés pour netoyer les chemins remplis de neige, et 400 chevaux pour l'accompagner' (Bibliothèque de la Ville d'Avignon (hereafter BVA.) MS 3188, fol. 302, the diary of Dr Brun, 19 February 1717: 'le Duc d'Ormond a écrit a Vice Légat ces nouvelles').

22 HMC *Stuart* III, 396, Mar to O'Rourke, 3 January 1717; 539, narrative by John Paterson of the journey of James III over Mont Cenis, undated (February 1717). For the presence of the Marchese di Cavaglià, see the diary of Dr Brun, 19 February 1717: 'Notre Archeveque a receu une lettre de son frère le Marquis de Cavaillac qui lui marque comme le roi de Sardaigne son maitre l'avoit chargé d'aller au devant du roi d'Angleterre pour luy offrir ce que depend de sa majesté. Il a ordre de le deffrayer et toute de suite, de luy faire rendre tous les honneurs, et de l'accompagner iusques à la sortie de ses Etats' (BVA. MS 3188, fol. 302).

23 BL. Add MSS 31260, fol. 20, Nairne to Gualterio, 23 February 1717; HMC *Stuart* III, 535, Paterson to Mar, 24 February 1717; HMC *Stuart* IV, 107, Mary of Modena to Mar, 7 March 1717.

24 HMC *Stuart* IV, 103, Paterson to Mar, 5 March 1717; BL. Add MSS 31260, fol. 24 and fol. 26, Nairne to Gualterio, 6 and 7 March 1717.

25 HMC *Stuart* IV, 107, Mary of Modena to Mar, 7 March 1717; 143, Dowager Duchess of Savoy to Mary of Modena, 27 March 1717.

of Sicily'.[26] As a result he had no choice but to accept the hospitality of Pope Clement XI, first of all at Pesaro, then at Urbino, and eventually in Rome.

While he was at Urbino James made one final attempt to influence the court of Turin. He had commissioned from Antonio David a three-quarter length portrait of himself showing him for the first time with the closed crown of a king (Figs 3.3 and 3.4). It was to be sent to his mother at Saint-Germain, but James had ordered a further ten copies as bust-length portraits to be distributed among his supporters in Italy. Nine of the ten were destined for various cardinals and princes in Rome, but the tenth was for the court of Turin.[27]

During his time at Avignon James had enjoyed good relations with the Archbishop, Paolo Francesco Gonteri di Cavaglià, whose family lived in Turin. The tenth bust copy was for the archbishop's sister-in-law, the Marchesa di Cavaglià.[28] It was sent with a frame from Rome to Turin in March 1718,[29] and exhibited at the court there. James III's private secretary was informed by the Marchesa's husband that 'the portrait was received with a great deal of pleasure, and that the painting did honour to Monsieur David at the court of Turin, where the Queen herself saw it with pleasure and praised it'.[30] The opinion of the King of Sicily, if he also saw it, was not recorded.

By 1718 Victor Amadeus was actively encouraging James III to get married and have children, so that the Queen of Sicily would no longer cause him embarrassment by remaining the Jacobite heiress presumptive.[31] Of course that is not the way Victor Amadeus put it when speaking to

---

[26] HMC *Stuart* III, 536, James III to Mar, 25 February 1717.
[27] BL. Add MSS 20313, fol. 269, note by Nairne: 'Liste des personnes pour qui le Roy a commandé des copies de son portrait à Rome', undated (March 1718).
[28] BL. Add MSS 31260, fol. 174, Nairne to Gualterio, 3 October 1717; BL. Add MSS 20312, fol. 96, Marchesa Anna Maddalena di Cavaglià to Nairne, 30 October 1717; BL. Add MSS 31260, fol. 224, Nairne to Gualterio, 25 November 1717. The archbishop's brother, Filippo Giacinto Gonteri, was the second Marchese di Cavaglià, who accompanied James III during his visit to Turin on 24 February 1717. The Marchese's second wife, Anna Maddalena (née Roero di Ternavasso), was a *dame d'honneur* to the Queen of Sicily and had the most important salon in Turin. I am very grateful to Dr Andrea Merlotti for giving me information about the Gonteri di Cavaglià family. For more information on *dames d'honneur*, see: Merlotti 2013a.
[29] BL. Add MSS 31260, fol. 248, Nairne to Gualterio, 16 December 1717; BL. Add MSS 31261, fol. 16, Nairne to Gualterio, 20 January 1718; BVA. MS 1725, fol. 43, Nairne to Gonteri di Cavaglià, 16 June 1718.
[30] BL. Add MSS 31261, fol. 103, Nairne to Gualterio, 21 April 1718: 'le portrait du Roy est arrivé a bon port et a été reçu avec beaucoup de plaisir, et la peinture a fait honneur a Mr David a la cour de Turin, ou la Reine elle meme l'a vû avec plaisir et l'a loué.'
[31] HMC *Stuart* V, 238, Mar to Dillon, 26 November 1717.

Figure 3.3 Antonio David, *James III*, oil on canvas, 1717, Palacio da Liria, Madrid, Fundacion Casa de Alba.

Figure 3.4 Antonio David, *James III*, oil on canvas, private collection. Photograph: author.[32]

Jacobite agents, some of whom regarded his recommendation of various German princesses as 'very kind and friendly'.[33] It is unlikely that James III

---

[32] In the summer of 1717 James III was painted in Rome by Antonio David. The three-quarter length portrait was the first to show James with both the Garter and the Thistle, as well as the closed crown of a king, which had never been included in any of his portraits before the accession of George I. In March 1718 the picture was sent to Queen Mary at Saint-Germain, but shortly after its arrival she died. The painting was therefore entrusted to the care of the senior Jacobites still living in the château there. It was the only one they had ever seen showing their king wearing the Order of the Thistle. Alexis-Simon Belle, who still had his *atelier* in Saint-Germain, was asked to make some copies for circulation among the Jacobites and their supporters in France, but in July 1718 a message was sent from the *Stuart* court in Italy that the king 'would not have any copies made of it' (HMC Stuart VII, 1, Mar to Dillon, 1 July 1718).

[33] HMC *Stuart* V, 223, Innes to Mar, 23 November 1717. See also BL. Add MSS 20298, fol. 20, Nairne to Gualterio, undated (early Feb 1718): the King and Queen of Sicily 'l'ont chargé avec beaucoup de bonté et avec une ouverture qu'on n'auroit pas attendu de [lui], de presser fortement S.M. de leur part de se marier au plutot. [The King of Sicily] a paru s'interesser vivement.'

was himself taken in, but he knew that George I would do all he could to prevent his getting married and having a Stuart heir, so it suited his interests to obtain diplomatic support for his plan to find a suitable princess. He also wanted to drive a wedge between Turin and London by starting a secret correspondence with the King of Sicily. He wrote to Victor Amadeus in February 1718 to thank him for the 'sincere friendship' he had shown in 'continuing to aid me' with his 'good counsels'.[34] In March he ordered General Sheldon, who was travelling to France via Turin, to tell the King of Sicily of 'the great esteem etc I have of him', though Sheldon was 'to take no notice of his having begun a [secret] correspondence with me'.[35] James and Victor Amadeus continued their correspondence about prospective brides during the early months of 1718,[36] and as late as the end of May James asked for a list of suitable princesses to be sent from Turin to Urbino.[37] It was shortly after this that James decided to marry Princess Maria Clementina Sobieska.

This was really the end of James III's attempts to obtain support at Turin. In June 1718 the Spanish invaded Sicily, captured Palermo and quickly overran the island. A few weeks later the marriage contract was signed with Prince James Sobieski, father of the Princess.[38] James III immediately dropped all his diplomatic efforts at Turin and declared his support for King Philip V of Spain. In August, before the Spanish were defeated off Cap Passaro, James's secretary wrote optimistically that 'the news from Sicily is excellent, and there is reason to hope that the King of Spain will soon be master of the entire kingdom'.[39] It clearly gave the Jacobites considerable satisfaction to see Victor Amadeus deprived of his Kingdom of Sicily and reduced to being a sovereign 'royal highness' again rather than a sovereign 'royal king'.

In the peace settlement of 1720 Victor Amadeus was compensated by being given the Kingdom of Sardinia instead of Sicily, which was acquired by the Emperor Charles VI. By then James had married Clementina Sobieska, and she gave birth to the long-awaited Stuart male heir in 1720, so that Anne Marie, now Queen of Sardinia, was no longer his heiress presumptive. James

---

[34] HMC *Stuart* V, 435, James III to Victor Amadeus II, 4 February 1718: 'Les differentes et etroittes liaisons qui sont entre nous, et l'amitié sincere que vous m'avés temoigné, m'en font avec justice esperer la continuation … Ce seroit pour moy un sensible plaisir et un singulier avantage, que de profiter de vos avis qui ne pourront qu'etre utiles au bien de nos deux familles.'

[35] HMC *Stuart* VI, 175, James III to Sheldon, 20 March 1718.

[36] HMC *Stuart* VI, 222, James III to Victor Amadeus II, 29 March 1718; 373, James III to Dillon, 27 April 1718.

[37] HMC *Stuart* VI, 497, James III to Victor Amadeus II, 30 May 1718.

[38] HMC *Stuart* VII, 77, James III's marriage contract, 22 July 1718. For the details, see: Corp 2009: 92; 2013: 152–3.

[39] BL. Add MSS 31261, fol. 189, Nairne to Gualterio, 7 August 1718: 'Les nouvelles de Sicile sont fort bonnes, et il y a lieu d'esperer que S.M.C. sera bientot maitresse de tout ce Royaume.'

made a point of not informing Victor Amadeus. In fact, he announced the news of his marriage to the court of Turin by ordering his secretary, the same man who had revealed the assassination plot of 1708, to send a letter to the Marchesa di Cavaglià, the lady who owned the copy of the portrait by Antonio David, so that she could show it to the Queen and the members of her court.[40]

By 1720 the exiled Stuart court was established in Rome, and thereafter there seems to have been little contact between James III and either Victor Amadeus or his son Charles Emmanuel, who did all they could to maintain good relations with both George I and George II.[41] During 1727, for example, James left Italy and went to live for a second time in Avignon.[42] When he decided to return at the end of December he once again travelled via Savoy and Piedmont, but this time he was not received at Turin. As the Marchese del Borgo explained, 'when he [James] made very strong instances to have had an Audience from the King [Victor Amadeus], tho' it were, he said, but for one moment, it was constantly denied him, and … he was not suffered so much as to pass thro' the Town'.[43]

The Duke of Parma, by contrast, disapproved of the way Victor Amadeus treated James III, so he invited the latter to visit him for ten days a few months later: 'immediately upon his arrival he was visited by the Duke and Duchess of Parma who are pleased it seems openly and publickly to pay him the civilities and honours due to the King of Great Britain';[44] 'in his own Box at the Opera he [the Duke] gave him constantly the Place of honour'.[45] The difference in the treatment of James III by the King of Sardinia and the Duke of Parma could hardly have been greater. When Victor Amadeus was told how angry George II was with the Duke, he hastened to disassociate himself from the latter's behaviour. Calling the British representative at Turin into an 'inner room', he asked him to reassure George of his goodwill: 'Pour nous autres (he added) Nous avons toujours bien fait.'[46] This, as we have seen, was equally true for the period 1712–20.

[40] BL. Add MSS 31261, fol. 344, Nairne to Gualterio, 16 September 1719.
[41] In 1766, the year of James III's death, when there was a danger that Corsica might be annexed by France, King George III suggested that the island should be given by Genoa to the King of Sardinia. Charles Emmanuel II responded by suggesting that the island be given to James III's elder son, Prince Charles Stuart. Neither suggestion appealed to the Genoese, who ceded the island to France in 1768.
[42] Corp 2011a: 193–5.
[43] NA. SP 92/33/Part 1/fol. 76, Allen to Newcastle, 13 July 1728. James III left Avignon on 20 December 1727 and reached Bologna on 7 January 1728.
[44] NA. SP 92/33/Part 1/fol. 47, Allen to Newcastle, 19 June 1728. James III was in Parma from 10 to 22 June 1728.
[45] NA. SP 92/33/Part I/fol. 76, Allen to Newcastle, 13 July 1728. The opera at the Teatro Nuovo Ducale was Vinci's *Medo*, and the cast included Farinelli who had been particularly patronized by James III in Rome and Bologna: Corp 2011a: 93–4.
[46] Corp 2011a. For the reaction of George II, who ordered the Duke of Parma's Agent in London 'to leave the Kingdom in two days', see NA. SP 92/33/Part 1/fol. 64, Newcastle to Allen, 1/12 July 1728.

Figure 3.5 Antonio David, *James III*, oil on canvas, 1730, copy of the lost portrait of James III painted by Martin van Meytens the Younger in Rome in 1725, Private collection, reproduced by permission of the Pininski Foundation, Warsaw.

It is not known what became of the portrait of James III by David which the Marchesa di Cavaglià presumably displayed in her salon.[47] At any rate, David does not seem to have received any subsequent commissions from the court of Turin. Yet it is worth mentioning that two of the other portrait painters employed by James III in Rome were immediately afterwards given important commissions by Victor Amadeus II and Charles Emmanuel II. Martin van Meytens (the younger) painted both James III (Fig. 3.5) and his wife Queen Clementina in 1725, and was then employed by Victor Amadeus (Fig. 3.6) before he moved on to become court painter in Vienna.

---

[47] Unlike King Victor Amadeus, the Marchesa di Cavaglià continued to receive the important Jacobites who visited Turin, such as the Countess of Inverness in 1724 (NA. SP 92/31/fol. 389, Molesworth to Newcastle, 9 September 1724; Corp 2011a: 159). From 1726 to 1727 James III's first cousin once removed, who was also first cousin once removed of Queen Anne Marie of Sardinia, lived in Turin. This was Charles Radcliffe (later 5th Earl of Derwentwater), whose mother was an illegitimate daughter of Charles II.

Figure 3.6 Martin van Meytens the Younger, *Victor Amadeus II, King of Sardinia*, oil on canvas, 1728, Reggia di Venaria.

Domenico Duprà worked for several Jacobites in Rome in 1739–40, and then for James III from to 1740 to 1744, when he became court painter to Charles Emmanuel in Turin.[48]

For the House of Savoy the disputed English succession after 1689, though occasionally a source of embarrassment, was little more than a very convenient bargaining counter to further its aim of acquiring a kingdom in the Mediterranean. Yet it may be considered how different things would have been if the Duke of Savoy had been assassinated in 1708, if Duchess Anne Marie had then been declared Regent of Savoy for her nine-year-old son and of course if James III had died unmarried at some time before 1720.

[48] See Yarker in this volume.

4 | The British Diplomatic Presence in Turin: Diplomatic Culture and British Elite Identity, 1688–1789/98

CHRISTOPHER STORRS

The eighteenth century witnessed crucial developments in the international sphere in Europe.[1] These included the emergence of a relatively small group of dominant states – Austria, Britain, France, Prussia and Russia – whose resources and ability to wage war on a large scale set them apart from the numerous second and third rank states. Among the many conflicts in which these so-called 'Great Powers' emerged was what has been called the Second Hundred Years War, at whose heart was an intermittent but near-constant struggle between the British state created by the Revolution of 1688 and its allies on the one hand, and on the other Bourbon France, the latter sometimes in alliance with Bourbon Spain. The role of Britain, and above all the way in which it funded successive alliances against France (and Spain) between the Nine Years War at the start of the long eighteenth century and the Napoleonic Wars at its close, and the peace treaties – particularly that of Utrecht concluded at the end of the War of the Spanish Succession in 1713 and that of Paris at the conclusion of the Seven Years War in 1763 – contributed to an admiration in continental Europe of British institutions which did so much to underpin a widespread Anglophilia.

Britain's success in the eighteenth-century international struggle has been measured very largely in terms of its colonial, commercial, maritime and transatlantic achievement, notably the expulsion of France from Canada (and India) in the Seven Years War. This approach has in some respects been reinforced in recent decades by the great interest in the Atlantic – broadly conceived by Anglophone historians in largely Anglophone and even Anglocentric terms – and even more recently by an enthusiasm for global history. However, while these enthusiasms reflect real eighteenth-century concerns, they run the risk of ignoring other areas, particularly in the Old World and not least what we know as Italy. The resources of the Atlantic world were largely valued in Europe not least for what they could contribute to the struggle for dominion, status, resources and territory in Italy and other parts of Europe. At the same time, Italy, or rather some of the

---

[1] McKay and Scott 1983; Brewer 1989.

Italian states, could play a key role in the larger European struggle. These considerations shaped the role that the Court of Turin could and did – and it should be said did not – play in the international struggle. They also shaped the objectives and character of British diplomacy in Turin – and the activity, attitudes and pursuits of successive British diplomats there – between *circa* 1690 and 1799.

The warfare which underpinned the emergence of the 'Great Powers' and the rise of Britain also transformed the Savoyard state[2] – a composite polity whose main components were the Principality of Piedmont, the Duchy of Savoy, the Duchy of Aosta, the County of Nice and between 1713 and 1720 the island Kingdom of Sicily, which was exchanged (permanently) in 1720 for the island Kingdom of Sardinia which henceforth identified the Savoyard state. That state also acquired new influence and importance. The rise of Savoy was very closely related to that of Britain. Thus, the acquisition by Victor Amadeus II, Duke of Savoy, of the Kingdom of Sicily in 1713 – and that at last of a royal crown – and at the same time of territorial adjustments in the west at the expense of France and in the east at the expense of Austrian Habsburg Milan (and of the Gonzaga Dukes of Mantua) was intimately associated with his collaboration in the peacemaking of Queen Anne's Tory ministry led by Robert Harley and Henry St John. This close connection was accompanied by closer diplomatic contacts between the two states. Indeed, this paper could not have been written if it was not for the existence of a substantial correspondence maintained with London by a succession of British diplomats resident in Turin in the eighteenth century and which are now housed in the National Archives at Kew in London, in the State Papers (SP 92, Sardinia) down to 1782 and thereafter in the Foreign Office series (FO 67, Sardinia).

British Diplomacy in Turin Post 1688

Before 1688, Tuscany and Venice figured more largely in British approaches to Italy than did the Savoyard state.[3] But Britain's emergence as a major power after 1688 depended not only upon its ability to field armies and float navies. It also depended upon the ability to put anti-French coalitions together. Without allies who could field larger armies British seapower was not always effective. The effectiveness of British diplomacy in finding

---

[2] Symcox 1983a; Storrs 1999.
[3] See the missions listed for the various states in: Bell 1990b.

allies depended in part upon the ability to offer support at sea and cash subsidies, an aspect of British influence which is largely taken for granted but rarely properly studied. Among the most frequent recipients of British subsidies in the century and more after 1688 were successive Dukes of Savoy/Kings of Sardinia: Victor Amadeus II (1675–1730), his son and successor, Charles Emmanuel III (1730–73), and his son and successor Victor Amadeus III (1773–96).[4] The new relationship between the two states was forged in 1690, largely by accident. William III was trying to mobilize the Swiss against Louis XIV (and his ally the Duke of Savoy), but the Swiss were reluctant, and Victor Amadeus, resenting French tutelage, was ready to join the anti-French coalition. An alliance was concluded between William and Victor Amadeus in the autumn of 1690 in which William (and the Dutch) promised the Duke a subsidy. This set the pattern for relations between the Courts of Saint James and Turin for the succeeding half century and more. The following year William sent Edmund Poley to Turin, the first of more than 30 British diplomats resident there between 1691 and 1799.[5] By the middle of the eighteenth century, if not before, the Savoyard state was thought of by most British policy-makers as almost an automatic member of any anti-French coalition,[6] and completely eclipsed the other Italian states as the focus and foundation of British diplomacy in Italy, although it never rivalled Versailles, Vienna, Madrid, Berlin or St Petersburg in its place in the larger British picture of Europe.

But what was the foundation of the new relationship? For British policy-makers the Savoyard state was above all valuable because of its strategic position, straddling the Alps between southeastern France and the Po valley and thus allowing – or denying – a route into France from the latter for Britain and its allies (perhaps linking up with a Huguenot revolt, although this became less and less likely); alternatively allowing – or denying – French forces into northern Italy. Throughout the eighteenth century British ministers dreamed of delivering what some hoped might be the knockout blow against France which could not be delivered in other theatres – Flanders and the Rhine. In 1692, indeed, Victor Amadeus II had led an allied invasion force into Dauphiné, and in 1707, too, an allied force operating out of Piedmont – and supported from the sea by British ships – attacked the great French naval base at Toulon. Both of these invasions proved abortive, but they suggested what might be achieved, and continued to haunt

[4] Symcox 1983b: 151–84; Storrs 2012: 87–126.
[5] See list of missions in: Horn 1932: 119–27.
[6] Scott 1989: 55–91.

British ministers and to make clear the value of the Savoyard alliance. But there was more to it than just the strategic issue, although this clearly distinguished the Savoyard state from most other Italian states. That state also seemed to be ruled by princes who were very effective rulers – we might call them 'absolute' using a simplistic shorthand – able, not least when aided by British subsidies, to mobilize relatively large numbers of troops to swell an allied army which, even if it did not involve force, obliged the French king to divert troops from other fronts. The fact that the Savoyard state was much weaker, especially at sea, that it was so distant and in some respects a dependent, also smoothed relations between the two states.[7]

These concerns shaped the activity of successive British representatives in Turin. In wartime, these ministers were expected to encourage and negotiate alliance, to maintain good relations between the two allied Courts, and to help co-ordinate allied strategy. This often involved seeking to resolve differences between the Court of Turin and other allies, which really meant the Court of Vienna whose prickly relationship with Turin sometimes seriously undermined the effectiveness of the allied war effort in Italy. British diplomats also had to maintain good relations between the two Courts, and kept their own Court informed of important developments in the Savoyard state, such that their correspondence with the Secretary of State in London is an invaluable source of information about all aspects of the Savoyard state. Of course, successive British ministers were expected to keep a very watchful, wary eye on the manoeuvring of Savoyard monarch and ministers, not least because the latter acquired a reputation for duplicity, double-dealing and the betrayal of allies, founded very largely on the conduct of Victor Amadeus in 1690, in 1696 (when Victor Amadeus made his own very advantageous peace with Louis XIV, ending the war in Italy at the expense of his allies) and in 1703 when, having allied with the Bourbons, Louis XIV and Philip V of Spain (in 1701) he instead joined the Grand Alliance against them. Thereafter, ducal or royal policy is far less easily convicted of such conduct but the reputation for double-dealing and the consequent deep suspicion – by no means peculiar to British ministers – persisted long after.[8]

British ministers in Turin also reported to London on many other matters. Turin was an excellent vantage point from which to secure intelligence about the French fleet at Toulon (often via the British consul in

---

[7] See: Storrs 2012 (and references there).

[8] In the summer of 1727, after more than a year seeking to pin Victor Amadeus down in alliance negotiations, the British minister declared that he was 'weary of endeavouring to hold an eel by the tail', Hedges to Newcastle, 14 June 1727, National Archives, Kew (London), State Papers [SP] 92 (Sardinia), volume 32.

Nice);[9] about the Jacobite Court in Rome and the activities of Jacobite sympathizers;[10] and last but by no means least, about the efforts of other powers to raise loans in neighbouring Genoa, and which might be the prelude to war in Europe.[11]

These primarily political, diplomatic and/or military concerns dictated the chronology and shape of British diplomacy and diplomatic representation. Thus, there was an initial period of intense wartime contact between 1690 and 1696, effectively broken off when the duke abandoned his allies in that year and another between 1700 and 1713. Contacts were interrupted thereafter, not least because the first Hanoverian, George I, was not so committed to the Tory peace of Utrecht of which Victor Amadeus had been such a beneficiary. Indeed, in response to the efforts of Philip V of Spain to overturn the Utrecht peace settlement and to recover what had been Spanish Italy by invading Sardinia and then Sicily, George's Whig ministers helped broker the deal which in 1720 forced Victor Amadeus to exchange Sicily for the smaller and poorer island of Sardinia whose only attraction for Victor Amadeus was the royal title which went with it. No episode so clearly demonstrates the real weakness of the Savoyard state when the other powers were bent on peace and not on war, but which historians mesmerized by the successful volte-faces of 1690, 1696 and 1703 have not sufficiently appreciated.

However, the prospect of another major European war – driven by Spain's revanchist aspirations in Italy – as the rival alliances of Vienna and Hanover squared up to each other from 1725, triggered a British diplomatic offensive in Turin aimed at securing Victor Amadeus's alliance, although war did not in fact materialize and relations again entered a quiet period. This only ended with the appointment of one of the only two ambassadors sent by London to Turin throughout this period, namely the Earl of Essex in 1732, following the accession of Charles Emmanuel III. Essex returned home in 1736. Thereafter, business in Turin was the responsibility of the man who had been Essex's secretary, Arthur Villettes, until the end of the War of the Austrian Succession, although most important matters went through the

---

[9] Successive British ministers in Turin, including Bristol, received and forwarded to London naval intelligence from Toulon throughout the Seven Years War. Thereafter, see Jackson to Fraser, 14 September and 10, 13, 17, 20, 27 and 31 October 1787, National Archives Kew (London), Foreign Office [FO], 67 (Sardinia), volume 5, and Trevor to Carmarthen, 1 April 1788, FO 67/6.

[10] Sherdley to Conway, 15 and 25 January and 23 April 1766, SP 92/72; Lynch to Rochford, 4 Sept. 1771.

[11] Jackson to Fraser, 19 March, 7 June, and 2 and 16 July 1788, and Trevor to Carmarthen, 22 October, 5 November and 27 December 1788, and 7 March and 1 April 1789. FO67/6.

very capable hands of the Savoyard representative in London, the cavaliere Ossorio.[12]

After 1748, the so-called 'Diplomatic Revolution', that is the alliance between the old enemies the Courts of Versailles and Vienna, transformed the international scene, and undermined the strategic importance of the Savoyard state. This was by no means the end of efforts by Britain to court the Savoyard state, as it did in both the Seven Years War and the American War of Independence. However, although some Savoyard policy-makers urged a more aggressive, opportunistic policy, some pressing Charles Emanuel III to intervene in the Seven Years War to press his claims on Piacenza following the succession of Carlo di Borbone king of Naples as king of Spain in 1759, fear of Austria and France and concern at the enduring debt built up during the War of the Austrian Succession ensured that between 1748 and 1789 the Court of Turin remained neutral and could even be said to be drifting into its pre-1690 status as a French satellite. Indeed, the only military adventure of that Court in this period was military intervention, in alliance with Louis XV of France and the canton of Bern against the Genevan revolution in 1782. Only with the French revolution, and the outbreak of war with revolutionary France from 1792 would the Court of Turin revert to the pattern which had developed between 1690 and 1748 of subsidy alliance with Britain against France, with disastrous consequences for the Savoyard state, which was effectively absorbed into the expanding French state by 1800. Once again, these developments had important implications for British diplomacy in Turin and the activities there of successive residents.

So far, the emphasis has been upon the largely political, secular concerns that drew the two Courts together. However, other issues divided them, or threatened to. Chief among them was that of religion. It is increasingly apparent that the old commonplace that religion disappeared as an issue in international relations after 1648 must at the least be modified. The relations between Protestant Britain and Catholic Piedmont/Savoy support this revisionist approach. British divines and politicians felt a sense of religious solidarity with the Protestant Waldensian (or Vaudois) subjects of the Dukes of Savoy/Kings of Sardinia. This was reflected in the instructions given to successive British diplomats sent to Turin, to take particular care of the Vaudois, in the way the subsidy paid in the 1690s was used to extract an edict of toleration on their behalf in 1694, which seriously complicated relations between Victor Amadeus II and the papal Curia, and in the way Queen Anne's ministers sought to protect the Huguenots who inhabited the French territory ceded to the Duke by Louis XIV in 1713.[13] British ministers were

---

[12] Storrs 2000: 210–53.
[13] Cozzo *et al.* 2005; Chauvard *et al.* 2015.

not always able to protect Vaudois or Huguenots as much as they would have liked, but without their vigilance and representations there can be no doubt that the plight of the Protestant community in Turin – where the minister's chapel offered a place of worship for local and visiting (British and other) Protestants – and the wider Savoyard state would have been much worse.

Many of these activities or duties continued in peacetime, when other aspects of their duties were more to the fore. Thus, while war did not completely halt the flow of British travellers to Europe, peacetime brought far more of them to Turin. Some of them were Grand Tourists, stopping off in Turin (a friendly Court) on their way to Rome and Naples.[14] In October 1789 Trevor thought the number of English visitors that year 'considerable', calculating that there were at that moment 40 in Turin. Indeed, he believed that there were too many for the inns of the city to accommodate such that they had to continue onwards to Italy fairly speedily.[15] The more distinguished of these visitors required proper handling by the British minister. In November 1786 Prince William Henry Duke of Gloucester briefly visited Turin (incognito) where he was presented to Victor Amadeus III and given a tour of the citadel.[16] But it was not only English visitors who necessitated looking after: in 1771 Sir William Lynch (Fig. 4.1) arranged the reception at the Court of Turin of Prince Augustus of Saxe-Gotha, nephew of the Dowager Princess of Wales.[17]

At the same time there was a small but growing British resident community in the Savoyard state (although we ignore this, focusing above all on the Grand Tour travellers). This British resident community also included a number of Catholics, for example a Mr Corby of Northampton, who was found a place in the Marquis of Cordon's regiment by Trevor but who died while in garrison in 1786.[18] But the great concentration of Britons in the Savoyard state was at Nice. In 1786, Trevor calculated that about 100 foreign families or households spent the winter there, about 86 of them were English (British?), totalling (including servants) about 250 people – this in addition to the men aboard the British squadron which sometimes put in there; Trevor calculated that these families spent there a total of 400,000 lire, a considerable sum.[19] But things were not always easy for these expatriates. In 1773–4 the fate of a Miss

[14] Black 2003.
[15] Trevor to Leeds, 24 October 1789, FO 67/6.
[16] Trevor to Carmarthen, 8 November 1786, FO/67/5. The Duke again passed through in June the following year, Jackson to Fraser, 2 June 1787, FO 67/5.
[17] Lynch to Weymouth, 4 September 1771, SP 92/76.
[18] Trevor to Carmarthen, 30 July 1786, FO 67/5.
[19] Trevor to Carmarthen, 19 April and 9 August 1786, Turin, FO 675, and 27 January 1787, FO 67/6.

Figure 4.1 Unknown artist, *Sir William Lynch, M.P. and K.B.* [Knight of Bath], pencil and brown wash, c. 1774, © National Portrait Gallery, London.

Mearns, daughter of a British shipwright in the king of Sardinia's employ at Nice, educated in a local convent, expressed a determination to abandon her Protestant faith and embrace Catholicism, and led to some of the most negative commentary by British diplomats in the eighteenth century regarding the Savoyard state and ruling élite – as Catholic and bigoted – and almost provoked a rupture of diplomatic relations between the two states.[20]

British subjects were drawn to Nice by the climate and by commercial possibilities as trade grew between the two states.[21] Efforts to develop trade were not always successful – witness the abortive attempts to export wine from Piedmont to London before 1789 – but reflected a new interest in

[20] Cooke to Rochford, 2 February and 14 August 1773, and Lynch to Rochford, 11 September, 27 October, 13 and 24 November 1773 and 26 February and 2 March 1774, SP 92/77.
[21] For Piedmontese trade with Britain, see the enclosure in Trevor to Carmarthen, 22 December 1786, FO/67/5. But see especially: Chicco 1995.

trade and commercial issues which characterized the diplomatic activity of most states in the second half of the eighteenth century. Here, too, was however a source of tension. For one thing, the Savoyard state depended enormously (too much, in fact) upon silk production and export, and was suspicious of, and determined to obstruct, the development of rival silk industries, including in Britain. At the same time, the efforts of the Court of Turin to develop its own woollen manufactures, and to restrict imports of these, also meant conflict with British interests. However, these never threatened to interrupt relations as did the religious issue.

There was one final respect in which Turin was British in the eighteenth century. Successive wars with France in the eighteenth century reflected but also stimulated a Savoyard patriotism. This in turn found expression in a marked Anglophilia. This is most easily traced among the Savoyard élite, and particularly among those who had visited Britain, many of whom became great admirers of Britain and its institutions. They included Conte Perrone, who having served as Savoyard envoy in London returned to Turin as chief minister of Victor Amadeus III,[22] and the Marchese Grisella di Rosignano, the first Savoyard envoy to Berlin (1774).[23] But this Anglophilia was not confined to the élite.[24] This is suggested by widespread anxiety regarding Britain's situation at the start of the Seven Years War and subsequent celebration there of British military and naval success even though the two Courts were not allies at that time.[25]

British Diplomats in Turin

These issues all influenced the character of British diplomacy in Turin and the quality and activities of the men sent there. The Court of St James was represented by 34 men in Turin between 1691 and 1799,[26] some of them – for example Essex – accompanied by their wives.[27] Their

[22] Dagna 1968: 9–46. On Perrone's cultural Anglophilia, see: Zoller in this volume; Bianchi 2015b.

[23] Lynch to Rochford, 26 November 1774, SP 92/77.

[24] See the contribution by Andrea Merlotti in this volume and references therein.

[25] Bristol to Fox, Turin, 26 June and 1 May 1756, SP 92/65; Pitt to Egremont, Turin, 23 October 1762, SP 92/69.

[26] What follows draws, unless otherwise indicated, on the work of Horn (1932: 119–27) and – where these exist – entries in the *Oxford Dictionary of National Biography* (*ODNB*). Surprisingly few of the British representatives in Turin in this period have entries in the *ODNB*, even the recently revised version.

[27] For Essex's art collecting in Turin, see Yarker in this volume.

Figure 4.2 After Michael Dahl, *Charles Mordaunt, 3rd Earl of Peterborough*, engraved by John Simon, London, Cooper, 1706, © National Portrait Gallery, London.

background, rank and so on can throw some interesting light on the British diplomatic 'service' and British diplomatic culture in the eighteenth century. In terms of diplomatic rank, only two of the 34 (the Earls of Peterborough and Essex) were appointed ambassador, whereas seventeen were sent to Turin as envoy extraordinary (Fig. 4.2). Various factors were operating here. Ambassador was the most prestigious rank and sending one was expensive but would clearly please the receiving Court and might be the only means to tempt an individual to go on diplomatic mission. The rank of envoy on the other hand was less costly, less hobbled by ceremony and not surprisingly was the rank most favoured by most Courts when sending men abroad in the eighteenth century. Most Savoyard ministers sent to London went as envoy, and most Courts practised reciprocity, giving the same rank as they received. (Some envoys were also given the rank of minister plenipotentiary, largely in order to supplement their salary as envoy.)

Socially, only the two ambassadors, plus Galway, Rochford,[28] Bristol and Cardiff/ Mountstuart were of distinguished noble rank, being earls and/or the sons of earls, Mountstuart subsequently becoming Marquess of Bute (Fig. 4.3),[29] while Hampden Trevor was the son of Baron Trevor and Viscount Hampden and himself subsequently succeeded as Viscount Hampden. The rest were men of far less distinguished birth, although Pitt was subsequently promoted baron and Liston was knighted. Indeed, and contrary to a view of diplomatic culture as aristocratic, the core of that of Britain at least was far from aristocratic. (This becomes clearer if we take into consideration the frequent absences or intervals between the higher-ranking appointments, which were filled by a secretary or charge.)[30] It should be pointed out that the representatives of other states were also often absent from Turin for long periods, suggesting that this was the norm in an age of more or less permanent relations and long-term residents.[31] As for nationality, while two of the men sent by the Court of St James to Turin might be thought of as Scots (Mackenzie and Liston), and one Anglo-Irish (Molesworth), the rest were English apart from three of French Huguenot origin (Villettes, Galway and Louis Dutens, the last two of rather humble standing) (Fig. 4.4).[32] A very few of these men were what we might call career diplomats, going on to other postings. For some at the top, Turin was followed by a posting to Madrid. For Rochford, it was a stepping-stone towards appointment as Secretary of State. But the career men were really to be found lower down the diplomatic hierarchy. They included both Villettes, who went on – despite writing despatches of such extraordinary length that he was in fact reprimanded for it by the Duke of Newcastle – to be sent as resident to Zurich (1750–60),[33] and most strikingly Robert Liston, who rose in the course of a number of missions (Turin, Madrid, Stockholm, Piladelphia, Constantinople) from secretary to envoy. In what sense were any of those sent to Turin especially well prepared? Most of them had no particular expertise or knowledge of the Savoyard state or its capital, although a number had already travelled in Italy and may have visited Turin. This was certainly true of the Earl of Essex, who was among the

---

[28] For Rochford, see: Rice 1989: 92–113.
[29] Bianchi 2012b.
[30] Lynch was absent from Turin from early 1772 to the summer of 1773. Trevor was absent from Turin between February 1787 and the autumn of 1788, the best part of two years.
[31] The French ambassador returned to Turin at the end of 1774 after an absence of fifteen months, Lynch to R, 24 December 1774, SP 92/77.
[32] For Molesworth, see Wolfe in this volume. On Dutens, see: Dutens 1806b.
[33] Storrs 2010: 181–205.

The Right Hon.ble John — — Lord Viscount Mountstuart.
Lord Lieut.t & Custos Rotulorum of the County of *GLAMORGAN*

Figure 4.3 After Jean-Étienne Liotard, *Lord Mount Stuart, John Stuart, 1st Marquess of Bute*, engraved by John Raphael Smith, London, 1774, © National Portrait Gallery, London.

many British aristocrats whose education had included a stint at the cele-brated Turin Royal Academy, where the sort of institutional education most appropriate to a nobleman was to be found in a way not available in Britain itself.[34] Indeed the Turin Royal Academy is a neglected aspect of British élite

[34] See the contribution in this volume by Bianchi and references therein; see Moore in this volume for Thomas Coke, a British aristocrat at the Turin Royal Academy. Unfortunately,

Figure 4.4 Unknown artist, *Louis Dutens*, engraved by Edward Fisher, London, 1777, © National Portrait Gallery, London.

education in this period. The Britons who went there for a 'noble' education included not only Essex, but also the Earls of Sandwich and Lincoln[35] – and a number of others – although their entries in the *Dictionary of National Biography* rarely acknowledge this. This meant that Essex had a familiarity with Turin, its Court and its nobility which to some extent eased his task but which by no means guaranteed success. In fact, his contacts may have distracted Essex from the business he was officially in Turin to pursue and he appears to have left even quite important business to be conducted

this institution is ignored by – or unknown to – most historians of the English elite and their education despite the fact that it appears in Lord Chesterfield's letters to his son. According to the Piedmontese nobleman, Count Vittorio Alfieri, himself a student there, the end of the Seven Years War saw an influx of foreigners, above all English (presumably British) to the Royal Academy. Alfieri 1987: 86.

[35] Henry Fiennes Clinton (1720–94), 9th Earl of Lincoln and 2nd Duke of Newcastle, arrived in Turin in October 1739 and promptly entered the Royal Academy. A year later, he went to Acqui for the waters, accompanied by his physician, Doctor Richa, 'an Oxford scholar devoted to the English', Villettes to Newcastle, Turin, 10 September 1740, SP 92/42.

by Villettes. Finally, while there was political and other work to be done, successive British diplomats in Turin did not neglect the ceremonial issues which were such an important aspect of diplomatic life and which may – in the absence of other more pressing political issues – have come more to the fore. In 1770 Lynch triggered an incident which mobilized the entire diplomatic corps in defence of its privileges when he returned late to Turin from a visit to the country and had difficulty getting into the city.[36] The following year Lynch reported to London on the French ambassador's formal public entry into Turin at the start of his diplomatic mission.[37] The relative lack of business may also have allowed successive British representatives in Turin greater freedom to develop cultural interests and social contacts (which may also however have been useful in a diplomatic sense).

Conclusion

The eighteenth century witnessed a remarkable coming together of the Courts of Turin and St James, the presence of a British resident contributing to a doubling or even trebling of the size of Turin's diplomatic corps between 1690 and 1786. This rapprochement was largely a matter of convenience and interest rather than a real meeting of minds or affections. Indeed, some British ministers articulated a fierce resentment of Savoyard wheeling and dealing. As late as the 1780s some British diplomats and visitors continued to disparage the Savoyard state and its rulers whose religion, government and character they had little sympathy for. In 1774, Lynch declared that 'vanity is the rock a Piedmontese splits upon, let him [Harris] angle with that bait and he may tickle him like a trout'.[38] By that time, too, the Savoyard state seemed under the rather weak Victor Amadeus III to be in decline. In October 1773, Lynch wrote to Rochford: 'My Lord, this country has imposed upon Europe long enough for its wisdom, its policy, and its police. I am the most mistaken man in the world if ever it can make a great figure again' (that is as it had under Victor Amadeus II and his son).[39] Such views were underpinned by the determined neutrality of the Court of Turin in both the Seven Years War and that

---

[36]   Lynch to Weymouth, 11 August 1770, SP 92/75.
[37]   Lynch to Weymouth, 24 April 1771, SP 92/76.
[38]   Lynch to Rochford, 26 November 1774, SP 92/77. Lynch's words were intended to help the British envoy in Berlin, James Harris, deal with the marchese Griselli di Rosignano, then on his way to the Prussian capital as the first resident envoy sent by the Court of Turin to that of Berlin.
[39]   Lynch to Rochford, 6 October 1773, SP 92/77.

of American Independence and its greater closeness to the French Court.[40] These developments – and a decline which culminated in the collapse of the Savoyard state after a disastrous[41] participation in the French revolutionary wars[42] – were a factor in the relegation of responsibility for the conduct of relations to a less distinguished collection of individuals, although their diplomatic rank and social background says a great deal more about British diplomatic culture in the later eighteenth century, suggesting that it was perhaps less aristocratic in tone than has been suggested hitherto.[43] That diplomatic presence was the tip of an iceberg, since many more Britons passed through and even resided in Turin and other parts of the Savoyard state in the eighteenth century, far more than have been acknowledged hitherto. Some of these accounts have been published, for example that of James Boswell who briefly sojourned in Turin in January 1765 (and saw John Wilkes there). But many more Britons' accounts of their time in Turin – in letters, journals and so on – still lie in numerous private and public archives awaiting discovery. Thus James Graham, 4th Marquis (later the 1st Duke) of Montrose visited Turin as part of his Grand Tour of Europe between 1698 and 1700, before moving on to Milan and Venice. The young nobleman spent only a few days in the Savoyard capital and did not meet Victor Amadeus (perhaps because there was no resident English diplomat to formally present him at Court) but he found out – and recorded in his journal – information about Turin, the Royal Academy and some very brief details of ducal revenues and army pay.[44] Until the many other similar accounts are discovered and their rich contents properly explored we will never fully grasp the astonishing phenomenon that was *Torino Britannica* in the eighteenth century.

---

[40] 'It is not probable that I may often have occasion to trouble you with Intelligence of much importance from a Court which bears no part in the great affairs now on the Tapis', Thomas Jackson to William Fraser, 6 August 1785, FO 67/4.

[41] For this description, see: Boswell 1791: 131–42

[42] Merlin *et al.* 1994: 741–834.

[43] Storrs 2010: 181–215.

[44] The marquess's journal is now in the National Archives of Scotland, Edinburgh, GD220/6/ 1748. I should like to thank Dr Nicola Cowmeadow for drawing the journal to my attention and for providing me with a transcription of that part of it relating to Turin. The Marquess's Grand Tour is not mentioned in his entry in the *Oxford Dictionary of National Biography*.

PART II

Turin: Gateway to Grand Tour Society

5 | The British at the Turin Royal Academy: Cosmopolitanism and Religious Pragmatism

PAOLA BIANCHI

A sojourn in Turin, as part of the traditional Grand Tour of Italy, has been described as the reflection of a political itinerary that emerged in a new light in the 1860s. After the proclamation of the Kingdom of Italy, Turin, Florence and Rome featured prominently on the international map for various reasons: Turin had lost the title of capital already in 1865, passing the baton on to Florence that, ultimately, was in turn superseded by Rome in 1871.[1]

However, Turin could boast of a long-standing and prominent role in contacts and exchanges with the rest of the European continent. Elsewhere I have demonstrated the profoundly cosmopolitan climate of the Piedmontese capital, whose appeal had matured in the late 1600s and would consolidate in the course of the following century.[2] While major Italian urban centres continued to be appreciated mostly as repositories of past glories, as early as 1700 Turin was perceived by many foreign observers as an exception on the Italian peninsula – a place of great social relevance by virtue of its political and cultural modernity. In this chapter, complementary to that by Paolo Cozzo in this same volume and expanding on the subject of Turin's sociability in the eighteenth century as reconstructed by Andrea Merlotti, also in this volume, I will focus on one aspect that contributed to bringing travellers and Grand Tourists to the capital of the State of Savoy: religious promiscuity.

Secular travel in the modern age was driven by the rise of a culture of reason and by the marked diversification of educational curricula for the élite as a consequence of the Protestant Reformation.[3] In this context, Turin had successfully avoided the significant decline in incoming foreign visitors that other Italian centres had witnessed due to the distinction of its educational traditions dating back to the Middle Ages. Since the late seventeenth century traditional enrolments at famous university centres in Italy had suffered a slowdown; this was not so, however, in the capital of the Sabaudian

---

[1] Brilli 2006: 185–6; 2010.
[2] Bianchi 2003a; 2007a; 2014.
[3] Maczak 2002: 323.

91

State – which had entered the scene almost a century after the Italian Grand Tour came into fashion. Turin had offered young gentlemen seeking to expand their educational horizons, including Protestants, the structure of a typical *Ritterakademie* and a political landscape characterized by manifest pragmatism. These elements would continue to augment Turin's fame throughout the eighteenth century.

As early as the 1630s – as noted by Franco Venturi – 'uno strano *modus vivendi* si era venuto stabilendo fra Roma e Londra' ('a peculiar modus vivendi had been established between Rome and London') and a growing number of British visitors travelled to the Italian peninsula. The policy implemented by Pope Innocent XI, due to his contempt for Louis XIV, had eventually – and not by chance – resulted in his indirect support of the Glorious Revolution.[4] Clearly, Rome would not cease to exert its well-known and powerful fascination on Britain in the following century, regardless of the connections that had resulted from the transfer to the papal city of the Jacobite court. At a time when Rome had lost the political charisma of the Holy See and, in the eyes of Protestant countries, had come to embody a new Babylon, Rome, so rich in archaeological and artistic treasures, nevertheless remained a fundamental meeting place for European travellers.[5] Turin was certainly lacking in all these aspects: a relatively small city, it was simply unable to compete with the tradition of the largest Italian cities of literary and artistic culture. Nevertheless, by the end of the seventeenth century, a connection had been established with many foreign aristocrats – including, but not limited to, Catholics – through the creation of the Accademia Reale or Turin Royal Academy. Before describing in greater detail this institution, which thrived throughout the eighteenth century, it is useful to provide an overview of the circumstances that led to its founding.

Religious Denominations in Turin at the Turn of the Eighteenth Century

It is difficult to assess how long Protestants had been residing in Turin. From early on the city had certainly welcomed followers of the Reformation among its troops, and as early as 1620 Charles Emmanuel I had established a 'fiera franca' or free-trade fair in Turin that was also open to non-Catholic

[4] Venturi 1973: 991–2.
[5] Marshall *et al.* 2011.

merchants.[6] However, the available data are not sufficient to identify this phenomenon from its inception, or to distinguish well between its various components (Lutherans, Calvinists, Waldesians), in terms of their level of cohesion, their activities or their provenance. On the other hand, the Protestant presence in Turin at the turn of the eighteenth century is well documented and provides a background for the experience of travellers in an atmosphere that reflected the economic and political context of the time.

The agreement reached between the House of Savoy and Anglican England had favoured, on the domestic front, an easing of tensions with the Waldesian communities. The campaigns of persecution that had periodically targeted those communities since the 1500s came to an end, significantly, at the time of the military campaigns of the War of the League of Augsburg, thus providing Britain greater contact with Piedmont, that would be consolidated in the eighteenth century.[7] The commercial and diplomatic pragmatism of the crown of England never lost sight of its relationship with the House of Savoy, not just in terms of the roadways that connected Turin to the Paduan Plains and the supply of Piedmontese silk, but also in light of the role the court of Savoy played in the international balance of power.[8] While the mercantilism implemented by Sabaudian rulers did not eliminate obstacles to the penetration into Piedmont of British imports and maritime communications through the port town of Nice (in fact, trade fell short of British expectations), the economic bond between the two States grew stronger. In this context, the Protestant community in Turin played a role that was far from marginal, particularly in three areas: 1) handicraft, trade and money-lending activities; 2) the army; and 3) diplomacy.[9]

The turning point came in the 1690s, when the events of the War of the League of Augsburg coincided with the consequences, in France, of the repeal of the Edict of Nantes (1685).[10] The clandestine assistance that, in the Savoy territories, had been provided to Protestants from Geneva and the Swiss cantons had been overridden, in those instances, by political agreements that favoured the coexistence of the 'religionari' (Protestants) with the Catholic population.[11] A decree issued in 1694 by Victor Amadeus II

---

[6] Archivio di Stato di Torino (hereafter AST), Corte, Provincia di Torino, Città di Torino, mz. 4, n. 13.
[7] Bianchi 2001: 73–117.
[8] See: Venturi 1956: 229 and *passim*; Levi 1967: 803 and *passim*; Venturi 1973: 1010–11; Chicco 1995; Chicco 2002: 155–84.
[9] Romagnani 2002: 423–51.
[10] Bianchi 2007b: 213–28; 2012a: 133–46.
[11] Carutti 1875–80: I, 432–43; II, 162, 517, 536.

had granted a level of supervised tolerance that paved the way for a new phase in the life of the Protestant enclave in Turin.[12]

The end of the War of the League of Augsburg (1696), however, brought this policy to a halt. Victor Amadeus II signed a separate peace agreement with Louis XIV and committed to expelling Huguenot 'refugees' in an attempt to contain the further dissemination of the Reformation. The Huguenot pastors and most Protestants who had settled in Turin were thus forced to leave the Duchy and to return to their countries of origin.[13] Dating to that same period, however, was also the official recognition of the extra-territorial status of the chapel available to the English Embassy, while the extent of constraints on Protestants who were living or travelling through the Sabaudian capital are unknown.[14] Nonetheless, the Reformed minority was not eliminated, in spite of the ban on professing 'heretical' ideas in public.

By this time, several 'religionari' members of the military had settled in Turin, and they provided a highly skilled reserve force that the Savoy troops would not renounce throughout the ancien régime. Indeed, in Piedmont foreign military officers were able to advance their careers because the State not only welcomed their precious contribution as war professionals (as was generally the case across Europe), but also saw them as a buffer against the old aristocracy that would otherwise have dominated positions of power among the troops and at Court. The honours bestowed by the Court of Savoy on a number of high-ranking officers of foreign origin and the assimilation of military units of Protestant religion (troops recruited in the Waldesian valleys to join the Savoy military Corps, and many Swiss and German regiments participating in major military campaigns) are two of the peculiarities that characterize the history of the Sabaudian State. Conversely, however, Sabaudian troops would also join foreign armies, with the migration flow directed mainly towards Germany between the seventeenth and eighteenth centuries.[15]

In this scenario, the facility that was home to those recently converted to Catholicism was transferred in the mid-1700s from Turin to Pinerolo, a town that had progressively evolved from a military outpost to a religious

---

[12] *Compendio de' sovrani provvedimenti* (no date, but post 1816), AST, Corte, Materie
       ecclesiastiche, cat. 38, Eretici, mz. 5 not inventoried; published in Duboin 1818–69: II, 257–9.
       On the controversy with the papacy, see: Viora 1930: 202–41; Rostain 1940: 29–30; Pascal
       1924: 186–210.
[13] Romagnani 2002: 426–7.
[14] Storrs 1999: 137.
[15] Bianchi 2012a.

bulwark to protect Waldesian enclaves.[16] While forced conversion had far from ended, in the heart of the State the government had opted for medi-ation with the Protestant powers, thus mitigating the intransigence of those Episcopal sees that were still persisting in encouraging conversion by deceiving unsuspecting children and young people.[17]

The number of Protestants in the Sabaudian capital can only be calcu-lated starting from 1724, the year in which the Savoy ruler launched an annual census of the urban population broken down by religious groups: up to that point the only distinction applied had been between Catholics and Jews.[18] In 1726, Turin counted 144 Protestants and 1,056 Jews out of a total population of 63,819. During the economic crisis of the 1730s, the num-ber of Protestants decreased significantly, and by 1751 the number ranged between a minimum of 45 and a maximum of 86 individuals. In the middle of the century the overall population started to increase, and the number of Protestants rose to between 150 and 200, with a peak in 1769–71 when the number reached 216. Another drop followed in the last decades of the century, when the number of Protestants in Turin stabilized at around 70 or 80 each year. It should be noted, however, that the surveys did not take into account military personnel and their families, diplomats and diplomatic legations, and all those who, for various reasons, were temporarily present at court.[19]

This Protestant segment of the population mainly consisted of merchants, shopkeepers and bankers, but there were also lawyers and 'aritmetici' or pro-fessional groups, as well as domestic help, labourers, errand boys, tailors, barbers and watchmakers.[20] The percentage of merchants and creditors was, however, quite high – a trait that connotes this community as belonging to the upper middle class.[21] When, in the mid-eighteenth century, hostil-ity started growing against this enterprising group, the government tried to expel them through an authoritarian act targeting the 'ginevrini' (peo-ple from Geneva). In fact, the ultimate target of this measure was quite a diverse group in terms of origin and religious denomination, while the town of Geneva was simply a crossroads between Turin, other Italian towns, and the Dutch, French and British markets. Eventually, the inevitable need to

---

[16] The Hospice of the Catechumens remained in operation in Turin until 1746. Allegra 1990: 513–73. On Pinerolo, see: Merlotti 2001b: 73–136.

[17] *Lettere, pareri ed altre scritture* (1773–4), AST, Corte, Materie ecclesiastiche, Eretici, mz. 1 not inventoried; *Lettere* (1774–6).

[18] Romagnani 2002: 428; Bianchi 2012a: 139.

[19] Balani 1987; Bianchi 2005a: 473–504.

[20] Balani 1995: 13–46; Pascal 1937: 18.

[21] Davico 1986: 109–33; Romagnani 2002: 436.

access safe credit led to the pragmatic decision to rethink any exclusionary plan, and it is important to note that, to forsake a rigid closure, a patronage system was organized by Rochford, the British Envoy to Turin, the Secretary of Foreign Affairs Ossorio and the Savoy Envoy to London Perrone di San Martino.[22] Thus a sort of 'interested tolerance' was established that deflected some of the hostility – more or less widespread – against the Protestants which would last for some considerable time even in the educated discussions of scientific and literary circles in Turin in the late eighteenth century.[23]

The Origins of the Turin Royal Academy

The self-interested tolerance that in the mid-eighteenth century had been created through specific commercial and military negotiations had thrived in the cultural climate of the late seventeenth century, which saw the presence in Turin, if only for a limited period of time, of a number of foreign gentlemen concerned with furthering their educations.

There is no significant evidence of a Protestant presence in research documents devoted to students living in Turin in the early modern period: not in the oldest schooling institutions, nor at the reformed university in the 1720s, nor in the colleges of the religious orders, for obvious reasons.[24] It is known that in the sixteenth century, some students in Turin were aware of writings by Protestant authors, but the very same students had been compelled to leave town to avoid censure and arrest.[25] The crisis of the *peregrinatio academica* – that between the sixteenth and the seventeenth centuries had deprived the most prestigious Italian universities (except for Padua) of their supranational status[26] – had not spared the town of Turin. None the less, Turin remained a fundamental stopping point on the itinerary of the Grand Tour. The Protestant question had arisen in the Sabaudian capital as the result of contact with the travellers, diplomats and young aristocrats who had been attracted to the city by the establishment of the Turin Royal Academy between 1677 and 1678.

---

[22] William Henry Nassau de Zuylestein, 4th Earl of Rochford (1717–81), British Envoy to Turin (1749–55), Ambassador to Madrid (1763–6) and Paris (1766–8), Secretary of State (1768–75). On Ossorio, see: Merlotti, 2013b. On Perrone, see: Bianchi, 2015b.

[23] Romagnani 2002: 446–8, 450–1.

[24] Catarinella and Salsotto 2002: 546–56. On the eighteenth-century reform of the university, see: Ricuperati 1968: 24 and *passim*; Roggero 1981; Roggero 1987; Bianchi 1992: 241–66; Bianchi 1993: 353–93; Bianchi 1995: 308–9; Balani 1996; Delpiano 1997; Carpanetto 1998.

[25] Platone 2003.

[26] See: Brizzi 1976a: 205; De Bernardin 1983: 65–72; Bianchi 1998: 166, 179–80; Zonta 2000: 35–6.

Starting in the second half of the sixteenth century the main urban centres in the Duchy of Savoy had seen the flourishing of colleges run by religious or secular masters, but study programmes were not available at all
levels from the lower ('umanità' or humanity) to the upper ('pieno esercizio'
or full exercise) in all of the towns.[27] At the turn of the century it was decided
that two new institutions would be established in the capital, also with a
view to redefining attendance intake: the Collegio dei Nobili (or College
of Noblemen), entrusted to the Jesuits, and the Accademia Reale (or Royal
Academy), organized and located within the Court itself. Both institutions
provided for the possibility – which was rare at the time – of finding accommodation at the school instead of requiring students to find private lodging,
but they targeted different élites: mostly Sabaudian for the former, foreign
for the latter. The advance publicity that the Dukes of Savoy devoted to the
'equestris Academia' in the *Theatrum Statuum Regiae Celsitudinis Sabaudiae
Ducis* was testimony to the European breadth that the two institutions were
intended to embody (Fig. 0.4). Significantly, in the extensive iconographic
corpus printed in 1682 by the presses of the Dutch publisher and cartographer Blaeu, the figurative approach had attached greater emphasis to the
Royal Academy than to the College of Noblemen, while both facilities were
being constructed at the same time.[28] The Academy became operational
between 1680 and 1685, before the inauguration of the chapel, the riding
school and the riding ground, all of which were designed later.

During the same months that the *Madama Reale* (Marie Jeanne Baptiste
Nemours) approved the establishment of the Royal Academy, a literary
academy was created following the express wish of Duke Charles Emmanuel
II. Although few traces of this remain, it was located in the building adjacent to the ducal Palace, and had been created to promote knowledge of the
Italian and French languages through regular gatherings of Piedmontese
and foreign noblemen. While the Royal Academy required the practice of
the knightly exercise of 'body and spirit', the literary academy encouraged
its members to participate in literary activities, outside of regular school
curricula, which were regarded as 'd'ornamento e d'utilità alla Corte et allo
Stato' ('an ornament and a useful asset to the Court and the State').[29] It is
unclear whether this facility was part of the Royal Academy, along the lines
of what was customary in *seminaria nobilium*.[30] Nor is it known to what

[27] Catarinella and Salsotto 1998: 523–67.
[28] Roccia 2000: II, tab. I, 13. For the seat of the Collegio dei Nobili, see: Dardanello 1993a: 175–
252. For the seat of the Royal Academy, see: Bagliani *et al.* 2000.
[29] Vallauri 1844: 113–22; Claretta 1878: 204.
[30] Brizzi 1976b: 227, 235–56.

Figure 5.1 After Charles Dauphin, *Victor Amadeus II before the Royal Academy of Turin*, engraving by Antonio de Pienne, 1675, Turin, Archivio Storico della Città di Torino, Collezione Simeom.

extent this undertaking by Marie Jeanne Baptiste was influenced by the contemporary activities of Christina Queen of Sweden, patron of several literary academies in the palaces that she resided in, in Rome. Whatever the case may be, in 1676, Paolo Negri, secretary to the Duke of Savoy in Rome, informed the Turin court that the academy inaugurated two years earlier by Christina of Sweden had 'già preso notevole incremento' ('already undergone some remarkable increase') (Fig. 5.1).[31]

In the seventeenth century Piedmont had already witnessed the flourishing of literary academies, including those sponsored by Cardinal Maurice in Rome and Turin.[32] At that time, no tensions had arisen due to religious conflicts, as instead was the case in the instance under examination here. A Jesuit, Carlo Maurizio Vota (1629–1715), played an active role in the literary

---

[31] Claretta 1892: 214; Rotta 1990: 99–174.
[32] Oberli 1999: 99–104, 115–16. On eighteenth-century conversations and salons, see Merlotti in this volume.

academy established by Marie Jeanne Baptiste and contributed significantly
to the opening of the College of Noblemen. Vota had made a name for himself
in Venice teaching rhetoric at the college of the Fondamenta Nuove, holding
lessons that were also open to noblemen of the Venetian Republic, apostolic
nuncios and German Protestant princes.[33] When he was in Piedmont, Vota
attended the first meetings of the literary academy sponsored by Marie Jeanne
Baptiste, calling extensively on his Venetian experience.[34] Documents attest
that the encounters continued until the second regent died (1724), and indicate that Vota – who had appointed Girolamo Brusoni (another important
trait-d'union with the Venetian cultural milieu) as first 'director'[35] – resorted
to all of his skills in mediation to overcome the complications raised by the
Holy See, provoked by the fact that Protestant princes were participating in
the Turin talks. Vota had suggested to the Duchess that the Academy also
welcome Protestants simply as temporary visitors, without any formal or permanent association.[36] From 1677 to 1681 Marie Jeanne Baptiste, supported
by the Savoy minister to Rome, Orazio Provana, and the Sabaudian Abbot
de Cagnol, had already repeatedly engaged in negotiations with the clergy
to reach a tacit compromise, that left the Protestant question *de facto* unresolved.[37] Similarly to the literary academy, the Royal Academy had, since its
inception, welcomed Germans from the Protestant States: aristocrats from
Pomerania, Silesia and Saxony.[38] Other British, German, and some orthodox
Russian noblemen also joined the academy in the course of the eighteenth
century, reinvigorating the cosmopolitan and multi-dominational climate
that had matured around the court of Turin.

The Turin Royal Academy in the Golden Age of the Grand Tour in Italy

The inspiration for the Turin Royal Academy derived from the chivalric
academies that had been established in various Italian and German courts

---

[33] See: Sommervogel 1890–1909: VIII, 919–21; Maylender 1926–30: I, 337–8; II, 105. For
   educational institutes in Venice, see: Del Negro 2003: 98–9.

[34] AST, Corte, Lettere di particolari, V, mz. 42, letter from Vota to Madama Reale, 1
   November 1678.

[35] Claretta 1873: 81–96.

[36] AST, Corte, Lettere di particolari, V, mz. 42, letter from Vota (December 1679). See
   also: Gilardi 1998: 116–18, 121; Silvestrini 2002: 1162.

[37] Claretta 1887: 135–42.

[38] *Notizie sull'istituzione dell'Accademia Reale* (1679), AST, Corte, Istruzione Pubblica, Accademia
   Militare (già Accademia Reale), mz. 1 not inventoried. The early 'manifesti' (1677, 1685) are
   found in AST, Corte, Istruzione pubblica, Accademia Militare (già Accademia Reale), mz. 1
   d'addizione, n. 1, published in: Duboin 1818–69: XIV, 790–4.

in the early modern age, as well as from the *seminaria nobilium* that were spreading across Europe. Peculiar to Turin was the connection with institutes for pages, resulting in a very close relationship with the Court.[39] The Academy depended on the organization of the Court, and, while ecclesiastical figures served as teachers, its administration was never entrusted to any religious order. Its institutional transformations can be summarized according to existing but rather scant documentation, which testifies to the adoption of a number of reforms mostly aimed at adjusting original seventeenth-century curricula to the cultural offerings of Turin in the eighteenth century.

Closed temporarily in 1690 during the War of the League of Augsburg, the Academy reopened in 1697. Lessons in the classroom associated chivalric exercises to theory, most notably in geometry, geography, 'cronologia delli Stati de' sovrani' ('chronology of the states of sovereigns'), mathematics and drawing.[40] From 1697 to 1713, owing to a number of conflicts at that time, the Academy was able to provide only riding activities to a limited number of attendees, including page boys.[41] After another interruption from 1703 to 1713, the courses resumed in earnest until the 1720s,[42] mostly benefiting various German princes.[43]

The reform in 1730 eventually allowed the Academy to go beyond this transitional phase and to inaugurate an educational programme that reflected more significantly material taught at the former institute for pages. The creation of the three 'apartments' also occurred at this time: the Academy no longer consisted of a single college, but of three distinct sections for boys and young men aged between ten and 30.[44] The first apartment was home to pages and those pursuing a chivalric career; the second to those who were training for a military career or preparing to enter university (with a special emphasis on the law), that they would subsequently attend in the nearby seat of the university; and the third was home to the youngest students, who started with the rudiments of the 'basse scuole'

[39] For an Italian comparison, see: Protopapa 2003: 27–44; Cont 2013.

[40] See: Duboin 1818–69: XIV, 796–9; AST, Corte, Istruzione pubblica, Accademia Militare (già Accademia Reale), mz. 1 addition, n. 2.

[41] *Recueil des piéces* (8 June 1807), AST, Corte, Istruzione pubblica, Accademia Militare (già Accademia Reale), mz. 1 not inventoried.

[42] See: Duboin 1818–69: XIV, 799–804; AST, Corte, Istruzione pubblica, Regia Università di Torino, mz. 1 addition, nn. 3–4.

[43] *Memorie* (1719), AST, Corte, Cerimoniale, Funzioni diverse, mz. 1 addition, n. 8. See: Bianchi 2010a.

[44] *Correzione del primo progetto dell'Accademia* (not dated, but *c.* 1734), AST, Corte, Istruzione pubblica, Accademia Militare, già Accademia Reale, mz. 1 addition, n. 11; Duboin 1818–69: XIV, 804–30.

(elementary teachings): grammar, geography, basic principles of science and history. Suspicions dictated by religious denominational concerns focused on the first apartment, which was directly linked to the Court, but that also offered privileged access to numerous socializing opportunities for the gentlemen attending. It was a sort of 'no man's land' that Vittorio Alfieri, *a posteriori*, when remembering his experience as an 'accademista' (academist') in the years 1758–66, characterized colourfully and ambiguously as a place of 'sfrenata e insultante libertà' ('unrestrained and insulting freedom') (Fig. 5.2).[45]

Some important changes to the regulations were made in the second half of the century. In 1759 a more detailed programme was defined for the second and third apartments, based upon the model of the Austrian Academy of Wiener-Neustadt, founded by the Empress Maria Theresa (1752). Starting in 1769, the cadets of the second apartment were allowed to leave the premises of the Academy to attend not only university courses, but also the lessons held at the Artillery School that were organized, in 1739, in Via della Zecca (today Via Verdi) and then transferred in the early 1780s to the Via dell'Arsenale.[46] The number of those enrolled in the third apartment decreased and, in 1778, the 'basse scuole' were eliminated, while the first and second apartments remained in operation until the interruption of the Napoleonic years that were an institutional watershed for the Academy.[47]

In this context, religious heterogeneity was preserved, if somewhat toned down by the compromise reached between the Sabaudian State and the Holy See. As has been documented, in the forefront of the 'politica della religione' ('politics of religion') the Savoy dominions adhered to a rather unstructured regulatory framework, while canon law was 'duttile ed elastico' ('flexible and elastic') and allowed for the 'mediare o dilazionare i conflitti di potere secondo logiche contingenti' ('mediating or deferring conflicts of power according to contingent considerations').[48] It is useful to note that in Piedmont the Apostolic Nunciature was only active for about a decade, between 1741 and 1753, and that inquisitors were dismissed early in the century, leaving inquisition tribunals in the hands of vicars. In the Sabaudian State, secular magistrates mostly interacted with bishops, whose appointment was regulated according to the concordat rules, that left the

---

[45]　Alfieri 1981: 27.

[46]　For the Royal Schools of Artillery and Engineering, see: Barberis 1988; Ferrone 1988; Bianchi 2002.

[47]　In the years of the Napoleonic occupation a secondary school (*liceo*) opened temporarily in the Royal Academy, before the building was turned into a higher institute for military officers of the Savoy and, later, the Italian Army.

[48]　Silvestrini 1997: 11.

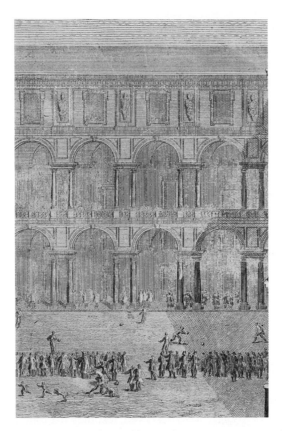

Figure 5.2 Benedetto Alfieri and Giovanni Antonio Belmond, *View of the Courtyard of the Turin Royal Academy, with Students Playing Hand-ball,* 1761, Turin, Archivio di Stato di Torino, Corte, Palazzi reali, Fabbriche regie, Disegni Alfieri c. 4.

application of Gallican customs to the discretion of its various territories (in Savoie, Nice, Aosta and the valleys of Pinerolo).

The prosopographical study of the Academy's writings illustrates in detail the impact of the Protestant (Anglican, but also Calvinist and Lutheran) presence and, to a lesser extent, that of the Orthodox presence (represented by a smaller group of Russians).[49] A quick overview of institutional documentation provides us with some interesting insights. A royal notice, addressed in 1730 to the Governor of the Academy, for example, recommended a close monitoring of the 'morale cristiana' (Christian morality): 'cristiana', not Catholic or Roman-Catholic.[50] In 1754 the Secretary of

[49] See Appendix III. For a partial identification of British attendees at the Academy (1758–66), see: Bianchi 2003b.
[50] Duboin 1818–69: XIV, 804–9.

the Academy referred to the obligation, dating back to 1730, for the butcher who supplied the institute to 'provvedere a giusto prezzo di tassa e a quelle condizioni prescritte dal controllore quella quantità di carne necessaria per la casa, non solo ne' giorni magri per servizio dei britannici nel primo appartamento, ma anche in ogni occorrenza per gli ammalati' ('provide, at a fair duty price and at the conditions prescribed by the comptroller, the adequate amount of meat necessary for the household, not only for the British on their lean days in the first apartment, but also, when needed, for the sick').[51] In this case, there is explicit reference to the religious sanitary practices of a non-Catholic group. The *Regolamento* or Regulation of the first apartment, dated 1760, stigmatized behaviours that encouraged heterodoxy in its widest sense: 'affectation de singularité tendante à blesser le respect de la réligion et de la morale chrétienne' ('show of individuality aimed at breaching the respect of Christian religion and morals'). 'Les académistes catholiques assisteront tous les premiers dimanches de chaque mois aux offices de la congrégation' ('Catholic academists shall participate, every first Sunday of the month, in the offices of the congregation'): the specification whereby Catholic students were required to make regular visits to the Chapel inside the Academy implies, in this context, the presence of students of other denominations.[52] Finally, in 1778, the spiritual directors of the Royal Academy appealed to the Pontiff for a pardon concerning the institute's oratory, that had been planned for a long time but the construction of which had been stalled by difficulties in negotiations. As reported to Victor Amadeus III by the Savoy Ambassador to Rome, Pietro Graneri, the delay was due to unresolved Roman suspicions about the 'mescolanza *sub eodem tecto* dei cattolici e dei protestanti' ('the mixing *sub eodem tecto* of Catholics and Protestants').[53]

This long-term coexistence was preserved through the actions of diplomatic cabinets, that included various ranks of representatives – ambassadors, plenipotentiaries, envoys extraordinary and representatives 'senza

---

[51] *Rappresentanza del segretario della Regia Accademia* (Representative of the Royal Academy Secretary) (1754), AST, Corte, Istruzione pubblica, Accademia Militare (formerly Accademia Reale), mz. 1, n. 15.

[52] *Regolamento dell'Accademia Reale di Torino pel primo appartamento* (Regulation of the Royal Academy of Turin for the first apartment) (Turin, Imprimerie Royale, 1760). In other regulations, that were printed and distributed, it was stated that one should not wander away 'da' doveri del Cristianesimo' ('from the duties of the Christian faith'). AST, Corte, Istruzione pubblica, Accademia Militare (formerly Accademia Reale), mz. 1, mz. 1 addition and mz. 1 not inventoried; Duboin 1818–69: XIV, 790–56.

[53] Letter from Graneri, 7 March 1778.

rango particolare' ('without any particular rank').[54] In some cases, these figures held prominent social positions,[55] but in general they were able to conduct delicate negotiations, at times in spite of complex personal vicissitudes related to religious matters. Significantly, for example, London had sent two Huguenots, Arthur de Villettes and Louis Dutens, to Turin: both were of French origin, both were exiled for religious reasons and living in Britain and charged with diplomatic missions, both eventually were sent to Piedmont, where the diaspora of the *réfugiés* had found one of its safest havens.

De Villettes (1701–76) lived in Turin, first as Secretary and then as British Resident, from 1734 to 1749. He was descended from an ancient, aristocratic French family whose members had served under various French Kings until the clashes between Catholics and Huguenots broke out. The family sided with the Protestants and eventually chose to move to Britain after the revocation of the Edict of Nantes. Trained in the arts of diplomacy, De Villettes was Minister Plenipotentiary of the British Crown for a number of years. He transferred from Turin to the Swiss Cantons, where he married a Genevan resident and retired from public life in 1762, spending his last years in the town of Bath.[56] In Turin, de Villettes closely followed the conduct of British gentlemen at the Royal Academy: these included, amongst others, in 1739–40, Henry Fiennes Clinton, 9th Earl of Lincoln (1720–94), the nephew of the Secretary of State of the Southern Department, the Duke of Newcastle.[57] Testimonials of his posting at the Savoy court are preserved in a memoir 'concerning the rights and privileges annexed to the character of residents', that argued in favour of the prerogative of the British Representative to attend a private chapel.[58]

[54] See the essay by Storrs and Appendix I in this volume. On hierarchy in the diplomatic corps, see: Horn 1932: I, 119–27; Bindoff *et al.* 1934: 118–22; Wynne 1996: 145–60.

[55] This was the case with John Stuart, Lord Mount Stuart, 1st Marquess of Bute (1779–83); see: Bianchi 2012b: 135–60.

[56] His second child, William Anne (1754–1808), was born in Switzerland. He was a cadet in a Regiment of Dragoons (1775), then aide-de-camp and secretary to William Pitt the Younger, Major-General (1798), Comptroller of the Household of the Prince of Kent (Prince Edward), Colonel of the 64th infantry regiment, and lastly Lieutenant-governor in Jamaica (1807), where he died and was buried. A monument in his honour was erected by his friends, including Giacomo Casanova, at Westminster Abbey. See: Bowdler 1815.

[57] Letter from Villettes to Newcastle (1740) in the British Library, Manuscripts, Add. 32802, fols 180, 217–20. See also: Black 1989.

[58] *Sentimento del signor procuratore generale* (Sentiment of the Lord Prosecutor General) (5 April 1742), AST, Corte, Cerimoniale, Ambasciatori e inviati, mz. 1 addition, n. 7. Villettes was regarded as a 'third-tier' minister (the first included ambassadors, the second envoys extraordinary), but the matter remained controversial. On the temporary presence of British representatives in the Ferrero d'Ormea Palace, see: Palmucci 2003: 466; Piccoli, this volume. In

Louis Dutens was a wealthy scholar of French origin who, in 1749, had fled from Tours – where he was born in 1730 into a Huguenot family – to join his uncle, a jeweller, in England (Fig. 4.4). After becoming a tutor, he became proficient in ancient Greek and other oriental languages, as well as modern Italian and Spanish. After taking his holy orders and becoming an Abbot and a naturalized British subject, he moved to Turin in 1758 as chaplain of the British Embassy. In 1761 he took over as chargé d'affaires, succeeding Stuart Mackenzie, when Mackenzie left Turin. In 1762, when the new ambassador, George Pitt, arrived in the Savoy capital, Dutens returned to England; but from February 1764 to September 1765 he was back in Piedmont as Pitt's replacement at the Embassy.[59] Once back in London, he turned down an offer to serve the powerful Duke of Northumberland, but he accepted a position to accompany the Duke's son Percy on his Grand Tour. After an extended stay in Tours, that allowed Dutens to return to the sites of his childhood, the two travelled to Genoa, Florence, Rome, Naples, Venice, Turin again (where they remained for more than six months), Geneva, Bern, Vienna and Berlin. The tour ended in 1772. From 1774 to 1776 Dutens was in Paris, where he worked as a publisher. In 1775 he was admitted to France's prestigious Académie des Inscriptions et Belles-lettres and became a Fellow of the Royal Society. In the years that followed, he divided his time between Britain and Italy, and he also returned to Turin, where he was appointed to a diplomatic post for the third time.[60] After another stay in Paris, he spent his last years in England, where he died in 1812. A very productive and cultured writer, he was also committed to defending Christianity against the claims of the *philosophes*, linking his name to an important edition of Leibniz's works and the translation into French, in 1790, of *Reflections on the Revolution in France* by Edmund Burke. He published three large volumes that appeared in an abridged version for the first time in 1782, and that were published in a more extensive form in 1806, in which he collected memories, literary portraits, and reflections on the social and cultural circumstances he had become familiar with during his travels across Europe. His time in Turin was described in detail: 'Le roi de Sardaigne est l'allié naturel du roi d'Angleterre aussi un ministre d'Angleterre est toujours bien

---

the nineteenth century the chapel of Protestant legations, under the protection of the British, Dutch and Prussian governments, was formally recognized in the palace of the Prussian Embassy. Chiavia 2003: 197–8.

[59] The correspondence sent from Turin is in the National Archives, State Papers, 92/68–9, 92/71. See also Yarker in this volume for Dutens relations with the court and a curious encounter with Victor Amadeus III.

[60] Talucchi 1960–1.

Figure 5.3 Carlo Sciolli, *The Turin Royal Academy*, lithograph, Turin, Doyen, 1836, Private collection, Turin.

vu à cette cour et n'a pas de peine à s'y faire aimer' ('The king of Sardinia is the natural ally of the king of England and a British minister is always well-regarded at this Court and has no trouble being loved'), he wrote, for example, in his notes dated 1775. Ministers, aristocrats and members of the upper classes, men of letters and science from Turin society, all spring to life in his pages.

Ce qui me plaisoit à Turin étoit la facilité d'y rencontrer les étrangers de distinction, qui y abordoient de toutes parts pour visiter l'Italie. Tous vont à Rome et passent par

Turin. Plus je restois à Turin, plus j'en aimois le séjour; j'y avois beaucoup d'amis, j'étois répandu dans la meilleure compagnie, et j'étois bien vu à la Cour [*sic*]

(What I liked about Turin was the ease with which I met distinctive foreigners, who came from all over to visit Italy. Everyone visits Rome and everyone passes through Turin. The longer I stayed in Turin, the more I enjoyed my stay; I had many friends there, I was surrounded by the finest company, and I was well regarded by the Court).[61]

This is how things stood in Duten's experience after spending time in Piedmont in the 1760s and 1780s. However, little remained of that cosmopolitan Turin by the early nineteenth century – the city was no longer a place where the court and institutions like the Royal Academy had been powerful catalysts. The context in which court life in the Sabaudian capital would resume after the Restoration would be quite different. And just as different would be the role played by the Turin Royal Academy, reborn as a military academy, reinventing a tradition dictated by what was, by that time, a national historiographic vision (Fig. 5.3).

[61] Dutens 1806a: II, 252–4.

6 | Thomas Coke in Turin and the Turin Royal Academy

ANDREW MOORE

Thomas Coke (1697–1759), who was to become 1st Earl of Leicester of the 5th creation in 1744, was abroad for almost six years, from 1712 to 1718, one of the longest grand tours undertaken by an Englishman (Fig. 6.1).[1] An invaluable record of his travels lies within the financial account books of the tour which provide an authentic record, day by day, of the young master's travels by post and chaise across Europe, following routes only recently established. A general overview of his journey reveals how a number of cities acted as vantage points from which to take excursions, and often return visits, that were not directly on the route.[2] He was just fifteen when he left England, returning in time to celebrate his majority at the age of 21 years old, just weeks before his arranged marriage to the wealthy heiress Margaret Tufton. One of the key centres for his time in Italy was Turin.[3]

The European tour in the early eighteenth century was to have an extraordinary impact upon early Georgian taste in collecting as well as architecture. The way that the tour contributed to education at this period resulted in an engagement with antiquity and late European Baroque culture that spread across the art forms – whether architecture, the collecting of sculpture, books, drawings or paintings, and even the taste for classical music and libretti based upon classical and mythological tales. This was an

---

[1] I wish to acknowledge the continuing support I have received from Lord and Lady Leicester during the course of my work on Thomas Coke's Grand Tour and its impact upon Holkham Hall. I am grateful also to Christine Hiskey, Archivist, and Suzanne Reynolds, formerly Holkham Library curator of manuscripts and printed books, for their unfailing responses to my enquiries about the Holkham collections in their charge. I am also grateful to Edward Bottoms and Anthony Smith for their help in establishing a conflated text of the two closely related versions of the Grand Tour accounts in Holkham Hall, Archives, F/TC 4 and F/TC 5 (Coke's travel accounts), which I am preparing for publication.

[2] For an overview of Coke's tour in Italy see: Ingamells 1997: 225–6.

[3] Coke's time in Turin is briefly considered in: James 1929: 185, 189–90; Lees-Milne 1986: 208, 210. The duration of Coke's time in Piedmont and Turin was: Wednesday 1 November 1713 (journey from Chambéry)–Saturday 2 December 1713 (Holkham Hall, Archives, F/TC 4 fol. 48); Monday 17 December 1714 (start of journey through Piedmont, page 96)–Sunday 30 December 1714; Tuesday 1 January 1715 (Holkham Hall, Archives, F/TC 4 fol. 98)– Tuesday 30 April 1715 (Holkham Hall, Archives, F/TC 4 fol. 109).

Figure 6.1 Francesco Trevisani, *Thomas Coke*, oil on canvas, 1717, © Holkham Estate, reproduced by kind permission of Lord Leicester and the Trustees of Holkham Estate, Norfolk.

all-pervasive aesthetic, which gave rise to a new interpretation of British Classicism, expressed through collections as well as architecture, leading to the ascendancy of the Amateur, whether as patron, collector or architect.[4] To follow Thomas Coke's European tour through the medium of his financial accounts is to witness the skeletal story of a young man's classical

---

[4] Amateur in England at this time reflected its French origin, denoting a lover of the arts who could also be a collector.

education that was complete of itself, and not simply the finale of an education undertaken at Eton and Oxford or Cambridge. The building of his new house at Holkham Hall (Fig. 6.2) in the county of Norfolk can be seen as entirely the outcome of Coke's experience of the Grand Tour.[5] It is in the minutiae of the account books, in the absence of any more expansive journal or correspondence, that I base this chapter.[6] My purpose is to establish just how Thomas Coke can be seen as an exemplar of the scholarly application of virtuosity, which was to result not only in his acceptance by his contemporaries as the virtuoso he believed he had become (by as early as 24 May 1714), but also the patron architect of his lifetime achievement, his grand tour seat at Holkham Hall.

Coke spent a great deal of the family's resources on works of art whilst abroad, all purposed for his new seat in the country – a project that must have grown in his mind with every palace he visited, especially in Rome during the years 1714, 1716 and 1717. In summary, Coke's travels proved to be the making of Holkham as one of the finest country seats in Britain, in terms of both architecture and contents. Coke's time in Piedmont, particularly while based at the Savoy Royal Academy (Accademia Reale), provided the environment for acquiring far more than simply military or social etiquette skills and demonstrates the importance of a leading centre among numerous others in northern Italy and also northern Europe during the course of an educative tour for which Rome was the principal but not necessarily exclusive goal.

Turin and Piedmont

Turin and Piedmont are in a sense just one of a number of northern European cities and states becoming established by 1700 as classic centres for the Northern European traveller.[7] Piedmont was special as a place of recuperation after a long and hazardous journey. The Piedmont plain was a

---

[5] Coke's tour ended in 1718. The Holkham landscape park was laid out during the 1720s, following initial design ideas sketched out by William Kent. Kent's involvement is not securely dated, the traditional dating of c. 1732 based upon the probability that it was at some point before the laying of the foundation stone in 1734, with a second phase of c. 1737 according to the estate accounts (Schmidt *et al.* 2005: 60–3). The final interior decoration was not actually finished until 1761, some two years after his death, but overseen by his dowager widow Lady Margaret.

[6] To date just seventeen letters written by Coke or his Governor are traceable for the entire period of their tour.

[7] For recent overviews of the tour, see: Chaney 2000; Sweet 2012; Chaney and Wilks 2014.

Figure 6.2 Holkham Hall, © Holkham Estate, reproduced by kind permission of Lord Leicester and the Trustees of Holkham Estate, Norfolk.

first welcome respite after crossing Mont Cenis, providing a chance to relax and recover. Coke was not alone, on arrival in Turin, in acquiring a wardrobe appropriate for this new stage of the journey, specifically the scarlet cloth for a bespoke brocade waistcoat and britches together with scarlet silk stockings, and new boots, presumably in order to be properly attired for a visit to the Academy, although he was not to register until the following year.[8] He also purchased powder and oil for his hair, bottles of burgundy and champagne – and plenty of chocolate.

Victor Amadeus II (Fig. 0.6) was well established at this time and introducing a number of administrative reforms. He was responsible for the new appearance of the city centre, with a large administrative area developed around the ducal palace, including the new military academy, the ministry of war, a mint and the customs house, effectively refocusing the militia system in 1714. During the War of the Spanish Succession, Victor Amadeus had switched allegiance to assist the Habsburgs and in consequence under the terms of the Treaty of Utrecht, became King of Sicily in 1713, but was later forced to exchange the title for that of King of Sardinia in 1720.[9] During Coke's two visits in 1713 and 1714/15 Turin was therefore an impressive combination of both French and Italian influence in architectural terms, while politically allied to the British and Habsburg lines. This was to have a

[8] See below.
[9] See Corp's chapter in this volume for an account of the historical and political context to this period of Turin's history.

seminal effect upon the young Coke, aiding an appreciation of architecture that allowed for influence and individuality rather than strict and rigorous interpretation of the Palladian model. Coke was soon to visit both Naples and Sicily, effectively surveying a continuation of Habsburg influence in conjunction with that of the House of Savoy.

Edward Jarrett's account books shed considerable light on the importance of Turin and Piedmont for the young traveller. His first visit was for just a fortnight in November 1713, having crossed Mont Cenis. There the party had hired strong carriers to take them by sedan chair, to reach Susa, and had then proceeded to Turin with the help of a guide by horse and chaise, hiring a mule for luggage and arriving on 7 November. His next visit was a year later, when the party arrived at Turin on 15 December 1714, and the city acted as a base for four months. These two visits were both when Thomas Coke was relatively young and it is important to remember that no matter how precocious he was deemed to be, his principal interests were youthful as well as educative under his tutor, Dr Thomas Hobart.[10]

Coke's First Visit to Turin in 1713

Coke's visit in 1713 is significant for his choice of sites in the limited time he had, the first being a visit by chaise to 'the King's Contrey House', as his valet Edward Jarrett describes it (14 November 2013). This was the Venaria Reale (Fig. 6.3), the King's 'hunting palace', already on the tourist itinerary. One English tourist, William Bromley, describes the palace as it was when he visited in 1691. The description in the second edition of his guidebook[11] would still have held in 1713, despite the building activity that bedevilled the site during this period:

It is in a good Country for it: Coming to the Palace there is a *Visto*, through handsome Uniform buildings, and the Sight is terminated on the Front of the Palace. In the great Hall are Pictures of many Ladies of the Family, astride on horseback, and in their hunting dresses. In the Rooms on each side are ma[n]y good Pictures. Below are the Duke and the Duchess their apartment, and for their Relations; all above Stairs are for the Courtiers. The Duke's Stables are well filled, and many of his Horses English.

---

[10] Coke's precociousness was commented upon by 'Mr Gullmann his Majesty's Resident in Frankfort' in a report in the Townshend papers dated 7 November 1715, who estimated his age at that time as 'peut avoir environ 23 ans'. He was actually just eighteen years old. British Library Add. MS 38507, fols 174r–175v.

[11] Bromley 1705: 244.

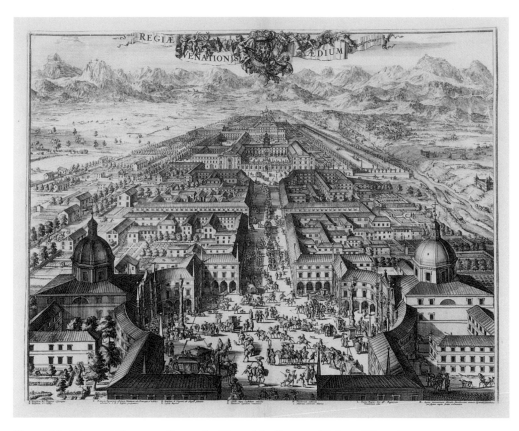

Figure 6.3 Giovanni Tommaso Borgonio, *View of the Town and Palace of Venaria*, in *Theatrum Statuum Regiae Celsitudinis Sabaudiae Ducis*, Amsterdam, Blaeu, 1682, vol. I, plate 37, Reggia di Veneria.

This, together with a second visit to the Venaria Reale in 1715, is typical of Coke's gradual and formative assimilation of the historic environment – including the recently built as well as developments under construction.

Coke's experience of Turin, even – or especially – for one so young, is important (as for any tourist newly arrived in Italy) for being an introduction to Italian culture. At this time that experience was modulated through the French influence of the House of Savoy, despite its status as an independent state. One payment records that he heard 'the King's music', those singers and members of the orchestra on the King's payroll. Musicians at this time would play at the Palazzo Carignano or alternatively in the city churches, as Juvarra and Alfieri's Regio Teatro was to be built only in 1740. Up to this point musical dramas were presented at the Court Theatre and at the recently built Teatro Carignano within the Palazzo Carignano (Fig. 6.4), one of the noblest buildings in Turin. The Teatro Carignano acquired its

Figure 6.4 Guarino Guarini, *The Facade of Palazzo Carignano*, c. 1679, engraved by Antoine de Pienne, in G. Guarini, *Architettura civile*, Turin, 1737, Reggia di Venaria.

own autonomy and specialized in hosting Italian and French comedies and operas, while the Court Theatre at this time was devoted to melodrama.[12]

Coke had one further experience unique to the city's reputation on this first brief visit when he paid a guard to let him see the *Sindone*, the Turin Shroud (20 November 1713), which had been repaired twenty years previously in 1694 by the priest Sebastian Valfrè, Confessor to Victor Amadeus of Savoy (Fig. 6.5). He must presumably have viewed the Baroque splendours of the urban centre, which was also at that time something of a building site in places, but the case for architectural and cultural influence must not be overstated for this first short stay. Nevertheless, it is important to note that enrolment at the Accademia Reale was not the only source of learning, but essentially provided an educative base for exploring the city and its environs. Coke's networks were to be more extensive during his second, longer visit (Figs 0.3, 5.1–5.3).

Coke's Second Visit to Turin, 1715

The return visit, arriving on 15 December 1714, can be seen to have been more significant in a number of ways. He was at the Academy on Christmas

---

[12] Thanks go to Francesca Sgroi of the Archivio Storico, Turin for her help in identifying performances Coke might have seen during the carnival seasons 1714/15 and 1715/16.

Figure 6.5 Giovanni Tommaso Borgonio, *View of the Chapel of the Holy Shroud*, in *Theatrum Statuum Regiae Celsitudinis Sabaudiae Ducis*, Amsterdam, Blaeu, 1682, vol. I, plate 19, Reggia di Venaria.

Eve and on 1 January 1715 he visited 'Prince Thomas'. This was presumably Prince Thomas Philip Gaston of Savoy (1696–1715), the son of Emmanuel Philibert, Prince of Carignano (1628–1709), who had commissioned the building of the Palazzo Carignano. Prince Thomas Philip was just a year older than Coke, but was to die later that year.[13] This was the first of numerous visits to the Carignano.

Thomas Hobart's aim for Coke's second stay in Turin was to enrol him in the Accademia Reale, a military institution that was one of the chief attractions of Turin, in William Bromley's words 'bring[ing] no small Advantage to Turin, by a great Concourse of Strangers'.[14] The academy had been created by Duke Charles Emmanuel II in 1669 to provide military personnel to reinforce the House of Savoy, although his early death meant that it was the Duchess Maria Giovanna Battista of Savoy-Nemours, the State Regent, who finally opened the Royal Academy in 1678, making it the first of its kind. Here Coke was to develop his riding and fencing skills. A long letter home survives which tells us something of Coke's feelings for his time there – at least at the start of his enrolment.[15] He had some trepidation but evidently enjoyed a protected status, having paid the princely sum of 368 Louis d'ors to register.

On 3 January 1715 in this one surviving letter from Turin, he writes to his grandfather:

I did intend to have desired you to defend me from being whip'd in this Academy, for a I hear'd a very ill character of it, but I, having a governour, am obliged to no rules, so I am very well contented to stay, for I divert myself extreamly morning and night at Court or in assemblys, and I like the company of the place very much. I am afraid it would have been an ungrateful demand to my guardians to avoid the place they had so much commended to me.

Nevertheless he continues:

I am sure you would not like me to be treated like a child, as the Piemontese are in this academy. I think of all the academys that I have seen, except at Rome and Naples, this is the worst, I have so very bad an opinion of the manner of riding, that I shan't much mind the master's instructions. The fencing master is excellent, and the only one that is tolerable here.

---

13 A second possible identification is Prince Thomas Emmanuel (1687–1729), Prince of Savoy-Carignan and Count of Soissons, the nephew of Prince Eugene of Savoy and a Knight of the Austrian Order of the Golden Fleece in 1712. Prince Thomas had recently married, in 1713, Princess Maria of Lichtenstein (1694–1772) and their baby son (born 23 September 1714) was called Prince Eugene John. I have found no reference to his being in Turin at this time.

14 Bromley 1705: 242.

15 Holkham Archive, F/G 2 (2), no. 463–4, 3 Jan. 1714/15, Turin.

This is not a ringing endorsement of formal military training by the young entrant but he stayed the course and reinforced his learning about the Court of Savoy and military imperatives. So successful, indeed, was his education moulded to the martial arts that later, in 1717, his tutor had to have him incarcerated when in Vienna, to prevent the young Englishman's headstrong attempt to join the Austrian armed forces under Prince Eugene of Savoy (Fig. 6.6), in a bid to keep his charge from coming to any harm.

Coke's admiration for Prince Eugene and his role in helping to end the Spanish Wars of Succession evidently made him predisposed to the Piedmont region. In Turin Coke's education was a combination of military and royal court, and his letter home also gives an indication of his growing cultural leanings, tutored by his recent journey through Italy. He writes: 'during my voiage round Italy, I have bought several of the most valuable authors that have writ in Italian or about the Country'. Coke explains his expenditure in the worthiest terms, saying that

if I miss'd the occasion of buying books while I am travelling, I should not be able to find the best of them and it's impossible to buy them to my mind unless I am myself present, and certainly one of the greatest ornaments to a gentleman or to his family is a fine library.

This is a timely reminder that Coke's learning came from his reading as much as his travelling. It is difficult to be sure from his library as it survives today quite what printed books he purchased in Turin, apart from one important two-volume work, the first French edition of Johan Blaeu's *Théâtre des etats de son Altesse royale le Duc de Savoye, Prince de Piémont, Roy de Cypre* published by Adrian Moetjens in 1700 (Fig. 6.7).[16] This major acquisition was probably the 'book of mapes' bought during his first stay in Turin on 21 November 1713, but it is much more than simply a book of maps. The first of the large folio volumes contains town plans and images of Piedmont, Turin, and the neighbouring towns and places, while the second volume covers Savoy and other areas under the rule of the prince of Savoy, including to the west of the Alps. This was a prestigious publication, based upon the work of Tomaso Giovanni Borgonio (c. 1620–83) and originally published as *Sabaudiae Theatrum* in 1682. Borgonio was official cartographer to Victor Amadeus II, Duke of Savoy (1675–1730) and had an extraordinary talent for making himself indispensable to the Duke, his numerous roles throughout his career including engineer responsible for fortifications and Secretary of Finance. The

---

[16]   Holkham Library BN 2789.

Figure 6.6 After Godfrey Kneller, *Prince Eugene of Savoy-Carignan-Soissons*, engraved by John Simon, 1712, London, British Museum, London, © The Trustees of the British Museum.

volumes contain some 50 of his own etchings, based upon his travels, and contributed towards Amadeus II's deliberate reinforcement of the prestige of the Savoy Court. Surveying the striking images in these volumes one can see why travellers were curious to tour the region and not simply treat Turin alone as a gateway to Rome. Some of the towns are shown in vertiginous locations and it is no surprise that some of the smaller mountaintop towns were not on the tourist track. The volumes successfully acted as a political statement that challenged the court of Versailles, demonstrating the extent of the wealth and territories of the Alpine principality, helping to overturn the notion of the Alps as geographically isolated.[17] By inference we learn of the influence of ancient Rome as well as geography on the region, with images that integrate the monuments and churches, while

[17] The young Duke Charles Emmanuel II had initiated the original publication in 1657, following the example of the similar volume on the cities of Flanders.

Figure 6.7 Gérard de Larisse, *Allegory of Piedmont* and *Allegory of Savoy*, engraved by Abraham Blooteling and Gérald Valk, in *Theatrum Statuum Regiae Celsitudinis Sabaudiae Ducis*, Amsterdam, Blaeu, 1682, vol. I, plates 1 and 2, Reggia di Venaria.

evoking urban and rural landscapes of wealth and prosperity, stretching from the Maurienne valley to Susa.[18]

Coke could not fail to be impressed by the architecture of the city of Turin. English tourists at the turn of the century were universally impressed by the town planning, William Bromley's comment being typical:[19]

the streets are straight and large, and the Buildings the most Uniform I have ever seen. They appear to be of stone but are most only Brick plastered. The Piazza san Carlo is very great, handsome Cloisters, and inhabited by the Nobility, to whose palaces it must be a lessening to have Shops under them, did not the frequent Practices of the like in Italy make it the less regarded: for I have seen the ground Rooms of many Noble Palaces converted into Shops.

[18] These two volumes could well have been among the box of books sent on from Turin Holkham Hall Archives, F/TC 4, 21 November 1713 'Paid for a book of mapes 21 00'. The bankers Messrs. William and Smith were later charged carriage. For an essay on the *Theatre des Etats* see: Bourdon 2009. See also: Roccia 2000.

[19] Bromley 1705: 241.

Bromley thought the Academy 'in which most exercises are learnt, [is] as well as [that] at Paris'.[20]

One palace in particular, Palazzo Graneri, interested Coke enough for him to pay 64 Louis d'ors for copying the plans of the Marquis della Roccia for his palace, then being remodelled.[21] An architectural competition (c. 1680) had been held by Graneri which had led to the final selection of the architect Giovanni Francesco Baroncelli (1643–94). These drawings were presumably available at the palazzo.[22]

Coke's interest does raise the question as to quite what it was that impressed him and whether this could have been reflected in any way in his building plans for Holkham. If there is a similarity of any description with the eventual form of Holkham Hall it is in the sober severity of this elegant palace. Commissioned by Marco Antonio Graneri (1629–1703), Abbot of Entremont, the palace was built over the period 1681–99. Coke was evidently captivated by its noble grandeur, rightly recognizing it as the archetype of Piedmontese Baroque, being heavily influenced by the neighbouring Palazzo Carignani by Guarini, notably in the application of compartmented bands on the street facade, together with an inner courtyard. It had been here that a victory dinner took place with Victor Amadeus II in honour of Prince Eugene of Savoy on 7 September after the siege of 1706.[23]

It was on the same day as Coke was recorded as copying the Palazzo Graneri plans, 25 April 1715, that Jarrett accounted for the hire of horses to take his young charge to the Venaria Reale once again, this time for dinner. There is little to give us any direct idea of Coke's experience of the Venaria but it was clearly at a time when he was seriously interested in architectural matters. Equally, there is little direct information of Coke's contacts in Turin, let alone who his dining companions were, but certainly one individual is recorded who is a reminder of the military and courtly circles in which Coke was spending his time at Turin, namely Theophilus Oglethorpe (1682–c. 1728). Educated at Eton, Oglethorpe had been in India and China (1700–5) and personal aide-de-camp to the Duke of Ormonde in Flanders in 1712. Having arrived in Turin in January 1714 he stayed on in an official capacity for four years. Coke was not alone when he wrote to his guardian in January

---

[20] Bromley 1705: 242.
[21] Holkham Hall Archives, F/TC 4, 25 April 1715 'Gave for Copying the plans of Marquis de la Roche for his palace 64 00'. The palace has been home to the Circolo degli Artisti since 1834.
[22] See: Dardanello 1993b; and also (more extensively), Castello 1991. The present whereabouts of these drawings, which included a project drawing attributed to Guarini, is unclear. I am grateful to Edoardo Piccoli for this information.
[23] See Corp and Merlotti in this volume.

1715 that he could make 'nothing at all' of Oglethorpe's official position, 'for he is one day Envoy, and the next not, but he is a very good nature'd man'.[24] They travelled together on an excursion from Turin to Milan in January 1715. During this period Oglethorpe became a Jacobite sympathizer and he is just one of a number of exposures Coke had to the Jacobite cause during his travels without necessarily falling into an ardent political stance himself.

Thomas Coke visited two more palaces in Turin. The first of these was the Castello di Valentino (Fig. 6.8), which had been modernized by Marie Christine of France (1606–63), wife of Victor Amadeus I, when in residence from 1630.[25] Horseshoe in shape, the palace reflects an architectural style that looks northwest across the alps rather than south to Rome. Here Coke would have seen the newly established (in 1713) Orto Regio, now the Botanical Gardens of Turin University. His next visit was an excursion (12 April 1715) via the recently completed direct route (completed 1711–12) to the Castello di Rivoli (Fig. 6.9), a royal residence since the sixteenth century.[26] Seriously damaged by the French army in 1693, Victor Amadeus had yet to call in Juvarra, but restructuring had taken place between 1703 and 1713 to the designs of Michelangelo Garove (1648–1713), who had died just before Victor Amadeus became King of Sicily. If these were the buildings with which Coke was most familiar, it is clear that this plurality of architectural influence is behind the unique contribution of Coke and Holkham to the history of the British Country house.[27]

Opera and Music

One last but very important aspect of Coke's time in Turin, which demonstrates that enrolment at the Accademia Reale provided more than a military education, was his attendance at the opera and theatre or playhouse. These years saw the birth of opera in Italy as a full costumed performance. Prior to arriving in Turin in 1713 he had visited playhouses to see comedy and masquerade, while the first performance identified in the accounts as opera that he had witnessed, was at Marseilles in September 1713. The opera was still closed in Turin during his brief stay in November 1713, but

[24] MS letter, Holkham Archive no. 463–4, Thomas Coke to his grandfather Sir John Newton, Turin 3 January 1714/15.

[25] Holkham Hall Archives, F/TC 4, 25 March 1715, 'Gave at seeing the House of Valentain 02 00'.

[26] At this time the residence of Victor Amadeus II, Duke of Savoy. Holkham Hall Archives, F/TC 4, 12 April 1715, 'Paid for a post horse from Rivoli to Turin 07 00'.

[27] See Wolfe's chapter in this volume for an analysis of an important letter to Alessandro Galilei by John Molesworth, Turin, 4 June 1721, concerning the plurality of interests to which the amateur patron architect aspired at this period.

he saw his first Italian opera at Venice shortly after he had left, hiring a box for the first night of the opera at San Giovanni Crisostomo.

Coke was evidently smitten and it was on his return to Turin that the opportunity presented to hire a box at the Carignano playhouse on 7 January, paying for new hangings and repairs. This was for the 1714/15 Carnival season, which lasted from 26 December until the eve of Ash Wednesday, with the presentation of just two principal works each season. Under the pressure of political and economic difficulties, the repertoire of the Carignano in 1715 was composed of pastoral fables and music dramas with some comic musical interludes. Here he renewed his acquaintance with the Opera, seeing a possible maximum of six performances from 7 January 1715 to 12 April 1715 – either plays or operas – and including the pastoral fable *Il trionfo d'amore o sia La fillide* (*The Triumph of Love or The Phyllis*).[28] This was the first performance of the woodland fairytale for music, by the young librettist Giovanni Antonio Giai (1690–1764) in collaboration with the composer Andrea Stefano Fiore (1686–1732). The Carignano was a formative aesthetic influence on the young traveller. Thereafter he visited a considerable number of opera and musical performances throughout Europe, but it was Turin where his love of the theatre and opera blossomed.

Coke's interest in music ran deeper than simply attending performances. That April in Turin he bought some music direct from Thomas Roseingrave (1690/1–1766).[29] Roseingrave became a leading English keyboard composer of the period, and Coke could well have been purchasing one of his early keyboard pieces such as a sonata for flute and harpsichord. Frustratingly, nothing remains at Holkham as evidence of the young man's purchase of musical scores, but a good number of such purchases are recorded throughout his travels, and he was learning to play the flute during his journey. It seems his music masters had instilled in him a deeper appreciation of performance as well as developing his facility with the flute. His final commission from the artist Sebastiano Conca on leaving Rome was to have him depicted as Orpheus with his lyre in the Elysian Fields. This was a typically learned reference to which William Kent may well have referred in his early design for the library at Holkham. An elevation drawing for an unexecuted design shows the figure of either Orpheus or possibly Apollo with his lyre as the central motif of the overmantel. On his return to England he was among the first subscribers, alongside Lord Burlington for one, to the new

---

[28] See: Basso 1976–88; in particular: Bouquet 1976; Viale Ferrero 1980; Bouquet *et al.* 1988: 96–9 ref. Il Teatro Carignano and 102 ref *Il trionfo d'amore o sia La fillide*.

[29] This was quite possibly harpsichord music, as Roseingrave was soon to leave for England to promulgate Domenico Scarlatti's harpsichord music in particular.

Figure 6.8 Giovanni Tommaso Borgonio, *View of the Castle of Valentino*, in *Theatrum Statuum Regiae Celsitudinis Sabaudiae Ducis*, Amsterdam, Blaeu, 1682, vol. I, plate 28, Reggia di Venaria.

Royal Academy of Music, founded in 1719.[30] Turin provides the first clear example of his musical tastes formed abroad. We can conclude that Coke would already have seen a number of the operas on his travels that were then imported to London. It is important to note that it was in Turin that Coke and Burlington quite possibly met.[31]

While Coke was in Turin he witnessed – or participated in – at least two performances, the nature of which is a reminder that the young milord's exposure to culture was not exclusively high-minded but could as well

---

[30] Handel was then Master of the Orchestra, responsible for adapting the new operas from abroad. The young Coke was associating with a group of aristocrats in whose circle he was only just gaining a foothold. For Coke's involvement in the new Royal Academy of Music on his return to London, see: Gibson 1987: 138–64.

[31] A payment for 'two physicians viz: for ye kings and ye Ld Burlingtons' is recorded on 16 March 1715. This is ambiguous but suggests a direct intervention by Coke on behalf of Lord Burlington, who was unwell for much of his first tour of Italy. See also: Moore 2014.

Figure 6.9 Giovanni Tommaso Borgonio, *View of the Town and of the Castle of Rivoli*, in *Theatrum Statuum Regiae Celsitudinis Sabaudiae Ducis*, Amsterdam, Blaeu, 1682, vol. I, plate 44, Reggia di Venaria.

involve letting off steam. The repertoire of dance music popular at this time included the 'quadrille', whereby groups of four dancers were corralled by strong men with thick ropes orchestrating the energetic dance. Performances of 'rope dancing' were held at the Teatro Carignano and a number of entries in the accounts indicate that Coke attended such dances.[32] Both the rope dance and the sword dance were favoured by Luigi Amedeo as part of court festivals in the Trincotto Rosso, the pavilion used for the game of *Trincotto* or *pallacorda* (real tennis, played with a cork ball) near the Carignano Palace, and Coke also played many games of tennis while he was in Turin.[33] The Trincotto Rosso was originally intended for a riding school, but in 1708 Prince Luigi Amedeo had four tiers of boxes built in the

[32] Holkham Hall Archives, F/TC 4, 10 February 1715, 'Paid at the Opra and Rope dancing 02 15'; 13 February 'Paid at the Rope Dancing and a Letter 01 12'; 24 February 1715, 'Paid at the Rope dancing 01 00'.

[33] A bill of 108. 06 Piedmontese livres, paid 19 March 1715 is a large sum, suggesting that it settles a long-standing account. On *pallacorda*, see: Merlotti.

pavilion to seat guests for performances and court festivals. One of Jarrett's references directly links the opera with rope dancing. The Savoy house, in common with all the royal houses, employed jugglers and theatre companies in their theatres, sometimes even requesting the creation of specially made performances for opera intervals. A troupe of acrobats could well have been allowed to perform in front of the Royal family, which would have appealed to the young princes.[34] A second payment three days later refers simply to the rope dance, with no mention of another attraction. This second payment may refer to the Teatro Carignano, or specifically the Trincotto Rosso, but could equally well indicate a street or possibly even a circus performance.

It is these moments that reveal something of the diverse, cultural, experiential and performative nature of Thomas Coke's travels at the heart of his eventual commitment to the creation of his country seat at Holkham.

Conclusion

The scholarly application of the virtuosity Coke acquired on his travels was made manifest in the creation of Holkham Hall, one of the finest neo-Palladian, or Roman, buildings in Europe. It is also as much the product of the owner-patron Thomas Coke, as it is of his advisers William Kent (c. 1685–1748), Richard Boyle (1694–1753), the 3rd Earl of Burlington and his executant builder Matthew Brettingham (1699–1769). Indeed, it was Colen Campbell's publication of the first volume of *Vitruvius Britannicus* (1676–1729) that established Holkham Hall as an archetype of neo-Palladianism within the literature of architectural studies. Yet Holkham represents so much more within the story of the architectural development of the English Country house than simply a neo-Palladian villa. The visitor is impressed on arrival by an exterior of classical austerity reminiscent of so many of the plates published to illustrate Palladio's writings. Once inside, the visitor is confronted by the Marble Hall (Fig. 6.10), which has elements that echo the choir of Palladio's Redentore church in Venice but is reminiscent not only of a temple, but also the palace chapel at Versailles, while also informed by Alberti's *Ten Books*, published in English in 1726.[35] Other rooms of parade are reminiscent of a Roman picture gallery or a Roman

---

[34] Thanks go to Andrea Merlotti for this suggestion.
[35] Coke's library included Alberti's original 1565 edition of *De re aedificatoria* as well as Giacomo Leoni's English translation (1726). Holkham Hall, BN 2537 and BN 2246. See also Schmidt *et al.* 2005: 100–1.

Figure 6.10 The Marble Hall, Holkham Hall, © Holkham Estate, reproduced by kind permission of Lord Leicester and the Trustees of Holkham Estate, Norfolk.

sculpture gallery.[36] The development of the collection was also extensively informed by the tour – just as much as the many architectural sites, modern and antique, that Thomas Coke encountered on his travels through Northern Europe as well as Italy informed his building plans. Together, they reveal the complexity and variety of influences upon Coke's development as a collector and virtuoso as well as an amateur patron-architect. Many of these influences are reflected in his growing and extensive library. The cultural influences that helped to form the taste for antiquity in Coke's mind included music and performance, which are significant in relation to his time in Turin.[37] Importantly, Coke's education was guided throughout his tour by the systematic approach of his governor, Thomas Hobart, and

[36] For example Palazzo Doria Pamphilij and Palazzo Farnese, Rome. See also, for an analysis of the sculptural display programme at Holkham: Angelicoussis 2001: 43–72.

[37] For the essentially scholarly nature of Coke's tour, notably his engagement with Livy and his publication of Thomas Dempster's *De Etruria Regali*, see: Gialluca 2014.

numerous tutors.[38] The experience of Turin and its environs, particularly the social and tutored accomplishments to be gained from attendance at the Accademia Reale, may be seen as an important moment in this process of exposure through travel, the narratives of which can be read through the pages of the financial accounts.

[38] Understanding of Thomas Hobart's influence upon Thomas Coke as his governor has been greatly advanced by Reynolds (2014).

7 'Never a more favorable reception than in the present juncture': British Residents and Travellers in and about Turin, 1747–48

EDOARDO PICCOLI

The aim of this chapter is to add to knowledge about travel and eighteenth-century Turin by concentrating on the city and its surrounding territory, as they are revealed by the archival sources relating to travel and travellers around the middle of the eighteenth century.[1] By placing the city, its roads and the built environment at the centre of this study, many issues will be highlighted that may be useful for enriching existing narratives about travel and mobility, including some found in this volume.

By following in the footsteps of the British envoys along the routes across Piedmont around 1748, the first part of this study uncovers a territory and a network of roads beyond the capital (Fig. 7.1). In the second part, the identification of specific places and buildings within the city allows for a discussion of some of the issues that influenced the housing choices made by foreign travellers and residents. It will also be proposed that the observation of British élites in Turin should take into account the complex relationships – also involving placement and proximity within the city – they had with their bankers.

The end of the war of Austrian succession may be considered an important starting point for our analysis, as the events following the treaty of Aix-la-Chapelle in 1748, whereafter an upswing in French and British travellers to the Italian peninsula is noted, led directly to the 'fantastic' increase in mobility that took place throughout Europe after the Peace of 1763.[2] Turin, during the final years of war, seems to have already been preparing for this acceleration. Between 1747 and 1748 at least three kinds of British travellers were touring Piedmont's roads: diplomats, 'who try to mend the cobwebs, perpetually undone by the *coups de main* and the skirmishes of the armies';[3] military men, engaged in missions and meetings with other military men and the courts; and even some privileged Grand Tourists, wealthy

---

[1] The archival research for this topic was conducted by the author and by Emilio Mazza (Università IULM, Milan), in part, in the context of a research project on Hume's travels in Turin and Paris. Mazza and Piccoli 2011a; 2011b.

[2] Dubost 2000: 236; Roche 2002.

[3] Venturi 1969: 60.

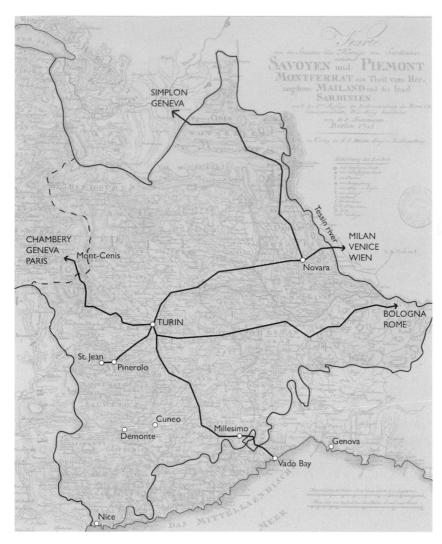

Figure 7.1 Piedmont, with the routes and the locations frequently cited by British travellers, c. 1748, highlighted on a map by D. F. Sotzmann, *Karte von den Staten des Königs von Sardinien,* Berlin 1795. Adapted by the author from an original digital file (wikimedia commons, Creative Commons Attribution-Share Alike 3.0 Unported license).

and powerful enough to disregard the constraints and risks of the ongoing hostilities. These various people made different use of time and space. Some were in Turin for just a few days, such as Augustus Hervey, a naval officer. Others, such as General Thomas Wentworth,[4] came and went, using the city as a station to buy goods and supplies during a military campaign,

---

[4] Major General Thomas Wentworth (1694–1747), special envoy to the King of Sardinia in 1747: London, National Archives (NA), SP 92/53; Edinburgh, National Library of Scotland

Figure 7.2 *Funerary Monument of Thomas Wentworth*, marble, 1748, Waldensian
Temple of Ciabàs, Angrogna, Photograph: author.

in the camps of Southern Piedmont (although the general had arrived in
the capital with his nephew, James Leigh, whose aim was to enrol at the
Royal Academy and therefore to stay in the city for at least one full season).
Others were confined to Turin for several months, such as General James
Sinclair and his delegation, sent to replace Wentworth following his sudden
death (Fig. 7.2). The general (who, among others, employed David Hume as
his aide-de-camp) arrived in the Piedmontese capital as the war was ending
and was literally forced to remain in the city during the lengthy renegotia-
tion of the conditions set by Britain for financing the Sardinian army.

On the Roads of a 'Little Known' Country

Since 1743 the British resident, Arthur Villettes, had been writing to
British travellers that the allied capital was an ideal destination for

(NLS), MSS Add 25704–25707; Stratford-upon-Avon, Shakespeare Centre Library and
Archives (SCLA), Local archives, Leigh of Stoneleigh, DR 18, DR 671.

them: '[We] can never expect a more favourable reception than [...] in the present juncture'.[5] The military alliance between the two countries, involving also the financing of the Sardinian army by Britain,[6] indeed favoured the *accueil* of British nationals, and allowed them seemingly absolute freedom of movement in Turin. Yet Turin was also the political centre of a vast territory, which the itineraries of the citizens of the 'three nations' sometimes reveal.

In 1747, the roads from Savoy and France were not open to the British. Even the most privileged among them, such as Lord Charlemont, who brazenly tried to obtain from the French authorities a permit for inexistent 'health reasons',[7] had to choose less travelled passes than the Mont Cenis. Therefore, all those arriving and departing had to find other routes: by sea; by land through Geneva and the Simplon; or along a sort of 'diplomatic road of the capitals', passing through the allied territories of Flanders to Vienna, and then back 'by way of Milan'.[8] This reversal of the usual path allows us to gauge the attitude of travellers towards some parts of Piedmont that were not included in the canonical routes of the 'Voyage d'Italie'. Apparently, in the absence of a literary precedent, the mechanism of travel description was not easily set in motion. If the Piedmontese plain was frequently crossed in these years, it was only rarely commented upon, with the exception of standard remarks about 'bad roads' or about the difficult crossing of the river Tessin. So in the words of David Hume, the plain of the Po in Lombardy is 'Classic Ground' ('we are now in Classic Ground; and I have kist the Earth, that produc'd Virgil, and have admir'd those fertile Plains, that he has so finely celebrated. [...] nothing can be more singularly beautiful than the Plains of Lombardy'),[9] but nothing is said about the Piedmontese side. The physician and antiquarian, John Clephane, during his 1744 journey with Charles Coote, later Earl of Mountrath, was similarly silent, providing an additional explanation of his motives: 'Our journey from Geneva hither was partly thro' a country

[5] Edinburgh, National Archives of Scotland (NAS), GD 125/26/3: 28 January 1743, Arthur Villettes, Turin, to John Clephane, Geneva.

[6] Storrs 2003.

[7] NA, SP 78/230, fol. 236; 24 September 1746, René Louis de Voyer de Paulmy, Marquis d'Argenson, Versailles, to Abraham Van Hoey: 'Cannot obtain passport for Viscount Charlemont and company to travel in France for health reasons, because of reports of maltreatment of French prisoners of war.'

[8] NLS, MSS 26705, c. 5v: Vienna, 14 April 1747, James Sinclair to Earl of Chesterfield, 'I am to set out tomorrow, and shall go by the way of Milan.' For a comparison with later travel itineraries, see: Bianchi 2012b: 153–60. On roads and routes to Turin: Sereno 2009.

[9] Greig 1932: I, 132. 11 May 1748, David Hume, Mantua, to John Hume of Ninewells. Mazza and Piccoli 2011a: 82–4.

little known, and hardly worth enquiring after, and partly thro' a country already well known to you I mean that part of the Milanese about the Lago Maggiore.'[10]

Some more unusual routes yield more interesting information. Savona, that is 'Vado Bay', where the British fleet was stationed in 1747, was another point of access to Piedmont during the war. From there to Turin, officers and convoys followed roads that in times of peace were rarely used because they were difficult, and because of the superiority of the roads from the port of Genoa.[11] And yet the speed with which the British crossed these mountains and reached the capital reveals the strategic quality of this passage, to the extent that, during the peace negotiations, Finale and Savona were mentioned as the most advantageous of Piedmont's access points to the sea. Savona, Hervey says, 'would be a most convenient place for the King of Sardinia if at the Peace he is allowed to keep it […] with Finale he will soon rival most of the trading ports of Italy'.[12] War, here, activated a potential relationship that would be developed in the *longue durée*, with the redefinition of Savona as an industrial port connected to Turin in the second half of the twentieth century.[13] In this territory, the comments of travelling military are clear and concise. To the officers who travelled between the sea and fertile plain near Turin, the territories of Southern Piedmont appeared quite poor. The area of Cuneo was for Hervey a 'sad, mountainous country' with 'filthy inns'. Wentworth, between Cuneo, Demonte and Limone, observed the vegetation, the state of the roads and noted the 'swelled throats'[14] of the peasants (goitre, due to iodine deficiency, was endemic in large parts of the Alpine regions), while in Liguria, the people are made miserable by war: 'as poor as rats.'[15]

The young men of the First Apartment at the Turin Royal Academy and their companions had other destinations and motives for travelling.[16] It is well known that the network of residents and ambassadors in the Italian peninsula functioned, for these young aristocrats, as a system of attraction points; a system where a 'bear leader', or tutor, was directly

[10]   NAS, GD 125/26/4: 3 January 1744, John Clephane, Turin, to Dr Richard Mead.
[11]   Raviola 2007. On itineraries in Southern Piedmont, see also: Battistoni 2009.
[12]   Erskine 2002: 54.
[13]   Bonino and Moraglio 2006.
[14]   NLS, MSS 25707 (Wentworth's private memoirs), c. 78r; see also c. 117v, where between Turin and Cuneo 'the country between Raconis and Savillian, is exceeding fine, well cultivated, and full of plantations'.
[15]   Erskine 2002: 54.
[16]   On the Turin Royal Academy, see Bianchi's chapter in this volume; also see: Bianchi 2003a; 2003b; 2005a.

responsible for the young man, and the local resident acted as assistant, and witness, in case of need. Thus, for Lord Charlemont and the other *milordi inglesi* enrolled in the Academy, Turin acted as a base station for a widespread mobility, albeit essentially limited to the roads leading to other British consulates and stations in Italy. Venice was a favourite destination, even for a few days or weeks. It was a place of easy emotions and adventures.[17] Bologna was a traditional stop on the way to Rome. We find Clephane and Coote there with their two servants ('tutti inglesi') in 1744, just after leaving Turin; due to fear of the plague in Messina, a bill of health was required to cross the border.[18] Livorno was another destination, due to the presence of a British community there and its importance as a port and logistical hub. Charlemont prepared there for his expedition to Constantinople and Greece, buying a French vessel captured during the war.[19] Milan was the marketplace of luxury goods, such as snuff-boxes that were exhibited while playing cards,[20] and also a marketplace for scientific instruments, such as lenses and binoculars.

Another path, where politics and international diplomacy played a more important role, led from Turin towards Geneva. The Swiss city is 'so near us',[21] writes Villettes to Clephane in 1743; even with the Mont Cenis road unavailable, it was just a few days away, while a letter took five or six days to cross the Alps and arrive in Turin. This proximity allowed for an easy passage of people and goods: money, documents[22] and books were exchanged between the British community in Turin and their contacts in Geneva. Hume, in Turin, was among the first readers of the *Esprit des Loix* in the autumn of 1748, thanks to a freshly printed copy likely obtained through the

---

[17] In July 1747 Tinkler Duckett, secretary to the deceased Wentworth, was involved with Lord Charlemont, 'an Irish Lord now at the Academy here [in Turin], happening to be then in Venice with his governor [Edward Murphy]' in a comic adventure involving shenanigans and thievery in Venice. The episode occupies pages of the private correspondence between General Sinclair and the British ambassador in Vienna, who clearly found it amusing. Robinson: BL, MSS Add 23829, c. 194–195: 3 August 1747, James St Clair, Turin, to Thomas Robinson.

[18] NAS, GD 125/23/6(20) and GD 125/23/7(3).

[19] The *Aimable Vainqueur*, a 200-ton 'frigate', set sail in April 1749 from Livorno/Leghorn. Stanford and Finopoulos 1984.

[20] Royal Irish Academy, Charlemont Manuscripts, 12 R 9, n.8: 12 March 1749, Charles Douglas, Turin, to Lord Charlemont.

[21] NAS, GD 125/26/3: 28 January 1743, Arthur Villettes, Turin, to Dr Clephane, Geneva. The letter is received by Clephane on 4 February. Carpanetto 2009.

[22] For ex. ASTR, Notarile, Mastrella, vol. 4171, 104–13; on 14 October 1749, a document was signed regarding an inheritance and different actors in Geneva, Turin and Nice (France). Elisabeth Antoine Gautier, widow of the *console di S. M. Britannica a San Remo*, François Dubruc, was involved. In Turin, the document, signed in the office of the bankers Torras, was supervised by Villettes. Cramer, in Geneva, signed a document of power of attorney.

Genevan agents of Villettes.[23] This connection, whose continuity in 1747–8 was ensured largely by the British resident, would be maintained even after the war, when, in redefining the borders between the Kingdom of Sardinia and Geneva, British diplomacy would play an important role. Proof of this triadic relationship emerges in 1752 when a group of Genevans dined at the British ambassador's residence, before being admitted to see the King and meet his First Architect Benedetto Alfieri to discuss the latter's design for the facade for the Genevan Temple of St Pierre.[24]

Only one of the habitual itineraries of the British in these years did not cross a state border: that was the road through Pinerolo leading to the Vaudois valleys. In the years of the War of the Austrian Succession, Arthur Villettes intervened frequently in favour of petitions or requests by the *religionari* of Luserna valley. Villettes travelled there at least once, for four days in 1744, and regularly received delegations of their 'Principal Ministers' in Turin.[25] Villettes was known in diplomatic circles as an 'artful man', a writer of long-winded and usually mild reports to his superiors in London. However, when the topic of the Vaudois was touched upon, his tone changed. References to the 'prevalent Bigotry, and the implicit Obedience that is paid here to the Pope and his Emissarys', or 'bigotted Fools of the Court of Rome'[26] were common, and leave no doubts about his personal dedication to the matter. The defence of these 'unfortunate people' in the difficult years when a new bishopric was being set up in Pinerolo[27] (where a new hospice for catechumens was also under construction) was not just 'one of the many elements of a complicated Diplomatic and military game' between states,[28] but a visible priority. The strength of this confessional link between Britain and the territories of the Vaudois communities was confirmed in a very explicit manner when an Englishman of high rank died in Turin. General Wentworth, Special Envoy to the King of Sardinia, died of a 'distemper' on a winter night in 1747. The fact that his funeral would take place 'in the valley of Luserne'[29] held a political significance that should not

---

[23] On 30 October 1748, Joseph Bouer sent to Turin from Geneva 'le livre intitulé L'esprit des Loix': ASTC, Lettere Ministri, Geneva, M.3, *Lettere orig.li dell'Agente Bover al Ministro*. See also: Mazza and Piccoli 2011a: 102–7.

[24] Piccoli 2012: 373.

[25] NA, Kew, SP 92/52–92/56, 'Letters from M.r Villettes to the Secretaries of State with Draughts to him.' Among other letters, see (SP 92/55) the *Mémoire des Protestans des Vallées de Piedmont, contenant leurs Griefs en matière de Religion, envoyé de Turin en Août 1744 par M.r de Villettes* (…). On Villettes' role, see the chapter by Bianchi in this volume.

[26] NA, SP 92/56; 28 September 1748, Arthur Villettes, Turin, to Lord Newcastle.

[27] Bernardi *et al.* 2001.

[28] Venturi 1956: 227.

[29] NA, SP 92/53: 4 December 1747, T. Duckett, Turin, to Lord Newcastle.

be ignored. Wentworth's expense accounts allow us to trace the itinerary of the cortége 'to St. John's and back again'.[30] The funeral procession started in Turin, where the corpse was lowered with a rope 'depuis la chambre à la basse court';[31] it proceeded through Orbassano and Pinerolo to the Vaudois temple of Ciabàs, at Luserna San Giovanni.[32] Here, the burial rites were performed by 'Appia the minister', which seems appropriate, as members of the Appia family had been educated in England at the beginning of the eighteenth century and were receivers of the subventions provided by the British monarchy to the ministers and schools of the valleys.[33] The small building of the Ciabàs would be endowed with significance, and to a certain extent protected, by the General's funerary monument: a sculpted tombstone in local Foresto marble, whose epitaph was engraved with a text sent from Oxford in the weeks following Wentworth's death.[34] The Sardinian authorities were vigilant in this entire matter (the funeral procession paid 'a la Garde a Pignerol, L. 48.15'), but silent: not one word about the burial or the sculpted memorial has yet emerged from the state archives.

From Vado Bay to Luserna, the constellation of roads, ports and cities that have been mentioned, with Turin at the centre, appears as a network of lines with few interconnections. To the British travellers in these years, Piedmont probably seemed a rather heterogeneous place, where one moved about with some difficulty (Wentworth had to pay for 'Odell the guide' to venture beyond Cuneo), and whose borders and limits were still not clearly defined. It was a region whose identity did not rely on established narratives and that was of interest not so much for what it contained – the goods produced in Piedmont are not discussed in these years whereas they are a focal point in other periods[35] – but rather for its strategic position.

---

[30] SCLA, Local archives, Leigh of Stoneleigh, DR 18, DR 671/98 (Wentworth papers).

[31] SCLA, Local archives, Leigh of Stoneleigh, DR 18/28/6: Bill of L.374.1 by Barthelemy Peyrot, 'Depense faite p.r S. E. Monsieur le General.'

[32] I am grateful to Gabriella Ballesio for her assistance in identifying the tombstone and the documents in the Archivio Storico della Tavola Valdese in Torre Pellice.

[33] Venturi 1956: 249–50. In 1755 the Minister 'Daniel Appia' declares having received L. 5687.6.8 of 'Carità del Re Brittannico': ASTR, Senato di Piemonte, Materie giuridiche, Rappresentanze e pareri Senato, M. 4.

[34] The author of the epitaph was Theophilus Leigh (SCLA, Local archives, Leigh of Stoneleigh DR671/98). I am grateful to Maurizio Gomez Serito, who identified the provenance of the marble. Other tombstones of British nationals are still inside the Ciabàs temple: Richard Shirley ('Ricardi Shirley nobilis Angli Baronetti Preston', 1681–1705); and Anne Stuart Mackenzie (14 August 1759, H. Walpole to H.S. Conway: 'You will be sorry for poor Mckinsy and Lady Betty who have lost their only child at Turin', Lewis 1974: 24); Canella 2005.

[35] Venturi 1956.

In Town

Italy, 'tis probable [...] has decay'd: But how many great cities does it still contain; Venice, Genoa, Pavia, Turin, Milan, Naples, Florence, Leghorn, which either subsisted not in antient times, or were then very inconsiderable? (David Hume, *Of the Populousness of Antient Nations*, 1752)

Although Englishmen rarely travelled across the Piedmontese countryside in the mid-eighteenth century, and only did so to specific destinations, a small community of them had been firmly established in Turin for many decades (Fig. 7.3). As a series of recent studies shows, they were well integrated into the rites of court diplomacy and aristocratic social life. The urban and suburban seats of the court, the Royal Academy and the *conversazioni* in private palaces, defined a topography in which the British presence was routinely registered.[36] Other places were mentioned in correspondence and diaries in 1747–8,[37] in connection with visits to fortifications, horseback rides outside the walls and, in summer, the stays at villas, or *vigne*, that provided an escape from the heat and unhealthy 'air of Turin'. These are all signs of a substantial freedom of movement that British citizens enjoyed, and reveal their familiarity (made easier by the relatively small scale of the city, in contrast with Paris or London) with the city and its surroundings.

With the exception of those staying at the Turin Royal Academy, however, it is not always possible to identify precisely where the *Inglesi* took up residence. The registers of incoming foreigners, once kept by the municipality, are lost, along with the notices and bookkeeping of the hotels. Regarding these establishments, it can be demonstrated that a few of them, such as the Bonne Femme or the Auberge d'Angleterre, did indeed welcome foreign travellers in this period.[38] To these locations, suitable for short stays, must now be added a small number of apartments throughout the city, rented for longer periods by British nationals. One of these came to light when in 1743 Count Lodovico Canera di Salasco declared the income of his rented property in the San Giacinto *isola* (block), situated in the new town, extending towards the river Po. The Count owned a large plot of land there on which he had built three houses: he lived in one with his family and he

---

[36] Merlotti 2004.
[37] Mazza and Piccoli 2011a.
[38] In 1741 Algarotti settled at the Auberge Royalle (ASTC, Materie politiche in rapporto all'estero, negoziazioni, Prussia, M. 1); the scarcity of information about Turin hotels is mainly due to loss of sources, such as the *Registro de Forestieri, che giongono in questa Città, e de loro alberghi* (ASTC, Archivio Alfieri, M. 94, Elenco dei 53 registri che tiene il Vicario nel 1746).

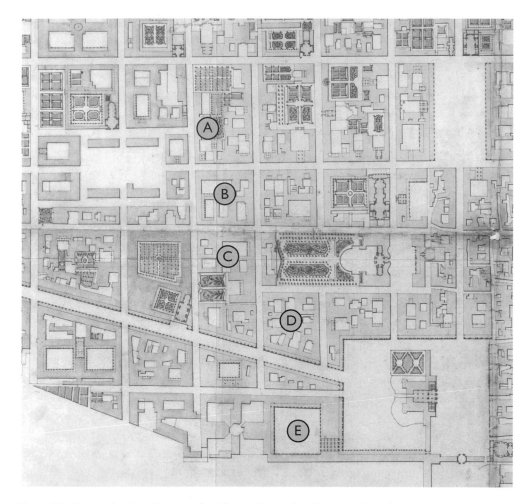

Figure 7.3 Turin, showing the area of residency of some British nationals in the city from 1743 to 1748:

A. Isola S. Giacinto, Villettes's Residence in the Palace of Count Canera di Salasco

B. Isola Beato Amedeo, The Old Ghetto

C. Isola S. Giovenale, The Location of the Bankers' Offices on the Graneri Property

D. Isola S. Federico, The Residence of Several 'religionari' (Protestant Families)

E. Royal Academy

Map: Detail from *Copia della carta dell'interiore della città di Torino che comprende ancora il Borgo di Pò* [eighteenth century], Turin, Archivio di Stato di Torino, Corte, Carte topografiche e disegni, Carte topografiche per A e per B, Torino, Torino 16.

rented the other two to eleven different tenants. The most expensive of the apartments for rent (650 Piedmontese lire per annum) was in the hands of 'Monsieur de Villettes'.[39] Besides revealing one of the centres of the British community, this information also introduces the question of money, and of its availability. The English in Piedmont – whether special envoys, diplomats or Grand Tourists – were usually well-off,[40] and some, such as Lord Charlemont, with his 'unlimited credit',[41] were exceptionally wealthy. In the six months he passed in Turin preceding his death, General Wentworth spent more than 30,000 lire. The greater part of this sum was spent on a number of personal and household goods and services: horses, saddles, silverware, clothes (and also copper and tin kitchenware, mattresses and sheets); rent and furnishing of a town apartment, stables and hillside *vigna*; and salaries for his entourage and Piedmontese cooks, servants and maids. Some expenses, such as the decoration of a coach with the General's coat of arms,[42] indicate that if Wentworth was a military envoy, the public character of his spending positioned him among the diplomatic élite, whom he rivalled to 'pay for the visible expression of majesty abroad'.[43] Even travelling with an envoy such as Wentworth was a well-paid business: David Hume refers more than once, in his correspondence, to the freedom that his pay as a secretary and aide-de-camp to General Sinclair would allow him, once he returned to England.[44] Even those who ranked at the lowest level in the hierarchy of royal representatives, the residents, were wealthy by the standards of eighteenth-century Italy. The daily allowance of £3 (the same for Villettes in Turin as for Horace Mann in Florence), or £1,065 per annum, plus extras, enabled a British resident in Turin to rent an apartment for an entire year[45] for the equivalent of less than two weeks' pay. Indeed, Villettes's apartment must have been among the best available, given its cost and the rank of his neighbours, Count Castelmagno and Countess Santus. But even in Turin, the residence of a diplomat of higher standing, such as an

---

[39] ASCT, Coll. V, vol. 591, 1743, vol. 2: *Consegnamenti di beni immobili*, c. 574, *Consegna per parte del Sig.r Conte Lodovico Canera della presente città nell'Isola di S. Giacinto un corpo di case compresa quella di sua propria abitazio*ne (…). In 1742, Villettes fought for the right to establish a chapel inside his residence (ASTC, Materie politiche per rapporto all'estero, Corti estere, Gran Bretagna, m.2 di 2a addizione).

[40] This is nearly a *lieu commun*; see: Hazard 1968: 2, 23.

[41] Thomas Adderley, Dublin, to James Caulfeild, Lord Charlemont, Turin, 30 May 1747; RIA, Charlemont Mss, 12 R 12.

[42] SCLA, Leigh of Stoneleigh, DR 18/5, DR 18/28.

[43] Jacobsen 2014: 12.

[44] Mazza 2012: 107–8.

[45] 640 Piedmontese lire, or £32. The cost is in line with other aristocratic apartments in Turin in 1743 (see the rental property declarations in ASCT, Coll V, vol. 590–4).

Envoy Extraordinary or Ambassador, would have been of a different magnitude: an entire palace, with a corresponding household, rent and management expenses. In 1758, Mann and Walpole exchanged opinions about the costs Lord Bristol faced:

I should have no ambition to supply his [Lord Bristol's] place at Turin. The climate, the Court, which occasions so great expense, and the example of such a predecessor are essential objections. Lord Bristol gives £500 a year for his house, and has everything in it equal to that expense. What could anyone do who has only his appointments to live upon![46]

Mann's estimate of '£500 a year' may have been exaggerated: for that sum, Lord Hertford, in 1763, had rented the entire Hôtel de Lassay in Paris, with its gardens overlooking the Seine.[47] When Bristol was replaced by Stewart Mackenzie in the same year, the new envoy rented Palazzo Provana di Parella for a more modest 4,500 lire per annum (approximately £225): still a substantial cost and seven times that of Villettes's apartment. In later years, William Lynch, Envoy Extraordinary, and Lord Mountstuart, Ambassador, resided in the best available residences (Figs 4.1 and 4.3). Palazzo Ferrero D'Ormea would house the Ambassador and a 40-person entourage in 1780; at that time, rent had reached 9,000 lire (£450) per year.[48] These fluctuations in cost and frequent changes of address were common in diplomatic practice: the seat of an ambassador needed to reflect the status of both the nation and the occupant,[49] and elevated status was also indicated by the purchase and display of luxury goods, such as plate (as Rothwell discusses in this volume), coaches and furnishings.

It was not only the quality of the house but also its location that mattered. In 1743, Villettes lived in a neighbourhood that seemed well-suited to his interests. Near the Piazza Reale and the Turin Royal Academy, his residence was also just a few steps from Palazzo Graneri, which housed the bank, or *comptoir*, of the Torras brothers. These merchant bankers

[46] See: Lewis 1955: 175; 11 February 1758, H. Mann, Florence, to H. Walpole.
[47] Mazza and Piccoli 2011b.
[48] BL, MSS Add. 37083, Bute Papers, v. IV c. 119, 'Le loyé de la Maison ou Demeure S. E. est de L. 9060 par année. On le paye a six mois selon la coutume de Turin, savoir L.4830 à la fin du mois de juin, et L. 4830 à la fin de Xbre'. See also NLS MSS 5527, Liston Papers. Bianchi 2012b.
[49] Jacobsen 2014: 37–74. Piedmontese envoys abroad had the same aims and problems: ASTC, Materie politiche, Negoziazioni con l'Austria, Mazzo 17, 2a addizione: 31 March 1748, René de la Chavanne, Aix la Chapelle, to Marquis de Gorzegno, Turin, 'trés mal a mon aise icy, mal logé, mal servi la moitié de mes domestiques en arriere dont je n'ay point de nouvelles. Sans hardes, sans bagage, Il est vray que les autres ne sont pas mieux (…) Milord Sandwich a cherché aussy une autre maison on luy demande pour la plus considerable seize mille florins d'Allemagne.'

belonged to the Protestant community (whose members lived, for the most part, in the adjoining *isola* of San Federico), and had interests as far afield as Geneva and London, and they were deeply involved in assisting Englishmen in Turin.[50] As can be now documented by references made by Dr Clephane in 1744, later by Lord Bristol in 1753,[51] and by Boswell in 1765, the Torras brothers systematically changed and managed money for foreigners. They also rented houses, for the likes of the Duke of Hamilton in 1750,[52] and Stuart Mackenzie in 1758.[53] In the 1770s they were neighbours of the British Envoy, William Lynch, when both were tenants in Palazzo Ferrero D'Ormea near the Arsenal. In maintaining these privileged relationships with English travellers, they were not alone. General Wentworth referred to two other 'Genevan' Protestant bankers in 1747: Isach Delachaux from Neuchâtel and his associate in commerce, Giovanni Dassier,[54] who lived, like the Torras brothers, on Graneri property in the San Giovenale *isola*. All of Wentworth's cash flowed through their office. When Delachaux was involved in a scandal – probably an attempted suicide – a powerful foreigner, George Keith, a Scottish friend of Hume and, at that moment, Governor of Neuchâtel, intervened to protect him.[55] Was there a strategy of proximity, characterizing the localization of these privileged 'foreign' communities? Wentworth arrived in Turin in June of 1747, by coach, followed by his secretary and servants. He initially settled at Villettes's, leaving his horses at the Auberge de la Bonne Femme. He then rented an apartment and stable for 520 lire per month, a cost that mirrored that of the other residents. The owner of the house, Marchesa Louisa Pallavicini,[56] came from a family that seemed to be well-introduced into the English community and its bankers. In the same summer months, a daughter of the Marchesa received Captain Hervey, who had just landed at Vado, at her house in Millesimo. Hervey, in turn, as soon as he had arrived

[50] Romagnani 2000.
[51] Goslings Bank Ledgers, account of George William Hervey, 2nd Earl of Bristol: Barclays Group Archives, Ref. 130/25. I am very grateful to James Rothwell for sharing this information with me.
[52] NAS, GD125/23/7(3); NAS, Douglas-Hamilton Family, Dukes of Hamilton and Brandon Archives, 332/C3/60.
[53] ASTC, Famiglia San Martino di Parella, m. 150; Cassetti 2005.
[54] ASCT, Vicariato, vol. 223, c. 64, *Stato dei religionari, che hanno il permesso di continuare la loro abitazione nella città di Torino per l'anno 1755*.
[55] ASTC, Materie militari, Imprese militari, M. 9 di addizione, fol. 10, *1758. Letters by Milord Giorgio Keith Maresciallo di Scozia, Governatore per S. M. Prussiana a Neuchâtel*, to Ossorio; 17 January 1758, 'je rens mil remerciments a Votre Excellence de ce qu'elle a bien voulu accorder sa protection a Lachaux'. Burton 1849: 67–8.
[56] SCLA, Leigh of Stoneleigh, DR 18/5, DR 18/28.

in Turin, promptly paid a visit to 'Madame Pallavicino'.[57] In October 1747, the Marchesa took out a loan with the Torras brothers.[58]

Bankers, salons, English apartments: lending 'to a member of an elite creates a relationship of reciprocity that implies extra-economic ties';[59] the same should be said of housing. These relationships were even more signifi-cant in the limited, dense, urban space inside the walls of Turin, and among élites already tied together by political and confessional affinities.

---

[57] Erskine 2002: 54–5.
[58] ASTR, Insinuazioni Torino, 1747, L. 7, c. 246. Loan by the brothers Torras to Marchesa Ludovica Pallavicina, 9 October 1747, 'nel contoir dei S.ri Torras infrasc.ti tenuto nel palazzo Graneri.'
[59] Pezzolo 2003: 412–13.

The British and Freemasonry in Eighteenth-Century Turin

ANDREA MERLOTTI

Very little is known of the origins of Freemasonry in the State of Savoy. This is principally due to the difficulty in locating adequate primary sources. The eighteenth-century archives of the main lodges of the State of Savoy have still not been traced. The paucity of studies on the subject also reflects some historiographical difficulties in understanding the institutional peculiarities of the State of Savoy. From the 1300s, Savoy was a composite monarchy that had ruled over two main regions: Savoie (Savoy), the cradle of the dynasty, and Piedmont, a term that identified the totality of the Italian dominions under Savoy rule and the political centre of the state, at least until the late fifteenth century. In 1720 Sardinia, after the brief reign of Sicily, was added to Piedmont and Savoy, earning the House of Savoy its royal title. In spite of this, the State of Savoy was remarkably cohesive. Service to the Crown was the source of a deep-set and profound sense of unity, particularly among the aristocracy. It is generally maintained that in the eighteenth century the Savoy portion of the State had been marginalized by its rulers, and yet throughout the century several key ministers came from this region[1] as did many high-ranking officers of the court and the army. The Italian Risorgimento would eventually break up the state, leading ultimately to the separation of Savoy and its subsequent annexation by France in 1860. Since then, the history of Savoy has been examined almost exclusively through the lens of French history studies, while Piedmont was examined by its Italian counterpart. However, an approach to the history of the State of Savoy in the modern age placing the concept of 'nation' at the centre has been a mistake in perspective: it has assumed the nineteenth-century outcome would project onto the past – an outcome that was by no means inevitable. By using such an approach, it has become difficult to understand the events that contributed to a highly complex and multifaceted political and dynastic scenario.

---

[1] From Pierre Mellarède, Minister of the Interior under Victor Amadeus II, to Victor Chapel de Saint Laurent, Minister of the Interior under Charles Emmanuel III, to Joseph Perret d'Hauteville, Minister of Foreign Affairs under Victor Amadeus III.

This is also true of the historiography of Freemasonry: it has maintained a distinction between the lodges of Savoy and those of Piedmont, presented at times as conflicting entities (which was not always the case) and considered the developments of the former solely relevant to the history of French Freemasonry and of the latter to Italian Freemasonry. Significantly, in 1937 Walter K. Firminger (1870–1940) in his *Freemasonry in Savoy*, wondered, 'Are we to look for the lodges of Savoy under France or Italy?'.[2]

The study of Freemasonry in the State of Savoy began in the early twentieth century in Savoy and Piedmont respectively, in both cases instigated by individuals outside the academic *milieu*. The first major study was that of the attorney François Vermale (1876–1970), who between 1909 and 1912 published works that remain pivotal to this day. In fact, he devoted very little attention to the Piedmontese lodges, despite the fact that many had not only originated from the lodge at Chambéry, but that many of its members must certainly have been 'brothers' from Savoy.[3] The librarian and Freemason Pericle Maruzzi (1887–1966) – 'il maggior competente italiano' (the most competent in Italy) – wrote the most complete study of Freemasonry in Piedmont.[4] Between 1928 and 1929, Maruzzi published his research about the Freemasons in Turin in the eighteenth century, work that is still unparalleled.[5] The approach followed by Vermale and Maruzzi a century ago set a high standard for eighteenth-century Freemasonry studies in the State of Savoy, both in terms of the importance of their work and of the scarcity of new archival documents discovered subsequent to their research, so that their contributions are regarded as near primary sources themselves. Both Carlo Francovich and Jean Nicolas in the 1970s, and, more recently, Vincenzo Ferrone, have provided studies dedicated to a more fully articulated interpretation of Freemasonry in the State of Savoy, unhappily, however, without uncovering new documentary material.[6]

---

[2] Firminger 1937.

[3] Vermale 1909; 1912.

[4] Francovich 1974: XII–XIII.

[5] See: Maruzzi 1928–9 (reprinted in 1990, from which I will cite). As early as 1922, however, Maruzzi had provided a first outline of the history of Freemasonry in Piedmont in the eighteenth century (Maruzzi 1922). It should be noted that Maruzzi himself did not hold Vermale in great esteem, and in his work he defined him 'trascurato' (careless). None the less, Vermale's work was immediately recognized and cited in European masonic literature, while Maruzzi's has been neglected for a long time: it was unknown to Firminger.

[6] See: Francovich 1974; Nicolas 1978; Ferrone 1991; Ferrone 1998; Ferrone and Tocchini 2006. In this sense, this essay is part of an ongoing effort on my part to locate new documents on Savoy masonry, to integrate the works of Vermale and Maruzzi: Merlotti 2003b; Bianchi and Merlotti 2013a.

The fact that Freemasonry in the eighteenth century cannot be viewed from a *national* perspective has also meant that, in the limited context of the State of Savoy, it has been less fully explored. It was, rather, something of a social movement that the continental states imported from Britain and in which foreigners featured quite prominently. This original feature was regarded negatively in a historiographical view that, at the turn of the twentieth century, attempting to retrace the steps of Freemasonry in eighteenth-century Italy, perceived it chiefly as the dawning of the Risorgimento, and therefore necessarily nationally rooted. This view left little room for the ideas spreading in from France under Napoleon, and even less room for the British ideas of that age. This eagerness to assert the Italian origin of both the Risorgimento and the cultural and political movements that had paved the way for it detracted from the study of Freemasonry, whose cosmopolitan origins were perceived as something of an embarrassment. Consider, for example, that the historian Renato Soriga (1881–1939) defined Freemasonry in 1919 as 'fra le più suggestive correnti ideologiche di origine esotica, che gradualmente snaturarono la realistica mentalità paesana della borghesia italica' ('one of the most evocative ideologies of exotic origin, that gradually distorted the realistic homely mentality of the Italian middle-class'), 'sorta fra noi per iniziativa straniera, ad uso di stranieri' ('established among us on the initiative of foreigners, for the use of foreigners').[7] This was all the more true under Fascism, when Italian lodges were declared illegal and accused of functioning as the *longa manus* of Britain and France on Italian soil.[8] In this sense Maruzzi's work is a welcome exception, in its striving to understand the European components of Freemasonry in Turin.

In this short chapter I shall analyse various aspects of the role of the British in the creation and development of Freemasonry in eighteenth-century Turin, focusing on the interesting Jacobite presence – that has been largely overlooked – and also on the Accademia Reale (Turin Royal Academy)[9] that united British, German, Polish and Russian nobility into an aristocratic international circle that undoubtedly had an impact on later Masonic developments.

[7] Soriga 1919: 14, 86.

[8] On the Fascist attitude towards Freemasonry see the useful work of Mola (1976) and more recently (each with an extensive bibliography): Conti 2003; Venzi 2008.

[9] On the Turin Royal Academy, that has been largely neglected in the study of eighteenth-century Turin, important contributions have come from Paola Bianchi, who reconstructed its Europe-wide role and value. See Bianchi 2003a; 2003b; 2010a; 2012b; as well as the chapter by the same author in this volume.

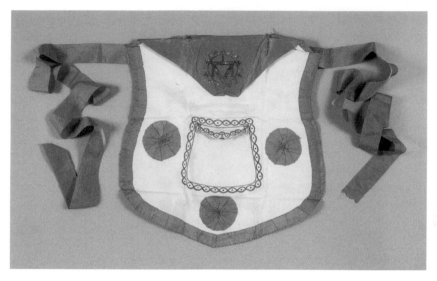

Figure 8.1 Apron of the Grand Lodge of Turin 'Saint Jean de la Mysterieuse', c. 1778, Turin, Archivio di Stato di Torino, Corte, Archivio Solaro di Moretta, mz. 5.

The Jacobite Presence in the Early Days of Savoy Freemasonry

According to the research carried out by Maruzzi, the Savoy Freemasonry was established in May 1749, when the Marquis des Marches Joseph François de Bellegarde (1687–1759) set up the lodge 'aux Trois-Mortiers', that would remain the main lodge in the State of Savoy for almost two decades. It was only sixteen years later, in 1765, that Turin, the capital of the State and the seat of the Court, would have its own lodge, 'Saint Jean de la Mysterieuse' (Figs 8.1 and 8.2).[10] Maruzzi, however, did not deny the presence of Freemasons in the Savoy capital even in previous decades. In Turin, he wrote, 'vi erano certo dei liberi muratori in numero ristretto, e è probabile che abbiano costituita, più o meno regolarmente, una loggia di breve vita e, forse, indipendente' ('there were certainly Freemasons in a limited number, and it is likely that they established, more or less regularly, a short-lived and, perhaps, an independent lodge').[11] This fact has been cited also by historians who later studied the same topic, from Francovich[12] to Ferrone and Tocchini.[13] It therefore seems useful to start with a few facts that are available on this subject.

---

[10]   On this event see: Maruzzi 1990. See also the works listed above in note 6 and the related text.
[11]   Maruzzi 1990: 9.
[12]   Francovich 1974: 174.
[13]   Ferrone and Tocchini 2006: 335.

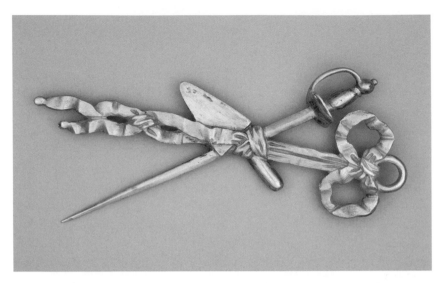

Figure 8.2 Badge of the Grand Lodge of Turin 'Saint Jean de la Mysterieuse', c. 1778, Turin, Archivio di Stato di Torino, Corte, Archivio Solaro di Moretta, mz. 5.

The earliest official document concerning Piedmontese Freemasonry is dated 12 June 1739 – the patent given to the Marquis des Marches from the Grand Lodge of London as 'Grand master of the States of the King of Sardinia'. The figure of the Marquis des Marches is central to understanding the relationship between Turin, London and the Jacobite world in which the first lodge of Savoy is likely to have been established. Joseph François Noyel de Bellegarde was a member of a prominent aristocratic family from Savoy. His ancestor, Janus (1634–1712), had served as Grand Chancellor of Savoy – the highest post in the State after the Sovereign – from 1687 until his death. His father, Jean François (1661–1742), had served as ambassador of Victor Amadeus II to France from 1716 to 1718, among other important roles. He had five children from his marriage to Catherine Françoise de Regard de Vars, three of whom would eventually play significant roles in the history of European Freemasonry.

Joseph François accompanied his father to the Embassy in Paris, where he came into contact with exiled Jacobites. In particular, he became a member of the circle that gathered around the Oglethorpe family, whose important role as supporters of James III is widely known. It is likely that in Turin Joseph François had encountered Sir Theophilus Oglethorpe (c. 1684–1737), who was a Member of the English Parliament from 1708 to 1713, and who had arrived in the Sabaudian capital after leaving Britain. Here he became 'the Jacobite representative at the court of the King of

Sicily'.[14] He continued to travel to Turin and Paris until at least 1720. Theophilus, however, was not the only member of his family in contact with the House of Savoy. His younger brother, James (1696–1785), after leaving England in 1715 and moving to France, served Prince Eugene in 1716: he fought at his side in the Balkans against the Turks and was his secretary and aide-de-camp until 1718. In spite of the fact that in February 1716 Victor Amadeus refused to give sanctuary to the English sovereign when he was forced to leave France, the Oglethorpe family continued to visit the Savoy capital regularly. In 1716 James Oglethorpe travelled to Turin and to Paris, where the Savoy ambassador at the time was the Marquis de Bellegarde.[15] At that time, Theophilus was in Turin certainly, from March to October of the same year. In a letter dated 9 October 1716, Lord Murray wrote that Victor Amadeus II 'shows Mr. Oglethorpe all manner of outward civility'.[16] After returning to the army and participating in the siege of Belgrade (July–August 1717), in the autumn he was in Turin with his brother Theophilus. The two remained for some time in the Savoy capital and there they met with the Earl of Mar, secretary to James III.[17] At the end of 1717, their sister, Françoise Charlotte d'Oglethorpe (1696–1762), known as 'Fanny', also resided in Turin for an extended period.[18]

There is no documentation about the relationship between the Oglethorpes and the Bellegardes. What is known, however, is that in Paris in December 1719, Joseph François Noyel de Bellegarde married Fanny d'Oglethorpe.[19] She was endowed with a dowry of 500,000 lire and two pensions, the first provided by the King of France and the other by James III.[20] Born in 1696,[21] the young bride had moved to France in 1713[22] and settled

---

[14] Aschbach Ettinger 1984: 9.

[15] Baine and Williams 1989.

[16] *Calendar of Stuart Papers*, III: 56.

[17] From Turin the two brothers travelled to Urbino to meet with James III at least on two occasions: Corp 2011a.

[18] *Calendar of Stuart Papers*, IV: 276. On Fanny, see: Kneas Hill 1977.

[19] The marriage contract was signed on 3 November 1719. The date is found in a notarial document contained in Mansord 1824: I, 229–30. The wedding was celebrated a month later, on 3 December. The wedding is also mentioned in: Dangeau 1860: 167.

[20] Clarke de Dromantin 2005: 118. According to other sources, the dowry amounted to the considerable sum of 800,000 lire: Dangeau 1860; and Fénelon 1999: 226.

[21] Born in February 1696, she died in Chambéry on 28 February 1762. She was buried with her husband in the Chapelle des Trois-Rois and in the register of the dead she was recorded as 'agée de 62 ans'. But already in the French years she would declare a younger age than was actually the case: Pérpechon 1895: 381.

[22] A document dated November 1719 states that she had 'passé en France il y a six ans' ('moved to France six years earlier'), therefore in 1713, and that she lived in Paris: Clarke de Dromantin 2005: 52.

in Paris, where she refused to take religious vows she had previously offered to take. In the French capital, Fanny engaged in intense political activity to support the Jacobite cause. She worked closely with her brothers, but more significantly, with her sisters, and for a long time was believed to have been James III's mistress.

While in later years Theophilus Oglethorpe and his sisters remained faithful to the Jacobite cause, James Oglethorpe sided – or at least appeared to side – with the Hanoverian front and returned to London, where he started the military career that would make him first Governor of Georgia. It was perhaps thanks to James, or for other unknown reasons, that the young Marquis Bellegarde des Marches travelled to London, where in 1723 he is reported to have been a member of the Grand Lodge of England. The patent given to Bellegarde in 1739 was therefore the outcome of almost twenty years of Masonic involvement. The names of the members of the Grand Lodge of London were public, and it is safe to assume that Charles Emmanuel III (Fig. 8.3), who from 1729 had depended upon a skilful and conscientious ambassador like Count Ossorio in London,[23] was unaware of the decisions made by the Marquis des Marches. However, had diplomacy failed to acquire this information, after Aachen, the documents produced by (or in the framework of) the Grand Lodge of London reported that the post had been assigned to Bellegarde.[24]

It would be impossible that in late 1736, when the sovereign appointed Bellegarde as a Gentleman of the Bedchamber, he was unaware of his Masonic membership and equally unaware of Fanny's loyalty to the Jacobite cause.[25] At that time, his younger brothers Claude Marie (1700–1755) and Jean François (1707–69) – following a path not rare among the Savoy aristocracy in the early eighteenth century[26] – went to serve Saxony, thus beginning careers that would take them to the highest ranks of the army and diplomacy. Claude Marie married the daughter of Augustus II the Strong and became the Ambassador of Saxony, first in Turin (1747–53), and then in France (1754–5).[27] Jean François had a brilliant career at Court and in the army that ended in 1768 when he was appointed Minister of War ('Staatssecretair im Kriegswesen').[28] It should be noted that both were prominent

[23] See, with extensive bibliography: Merlotti 2013b.

[24] See, for example: Scott 1754: 116–17; Anderson 1756: 333; which reported that in 1739 the Marquis des Marches had been appointed 'Grand Master for Savoy and Piedmont'.

[25] Archivio di Stato di Torino (hereinafter: ASTo), Sezioni riunite, *Patenti Controllo Finanze*, reg. 12, c. 176.

[26] Bianchi 2008.

[27] A biography is found in *Neue Genealogisch-historische* 1756: 455–6.

[28] A biography is found in *Fortgesetzte Neue Genealogisch-historische* 1769: 282–5.

Figure 8.3 After Maria Giovanna Battista Clementi (La Clementina), *Portrait of Charles Emmanuel III, King of Sardinia*, engraved by Thomas Burford, London c. 1735, British Museum, London, © The Trustees of the British Museum.

Freemasons. Claude was a Brother of the Grand Lodge of Paris as early as 1737.[29] Jean François was among the highest-ranking members of the Saint-Jean des Voyageurs lodge of Dresden, one of the most important in Europe, as described by Pierre-Yves Beauripaire.[30] The Bellegarde brothers were therefore part of a Masonic network that connected the Sabaudian capital to Dresden, London and Paris, and that was reflected most accurately in the paths of the students of the Turin Royal Academy – an aspect that certainly calls for further investigation.

At the time the Marquis Joseph François became a member of one of Britain's most important lodges, the Jacobite presence in the lodges of Europe was increasing. We know that after James III moved to Rome and

[29] Chevallier 1964: 105.
[30] Beaurepaire 2003: 166–7.

married Maria Clementina Sobieska in 1719, the Jacobite court had inaugurated a new political strategy that involved the creation of more Masonic
lodges whose members were *brothers* who supported the cause of James III.
The birth and growth of Freemasonry in Italy must be considered against
this rather nebulous background. While the distinction between Jacobites
and Hanoverians did not exactly coincide with the distinction between
Catholics and Protestants (many Protestants actually embraced the Jacobite
cause), members of both parties happily coexisted within the same lodge.

With regard to this chapter, the Jacobite presence in the State of Savoy is
a subject that deserves further serious consideration. It has formerly been
considered irrelevant because of Victor Amadeus's refusal to allow James
III to settle in the Savoy territories. However, the actual scenario was far
more complex and merits ad hoc research. An examination of the court of
the Princes of Savoy-Carignan, for example, reveals that its ranks included
Charles Stourton (1671–1724), who belonged to one of England's most
prominent aristocratic families and who supported the Catholic side. He
had begun to serve the Princes of Carignan as early as the 1690s and had
fought with Prince Eugene. In 1702 he went on to serve Louis Thomas,
Count of Soissons, while his brother, Matthew, remained with Prince
Eugene and died in the battle of Luzzara. Upon the death of Louis Thomas,
Charles was made 'Master of the Horse' by Princess Louise of Carignan
and, most notably, governor of the Princes Emmanuel, Maurice and
Thomas of Savoy-Soissons. It should be noted that Charles Stourton was
related to Baron Stourton (1665–1720) who had been 'Grand Master of the
Stable' at the court of James II and who, after moving to Saint Germain-en-
Laye, had remained there even after the Stuart court left for Italy.[31] More
closely examining the ranks of the courts of Carignan and Soissons leads to
some interesting surprises. What should also not be forgotten is the bond
between Prince Eugene and the Duke of Ormonde.[32] In 1712, during the
Prince's visit to London, his nephew Maurice, *le chevalier de Soissons*, died
suddenly at the young age of 22 and was buried in Westminster in the tomb
of the Dukes of Ormonde. Four years later, in February of 1716, after siding
with the Jacobites, the Duke accompanied James III on his travels through
Piedmont.

Even at the court of Anne Marie d'Orléans (until 1720 successor to the
throne of James III)[33] the Jacobites were a presence. As reconstructed by

---

[31] Wynne 1994: 158.
[32] Jori 1942: 194.
[33] See the chapter by Corp in this volume.

Wynne and McDonnell, an Irish aristocrat named Marie MacNamee (*rectius* MacNamara), who had moved to Turin from Saint Germaine-en-Laye, was among the ladies attending on the Queen of Sardinia in 1725.[34] There is no mention of her name in the court's financial accounts, indicating that it was the Queen herself who provided for her payments through her private funds. This is an interesting circumstance, because it could suggest an attitude on the part of Anne Marie d'Orléans in favour of the members of the Jacobite court. If such favour existed it has remained unmentioned until now, but cannot be substantiated by investigating the official documents of the Savoy Treasury. The Treasury was the only office that kept registers of court members, for the purpose of paying their salaries. The presence of Marie MacNamee was neither casual not momentary, as witnessed by the Queen's determination to keep the Irish noblewoman at court. In 1725 Madame Helene MacMahon,[35] another Jacobite noblewoman who had remained in Saint Germain-en-Laye, contacted Anne Marie d'Orléans to request that the young Irish aristocrat be allowed to leave for France to marry Randal MacDonnell (1689–1740). MacDonnell belonged to a family that had come to France with James II: his father, Captain Randal Sr (d. 1711), had been 'groom of the bedchamber' of the two sovereigns from 1689 until their deaths. The same post was held by his younger brother, Daniel (d. 1734), until 1717. At court Randal was educated as a page of honour and later became a squire. In 1717, instead of following the court to Italy, he served in the Spanish army. There is no doubt that these families had been close to the Jacobite court for centuries. In spite of the insistence on the part of MacDonnell and MacMahon, who sent a representative to Turin, Anne Marie d'Orléans refused to be parted from her lady-in-waiting.

In that same year, 1725, Marie MacNamee was therefore present at the Savoy court when Charles Radcliffe (later 5th Earl of Derwentwater, 1731), one of the most prominent figures of the court of James III and of Jacobite Freemasonry, arrived in Turin. He had already spent some time in Turin in 1725, on his way to Paris where he then founded the Grand Lodge in that city.[36] He also made a stop in the Savoy capital on his way back from France, remaining in Turin for several months between 1726 and 1727. It was at

---

[34] See: Wynne 1995; Wynne 1996; and, especially: McDonnell 1996: 88–9.

[35] Born Maguire of Inniskillin, she married Eugene MacMahon, captain of an Irish regiment serving the French crown. In 1723 she travelled to Italy to visit James III and her husband entered the service of the Grand Duke of Tuscany and become governor of Pistoia. I owe this information to the courtesy of Edward Corp.

[36] On the creation of Freemasonry in France, a seminal work remains that of Chevallier (1964), who devotes a number of pages to Derwentwater's works. On this work, however, see the remarks in: Le Bihan 1967.

that time that his wife, Lady Newburgh, gave birth to their first daughter, Charlotte (1726–1800).[37] No concrete information about Derwentwater's contacts in Turin has yet emerged. Recently, Marsha Keith Schuchard, in her extensive biography of Swedenborg, suggested that in 1727 Radcliffe may have founded a Jacobite Masonic lodge in Turin.[38] This is a tantalizing theory, and a plausible one at that, but for the moment there is no evidence to support it. There is no doubt that a Jacobite lodge did exist in the early 1730s. It was, in fact, so active that it was a source of concern for the English Prime Minister, Robert Walpole, who published an article in a Masonic paper in London in 1734 explicitly accusing the Turin lodge of playing a role in pushing Charles Emmanuel III towards France in the War of the Polish Succession.[39] The journalist – and Walpole behind him – warned the Savoy ruler and the Hanoverians 'about the masonic activities of the Masons of Turin'.[40] The English ambassador in Turin from 1732 had been William Capell, third Earl of Essex (1697–1743) and Gentleman of the Bedchamber to George II.[41] A close ally of Sir Robert Walpole, the Earl of Essex was not only a Freemason, but also a member of Walpole's lodge at Houghton Hall – the lodge that would host the elevation of Francis, Duke of Lorraine, future Grand Duke of Tuscany and Holy Roman Emperor in 1731. It is 'quite likely' that the ceremony was attended also by Essex, before he was sent to Turin as ambassador.[42] Through his ambassador, Walpole was well aware of what was happening in Turin on the masonic front, especially since Essex was intimately familiar with the state of affairs in Turin, having attended the Royal Academy as a student years earlier.[43]

The years between 1737 and 1739 were crucial in the history of Freemasonry and its fortunes in Catholic countries. In August of 1737 Fleury launched an attack against the Grande Loge de France, forcing Derwentwater to concede his role as Grand Master to the Duke of Antin, a Hanoverian. Also significant in this context, in the effort to remove Jacobite elements from the masonic world, were the Bull *In Eminenti* issued by Pope Clement XII (April 1738) and the creation of the Ancient and Accepted Scottish Rite (*Rite écossais Ancien et Accepté*) by Ramsay, introduced to France in that same year from the Castle of Saint Germaine-en-Laye. The

---

[37] Derwentwater sent a letter to James III from Turin on 18 January 1727. See: Arnold 1959: 186.
[38] Schuchard 2011: 258; Lewis 1961: 86, 96.
[39] Schuchard 2011: 258–9.
[40] Schuchard 2011: 258.
[41] Black 2001: 21, 54–5, 78, 105, 112.
[42] Daynes 1924: 129.
[43] Black 2001: 21, 202.

presence in Turin of a number of Freemasons, from both political fronts, was therefore hardly accidental.[44] Furthermore, the fact that diplomatic relations between Rome and Turin at this time were rather strained (following the Pope's revocation of the 1727 Concordat on 6 August 1731) may have provided an additional element in favour of Turin as the ideal choice for visiting Freemasons.

It is interesting to note that in the same years, 1737–9, documents attest to the presence at the Turin Royal Academy of several supporters of James III. In 1737, for example, the Honourable John Forbes was there for several months. He was loyal to James III and was also a 'visiting brother' of the Jacobite lodge in Rome.[45] Between 1738 and 1739 the Catholic William Stafford-Howard (1718–1751, 3rd Earl of Stafford, *de jure* 4th Baron Stafford) was at the Academy for a few months in the early days of his Grand Tour of Italy that would continue until 1740.[46] His family was one of the most influential at the court of Saint Germain-en-Laye. His ancestor, John (†1714), had been Comptroller of the Household under James II from 1696 to 1700, and he later became Vice-Chamberlain to Mary of Modena from 1700 to 1714 (in addition to being her private secretary from 1711). Another ancestor, Mary Southcote, was Under-Governess to James III from 1692 to 1694, and then Governess of Princess Louise Marie from 1694 to 1700.[47] His uncle, John Paul (1700–62), was Under-Governor of the Duke of York from 1729 to 1730.[48] It is not surprising, therefore, that during his stay in Rome, Stafford received a warm welcome from James III and made no secret of his Jacobite inclinations.

At this time the Jacobite lodge in Turin was still active, as witnessed by the presence in the Savoy capital in April 1738 of Swedenborg, who was serving James III.[49] In those same years the Turin Royal Academy was also home to Hanoverian English Freemasons. Between 1736 and 1737, for example, Lord Sandwich and his tutor – and later private secretary – the Carinthian Johan Jakob Frolich (1699–1774), were at the Academy. Frolich, as reconstructed by Nicolas Hans, had been a member of the Hanoverian lodge of Florence since at least 1732.[50] The total lack of archival documentation

[44] Francovich 1974: 173.
[45] Hughan 1910: 13, 19, 48. A different view on the lodge at Rome and, in general, on Jacobite freemasonry is found in: Ferrer Benimeli 2010.
[46] Ingamells 1997: 885.
[47] Corp 2004a: 360, 364, 265. Francis Stafford, John's younger brother, was 'groom of the bedchamber' of James II from 1689 to 1700. See Corp 2004a: 359.
[48] Edward Stafford († 1746), another uncle, was allegedly a Gentleman of the Prince of Wales from 1743 to 1744. See: Corp 2011a: 197, 363–4, 366, 368.
[49] On Swedenborg's stay in Turin, see: Tafel 1877: III, 104–5.
[50] See: Hans 1958; Francovich 1974: 49–85; Ferrer Benimeli 1985; Bertini 1989.

permits us, for the time being, only to speculate on these matters of contacts and networks, but the subject is of remarkable interest even if we can not yet offer firm substantiation.

It is significant that the patent of 'Grand Master for the States of the King of Sardinia', given to the Marquis des Marches by the Grand Lodge of London, on 12 June 1739, followed the arrest, a month earlier, of Tommaso Crudeli and the attack against masonry in Florence, close as it was to the Hanoverian camp. The 'Primo sorvegliante' of the Florentine Lodge was the Reverend Robert Spence (1699–1768), an Oxford professor who often accompanied young English gentlemen on their Grand Tour of Italy.[51] He had been admitted to the Lodge in 1732, when he was in the Tuscan capital as tutor of Charles Sackville, Earl of Middlesex (1711–69),[52] one of the most prominent members of the Lodge of Florence during the year he spent there. Spence subsequently returned home and left again in September 1739, this time as tutor of Henry Clinton, 9th Earl of Lincoln (1720–94).[53] They arrived in Turin in October, where the two remained for a year, until September 1740. The fact that the Royal Academy of Turin had provided accommodation for a member of the Lodge that had been made the object of such drastic Papal measures was a fact that simply could not have gone unnoticed by the ever-vigilant Savoy police. Between 1730 and 1740 the masonic presence in the State of Savoy was a given – and a central role had been played in this presence, as is clear, by the British.

This fundamental role also emerged as the result of events that occurred at a military lodge in August 1742. The Bishop of Nice, Mons. Carlo Enrico Cantono, addressed a concerned letter to Charles Emmanuel III in which he reported 'the introduction' into his diocese 'della congregazione dei *francs maçons*'[54] ('of the congregation of the Freemasons'). According to Monsignor Cantono the information he had become privy to regarded an affiliation ceremony in which English and Swiss officers had accepted Piedmontese military officers and civilians into their lodge.[55] The role of the British as the instigators of this initiative also appears clearly from a report drawn up by the Papal nuncio, Monsignor Merlini, who wrote about a

---

[51] On Spence, see: Ingamells 1997: 881. On his second stay in Turin he wrote for Clinton a *memorandum* on the institutional organization of the State of Savoy. Black 1989.

[52] Ingamells 1997: 657–8.

[53] Ingamells 1997: 601–2.

[54] Cauda to S. Laurent, 22 August 1742, in ASTo, Corte, *Lettere di particolari*, «C», mz. 48.

[55] Mazé to S. Laurent, 31 October 1742, in ASTo, Corte, *Piemonte giuridico*, reg. 21. On the importance of military lodges as the 'modello di disseminazione e di contagio più importante' ('most important model of dissemination and contagion') for Freemasonry, see: Giarrizzo 1994: 101–5.

masonic gathering 'd'undici eretici, fra quali otto inglesi' ('of eleven heretics, including eight Englishmen') who, together with a number of Piedmontese aristocrats, had 'a porte chiuse fatto diverse operazioni che non si sanno, con impressione di figure sul pavimento che non si sono potute distinguere che cosa fossero' ('accomplished behind closed doors several operations that remain unknown, designing figures on the floor that could not be distinguished for what they were').

Charles Emmanuel III was in Imola at the time, where the Savoy troops had been deployed to fight in the War of the Austrian Succession. Also in the field was Giacomo Antonio Cauda, a lawyer, who was the liaison to Count Chapel de Saint Laurent, Secretary of State for Internal Affairs, who had remained in Turin. Charles Emmanuel III, wrote Cauda, believed that 'quantunque non vi sia propriamente in chi ha formato l'idea di questo istituto cosa che ripugni alla religione o allo Stato, si è però fissata la massima di non soffrirne l'introduzione ne' suoi Stati, meno che alcuno ne parli'[56] ('while there is not truly, in those who conceived the idea of this institute, anything against religion or the State, the custom has been adopted not to suffer its introduction in one's State, nor to make reference to it'). The minister, moreover, should have ordered the commander in Nice to send for the officers that the bishop indicated as 'francs maçons', and give them notice that they would be 'carcerati e castigati' ('imprisoned and punished') if they were to 'conoscere d'essere del numero' ('let it be known that they were members') of the Freemasons or to refer 'in qualunque maniera' ('in any fashion') to the secret society.[57] As we can gather from the letter, there is a difference between the principle of 'non soffrire l'introduzione' ('not suffering the introduction') of the Freemasonry in Piedmont, and the fact of simply warning Freemasons to keep a low profile. Maintaining, just four years after the Papal Bull *In eminenti*, that those who had founded Freemasonry held nothing against religion was, in itself, a revealing point. Cauda also noted another important fact: the orders issued by Charles Emmanuel III were not a new development, 'così avendomi detto Sua Maestà di aver fatto praticare in Torino per mezzo del signor governatore in una simile occasione' ('having His Majesty told me that he had allowed the practice in Turin through the lord governor in a similar occasion'). While no evidence has been found of the occurrence in Turin to which Cauda refers, this lack of documentation surely provides further confirmation of a tacit masonic presence in Turin in the 1730s.

[56] Cauda to S. Laurent, 22 August 1742, in ASTo, Corte, *Lettere particolari*, C, mz. 48.
[57] Quoted from *ibid*. See also S. Laurent to Cauda, 26 August 1742, ASTo, Corte, *Piemonte giuridico*, reg. 21.

Instead, several testimonies from the 1740s survive. Only two years after the events in Nice in 1744, another lodge was discovered in Piedmont, that included Swiss, Irish and other military officers.[58] In that same year, in the preface to the second edition of his *Chansons*, Naudot reported that a Lodge had been established in Turin. In 1746, Valerio Angiolieri Alticozzi wrote about the nocturnal disturbance caused by the 'fratelli muratori' ('mason brothers') of the 'principale loggia di Turino' ('main Lodge of Turin'), who 'al sommo rallegrati dal vino e dal canto, lacerarono da capo a piedi la tonaca e la cocolla ad un romito inglese, in quella città dimorante e membro del ceto muratoriano ('most euphoric from wine and chanting tore from head to toe the habit and the cowl of an English hermit, who resided in that town and who was a member of the masonry').[59] This intense activity of military Lodges – whose membership, it should be noted, was not limited to army officers, but also open to civilians, as was the case in Nice in 1742 – may help to explain why the Marquis de Bellegarde waited until May 1749 to create the Lodge in Chambéry 'aux Trois-Mortiers', that was from 1751 the *Grande loge maitresse* of all the States of the King of Sardinia.[60]

An Englishman from the Turin Royal Academy at the Lodge of Turin Saint Jean de la Mysterieuse (1778)

In subsequent years, the major event in the world of Savoy Freemasonry surely was the creation in Turin of the Saint Jean de la Mystérieuse Lodge, in December 1765. In its early years this lodge remained under the Lodge of Chambéry. In 1771 the Marquis Carlo Gabriele Asinari di Bernezzo (1724–1803) was elected Grand Master and, in the same year, he was also appointed as major-domo to Charles Emmanuel III (once again it should be noted, as was the case with Bellegarde, that the highest-ranking officers of the Lodges were very close to the sovereign, who in fact appointed them to important posts at court).[61] Bernezzo endeavoured to breathe new life into the Saint Jean de la Mystérieuse Lodge by accepting new members and making it independent from the Lodge based in the Savoy region. On 3 April 1774, the Grand Lodge of London recognized the Mystérieuse as the provincial Lodge for Piedmont (in spite of the opposition of the Trois Mortiers).

[58] Giarrizzo 1994: 103.
[59] Angiolieri Alticozzi 1746: 48–9.
[60] Vermale 1912: 5; Maruzzi: 1990.
[61] On Bernezzo in addition to Maruzzi (1990), see also: Bianchi and Merlotti 2013: 286–9, 292.

It is significant that in this period the Lodge of Turin accepted as a 'brother' an English student of the Turin Royal Academy. As previously noted, the archives of the Saint Jean de la Mysterieuse Lodge appear to have been lost. The only documents available attesting to the Lodge's activity and, more specifically, to the list of the Lodge's brothers, remain those that Maruzzi located in an unspecified 'archivio di Borgognas' ('Burgundy archive'), deposited with the *Modestia cum libertate* Lodge in Zurich, from which he extracted a partial list of Turinese brothers in 1765 and in 1768. However, recently, in the archives of the Solaro di Moretta family, I have uncovered further references to the Saint Jean de la Mysterieuse Lodge. These references comprise documents that belonged to Count Gaspare Solaro di Moretta, who was the Lodge's treasurer in 1778. Among the most interesting finds is a 'Compte courant de moi F∴comte de Challant avec la T∴R∴de Saint Jean de la Mysterieuse', signed by Count Maurice of Challant.[62] According to the *Compte courant* (the list of brothers), dating from between June and December 1778, seven new brothers were accepted to the Lodge, an average of one per month. Among these new members, in addition to individuals from the highest Sabaudian aristocracy – like Giuseppe Solaro del Borgo, 'un jeun maçon extremement vif' ('an extremely enthusiastic young mason') who would soon leave to study law in Leiden – appears also the name of a young Englishman: James Roper Head (1757–1814).

Date	Brother
29 June	B∴Du Bourg
29 June	B∴St. Severin
29 July	B∴de Pamparà
18 August	B∴de S.te Rose
9 September	B∴Roper Head
17 December	B∴Cavalchini
	B∴Biandrà

Roper Head, who was 22 at the time, was attending the Turin Royal Academy, where he was registered as one of the students of the 'Primo appartamento' (first apartment) from September 1778 to August 1779,[63] and then

---

[62] See ASTo, *Corte*, Archivio Solaro di Moretta, mz. 5, f. 1. As regards Challant, this should be François Maurice Challant de Châtillon (1756–96), gentleman of the mouth to the king and amateur scientist. His affiliation to Saint Jean de la Mysterieuse, as was the case with Solaro di Moretta, was unknown to Maruzzi.

[63] See: Ingamells 1997: 481; and also the list of students presented in this volume by Bianchi, p. 404.

again in March 1780, when he was presented to Victor Amadeus III, along with the poet Robert Merry.[64] Roper Head was educated at Eton from 1772 to 1774, moving on to Trinity College in Oxford, and on 1 November 1776 he joined the sixth regiment of the dragoons of H.R.M. as a cadet. He then left for his Grand Tour of Europe, during which he resided for an extended period in Turin, as was the norm for many British tourists. Further archival research will demonstrate whether Roper Head's admission to the Lodge Saint Jean de la Mysterieuse was an isolated case or not. None the less, the fact that a young student at the Turin Royal Academy had been accepted to the main Lodge of the Sabaudian capital is an important fact in and of itself. It is even more significant that this happened not at the end, but at the very beginning of Roper Head's sojourn in Turin, indicating that this step was a necessity to his education. Furthermore, and even more significantly, Roper Head's admission to the Lodge may well be evidence that direct ties existed between the British, German, Russian and Polish students who gathered in the halls of the Academy and the Sabaudian world of Freemasonry.

Even more fascinating, however, is the fact that Roper Head's true family name was Mendes. His father was Moses Mendes (c. 1690–1758), a well-known writer in London under George II, who descended directly from Fernando Mendes (c. 1645–1724), a Portuguese Jewish physician to the Queen of England, Catherine of Braganza. After converting to Anglicanism, Moses married Anne Gabrielle Head (d. 1771), the daughter of a Baronet, and they had two children, the younger of whom was Roper Head, the student at the Turin Royal Academy. The change in family name occurred after Moses Mendes's death, when in 1760 his widow remarried Captain John Roper, son of Lord Henry Teynham. In 1770, Anne's children took the Captain's name (after the issuance of a special royal licence dated 11 May of that year), adding their mother's maiden name, resulting in Roper Head.

The Turin Royal Academy, a meeting place for young tourists on the Grand Tour, with its vast 'colluvie di Boreali, inglesi, principalmente, russi e tedeschi' ('muddle of Northerners, mostly English, Russian and German'), as famously described by Vittorio Alfieri,[65] was an ideal environment for the flourishing of Freemasonry and other similar forms of sociability. The introduction into the Sabaudian capital of the rite of Strict Observance further increased the masonic ties with the world of the lesser German Princes who played a major role in Turin. The Court of Savoy – the House of the

---

[64]   Bianchi 2012b: 154.
[65]   Alfieri 1981: 27.

Princes of the Empire –[66] and the Turin Royal Academy were a constant point of reference in Italy in the eighteenth century. If Turin in the 1760s and 1770s was, along with Naples, the main masonic centre of Italy, this was due in large part to Savoy's long history of hosting secret societies, as well as to the lively presence of the highly cosmopolitan students in attendance at the Royal Academy.

---

[66] See the essays collected in: Bellabarba and Merlotti 2014.

PART III

Torino Britannica: Diplomacy and Cultural Brokerage

9 | John Molesworth: British Envoy and Cultural Intermediary in Turin

KARIN WOLFE

On 4 June 1721, John Molesworth, British Envoy Extraordinary and Plenipotentiary to the Savoy royal court of Victor Amadeus II in Turin, sent a long letter to his friend and protégé Alessandro Galilei (1691–1737), 'principal engineer and architect to his royal majesty of Florence' (Fig. 9.1).[1] This letter forms part of a copious correspondence entitled 'Fogli inglesi' in the Galilei papers in the *Archivio di Stato* in Florence, extracts of which were first published in 1952 by Ilaria Toesca.[2] Though numerous scholars have referenced the correspondence since that date, it remains largely unpublished.[3] However, Molesworth's letter to Galilei merits serious consideration as it contains passages of extraordinary importance as to his sensibility to the arts and to the cultural rapport between Britain and Italy, while also revealing his exposure to the architectural brilliance and entrepreneurship of the royal architect in Turin – the Sicilian, Filippo Juvarra (1678–1736). In a section that has never been cited in its entirety, Molesworth writes:

Sir, I have been considering, in relation to your future wellfare in our Country, that one may venture to lay down as a Maxim that no man ever made a fortune by excelling in his profession unless in those which are of absolute necessity to Mankind, for those which conduce only to the pleasure of the Rich as Architecture etc. whoever would thrive by them, must look one way and row t'other as our Seamen's proverb is: I mean that they must acquire a competent Skill in some other Art, under the Covert of which they may introduce their own. Thus you Saw that D.r Garth by being a good Poet. D.r Wellwood by excelling in History, carry'd on their business in Physic; as S.r John Vanbrook commenc'd Architec[ture] by writeing Comedies. This being granted, I should think that you have now leisure and an excellent Opportunity to put this rule in practise. You may chuse out of several Elegancys which Italy is fam'd for, one besides your own, to excell in; and a little Study would easily make you Master of any, especially those that have some relation to what you allready possess.

---

[1] Archivio di Stato di Firenze (ASF), Carte Galilei, b. 21, ins. 1, fols 37r–38r, Turin, 4 June 1721, Molesworth to Galilei (for the full transcription of this letter see Appendix IV.3.)

[2] Toesca 1952.

[3] In particular: Kieven 1973. See also: Kieven 1975; Connor 1998; Cusmano 1998; McParland 2001; Kieven 2008a; Giusto 2010; Molesworth 2010; Sicca 2011.

Figure 9.1 Antonio Francesco Selvi, *Medal depicting John Molesworth*, bronze, 1712, Collection Viscount Molesworth.

I will mention the knowledge of Medals; the Skill of conducting water and contriving Fountains; Painting, especially Landskape or Pictoresc Architecture with Ruines, Caverns etc; Scenical Architecture with th'invention of Machines etc in Bibiena's stile: Criticism in Pictures, drawings, Basso rilievos etc with the distinction of the hands of the Several Masters; the disposition of Gardens, Grottos, Labyrinths etc., to which purpose you might take the Sketch of any remarkable pieces you could observe at Florence, Rome, France or elswhere in your travels. These or indeed any more important operations in Geometry would be in … your pursuit; and would serve to recommen'd you to the Great Men while you should dissemble your Skill in Architecture till their good opinion of you in other Matters should open their Eyes.

I have dwelt long upon this Subject and been even tedious in explaining it because I am really convinc'd that such a comendable artifice would much conduce to your gaining access to the Genius of our Nation which is yet in the dark as to Building: but if ever it recover from the dreadfull Abyss it is now plung'd in, I believe we shall be less wanton and consequently more Apt to hear good Advice as well in matters of taste, as of prudence.[4]

Molesworth's considerations 'in matters of taste' centre primarily on the contemporary state and shortcomings of the architectural profession in Britain. His words convey his vision of an ideal modern architect – highly cultivated, cosmopolitan and multi-disciplinary – a challenge he hopes Galilei will take up and, indeed, a challenge he wishes to set for future British

---

[4] See Appendix IV.3.

architects to attain a national level of excellence. In order to understand how such exacting aesthetic considerations and philosophical advice came to be written to an Italian architect in Florence by an Anglo-Irish diplomat posted to Turin, it is necessary to give a brief overview of Molesworth's career to that date, taking into account both the British and Italian cultural milieus in which he operated.

Born in 1679, John Molesworth was the eldest son of the prominent Whig politician and diplomat, Robert Molesworth (1656–1725), future Viscount of Swords (1716), known for his writings on politics and social reform, and an enlightened landowner.[5] John was brought up between the family's country residence of Breckenstown in Ireland, and London, where he was educated, excelling in classical literature.[6] Thanks to his paternal contacts, he was awarded a series of political and diplomatic appointments, culminating in a posting to Florence in 1711 as Envoy Extraordinary to the Medici court. Arriving on 14 March, he spent three years in Florence, a period of enormous benefit for the enrichment of his taste and for his interests in architecture, art, music, literature and poetry, as well as for the lasting friendships he formed with prominent Florentine intellectuals and artists.[7]

While the list of his Florentine contacts is long, it included, most importantly, the celebrated Greek and Latin scholar and linguist, the Abate Anton Maria Salvini (1653–1729).[8] Salvini translated Joseph Addison's *Cato, A Tragedy* into Italian in 1715, a project Molesworth directly supported and which helped to garner Salvini the distinction of being elected to the Royal Society on 5 April the following year.[9] Significantly for his developing enthusiasm for art criticism and connoisseurship, Molesworth frequented, and was in turn esteemed by, the nobleman diplomat, collector and compiler of artist biographies, Francesco Maria Gaburri (1676–1742). But most importantly for his lifelong cultural undertakings, Molesworth formed a close alliance with the architect Alessandro Galilei, who had originally trained as a mathematician, and who was a distant relative of the scientist Galileo Galilei.[10]

---

[5] See: Molesworth 2010. I am indebted to William Molesworth, who very kindly shared access to his unpublished thesis, which includes much new biographical information on John Molesworth and the Molesworth family, and to Edward McParland, who alerted me to this study.

[6] Molesworth 2010: chapter 1.

[7] For the cultural situation in Florence in relation with that of London, see: Kieven 2008a: 1–6.

[8] On Salvini, see: Paoli 2005.

[9] Paoli 2005: 27.

[10] On Molesworth and Galilei in Florence, see: Kieven 2008a.

Despite the fact that he was only twelve years Galilei's senior, Molesworth developed an almost paternal relationship with the architect, mentoring him in his professional development and sharing with him an intense interest in architecture and architectural theory that continued throughout their friendship.[11] He sponsored a one-month study trip to Rome for Galilei in 1714, joining him there for part of the time, to tour and measure the most important examples of antique and modern architecture, as well as the most celebrated collections of art.[12] The extent of their friendship is underlined by the fact that by the time Molesworth concluded his diplomatic service at the Florentine court in April 1714 he had persuaded Galilei to travel to London in the same year, intending to introduce him to the city's dynamic professional world of architecture, which offered such free-market opportunities as the ambitious scheme for the building of 'Fifty New Churches', set up by Act of Parliament in 1710.[13]

Well before their arrival in London, Molesworth and Galilei had nurtured a shared passion for architectural aesthetics at a heady moment when the British architectural scene was in the midst of significant transformation. This sea-change was determined by an anti-Baroque current first set in motion by John Evelyn in the seventeenth century and then promulgated by Anthony Ashley Cooper, 3rd Earl of Shaftesbury (1671–1713). Shaftesbury was an intimate friend of Molesworth's father, and of John, who had hosted him in Florence in 1711 – precisely at the time Shaftesbury was formulating the ideas and aesthetic principles he set down in 1712 in *A Letter Concerning the Art or Science of Design*.[14]

Contrary to the newly fashionable and widely admired model of neo-Palladianism articulated by the Scottish architect Colen Campbell (1676–1729) in the first two volumes of *Vitruvius Britannicus*, published in London in 1715 and 1717 – an architectural model subsequently embraced by the influential taste setter Richard Boyle, 3rd Earl of Burlington – Molesworth and Galilei's vision for architecture constituted a far more severe and

---

[11] Inviting Galilei to Pisa, Christmas 1722, Molesworth wrote: 'Pray bring some book of the rudiments of Architecture and your Case of Instruments, for I intend to revive my lost Ideas of that noble science', ASF, Carte Galilei, b. 21, ins. 1, fol. 66, Pisa, 16 December 1722, Molesworth to Galilei.

[12] For Galilei's Roman diary of 8 January–4 February 1714, see: Cusmano 1998: 97–9; Giusto 2010: 29–33.

[13] On Galilei in Britain and Ireland, see: Toesca 1952: 189–220; Kieven 1973: 210–12; McParland 1994; McParland 1995: 160–5; McParland 2001: 7–15; Arciszewska 2005: 135–45; Kieven 2008: 1–31a; Giusto 2010: 29–86.

[14] Among his considerations, Shaftesbury (1790: 115) wrote: 'It is evident beyond doubt that the arts and sciences were formed in Greece itself.'

abstract concept of 'Greek' purity of design.[15] Their ideal architectural aesthetic served as a synonym for simplicity and plainness and admitted the
ancient architectural examples visible in Rome and those of renaissance
Florence, especially those of Michelangelo. This model was conditioned
by Molesworth and Galilei's Florentine cultural grounding in the 'Tuscan
Athens',[16] as defined by the literary group of Salvini and his circle, a position that also absorbed the views on Greek cultural superiority advanced
by Shaftesbury.

Indeed, in 1717, three years after John Molesworth and Galilei arrived
in London, Robert Molesworth was to refer in a letter to a 'New Junta for
Architecture',[17] undoubtedly an attempt to launch a new style of architecture
in Britain, formulated by a 'clique', as Edward McParland has described their
group, of 'precocious neo-classical tastes'.[18] Aside from the Molesworths and
Galilei, this ideal was also embraced by the architects Sir Thomas Hewett
(1656–1726) and Edward Lovett Pearce (1699–1733), both of whom openly
called attention to the 'Greek' qualities of their own architecture.[19] John
Molesworth and his father's concerted, and ultimately failed efforts over
four years to establish Galilei professionally in Britain and Ireland are well
known from several studies dedicated to the architect's travails.[20] In a letter
of June 1719 from Robert Molesworth to Galilei – and which also surely
reflects John's opinion – Robert writes, disheartened, 'Sir, We have no taste
in this Country of what is excellent in any of y fine Arts, and I doubt shall
not have for severall years yet to come.'[21]

As if to bear out this gloomy prediction, following the departure of
Galilei from the British Isles, in 1719, to take up a post as court architect
to Duke Cosimo III in Florence, and the departure of John the following
year to take up the role of envoy to the Savoy royal court in Turin, the 'New
Junta for Architecture' lost its principal actor and director, as well as its
momentum. Molesworth's diplomatic appointment to the Savoy court,
however, brought him directly into the artistic orbit of Filippo Juvarra,
whose dynamic approach to the wider profession of architecture would

---

[15] McParland 1995.
[16] Paoli 2005: 28–9.
[17] McParland 1994.
[18] McParland 1995: 161–3.
[19] McParland 1995: 161.
[20] McParland 1995: 160–5; Kieven 2008a. John Molesworth continued to try to secure work for
      Galilei in Italy and in Britain, see Appendix IV.7 and Appendix IV.8.
[21] McParland (2001: 9), citing this phrase, underlines Robert Molesworth's preoccupation
      specifically with Ireland's cultural standing (the letter was written from Breckdenstown,
      County Dublin to Galilei in London).

influence the envoy's aesthetic and refine his concept of what constituted the ideal architect.

Arriving in Turin on 29 December 1720, Molesworth came face-to-face with an extraordinary city-wide programme of dramatic architectural and urban renewal and restoration.[22] Under the aegis of Victor Amadeus II, who exploited monumental architecture and urbanism as a medium to enhance and consolidate his sovereignty, vast construction projects for churches, palaces, squares and streets were underway, or in their final planning stages.[23] These included Palazzo Madama (Fig. 9.2), the twin churches of Piazza San Carlo, the Venaria Reale and the royal church and mausoleum of Superga, as well as whole tracts of the city that were being revamped for military quarters. This spectacular renovation of the Savoy capitol, also including extensive interior decoration, comprising painting, the court arts of furniture and silver, and even remarkable ephemeral manifestations, was all designed and overseen by one man, Juvarra, who at that moment was the most qualified specialist of his kind in Europe, embodying the figure of the universal, multi-disciplinary architect and director of the arts.[24] Molesworth, by now highly culturally attuned to shifts in taste, felt compelled to advise Galilei on what he discerned were modern professional prerequisites for an architect.

Written six months after he was received at court in Turin, the letter to Galilei of 4 June 1721, cited at the start of this paper, was undoubtedly prompted by Molesworth's personal experience of Juvarra's genius for designing and directing all manner of building and artistic projects.[25] Tellingly, Molesworth singles out talents unique to Juvarra, such as 'Painting, especially Landskape or Pictoresc Architecture with Ruines [or] Caverns and Scenical Architecture with th'invention of Machines in Bibiena's stile'. These were well-known specialities of the Sicilian architect, particularly his sketches of landscape and architectural *capricci* – a genre that anticipated the work of this type by Giovanni Paolo Panini and Giovanni Battista Piranesi – not to mention Juvarra's noted theatre designs, inspired by the work of Ferdinando and Francesco Bibiena.[26]

---

[22] Molesworth 2010: 100, n. 601. Molesworth was presented to Victor Amadeus II on 7 January 1721; see: Molesworth 2010: 100, n. 605.

[23] For the urban reconstruction of Turin, see the various contributions in the volume edited by Kieven and Ruggero (2014), with previous bibliography.

[24] For the architectural projects Juvarra realized for the Savoy court, see Gritella 1992. For Juvarra's role as pictorial adviser to the royal court, see Wolfe 2014a; Wolfe 2014b.

[25] Documented as in Rome on 15 December 1720, Juvarra only returned to Turin in early April 1721, see: Manfredi 1995: 290, n. 14.

[26] In an earlier letter (15 January 1721) Molesworth advises Galilei to apply himself to the study of theatre architecture as a new theatre had been mooted for the opera in London. It cannot be

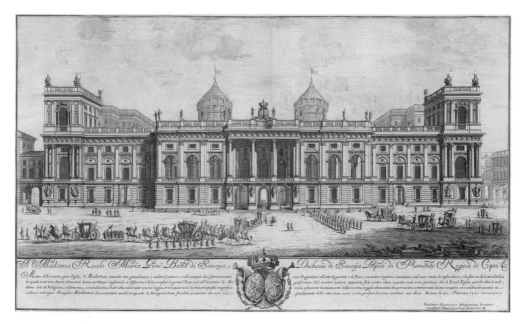

Figure 9.2 After Filippo Juvarra, *Project for Palazzo Madama*, engraving by Filippo Vasconi, Rome, 1721, Private collection.

Molesworth's commendations regarding 'Criticism in Pictures, drawings, Basso rilievos etc with the distinction of the hands of the Several Masters', on the other hand, demonstrate his own knowledge of, and interest in, connoisseurship as practised by the wider literary and intellectual circles of Florence and London. In particular, he had direct experience of the connoisseurship of his friend Gaburri, a noted collector of drawings, and also of Shaftesbury's writings on criticism. And Molesworth would have been familiar, too, with the work of Jonathan Richardson (1665–1745), including his recently published *Essay on the Theory of Painting* (1715) and *Essay on the Whole Art of Criticism as it Relates to Painting*, and *Argument in Behalf of the Science of the Connoisseur* (both 1719).

The letter of 4 June 1721 reveals Molesworth to be at the forefront of both continental and national matters of culture and taste, which goes some way to explain why he was known in Turin as the 'virtuoso', an honour that distinguished him from the other envoys.[27] While the political

coincidental, that at that time in Turin, plans under Juvarra's direction were in progress for the refurbishment of the royal theatre in Palazzo Reale, ASF, Carte Galilei, b. 21, ins. 1, fols 33r– 34r, Turin, 15 January 1721, Molesworth to Galilei, see Appendix IV.1.

27 Molesworth 2010: 114.

situation of British diplomacy at the Savoy capitol and the foregrounding of the critical role played by Victor Amadeus II in the Piedmontese-British political sphere has been charted,[28] Molesworth's role as a diplomat requires further research. Nevertheless, his cultural persona emerges clearly not only from his surviving correspondence and commissions, but also from accounts given by his contemporaries and travellers in Turin. At the countryside villa of his friend Giambattista Balbo Simeone, the Count de la Rivière,[29] where Molesworth soon moved on account of his chronic respiratory ailments, he met the officer Charles De Saint-Maure, in December 1721, en route to the Middle East. While in Turin, Saint-Maure was invited daily to supper with Molesworth, who introduced him to the Marchese Francesco Giuseppe Wilcardel de Fleury di Trivero, the first envoy and later Savoy ambassador to the British royal court in London. In his travel memoirs Saint-Maure later described di Trivero as 'the most accomplished man in town', while of Molesworth he wrote, 'he is the Delight of this whole court'.[30]

In the vivacious international atmosphere that characterized the Savoy capitol, Molesworth participated in an intense round of representational court appearances, necessitated by the King's active pursuit of political diplomacy. Alongside these, he enjoyed a hectic social life of *salotti*, *conversazioni* and musical entertainments. The Dutch traveller and music connoisseur Jan Alensoon (1683–1769), resident in Turin during Molesworth's tenure, documents the range of musical spectacles on offer in the city, making particular note of a chamber concert that Molesworth hosted for the occasion of the birthday of the Prince of Wales (George Augustus, later George II) in November 1723.[31] Alensoon also enthusiastically writes of meeting the 'great architect' Juvarra, who accompanied him on tours of Turin.

Juvarra is also frequently nominated in Molesworth's correspondence to Galilei.[32] Having solicited Galilei's advice for a Florentine fresco painter for a commission for an unnamed nobleman in Turin, Molesworth recounts in a letter to Galilei (3 January 1725) how he advanced the cause of this artist:

Sir, since the arrival of the Court in town, I have spoken about the Painter [the Florentine painter] and was answer'd that as Don Filippo the King's Architect [Juvarra] was to pass through Florence soon in his return from Venice and Rome, he

[28] See Christopher Storrs, Chapter 4 in this volume.
[29] I wish to thank Paola Bianchi for information on Giambattista Balbo Simeone (1703–77).
[30] De Sainte-Maure 1725: 137–8.
[31] Vlaardingerbroek 1991: 539–42.
[32] Manfredi 2014.

should be desir'd to view some of that Painters works where they are finish'd in their Several Situations at the Palaces you mention, and upon his report this Nobleman would take his resolutions. I took an opportunity of mentioning the painter to the King himself, who has some rooms to finish at Rivoli [the royal Castle at Rivoli]; so that I am of Opinion it would be for his service to send me a Couple of Sketches in Oil to Show. He may chuse the subjects and the dimensions, provided they be such as will admit of Noble designs. My thought is that two Storys of the Roman History, both relateing to the Great Camillus, might be express'd with vast dignity.[33]

Though the Florentine painter in question has not been identified, Giovanni Domenico Ferretti (1692–1768) is a likely candidate, considering his contacts with Molesworth's acquaintances in Florence and his thriving career as a fresco painter. Significantly, the letter confirms to what degree control of artistic matters in Turin was delegated to Juvarra, and not exclusively for royal patronage, but also, as in this case, for local noble commissions. Equally, the letter demonstrates Molesworth's desire to influence artistic developments at the Savoy court. His erudition and refined taste, which originated in his British education centred on the moral lessons of classical literature, which he had actively cultivated in Florentine intellectual circles, ultimately served him to promote his role as cultural intermediary in Turin.[34]

By 2 May 1725, Juvarra was back in Turin, and Molesworth informed Galilei of their collaboration:

Don Philippo appear's very well satisfy'd with the Painter's [the Florentine painter's] performances, and tell's me he has settl'd the Conditions on which he is to come hither. Perhaps his Recommendation may suffise to establish that Artists reputation here: however I would have him [the painter] continue those Sketches I gave him the Subjects of; for a Sample of a Man's Capacity has ever a more forcible effect that any fame by Hearsay: and after they have been sufficiently consider'd; if the King does not seize them I intend to take them my self [the sketches]: the sooner they are sent the better.[35]

As a collector and patron Molesworth was severely handicapped by financial constraints. Already during his tenure in Florence, he suffered economic hardship due to non-payment of his salary as envoy – a common problem for diplomats abroad at the time – and his monetary situation

---

[33] ASF, Carte Galilei, pezzo 21, inserto 1, fol. 163rv, Turin, 3 January 1725, Molesworth to Galilei, see Appendix IV.6.

[34] Molesworth may have proposed the subject of Camillus to commemorate the important Savoy victory at the Siege of Turin, 1706.

[35] ASF, Carte Galilei, pezzo 21, inserto 1, fol. 174r, Turin, 2 May 1725, Molesworth to Galilei, see Appendix IV.7.

worsened in Turin on account of his family's investment in the South Sea Bubble debacle. Even so, this in no way dampened his desire to acquire art, as he stated in a letter of 21 June 1724, lamenting that he would prefer 'to spend his money for the beautiful things to be found in Florence', rather than for Savoy diplomatic protocol.[36] Though it is unlikely that he ever got hold of the sketches for Rivoli featuring Furius Camillus he had promoted and which he hoped to receive gratis, Molesworth nonetheless commissioned two important sets of artworks from Florentine artists, which characterize his aesthetic ideals as a patron and define the refined, classically derived taste he worked hard to endorse.

Through the offices of Gaburri, Molesworth ordered two Roman history pictures *en pendant* from Tommaso Redi (1665–1726), Gaburri's protégé.[37] These *pendants* have not been traced, but they are well documented from 1757, when Giovanni Gaetano Bottari (1689–1775), in the second volume of his *Raccolta di lettere pittoriche*, published three of Molesworth's letters about the commission which he had written to Gaburri over the course of five months in 1724.[38] Bottari included Molesworth's letters on account of their importance as examples of art criticism and his admiration for Molesworth, whom he knew personally, as expressed in his notes: 'It is from these particulars that one can see he was a man of letters and of a highly refined discernment. How many are bereft of such sensibility and how few know to differentiate between these two questions, i.e. erudition and artistic sensibility?'.[39]

Molesworth selected as the themes for his *pendants*, *Cincinnatus Called from the Plough* and *The Ghost of Caesar Appearing to Brutus*, in line with his ideals regarding the republican virtues of ancient Rome as precursor to a new Augustan age.[40] In his dealings with Redi, Molesworth set out to exercise tight creative control over how the subjects should be portrayed, the exact moment and emotions to be depicted, the scale and poses of the

---

[36] 'La nostra corte parte per la Savoia verso la fine di questo mese, e io credo d'essere obbligato a seguitarla per vedere celebrar le nozze del principe di Piemonte con la principessa d'Hassen Rhinfeltz. Ecco, oltre una gran fatica, una spesa considerabile per me. Io amerei meglio d'impiegare il mio danaro in queste belle cose che si trovano in Firenze. Pazienza'. Torino, 20 giugno 1724 (Bottari 1757: 28).

[37] On Redi and his British patrons, see: Monbeig Goguel 1994.

[38] See: Bottari 1757: II, LXIV 127–8 (21 June 1724); LXV 129–30 (18 October 1724); LXVI 131–3 (22 November 1724).

[39] See: Bottari 1757: II, 127. Bottari probably met Molesworth through his mentor Salvini, and via Gaburri, who supplied Bottari with Molesworth's letters.

[40] Thomas Coke (1697–1759) – who may have met Molesworth in Italy in December 1713 – commissioned a *Cincinnatus Called from the Plough* from Luigi Garzi in Rome in 1716; on the vogue for subjects by Livy and Virgil, see: Bulman 2003.

figures, and even the palette. Perhaps not surprisingly, the artist was either unable or unwilling to fulfill this exacting brief, and when Molesworth finally received the finished pictures, sometime between June and July of 1724, he was extremely disappointed. As the letters that Molesworth wrote to Gaburri with his critiques for the painter were translated into Italian by Bottari when he published them in 1757, it suffices to cite a passage summing up the circumstances, from a letter Molesworth wrote to Galilei on 11 October 1724:

Sir, I don't know whether you ever saw the pictures done by my Orders at Florence. I took a good deal of pains to instruct the Painter Rhedi in several little Criticisms which I find he has not carefully Observ'd, since the Pictures are rather done according to his first thought than according to what was afterwards settl'd between us. I could specify many particulars, but I wonder chiefly at the Errors in design: that is what I Thought him incapable of: they are however Evident in the figure of Brutus where he has quite miss'd the true torso or turn of the body and that right arm has no shoulder, while the left arm from the Elbow upwards seems a little too short.[41]

It is likely that a surviving drawing by Redi for the seated *Brutus*, which belonged to Gaburri and which bears his annotations, was kept by the connoisseur specifically to discuss Molesworth's sustained criticism of the figure's pose with the artist (Fig. 9.3).[42]

Paradoxically, Molesworth's most important art commission, and the one that most perfectly embodies his aesthetic ideals as they matured in Florence, has never been properly considered in context. By a new reading of the Molesworth correspondence, it is now possible to ascertain that the commission to the Florentine sculptor Antonio Montauti (1683–1746) for a pair of large marble sculptures of *Ganymede with the Eagle of Jupiter* (Fig. 9.4) and *Hebe* (Fig. 9.5)[43] dates from Molesworth's first tenure in Italy,

---

[41] ASF, Carte Galilei, pezzo 21, inserto 1, fols 153v–154r, Turin, 11 October 1724, Molesworth to Galilei, see Appendix IV.5.

[42] Two drawings for the Redi *pendants* survive: one, pictured here (Figure 9.3), is a study for *Brutus* (red chalk and heightening on buff paper, 340×220 mm), which belonged to Gaburri and was inscribed by him on the verso 'Di Tommaso Redi/Bruto in atto di voltarsi all'ombra di Cesare. Questo quadro il d. Redi lo fece a olio al Sig. Moleswort inviato britanico alla corte di Toscana et ora e in Ingliterra'; the other is a study for the figure of *Caesar's Ghost* (National Gallery of Scotland, RSA 305, black chalk with highlights, 38.5 × 23.6 cm, also inscribed by Gaburri). For the drawings, see: Molesworth 2010: 142–3 (with previous bibliography).

[43] On Montauti generally, see: Bellesi 2012, *ad vocem* (who, however, does not include these sculptures). They were sold at Christie's King Street, 9 July 2009, lot 114 (*Hebe*, 139.7 cm) and lot 115 (*Ganymede*, 142.2 cm). See also: Zikos 2005.

Figure 9.3 Tommaso Redi, *Study for Brutus*, red chalk and heightening on buff paper, © Christie's Images Limited (2005).

when he was envoy to the Medici court from 1711 to 1714, and not from 1721, as has been previously assumed.[44]

[44]   As Molesworth continued to correspond with Galilei about the progress (and costs) of these sculptures for some years, including after his return to Italy, as envoy to Turin from 1721, scholars have presumed the commission originated later, see: Molesworth 2010: 115–32 (who dates the commission to 1721, proposing that Molesworth acted only as an intermediary; however, in all correspondence about the statues Molesworth refers to them as 'my sculptures'; see note 48 below); Sicca 2011: 56 (who also presumes the commission dates to early 1721). Rather, Molesworth wrote to Galilei on 16 April 1721 from Turin, to remind him to calculate the monies he had already paid toward the Montauti statues before he left Florence, alongside the amount still outstanding: 'it must be remember'd that I furnish'd the money for buying the marble which together with what other Summs Montauti had from me, or M.r Gould since my departure, should be accounted for', see Appendix IV.2. It is also worth stating, that the process of ordering and quarrying blocks of marble and then designing and carving them, could not have come about so speedily after Molesworth's return to Turin, and Montauti was notoriously slow (see note 48 below). Significantly, Galilei observes that the sculptures were Montauti's 'first works', see note 51, below. Montagu (1975: 20, n. 15), without knowing of the existence of the sculptures, linked the fact of Molesworth's commission to a Montauti bronze of *Ganymede*

Montauti's earliest biographer, Gaburri, describes with what diligence the young sculptor studied ancient Greek sculpture – albeit via Roman copies – together with the works of Michelangelo.[45] Salvini, Montauti's protector, directed these studies, both artistically and through his knowledge of antique literary sources, dedicating 36 letters (written for publication) to Montauti's cultural education.[46] The rarefied effect of this tutelage is apparent in the overtly accentuated classicism of the figures, as well as in the recherché choice of subjects. While the lithe figure and pose of the nude *Ganymede* derives from a fusion of antique examples and the renaissance sculpture of *David* by Donatello – as close to a 'Greek' ideal as was possible to view in Florence – *Hebe* is an awkward attempt at a neo-classical ideal of female beauty. Aspects of the fleshy corporality of Michelangelo are wed to a delicately beautiful, classically modelled head, based on the Medici Venus and anticipating similar models by Canova, yet the figure is swathed in swirling folds of drapery still dependent on Baroque prototypes.[47]

Ultimately, due to Molesworth's deteriorating financial situation, he was unable to pay the outstanding costs of the sculptures, including their transport to Britain,[48] and he lost them to his acquaintance, the collector Thomas Parker, 1st Earl of Macclesfield (1666–1732).[49] Hidden at Shirburn Castle since they were acquired by the Earl after 1723, the pair of sculptures have remained practically unknown to modern scholars.[50] This most important of Molesworth's art commissions has not been considered in the framework

(Galleria Nazionale d'Arte Antica, Rome) based on a letter of Galilei of 1 May 1721 in the Molesworth papers, Clements Coll. Ireland – now lost, but saved on microfilm, National Library of Ireland. This letter, transcribed by Kieven (1973), also states that the sculptures were Montauti's first works.

[45] Bellesi 2012: 1.

[46] Paoli 2005: 29–31.

[47] That the head of the Medici Venus was widely considered 'the true Grecian face' is evidenced by the comments of the Scottish painter, William Aikman (1682–1731), upon his return from the Eastern Mediterranean by April 1710, see: Ingamells 1997: 11.

[48] ASF, Carte Galilei, pezzo 21, inserto 1, fol. 118r, Leghorn, 9 August 1723, Molesworth to Galilei: 'Sir, it is a strange thing that after my pressing Montauti to finish my statues, he should be near three weeks doing one single lock of hair, by wch unaccountable laziness I have lost the Opportunity of sending them by Man of War with great Safety and no charge. In all probability the carriage will now cost me 30 or 40 crowns besides the risk of having them broken or spoli'd by lying under weighty goods or some other accident. I had long ago order'd Mess.rs Gould and Comp.y to pay him the remainder of 500 scudi upon receipt of the Statues in good condition, and he may depend on it he will not receive the money together wth the charges for Cases etc till they arrive at the Consul's house in this town. Is it impossible for an Italian Workman ever to make haste, or finish any thing?'

[49] On Molesworth's rapport with Parker, see: Connor 1998: 23–4, 2005. Precisely when and under what circumstances the sculptures passed to Parker is not known.

[50] See: Molesworth 2010: 115–17.

Figure 9.4 Antonio Montauti, *Ganymede with the Eagle of Jupiter*, marble, © Christie's
Images Limited (2009).

of his patronage and cultural milieu in Florence, in sculptural studies of the
period, nor in the context of Montauti's career, although they are surely,
as Galilei noted, 'the first works by the artist'.[51] It is now evident how his-
torically and culturally significant Molesworth's commission to Montauti

---

[51] 'Per avervi il detto Montauti usato molta diligenza nel terminarle quantunque esse siano le sue
prime opere', ASF, Carte Galilei, pezzo 21, inserto 1, fol. 48r [1721], Galilei to Molesworth, see
Appendix IV.4.

Figure 9.5 Antonio Montauti, *Hebe*, marble, © Christie's Images Limited (2009).

for the *Ganymede* and *Hebe* sculptures was. This commission was an art and patronage enterprise which spanned Molesworth's two sojourns in Italy and which demonstrates his continuing commitment to the antiquarian-oriented literary climate of Florentine culture, that of a classical 'Greek' ideal as refracted through Shaftesbury's writings and the renaissance lens of Donatello and Michelangelo.

The Molesworth-Galilei correspondence that survives in the Galilei papers in the *Archivio di Stato* in Florence, considered together with

Molesworth's art commissions and his active participation in the social, intellectual, cultural and artistic life of Florence and Turin, reveal him to be a crucial figure in the artistic and architectural exchanges that took place between Italy and Britain in the second and third decade of the eighteenth century. Though he was unable to pursue collecting on an important scale owing to a lack of resources, Molesworth nonetheless engaged fully in the most important artistic debates of his day and his letters indicate a strong desire to make a lasting – perhaps even literary – contribution. Sadly, the refined antiquarian taste for art and architecture that Molesworth promoted was ahead of his time; and indeed, after he returned to Britain in July 1725, in one of his last letters before his death in February 1726, he wrote a poignant memorandum to Galilei warning the architect to prepare for the triumph in Britain of neo-Palladianism, which, together, they had sought to contain only a few years earlier:

I must give you one piece of necessary advice w.ch is in the mean time to take the first possible opportunity of engageing some of our travellers to carry you with them into Lombardy, particularly to Venice and Vicenza: for here the reigning taste is Palladio's style of building, and a man is a Heretick that should talk of Michael Angelo or any other modern Architect. You must diligently Copy all the noted fabricks of Palladio, for those very draughts would introduce you here, and without them you may despair of success.[52]

---

[52] ASF, Carte Galilei, pezzo 21, inserto 1, fol. 190v, London, 13 Jan 1725/6, Molesworth to Galilei, see Appendix IV.8.

10 | Silver from London and Turin: Diplomacy by Display and George Hervey, Earl of Bristol, Envoy Extraordinary to the Court of Savoy, 1755–58

JAMES ROTHWELL

There survives at Ickworth House in Suffolk, a vast collection of silver (Fig. 10.1) assembled by the Hervey family, Earls and subsequently Marquesses of Bristol. It includes some 70 pieces made in Turin in the mid-1750s which constitute perhaps the largest remaining collection anywhere in the world of eighteenth-century Turinese silver of one period and one patron.[1] That patron was George William Hervey, second Earl of Bristol (1721–75) (Fig. 10.2), who served as envoy extraordinary to the King of Sardinia from 1755 to 1758 and had, earlier in the decade, commissioned much of the rest of the collection from one of the principal goldsmiths of London. The combined hoard, all of the highest quality, style and exuberance of form and extending to nearly a thousand individual pieces, was an essential part of his diplomatic and political armoury and went on to be used for the remainder of his high-ranking career. Its survival, virtually intact, along with the extensive evidence of Lord Bristol's time in Turin, sheds light on aspects of the craftsmanship, fashion, politics and social history of the two courts.[2]

George Hervey was born into an immensely wealthy and politically ambitious family who had, by the 1730s, firmly established themselves at the heart of British court affairs. His grandfather, John Hervey (1665–1751), received a barony in 1703 thanks to the patronage of the Duke and Duchess of Marlborough and adroit support of the Hanoverian faction later in Queen

---

[1] Turinese royal and noble collections of silver largely succumbed during the Napoleonic Wars. See, for instance: Griseri and Romano 1986: 180. The other major survival, in addition to Ickworth, is the 1780s 'Turin Service' commissioned by Prince Golitsyn which originally consisted of 220 pieces (not all Italian) but is now reduced to 44 (all Italian, divided between the Hermitage and the Kremlin Armoury Museum). Information from Natalie Abramova.

[2] The principal components of the Ickworth collection, including the silver, were accepted by the Treasury along with the house and the park in lieu of Death Duties and transferred to the National Trust in 1956. This was the first occasion that a complete collection of silver was so treated.

Figure 10.1 Part of the second Earl of Bristol's collection of silver laid on the dining table at Ickworth. The mid-eighteenth-century Italian giltwood side-table in the background is one of a series probably brought back from Turin, National Trust (Bristol Collection), Ickworth, © National Trust, Photograph: David Kirkham, Fisheye Images.

Anne's reign led to his advancement to the Earldom of Bristol on George I's accession in 1714. It was with the future George II and Queen Caroline, however, that the importance of the Herveys really flourished: the earl's eldest son, Carr, Lord Hervey, was appointed a Groom of the Bedchamber to the then Prince of Wales in 1714, and the Countess of Bristol became a Lady of the Bedchamber to the Princess four years later. George Hervey's father John, who succeeded as Lord Hervey on Carr's death in 1723, proved the most successful of all. He was a favourite of Queen Caroline, and as Vice-Chamberlain of the Royal Household from 1730 he had his own quarters in the various royal palaces, being, in his own words, 'continually in attendance' on the King and Queen. In 1740 he rose to be Lord Privy Seal, one of the five principal offices of state, and he held the post until shortly before his untimely death three years later.[3]

The Francophile Lady Hervey, born Mary Lepel, was also prominent at court, and highly popular, being eulogized by Pope, Gay and Voltaire. The golden couple resided almost permanently in London to be near the court and society and they sent their eldest son and heir, George, to a French school there from the age of five, and then to Westminster. Whilst at the latter he had three years of special tuition in speaking and writing French from a Monsieur Pélissier, and no doubt also fencing and dancing lessons, as had his numerous uncles previously.[4] On 7 September 1738 the first

---

[3] Halsband 1973: 8, 20, 34, 96–7, 255.
[4] Hervey 1894: 188–9.

Figure 10.2 Johann Zoffany, *George William Hervey, second Earl of Bristol*, oil on canvas, National Trust (Bristol Collection), Ickworth, © National Trust Images.

Earl of Bristol recorded in his diary 'My hopeful grandson George [then aged just seventeen] sett forward from London on his journey towards Geneva (by Paris) to study there.'[5] Geneva, then an independent city state, was a popular destination for young British aristocrats, having a cultured, French-speaking élite with close ties to Paris but without the disadvantage of Catholicism.[6] Hervey stayed there for two years and then travelled in

---

[5]   Hervey 1894: 85.

[6]   Black 1999: 37.

Italy. He is likely to have at least passed through Turin, the Mont Cenis pass to its north being the easiest and most frequented route when approaching from the west, and he proceeded to Venice, Bologna, Reggio, Rome and probably also Naples. Upon being made a captain in the 34th Regiment of Foot he departed for England from Florence in May of 1741.[7] His grandfather, Lord Bristol, did not approve of an army career, however, and neither did his health ideally suit it – Walpole later described him as 'the delicate Lord' and he was often at death's door.[8] In October 1742, encouraged by his father who had in turn been bribed to the tune of £10,000 by Lord Bristol, he gave up his commission and concentrated on a life at court.[9]

George Hervey had, as might be expected of the heir to an immensely wealthy landed family, been surrounded by silver from birth. He was the godson of King George I and as custom dictated his father was entitled to 80 ounces of silver gilt which, according to the Jewel Office records, he took in the form of a 'Gilt Ewer Enchased'.[10] John, Lord Hervey was, like the first Earl of Bristol, a discerning and prolific patron of goldsmiths, and in the 1720s and 1730s he acquired pieces by such fine makers as Paul Crespin, Paul de Lamerie and John Hugh Le Sage. The few that remain, including a bread basket of 1731–2 by de Lamerie (Fig. 10.3), show that, as might be expected of a dedicated Francophile, he embraced the sophisticated *Régence* style promulgated by the Huguenot goldsmiths who dominated the London market in the first half of the eighteenth century. All of his silver passed to George on Lord Hervey's untimely death in 1743, as well as a seat in the House of Lords and use of the family's town house in fashionable St James's Square.[11] In 1751, when his grandfather died, some 30,000 acres in East Anglia and Lincolnshire were added together with another vast quantity of silver. Once again only a small number of pieces survive, most impressive amongst them being a huge cistern of 1682–3 by Robert Cooper, bought secondhand in 1697. With what does remain, along with detailed surviving accounts, a clear picture is given of a typical and plentiful aristocratic collection. The Earl kept his diary and accounts in a single volume, the diary on the left page and the accounts on the right.

[7] Brinsley Ford Archive, Paul Mellon Centre, London, Notes on George William Hervey.
[8] Erskine 1953: xvi.
[9] Halsband 1973: 276.
[10] National Archives, LC 9 44, Jewel Office Delivery Book September 1698 to February 1731/2, fol. 265. The ewer does not survive. Royal Christening gifts, always silver-gilt, were graded in weight according to the rank of the father. As an untitled gentleman in 1721, Hervey received the lowest weight.
[11] Suffolk County Record Office (Bury St Edmunds) (henceforth SCRO), Hervey MSS, HA 507/ 5/7, Will of John, Lord Hervey, 23 June 1743, proved 18 August 1743.

Figure 10.3 Bread basket, Britannia standard silver, Paul de Lamerie, London, 1731–2, the gilding c. 1752, National Trust (Bristol Collection), Ickworth, © National Trust Images, Photograph: Robert Thrift.

Amongst the constant stream of payments for silver was, for example, one of £67 in 1726 to David Willaume II for various items including a kettle, almost certainly that marked for 1726–7 and by Peter Le Chouabe, which remains at Ickworth.[12]

Survivals of Lord Hervey's and the first Earl's silver are the exception rather than the rule as a result of the fact that George Hervey, as soon as he became second Earl of Bristol and was without his grandfather's cautious control, wasted little time in having the bulk of his collection of plate sent to that most effective interpreter of the Rococo amongst London goldsmiths, Frederick Kandler, to bring it up to the latest fashions.[13] The first Earl's sober round dinner plates of 1703 by John Jackson were turned inside out and given a suitably wavy outline with gadrooning, in line with the most popular form of the mid-century,[14] whilst what must have been Lord Hervey's oval meat dishes of the 1730s, by Crespin, were made fashionable by the addition of prominent shell handles (Fig. 10.4), following a pattern set by

[12] SCRO, Hervey MSS, 941/46/13, first Earl of Bristol's accounts and diary. The purchase of the cistern is recorded on the 7 May 1697.

[13] No archival references survive relating to Lord Bristol's turning in of his old plate but there is ample physical evidence amongst the pieces provided in its stead.

[14] Lomax 1992: 94, 99.

Figure 10.4 Large oval meat dish from a set of ten in three sizes, sterling standard silver, Paul Crespin, London, 1733–4, the shell handles probably added by Frederick Kandler c. 1751, National Trust (Bristol Collection), Ickworth, © National Trust Images, Photograph: Robert Thrift.

such makers as Paul de Lamerie and George Wickes in the early 1740s.[15] The great majority of Lord Bristol's newly transformed collection was associated with dining, and there were also soup plates, sauce boats, entrée and second course dishes, salts, scallop shells for gratin fish dishes and flatware and cutlery. To create the key elements of a dessert service his father's bread basket and the central dish from a dismantled epergne, also by de Lamerie and in the *Régence* style, were gilded and exact copies were made of each of them by Kandler.[16]

The new Lord Bristol had shown a partiality for the rococo in what is likely to have been one of his earliest acquisitions, before inheriting the earldom and in his mid-twenties: an inkstand of 1746 by Paul Crespin, with a cast border and engraving positively frothing with C-scrolls and shells. This piece was, however, extremely tame in comparison to the most significant outcome of Lord Bristol's re-casting of his plate in the early

---

[15] Barr 1980: 23. The plates and dishes bear signs of their alteration, Kandler presumably preserving the old hallmarks to disguise his dodging of Plate Duty, due on any piece worked upon. The first Earl of Bristol's accounts (see note 12 above) records the purchase of three dozen plates, amongst other items, on the 23 June 1703.

[16] Two further copies of each were added in 1766, also made by Frederick Kandler.

Figure 10.5 Oval tureen (left), sterling standard silver, Frederick Kandler, London, 1752–3, and circular tureen (right), silver, Turin, mark of assay master Giovanni Battista Carron, c. 1755, National Trust (Bristol Collection), Ickworth, © National Trust Images, Photograph: Robert Thrift.

1750s: a pair of oval tureens (Fig. 10.5) of a rococo extravagance scarcely exceeded by any other English examples of the period. They bear Frederick Kandler's mark and the date letter for 1752–3 and are a tour de force of the silversmith's art. There is so much cast ornament, including in the Bristol coat of arms and the ounce (snow leopard) crest, which forms the handle, that they have a combined weight of just over 14.5 kilograms (468 troy ounces).

Lord Bristol had determined upon a diplomatic career immediately upon inheriting in 1751, stating to his brother Augustus in October of that year that 'he had asked to go Envoy to Portugal, and that the Duke of Newcastle had hinted the Embassy to Spain one day or other'.[17] A magnificent table was a prerequisite for such an occupation and the earl's silver acquisitions could well have formed part of the strategy. Certainly his stance in the House of Lords did, as by being prepared to vote against the administration on occasion he outmanoeuvred the Hervey family's longtime adversary, the all-powerful political fixer, the Duke of Newcastle. The Duke had previously blocked the careers of Lord Bristol, and before him

---

[17] Erskine 1953: 115–16.

that of his father,[18] some suspicion perhaps resting on the family because of Mary, Lady Hervey's dalliance with Jacobitism.[19] The Earl was firmly of the establishment, however, and upon offering his proxy vote in the House of Lords should he be absent abroad, the Duke deftly changed stance.[20] Following the death of Lord Albemarle, Groom of the Stole and First Gentleman of the King's Bedchamber, in December 1754, the Earl of Rochford was recalled from Turin to fill the post and Bristol was sent in his stead, as Envoy Extraordinary. That did not entitle him to a grant of silver from the Jewel Office, as did his later appointment as Ambassador to Madrid, but he must have considered himself well provided for anyway and only seems to have made a few last-minute additions, including extra meat dishes, a pair of bread baskets of 1754–5 by John Robinson, a set of waiters and some flatware, before travelling via Paris to Turin where he arrived on 15 June 1755.[21] Once there he established himself in what must have been palatial accommodation, Sir Horace Mann suggesting that he paid rent of £500 a year[22] and his own bank account indicating a figure closer to £1,000.[23]

In the mid-eighteenth century Turin was considered amongst the politest courts in Europe, its academy a favoured destination for the sons of the British aristocracy and its diplomats, according to Lord Chesterfield writing in 1748, 'the ablest, the politest and les plus déliés' ('most free/untied') in Europe.[24] Lord Bristol had been reported upon favourably by his opposite number in London, Count Perrone, as 'très noble et fort riche, mais qu'il a aussi beaucoup d'esprit et un caractère fort doux et honnête'[25] ('very noble and very rich but he also has much spirit and a very gentle and honest

[18] Ilchester 1950: 3.

[19] Erskine 1953: 105, 112. She exasperated her eldest son by teaching his sisters 'to reverence the Pretender'. A Capodimonte scent bottle of 1753–5 in the Fitzwilliam Museum, Cambridge, bears both Lady Hervey's arms and the Young Pretender's portrait. See: Manners 2007: 452–4, figs 59 a and b. I am grateful to Patricia Ferguson for this reference.

[20] Erskine 1953: 181, note 1.

[21] The National Archives (henceforth TNA), SP 92/63, Earl of Bristol to Earl of Holdernesse, 21/6/1755.

[22] Lewis 1937–83: XXI, 175. 'Lord Bristol gives £500 a year for his house, and has everything in it equal to that expense.' I am grateful to Edoardo Piccoli for drawing my attention to this reference; the residence of Englishmen in Turin in the eighteenth century, including Lord Bristol, is dealt with in detail by Piccoli in this volume.

[23] Barclays Group Archives, Goslings Ledgers, ref 130/25, fols 77–80, the Earl of Bristol's account 1754–7. There are payments of £337 a quarter to Count Viry (Sardinian envoy to Britain) which may represent rent for his Turin palazzo.

[24] Woolf 1961: 211.

[25] Archivio di Stato di Torino, Sezione Corte (henceforth AST), Materie Politiche Estero, Lettere Ministeri, mazzo 59/1, Count Perrone to King Charles Emmanuel III, 20/2/1755.

character') and neither the King, Charles Emmanuel III, nor his chief minister, the Cavaliere Giuseppe Ossorio, proved disappointed in him, sending rapturous reports back to Perrone after the Earl's arrival.[26] Rank was of great importance, and when a replacement was needed for Perrone later in the year Charles Emmanuel took care to send Count Viry, 'a Person who might in all Respects be the most acceptable to the King [George II]' including being of equivalent status to the Earl.[27] There were existing and highly advantageous personal connections between Lord Bristol and Turin as well, Ossorio having been friendly with Lord and Lady Hervey during his term as Envoy to the Court of St James from 1730 to 1749,[28] and thereafter retaining an obligation of gratitude to Lady Hervey, as he expressed it in a letter to Viry in October 1755.[29] The Turin court was even more delighted with the appointment the following month when Henry Fox (later Lord Holland), who had been Lord Hervey's intimate friend, became Secretary of State for the Southern Department (effectively Deputy Prime Minister) and Leader of the House of Commons. Count Viry informed Ossorio that 'Mr Fox est fort dans les interests de Milord Bristol' ('Mr Fox is strongly in the interests of Lord Bristol').[30]

Irrespective of the support he received through personal connections and the status brought by his rank and wealth, Lord Bristol was quite clearly a highly able diplomat, winning the approbation of both George II and Charles Emmanuel III, as well as their ministers, and managing with comparative ease to smooth over such difficult situations as British boats firing mistakenly on Sardinian vessels following the outbreak of the Seven Years War in 1756.[31] He was acutely sensitive of the need not to offend the devout court of Savoy over religious matters by strident expressions of Protestantism and he also proved a highly effective spy master, sending agents into southern France to gain information on French naval and army manoeuvres. That brought especial compliments from George II and Henry Fox though sadly they did not take sufficient notice of his strong report of an intended invasion by France of British-controlled Minorca, sent in early April 1756, three months before the actual event.[32] There was no real

---

[26] *Ibid.*, mazzo 59/2, Cavaliere Ossorio to Count Perrone, 21/6/1755 and King Charles Emmanuel III to Count Perrone, 21/6/1755.

[27] TNA, SP 92/63, George Charles to Sir Thomas Robinson, 12/4/1755.

[28] Halsband 1973: 260.

[29] AST, Materie Politiche Estero, Lettere Ministeri, mazzo 59/4, Cavaliere Ossorio to Count Viry, 4/10/1755.

[30] *Ibid*, mazzo 59/3, Count Viry to Cavaliere Ossorio, 20/11/1755.

[31] TNA, SP 92/65, Earl of Bristol to William Pitt, 21/9/1757

[32] TNA, SP 92/64, Earl of Bristol to Henry Fox 6/3/1756.

prospect of an open alliance between Britain and Sardinia because, as the King expressed to Lord Bristol through Ossorio, his country would not stand a chance, being sandwiched between France and its equally mighty ally, Austria.[33] The maintenance of Sardinian neutrality, however, was of very great import to British chances of success and Lord Bristol's intimacy with Ossorio and Charles Emmanuel proved invaluable, being in striking contrast to their relationship with the French who tended to resort to bullying.[34]

Fully entering into the busy social life of Turin was as important a part of effective diplomacy as charming the king and his ministers, and spying. As well as attending at court, Lord Bristol would have been present at a constant round of visits, dinners, balls and at the opera, where he kept a box.[35] He would also have given entertainments himself, as had the Earl of Rochford whose countess gained permission from the Sardinian king to hold a ball in 1752.[36] Such events were reported back to their respective nations in detail by diplomats and one of Perrone's most extensive letters to Ossorio from London in 1755 was a description of the lavish fête for 250 guests put on by the Russian Ambassador at Somerset House on 5 February to celebrate the recent birth of a Romanov prince (the future Tsar Paul I). He made particular note of the ladies wearing jewels to the value of £50,000 and the attendance of 'toute la famille Royale' who 'assisté a cette fête' and supped at a table of eighteen covers.[37] Such grand and extravagant affairs were, inevitably, comparatively rare and the main means of showing off the wealth and the taste of the home nation, as well as of the diplomat himself, was through dinner which also provided an opportunity for gleaning information and influencing. It was an especially potent weapon in the diplomatic armoury and silver, with which the table should ideally be laden, played a critical part. Bristol found that a high standard had already been set by his chief rival in Turin, the indubitably haughty Marquis de Chauvelin,

---

[33]   TNA, SP 92/65, Earl of Bristol to William Pitt, 9/3/1757.
[34]   Shortly before Lord Bristol's arrival, for instance, the French had violated Sardinian sovereignty by sending in their forces to seize a troublesome brigand and smuggler, Louis Mandrin, TNA, SP 92/63, George Charles to the Earl of Holdernesse, 24/5/1755 and 7/6/1755. They then compounded the insult by the publication of the private conversation between the Ambassador Extraordinary sent to appease, the Comte de Noailles, and Charles Emmanuel III, TNA, SP 92/63, Earl of Bristol to Sir Thomas Robinson, 13/9/1755.
[35]   TNA, SP 92/63, Earl of Bristol to Henry Fox, 13/12/1755.
[36]   AST, Materie Politiche per rapporto all'interno, Ceremoniale, Ambasciatori e Inviati, mazzo 14.
[37]   AST, Materie Politiche Estero, Lettere Ministeri, mazzo 1, Count Perrone to Cavaliere Ossorio, 6/2/1755.

Ambassador from France.[38] Dinners given at his house in April 1755 for the Duc de Penthièvre, Louis XV's cousin, were described by George Charles, the embassy secretary who held the fort prior to Bristol's arrival, as consisting 'daily of about Twenty five Covers, the Company being chiefly, besides Foreign Ministers, Officers of Distinction and the Principal Servants of His Sardinian Majesty's and his Royal Family's Household'.[39] Lord Bristol, who had his own reputation at home for stately manners and excessive pride, was quite clearly not to be outdone and his focus was certainly not clouded by personal affection. He loathed Chauvelin from the start, sending an assessment on the Frenchman's character within three months of his arrival in Turin: 'by the best judgment I can form of him, he has pride without Dignity, he flatters without persuading, is Verbose without meaning and never scruples to assert an untruth … his private [character] is Vain, frivolous and false.'[40]

It may well have been a need to keep up at the dinner table in this feverishly competitive atmosphere, in a city where Lord Bristol also found 'a vast deal of magnificent Appearances in the Palace',[41] that led to him commissioning a significant quantity of additional silver from the principal Turinese makers of the 1750s, Andrea Boucheron and Paolo Antonio Paroletto.[42] This included 48 extra dinner plates, which increased the total available to 120, and thereby allowed for up to 40 guests to be catered for (assuming three plates each for the principal courses). There were also four exquisite silver-gilt sugar sifters, six soup plates, a tumbler cup which must have been for Lord Bristol's personal use – perhaps for those countless carriage journeys to and fro the palaces – and a pair of huge, curvaceous salvers (Fig. 10.6) with an elegant band of rococo decoration engraved around a bold representation of the Earl's full heraldic achievement. The salvers were probably for the service, with suitable grandeur, of tea which would have been taken after dinner and also served to visitors at other times of day. Most spectacular of all amongst the Italian augmentations to the Earl's plate, however, were two circular tureens (Fig. 10.5) which complemented their oval British progenitors. All four were provided with

---

[38] François Claude Bernard Louis de Chauvelin (1716–73), Marquis de Chauvelin was a crony of Louis XV and his death at the King's gaming table inspired Alexandre Dumas's novel, *Le Testament de M. Chauvelin* (1861). His son, Bernard-François, served as Ambassador from Republican France to Britain and also inspired a literary character – the villain in Baroness Orczy's *Scarlet Pimpernel* novels.

[39] TNA, SP 92/63, George Charles to Sir Thomas Robinson, 12/4/1755.

[40] *Ibid.*, Earl of Bristol to Sir Thomas Robinson, 30/8/1755.

[41] TNA, SP 92/63, Earl of Bristol to Henry Fox, 27/12/1755.

[42] I am grateful to Gianfranco Fina for confirming the identity of the makers from their marks.

Figure 10.6 One of a pair of stands or tables, silver, Paolo Antonio Paroletto, Turin, c. 1755, National Trust (Bristol Collection), Ickworth, © National Trust, Photograph: Robert Thrift.

stands matching the existing meat dishes (Fig. 10.4), and Lord Bristol was no doubt influenced in acquiring such articles, which were not yet in general use in England, by the up-to-the-minute French fashions which he would have seen at royal and noble Turinese tables as well as at that of the Marquis de Chauvelin.[43] Stands for tureens had been commonplace in France since at least the early 1730s and Turin was never far behind, Charles Emmanuel III being supplied by Andrea Boucheron in 1731 with 'due pot a oglia due piatti da mettersi sotto' ('two tureens with two plates to go under them').[44]

For an Englishman to be commissioning silver abroad in the eighteenth century was remarkably rare, the quality of what they could get at home

[43] The only Turinese items not mentioned here are two ladles (Ickworth) for the round tureens, cast from moulds taken from Frederick Kandler's pair of 1752–3 which were made for the oval tureens, and a pair of ragout spoons (private collection) matching a set of four (Ickworth) by Elias Cachart, 1751–2 and 1754–5.

[44] Fina 1997: 62. The tureen and *pot à oille* were not generally differentiated in England, the former name being used for both in most instances.

being so very high, and import duties also playing their part, though less so for diplomats. Exceptions were primarily restricted to the inevitable desire to seek French fashions, especially as the direct impact of Huguenot immigrants began to wane after the mid-century. Thus the fourth Duke of Bedford and the first Earl Harcourt, both ambassadors in Paris, patronized François-Thomas Germain and Robert-Joseph Auguste in the 1760s,[45] and George III commissioned a huge service for Hanover, also from Auguste, the following decade.[46] From the outbreak of the Seven Years War, however, which occurred in 1756, the year after Lord Bristol's arrival in Turin, access to Paris was restricted. Fortunately for the Earl, Turin's cultural links with France could not have been closer and Andrea Boucheron had been apprenticed to the pre-eminent Parisian goldsmith of the rococo, Thomas Germain.[47] Lord Bristol could even conceivably have had a pre-existing awareness of Turinese silver, and of Boucheron in particular, through his patronage in the 1740s of Paul Crespin and Nicholas Sprimont, the London goldsmiths who may have had some connection with the Turin master, yet to be fully clarified.[48] Further evidence of British patronage of Turinese goldsmiths, during previous hostilities with France, has been discovered by Edoardo Piccoli amongst the papers of General Thomas Wentworth, special envoy to the King of Sardinia in 1747.[49]

The Earl of Bristol's commissions were, in the main, for copies of his English pieces to augment what he already had and it is only really in the tea salvers, the sifters and the tureens that the stylistic influence of France and Turin can be overtly seen. A comparison of the English-made tureens and those of Turin is particularly instructive (Fig. 10.5). The English tureens, of 1752–3 by Frederick Kandler, are technically superior, with a thicker gauge of silver employed for the raised elements and the complex-shaped parts fitting together more precisely, but the Turin versions are freer artistically, clearly more directly influenced by Paris and the Germains, and show up a certain constraint or stiffness in the English design, despite the exuberance of its rococo ornament. Unfortunately there is no maker's mark on the Turin pair, but given their sophistication and the authorship of most of the other pieces

[45] Clifford 2004: 168–70.
[46] About half of the Hanover service is now at Waddesdon Manor, Buckinghamshire.
[47] Fina and Mana 2012: 222.
[48] Jones and Garibaldi 2006: 30–3.
[49] See the number of references to General Wentworth's purchase of silver in Turin amongst his papers (Stratford-upon-Avon Record Office), including a bill from the goldsmith Giacomo Antonio Serafino, ref. D 18/5/28. See also Piccoli in this volume.

it is highly likely that they are by Boucheron and/or Paroletto. Furthermore, two tureens bearing Paroletto's mark and post-dating 1758 have a number of strikingly similar elements.[50] In terms of usage rather than style, Lord Bristol's acquisition of stands for his tureens is particularly momentous in the history of silver as it represents a comparatively rare instance of their incorporation into a British dinner service and it could thus have been partly through him and via Turin, as well as directly from France, that such objects were introduced to the British table in the mid century.[51]

Lord Bristol left Turin in August 1758 to take up the post of ambassador extraordinary and plenipotentiary to the court of Madrid, though on the lesser remuneration of an ambassador ordinary thanks to the proverbial stinginess of George II.[52] The Earl, with six servants, and one of the king's messengers, was transported from Genoa by his brother, Captain the Honourable Augustus Hervey, on H.M.S. Monmouth. Another fifteen servants plus all the Earl's goods were loaded, as Captain Hervey recorded in his journal, onto 'a great Dutch ship he [the Earl] had hired for the purpose'.[53] Amongst those goods must have been all the silver, including the Turinese pieces, and also the portraits and portrait miniatures of Charles Emmanuel and the Duke and Duchess of Savoy.[54] These are still at Ickworth, as too is a group of massive giltwood side-tables and associated mirrors (Fig. 10.1) which appear to be of Turinese manufacture and probably furnished the state rooms of Lord Bristol's palazzo in Turin. The Earl had quite clearly enjoyed his time as envoy and had what appears to have been a genuinely warm and mutually affectionate relationship with both the chief minister, Ossorio, and the principal members of the royal family. There was a tinge of regret in his final report to the Secretary of State in London, written on 14 August, and his statement that 'I have had the Honor of being so particularly distinguish'd by the King of Sardinia, the Duke of Savoy and every one of the Royal Family' does not come across as being entirely courtly flummery.[55]

The principal legacy of Lord Bristol's patronage of goldsmiths in Turin, and his exposure to prevailing French and Turinese fashions whilst there, can perhaps be seen in his commissioning of the magnificent set of twelve

---

[50] Fina and Mana 2012: figs 296–7.
[51] This suggestion was made to me by Christopher Hartop.
[52] His allowance was only raised to the correct level following the accession of George III in 1760.
[53] Erskine 1953: 286–91.
[54] There are three oil portraits, that of Charles Emmanuel III is by Maria Giovanna Clementi and studio whilst those of the Duke and Duchess of Savoy (the future King Victor Amadeus III and Queen Maria Antonia) are after Domenico Duprà. The two miniatures are of Charles Emmanuel (Italian school) and Victor Amadeus (after Duprà). For the royal portraits by Duprà and copies of these, see also Yarker in this volume.
[55] TNA, SP 92/66, Earl of Bristol to William Pitt, 14/8/1758.

candelabra by Simon Le Sage (Fig. 10.7) as part of his official allocation of plate as ambassador to Spain, which amounted to 6,959 troy ounces (216.45 kilograms) of silver and silver-gilt. Comparable creations are proudly accentuated in the portrait of Andrea Boucheron[56] as well as in that of his erstwhile master, Thomas Germain.[57] The Earl had, however, already proved that he needed little encouragement to choose exuberant Rococo forms. In the other direction, his London pieces certainly seem to have rubbed off on Paroletto if a surviving meat dish made by him post-1758 is anything to go by.[58] It has an overall shape, gadrooned border and shell handles, all very close indeed to the pieces Paroletto and Boucheron copied for Lord Bristol in the mid-1750s. Gadrooning was particularly favoured by the British, whereas the French and the Turinese had generally eschewed it by the mid-eighteenth century in favour of either bold, plain mouldings or reed and ribbon-tie borders. Only a handful of items amongst the extensive acquisitions of silver by the Kings of Sardinia between 1730 and 1796 are referred to as 'godronati', meaning gadrooned,[59] and the huge travelling service provided to Louis XV in 1752 was described as being bordered by 'un cordon de feuilles' (a cordon of leaves).[60] There are also, as previously discussed, the similarities between the Bristol tureens from London and Turin, and Paroletto's pair of post-1758, but any influence from the Earl's pieces can only at most have affected details as the overall concept of both designs clearly comes from France and Germain. Any further conclusions are limited by the paucity of survival of mid-eighteenth-century Turin silver.

Although evidence of artistic cross-fertilization as a result of Lord Bristol's term as envoy in Turin is limited, his success as a diplomat in that most courtly of European capitals is clear and it prepared him perfectly for what proved to be a successful and high-ranking career. He went to Spain as Britain's senior diplomat and was the nation's only ambassador during the most intense period of the Seven Years War. In 1766 he was appointed Lord Lieutenant of Ireland and a Privy Councillor, after which he became Lord Privy Seal (from 1768 to 1770) and then Groom of the Stole and First Lord of the Bedchamber to George III, dying whilst still in post in March 1775.[61] Lord Bristol's great assemblage of silver, a harmonious blend of pieces commissioned in London and Turin, continued to play its part throughout that

[56] Bargoni 1963: figs 222, 224.
[57] The portrait of Andrea Boucheron (unknown artist) is in the Palazzo Madama, Turin. That of Germain and his wife, by Nicolas de Largillière, is in the Gulbenkian Museum, Lisbon.
[58] Bargoni 1963: 24, fig. 45.
[59] Fina 1997: including 81 and 91.
[60] Babelon 1993: 102.
[61] Goodwin 2008.

Figure 10.7 One of twelve candelabra, sterling standard silver, Simon Le Sage, London, 1758–9, National Trust (Bristol Collection), Ickworth, © National Trust Images, Photograph: Robert Thrift.

time and was thereafter treasured by the Earl's successors at Ickworth. It survives almost entirely intact, is on display in the house, and ranks as perhaps the most important collection of plate in the National Trust, as well as the most significant group of Turin silver anywhere in the British Isles.[62]

---

[62]   The only other substantial group of Turin silver in the United Kingdom is in the Victoria and Albert Museum, being the surviving pieces of altar plate from the former Sardinian embassy chapel in London: pair of cruets, salver for the cruets, altar cross, censer and incense boat (refs LOAN: ST ANSELM.1–5). All but one bear the mark of Andrea Boucheron and they were commissioned by Count Viry c. 1759 (Oman 1966). The same museum also holds a pair of candlesticks with the mark of the Turin assay master, Giovanni Battista Carron (in post 1753–78) which may be by Boucheron (ref. 896:1882). Another Boucheron object is to be found in the Royal Collection, being the shell base and perhaps also the tureen which form part of the Neptune Centrepiece by Paul Crespin (refs XQG 1988 114, 118 and 119).

11 | The 'Savoyard': The Painter Domenico Duprà and his British Sitters

JONATHAN YARKER

In most Italian states during the eighteenth century British diplomats – Consuls, Residents and Minister's plenipotentiary – used their position to become de facto art dealers and brokers. But despite being the 'gateway' to the Grand Tour, Turin was a notable exception; Britain dispatched to Savoy professional diplomats, not *marchand amateurs*. Some were *virtuosi* of great repute: Dr William Aglionby, author of *Painting Illustrated in Three Dialogues*, the first systematic treatise on the history and theory of painting in English, was Envoy in 1694, and Paul Methuen, who served as Envoy in 1705–6, assembled an important group of Italian pictures, but they were principally acquired in London and Paris, not Italy.[1]

As is discussed elsewhere in this volume, some diplomats did use the position to facilitate artistic acquisitions.[2] William Capell, 3rd Earl of Essex, for example, formed a fine collection of contemporary Turinese pictures along with works by Canaletto and Bartolomeo Nazari.[3] James Stuart-Mackenzie helped his brother, the Prime Minister and collector, John, 3rd Earl of Bute, to execute commissions and correspond with his other agents. But the strategic importance of Savoy, particularly during the first half of the century following the War of Spanish Succession, made it too valuable a political position to leave to *virtuosi* such as Horace Mann and Sir William Hamilton, or mercantile opportunists such as Joseph Smith or Sir John Dick. But there was the other reality, that Turin offered comparatively little in the way of 'classic' souvenir purchases, these were the preserve of more traditional 'Grand Tour' cities.

---

[1] For details of the collecting habits of several British diplomats in Turin, see Wynne 1996; for the British envoys to Turin, see Appendix I in this volume.

[2] See Wolfe's discussion of the collecting activities of John Molesworth in this volume; see also Rothwell's discussion of the commissioning of silver in Turin by George Hervey, Earl of Bristol, in this volume.

[3] For Essex's acquisitions in Italy see: Watson 1950. The posthumous sale of his collection, held at Christie's, 31 January 1777, contained works attributed to Francesco Solimena, Gaspar Van Wittel, Francesco Trevisani and Giovanni Paolo Panini, and were probably acquired whilst Essex was based in Turin. Certainly Essex's wife, Lady Jane Hyde, used Turin as a base to collect works from other parts of Italy, purchasing canvases by Canaletto through the Consul Joseph Smith in Venice. Smith's correspondence to Lady Essex is preserved in the British Library, Add MS.27733 fol. 80.

This last statement demands qualification. Recent examinations of the patterns of acquisition made by travellers in Italy have begun to make a distinction between a primary market – consisting of 'celebrated' old masters and antique sculpture – and what I would term a secondary market: of modern copies, casts, reproductive engravings and antiquarian publications.[4] The two were intrinsically tied to cities firmly on the itinerary of foreign travellers: principally Florence, Venice and Rome. Whilst Savoy with its largely 'modern' architecture and 'foreign' collections – the most celebrated painting in Turin during the century was Gerard Dou's *Dropsical Woman* now in the Louvre – had few dealers or craftsmen who catered for a specifically 'Grand Tour' clientele.[5] But there were primary markets which were contiguous, but distinct from the market for old masters and antiquities, particularly for landscape painting and portraiture. Turin produced at least one artist who fits into this model: the portraitist Domenico Duprà who forms the subject of this chapter.

Duprà, like many Italian artists during the century, had a varied, international career.[6] Born in Turin in 1689 he trained in Rome before spending some eleven years in Portugal at the court of King John V. On his return to Italy, he worked in Rome for a number of patrician families as well as foreigners, before being recalled in 1750 to Turin, where he became court painter to Charles Emmanuel II. Duprà was primarily a commercial painter, whose adaptability and diversity led to considerable professional success but has resulted in concomitant critical neglect.[7] This is in part because the practical demands of servicing a court meant that the artistic product was often rather uninspiring. First, because on the whole rulers required hieratic depictions of themselves and their families, unequivocal statements of their position and dynastic authority; and second, because these images needed to be disseminated widely, as a result of which court painters were required to produce numerous copies of their works. Despite these constraints, this chapter will show that Duprà was a fine painter, whose range of commissions sheds important light on the market for portraiture in mid-eighteenth-century Europe and the commercial realities of practising as a

---

[4] For example, see: D'Agliano 2008; Wilcox and Sánchez-Jáuregui 2012.

[5] Most eighteenth-century accounts of Turin mention only three or four famous paintings.

[6] In this context it is instructive to note the peripatetic life of the architect Giovanni Battista Borra – see Zoller in this volume; for John Molesworth's advice to the architect Alessandro Galilei, see Wolfe in this volume.

[7] Duprà has been the subject of only two articles: Busiri Vici 1977; de Carvalho 1958. But he has received comparatively little notice in surveys of Italian painting during the eighteenth century. A notable exception is: Petrucci 2010, I and II.

portraitist at this date. More than this, Duprà's works illuminate a significant aspect of British patronage of Italian artists outside the usual list of 'Grand Tour' painters.

Duprà moved to Rome whilst young, probably in 1717, where he entered the studio of Francesco Trevisani.[8] At this date Trevisani was much in demand from both Roman and an international circle of patrons, and as a result he had a large and productive studio.[9] Although principally remembered for his religious and historical work, Trevisani had a considerable contemporary reputation as a portraitist, and Duprà arrived in his studio as he was completing his famous depiction of *Thomas Coke*, later 1st Earl of Leicester.[10] It was probably through Trevisani, or his friend and colleague, the architect Filippo Juvarra, that Duprà secured an invitation to Lisbon, to become portraitist to John V of Portugal.[11] It has not been noticed before, but Duprà possibly travelled to Lisbon with another of Trevisani's pupils, the Portuguese artist Vieira Lusitano, who is recorded joining the Company of St Luke in Lisbon, the local painters guild, six days before Duprà in May 1719.[12] Duprà was given a studio in the Paço Real da Ribeira and rapidly established himself as a significant part of John V's campaign to add Italianate sophistication to his court.[13]

It was in Portugal that Duprà first made contact with British clients. In 1724 Duprà married a Portugese woman, Gervasia Maria Rodriguez with whom he had a son and a daughter. The baptismal records of Duprà's son, Antonio Sabino, shows that one John O'Brien, an Irish merchant, stood as godfather.[14] Comparatively little is known of Duprà's life in Lisbon, in part because much documentary material and many of his paintings were destroyed in the Lisbon earthquake of 1755.

One episode from Duprà's time in Portugal is illustrative of the kind of concerns that governed 'official' portraiture of the period. In 1725 a double royal marriage was negotiated between the Portugese and Spanish reigning houses and Duprà was given the task of painting the Portugese children –

---

[8] Busiri Vici 1977: 2. Busiri Vici also detects French influence in Duprà's earliest portrait work.

[9] On Trevisani's studio practice, see: Wolfe 2007.

[10] For Trevisani's work for British patrons, see: Wolfe 2011.

[11] Trevisani completed a number of pictures for Portughese clients including the high altarpiece at Mafra, *Virgin and Child with St Anthony of Padua*, for John V, but this was not completed until 1730; see: Wolfe 2014a. Despite being employed as the principal architect to Victor Amadeus II of Savoy, Juvarra made a brief trip to Lisbon to plan a new patriarchal church and palace. See: Delaforce 2002; Manfredi 2014; Raggi 2014; Rossa 2014; Sansone 2014.

[12] De Carvalho 1958: 81. For Vieira Lusitano see Delaforce 2002: 345–6.

[13] For John V, see: Delaforce 2002: 29–66.

[14] Skinner 1958: 12.

Figure 11.1 Domenico Duprà, *Maria Barbara de Braganza*, oil on canvas, 1725, Museo del Prado, Madrid, © Bridgeman Images.

Maria Barbara, Princess of Brazil and Jose, Prince of Brazil – for the Spanish court (Fig. 11.1).[15] The nuptials required delicate negotiation, and Duprà, or 'the Savoyard' as he was known, appears frequently in the correspondence of the Spanish Ambassador, the Marquis of Capeccelatro, who observed on the completion of his portrait of Maria Barbara, Princess of Brazil: 'the one of the Infanta does not resemble her at all as, besides concealing the pitting of the small-pox too much, it enhanced excessively the eyes, nose and mouth making her look bigger and older'.[16] In the complex world of diplomatic portrait painting, Duprà was required to mediate between a flattering likeness and deception. A remarkable document preserved in the Bibliothèque Nationale in Paris states that John V, on the eve of Duprà's return to Rome, gave him '12 gold bars weighing 50 marks as reward to the painter who had portrayed the prince of Brazil and the Infanta'.[17]

Duprà returned to Rome in 1731 with the Papal nuncio to Portugal, Vincenzo Bichi. This came at the end of a period of political hostility between John V and the papacy. In brief, the King wanted the diplomatic honour accorded to the Catholic monarchs of Austria, Spain and France, namely that any nuncio on leaving his post in Lisbon be automatically made a Cardinal.[18] Initially Pope Benedict XIII resisted, recalling Bichi

---

[15]   The correspondence is preserved in Madrid; a digest was published by de Carvalho (1958: 80–1).

[16]   De Carvalho 1958: 81.

[17]   See: De Santarem 1842–60: V, 11, no. cclx '12 barras de ouro de peso de 50 marcos'.

[18]   For the political dispute between Portugal and the Papacy, see: Miller 1978: 28–106.

from Portugal and dispatching his replacement. Bichi remained in Lisbon, and John V ended diplomatic relations with Rome, recalling his own Ambassador from Italy. In the end it was Pope Clement XII who eventually relented and, despite a great deal of domestic opposition, made Bichi a Cardinal. Duprà commemorates his elevation with a fine portrait which recently appeared on the art market.[19] At the same date Duprà painted an imposing portrait of *Giovanni Antonio Guadagni*, who was made a Cardinal with Bichi.[20] Guadagni is shown dressed in the distinctive costume of the Discalced Carmelites.

This early curial patronage allowed Duprà to establish himself in a large house and studio on the Via Trinitatis in Rome, where according to the Parish registers, he was joined by his brother, Giuseppe.[21] Fourteen years Domenico's junior, it has always been assumed that Giuseppe Duprà trained with his elder brother, but a reference in Giuseppe Bottari's *Raccolta di lettere sulla pitture* of 1766 states that he was the earliest of 'gli scolari' of Marco Benefial.[22] From this date on, Giuseppe became an essential part of the studio operation, acting as Duprà's drapery assistant and aiding in the production of replicas of his more important portraits.

It was not until the late 1730s that Duprà began to paint portraits of British sitters, the majority of whom were linked to the exiled Stuarts. As Edward Corp has persuasively demonstrated, the Stuart court – based in Palazzo del Re at the north end of the Piazza dei Santi Apostoli – acted as a powerful centre for English, Irish and Scottish travellers regardless of their political persuasion.[23] Grand Tourists gravitated to the circle of cultured and well-connected British exiles who congregated around James Francis Edward Stuart, Jacobite claimant to the English throne, and would undoubtedly have sought advice on innumerable practical matters, including whom to employ as a portraitist. It is perhaps not surprising therefore to find Duprà's earliest British sitters were committed Jacobites. Amongst the first datable of his British sitters is a portrait of the distinguished economist *Sir James Steuart Denham* (Scottish National Portrait Gallery, Edinburgh) who became the Jacobite Ambassador to France in the crucial year of 1745

[19] See: Petrucci 2010: I, 229–30.
[20] Reproduced in: Petrucci 2010: I, 224.
[21] Busiri Vici 1977: 2.
[22] Marco Benefial, a fact confirmed by a reference in Giuseppe Bottari of a letter dated 22 July 1764 from Giovanni Battista Ponfredi describing Benefial's earliest pupils: 'pochissimi furono gli scolari che continuassero a star secco… il primo che mi viene in mente è il Signor Giuseppe Duprà, che attualmente e impiegato al servizio di S.M. il Re di Sardegna'. Bottari, V. 22.
[23] As Corp has written: 'national and linguistic affinities eroded the political and dynastic differences that divided British people when in England'. See: Corp 2011b: 39.

(Fig. 11.2). The portrait of Denham is dated 1739 and shows Duprà was conscious both of the sitter's learning – his left hand rests on a book – and the then still nascent conventions for depicting cultured travellers in Italy: Denham is shown seated, informally attired and draped with a splendid blue cloak suggesting a classical toga, and the book is identifiable as a volume suggestive of on-the-spot reading, Suetonius's *Twelve Caesars*. This was a format which would reach its height in the works of Pompeo Batoni in the following decades. It is quite distinct from the more traditional, late Baroque format Duprà used to depict Roman nobleman such as his portrait of *Sigismondo Chigi* (Palazzo Chigi, Ariccia), and, crucially, the members of the Stuart family.

Denham was in turn responsible for collecting a series of bust-length portraits of his Jacobite friends in Rome. Five paintings are now identifiably part of this group, noted by the long inscriptions Denham had added to the reverse of each.[24] To quote just one example, that of *James Carnegie of Boysack*, now in Glasgow:

Done for James Carnegie Esqr of Boysac from Scotland, one of the Society of Young Gentlemen Travellers at Rome in the year 1739, and given to Sir James Stewart of Coltness Bart to whom he was a firm and intimate friend from about the year 1730 till the year 1760, that Mr. Carnegie dyed singularly regretted by Sir James.

The 'Society of Young Gentlemen Travellers' was the name given to the specifically Jacobite Freemasons Lodge, which was formed by two of the sitters, Sir William Hay the Old Pretender's *maggiordomo* and Dr James Irwin, his physician in 1739, from the remains of an earlier lodge (Fig. 11.3).[25] These reduced, head and shoulders portraits, have none of the surface complexity or refinement of Duprà's finest works from this period and it seems likely, given the inscriptions on the reverse, that they were copies of existing compositions made specifically for Denham. There is some visual evidence to confirm this supposition. A fine portrait of *James Drummond, Titular Duke of Perth* in a splendid gold-embroidered jacket was on the art market in the 1990s and seems to have acted as the model for the bust-length

---

[24] This series was discussed in an article by Skinner (1958). The surviving portraits comprise: *Captain William Hay of Edington*, Scottish National Portrait Gallery, Edinburgh; *Dr John Irwin*, Scottish National Portrait Gallery, Edinburgh; *James Drummond, Titular Duke of Perth*, Scottish National Portrait Gallery, Edinburgh; *James Carnegie of Boysack*, Glasgow Museums; and *Bellingham Boyle*, formerly in the collection of Ralph Holland, Sotheby's, London, 5 July, 2013, lot. 361.

[25] For the Jacobite lodges in Rome see: Corp 2004b; 2011b: 42–3.

Figure 11.2 Domenico Duprà, *Sir James Steuart Denham*, oil on canvas, 1739, Scottish National Portrait Gallery, Edinburgh, © National Galleries of Scotland.

version.[26] Even more suggestive is the fact that the bust-length portrait of *Drummond* exists in multiple versions.[27]

[26] The fine, three-quarter length portrait was with Chaucer Fine Arts, London. It was inscribed on the reverse 'D. Dupra pingebit Roma 1737' and almost certainly depicts James Drummond, 3rd Duke of Perth.

[27] Another apparently autograph version of the portrait is in the collection of Lady Willoughby de Eresby at Drummond Castle, Perthshire; possibly later copies are recorded in the collection of Lord MacDonald, Armadale Castle, Isle of Skye and Murthly Castle, Perthshire.

Figure 11.3 Domenico Duprà, *Captain William Hay of Edington*, oil on canvas, 1739, Scottish National Portrait Gallery, Edinburgh, © National Galleries of Scotland.

This group of works undoubtedly led to Duprà's direct employment by the Old Pretender, who commissioned him to paint two sets of portraits of his sons – Prince Charles and Henry, Duke of York – in 1740. For the next decade, until his return to Turin in 1750, Duprà was central to the pictorial presentation of the Stuart family. Corp's digest of the Stuart's household accounts offers an important insight into how much Duprà charged for his portraits at this date and the practicalities of serving as a 'court painter' – particularly of a court in exile attempting to maintain the loyalty of a diaspora of supporters – where multiple copies were requisite.[28] Duprà was paid on average 40 sequins or about £20 for an original composition and the same price for a pair of copy-portraits (either of the two young Stuart princes or James and his late wife Clementina Sobieska).[29] This pricing structure

---

[28] Corp 2011a: appendix C, 373–5.
[29] Corp 2011a: appendix C, 374. The payment for the Duke holding a miniature of the prince was 40 *scudi*.

precisely reflects contemporary customs across Europe and given the number of copies which are recorded in the accounts – five sets at least – would have required Duprà to have employed a number of assistants.

The need to project the young Stuarts as military figures was even more important to the stateless, exiled court than in Portugal (Fig. 11.4). Duprà's portraits of the two princes in armour, holding batons, were therefore widely disseminated not only in same-size copies, but replicated in miniature for the discreet distribution to loyalists. Numerous portrait heads of the Stuart family by miniaturists such as Veronica Telli made after Duprà's 1742 portraits survive.[30] But more importantly Duprà's pictures of the younger Stuarts were engraved in Paris by Jean Daullé and Johan Georg Wille, becoming the official images of the two princes on the eve of the rebellion of 1745. This aspect of Duprà's career has already been covered in literature on the iconography of the Stuarts, but it is worth pointing out the link with John O'Brien, who acted as Duprà's son's godfather, he was possibly connected to a known Jacobite who is mentioned as a potential donor to the cause and living in Malaga.[31] This needs greater investigation, but it raises the possibility that Duprà had a link to the Stuart court before he even left Lisbon.

Throughout this period Duprà also painted non-Jacobites (Fig. 11.5).[32] One of his most engaging portraits of a British sitter is a three-quarter-length of *James Stuart-Mackenzie* (Mount Stuart), brother of George III's governor, John Stuart, 3rd Earl of Bute. As with the portrait of *Denham*, Duprà shows *Stuart-Mackenzie* as a 'tourist', his magnificent red travelling cloak arranged across his body in a manner suggesting a toga. It seems likely that Giuseppe Duprà, as the drapery painter, was responsible for the intricate pattern of folds and the inclusion of the ring with the red-cabochon stone, which is similar to one worn by Guadagni.[33] The survival of a bust-length version of the same picture, formerly in a collateral branch of the Stuart family, once more suggests the importance of replication as a commercial element in Duprà's career.[34]

---

[30] For a list of Telli's miniatures after Duprà's portrait see: Corp 2011a: 109.

[31] Corp 2011a: 372.

[32] On this point Busiri Vici was confused: 'Ma se ne ha invece notizia di quelli di James Stuart Mackenzie of Rosehaugh, di Sir Hew Dalrymple, di William Henry Earl of Rochford, e dell'irlandese Bellingham Boyle, tutti strettamente associati ai Giacobiti in esilio.' James Stuart Mackenzie was certainly not a Jacobite. See: Busiri Vici 1977: 14.

[33] An inventory of the collection of the Marquises of Penalva in Lisbon, made by the Portugese painter Lusitano, confirms the division of labour which Duprà practised, he describes a picture as: 'Portrait of the old Duke of Cadaval, the head only having been made by Monsieur Duplat'. See: Delaforce 2002: 247.

[34] The copy was in the collection of Lt Colonel Howard when it was sold attributed to Allan Ramsay at Christie's, London, 24 July, 1969, lot. 76.

Figure 11.4 After Domenico Duprà, *Prince Charles Edward Stuart*, engraving by Gilles Edme Petit, London, c. 1740, British Museum, London, © The Trustees of the British Museum.

A letter from Cardinal Alessandro Albani in Rome dated 1 April 1750, addressed to the Marchese di Gorzegno, Minister of State at Turin, recommended the bearer – 'il Signor Duprà eccellente ritrattista' – explaining that he had been called to Turin to paint the newly married Victor Amadeus (III), Duke of Savoy and his wife the Infanta Maria Antonietta of Spain.[35] The letter makes it clear that Duprà had for some time been working for Albani ('egli antico mio dipendente'), although thus far it has not been possible to ascertain precisely what this entailed.[36] It is a suggestive corollary to Duprà's success amongst British sitters in Rome, as Albani was not only an active Anglophile – representing the interests of British travellers and encouraging British artists – but an advocate of the papacy recognizing the

---

[35] For an account of this episode see: Pinto 1987: 73–4.
[36] Transcribed and published in: Baudi di Vesme 1986: II, 438.

Figure 11.5 Domenico Duprà, *Duke of Hamilton*, oil on canvas, 1752, Lennoxlove House, Scotland, © Lennoxlove House Ltd.

Hanoverian succession. In his extensive correspondence with the British Minister in Florence, Horace Mann, Albani frequently brokered commissions for British patrons in London, and it is likely that in Rome he introduced Duprà to some of his British sitters, particularly the non-Jacobites.[37]

---

[37] It is unclear precisely what work Duprà undertook for Albani. For Albani's work for British clients, see: Lewis 1961.

Three days after Albani's letter, Gorzegno received one from the Piedmontese Ambassador in Rome, the Conte di Rivera, alerting him to the arrival of 'I fratelli Duprà piemontesi, celebre ritrattista, l'uno, e l'altro assai buon pittore di figure'.[38] It is the first time we have a clear reference to the break-down of the brothers' roles: Domenico was the portraitist and Giuseppe the figure and drapery painter. This was an entirely typical division at this date, although it is rare to have it stated so categorically. The brothers re-established themselves in their native city and in September of 1750, Charles Emmanuel, King of Sardinia, made Duprà his *Reale Pittore per li Ritratti*.[39] Duprà's official career in Turin is remarkably well documented: accurate records were kept of payments made for portraits of members of the Royal family.[40] From March 1751 this meant a considerable number of copies of the new ducal portraits, destined for foreign courts and for palaces and towns throughout the Savoyard territories including Moncalieri, Stupinigi, Racconigi and Venaria Reale. As with the Stuart accounts, we know the brothers were paid 195 livres or about 40 sequins for each pair of portraits; in other words, precisely the same amount that they had been charging Jacobite followers in Rome for copies.[41] One of the earliest iterations of the picture of *Victor Amadeus* was given to a British traveller, James, 6th Duke of Hamilton who was in Turin in 1752.[42]

This brings us neatly to Duprà's British patronage in Turin. As a centre for young travellers, Turin offered Duprà a clientele beyond the royal family and members of the court.[43] The Duke of Hamilton, for example, spent a considerable period in the city becoming the *cicesbeo* of one of Turin's most fashionable hostesses, the Comtesse de St Gilles (Fig. 11.5).[44] As a result he was himself painted by Duprà in this fine portrait which is inscribed and marked 'Turin 1752' and which remains in the collection of the Duke of Hamilton at Lennoxlove. The style of the portrait is quite different from Duprà's Roman portraits of 'Grand Tourists'. Hamilton is shown without a

[38]   Baudi di Vesme 1986: II, 438.
[39]   Baudi di Vesme 1986: II, 438.
[40]   Baudi di Vesme 1986: II, 438–43.
[41]   Baudi di Vesme 1986: II, 439.
[42]   The portrait remained at Lennoxlove until it was sold erroneously as a portrait of 'Charles Emmanuel I', Sotheby's London, 8 July, 1987, lot. 190.
[43]   At least one portrait of a young traveller from Holland survives. A portrait of *Aernout Leers* is inscribed on the verso 'Dominicus Duprà fecit. Torino 1755' and is in the Historisches Museum Rotterdam.
[44]   James Boswell noted in his diary of a visit to the Comtesse de St Gilles: 'she talked of Duke Hamilton, who had been a great gallant of hers': Wain 1991: 132. For the important role of the Comtesse de St. Gilles in the Turinese aristocratic sociability, see: Merlotti 2004.

Figure 11.6 After Domenico Duprà, *Earl of Rochford*, engraving by Richard Houston, 1775, British Museum, London, © The Trustees of the British Museum.

cloak against a simple background; the most striking feature of the picture is the richly embroidered jacket, which is very finely painted.

At about the same date, Duprà executed a portrait of the British Envoy, William Henry Nassau de Zuylestein, 4th Earl of Rochford (Fig. 11.6). Sadly now missing, it is known only from a mezzotint by Richard Houston.[45] Rochford was appointed in 1749 and Duprà's portrait probably dates from shortly afterwards, given its similarity to the portrait of Hamilton (Duprà depicts him wearing a similarly embroidered waistcoat and jacket). Turin at this date was famous for the production of raw silk and silver and gold threads; it was an industry illustrated in a print from Awnsham Churchill's *Collections of Voyages and Travels* published in London in 1745.[46] The result

[45]   Portraits of the Earl and Countess of Rochford by Jean-Baptiste Perronneau were sold at Sotheby's, 11 July 2001, lot. 210, but there is no record of the portrait of Rochford by Duprà.

[46]   Churchill 1745: 584.

Figure 11.7 Domenico Duprà, *Victor Amadeus III as Duke of Savoy*, oil on canvas, 1755/58, National Trust (Bristol Collection), Ickworth,© National Trust Images.

was an extravagance and formality in dress, similar to that at the French Court, which was much commented upon by British travellers. But it seems likely that this shift in Duprà's style from his Roman portraiture also reflected his greatly increased volume of business, particularly as the official Royal portraitist; it seems likely that Duprà simply painted the face, whilst Giuseppe, or another unknown drapery painter, completed the body.

Rochford also commissioned a portrait of his wife, Lucy. The original picture remains in a private collection and a copy – of studio quality – is preserved in a collateral branch of the family at Kasteel Heeze in Brabant. This is the only portrait of a British female sitter, and it shows Lady Rochford in much the same register as earlier female portraits, in generalized, loose costume, rather than a particular dress, in contrast to her husband's modish appearance.

As well as painting portraits of resident diplomats Duprà, in his capacity as *Reale Pittore per li Ritratti*, was called upon to paint pictures as diplomatic gifts. It was a convention which saw versions of Duprà's portraits of *Victor Amadeus III* and his wife given to several British visitors (Fig. 11.7). Throughout Europe there was an established tradition of reigning monarchs presenting their portraits to foreign ambassadors. Turning to just one unpublished example as a precedent: a miniature of *Victor Amadeus II* by the Swedish enamellist Charles Boit was given in 1706 to Paul Methuen who had arrived in Savoy as Minister shortly after the conclusion of the siege of Turin. We have already seen that the Duke of Hamilton acquired a version of Duprà's portrait of *Victor Amadeus III* and Duprà's portraits of the young Duke and his wife became a staple gift for retiring British diplomats.

In the *Registro de' ceremoniali del conte Carlo Amedeo Salmatoris*, the four-volume manuscript account of the official diplomatic life at the court of Charles Emmanuel III kept by his Master of Ceremonies, Carlo Amedeo Salmatoris di Roussillon, and preserved in the Biblioteca Reale, several entries testify to this practice during the eighteenth century.[47] The volumes only cover one departing British Minister, the Earl of Rochford, but the gifts he received can be seen as representative of the whole period up to 1800.[48] According to the volumes, Rochford took his final leave of the court on 30 January 1755 but remained in Turin for a further two weeks before setting out for London on 12 February. Before leaving, Salmatoris records that Rochford was presented with portraits of Charles Emmanuel and his son framed with diamonds.[49] Rochford's magnificent gift can no longer be traced, but some idea of their appearance is offered by a pair of miniatures and bust-length portraits, all by or after Duprà, which survived in the collection of Rochford's successor, George Hervey, 2nd Earl of Bristol, and are now preserved at Ickworth House, Suffolk.[50]

But Salmatoris's records prove that such diplomatic gifts were by no means a certainty. Something also testified to by contemporary accounts, the British *chargé d'affaires*, following the departure of James Stuart Mackenzie in 1761, was Louis Dutens, who recounted the expectations surrounding such diplomatic gifts in his vivid *Memoirs of a Traveller* (Fig. 4.4). On the eve of his return to Britain in 1766, Dutens[51] called on the first Minister, the Comte de Viry, who he records was 'desirous of giving me an unequivocal proof of the friendship he had always entertained for me'. After a delay of some days,

[47] Turin, Biblioteca Reale di Torino (BRT), Storia patria 726/7-4.
[48] The volumes cover the period from 1738 to 1758.
[49] BRT, Storia patria 726/7-4, f.151.
[50] See Rothwell in this volume.
[51] Dutens 1806b: II, 90.

Dutens was granted an audience with Victor Amadeus III. 'In consequence of this,' he explained:

I expected nothing less than a magnificent portrait, or some rich present, which the Count de Viry, in the plentitude of his friendship, might have suggested to the King that it would be proper to give me. I presented myself to the King; and had the honour to be admitted to a private audience, which lasted three quarters of an hour. While His Majesty was conversing with me, with that affability which was so peculiar to him, he pulled out a gold snuff-box, which I supposed contained his portrait, and was intended for me; but after he had taken a pinch of rapee, he put it back into his pocket. A quarter of an hour after, the King put his hand into another pocket, and drew out another snuff-box, which I would have sworn was the one destined for me. I had already thought of the acknowledgments which I was to make; when his Majesty took a pinch of Spanish snuff, shut the box and dismissed me.[52]

Dutens's lack of gift may be explained by his rank, as a Frenchman temporarily made the British *chargé d'affaires*, and never officially a member of the diplomatic 'service', he occupied an ambiguous position in the status conscious Savoy court.

Throughout the eighteenth century British Ambassadors would have taken substantial equipage on their embassy, including a canopy of state and portrait of the reigning monarch, as well as plate and splendid personal effects.[53] But during the eighteenth century Britain only sent Consuls and Ministers Plenipotentiary to Turin, and only twice full Ambassadors.[54] Envoys required none of this apparatus, although the complexity of the situation was one that even confused contemporaries. George Pitt – who was painted by Duprà in Rome in 1741 – was appointed Minister in 1761. He promptly ordered a copy of George III's recent state portrait from Allan Ramsay, only to discover he was not entitled to one. A letter from Robert Wood, Under-Secretary of State dated April 1763 and preserved in the Stratfield-Saye manuscripts, explained: 'I am sorry to find out that Ambassadors only have a right to the King's Picture, Ramsay had proceeded upon one for you but it may do for Lord Sandwich. I suppose you wont chuse to buy one.'[55]

---

[52] Just such a gold snuff-box, containing miniature copies of Duprà's portraits of Victor Amadeus and Maria Antonia was on the art market in 1997: Sotheby's Geneva, 19 and 20 May, 1997, lot. 396.

[53] The plate of the Earl of Bristol which is preserved at Ickworth House is discussed elsewhere in this volume by James Rothwell.

[54] See Storrs in this volume.

[55] Simon 1994: 452.

Duprà and his brother spent the remainder of their lives executing portraits of the Royal family for their multiplying palaces, but most of these Turinese works lack the vigour of their earlier paintings. Duprà died aged 81 in 1770 and was honoured for his service by burial in the Regia Cappella.[56] Giuseppe continued to paint in Turin becoming one of the professors at the Turin Royal Academy of Painting, and he also died aged 81, in 1784.

Forming an assessment of Duprà's work is not an easy task. Like many painters during the eighteenth century, he developed a distinctive formula for completing different types of portraiture. His royal portraits remain consistent from his earliest depictions of King John V and his family from the 1720s to his work for Charles Emmanuel. Comparing the picture of John V's son, the Prince of Brazil, painted in 1721 and now in the Villa Vicosa in Portugal, and an engraving made in Paris by de Poilly in 1746 of *Prince Charles*, the visual similarity is clearly legible. This continuity is reinforced when viewing the portrait of *Henry Benedict Stuart* next to the portrait of the young *Victor Amadeus* given to the Duke of Hamilton: one need only replace the Savoyard order of the Annunciation with the Saltire of the Order of the Thistle to have the portrait of *Henry Benedict*. This was a natural corollary of fulfilling the political and practical demands of royal portraiture. In depicting British tourists Duprà tended to shift register and follow the emerging conventions of tourist portraiture. Artistically he owed a great deal to his early training with Trevisani, but his Roman training was tempered with a softness, particularly in the handling of faces and hair, which owes something to French painting. As was intimated at the beginning of this chapter, it is perhaps possible to make a distinction during the eighteenth century between artists who catered specifically for the tourist market in Italy – such as Antonio David or Pompeo Batoni – and those whose careers were more inherently international. Duprà was an itinerant court painter, whose work reflected the practical and commercial demands of such a position. Recovery of his work and career is important for understanding the status of such painters during the eighteenth century.

---

[56] Baudi di Vesme 1986: II, 441.

12 | The Culture of Confession: The Sardinian Chapel in London in the Eighteenth Century

PAOLO COZZO

The history of the Sardinian embassy chapel in London is not well known in Italy. While Italian scholars have paid relatively little attention to the events surrounding this religious site,[1] the same cannot be said of academics across the Channel. At various times and in different ways, British scholars have given a certain amount of scholarly attention to exploring the history of the Sardinian Chapel,[2] highlighting its role and importance in the context of London's churches with particular regard to its relationship with the sites of worship that belonged to other diplomatic missions. As a matter of fact, several Catholic countries maintained embassies in eighteenth-century London that were endowed with their own chapels. The most long-standing of these were the French and Spanish embassies, as well as the Florentine, Venetian (located in the Haymarket), Portuguese (originally in Golden Square before being moved to South Street, Grosvenor Square), Austrian (on Hanover Street), Neapolitan (in Soho Square), Bavarian (on Warwick Street) and, finally, the Sardinian Chapel, built in Lincoln's Inn Fields on what was originally called Duke Street, but later renamed Sardinian Street.[3] In 1766, the *Gazetteer* and *New Daily Advertiser* listed eight 'public Roman Catholic chapels' in London: the Sardinian (mentioned earlier), French, Spanish, Bavarian, Neapolitan, Portuguese, Farthing-hatch and Mint chapels.[4]

If the existence of a church of the House of Savoy in London is not by any means a fresh discovery, it nevertheless seems worthwhile to try to understand why it 'was probably the best known of all the embassy chapels'.[5] Indeed, the fame that the Sardinian church acquired during the eighteenth century should be interpreted in the context of the diplomatic relations that existed in that period between the courts of Turin and London, and as the outcome of a foreign policy in which religious issues were always of primary importance.

---

[1] There are some references in: Molle 2014.
[2] Harting 2012.
[3] Evinson 1998; Symondson 2003: 14.
[4] Gilman 2013: 445.
[5] Evinson 1998: 85.

The Savoy chapel was built on a site that had already been set aside for Catholic worship at the end of the seventeenth century, when Franciscan friars had apparently had a chapel built there in Lincoln's Inn Fields during the reign of James II. After the fall of James II, this property was destroyed and perhaps subsequently ceded to the Portuguese diplomatic mission, which had its headquarters in that same neighbourhood.[6] In 1715, however, the church was registered as belonging to the Embassy of the Kingdom of Sicily, having been acquired by the House of Savoy only two years earlier, in 1713, when the Savoy dynasty finally gained the royal crown under the Treaty of Utrecht.[7] As scholars have noted, the House of Savoy's domination of Sicily lasted only five years. After losing Sicily, the House of Savoy acquired Sardinia in 1720, following the War of the Quadruple Alliance, and Sardinia went on to lend its name to Savoy rule, as Piedmont-Sardinia, until the mid-nineteenth century.[8]

The church's first inventories, dating to the period 1719–22, confirm the idea that the Turinese court chose to establish this site of worship in London as part of the propaganda campaign it formulated after having acquired the royal crown. This achievement essentially meant that the House of Savoy had gained a full and recognized place on the international stage of the period, given that it was 'in a very striking way caught between England and Spain'.[9]

Featuring a large gallery and directly connected to the residence of the ambassador of Savoy, the chapel had two doors that opened onto Duke Street.[10] The building's interior, which displayed the House of Savoy coat of arms, was quite spacious (indeed, it was capable of holding up to 600 people, a hundred of them in the gallery alone, and was equipped with six confessionals) and served by five chaplains and a head chaplain.[11] These numbers alone suggest that this site of worship had the potential and

---

[6]   Riley and Gomme 1912: 81–4.

[7]   Perrillat 2013.

[8]   Girgenti 1994; Bély 2013.

[9]   Storrs 2003: 233.

[10]   This is confirmed by a report by the Savoy special envoy to London, the Marquis of Cortanze: 'The aforementioned chapel, which (including galleries) can hold over 600 people, was adjacent [to the embassy] and connected to my residence via a wooden bridge. It had two large doors facing the street, one of which opened onto the passageway and the other the chapel itself'. Archivio di Stato di Torino (hereafter ASTo), Corte, Materie Ecclesiastiche (hereafter ME), Benefizi di qua da monti, mz. 17, Londra, Cappella Regia, fasc. n 2. 1721, July 1, *Stato e regolamenti della capella cattolica di Sua Maestà in Londra fatto dal marchese di Cortanze.*

[11]   *Ibid*, fasc. n. 1, *1719 in 1722, Inventario de mobili esistenti nella capella cattolica di Sua Maestà in Londra.*

ambition to attract a number of worshippers much greater than the rather limited group of Savoy subjects living in London. In fact, the first reports written by the diplomatic representatives of Piedmont clearly indicate that the church displayed all the characteristics of a parish in the post-Council of Trent style: specifically, baptism and marriage records were preserved in the archives, and the chaplains carried out all the liturgical and sacramental duties normally associated with the 'care of souls'.[12] As mentioned above, the population of individuals who received these spiritual services – and this brings us to the most interesting issue – extended beyond the subjects of the King of Sardinia alone. This fact can be deduced from a report by the ambassador of Savoy, the Marquis Ettore Tommaso Roero di Cortanze,[13] in which he states that the Catholic authorities of other countries – first and foremost England – also recognized the validity of baptism and marriage certificates provided that they displayed the official seal composed of the white cross of Savoy and the inscription *Capella Regia Sardiniae Londini*.[14] It should therefore come as no surprise that the church of Savoy hosted the marriages of personages such as the dancer Eva Marie Veigel and the actor David Garrick in 1749,[15] Giuseppe Novello and Joan Wins (future parents of the musician Vincent Novello) in 1772,[16] the writer Frances 'Fanny' Burney (daughter of musician and music historian Charles Burney and a French Catholic) and the French exile Alexandre d'Arblay in 1792, to name just a few.[17]

The claim that 'generations of London Catholic families'[18] worshipped in this space seems well supported by the historical record if we consider what was said about this church in London circles in the mid-eighteenth century. Indeed, the Knight Giuseppe Antonio Ossorio, Secretary of State for Foreign Affairs,[19] who was quite familiar with the English context and the

---

[12] The baptism (from 1731), marriage (from 1729) and death (from 1858) records are stored in the collection Sacramental registers of the Westminster Diocesan Archives. Twelve volumes of baptism records, for the years 1772 to 1841, have been transcribed and made available on CD ROM (http://www.catholic-library.org.uk/registers.html).

[13] The Marquis of Cortanze was special envoy to London from 1719 to 1725 (Raviola 2005: 89).

[14] ASTo, ME, Benefizi di qua da monti, mz. 17, fasc. Londra, Cappella Regia, fasc. n 2. 1721, July 1, *Stato e regolamenti della capella cattolica*.

[15] These two public figures (the first Catholic, the latter Protestant) were married with two separate ceremonies in two different churches, one of which was the Sardinian Chapel (Gilman 2013: 34).

[16] Palmer 2006: 12.

[17] Harting 2012: 29.

[18] Gilman 2013: 34.

[19] The Sicilian Giuseppe Antonio Ossorio Alarcon, one of the leading figures of Savoy diplomacy during the reigns of Victor Amadeus II and Charles Emmanuel III, was special envoy to London for approximately twenty years, from 1730 to 1750 (Merlotti 2013a).

'Sardinian Chapel' itself, received a report in 1750 describing the church as being 'like the Catholics' Metropolitan' and 'The Roman chapel par excellence', so much so that 'it is what sets the tone for all the others'.[20]

Why did this Chapel come to occupy such a distinguished and pre-eminent place in the sphere of London Catholicism? An explanation can be found in the correspondence of the chief Savoy diplomat, who was invested as Knight of the Grand Cross of the Order of St Maurice on 7 April 1731 in this very church.[21] The Sardinian Chapel had various factors in its favour, including its size (which made it easy for the faithful to attend services there), its large staff of priests and chaplains (which made it possible to celebrate Mass every day, at noon) and its location, which remained the same for many years and was considered quite strategic. 'It is known', as stated in a report that the Abbot Giovanni Antonio Palazzi of Selve, the Bursar of the troppe maiuscole,[22] sent to Sir Ossorio in 1757, that London

is composed of two cities: one called the Liberty of Westhminsther, wherein is located the royal palace and where most members of parliament reside, and the foreign ministries that have various semi-public or private chapels; the other city, London proper, stretches for miles along the Thames, with seafarers disembarking around its midpoint, and in this huge population there is not a single chapel. In Linkolfields square – continued Abbot Palazzi – where these two cities converge and approximately two miles from the palace, there is located the chapel maintained by the ministry of His Majesty: and whereas the other ministries provide offices in the jurisdiction of Westhminsther, close to the court, more comfortable and less expensive, his Majesty has always obliged his ministry to maintain the residence located there at the chapel, (to their severe expenditure and discomfort), so that all the Catholics in London and some of those in Westhminsther may have the convenience of attending mass, and receiving the sacraments, above all in moments of illness, and that both prisoners and those facing execution might always be served by our chaplains, as indeed they are, and without which all of them would find it impossible to exercise their religious beliefs.[23]

Bishop Richard Challoner (the Apostolic Vicar of London and a leading figure of eighteenth-century English Catholicism), likewise acknowledged

---

[20] ASTo, ME, Benefizi di qua da monti, mz. 17. 1, Londra, Cappella Regia, *1755 in 1787, Memoire touchant la chapelle du roi a Londres, avec une pièce latine qui y est citée, reçue par le chavalier Ossorio avec le dêpache du roi du 11 mars 1750.*

[21] Merlotti 2013a.

[22] Regarding Abbot Palazzi, see: Dell'Oro 2007: 289–90.

[23] This is a passage from *Memoria per la Regia Capella di Londra da trasmettersi a Sua Santità* attached to a letter from Abbot Palazzi to Sir Ossorio, dated June 14, 1757 (ASTo, ME, Benefizi di qua da monti, mz 17. 1, Londra, Cappella Regia, *1755 in 1787*, fasc. 4).

Figure 12.1 Unknown artist, *The Right Reverend Richard Challoner performing Mass in the Sardinian Chapel* (in the background, Claudio Francesco Beaumont's *Deposition* over the altar), engraved by James Peter Coghlan, London, 1784, © National Portrait Gallery, London.

these explanations of why the Sardinian had become 'the best known, the most frequented' of London's chapels (Figs 12.1 and 12.2), in that it was:[24]

the most commodiously situated for the body of Catholicks of all the chapels in the town, the rest being mostly in the court end or just upon the skirts of the suburbs, so that this chapel has been above fifty years the chief support of religion in London.

Another factor that helped increase the church's prestige and influence among English Catholics was a purely political consideration: unlike other Catholic powers represented in the British capital whose diplomatic relations could (and frequently did) suffer serious upheaval, it was quite unlikely that relations between the courts of Turin and London could reach such a

---

[24] Burton 1909: 19–20.

Figure 12.2 John Buck, *The Roman Catholic Chapel, Lincoln's Inn Fields*, in Ackermann's *Microcosm of London*, 1808, the Stapleton Collection, © Bridgeman Images.

low level that the King of Sardinia would be forced to recall his ambassador and therefore suspend the religious services offered by the embassy.[25] As a matter of fact, the British government clearly regarded the House of Savoy with sympathy and appreciation, encouraging the local populations to respect it as well (and thus its offshoots, such as the church associated with the diplomatic mission as well). The confirmation of this state of affairs occurred in 1750, in the tense atmosphere of one of the many revolts that shook London in the eighteenth century. On this occasion,

when in all the other chapels mass was recited behind closed doors and without noise, the priests leading the services not daring to set foot outside the residences of

---

[25] 'It is unlikely events could occur that would force the King of Sardinia to recall his ambassador without replacement, whereas other Catholic powers that have chapels in London might easily enter into intense conflict with England' (ASTo, ME, Benefizi di qua da monti, mz 17. 1, Londra, Cappella Regia, *1755 in 1787, Memoire touchant la chapelle du roi à Londres*).

the ambassadors [in the chapel of the King of Sardinia] mass has always been sung with open doors and its priests have continued to handle their affairs in the city as before, without anything ever happening, having even obtained permission to convoke and aid Catholics imprisoned for having rebelled against the government.[26]

In fact, this privileged status enjoyed by the Sardinian church was actually documented as early as the end of the reign of George I, when the court included a significant number of important figures who looked upon this site of worship with particular tolerance. One of these was Thomas Parker (1st Earl of Macclesfield), Lord Chancellor of England from 1718 to 1725 who, residing in the vicinity of the church, was able to see for himself – according to the Savoy envoy, the Marquis Tommaso Roero di Cortanze – the tone and character of the ceremonies performed there. When his daughter-in-law fell ill, Lord Macclesfield asked the Piedmontese ambassador to limit the amount of singing and organ music used during services; when she recovered, the Lord Chancellor informed the Sardinian diplomat, thanking him for his diligence and telling him they could resume singing and playing music 'as usual'.[27]

In light of these special conditions, it should not be surprising that English Catholics flocked to the Sardinian church, which – it was observed at the end of the 1750s – was attended 'more than any of the others in the city', so much so that more than half of all the Catholics in London and Westminster (which at that point must have been approximately 20,000[28]) were estimated to have made their way there for religious holidays.[29] These individuals ('artisans, merchants, workers and sailors who do not have the convenience of carriages and furthermore may go to church only during certain hours') were motivated to use the Sardinian Chapel 'for its greater proximity, lacking the time to go as far as the others',[30] but there were also worshippers who preferred it for other reasons, such as the high quality of the musical services it offered. If 'the music of the Sardinian Chapel was its glory' and 'the finest instruments in Britain were heard here', it is easy to understand why 'hundreds of non-Catholics attended services to

---

[26] *Ibid.*

[27] This is a passage from a statement by the Marquis Tommaso Roero di Cortanze (ASTo, ME, Benefizi di qua da monti, mz. 17, Londra, Cappella Regia, fasc. n 2. 1721, July 1, *Stato e regolamenti della capella cattolica di Sua Maestà*).

[28] 'According to an estimate made in 1786, the Catholic population of all England numbered 60,000. One third of these were in London' (Gilman 2013: 462, note 2).

[29] ASTo, ME, Benefizi di qua da monti, mz 17. 1, Londra, Cappella Regia, *1755 in 1787*, fasc. 4, *Memoria per la Regia Cappella di Londra*.

[30] ASTo, ME, Benefizi di qua da monti, mz 17. 1, Londra, Cappella Regia, *1755 in 1787*, fasc. 4, *Memoria per la Regia Cappella di Londra*.

listen'.[31] Indeed, the best Catholic musicians of eighteenth-century England (from Thomas Arne to Samuel Webbe, from George Paxton to John Francis Wade – whose creation of a 'Missa Sardonica' unmistakably indicates his deep connection to the Sardinian Chapel[32] – as well as Vincent Novello, who began his musical career there as a chorus member[33]) assumed the role of organist in the Savoy church, and the Catholic élite of the city came to hear them play. One visitor, for example, was the wealthy wool merchant William Mawhood (1724–97), 'well known and respected by all the leading Catholics of his day, especially by the clergy, who sought his advice in many important matters'; on more than one occasion Mawhood, a music lover, played the organ in the 'Sardinian Chapel' where he regularly attended mass.[34]

In part to cope with the growing influx of worshippers ('the crowd on feast days in this chapel comes close to twelve thousand souls', noted a London-based observer[35]), officials in Turin decided to increase the number of chaplains, bringing the total to seven. Indeed, the number of clerics (five chaplains and a head chaplain) who had originally served the church was low compared to the eight posted at the chapels of the Spanish and Portuguese legations, sites which were also much less heavily attended by the faithful.[36]

In many ways, the staff serving the Chapel (in addition to the six chaplains, there was also a choirmaster, sacristan, door-keeper and attendant hired to 'sweep the chapel'[37]) represented the most problematic aspect of managing a church whose 'pre-eminence', acknowledged in the world of London Catholicism, required constant vigilance to ensure that it would continue to constitute a model for others without ever providing Protestants with instances of controversy or scandal. It was the clerics themselves who presented the most serious risk: as a matter of fact, they were regulars of religious orders (mainly Jesuits and Dominicans) and British (English, Irish and Scottish) rather than Savoy subjects. Irish clerics held the pre-eminent position within this group and the head chaplain was usually chosen from among their ranks. At mid-century, for example, the 'senior chaplain at the

---

[31] Gilman 2013: 34.

[32] Muir 2008: 70.

[33] Palmer 2006: 14.

[34] Gilman 2013: 447.

[35] Gilman 2013: 447.

[36] ASTo, ME, Benefizi di qua da monti, mz 17. 1, Londra, Cappella Regia, 1755 in 1787, *Osservazioni sopra il disegno della capella da farsi in Londra*, Turin, 1 July 1762.

[37] ASTo, ME, Benefizi di qua da monti, mz. 17, Londra, Cappella Regia, fasc. n 2. 1721, 1 luglio, *Stato e regolamenti della capella cattolica di Sua Maestà*.

Sardinian Chapel' was the Bishop of Derry, the preacher Patrick Brolaghan (O'Brullagahan). Brolaghan was a Dominican friar named Bishop by Pope Benedict XIV. He was granted Episcopal ordination on 3 March 1751 by the Bishop of Ossory, James B. Dunne, in the Chapel.[38]

The decision not to use secular clergy was indicative of the fact that Turin, inspired by Rome, viewed England as a missionary destination, in that 'of all the great losses suffered in the sixteenth century by the Catholic religion, and with it the Holy See, the most significant – as everyone knows – is that of the kingdoms of Great Britain, a loss all the more sensitive given that the incompatibility, intolerance and repeated interdiction of Catholicism would seem to render it unrecoverable'. The chapels of diplomatic missions were therefore 'the only means' remaining to 'the zeal of the greatest popes' to 'provide spiritual aid to the considerable number of families and individuals of every rank and condition who, despite the many obstacles, still maintain the ancient religion'.[39] This missionary aspect is evidenced by the *cursus* required of the clerics attached to the London-based churches, which involved several years of training in Catholic countries (with an almost obligatory period spent in Rome) in which the clergy had the opportunity to perfect their Latin and learn other languages. This was necessary because the religious services at the diplomatic mission chapels were not supposed to be held in English. Indeed, for many years, mass at the 'Sardinian Chapel' was recited not only in Latin but also in Flemish and French.[40]

By effectively preventing the serving clergy from putting down roots in the places where they worked, this itinerant course of training risked exacerbating the climate of conflict arising from the fact that the chaplains all belonged to different 'nations' (England, Ireland, Scotland) whose relationships were often characterized by mutual hostility. In this context, the primacy of the Irish was viewed as an insurmountable obstacle to harmonious relationships among the clergy: 'as long as there is a senior chaplain from this latter nation' – feared officials in Turin – 'it will not be possible or even advisable to seek to make the British commingle, as peace would no longer reign among the chaplains'.[41] Many advocated a plan to create the conditions for these chaplains to live a communitarian life, forming a sort

---

[38] Gilman 2013: 463.
[39] ASTo, ME, Benefizi di qua da monti, mz 17. 1, Londra, Cappella Regia, *1755 in 1787*, fasc. 4, *Memoria per la Regia Capella di Londra*.
[40] ASTo, ME, Benefizi di qua da monti, mz. 17, Londra, Cappella Regia, fasc. n 2. 1721, 1 July, *Stato e regolamenti della capella cattolica di Sua Maestà*.
[41] ASTo, ME, Benefizi di qua da monti, mz 17. 1, Londra, Cappella Regia, *1755 in 1787*, fasc. 9, 1755, *Regole proposte ad osservarsi dai cappellani*.

of convent adjacent to the Savoy Embassy and subject to the local ecclesiastical authority, that is, the Apostolic Vicar of London. However, the clergy members' inability to be together 'without jealousy and dissension' made such a project wholly unfeasible.[42] Uniting the chaplains and aggregating them in a single space adjacent to the Sardinian embassy would have presented many potential advantages. First, the clergy would have been protected from possible resurgences of anti-Catholic sentiment: if, it was said, such sentiment were to potentially originate from the British government, it might much more easily emerge from public opinion. Furthermore – and this was the most important aspect for the court in Turin – the chaplains would be subject to more rigorous oversight by the ambassador and head of the diocese, putting them in a position to be able to censor any possible 'trafficking in religion' and, at the same time, ensure that the chaplains met the residence requirement.[43]

The absence of a proper parish also made it impossible to locate the chaplains in those crucial moments, such as in the event of extreme sickness, when they absolutely needed to be present to administer the sacraments of confession, communion and extreme unction. This less concentrated arrangement moreover fostered a certain moral laxity that was expressed in their attending or spending time at cafes, theatres, hotels and theatrical performances, the decency of which was difficult to guarantee in a city as large as London. The chaplains had also acquired the habit of 'begging lunches at the homes of their penitents'[44] who, coming from all over London, might be located quite far from the church. As a result, the church personnel were often absent from some of the Sunday services (such as high mass and vespers) that called for the participation of all the clergy members, or present in limited numbers at other ceremonies such as baptisms and weddings. To avoid such problems, a supplementary sum of 42 pounds per person was added to the chaplains' previous wages in 1757 to enable them to purchase 80 non-workday meals.[45]

It was certainly no secret at the court in Turin that economic issues were the cause of many of these problems. In 1749, the Sardinian Minister, Count Perron, pointed out that the frequent appeals to Catholic Londoners for donations to support the church – 30 pounds had been collected that year to maintain the organ and a thousand for work to expand the building,

---

[42] Ibid, fasc. 4, *Memoria per la Regia Capella di Londra.*

[43] ASTo, ME, Benefizi di qua da monti, mz 17. 1, Londra, Cappella Regia, *1755 in 1787, Memoire touchant la chapelle du roi à Londres.*

[44] Ibid, fasc. 4, June 2 1757, *Lettera dell'abate Palazzi economo generale de' benefici vacanti.*

[45] Ibid.

that had been carried out a few months earlier – had produced some 'talk' around town, exacerbated by the widespread belief that the alms collected at the end of services went not to fund charity for the poor but rather to manage the church itself.[46] What was at stake in this case was the prestige and credibility of a foreign court that risked giving the impression of being unable to fulfill the duties, both material and spiritual, associated with its own diplomatic mission, and for this reason the Bursar General of the troppe maiuscole ended up addressing this problem. In that period (the data refer to 1757) it cost the Savoy government a total of 5,000 pounds to maintain the church. Only a small part of this sum was needed to pay the chaplains, who earned one and a half pounds a month, or two pounds in the case of the head chaplain. The Abbot Palazzi therefore decided that these wages should be transformed into ecclesiastical pensions (to be increased to two and three pounds respectively) which would be funded by drawing on the income generated by the ancient Benedictine Abbey of Casanova in Piedmont.[47]

In addition to these economic problems, there were also legal complications. In compliance with the dictates of the Treaty of Trent, this church was supposed to be subject to the authority of the head of a diocese just like any other parish, in this case, specifically, the Apostolic Vicar who – as pointed out to the court of Turin – 'has the authority of the Bishop of London' and, as such, performed 'the sacrament of confirmation in pontifical dress and mitre'. It was for this reason that, at the end of his diplomatic mission, Count Roero reported that he had once allowed

the vicar apostolic to visit the chapel and examine not only the implements and all that related to the administration of the sacraments, but also the baptism and marriage records, as do the bishops in a parish church.

The Sardinian diplomat was quick to point out, however, that 'In order to avoid establishing it as a right, he had visited by presenting the head chaplain with a letter from myself in which I communicated to the head chaplain that I had authorized Monsignor the Apostolic Vicar to visit the chapel'.[48] This desire to assert the Sardinian Crown's authority over the church, representing as it did an offshoot of the Crown's diplomatic mission, raised a series of complex legal issues. In proclaiming that the church

---

46 *Ibid, Copie de lettre de M. le comte de Perron à M. le marquis de Gorzegne en date du 6 novembre 1749.*

47 *Ibid*, fasc. 4, 2 June 1757, *Lettera dell'abate Palazzi economo generale de' benefici vacanti.*

48 ASTo, ME, Benefizi di qua da monti, mz. 17, Londra, Cappella Regia, fasc. n 2. 1721, 1 July, *Stato e regolamenti della capella cattolica di Sua Maestà.*

was subject to its ambassador in London (specifically defined as 'the chapel's main director'), the court in Turin potentially opened the way to claims that the church fell under the spiritual jurisdiction, not of the local regular clergy, but rather the official whose scope of authority included the court itself, that is to say the Grand Almoner,[49] thus ensuring that jurisdiction was retained by a Savoy subject. The question was far from trivial because, as other considerations expressed at mid-century clearly show, the chaplains' discipline was anything but iron-clad:

Although there is a Catholic bishop in London, the priests do not believe they have to look to him and, despite what the ambassador says, they try to avoid any form of dependence. This bishop has issued manca, il ... the direction of the chapels. These rules are posted in the sacristy but, seeing as the ambassador does not have the time (and perhaps does not understand well enough) to ensure that they are complied with, the priests often act in a manner that is wholly contrary to the regulations: allowing foreign priests to say Mass in the chapel without written permission from the bishop, for example, or celebrating marriages without requiring the couple to confess beforehand, and so on, too often operating in a manner that runs counter to ritual.[50]

The Turin Court's ambitious and challenging plan to force the clergy incardinated to the Sardinian church to lead a communitarian life was halted, however, by the misfortune that struck the church on 30 November 1759: the entire building was destroyed by a serious fire, perhaps caused by the carelessness of the domestic workers in the adjacent ambassador's residence. The Chapel remained closed for about four years – indeed, it was not until 31 July 1764 that the Savoy ambassador, Count Antonio Ferrero della Marmora, was able to notify Turin that the building work had been completed.[51] The reconstruction was supervised directly by the court in Turin, with input from the Propaganda Fide in Rome and the Pope himself. The Pope specifically expressed his desire that the church be rebuilt in a location 'as close as possible to that one while being equally convenient for Catholics'. In part due to this interest expressed by Rome, the Savoy authorities drew on the expertise of Giovan Battista Borra, an architect who was familiar with British architectural developments,[52] in an effort to ensure that the new church would be 'airy and high-ceilinged', given that 'in the previous

---

[49] Merlotti 2012: 1025–6.
[50] ASTo, ME, Benefizi di qua da monti, mz 17. 1, Londra, Cappella Regia, *1755 in 1787, Memoire touchant la chapelle du roi à Londres.*
[51] *Ibid, Stati delle spese annue che li ministri di Sua Maestà in Londra hanno di tempo in tempo fatto per la cappella regia in Londra,* letter from Count della Marmora 31 July 1764.
[52] Zoller 1996b.

Figure 12.3 Andrea Boucheron, Pair of Cruets, glass, silver-mounted, c. 1759, property of the Church of St. Anselm and St. Cecilia, Kingsway (on loan to the Victoria and Albert Museum, London), © Victoria and Albert Museum.

one, the great crowds of people frequently caused episodes of fainting'.[53] In fact, the chaplains themselves had brought up this problem of overcrowding, claiming that allowing 'all kinds of people, without distinction' to enter had in turn caused attendees possessing 'any rank or social status whatsoever and those of a delicate temperament' to desert the Chapel, which had come to host more and more indecencies of various kinds and even some instances of theft.[54]

The Savoy diplomatic corps was undoubtedly concerned about these issues since English public opinion began to gradually turn against the church and against manifestations of Catholic worship generally towards the end of George II's reign. In 1755 the Sardinian ambassador reminded the chaplains of the need to make sure that the marriages they officiated took place exclusively in the church. He also forbade them to celebrate

[53]   The *Osservazioni sopra il disegno della capella da farsi in Londra*, Turin, 1 July 1762 are signed by Giovanni Battista Borra (ASTo, ME, Benefizi di qua da monti, mz 17. 1, Londra, Cappella Regia, *1755 in 1787*).

[54]   ASTo, ME, Benefizi di qua da monti, mz 17. 1, Londra, Cappella Regia, *1755 in 1787*. The letter from the chaplains dates to the 1870s.

Figure 12.4 Andrea Boucheron, Incense boat, silver, c. 1760–2, property of the Church of St. Anselm and St. Cecilia, Kingsway (on loan to the Victoria and Albert Museum, London), © Victoria and Albert Museum.

Midnight Mass on Christmas Eve ('because the Protestant population will flock to you and it could cause unrest and scandal'), and instructed them to perform the Good Friday rites strictly within the church itself and with the utmost discretion.[55]

When George III took the throne, the situation took a more critical turn. While as early as 1767 the chaplains had been on guard against the dangers of 'an English populace that is already dangerous in and of itself, and even more so for being a sworn enemy of our faith', in June 1780, the church, with its rich furnishings and sacred implements (Figs 12.3 and 12.4)[56] became a favourite target of anti-Catholic violence as part of the Gordon riots (revolts against the Catholic Relief Act passed two years before). Like other sites of Catholic worship, the Sardinian Chapel was attacked and severely damaged. On the night of 2 June 1780,

the Sardinian ambassador offered 500 guineas to the rabble, to save a painting of our Saviour from the flames, and 1000 guineas not to destroy an exceeding fine

[55] *Ibid*, fasc. 9, 1755, *Regole proposte ad osservarsi dai cappellani di Sua Maestà*.
[56] See: Oman 1966; Rothwell in this volume.

organ: the gentry told him, they would burn him self if they could get at him, and destroyed the picture and organ directly.[57]

The British court took a strong stand against the episode and, describing the events as a disgrace for the whole nation, hastened to write to Turin of the disgust that George III felt on seeing 'his best and dearest allies' struck in such a way; the court added that the Savoy ministry was 'universally esteemed and respected in this country' and enjoyed the regard of the king, who had shown himself determined to take charge of repairing the damage to the church and locating and punishing the parties responsible.[58]

Once it was rebuilt, the Sardinian Chapel went on to operate in the service of the embassy of Sardinia until the end of the eighteenth century. The Chapel was closed in 1798, the year the French occupied Turin, and its premises offered for sale; in response, a call for donations was launched and promoted by the Apostolic Vicar of London, Bishop John Douglass, and supported by the Savoy court, which had taken refuge in Cagliari. With the proceeds of this donation drive, officials were able to reopen the church on 13 August 1799.[59] Since that time, although the 'Royal Sardinian Chapel' maintained its (more and more tenuous) ties with the diplomatic mission of Sardinia until the eve of Italian unification,[60] it took pains to emphasize its identity as a city parish, a shift formalized by the church taking the new name of St Anselm and St Cecilia in 1861.[61] These hagiographic references were not accidental: while the name St Cecilia emphasized the leading role the church came to occupy in London's musical scene, eleventh-century St Anselm, who was born in Aosta and died in Canterbury (having become Archbishop of the city in 1095), symbolically expressed the long-standing nature of the ties between England and the House of Savoy that proved so essential to achieving the unification of the Italian peninsula under the Savoy monarchy.

In light of this, it is not irrelevant to note that the first Protestant church in Turin, built with the approval of the government of Piedmont and under the auspices of the British Crown, also opened its doors in that period.[62] In London as in Turin, diplomatic missions with their places of worship

[57] Carey 2012: 148.
[58] ASTo, ME, Benefizi di qua da monti, mz 17. 1, Londra, Cappella Regia, 1755 in 1787, fasc. 11, *Extrait d'une dépache de Lord Hillsborough en date du 13 juin 1780 à Lord Mountstuart ambassadeur à Turin*.
[59] Evinson 1998: 86.
[60] Gilman 2013: 446.
[61] Farrell 1967; The Church 2009.
[62] Cozzo *et al.* 2005.

internal to the embassy, but open to the public, had long functioned to guarantee the exercise of religious freedom, and governments began to count on that right as a privileged terrain of political negotiation. Scholars have come to agree that religious elements played a key role in inducing Piedmont to seek support from Britain as part of the project of Italian unification, and in convincing the British to grant it. In light of this, it seems quite relevant to note that one factor that contributed to cultivating this awareness (both religious and political) was the need to manage the religious presence of 'friendly' countries, presences such as that located for a century and a half in the *Capella Regia Sardiniae Londini*, right at the heart of British power.

PART IV

Turin and Britain: Architectural Crossroads

13 | Architects and Kings in Grand Tour Europe

TOMMASO MANFREDI

At the beginning of the eighteenth century, in the majority of European countries, the post of royal architect was conferred by rulers based upon subjective artistic and professional criteria, without making exceptions for specializations or for nationality. In France and Britain, however, the *premiere architecte du roi* and the *Surveyor of the King's Works* were chosen within ingrained bureaucracies that were part of their respective political systems, essentially inaccessible to foreigners, including the Italian architects and workforce that fuelled a centuries-old migration to the rest of Europe. And it is from the point of view of two famous and cosmopolitan Italian architects, Alessandro Galilei and Filippo Juvarra, that this chapter opens a perspective onto the role of court architect in the Europe of the Grand Tour.

King's Architects in France and Britain

In the nation states of Europe, even by the end of the seventeenth century, France best exemplified the most well-defined model of the royal architect, understood as a single figure who was responsible for running and designing the properties of the crown. The *Premier architecte du Roi*, in the person of Jules Hardouin-Mansart (Fig. 13.1), employed in this role for 27 years, from 1681 until the year of his death, 1708, was the quintessential expression of this system of pyramidal and bureaucratic power consolidated by Jean-Baptiste Colbert at the time of Louis XIV.[1]

Hardouin-Mansart was an architect with a specialized background who directed a bureaucracy that was strongly integrated with the French corporate and didactic system represented by the *Académie Royale d'Architecture* that had been placed under the direction of the *premier architecte* by Colbert from the time of its founding in

---

[1] For Hardouin Mansart, see: Jestaz 2008; Gady 2010b. On the role of *premier architecte*, see: Mignot 2010; Ringot and Sarmant 2010. For a general overview of the situation of the professional architect in Paris in the eighteenth century, see: Gallet 1995: 5–20 (and *sub vocem* for the individual architects).

Figure 13.1 After Joseph Vivien, *Jules Hardouin-Mansart*, engraving by Gerard Edelinck, before 1707, Private collection.

1671.[2] He was the head of the *Bureau des dessins*, that was, in turn, divided into many departments corresponding to the various royal properties, each run by an architect of the Bureau. The *Académie d'architecture* consisted of first- and second-class architects, all royally appointed, to whom the title of *architecte du roi* was exclusively applied. All of this bureaucracy was under the control of the *directeur de Bâtiments royales*, a role that Hardouin-Mansart held from 1699 until his death, exercising a virtually absolute power over the entire architectural system of the state, in a role that prudently, after his demise, was never again assigned to an architect.

Every *architecte du roi* enjoyed a reflection of the authority of the *premier architecte*. And when one among them, Jean-Baptiste Alexandre Le Blond,

---

2 For the organization of public architects, see *Procès-verbaux* 1911–26, and specifically the introduction to the first volume (pp. VII–LXIII).

accepted an invitation from Peter the Great to go to St Petersburg in 1716, he was immediately granted the unprecedented title of 'general architect', positioning him above all of the other architects active in the Tzar's service.[3] The idealistic program for the urbanization of Vasilyevsky Island drawn up by Le Blond in St Petersburg, was a perfect example of the rigidity with which royal French architects tended to impose their classicizing aesthetic concepts, supported by the academic dialectic, everywhere. But this attitude was not always looked upon favourably by foreign rulers, many of whom preferred the Roman school type of architect embodied by Nicola Michetti, an architect less cultured than an academically trained *architecte du roi*, but no less gifted from the point of view of design in the broader sense of design as a creative instrument, and certainly more inclined to stylistic and cultural compromises.[4]

Compared to the French top-down and bureaucratic system, the British system reflected a character more diffuse, pragmatic and complementary to the organs of politics, corresponding to less formalized aesthetic concepts. The Surveyor of the King's Works, in the person of Christopher Wren (Fig. 13.2), in charge for 49 years from 1669 until 1718, who served under six sovereigns, acted in coordination with the Comptroller of the King's Works.[5] While in charge of the most important public office for building materials, the Office of His Majesty's Works, the Surveyor was not formally first architect to the King and need not necessarily have been an actual architect. Wren, a scientist by training, evolved into an architect in the long years during which he ran the office, dealing with huge companies involved in the reconstruction of London after the Great Fire of 1666.[6] In turn, the Office, with Wren at its helm, partially took on, in an empirical way, training functions, as a way of compensating for the lack of a British royal academy such as that which would be founded much later in 1768.

Until that time, an educational system, like that in France through the *Académie Royale d'Architecture* that determined the codification of a

---

[3] Medvedkova 2007.

[4] Michetti, one of Carlo Fontana's brightest students and collaborators, was chosen in 1718 by Peter the Great's agent in Rome, Kolagrivov, to work alongside Le Blond in St Petersburg (Pinto 1992; Androsov 2011). Michetti remained in Russia for just five years – the minimum stay for such a project – but he left behind his collaborator, Gaetano Chiaveri, who acted as Russian Imperial Architect until 1729. Thereafter, Chiaveri transferred to the service of Augustus II of Poland (Caraffa 2006). For the larger European context, see: Pinto 2000. On Le Blond specifically, see: Medvedkova 2007; and in general: *Les Français à Saint-Pétersbourg* 2003.

[5] On the importance of the Office of His Majesty's Works for the history of the profession of the architect in Britain, see: Colvin 1995: 32–4.

[6] For Wren, see in the first instance: Downes 1982; Geraghty 2007.

Figure 13.2 After Godfrey Kneller, *Christopher Wren*, engraving by John Smith, 1713, © National Portrait Gallery, London.

national style of royal emanation, but that also imposed regulations and requirements of all types, from the Ionic capitol to fire prevention systems, considered equally useful both for the design of large royal complexes as well as for their operation and maintenance, did not exist.

In Britain, in stark contrast to the well-defined guild of master builders and building contractors, the figure of the architect was quite changeable, even at the highest levels of the profession. Wren had a background in medicine and astronomy, while John Vanbrugh, who held the office of Comptroller of the King's Works from 1702 until 1726, had a background in the military and in the dramatic arts, and tended to represent himself as an erudite gentleman rather than as a professional architect.

If Wren could only boast of a bookish knowledge of architecture before receiving the commission to rebuild St Paul's Cathedral or plan the city of London, it was obvious that, in the opinion of the British rulers, his personal qualities outweighed any lack of professional specialization. In the period between the seventeenth and eighteenth centuries among holders of public office, only Nicholas Hawksmoor was an architect by training, fully capable of managing every phase of the creative and executive process, employing styles of various chronological and geographic derivation with extreme self-confidence.[7] It is significant that after his 1718 dismissal from the position of Secretary to the Board of Works in favour of the gentleman and dilettante architect William Benson, Vanburgh regretfully questioned what Colbert could have done in France with such a man as Hawksmoor.[8]

In a context in which a noble architectural dilettante could have prevailed over a professional such as Hawksmoor in a primarily technical capacity, the British model of royal architect was not yet exportable to the rest of Europe. In contrast, the authoritarian and specialized model of 'first architect' to the French king was an ideal model for all other absolute sovereigns. However, the effective spread of such a model was never advanced because the training of the *architecte du roi* was professionally and linguistically too closely tied to the French system to be adapted to local conditions elsewhere. More than French architects themselves travelling around the courts of Europe, it was their projects that were sent from Paris to the various courts. Hardouin-Mansart's pupil and successor, Robert De Cotte, sent many architectural projects abroad, on occasion securing the success of his work by also transferring architects from his *bureau*, to follow up these projects in situ.[9]

In France, as in Britain, the self-referential political management of the building system was a direct consequence of self-sufficiency in the basic production system, completely independent of foreign contributions including those of the Italians. Unlike the plasterers and decorators, who in general still enjoyed their technical supremacy, the Italian master masons had little success in these countries, clashing with corporate systems that were consolidated and quite impenetrable and that even targeted Italian architects. A lapidary notice composed by Francesco Maria Gaburri testifies to this situation, describing the experience in France of the Florentine architect Ferdinando Ruggieri: 'He saw Paris, where however he did not prosper.'[10] Similarly, the thoroughly documented and pitiful experiences in

---

[7] For Hawksmoor, see: Downes 1959; Vaughan 2002.

[8] 'Poor Hawksmoor […] What a Barbarous Age have his fine, ingenious parts fallen into. What wou'd Monsr: Colbert in France have given for such a man?' (Colvin 1995: 475).

[9] On De Cotte in relation to the organization of the *Bureau des dessins*, see: Neuman 1994; Fossier 1997: 25–94; for the architectural projects that De Cotte sent via correspondence, see: Gady 2010a.

[10] 'Vide Parigi, con fortuna, non troppo prospera': F.M.N. Gabburri, *Vite di Pittori*, 1676–1742, manuscript, Biblioteca Nazionale Centrale di Firenze, Fondo Palatino E.B.9.5, t. II, fol. 227r.

Britain of Ruggieri's fellow countryman, Alessandro Galilei, and that of the Venetian Giacomo Leoni, can be recounted.[11]

Leoni came to Britain in 1713 from the Palatine court in Dusseldorf, boastful of his title of architect to the Elector Johann Wilhelm (1690–1716).[12] While he cultivated a reputation as a champion of Renaissance culture with his revised edition of the *Quattro Libri* by Andrea Palladio (1715–20), and later by editing the English version of Leon Battista Alberti's *De Re Aedificatoria* (1726–30), he never managed to achieve professional success, only gravitating to the fringes of noble patronage, while dying in abject poverty.

Arriving in London in 1714 from Florence, having studied at the school of Giovanni Battista Foggini, Galilei was a court architect by formation and vocation. He participated in the refined collective of the 'New Junta for Architecture' sharing purist neo-Greek and neo-Renaissance ideals with his mentor John Molesworth, together with Molesworth's father Robert, who stimulated his unlimited ambitions with no less a project than that of a new royal palace. But ultimately, Galilei succumbed before the ostracism shown by the British professional world to foreigners, the result of a much broader cultural prejudice of British patrons, clearly reflected in a letter Galilei wrote to his brother Filippo, in Florence, 19 February 1716:

here the English do not do as we do in Italy where, if a foreigner with no talent comes on the scene, they all run to him and leave behind the patriots who have twenty times the ability he has, here it's the opposite because they want to employ their countrymen even if they are jackasses.[13]

On 10 August 1719, while Galilei was leaving London to return home to Florence to take up a post as architect to Grand Duke Cosimo III de' Medici after failing in his bid to succeed as an architect in Britain, Filippo Juvarra (Fig. 13.3), architect to Victor Amadeus II in Turin, was just arriving in that city.[14] The end of a dream for Galilei of creating a classical, Mediterranean Renaisssance on British soil overlapped with Juvarra's burning desire to tap directly into an architectural culture known only indirectly in Italy. Nevertheless, Juvarra had managed to forge close ties to the world of British

---

[11] For Galilei's and Leoni's British contacts and projects, see: Toesca 1952; Kieven 1973; Kieven 1975; Hewlings 1985; Arciszewska 2005; Kieven 2008a; Woodhouse 2008; Giusto 2010: 29–86.

[12] This title belonged to Leoni's teacher and fellow citizen Matteo Alberti (c. 1646–1735) (see note 11 above).

[13] 'Qui gli inglesi non fanno come si fa noi costà in Italia che se viene un forestiero che abbia una benché poca abilità tutti corrono da lui e si lasciano indietro i patriotti che hanno venti volte più abilità di quello, qui è tutto il contrario p[er]ché vogliono impiegare i loro paesani con tutto che sieno grandissimi asini': Toesca 1952: 208; Giusto 2010: 76 n. 171.

[14] See: Manfredi 2012a: 49–50; Manfredi 2014: 229–30.

patrons. Specifically, at the urging of Victor Amadeus II, Juvarra had drawn up a project for Henry Grey, 1st Duke of Kent, between 1716 and 1717, that clashed with the difficult Baroque legacy of a noble class devoted to the sober expressions of monumentality that Galilei had tried unsuccessfully to interpret.[15] Notwithstanding Galilei's different artistic conception from Juvarra, the Sicilian architect still represented the most illustrious example of a royal architect in Italy. Indeed, the long and controversial relationship that prevailed between the two architects in Rome, London, Paris, Turin and Florence assumes the significance of an unprecedented debate about the implications of just such a role as court or royal architect, as well as the relationship between architecture and power in the most emblematic locations of the European Grand Tour.

Juvarra and Galilei: from London to Turin

Juvarra and Galilei first met in Rome at the beginning of 1714, when Juvarra was concluding his service as court architect to Cardinal Pietro Ottoboni, and when Galilei travelled to Rome to study ancient and modern monuments at the urging of John Molesworth in preparation for a possible career in Britain.[16] After fruitless attempts to enter into the service of various European sovereigns, finally in 1714, Juvarra was called as first architect to the strong-willed and enterprising regent, Victor Amadeus II.[17] It was in this capacity that Juvarra subsequently travelled to Lisbon and enjoyed a triumphant sojourn at the court of Giovanni V of Portugal, planning the patriarchal church and the royal palace.[18] Awarded the prestigious title of Knight of the Order of Christ by Giovanni V along with a pension of 1,000 crowns, as well as another 1,000 crowns for a trans-European journey, Juvarra was not simply a court virtuoso loaned from one king to another, but a sort of Grand Tourist, free also to visit London for several months and also to visit Paris, without constraints or obligations.

Juvarra arrived in London while King George I and much of his court were absent for their periodic sojourn in Hanover. However, on account of

[15] Manfredi 2011: 212–13; 2012a: 47–50.

[16] Manfredi 2012a: 42. On Juvarra's sojourn in London, see: Manfredi 2012a; 2012b; 2014: 230–5.

[17] For the failed attempts by Juvarra to attract the attention of Karl I, Landgrave of Hessen Kassel in 1707, of Frederick IV of Denmark and of Louis XIV in 1709, and of Joseph I of Hapsburg in 1711, and for the circumstances of his employment on the part of Victor Amadeus II, in 1714, see: Manfredi 2010.

[18] For Juvarra's trip to Portugal in the service of John V, see: Raggi 2014; Rossa 2014; Sansone 2014.

Figure 13.3 Francesco Trevisani, *Filippo Juvarra*, oil on canvas, Galleria dell'Accademia di San Luca, Rome.

Juvarra's friend James Gibbs, Richard Boyle, 3rd Earl of Burlington, and to other noble English visitors to Rome that Juvarra had frequented previously, he managed to briefly, but intensely familiarize himself with the architectural and artistic environment of London and its exponents. Among these personages were the elder Wren, Vanbrugh and Hawksmoor, who was the British architect closest to Juvarra in terms of sensibility, as well as in terms of poetic interpretation of the past. In the space of just a few days, Juvarra could have come into contact with the most significant protagonists of the British hierarchical architectural system more successfully than Galilei had managed to do over the course of five years.

Arriving in Paris, between August and September of 1719, in quick succession of one another on the way back to Italy, Galilei and Juvarra shared in an atmosphere of social rebirth fostered by the return of the court from Versailles to the capital city at the behest of Philippe the Duke of Orleans, who had been regent to the throne from the time of the death of Louis XIV until the crowning of the adolescent Louis XV (1715–23).[19] Galilei, following the instructions of his Florentine patrons, studied the monuments of Paris and Versailles as inherent to his role as the creator of an updating of the formal language of the Medici court. Juvarra, meanwhile, took the opportunity to explore fully and directly the origins of the modern concepts of architecture and of the role of court architect that had inspired him since his youth in Messina. Nor is it a coincidence that Juvarra's first encounter with the *premier archi-tecte du roi*, De Cotte, was emphasized in the biography written by his brother Francesco, and evidently based upon the architect's vivid memory of the event:

he was treated with great honor, and by the Ambassador of Portugal as ordered by the King and by the first architect who took him along with him to see the magnificent things of that city, and of Versailles, and he was asked by the architects of his country about their much-praised buildings, though they were dry and lacking grandeur, he gave a wonderful answer that, having been ordered by that great King, they did not know how to take the idea from the ancient emperors, in order to allude to their splendour.[20]

For Juvarra, the symbolism inherent in De Cotte's introduction to him of the 'magnificent things' of Paris and Versailles – and the cultural and professional respect this intimated – extended far beyond the normal etiquette that could have been shown him as Savoy court architect, subject to the sphere of influence of France. The bold statements of Juvarra that the projects executed for Louis XIV by great architects such as Le Vau, Perrault,

---

[19] Galilei remained in Paris for almost two weeks, from 26 August–8 September 1719; Juvarra arrived on 7 September, staying until the 24th of that month; see: Manfredi 2014: 235–44.

[20] 'Fu trattato con grande onore, e dall'ambasciadore di Portogallo secondo gli ordini di quel Re e dal primo Architetto di Luiggi XIV, che lo portò seco vedendo tutte le cose magnifiche di quella città, e di Versaglia, et interrogato dagl'architetti del suo paese su le lor fabbriche le lodò molto, ma per esser secche, e senza grandiosità gli diede una bella risposta, che essendogli state ordinate le fabbriche da quel gran Re non avevano saputo prendere un idea dell'Imperatori antichi, per alludere alla grandiosità': Vita 1981 [1736]: 285–6.

Hardouin-Mansart and De Cotte himself were not worthy of such a patron since they were 'dry' and lacking any idea that alluded to the 'grandeur' of the 'ancient emperors' is testament to this.

An architectural gem of the grandeur appropriate to the Sun King in its emulation of the ancient Roman emperors is Juvarra's noted project for a 'royal tomb' bearing the emblematic lilies of France, one of the architect's most enigmatic architectural creations, celebrated by engravings which were published in 1739, three years after the death of the architect at the behest of his brother, Francesco, in Rome (Figs 13.4–13.6).[21] Despite the abstract quality of the project – further accentuated by the absence of any topographic references at all – this project is datable to the period of Juvarra's trip to Paris in 1719, when the demolition of the unfinished Valois chapel, annexed to the Abbey of Saint Denis, and location of the tombs of French sovereigns, had given new impetus to the idea of a Bourbon mausoleum, already designed by Jules Mansart and Gian Lorenzo Bernini in 1665.[22] The powerful symbolism of the project is concentrated in the main chapel, conceived of as a combination, respectively in plan and elevation, of two famous Roman imperial monuments: the Christian mausoleum of Constantina (Santa Costanza), and the Pantheon, a temple converted to Christian use, whose symbolically stepped dome, surmounted by a *tholos*, is emblematically connected to the two large pyramid obelisks that characterize the main facade.

To De Cotte, to the architects of his office, and to any other cultured connoisseur it must have been clear that Juvarra had understood the most effective manner to represent the glory of the King of France, uniting the most courtly and significant historical references in a project based as much on the geometrical canons of the Italian sixteenth century, as on the rigid spatial verticalism of French seventeenth-century architecture. Overall, it respected the grandiose and poetic vision of the antique that he had already begun to cultivate in the imaginative drawings he executed at the beginning of his stay in Rome, replete with the courtly references that had gained him the favour of Victor Amadeus II and Louis XIV, who was no less eager to align the architecture of his realm with the canons of imperial magnificence.

---

[21] For a detailed analysis of Juvarra's original drawings, now in the Staatliche Museum zu Berlin, Kunstbibliothek, Hdz 1118–20), also in reference to the previous bibliography, see: Manfredi 2014: 241–4.

[22] The author (Manfredi 2014: 241–4) accepts the hypothesis of collocating the project for the mausoleum during Juvarra's sojourn in Paris, recently put forward by Erika Nagiski (Nagiski 2009: 43–6), although the dating of 1718 is incorrect – as we now know the trip took place in 1719 – therefore within the immediate circumstances surrounding the debate over the Valois chapel.

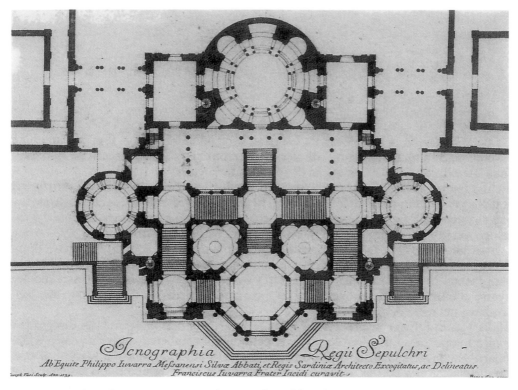

Icnographia *Regii Sepulchri*

Ab Equite Philippo Iuvarra Messanensi Silvæ Abbati, et Regis Sardiniæ Architecto Excogitatus, ac Delineatus.
Franciscus Iuvarra Frater Incidi curavit.

Figure 13.4 After Filippo Juvarra, *Project for a Royal Sepulchre*, plan, engraving by Giuseppe Vasi, 1739, Private collection.

At the beginning of October in 1719, when their paths crossed in Turin on their return from France, Juvarra and Galilei had the opportunity to discuss royal architects' roles and projects. Galilei exploited his sojourn in the Savoy capital to visit Juvarra's building sites – among which was that of the Venaria Reale – as an addendum to the Parisian architectural reconnaissance mission he had carried out as a function of his impending job as grand-ducal architect in Florence.[23] But ultimately, Galilei's glorious expectations as architect went unfulfilled. The appointment to Cosimo III, beyond the prestigious title of 'Architect and Engineer to His Royal Highness' ('Architetto e Ingegnere di Sua Altezza Reale'), revealed itself to be as devoid of commissions as it was full of bitterness, fuelling hopes for a change of post expressed in his heartfelt letters to John Molesworth who had, in the interim, become British envoy to Turin (1720–5). Galilei and

---

[23] Galilei arrived in Turin on 21 September 1719, and remained there for about a month, as his first-born child was born there. He preceded Juvarra's return from France by approximately two weeks (Manfredi 2014: 244).

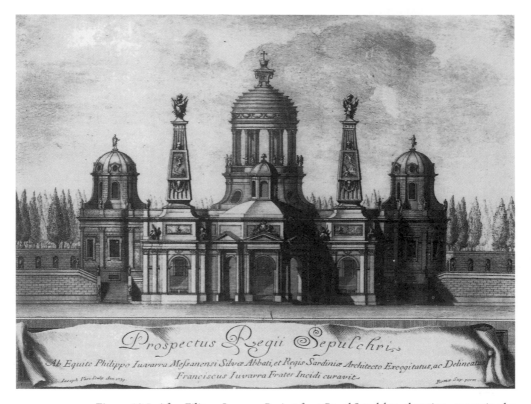

Figure 13.5 After Filippo Juvarra, *Project for a Royal Sepulchre*, elevation, engraving by Giuseppe Vasi, 1739, Private collection.

Juvarra probably met again during Juvarra's stay in Lucca between the end of 1723 and the beginning of 1724,[24] and almost certainly in the early days of April 1725, when Juvarra passed through Florence returning to Turin from Rome to evaluate the work of a Florentine painter for a commission at Rivoli, with Molesworth and Galilei acting as intermediaries.[25] A letter from Molesworth to Galilei dated 2 May 1725 confirms this contact, while alluding to a possible major turning point in Juvarra and Galilei's respective careers as court architects:

[24] On 22 December 1723 Molesworth wrote to Galilei about Juvarra's imminent departure for Lucca: Archivio di Stato di Firenze (ASF), Carte Galilei, fol. 125r, Turin, December 22 1723 N.S., Molesworth to Galilei.

[25] On 3 January 1725, Molesworth wrote to Galilei about Juvarra's impending arrival in Florence, as Juvarra was returning from Rome (*ibid.*, fol. 163v). Regarding the question of a possible Savoy royal commission to a Florentine painter for Rivoli, see Karin Wolfe in this volume, Chapter 9. For the circumstances of Juvarra's trip to Venice, see: Manfredi 2014: 222, 249 note 22.

Ab Equite Philippo Iuvarra Messanensi Silvæ Abbati, et Regis Sardiniæ Architecto Excogitatus, ac Delineatus
Franciscus Iuvarra Frater Incidi curavit

Figure 13.6 After Filippo Juvarra, *Project for a Royal Sepulchre*, section, engraving by Giuseppe Vasi, 1739, Private collection.

I am sorry to hear you have so many just reasons of Complaint, and entirely agree with you that the Climate you now live in is absolutely to be chang'd. As to this place, I do no see it will be praticable to procure you the Post Don Philippo fill's. I find he is very uncertain of Employment at Rome, and probably will not quit but upon very advantageous & sure terms. I hope the other project of seeing England again is much more likely to succeed, and I have Allready begun to take measures for it, but it will require some time to bring them to bear.[26]

Galilei had been informed by Juvarra personally about the possibility that he might move permanently to Rome to take up a role as architect to the *Fabbrica di San Pietro*, a role that had just been awarded to him, at which point Galilei hoped to substitute Juvarra as architect to the House of Savoy, rather than considering a return to England as requested by

[26] ASF, Carte Galilei, fols 174r–v, Turin, May the 2d 1725 N.S. In this letter Molesworth thanks Galilei for the copies of engravings of a catafalque designed by the Florentine in honour of Cosimo III, that he had received from Juvarra: 'Don Philippo has brought me the prints of your Catafalco which are very pretty and well engraven; I give you many thanks, but you are too liberal of them in sending so many' (174r).

Molesworth.[27] But the gratification of the important Vatican office, previously held by Bernini and by Carlo Fontana, was not enough to make
Juvarra abandon his secure post for an uncertain one and return sooner
to Rome, where, according to his friend Scipione Maffei 'he made diverse
acquisitions, in preparation for his old age there'.[28] Galilei, finally, did not
have the financial or patronage prospects to leave his Medici appointment
and to face the unknowns of a second trip to England, especially after
Molesworth's death in February of 1726.

Following Molesworth's death, the only documented contact between
Juvarra and Galilei is the exchange of recommendations in March 1726 in a
friendly correspondence for the English nobleman Simon Degge who was
visiting Turin, and for the painter and architect Carl Hårleman on his way
through Florence.[29] When the architects met again, in February 1732, it
was in the Rome of Clement XII Corsini, and their relationship would be
marred again by rivalry in the shadow of political conflict between the Holy
See and the Kingdom of Savoy.

---

[27] The hypothesis that Juvarra returned to Rome on another occasion is documented by a
letter from the French painter, Nicolas Vleughels, director of the French Academy in Rome
(Manfredi 2013: 109).

[28] 'Andava facendo diversi acquisti, con fine di terminarvi in vecchiezza i suoi giorni': Maffei
1738: 199.

[29] This and other interesting facts are contained in a lettter written by Degge to Galilei on
10 March 1726: Archivio di Stato di Firenze (ASF), Carte Galilei, b. 21, ins. 1, fols 168r–v,
Milan March 10th 1725 [ma 1726]: 'I went to visit Don Filippo in your name, who has been
extremely civil to me upon your account. It was such cold weather, I could not go to see his
new church, nor any thing else out of Turin, he has given me the two prints of the Palace
and the Piazza. He had no others that were done by him; I found at a printshop, some french
Prints, that were designed by him, and ingraved at Paris. They are mighty bad ones, but
having bought two sets, where I have an opportunity, I shall send one to Florence. He is now
making a design of some new scenes, by the Kings Order, he has succeeded very well in those
at Rome, as he himself says, there is to be something not common in these. He says he has
recommended a Swedish Gentleman to you, who draws very finely, and is now upon the road
to Florence. I am now taking the benefit of the four days of reprieve of poor Carnival, the
opera is a very good one, but does not come up to that of Turin. […] I have light on out very
few prints, in my journey: but I have had the fortune to light on a Vignola at Parma, for 14
pauls. I have shown to Don Filippo who says it is vero vero, it is very well preserved, and by
the by I believe it came out of the D. of Parma's Library without asking leave.' In a previous
publication (Manfredi 2013: 109) I followed the erroneous attribution and date of this letter,
as published by Hyde Minor (2010: 248). The engravings (printed in Rome, 1721) given by
Juvarra to Degge were for the projects for the Palazzo Madama and for the twin churches of
Piazza San Carlo. The Swedish gentleman recommended to Galilei can now be identified as
Carl Hårleman, travelling from Turin to Florence, as part of a study tour from Paris to Rome,
following his father's intentions for Carl's future career as court architect (Manfredi 2013: 109).
The printed engravings mentioned by Degge regard the ephemeral decorations which Juvarra
planned in Turin in 1722 (Manfredi 2014: 236, 250, n. 36).

Galilei had moved to Rome a year before in 1731 and was serving as Papal Architect thanks to the mediation of the pope's nephew, Cardinal Neri Corsini, and thanks also to the consent of the Grand Duke Gian Gastone de' Medici. Juvarra returned seven years after his previous sojourn with a six-month permit given to him by Charles Emmanuel III with a view to under-taking the project of the new sacristy at the Vatican based upon his lofty old designs.[30] But such a possibility was soon deemed unlikely in the face of the clear preference on the part of both the Pope and his cardinal nephew for the more modest and less expensive design by Galilei. Juvarra managed to stymy his rival's project, which he referred to as 'one of the greatest blunders in architecture', with the result that the project was shelved.[31] However, he could do nothing to prevent the triumph of Galilei in the competition for the design of the facade of San Giovanni in Laterano, for which he indignantly refused to be a judge, predicting an outcome favourable to the 'Florentine stars'.

Juvarra attributed the failure of his mission to Rome both to the prevailing situation in the papal court, 'composed of people without civilization, propriety, or respect', and to prevailing adverse attitudes towards the 'Savoyards'; 'we must conclude that it is original sin and the deep-seated resentment that nourish hatred toward us.'[32] He had, by now, attributed to his role as royal architect a diplomatic meaning that went far beyond the role of artistic ambassador that had brought him to the court of Lisbon, raising him to a very prominent position on the European professional stage. And we must believe that it is in this spirit, at the beginning of 1735, that he undertook his last mission to the court of Madrid, to build a new royal palace for the Bourbon King Philip V, symbolically ending his own professional and life trajectory a year later, in the presence of the sovereign he had celebrated spectacularly in Messina when he came to the throne in 1701 at the beginning of his reign.[33]

[30] For Juvarra's Roman sojourn from 15 February to 31 August 1732, see: Manfredi 2001.
[31] Manfredi 2001: 190.
[32] Manfredi 2001: 190.
[33] For Juvarra's Madrid sojourn in the service of Philip V, see: Sancho 2014 (with previous bibliography).

14 | A Homage from Turin: Filippo Juvarra's Sketches for Lord Burlington

CRISTINA RUGGERO

In August 1944, Rudolf Wittkower uncovered an exceptionally fine album of sketches in the 10th Duke of Devonshire's collection at Chatsworth.[1] Drawn and coloured by Filippo Juvarra (1678–1736), court architect to the Savoy family in Turin, the sketches were intended for Richard Boyle, 3rd Earl of Burlington (1694–1753). Wittkower wrote on the inner fold of the cover of the album:

I find that the book of drawings given by Juvara to Lord Burlington has slipped the attention of scholars … The book was not even known in Juvara's own days. It is not mentioned in the Catalogo … Sacchetti. Sacchetti lists, however, under the year 1716: 'Disegno di più idee fatti per diversi Milordi Inglesi'. This may possibly be connected with the Chatsworth drawings, as no other work by Juvara for 'Milordi Inglesi' is known. Lord Burlington may have met Juvara in Rome in October and November 1714, and again during the winter of 1720/21, when Juvara stayed in London for about a month.[2]

Wittkower twice published aspects of the discovery of the album: in 1949 and in 1975, comprising reproductions of all the sketches.[3] In the nearly 70 years since then, Wittkower's findings have led to the correction of some errors of dating regarding contact between Juvarra and Lord Burlington; furthermore, recent research and studies have helped to define scholarly questions regarding the relations between Juvarra and Lord Burlington in Britain and in Italy, as well as leading to the identification of architectural commissions to Juvarra from other English aristocrats.[4]

---

[1] Edward William Spencer Cavendish (1895–1950): Album 30, Chatsworth, Devonshire Collection. For the research for this paper, I would like to thank Charles Noble (Curator, Collections Documentation, The Devonshire Collection, Chatsworth), Diane Naylor (Photo Librarian, The Devonshire Collection, Chatsworth), Hugo Chapman (Keeper of Prints and Drawings and Curator of Italian and French drawing pre-1800, The British Museum, London), Richard Hewlings (Senior Historian at English Heritage), Ricky Pound (Researcher and Guide at 'Pallas Tours and Lectures') and Roy Graf (Conservator of Fine Drawings) for the help and informative discussions.

[2] Wittkower signed his inscription: 'Note by Dr. Rudolf Wittkower, Aug. 1944.'

[3] Wittkower 1949; 1975.

[4] See: Friedmann 1988; Manfredi 2011; Manfredi 2012a; Manfredi 2012b; Manfredi 2014; and the essay by the same author in this publication.

Figure 14.1 Filippo Juvarra, *Architectural Capriccio*, 1729, Album 30, Frontispiece, Chatsworth, reproduced by permission of Chatsworth Settlement Trustees.

The album, which contains 30 folios of sketches featuring architectural fantasies, is dated '1729' and signed 'Cav. Juvarra'.[5] The title page bears the dedication: '*PROSPETIVE DISEGNATE DALL CAVAL DON FILIPPO YUVARRA E DEDICATE All'Eccellenza di Riccardo Conte di Burlington MDCCXXX*' (Fig. 14.1).[6] The sketches are set into the album horizontally on support folios (the sketches are not glued to the supports), which are bound to the inner spine: the spine and cover are of Morocco leather, decorated on the outside with gilding.[7]

Analysing the iconography and the technical data of the individual sketches, Wittkower pointed out that of the 30 folios the last ten were primarily sketches of ruins and archaeological sites. He also recorded the

---

[5] The album measures 12.18 x 17.10 inches; the support folio 12.6 x 17.2 inches; the folio with the sketch 8.15 x 13.6 inches.

[6] *Perspectives drawn by the Knight don Filippo Juvarra and Dedicated to his Excellency Richard, Lord of Burlington MDCCXXX.*

[7] All three unbound borders of the folios are gilt. Roy Graf and Charles Noble believe that the inlaying of the drawings on the paper supports and the gilt borders were fashioned in Britain by a single individual, concluding that Juvarra must have gifted the sketches as loose sheets.

differences in technique: sepia (folio 1 to 20) and bistre (title page and folios 21 to 30). Before entering into a detailed discussion of the separate subjects represented in the sketches, Wittkower advanced his thoughts on the album as a whole, writing: 'The Chatsworth volume, however, has nothing very new to offer in the way of either invention or style.'[8] This judgement surely influenced Wittkower's contemporaries negatively, as thereafter architectural historians took no interest in the album. Lastly, Wittkower also put forward an explanation for Juvarra's gift of the album to Burlington:

If it were not for the coincidence in the dates of Burlington's publication of Palladio's *thermae* and of Juvarra's dedication, one might simply think that the latter was a belated thank-you from Juvarra for the hospitality he had enjoyed at Burlington House. Dedications are a useful barometer of a man's fame. In the years preceding 1730 and up to 1740, not a year passed without Burlington receiving some flattering dedication or other … Burlington saw in Juvarra's drawings exactly what the latter wanted him to see: a modern realization of ancient grandeur … They were certainly both moved by the art of the ancients.[9]

However, as is intended to be demonstrated in this chapter, Wittkower's hypothesis regarding the motivations of Juvarra's gift of the album may be incorrect.

The sketches in Juvarra's album are imbued with a heightened sensibility for ancient and contemporary Roman art and culture, represented by imposing buildings and renowned sculptures. Juvarra's passion as a draftsman was for livening up architectural and landscape scenes with figures carrying out various activities, mostly related to construction. Majestic urban landscapes characterize the first two-thirds of the album, including palaces, monumental steps, breathtaking bridges, shorelines and bodies of water. The scenes are depicted from extravagant viewpoints, with perspectives reminiscent of pseudo-classical theatre sets.

Born and brought up in Messina, Sicily, Juvarra had drawn harbours and quays countless times before, particularly for theatrical scenery.[10] Arriving in Rome in 1704 as a young architect, Juvarra explored a city landscape whose development was in part shaped by the course of the Tiber, beginning with the ancient and legendary Isola Tiberina (the Tiber Island, known as the 'rocky ship'), continuing with the contemporary monumental port of the *Ripetta*, under construction in that year by Alessandro Specchi

[8] Wittkower 1975: 205.
[9] Wittkower 1975: 207, 210.
[10] Viale Ferrero 1970.

(1688–1729),[11] and also the harbours of the Vatican State on the shores of the Adriatic and the Lazio region.[12] In 1715, Victor Amadeus II, King of Sicily, commissioned Juvarra to redesign the harbour in Messina (a project that was never realized). In 1719, John V of Portugal commissioned Juvarra for 'un disegno in prospettiva con veduta del Porto, e parte della città di Lisbona, che si scuopre da quel sito',[13] as well as 'un disegno per il fanale che pensava fare per il Porto',[14] as documented in the biography written by the architect's brother, Francesco.[15] Moreover, the first half of the eighteenth century was characterized by a common European interest in maritime themes, due to the growing development of port construction – an interest which took hold even outside naval architectural projects and influenced contemporary painting and scenic and graphic design.[16] The design of harbours became a topical subject artistically and was selected on more than one occasion as a theme for the *Concorso Clementino* of the Accademia di San Luca in Rome in 1728, 1732 and 1738.[17]

The architectural fantasies that Juvarra designed, sited near the water, with majestic and representative buildings rising from the shoreline, suggest the presence of an imposing imaginary city, filled with magnificent palaces, religious edifices and antique ruins, that together create an architectural landscape where past and present, ancient and contemporary, commingle. Juvarra peopled the scenes with simply sketched figures who bring these otherwise 'ghost towns' to life. Folio 9 shows docked boats that transport goods and provisions that have been unloaded from larger ships and that are to be delivered to the entrance of the large building characterized by a jutting facade and by a monumental staircase.[18] The triumphal bridge and shipyard of folio 25 are both drawn with a wealth of details, the gondolas docked one by one between the intercolumniation of a building that rises alongside the water (Fig. 14.2).[19] The left-hand border of this sketch

[11] Marder 1980. Specchi succeeded in creating an unprecedented dialectic relationship between the urban centre of Rome, the Tiber and the contiguous suburbs.

[12] For example, the harbours of Ostia, Civitavecchia, Anzio, Terracina, the 'Claudio' or 'Traiano' harbour. See: Simoncini 1994 (and especially vol. IV, *Lo Stato pontificio*).

[13] 'A sketch in perspective with a view of the harbour, and part of the city of Lisbon, that you can see from that location.'

[14] 'A sketch of a lamp for the harbour.'

[15] Marabottini 1981: 283, 284.

[16] For example, see the many subjects depicting maritime themes in the paintings and drawings of Viviano and Niccolò Codazzi, Claude Lorraine and Pierre Puget.

[17] Garms 1969; Marconi *et al.* 1974; Cousins 1982.

[18] Wittkower 1975: 192, fig. 253.

[19] The triumphal bridge was another theme that fascinated Juvarra. On folio 23 (Wittkower 1975: 199, fig. 267) an architectural perspective stretches out on the folio, in front of a partly

Figure 14.2 Filippo Juvarra, *Architectural Capriccio*, 1729, Album 30, folio 25, Chatsworth, reproduced by permission of Chatsworth Settlement Trustees.

is demarcated by the edge of a building where rings tied with thick ropes, which were probably used to bar access to the harbour are delineated. On the upper level a hoist is visible, used to lift heavy weights, while on the right-hand side of the drawing the corner of a pedestal – perhaps a triumphal monument – sporting a relief of a maritime figure with a large commemorative statue is pictured.

In the same drawing a rostral column is featured in the foreground – a device used by the Romans to commemorate naval victories and their dominion of the seas, with typical motifs, including dolphins, a trident (a symbol of Neptune), anchors and the rostra of the enemy ship placed atop the column. The acronym of S.P.Q.R. (Senatus Populusque Romanus) identifies the setting as Roman, although the scene has Venetian connotations.[20]

mountainous landscape, and this is joined to the terrain on the left. The perspective is created by three arches and buttresses that descend into the water. By keeping to Marshall's suggestions (Marshall 2003), one could suggest that what we see is a triumphal bridge, inspired perhaps, by the *pons neronianus*.

[20] This drawing may show the influence of Juvarra's visit to Venice in February 1729, when the architect contacted and instructed the artists who later would be working at the *Peota*, the

But, in any case, Juvarra habitually included vessels about to dock in his sketches (fol. 7).[21]

Folio 7 displays a *monopteros* on the shore, a circular-shaped temple with no solid walls, so the statue of Neptune within was visible to disembarking travellers through the columns. Three main figures, characterized by long flowing vestments, ascend the steps, while the figures following genuflect below. The poses, clothes and solemn gait of the figures imply that they are of noble lineage. However, a sketch found in the Biblioteca Nazionale di Torino (Riserva 59.4) suggests otherwise: the drawing is an elaboration of a subject initially conceived for a specific piece of theatre, a sketch for the first scene of *Iphigenia in Tauris* (1713).[22] This is one of the many cases where iconographic and formal correspondences and analogies in Juvarra's work can be found in subjects originating from different genres, making it difficult to assign a drawing to a specific category.

Nonetheless, the three main categories of Juvarra drawings are the projects for royal commissions, the architectural sketches or fantasies and the scenic sketches.[23]

The drawing of folio 22 is laid out on two levels, starting with a cluster of ruins in the foreground, with architectural remains, trabeated cornices and vases (Fig. 14.3). A pedestal is placed at the centre of this architectural 'still life': a majestic statue representing the personification of a river, with an oar and a cornucopia, lying in a semi-supine position, sited on the back of a smirking sphinx, is the crowning element. The model for this statue is the *Recubantes* of the Capitoline Hill.[24] The pedestal is further decorated with an inscription with a relief of a crocodile, of which only the word 'NILVS' can be recognized. This heterogeneous composition is set against the backdrop of another, visionary landscape of ruined buildings, reminiscent of an amphitheatre with arched openings, an aqueduct, pyramids with busts perched on their pinnacles, sphinxes, a spiral-shaped building (a *mixtum* between the spire of Borromini's church of Sant'Ivo, a tower of Babel, a lighthouse and a 'spiral' Coliseum) and a triumphal bridge adorned with the spoils of victory. The scene is enclosed within an ideal garden, demarcated by a parapet. The garden is accessible via steps and a portal whose tympanum is adorned with a brazier. This whimsical garden is divided from

---

sumptuous vessel prepared for the Savoy king, which had been designed following models of Venetian *bucintori*. See: Griva 1995; Griseri 2004; De Blasi 2012; Ballaira *et al.* 2012.

21 Wittkower 1975: 191, fig. 251.
22 Biblioteca Nazionale di Torino, Ris. 59.4, fol. 85. See: Grant 2011: 227, fig. 16.1.
23 This argument was advanced by Scott Munshower 1995: 24; see: Hatfield 1981.
24 Haskell and Penny 1981: 258–9, 272–3, 310–11.

Figure 14.3 Filippo Juvarra, *Architectural Capriccio*, 1729, Album 30, folio 22, Chatsworth, reproduced by permission of Chatsworth Settlement Trustees.

the 'still life' of ruins by a stream, along which small sailing ships and barges float. The imaginative arrangement of this background resembles the mixed collection of ancient buildings illustrated a few years earlier by Fischer von Erlach in his *Entwurff einer Historischen Architektur* (1721), including such structures as Egyptian pyramids and the lighthouse tower erected by King Ptolemy at the harbour of Alexandria.[25]

The Chatsworth album sketches are primarily of a type known as a *capriccio* – drawings of curious historical and topographical references, for example, that of the monumental sculptural group of the *Dioscuri* in front of the Quirinal Palace (Fig. 14.4). In this drawing Juvarra depicts the layout of the square as commissioned by Pope Sixtus V (1589–91), who had ordered statues on pedestals with a fountain between them, a project realized by the architect, Domenico Fontana. Furthermore, the granite trough for watering animals is shown with half-a-dozen horses surrounding it, a picturesque allusion to the site of the Quirinal Hill, known as Monte Cavallo (the Hill of Horses). References to other well-known antique and

---

[25] Fischer von Erlach 1721: plates IV, XII–XVI and VIII.

Figure 14.4 Filippo Juvarra, *Architectural Capriccio*, 1729, Album 30, folio 6, reproduced by permission of Chatsworth Settlement Trustees.

Renaissance sculptures can be recognized in the album, including homages to the equestrian statue of *Marcus Aurelius* (folios 2, 5, 17, 20), to the *Medici lions* (fol. 15), to the statue of a *River God* (fol. 2), to the *Jason with the Bull* (fol. 28), to the *Lion attacking a Horse* (fol. 29) and to the *Capitoline Wolf* together with the *Horses of Saint Marks Basilica* (fol. 30).[26]

These drawings, testament to Juvarra's extravagant creativity, are realized as delightful scenographic landscapes, set on paper with quick, decisive strokes. Buildings, sculptures, architectural details and figures intermingle, imparting spontaneity and naturalism to the sketches, demonstrating Juvarra's pictorial ability to render imaginary spaces. Moreover, the graphic and artistic value of the drawings point to the character of the recipient of the gift of the album – Lord Burlington – and the cultural context of early eighteenth-century Britain. However, the aim of this chapter is not limited to retracing Juvarra's sources of inspiration or to pinpoint Juvarra's favourite theme. In over 30 years, Juvarra continued to combine architectural styles and designs from various eras, albeit with varying degrees of

[26] Wittkower 1975. For a comparison with Roman antiquities, see: Haskell and Penny 1981.

intensity, modes and intentions, in scenic and architectural sketches.[27] The aim here is to focus on researching the question of why ancient and contemporary Roman history and art represented a source of inspiration for eighteenth-century Britain, including the suggestion that Britain identified with antique ideals. It is also intended to focus on the methods Juvarra used to represent the concept of 'romanitas' through his skills as an architect, set designer and creator of ephemeral structures.

Describing the Chatsworth album, Wittkower suggested that Juvarra may have had several finished drawings, that were recovered and integrated together with new folios (sketched differently), with a new title and dedication page, making up the small collection with its architectural *capricci*.[28] The album forms part of the Chatsworth collections, because Charlotte Elizabeth (1731–54), the last of Lord Burlington's three daughters and his only heir, married William Cavendish in 1748 (later 4th Duke of Devonshire, 1720–64).[29] Although the album may have been kept at Burlington House in Piccadilly initially, it was then probably kept in the library at Chiswick House, London, from 1733. This is the date when Lord Burlington 'moved all his paintings and library from Burlington House to Chiswick, which he made his principal seat and where he and his family lived for more than fifteen years'.[30] The album might have been shelved together with those works dedicated exclusively to architecture, antiquity, sculpture and topics relating to British history, or left out on one of the four large tables that furnished the room.[31] It is even possible that the album was kept in the old Jacobean House adjacent to Chiswick – more specifically the *Bagnio* or *Casino*, a spacious structure in the garden that Burlington used as a studio where he drafted his architectural projects.[32] Nonetheless, the 1741/2 catalogue of Burlington's collection (which records nearly 2,000 titles, of which 83 per cent were not older than a hundred years old) does not contain references to Juvarra's album.[33] The binding of the folios on the long side – not in correspondence with the direction of the reading of the

---

[27]   Myers 1975: 29.

[28]   Wittkower 1975: 207. Volume I of the collection of Juvarra albums at the Museo Civico d'Arte Antica di Palazzo Madama, Turin, contains many drawings similar to those of the Burlington album, particularly those signed and dated 1728 and 1729.

[29]   Besides the collections belonging to the inheritance of the Dukes of Devonshire, there is also Burlington House and Chiswick House in London; Londesborough Hall and Bolton Abbey in Yorkshire; Lismore Castle and County Waterford in Ireland.

[30]   Rosoman 1985: 664.

[31]   Ayres 1992: 114, *passim*.

[32]   I would like to thank Ricky Pound for this suggestion.

[33]   *A Catalogue of The Earl of Burlington's / Library, / At His Lordships Seat at Chiswick; /January, 1741/2.* See: Ayres 1992: 113; 1997: 108, 168–71.

sketches – may have been necessary so that the album conformed to other volumes in the library. These volumes had been regularly and uniformly bound with calfskin covers with gilt decorations – a process that continued until the third decade of the eighteenth century.[34]

There are many strands which weave themselves into the fabric of the story of the sketches, before they finally arrived in England. Several issues should be considered: the identity of the artist, the recipient of the album, the iconography of the sketches, the purpose for which they were drawn in the first place, how they were sent and the relationship between Juvarra and Lord Burlington. Was theirs a long-standing friendship or an occasional acquaintance? We can speculate that the most probable years for an encounter between the two were 1714 and 1715 and the summer and autumn of 1719, since both men travelled and sojourned abroad during these periods.

The twenty-year-old British lord travelled to Italy on his grand tour between 17 May 1714 and 2 May 1715. He visited Turin, was obliged to stay in Rome for longer than four months (28 September 1714 until 4 February 1715), as he fell ill and then had to convalesce there (3 October to 27 December 1714).[35] Juvarra arrived in Rome in mid-January 1715 to take part in the competition to decorate the Vatican sacristy,[36] which would have allowed him an opportunity to meet Lord Burlington.

In 1719, after Juvarra had travelled to Lisbon to work at the court of John V, and before returning to Turin, he decided he would 'tour England and France'.[37] He visited London, arriving on 10 August 1719, as a guest of the Portuguese ambassador, and then travelled on to Paris; it was during autumn of 1719 that Lord Burlington decided to travel to Italy a second time, leaving from London (perhaps even accompanied by Juvarra and Alessandro Galilei, whom he could have also met on his trip there, most likely in France).[38] Burlington then travelled to the Veneto to study examples of Palladio's architecture. On his return to England, he stopped in Turin on 6 November 1719.[39] However, Burlington may have made other unofficial trips abroad for non-artistic reasons using the pseudonym 'Mr Buck': several scholars have expressed their views that Lord Burlington was a friend to

---

[34] Ayres 1992: 123–6.

[35] Aside from the four months he spent in Rome, Burlington's other long sojourns abroad include The Hague (22 days) and Paris (35 days), whereas he stayed in Turin and Venice for only six and five days, respectively. Chatsworth Library, *Travel account book*, MS 25A.

[36] Hager 1970.

[37] 'Il giro per l'Inghilterra e la Francia.'

[38] Manfredi 2012a; 2012b; 2014. And see the essay by Manfredi in this publication.

[39] See the bibliography in note 38 above.

the Jacobites (but posing as a Whig) – a supporter of the Stuarts who lived in Italy under the protection of the Pope.[40]

Until Juvarra was called to the Madrid Court in 1735, no other travels abroad are documented for him.[41] There do not seem to have been any sojourns, for either of the two men, in 1730, and there are no paper trails recording a meeting between the two, when the album may have been handed over. It is more likely that the album reached Lord Burlington via travelling artists and British diplomats to the court in Rome and Turin, or even via Italians working for Lord Burlington or active on the London artistic scene. It is only because of the dedication on the title page that the album can be identified as a gift. As Wittkower noted, the album may have been a 'belated thank-you' from Juvarra for the presumed hospitality he received in London eleven years earlier. An exchange of gifts between Burlington and Juvarra is, however, mere speculation: Burlington may have sent his publication on *Roman Baths* (1730)[42] to the architect, receiving the 'Perspectives' in return.[43] The second decade of the eighteenth century was a successful period for both men on a personal level, as well as being interesting years in terms of developing architectural projects against an international backdrop of thriving production and cultural exchange.[44]

A longer-lasting relationship over the course of the years between Juvarra and the British world can be posited with Burlington, or, more probably, with William Kent (1675–1748),[45] Burlington's future architect who had lived and studied in Rome at the same time as Juvarra (1709–19). Kent took part in the cultural and artistic activities at the court of Cardinal Ottoboni in the Palazzo della Cancelleria, but he never really took to Burlington's Palladian ideas.[46] As an architect and painter, Kent instead promoted a style which mirrored the Renaissance, Mannerist and Baroque traditions of central Italy rather than the Venetian, most probably because of the strong influence exerted upon him by the collector and antiquarian, John Talman

[40]   Clark 1989a; Clark 1989b; Corp 2003; Pound 2009.
[41]   See: Sancho 2014 (with previous bibliography).
[42]   *Fabbriche Antiche disegnate da Andrea Palladio Vicentino e date in Luce da Riccardo Conte di Burlington*, London 1730.
[43]   Wittkower 1975: 207.
[44]   For other gifts sent to Lord Burlington during these years, see: Lees-Milne 1962: 120; Wittkower 1975: 207. For additional information on Lord Burlington's various activities, see: Barnard and Clark 1995; Corp 1998.
[45]   Brindle 2013.
[46]   Sicca 1986.

(1677–1726), who had collected 200 volumes of drawings, mainly focusing on architecture. This influence would last at least until the mid-1720s.[47]

To approach the content of the album, key principles found in Juvarra's drawings must be followed up, especially when considering the interest of the people involved in this singular cultural transfer. Palladian architecture was well known in England thanks to publications by Giacomo Leoni (1686–1746)[48] and Colen Campbell (1675–1729),[49] and as the result of the strong influence exerted by Talman. This influence saw Lord Burlington dedicating himself to a personal and national cause which earned him the title of 'our contemporary Palladio and Jones'.[50] However, Juvarra does not seem to have considered this revival in his drawings: Rome's virtues are extolled in preference to the culture of the Veneto of the sixteenth century, and its greatest exponent, Andrea Palladio. Juvarra does not depict the villas of Venetian or British nobility, but passes on the lessons which emerge from the Roman ruins, echoing Inigo Jones's sentiment expressed in the title of his 1614 Roman sketchbook: 'Rome, I find no other joy beyond you.'[51] The Italian architect had interpreted the significance of the ancient classical world of Rome for Burlington through refined, scenic sketches. However, the London drawings do contain several reinterpreted motifs typical of the traditions of the Veneto, particularly of Venice, with her lagoon and reflecting the reality of a city coexisting in the presence of water (as did the cities of Rome, Turin and London).[52] Juvarra had been to Venice in December 1724 and February 1729,[53] and by sketching these maritime settings he might have been referencing the cultural and artistic ties the British had to Venice. The city had hosted notable British personages such as consul Smith[54] and the theatre agent Owen McSwiney[55] during the 1720s, as did Turin and Rome. The capital of the Kingdom of Savoy, Turin was accustomed to hosting a contingent of British gentlemen who passed through the city on their Grand Tour,

---

[47] Kieven 2008b. See also the project on Talman's drawings: *John Talman an early-eighteenth-century collector of Drawings*, a collaboration of the universities of Pisa, Signum S.N.S. and the Getty Grant Program: http://talman.arte.unipi.it/IT/biblioteca_01.html.

[48] Leoni 1715.

[49] Campbell 1715–25.

[50] 'Palladio e Jones de' nostril tempi', as written in the dedication prefacing Pompei 1735, now conserved at Chatsworth, 80D.

[51] 'Roma, altro diletto che imparar non trovo'; Chaney 2006.

[52] On Turin, see: Griseri 2004.

[53] Juvarra's presence is confirmed in a letter dated 29 January 1729, written by Marini, from Venice, to the Minister to Turin, Solaro del Borgo: 'I am also waiting for Juvarra, who has stopped in Brescia'; see Marinello 2012: 81.

[54] Vivian 1990.

[55] Mazza Boccazzi 1976.

including *residents* at the Royal Academy of Italy and diplomats such as John Molesworth.[56] In Rome, however, Cardinal Pietro Ottoboni, a Venetian, was in charge of one of the most active cultural circles of the time. Furthermore, the English community in Rome was large and important: the court of the Cardinal included British artists and intellectuals such as Kent, Talman (who was also an 'Arcadian shepherd'), James Gibbs (1682–1754), Thomas Coke (1697–1759) and Lord Shaftesbury (1671–1713).[57] However, the opposite was also true; there were numerous artists, especially painters and musicians, who went to London from Rome or Venice. Juvarra knew them extremely well because some of them had been to the Accademia di San Luca, where Juvarra had taught for some years, or because they had been called by him to work at construction sites in Turin.[58] An interesting figure amongst these is that of Francesco Bianchini, a humanities scholar from Verona, who was also active at the Cardinal's court – he might even have unknowingly inspired Juvarra's trip to London, thanks to his accounts published as *Iter in Britannia* and the *Cose più cospicue di Londra* of 1713.[59] However, one could also posit a direct experience by the Sicilian architect of modern British architecture. He may have visited Chiswick House which was being completed in those years. This direct contact could explain to some extent the diversity of the drawings in the album.[60] Juvarra could have depicted the essence of Roman culture and art interpreted in light of what he had seen in London. However, unlike his Paris and Dresden sketches, these drawings almost never include designs for more 'royal' architecture. Aristocracy is what moved London, and he imagined it as an aristocratic setting: 'It would be the oligarchy who would make the new Roman Britain, with private money.'[61]

His Roman experience, together with the ideas offered by the sketches of this album, might have made Lord Burlington reflect upon his role as a true 'virtuoso', as befitted and was expected of an English gentleman of the time.[62] When speaking of architecture, it was believed, following the examples of Lord Shaftesbury and others, that a noble construction reflected the morality and freedom of the society that produced it.[63] Burlington achieved

---

[56] See the chapters by Bianchi and Wolfe in this volume.

[57] Anthony Ashley Cooper, Earl of Shaftesbury (1671–1713).

[58] Many of these are taken up by Juvarra in the *Memorie Sepolcrali* from 1735: Ruggero 2008. For Juvarra's presence at the court of Ottoboni, see: Manfredi 2010; while for his work as an architect, see: Gritella 1992.

[59] Manfredi 2012a; 2012b.

[60] Wittkower 1975.

[61] Ayres 1997: 123.

[62] To read an analysis of Lord Burlington's role as a gentleman, see: Wilton-Ely 1984.

[63] Sicca 1987: 89.

this lofty goal of virtuosity in several stages: first through music, theatre, painting and then landscaping, which captured his attention and made him into a real 'Apollo of the Arts'. Proof of this is Chiswick House which was considered a true temple of the arts as well as a meeting place and entertainment venue.[64] Burlington and Kent combined different experiences and styles by incorporating their knowledge of theatre into architecture, as Juvarra also had done. They both realized, for instance, that gardens based on the perception and management of spaces and perspectives, similar to that used when setting a scene,[65] allowed the observer to become an 'active' participant, nearly a lead actor, in this artistic experience.[66] By his architectural compositions, Juvarra conceived them as if he were setting the scene for a play.

The theatrical aspect and the scenic conceit are extremely important and essential aspects of architecture. One must not forget that many architects, including Jones, Juvarra and Kent, began their professional careers in these so-called minor roles as scenic designers and theatre architects. 'Minor' even though they required extreme versatility, skill in managing and representing limited spaces, perspective and compositional creativity. Indeed, the profound connection between theatre and architecture was also frequently expressed in the titles of important publications,[67] or in the urban fabric of the city itself with its outdoor building sites and the numerous festive occasions that required the presence of stages, with their ephemeral architecture and important role in the visual arts, especially in the seventeenth and eighteenth centuries. These 'ideal' building sites are represented in Juvarra's folios (Fig. 14.5).

As has been highlighted, despite the architectural style of Lord Burlington and Juvarra, they had little else in common.[68] In fact, it was only their mutual admiration for ancient buildings that they shared as common ground. Lord Burlington probably appreciated seeing the ancient world in the work of the architect. In the seventeenth and eighteenth centuries, the concept of 'ancient' was characteristic of the British, who considered themselves 'virtuous Romans' in the aftermath of the Glorious Revolution of 1688. They had rejected the absolute political restoration of Catholicism, desired by Charles

---

[64] Hewlings 1994.

[65] Hatfield 1981; Sicca 1987: 91; Grant 2011.

[66] Sicca 1987: 92.

[67] For example the *Nuovo Teatro delle fabbriche et edificij in prospettiva di Roma moderna sotto il felice pontificato di N.S. Papa Alessandro VII*, published in 1665 by Giovanni Giacomo Rossi for Giovanni Battista Falda. On this, see: Scott Munshower 1995: 252.

[68] Carré 1994: I, 302.

Figure 14.5 Filippo Juvarra, *Architectural Capriccio*, 1729, Album 30, folio 19, Chatsworth, reproduced by permission of Chatsworth Settlement Trustees.

II and James II, in favour of a constitutional monarchy, controlled by the aristocracy, gentry and the bourgeois. This rejection allowed them to establish constitutional principles of freedom, even if based upon an idealized image of Republican Rome, enhancing the analogies and sustaining an 'oligarchy of virtue'.[69] Amongst the many important implications of such an inspiration was the belief of the aristocracy that they shared the values of the ancient, classical world, especially those of the pre-Augustan Roman Empire. This connection expressed itself in a subtle, yet complex, form of nostalgia for the ancient, promoting a debate that encompassed all of the arts, sustained especially by Burlington.[70] Indeed it engendered an illusion of a Roman Britain, supported by the activities of 'neo-archaeologists', that could be rebuilt on the ashes of the old.[71] Between 1720 and 1730, the studies carried out into Roman Britain were the most prestigious antiquarian research of the time.[72] The neo-archaeologists reimagined a Britain full of cities, castles, temples and harbours, the vestiges of which were to be found among the ancient ruins

[69] See: Ayres 1997: XIII and chapter 'Virtue made visible', pp. 48–83, *passim*.
[70] *Apollo of the Arts* 1973.
[71] There are many publications on these themes beginning in the second half of the sixteenth century. See: Ayres 1997: chapter on 'Britannia Romana', *passim*.
[72] Ayres 1997: 92.

and monuments in the country. All this indicated that Britain had enjoyed one of the most significant, ancient heritages, second only to Rome.[73] By declaring that the nation possessed this refined taste, England came to be seen as the true home of the Muses. London was thus Apollo's favoured residence and the 'Augusta of Britain' was destined to become the *altera Roma*.[74] As Vitruvius had been the main architect during the reign of the Emperor Augustus (whose bust was placed above the entrance to Chiswick House), so Burlington's main architect was Kent, after Palladio and Jones.[75]

Lord Burlington trained as an architect mainly by studying engravings and drawings, including those of ancient buildings,[76] which he collected via the intermediary figures of antiquarians such as Talman.[77] Because of imprecise and superficial translations, there was little knowledge of 'classic' architecture texts in England. Scholars had to make do with 'images' that needed to reproduce and convey the theories behind the architecture they illustrated. In this way, Juvarra, using the only language he had mastered – that of drawing – had tried to represent what 'real architecture' was. He recognized, as Palladio had perceived before him, that graphic transmission was as important as any written theory.[78] The vitality of Juvarra's imaginary scenes, even though only an interpretation and not literal copies, must have offered a glimpse of the grandeur that could be achieved by adopting an architectural style befitting a British Lord. Juvarra employed a language that went far beyond the apparent 'agreeable Disorder' of his compositions.[79] After all, his contemporaries coveted his drawings for the immediacy of their representation. They not only avidly collected them (as they did with Michelangelo's drawings), but they also framed and displayed them, giving them the status of true works of art. By means of his drawings, Juvarra spurred Lord Burlington to look to the grandeur of ancient Rome to enhance the virtue that would bestow eternal glory on his efforts, just as Talman had suggested to Giuseppe Andrea Grisoni in 1716 in the registry of the University of Padua below his signature (Fig. 14.6).[80]

---

[73] Ayres 1997: 96.

[74] Ayres 1997: 101.

[75] This tradition was also recorded by Juvarra in the dedication preceding his *Studio di architettura civile* for his friend, the Marchese Carlo Giacinto Roero di Guarene (24 December 1725). See: Manfredi 2011: 209.

[76] Burlington owned primarily works of the sixteenth to seventeenth centuries, but he also owned Etruscan, Greek and Egyptian items. See Carré 1994: II. 300–2.

[77] See: Sicca 1987: 81–137, *passim*.

[78] Wittkower 1974a.

[79] Castell 1728: 32. Robert Castell dedicated the publication to Lord Burlington in 1728.

[80] Giuseppe Andrea Grisoni, *Virtù che incorona l'aristocrazia*, 1716, Padova, Biblioteca del Seminario Arcivescovile, in: Sicca 2008: title page.

Figure 14.6 Giuseppe Andrea Grisoni,*Virtue Crowning the Aristocracy*, 1716,
Biblioteca del Seminario Arcivescovile, Padua.

Furthermore, by making such a particular gift, Juvarra clearly hoped
to work as an architect for Lord Burlington, though this did not happen.
Juvarra's failure to do so can be viewed as the confirmation of what Galilei
wrote about the British: that they preferred to use their compatriots, even if
'great dunces',[81] instead of using foreigners.[82] Burlington commissioned projects from Kent during those years.[83] Kent had trained with Juvarra in Rome,
and he had egregiously competed for the Concorso Clementino of 1713. He
had also learnt much from the Sicilian architect,[84] ensuring that the Italian
'buon gusto' of Lord Burlington was praised even by Daniel Defoe as 'our
modern Vitruvius, …, who to the Strength and Convenience of the English
Architecture, has added the Elegance and Politeness of Italian Taste'.[85]

[81] 'Grandissimi asini.'
[82] Toesca 1952: 208.
[83] Wittkower 1974b.
[84] Grant 2011.
[85] Defoe 1748: II, 54.

15 | Crossing Borders: The Pioneering Role of the Architect-Engineer Giovanni Battista Borra between Piedmont and Britain

OLGA ZOLLER

In his native Piedmont, the reputation of Giovanni Battista Borra (1713–70)[1] as a practising architect rests almost exclusively on his transformation, from 1756 to 1760, of the baroque Castello di Racconigi in the province of Cuneo into a neo-classical summer residence for his patron, Prince Luigi Vittorio of Savoy Carignano. The commission to Borra heralds the Prince's avant-garde taste, which was in direct contrast to the prevailing baroque and French rococo architectural traditions of the Savoy region.[2] Such a highly prestigious royal architectural commission would have been inconceivable given Borra's practically non-existent Italian building career up to that date, if it were not for the excellent reputation he previously established in Britain. Indeed, Borra advanced his professional career in Piedmont by leaving Italy to work as an architectural draftsman for British scholars and archaeologists abroad, only returning to local acclaim in his homeland later, bringing British cultural advances in exchange.

Borra's professional development while he was associated with the Irish classicist Robert Wood (1717?–71),[3] along with his subsequent work in Britain for various patrons, has excited interest amongst scholars in England, long before his career has come to be appreciated in Italy.[4] This is primarily due to the important archaeological expedition to the Levant, led by Wood, accompanied by Borra as his architectural draftsman, which resulted in the publication of two exemplary illustrated scientific volumes: *The Ruins of Palmyra, Otherwise Tedmor, in the Desart* (1753), and *The Ruins of Balbec,*

---

[1] Borra, generally known as 'Giambattista' Borra, as he signed his name that way, was born in Dogliani in the province of Cuneo. On Borra's life and work, see, in the first instance: Colvin 1995: 144–5; Zoller 1996b.
[2] See: Gabrielli 1972; Zoller 2001: 277–9; Aprile *et al.* 2007: 241–64; Dardanello 2013a; 2013b.
[3] See: Courtney 1900: 373–5; Ingamells 1997: 1015–16; Parker 2004a; White 2004.
[4] See the entry on Borra in: Colvin 1995: 144–5. Borra's British career only came to the notice of Italian scholars after the 2001 conference, 'Sperimentare l'architettura. Guarini, Juvarra, Alfieri, Borra e Vittone'; see: Zoller 2001. See also the conference proceedings on Borra's importance as an intermediary of neo-classical architecture: Zoller 2012, 2013 Dardanello 2013a.

Otherwise Heliopolis in Cœlosyria (1757).[5] The extraordinary significance of these publications has been described as, 'by all accounts a triumph such as no English architectural book had ever before achieved. This material was intended to serve lovers of antiquity, scholars, artists and architects, regardless of nationality or interest', bringing fame to Wood and his travelling companions and, significantly, placing Britain firmly 'in the forefront of archaeological studies.'[6]

The contemporaneous international success of these publications can be explained as the result of a complementary, synergistic process of finding and following a new methodological approach to the exploration of antiquity. This new approach was based on a comparison of ancient sites as described in classical Greek and Roman texts, with their actual state. The present chapter will argue that this new type of archaeological survey and reconstruction was as much a creation of the editor and intellect behind the expedition, Wood, as of Borra, the university-educated architect and talented draftsman. Borra was the first Italian to be professionally engaged to explore classical antiquities outside Italy, while his knowledge of and training in the 'practical' disciplines of architecture and engineering, specific to Piedmont, were necessary to implement the ambitious British exploration and publication project Wood envisioned.

Wood's specific route and sojourn through the Levant from 1750 to 1751 are not the subject of this chapter, but rather it is the preparations for the tour that will be analysed, as well as the successful results of this British-Italian collaboration. Borra's role as a true pioneer for the study and presentation of classical ancient architecture will be examined from the point of view of his innovative archaeological renderings and the neo-classical building projects he later realized as architect. Moreover, Borra's significance as an exponent of a new type of architect-engineer, a figure emerging in the first half of the eighteenth century in Piedmont, will also be reviewed.

The British travel party to the Levant comprising Wood and two patrons and gentlemen-connoisseurs, James Dawkins (1722–57)[7] and John Bouverie (1722?–50),[8] surely first made contact with Borra via James Caulfeild (1728–99), 1st Earl of Charlemont (1763)[9], another traveller of Irish origin,

---

[5] Wood 1753; 1757. For detailed information on Wood's publications on Palmyra and Baalbek, see: Wiebenson 1969: chapters II–III, and appendix II; Harris and Savage 1990: 491–4; Middleton 1998a; Middleton 1998b.

[6] Harris and Savage 1990: 491.

[7] Having inherited a vast fortune from his father, who owned a sugar plantation in Jamaica, Dawkins was one of the wealthiest men in mid eighteenth-century Europe. On Dawkins, see: Hughes 1901: 119–20; Ingamells 1997: 283; Parker 2004b.

[8] Turner and Plazzotta 1994: 22–4; Ingamells 1997: 110–11.

[9] For Lord Charlemont, see: Craig 1948; McCarthy 2001.

who was well known to Wood. Lord Charlemont travelled from Turin to Rome at the end of October 1748, spending the winter and early spring of 1748–9 in Rome and Naples.[10] A meeting with Wood, Dawkins and Bouverie probably took place soon after Caulfeild's arrival in Rome, when he informed them about how his plans to engage the talented Piedmontese architect, Borra, had fallen through on account of Borra's hesitancy over financial compensation.[11] Wood and his companions, however, were not dissuaded by Borra's refusal to work for Caulfeild, and they roped Caulfeild in for help in contacting Borra again, making the architect what must have been a more attractive offer that likely included not only a generous and guaranteed payment, but also the irresistible proposal of participating in an unprecedented foreign expedition and the opportunity to contribute to an ambitious publication project.[12]

Alongside the financial reward, Borra would have been aware that the chance to accompany a travelling team of foreigners, dedicated to a new scientific standard of study, to far-flung antique sites outside Italy, would open new professional possibilities to him. Given the contemporary developments and new challenges facing Piedmontese architects in an increasingly competitive market among professional colleagues at home,[13] collaboration with an Anglo-Irish expedition team safeguarded Borra's future international career. Borra soon left Turin for Rome, where the group passed the winter together planning their expedition.[14]

The instigators and financiers of the tour, the young Oxford students Dawkins and Bouverie, would have been well informed about Wood's reputation as an experienced, competent traveller and tutor, and, indeed, Wood's role as guide to the expedition through mostly unknown antique sites in the Levant was conceived from the outset.[15] Wood was not only a noted classical scholar with an extensive knowledge of ancient history, literature and topographical descriptions,[16] but also an accomplished bear-leader, having led 'different tours through France and Italy'.[17] Just as

---

[10]   Craig 1948: 44.

[11]   King Charles Emmanuel III had personally endorsed Caulfeild's offer to Borra, but at the last moment the architect withdrew over concerns he would not be paid regularly, see: O'Connor 1999: 20–1.

[12]   'We accordingly wrote to Borra, and fixed him for the voyage.' See: Wood 1753: a(r).

[13]   More than 731 architects and engineers active in seventeenth- and eighteenth-century Piedmont are listed in the indispensable catalogue of Brayda and his colleagues (1963).

[14]   Wood 1753: a(r).

[15]   As secretary to Joseph Leeson. For information on Wood's career, see: Ingamells 1997: 1015–16.

[16]   As evidenced by Wood's reflexions on Homer. See: Wood 1775.

[17]   Wood 1753: a(r).

Dawkins and Bouverie sought to profit from Wood's expertise in antiquity, so all three may well have benefited from the ideas of James Stuart (1713–88) and Nicholas Revett (1720–1804), who were at that time planning an expedition to study the antiquities of Athens.[18]

While Dawkins's and Bouverie's particular interest was architecture, Wood's main interest was ancient history as recorded by ancient writers, above all that written by Homer.[19] The combined enthusiasms and talents of the group were focused on the common interest of all parties in ancient architecture in those countries where it 'had its origin, or at least arrived at the highest degree of perfection it has ever attained'.[20] Wood planned the route they would follow and the method for investigating and recording the antique sites, comprising renderings of the architectural and ornamental details of the monuments. It was Wood's proposal that the expedition provided a first-hand record of the surviving ancient architectural monuments based on scientifically conducted and empirically verifiable studies conducted on site, as opposed to simply identifying the ruins based on historical and literary descriptions. This novel approach was adopted to prevent their planned publication from containing errors of documentation, which Wood had identified in previous accounts of several other 'Brother Travellers', whom he satirized in an unpublished manuscript, that, in part, may be considered a draft of the beginning of his address 'To the Reader', of the *Ionian Antiquities* (1769).[21] This manuscript reveals that Wood identified integrity as the fundamental principle of an intellectual's work in providing facts for public interest based on investigation and documentation.[22]

---

[18] See: Stuart and Revett 1762; see also: Pinto 2012: 230. I am indebted to Martin Postle, Deputy Director of Studies, Paul Mellon Centre for British Art, for drawing my attention to this publication.

[19] Wood 1775.

[20] Wood 1775: a(*v*).

[21] Chandler *et al.* 1769: b.

[22] Wood [n.d.]: 25–6). 'Chance made the Traveller, and the Traveller has made the Author; I must indeed own that to the great variety of impertinence with which the Public is pester'd, non contribute more largely than my Brother Travellers, some, out of pure goodnature and an inclination to please, knowing that their Readers will not be much entertain'd by having things told as they really are, give an account of them as they really are not, from whence the word Traveller has been prostituted to mean something very different from a Person who has been in many Countries. Others, (who did they but confine themselves to tell plainly what they had seen, would be very tolerable) break loose into ingenious reflections upon the government, religion, Police, Manners, Antiquities become quite the Monkey in the China Shop. The Title page of these Gentlemen is only a modest declaration of the Author to the Public that he is Antiquarian, Politician, Philosopher, Divine etc, and like a Mountebank's haranque makes me suspect that to be good for nothing which is said to be good for every thing. Others from the moment they set out to begin to look upon themselves as the Hero of the piece and may be rather said to write their own lives than an account of the Countries they have seen; they take

As he wrote in the preface to *The Ruins of Palmyra*: 'As the principal merit of works of this kind is truth, it may not be amiss to prefix to this, such an account of the manner in which it was undertaken, and executed, as will give the publick an opportunity of judging what credit it deserves.'[23]

In the same publication Wood refers to Antoine Desgodetz's *Les édifices antiques de Rome* (1682), and specifically to Desgodetz's method of meticulously surveying ancient buildings,[24] as a model he planned to follow to record what remained of the architecture of the still largely unknown classical sites of the Eastern Mediterranean. The scientific studies to be carried out in situ were intended from the start to be published in the form of lavish, instructional volumes. In creating an aesthetically pleasing publication comprising fine engravings, rather than just a volume of written reports, Wood and his young investors hoped to attract a public of wealthy subscribers and readers.

Because of his practical experience as an architect, but equally because of his wide-ranging educational qualifications, Wood and his colleagues identified Borra as ideally suited to the expedition and publication project. In fact, before Borra completed his university education in architecture in 1741,[25] he had apprenticed at the studio of Bernardo Vittone (1704–70), soon after Vittone returned from Rome, awarded first prize by the Accademia di San Luca (1733).[26] Borra's university training also comprised engineering – the result of radical educational reforms first introduced under Victor Amadeus II (1666–1732) in 1720, reforms that were instituted and confirmed by his heir and successor, Carlo Emanuele III (1701–73), between the end of the Thirty Years War and the beginning of the War of the Austrian Succession in 1740. Both sovereigns sought to bring the educational system of the Savoy court into line with the many new challenges facing the developing Savoy polity.[27] The functional orientation of new

care not only to entertain you with elaborate descriptions of their hairbreadth scapes from Plagues, Storms, Earthquakes and Arabs, but the distress of a bad lodging or an exorbitant reckoning are now and then circumstantially dwelt upon, from not considering that a circumstance extremely important to ourselves may be perfectly indifferent to the Reader.'

[23] Wood 1753: a(*r*).

[24] Wood 1753: a(*v*); Desgodetz 1682.

[25] Zoller 1996a: 22.

[26] Oechslin 1972. Vittone settled in Turin in the palace of his patron and sponsor Carlo Francesco Vincenzo, Marchese d'Ormea (1680–1745), see: Canavesio 1997; on d'Ormea, see: Merlotti 2003a.

[27] *Regolamento per gli Ingegneri civili, e militari e Misuratori ed Estimatori*, Archivio di Stato di Torino, Sezione Riunite, Ufficio Generale delle Finanze, I Archiviazione, II, mazzo 1, *Misuratori, Sensali e Zavatini*, n. 3, 1724; Duboin 1818–69, tomo 14, lib.VIII, tit. XI, capo VI, art.VI, 10. Febb. 1741: 767; Zoller 1996a: 29–37.

science and technology disciplines in direct rapport with the moderniza-
tion of the state demanded appropriately educated and qualified specialists,
trained in the improvement of urban infrastructure, including sanitation,
water supply and roadways. Most importantly these specialists were to be
qualified for the improvement of national defence structures, including
civil and military buildings.

Borra was the author of an engineering treatise, published in Turin in
1748, a work which reflected an education mired in the practical sciences
of architecture and construction, and which satisfied the newly introduced
official mandates.[28] Borra's publication was conceived as an instructive text
book or manual on statics, comprising the largely forgotten science of dura-
ble construction techniques,[29] rather than as simply an architectural treatise in the theoretical tradition. The preface to Borra's manual demonstrates
that from the start of his career he appreciated the surviving remnants
of Egyptian, Greek and Roman architecture.[30] With reference to classical
Renaissance architects, Borra called attention to the exemplary status of
their art and to the scientific aspects of their constructions, knowledge of
which needed to be preserved as a canon for future architects. Regarding
his study of antiquity as a subject of university research, Borra surely profited from the work of Francesco Scipione, Marchese di Maffei (1675–1755),
a Veronese antiquarian, who had founded the Museo Lapidario di Torino,
and who also established historical research and archaeology as independent and state-funded disciplines at the University of Turin.[31]

Borra's interest in statics demonstrated his deep-standing respect for
ancient monuments and the long-lasting stability of the architectonics
with which they were designed and built, features he wanted to personally investigate while studying and sketching ruins at archaeological sites.
For Wood and his colleagues, Borra perfectly embodied the prototype of
the modern Piedmontese architect, university trained and scientifically
educated. Moreover, the travellers – acquainted with Borra's recently
published *Vedute principali di Torino*[32] – were surely also interested in
his talent for *vedutismo* as an artistic genre. Indeed, it may have been
their British enthusiasm for ancient topography that stimulated Borra to
produce fine panoramic views of such sites as the Palatine Hill in Rome
and Hadrian's Villa at Tivoli, comprising landscape embellishments with

---

[28] Borra 1748.
[29] Borra 1748 [1*v*]). 'di fabbricare all'eternità'.
[30] Borra 1748.
[31] Romagnani 2007.
[32] Borra 1749.

Figure 15.1 Giovanni Battista Borra, *The Palatine Ruins at Midday*, pen and black ink and grey wash over graphite, c. 1749/1750, Private collection, London, reproduced courtesy of the owner.

figures added for *staffage* (Fig. 15.1).[33] Lastly, the fact that Borra was a free agent architect-engineer signified that he could be engaged to pursue an independent career.[34]

Following the return of the Wood expedition from the Levant to Britain in August 1751,[35] Borra began to prepare the drawings for *The Ruins of Palmyra*, employing the many sketches, notes and measurements he had made, along with those measurements provided by Wood and Dawkins, who together had taken on the mantle of archaeologists after the death of Bouverie in September 1750. Even before Borra and the engravers had completed their plates for *The Ruins of Palmyra*, the drawings and engravings were advertised for viewing to subscribers in various newspapers in London: 'The Drawings and Engravings, as fast as they are finished, may be

---

[33] For Borra's Roman drawings, see: McCarthy 2007.

[34] Brayda 1963.

[35] Departing from Smyrna, with a stopover at the Grecian Porto Leone (the former Lion's Port of Piraeus) they returned to England, arriving 'off Dover' on 7 August 1751; see *The General Advertiser*, London, Friday 9 August 1751 (Issue 5243).

seen at Mr. Wood's, at the Corner of Lancaster Court in the Strand.'[36] British connoisseurs marvelled at Borra's talent not only for architectural site plans and overall views of ruins, but more importantly for the new method he utilized of meticulously rendering restored versions of individual buildings and their architectural ornament, based on precise measurements made in situ. Resident in London,[37] Borra soon distinguished himself as one of the most well-informed architects and artists of classical and ancient architecture in that city.

In 1752, Richard Grenville, 1st Lord Temple (1711–79), who was introduced to Borra's work at the subscribers' exhibition, commissioned the architect to design an ambitious project for the renovation of his country seat at Stowe, based on Borra's study of ancient architecture.[38] Although Borra's design for the main facade of Stowe was never realized, he nonetheless designed classicizing alterations for several important garden structures at Stowe, including the Palladian Bridge and the Grecian Temple.[39] An ink wash drawing from the West Yorkshire Archive, Leeds, for a hexagonal portico with a pediment of an Ionic temple *in antis*, which exactly corresponds to the (enlarged) main front of the Grecian Temple at Stowe, and which, moreover, features an unusual combination of a peripteral and a prostyle portico, can now be attributed to Borra (Fig. 15.2). This attribution finally confirms that Borra was the first architect to propose neo-classical designs for garden monuments in Britain.[40] Moreover, another drawing from the West Yorkshire Archive – also pen and ink with grey wash, and signed by Borra – may now be proposed as a sketch for the never-realized third Triumphal Arch – to represent the Ionic Order – to be erected alongside the Corinthian Arch (built in 1765 by Thomas Pitt, 1st Lord Camelford) and the Doric Arch (built in 1767 by Thomas Pitt and/or Richard Grenville, Lord Temple) for the Stowe gardens (Fig. 15.3).

[36] *London Advertiser*, 16 January 1752 (Issue 5380).

[37] Borra was in Britain from 7 August 1751 (note 35 above) to 1756 (the end of June?). For the earliest extant document, of 2 July 1756, which gives evidence of Borra's activity as military architect in Piedmont and his probable commission the same year for the rebuilding of Racconigi castle, see note 49 below.

[38] For Borra's works at Stowe, see: Whistler 1957; Clarke 1973; Zoller 1996a: 129–47; Rowan 2013b.

[39] At the end of the Seven Years War (1756–63) the Grecian Temple was renamed the Temple of Concord and Victory. As Michael Bevington writes: 'the Temple was started in 1747 when the Grecian Valley in front was laid out by Capability Brown and may itself be one of his designs' (see: Bevington 1994: 97). In 1752 Lord Temple wanted to 'rectify' parts of the 'Grecian' Temple, erected under Richard Temple, 1st Viscount Cobham (1675–1749), which was of a Roman rather than of a Greek order (see Benton Seeley's perspective view – after George Vertue – of Cobham's *Grecian Temple*: Seeley 1750).

[40] Bevington 1994: 97.

Figure 15.2 Attributed to Giovanni Battista Borra, *Design for the Southern Front of the Grecian Temple at Stowe*, pen and ink with grey wash, c. 1752, West Yorkshire Archive Service, Leeds.

Aside from the circular temples designed by William Chambers (1723–96) for Kew (1761) and by Henry Flitcroft (1697–1769) for Stourhead (1765), based on plates XLII–XLIV of *The Ruins of Balbec*, no other entire monuments directly derived from Wood's publications are known in Britain. However, the ornamental details illustrated in these volumes were copied by many British architects. The detail most commonly adopted was the Palmyran motif (plate XIX) from the largely destroyed Bel Temple (Temple of the Sun at Palmyra), showing a coffered ceiling decorated with a central rosette, surrounded by a meandering band set in a rectangular frame of octagonal coffering, with each coffer featuring a smaller centre rosette (Fig. 15.4). Well-known examples of this ceiling decoration include that designed by Borra himself at Stowe for the ceilings of the Palladian

Figure 15.3 Giovanni Battista Borra, *Design for a Triumphal Arch of the Ionic Order*, signed 'Borra del:', pen and ink with grey wash, West Yorkshire Archive Service, Leeds.

Bridge and of the Garter Room,[41] that by Flitcroft at Woburn, and that by Robert Adam (1728–92) at Osterley and at Syon. It is worth noting that Wood's two volumes exerted considerable influence on Adam, notwithstanding the sustained criticism Adam levelled at the publications,[42] for the

[41] See the ceilings of the Palladian Bridge in Stowe Garden and of the Garter Room (former State Bedchamber at Stowe House); for further Palmyran motifs, designed in various media; see: Zoller 1996a: 157–63.

[42] See Robert Adam's letter (1 November 1757) to his brother James excoriating Borra's depictions as 'hard as Iron, and as false as Hell'; Wiebenson 1969: 96–7.

Figure 15.4 After Giovanni Battista Borra, Palmyran motifs, from an engraving by Paul Fourdrinier in Robert Wood (ed.), *The Ruins Of Palmyra, Otherwise Tedmor, In The Desart*, London 1753, Plate XIX, Heidelberg University Library.

enormous success of the books commanded his admiration and he borrowed from them.[43] However, the writer who first referenced and identified a 'Palmyran' decoration in Britain was Horace Walpole, who in his *Journals of Visits to Country Seats* recorded that the ceiling in the State Bed Chamber at Woburn was similar to 'one of those from Palmyra'.[44]

It was Borra's Piedmontese origins and the traditions of Italian baroque and rococo design, rather than his rapidly growing reputation in England as

---

[43] Adam 1764: 4. Adam's designs for the ceiling decoration, as well as for the carpet pattern of the Drawing Room at Osterley Park House are directly derived from the Palmyran ceiling decoration illustrated on Tab. XIXB of Wood's *Ruins of Palmyra*. While Wood certainly intended to instruct his general readership about ancient architecture and to influence contemporaneous architectural design, nonetheless, there is no reason to believe that he anticipated that his books would serve as pattern manuals for fashionable interiors, for interior stucco decorations, or for textile production.

[44] Toynbee 1928: 19.

an expert in antiquity, however, that recommended him to Edward Howard, 9th Duke of Norfolk (1686–1777) and his wife, Mary, née Blount (c. 1712–73), who sought an architect for the new interiors they planned for their London residence, Norfolk House.[45] She and the Duke probably met Borra through Grenville, c. 1752, as they frequented the same social circle that gravitated around Frederick, Prince of Wales, who himself preferred the French rococo over the Palladianism increasingly favoured by the Whigs. The numerous visitors invited to the opening of the newly decorated Norfolk House in February 1756 would have been surprised at the contrast between Borra's baroque and rococo transformation of the interiors and the plain neo-Palladian exterior of the house, designed by Matthew Brettingham. Initially describing the decorative scheme as 'whimsical', Walpole later, in a letter to H.S. Conway of 12 February 1756, wrote admiringly:

> The Duchess of Norfolk has opened her new house: all the earth was there last Tuesday. You would have thought there had been a comet, everybody was gaping in the air and treading on one's other toes. In short, you never saw such a scene of magnificence and taste. The tapestry, the embroidered bed, the illumination, the glasses, the lightness and novelty of the ornaments, and the ceilings, are delightful.

Although it no longer survives, Borra's design for the decoration of the 'Italianate' staircase at Norfolk House reveals the Palmyran influences which had crept into the predominantly late baroque and rococo program of the interiors. The stucco-decorated dome featured another Palmyran motif (Fig. 15.5), specifically the ornament of the ceiling of a burial chamber (Fig. 15.6),[46] which was repeatedly copied and re-interpreted in Britain. Subsequently this decorative device appeared in Piedmont, where, thanks to Borra, it found admirers at both the Savoyard royal residence of Racconigi and at the private seat of the architectural dilettante Francesco Ottavio Magnocavalli, Conte di Varengo (1707–88) at Moncalvo.[47]

By June 1756, when Borra finally returned to Italy, he began work on the most prestigious commission of his architectural career – that for the renovation of Racconigi Castle, for Prince Luigi Vittorio of Savoy Carignano, as stated at the beginning of this chapter.[48] At Racconigi, Borra succeeded

---

[45] See the first and indispensible monograph on Norfolk House by Fitz-Gerald (1973). As a staunch Jacobite, the Duchess may have preferred to engage an architect who came from the Catholic country that welcomed and protected the Stuarts.

[46] Wood 1753: 48, tab. XLII C.

[47] Zoller 1996a: 204; fig. 85. On the life and work of Magnocavalli, see: Associazione Casalese Arte e Storia *et al.* (2005).

[48] After his return to Piedmont, Borra also proved himself as an experienced engineer and expert in statics, consulted for the important military fortification project at Alessandria. See Borra's

Figure 15.5 Photographic view into the ceiling design of the great staircase of Norfolk House, St James's Square, London, 1937, in *Survey of London*, volume 29: St James Westminster, 1 (1960), plate 154, Photograph: London Metropolitan Archives, City of London.

in integrating a variety of architectural 'styles' from different eras and origins together under one roof, a process inspired by the recent building work he had directed and that he had witnessed taking hold in Britain. The reception room at Racconigi, the Sala di Diana, located behind the neo-Palladian entrance hall of the villa, the Sala d'Ercole, is a case in point: Borra introduced a 'whimsical' British reference in the ceiling decoration by importing the contemporary enthusiasm for Palmyran architectural ornamention which he himself had imported to England by way of Wood's publication.[49]

'Osservazioni sovra le Resistenze delle volte', Turin, 2 July 1756. In Archivio di Stato di Torino (AST), Sezione Corte, Materie Militari, Imprese, mazzo 13, n.10. See: Zoller 1996a: 234–48. As to Borra's engineering activities in Piedmont up until 1769, see: Zoller 1996a: 165–257.

[49] Gabrielli 1972: 42–51; Fitz-Gerald 1973: 42–56; Zoller 2001: 277–9.

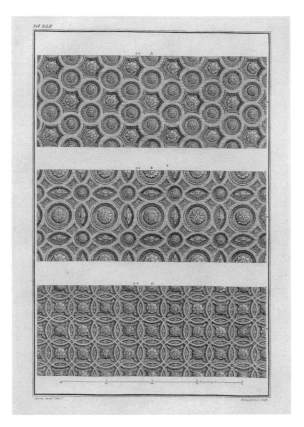

Figure 15.6 After Giovanni Battista Borra, Palmyran motifs, from an engraving by Paul Fourdrinier, in R. Wood (ed.), *The Ruins of Palmyra, otherwise Tedmor, in the Desart*, London, 1753, plate XLII, Heidelberg University Library.

Borra's British career had also come to the attention of the anglophile Piedmontese count, Francesco Baldassare Perrone di San Martino (1718–1802), who served as Savoy envoy in London from 1749 to 1755. Indeed, the friendly diplomatic relations between the Savoyard State, represented by Perrone di San Martino, and the British State, represented by Thomas Robinson, 1st Baron Grantham (c. 1695–1770), led to a cultural exchange of sorts, via Borra's activity as an architectural and cultural intermediary. Upon retiring from diplomatic service and returning to Piedmont, Perrone, a passionate collector and antiquarian, set out to redesign the small park at his palace in Ivrea in the taste of an English landscape garden *en miniature*.[50] Perrone commissioned Borra to design this project,[51] but the garden

---

[50] For Conte Perrone's English garden at Ivrea, see: Zoller 2013: 109–10.

[51] During this period Borra was involved also in the design and the construction of a new town-hall for Ivrea; see: Zoller 1996a: 192–4.

Figure 15.7 Thomas Robinson, *View of the House and Garden of Count Perrone at Ivrea*, detail, pen and black ink with grey wash, 1759, West Yorkshire Archive Service, Leeds.

no longer survives. However, Borra's pioneering landscape project is known from a letter which references it, written by the architectural dilettante, Thomas Robinson junior (the future 2nd Earl Grantham, 1738–86), and also by a drawing Robinson made, showing the garden as realized after Borra's lost design (Fig. 15.7). During the last nine months of his sojourn in Piedmont, from June 1758 to September 1759,[52] Robinson had been a pupil of Borra at the Royal Academy,[53] one of the final contacts Borra had with Britain.[54]

Thanks to the editorial and publishing efforts of Wood and Dawkins, Borra's archaeological drawings became widely known in Britain, and had a more significant impact on British taste for 'neo-classicism' than his work would ever have for Italian architectural developments. Thus far, in Italy, Borra's pioneering role as a catalyst for a new empiric approach to ancient architecture has been undervalued, both from the point of view of what an exceptionally talented draftsman and highly qualified architect he was – a product of the Piedmontese state system – as well as with a view to the

[52] See the *Robinson Papers* at the West Yorkshire Archive, Leeds.
[53] For detailed information on Perrone's contacts with Borra, particularly his persuasive influence on the architect to mentor the young Robinson, see: Zoller 2013: 106–10.
[54] Borra's final association with the British architectural scene was a commission for drawings for the reconstruction of the Savoyard royal chapel in Lincoln's-Inn-Fields in London, which had been destroyed by fire in 1759 – a project researched and analysed by Cozzo in this volume (Chapter 12). I am indebted to Paolo Cozzo for sharing original research regarding Borra's involvement in the project for the rebuilding of the chapel, and wish to thank also Edoardo

importance of the spread of the new scientific method by which he rendered antique architecture and ornament. His British-inspired neo-classical designs for the Savoy royal residence at Racconigi were exceptional, but alongside his classicizing projects for the new parish church at Trinità, in the province of Cuneo, in 1759,[55] and for a new facade for San Sudario in 1763,[56] a chapel that was part of the Senate House at Nizza-Marittima,[57] his innovations were never fully taken up in mainstream mid-eighteenth-century Piedmontese architecture. Moreover, it is likely that despite the cultural exchange between Britain and Piedmont during Borra's lifetime, there were far fewer copies of Wood's publications, *The Ruins of Palmyra* and *The Ruins of Balbec*, circulating in the Savoy State than in Britain,[58] notwithstanding the talents of an architect of the 'caliber of Borra'.[59]

Piccoli for providing me with copies of the relevant documents at the AST. See also, Pyne and Combe (1904): 115.

[55] Zoller 1996a: 196–201; Caterino 2013b: 135.

[56] Foussard and Barbier 1988: 204–7; Zoller 1996a: 224–6.

[57] From 1761 to 1765 Borra was also commissioned for engineering works at the seaport of Porto Limpia at Nizza-Marittima (Nice) and for road building for the same county; see: Zoller 1996a: 229–33.

[58] For the entries on Wood's publications on Palmyra and Balbec, see: Cicognara 1821: (n. 2722–2723).

[59] Pinto 2012: 19.

PART V

Britain and Turin: Chinoiserie as an International Aesthetic

16 | Chinoiserie in Piedmont: An International Language of Diplomacy and Modernity

CHRISTOPHER M.S. JOHNS

In the Dutch city of Utrecht in 1713, the European powers met to end the overlong War of the Spanish Succession, an international conflict that began in 1701 and that devastated much of Germany, Spain, the Netherlands and northern Italy.[1] Victor Amadeus II, Duke of Savoy, had been a relatively minor player in the conflict, but his strategically located territories in south-eastern France and northwestern Italy were crucial to the military strategies of both major protagonists, Bourbon France and Habsburg Austria. The Savoyard Duke played both powers against one another, even changing sides at one point in the war, and his diplomatic skills did much to augment his dynasty's influence at the conflict's conclusion. The most important and enduring result of the Treaty of Utrecht for the Savoyards and the entire Italian peninsula was the recognition, at long last, of the Dukes of Savoy as kings, and Victor Amadeus was given the title King of Sicily. Political and military complications forced him to surrender the rich but distant island of Sicily in the Treaty of London in 1718, but he received another large island, Sardinia, in return. Although a comparatively poor place, Sardinia, like Sicily, possessed the royal title, and the Kingdom of Piedmont-Sardinia was established definitively. By 1720, the Savoyards were numbered among the élite fellowship of European monarchs, and they took up their hard-won role with enthusiasm. The establishment of the new monarchy in the Piedmontese capital at Turin was the beginning of a political phenomenon that would, in 1861, result in the creation of the Kingdom of Italy under Savoyard sovereignty. In 1866 Venice and the Veneto, and, in 1870, Rome, were annexed to the Piedmontese state, completing the unification of the peninsula under Savoyard rule.[2]

---

[1] I am grateful to Dr Karin Wolfe for inviting me to participate in the 2013 conference 'Torino Britannica: Political and Cultural Crossroads in the Age of the Grand Tour', from which this paper derives, and for many scholarly courtesies over the years. I am also deeply indebted to Dr Cristina Mossetti for sharing her great knowledge of Piedmontese Chinoiserie and especially for introducing me to the Villa della Regina. For the conflict, see: Kamen 1969. For the final years of the war and the Utrecht Treaty, see: Kamen 2001: 79–119 (with additional bibliography).

[2] On the Savoyard family, see: Mannucci 2012 (with bibliography); Symcox 1983c.

Victor Amadeus II and his successor Charles Emmanuel III reigned as kings of Piedmont-Sardinia from 1720 to 1773. Both monarchs understood that in *ancien régime* Europe it was not enough simply to be a king, but one had to radiate royal status by creating a splendid visual setting for sovereignty. In the first half of the eighteenth century, these two Savoyard rulers transformed their backwater capital Turin into one of Europe's most beautiful and impressive cities.[3] The visual transformation of the capital was accomplished through an extraordinarily ambitious building programme that encompassed palaces, churches, villas and hunting lodges such as the splendid Venaria Reale. But exterior impressiveness also had to be complemented by internal opulence, and in the arena of interior decoration, the Piedmontese kings endeavoured to create ornate, fashionable spaces worthy of their freshly minted royal status. An emphasis on cultural and artistic modernity was the order of the day. It was essential to impress not only their subjects, but also the waxing numbers of foreign diplomats, tourists, students, artists and cultural luminaries who flocked to Turin in ever greater numbers as the importance of the Savoyard polity increased during the course of the eighteenth century.

Chinoiserie is one of the visual strategies of display seen almost everywhere in the dynasty's new, spectacular constructions. While the taste for Chinoiserie began as an attempt by European artists in a variety of media to emulate the wildly popular artistic productions of East Asia, especially those of China and Japan, by the early years of the eighteenth century, however, 'Chinese' subject-matter became frivolous and feminized, above all the depiction of Asian males, including the emperors. I have argued that this sea change in Chinoiserie, from a respectful emulation to a culturally degrading fantasy with little basis in actual Chinese art or society, is partly due to the closing of the Christian missions in the Qing Empire and the rejection of equal trading practices between China and Europe.[4] The debasement of Chinese men, social and court practices, imperial hierarchies, art and architecture is seen especially in Chinoiserie objects produced by artists and artisans in Roman Catholic countries.

In essence a late Baroque and Rococo exoticist aesthetic vaguely based on authentic Chinese objects, Chinoiserie was in fact far more interested in trivializing East Asia to demean it aesthetically and culturally in relation to a 'superior' Europe than in visualizing an authentic alien civilization. As an

---

[3] For an introduction to Turinese urbanism, see: Griseri and Romano 1989; Cornaglia 2012a; Cardoza and Symcox 2006: 120–4, 137–41; see also: Kieven and Ruggero 2014.

[4] Johns 2016.

international artistic style that was both chic and fashionable, Chinoiserie was also perceived to be cosmopolitan and progressive. Moreover, it was widely considered authoritative, not in and of itself but in relation to its deployment in the residences and public buildings of Europe's ruling classes. It connected Turin to Paris, Vienna, Naples, Madrid and other major European centres visually and culturally and was almost everywhere in evidence in royal décor. Spectacular examples survive in the Porcelain Room at the Capodimonte Palace commissioned by the Neapolitan Bourbons; the Chinoiserie suite at the University of Coimbra in Portugal, patronized by the Braganza monarchy; and the Spanish Bourbon Chinese Room at the Aranjuez Palace, among many other significant examples. It was important to the Savoyard kings that their palaces, villas and hunting lodges looked like monarchical abodes elsewhere, and they were cognizant of the fact that Chinoiserie could help promote their political agenda as well as advertise their sense of taste and splendour. Chinoiserie was a major player in the performance of monarchy in eighteenth-century Europe.

The British connection to Chinoiserie, however, had an especially significant appeal to the new royal establishment in Turin. Although the dynasty's international politics were more directly concerned with placating and containing Austria and France, because both Habsburgs and Bourbons coveted Savoyard territories, secondary powers like Piedmont-Sardinia looked to Great Britain as the key to maintaining a continental balance of power and to helping ensure the kingdom's independence. Seen in this light, it could be argued that Chinoiserie was a major feature of Turinese diplomacy. This chapter examines a select group of Chinoiserie interiors and decorative objects produced for the Piedmontese royal family and the aristocracy interrogated primarily in terms of their function in the rituals of *politesse* that dominated élite European sociability in the age of the Grand Tour. In this international context, there is one aspect of the British connection that should be kept in mind. The Hanoverian court was much less culturally ambitious before 1760 than its continental rivals.[5] Indeed, the aspirations of the Savoyards in terms of art, architectural and cultural patronage were far greater than their notably richer British counterparts. Chinoiserie in

[5] The lack of royal leadership in artistic, architectural and cultural patronage has been widely noted by scholars. Neither George I (1714–27) nor George II (1726–60) showed particular interest in the arts. The exception to Hanoverian indifference before the advent of George III in 1760 was Frederick, Prince of Wales, who did much to promote the Rococo style in England and patronized important continental artists such as Jacopo Amigoni, Etienne Liotard and Jean-Baptiste van Loo; among others, see: Newman 1958. Lack of interest in the arts may help explain why Great Britain had no official arts institution until the establishment of the Royal Academy in 1768 by George III (1760–1820).

the British Isles was, however, a major decorative feature of aristocratic town and country houses, but less so in royal residences. It was precisely the British aristocrats and their cohorts who inhabited such imposing rural mansions and palatial houses in London that the Savoyards wished to impress when they came to Turin. In sum, to upper-class Britons, their domesticated, aristocratic version of Chinoiserie preconditioned them to see the style abroad as a cosmopolitan visual language that indicated shared élite values and tastes. My chief assumption here is that British visitors to Piedmont-Sardinia would have felt quite at home in Savoyard Chinoiserie interiors. Indeed, I believe they would have been surprised had they not encountered them there.

Many scholars from a wide array of disciplines have argued convincingly that the decline of the cultural and artistic authority of Louis XIV's colossal baroque château at Versailles during the years of the War of the Spanish Succession was at least partly responsible for the genesis of the Rococo style, at the time significantly called *le goût moderne*.[6] One of the primary features of the new mode was a rejection of the grand interior salons, galleries and antechambers of the seventeenth century in favour of much smaller, more intimate and domesticated spaces in which conversation, light dining, card playing and small group sociability could reign. Although not decorated in the Chinese style, the famous Salon de la Princesse designed by the architect Germaine Boffrand in the Hôtel de Soubise in Paris is arguably the best-preserved example of an intimate early Rococo interior (Fig. 16.1).[7] The room features some of the major architectural and decorative characteristics of the new style that were influential throughout Europe, especially in the Italian and German states and, a bit later, in tsarist Russia. The floor plan of the room is an oval, and there is a marked tendency to obscure the traditional delineation between the walls and the ceiling; in this instance the two architectural elements are separated with an irregularly shaped cornice camouflaged by framed oil on canvas paintings with mythological themes. Stucco vine tendrils in gold gilt add a sense of richness and elegance without the heavily encrusted, classicizing cornices and entablatures of seventeenth-century baroque design. Unfortunately, the room's original furniture is no longer in situ, but the large mirrors placed between the windows add to the sense of airiness and allowed conversational groups to spy on one another discreetly, further underscoring notions of domesticity and

---

[6] For the rise of the Rococo, its aesthetic premises and the development of intimate spaces in domestic architecture and design, see especially: Scott 1995 (with additional bibliography).
[7] On the oval Salon de la Princesse in the Hôtel de Soubise in Paris, see: Béchu and Taillard 2004: 346–73.

Figure 16.1 Germaine Boffrand, *Salon de la Princesse*, Hôtel de Soubise, early 1730s, Paris, © RMN-Grand Palais/Art Resource, New York.

intimacy that were of such fundamental importance to *le goût moderne*. It should be noted that French mirrors and furniture were major luxury exports and were frequently encountered in élite interiors in Piedmont-Sardinia and throughout Europe. The vital importance of Rococo mythological narratives in a modern domestic space like those in the Salon de la Princesse will be combined with the Chinoiserie style in Filippo Juvarra's Chinese Room in the Palazzo Reale in Turin, a highly significant royal cabinet that will be considered in detail shortly.

Objects imported from East Asia, above all silk and porcelain, began arriving in Turin in the late sixteenth century, and their popularity soared throughout the baroque era. By the time of the establishment of the Savoyard kingdom, such exotic, luxurious commodities were also being imported from other parts of Europe in the form of Chinoiserie imitations of Chinese and Japanese originals. Eventually East Asian imports began to be imitated in local manufactories, a phenomenon also seen in other European states. As art historian Francesco Morena has observed, during the reign of Victor Amadeus II Chinoiserie decorations produced in Piedmont were often encountered in Turin, as a bed hanging with 'Chinese' figures dated circa

1720 indicates (Fig. 16.2).[8] The embroidered design shows a central male figure wearing a sunhat elevated above two suppliants, all contained in a baldachin-like structure made of gold thread. The central figure has been identified as an emperor, but is more likely derived from representations of Buddhist Immortals studied by western artists from Chinese originals, and the man's costume and commonplace sunhat argue against an imperial depiction. Several soapstone statuettes of the Immortals formed part of the Savoyard art collections by 1700, and may have served as one of the sources for the design. The fabric of the bed hanging is Piedmontese, but unfortunately its patron and destination are, to my knowledge, unknown. In any event, such a costly, sumptuous object strongly argues for either a royal or at least a rich buyer, and the ubiquity of such objects testifies to the wide dissemination of Chinoiserie design in Piedmont-Sardinia by the early decades of the Settecento.

This splendid Chinoiserie fabric also tells us something about the aesthetic and stylistic influences on northwestern Italian Chinoiserie in the first half of the eighteenth century. East Asian potentates or deities being adored by a pair of suppliants are a compositional motif also encountered in early French Rococo design. Antoine Watteau's famous *Chinese Deity adored by Two Devotees*, an engraving of the now-lost wall decoration for the château de la Muette near Paris, the original dating about 1714–15, is a case in point (Fig. 16.3).[9] The La Muette decorations were famous in their time and date only a few years before the triad appears in the Piedmontese bed hanging, but a direct connection between Watteau and the Italian fabric designer is speculative. In any event, similar narratives were widely disseminated by the early eighteenth century.

A salient feature of Enlightenment-era personal interaction was a vastly augmented emphasis on intimate conversation. This was true in both official diplomatic discourse and in domestic exchanges. The grand ceremonies celebrating peace treaties, royal births, deaths and marriages were little altered from baroque practices, but the business of government and élite sociability became a much more private affair. Visual culture responded to this sea change by creating smaller rooms, more comfortable furniture and elegant décor that relaxed protocol and blurred hierarchical distinctions. The most important papal audience of the eighteenth century, for example,

---

[8] For a brief survey of Piedmontese Chinoiserie in the late seventeenth and early eighteenth centuries, see: Morena 2009a: 152–77 (with additional bibliography). The bed hanging is discussed briefly on p. 154. For an idea of the type of Asian art collected in Piedmont by the royal family, see: Caterina 2008b: 127–32.

[9] For the château and its Chinoiserie images, see: Scott 2003: 189–248.

Figure 16.2 Anonymous, *Detail of a bed hanging showing a Chinese Deity with two supplicants*, embroidered silk, gold and silver thread, c. 1720, Photograph © Staatliche Schlösser und Gärten Baden-Württemberg Schloss Solitude.

was held in a very small pavilion chamber of Benedict XIV's new Caffeaus in the Quirinal Gardens in Rome in 1744, an event made famous by Giovanni Paolo Panini's highly mediated painting.[10] After a victory over the Austrians in the battle of Velletri near Rome, King Charles of Naples asked the Pope to receive him in audience, and the event took place in a small but elegant room with only the two leaders present. They sat in identical French armchairs and there were virtually no emblems of rank or hierarchy in evidence. East Asian and Saxon (Meissen porcelain was usually designated 'Saxon' during the eighteenth century) porcelain, oil on canvas paintings, Chinoiserie figurines and delicate gilt stucco surrounded Benedict and the Bourbon monarch. They sat beside a cosy fireplace, since the encounter took place in November. Such a high-level diplomatic meeting in so private and domestic a setting would have been almost inconceivable in the previous century. My

[10] For Panini's painting, see: Arisi 1986: 414.

Figure 16.3 After Antoine Watteau, *Adoration of the Goddess Ki Mào Sào in the Kingdom of Mang in the Country of Laos*, engraving after a lost painting from the Château de la Muette, near Paris, early 1710s, © akg-images.

point here is that small rooms with exquisite furnishings created for comfort and privacy rather than bombastic effect and pretentious splendour increasingly became the norm for the business of government. This was a lesson the Savoyard monarchs learned well.

By the 1720s, Piedmontese interiors, both royal and aristocratic, began to feature Chinoiserie as a crucial design element of the elegant informality modern sociability demanded. Three examples will help support my argument. Decorative arts historians Catherine L. Futter and John Twilley have recently investigated the restoration and reinstallation of a Chinoiserie cabinet dating circa 1740 and now reinstalled in the Nelson-Atkins Museum in Kansas City, Missouri (Fig. 16.4).[11] This lovely *gabinetto* was made for a 'Chinese' room in the Villa Vacchetta at Grugliasco, a suburb of the capital very near two royal residences. Its décor is in the fashionable Chinoiserie

[11] Futter and Twilley 2010: 137–55. See also: Futter 2008: 567–73.

style and is comprised of over 30 panels executed in imitation lacquer work, called japanning in the eighteenth century. The figural elements consist of 'exotic' landscapes containing pagodas, human figures, garden pavilions, birds and large flying insects rendered in gold and silver paint on a deep reddish background. In addition, several narrow panels painted in pastel colours depict flowers, birds and insects on a black ground done in imitation of East Asian cinnabar lacquer. Wood embrasures, or *boiseries*, another decorative feature of French derivation, surround the *faux* lacquer panels. The preparatory drawings for the images, very likely by the prominent Piedmontese Chinoiserie painter Pietro Massa, are preserved in the Museo Civico in Turin. The Kansas City *gabinetto* is a typical Rococo exoticist period interior and its scale and décor were clearly designed to promote quiet conversation and to entertain small groups of intimate friends. Unfortunately, its original furniture does not survive, an all-too-common phenomenon for eighteenth-century interiors that presents major challenges to scholars of the decorative arts.

The four Chinese rooms dated 1732 in the Villa della Regina near Turin are especially elegant examples of Savoyard Chinoiserie deployed in a building with both a political and domestic character. The elegant suburban pleasure house was built in the late sixteenth century, but was expanded, modernized and wholly refurbished by King Charles Emmanuel III's consort, Polyxena, Landgräfin von Hessen-Rheinfels-Rottenburg, who he had married in 1724 when still heir to the throne. The Villa della Regina was so designated because it was the favourite residence of Queen Anne-Marie d'Orléans, wife of Victor Amadeus II and grandmother of the future King Louis XV. When she died in 1728, her daughter-in-law, Queen Polyxena, purchased the property and hired the family architect, Filippo Juvarra, to oversee its ambitious restoration and redecoration.[12]

Of the four Chinese rooms, three of which have been recently restored, The Queen's Apartment, designated 'Gabinetto verso mezza notte, e Ponente alla China', is the most impressive, both in its design by Juvarra and in its imaginative decoration (Fig. 16.5). It was intended to be open, charming and intimate, visualizing the more relaxed and informal style of Settecento monarchs. As I have indicated, the transferral of important meetings to relatively private, more intimate settings was characteristic of Rococo-era diplomacy in general and Italian practices in particular.

---

[12] For Juvarra's work at the Villa della Regina, see: Dardanello 2008b: 59–70 (with additional bibliography).

Figure 16.4 Attributed to the workshop of Pietro Massa, *Gabinetto*, removed from the Palazzo Parato or Gastaldi, Gerbido (now part of Grugliasco), c. 1740–50, poplar with paint, gilding and varnish, The Nelson-Atkins Museum of Art, Kansas City.

The Chinoiseries at the Villa della Regina, executed at almost the same time as the mythological decorations in the Hôtel de Soubise in Paris, have strong formal affinities to the lacquer cabinet from the private villa in Grugliasco now preserved in Kansas City. Indeed, the Villa della Regina decorations must have been a major influence on the *gabinetto*, and provide a strong argument for Pietro Massa's direction of the project, for he also worked extensively under Juvarra for Queen Polyxena. Massa was the leading Chinoiserie decorator in Turin during the middle decades of the eighteenth century and was much employed by the Savoyard family in their large-scale architectural projects. The Villa della Regina paintings are coated in lacquer and are contained in *boiseries*. The objects depicted include large birds, garden pavilions, Chinese figures in landscapes, topiary trees, rock formations and other natural forms treated in a highly inventive, fanciful manner typical of the international Rococo aesthetic. The Chinoiseries at the Villa della Regina are of the highest quality, both in terms of invention

Figure 16.5 Filippo Juvarra, Pietro Massa and studio, Giovanni Maria Andreli *et al.*, *Gabinetto verso mezza notte, e Ponente alla China,* The Queen's Apartment, c. 1732–5, Villa della Regina, Turin, courtesy of the Ministero dei Beni e delle Attività Culturali e del Turismo – Soprintendenza Archeologia Belle Arti e Paesaggio per la Città Metropolitana di Torino.

and execution, and are arguably the zenith of the Piedmontese version of the Chinese style.

Art historians Lucia Caterina and Cristina Mossetti, the leading authorities on Piedmontese Chinoiserie, have documented 27 interiors *alla Cina* in Turin and its environs, making the capital city arguably the most important centre for the style in the Italian peninsula.[13] Massa's Chinoiserie creations are a combination of exoticist fantasy and accurate detail, since he undoubtedly used authentic Chinese objects available to him either in person or through prints to inform his visualizations of East Asia. *Landscape with an Empress seated on a Deer* of c. 1759 is a case in point (Fig. 16.6). Probably

---

[13] For the Chinoiserie decorations of the Villa della Regina and the style's development in Turin, see the fundamental studies by Caterina and Mossetti (2005a; 2005b).

Figure 16.6 Pietro Massa, *Landscape with a Chinese Empress Seated on a Stag*, oil on canvas, c. 1759, Pelham Galleries, London, photograph courtesy of Pelham Galleries.

executed for the villa of the Marchese Medici del Vascello, the oil on canvas image is over nine feet high. Details of costume and architecture are convincing and largely authentic, but the notion of any lady of rank, above all a Qing dynasty empress being depicted astride a deer, is pure orientalist fantasy.

A final superb example of Savoyard Chinoiserie interior decoration is found at the Palazzo Reale. It shows Filippo Juvarra to advantage as a proponent of the style. The Chinese Room (Fig. 16.7), a small square cabinet designed in the early 1730s and installed in 1736–7, is the finest of a number of Chinoiserie chambers in the Royal Palace executed during the middle decades of the century. While in Rome, Juvarra purchased a considerable number of original Chinese lacquer panels on behalf of King Charles Emmanuel to be used in the small *gabinetto* for which the royal architect was also making drawings. The décor includes both East Asian originals and Chinoiserie confections by Pietro Massa surrounding four large mirrors in irregular frames of gilded wood, all designed by Juvarra. The focal point of the ceiling is a mythological painting, *The Judgment of Paris* by Claudio Francesco Beaumont, the leading court artist in Turin during the early years of the Settecento.[14] The ceiling's *galante* subject complements the whimsical *fantasia* of the overall decoration beautifully. Juvarra's Chinese cabinet has a decidedly exoticist feel. The abundance of black lacquer, reflective mirrors and gold gilt creates a rich, sumptuous, yet intimate effect. The *gabinetto*'s decorative delicacy is an outstanding example of Piedmontese interior decoration and the room is an attractive example of the detailed, intimate style used by Juvarra in the smaller rooms of the Palazzo Reale. It stands in remarkable contrast to the formal opulence and ceremonial grandeur of the official reception rooms. Since important Grand Tourists and foreign diplomats doubtless visited the room, or at least passed through it during their tours of the palace, we may assume that the cabinet witnessed a number of important meetings in addition to its function as a small reception space leading to the enfilade of royal apartments.

The Kansas City red lacquer *gabinetto*, the Chinese Rooms of the Villa della Regina and Juvarra's Chinese Room in the Palazzo Reale are prominent examples of the deployment of Chinoiserie design in Turinese royal and aristocratic residences in the middle years of the eighteenth century. Many others could be considered, including the elegant Game Room (originally called the Camera Longo) of the Palazzina della Caccia di Stupinigi (Fig. 16.8) executed in 1765, with its light, delicate paintings that seem to be

---

[14] For Beaumont, see: Dardanello 2011.

Figure 16.7 Filippo Juvarra *et al.*, *Chinese Room*, 1736–7, Palazzo Reale, Turin, Ministero dei Beni e delle Attività Culturali e del Turismo – Polo Reale di Torino.

an intelligent mixture of the more florid Chinoiserie of the 1730s and 1740s joined to emerging Neoclassicism.[15] Unfortunately, the original furnishings of the Chinese rooms in the Palazzina have been obliterated.

There are several scholars whose incisive and magisterial publications on Piedmontese architecture and design, far too numerous to mention here, have been of enormous help to me in my attempt to place the Savoyard Chinese style in a British and, more broadly, a European political and social context. The international appeal of Chinoiserie as a signifier of modernity and global, as opposed to parochial, thinking must have been remarkably attractive to Europe's newest monarchy as it began to construct its visual identity in the 1720s. Moreover, it is no accident that Chinoiserie became popular in Piedmont-Sardinia at the same time that other élite Europeans began to demand scaled down, intimate spaces for new types of political

---

[15] For this elegantly understated Chinoiserie gallery, see: Caterina and Mossetti 2008: 530–3 (with archival and bibliographical sources).

Figure 16.8 Christian Wehrlin and Giovanni Pietro Pozzo, *Chinoiserie Landscapes and Grotesques*, 1765, 'Camera Longa', Palazzina di Caccia, Stupinigi, Archivio Storico, Fondazione Ordine Mauriziano.

and cultural exchanges that emphasized conversation and small group social dynamics. Any convincing account of the diplomatic, political and modernizing ambitions of the Kingdom of Piedmont-Sardinia must, in my view, take the ubiquity of *alla Cina* interior decoration into account.

Although Chinoiserie rooms in royal and aristocratic residences have received the lion's share of attention from art historical scholarship, component objects of these and other interior spaces should also be considered in this context. Furniture, draperies, screens, dressing gowns, porcelain, silver and other practical objects of visual culture were often designed in the Chinoiserie style. Such items were sometimes displayed in close proximity to luxury imports from China and Japan, since lacquer panels, desks, cabinets and silk screens, among other things, had long been collected in

Turin and continued to be imported throughout the Settecento. One of the myriad problems confronting researchers interested in such decorative arts productions is the fact that only rarely are they in the locations in which they were originally displayed. More often than not, they now are preserved in museums, and in many cases their early provenance is either unknown or poorly documented. Two examples, one Piedmontese and one English, will I hope shed light on the idea of *alla Cina* interiors as spaces of intimate exchange, both political and social, and call attention to the dramatically altered patterns of élite living in the eighteenth century that were as much in evidence in Piedmont-Sardinia as they were in Great Britain.

Small, delicate cabinets produced by Europe's finest *ébénistes* gradually came to replace the enormous, hulking cupboards and *secretaires* that held sway in upper-class interiors in the sixteenth and seventeenth centuries. An especially noteworthy example is the diminutive cabinet largely composed of *faux* lacquer panels with Chinoiserie themes long preserved in the Palazzo Madama in Turin but that has recently returned to the place for which it was intended – the Villa della Regina (Fig. 16.9).[16] Dated c. 1740 and produced in Piedmont, the body of the cabinet is perched on slender cabriole legs partly covered in gilt metal. They support a rectangular chest with two doors that open to reveal ten small compartments used for storing letters, writing papers, blotters, sealing wax and quills, along with other small objects of domestic use. The *alla Cina* iconography is rich and detailed, but on a miniature scale demanding close scrutiny, the type of looking that could only be accomplished in a space with a very limited number of viewers. Although the cabinet is unfortunately in a poor state of preservation, it nonetheless gives a good idea of the Chinoiserie mode popular in Piedmont-Sardinia. Elegant cabinets in a variety of styles were ubiquitous in posh eighteenth-century interiors and embodied sophisticated, progressive tastes. The exterior doors of the Villa della Regina cabinet were sealed with a key that could be inserted into a metal serrature and turned, exposing the small compartments, some of which could also be kept private with a second lock. These expensive pieces of furniture could in theory only be opened by the owner who had the key, eliminating the need to have servants fetch the items that in previous eras would have been kept in more imposing, and less private, places. Indeed, the desire to trim down the number of servants necessarily attendant on persons of rank was a major feature of the movement for greater personal privacy, above all in the domestic sphere. Interior décor in the Chinoiserie style even extended

---

[16]   Morena 2009a: 167–8.

Figure 16.9 Chinoiserie cabinet, with faux lacquer (*lacca povera*) panels, wood and gilt metal, c. 1740, Villa della Regina, Turin, Soprintendenza Archeologia Belle Arti e Paesaggio per la Città Metropolitana di Torino.

to such small decorative details as wainscoting, as an example by Pietro Massa in the Palazzo Reale indicates (Fig. 16.10). This sumptuous black lacquered object is decorated with Chinese figures, a large ho-ho bird, a rocky outcropping, flowers and, in the centre panel, an enormous butterfly that hovers over a gentleman holding a sun shade being entertained by a lute-playing lady. The existence of such an exquisite architectural detail indicates how pervasive Chinoiserie decoration had become in Turin by the third decade of the Settecento.

My final example is a work in metal produced in England that similarly visualizes new social practices in the era of the Grand Tour. The association of small group conversation with increased intimacy in sociability and the signification of progressive, modern sensibilities are seen to advantage in a

Figure 16.10 Pietro Massa, Lacquered wainscoting with Chinoiserie landscape, figures, plants, birds and insects, c. 1722, 'Gabinetto del Poggiolo', Palazzo Reale, Turin, Ministero dei Beni e delle Attività Culturali e del Turismo – Polo Reale di Torino.

stunning Chinoiserie *epergne*, probably designed by the English metalsmith Thomas Pitts about 1761 (Fig. 16.11). Unfortunately, the circumstances of its creation are not known. The combination of elegance and functionality executed in the fashionable Chinoiserie style marks the object as something remarkably modern. Executed in silver, the *epergne* is a miniaturized, pagoda-like structure whose trays are supported by elegant, Rococo arms highlighted with arabesques and other ornamental features. The trays are indirectly connected to small bells that tinkled gently when a guest lifted an exquisite edible from it. Pitts placed the *epergne*'s bells in imitation of those hung from the eave points of an actual pagoda, an architectural idea widely recorded by visitors to China and that was much imitated in Chinoiserie garden structures in the West.[17] The summit of the *epergne* has a sunhat-like

[17] The most famous Chinoiserie garden pagoda is William Chambers' structure in Kew Gardens, London (1761–2). The monument was inspired by Chambers' study of Chinese architecture during two trips to East Asia in the 1740s. See: Bald 1950.

Figure 16.11 Thomas Pitts, *Epergne*, 1761, silver, The Nelson-Atkins Museum of Art, Kansas City.

superstructure crowned by a pineapple, a traditional symbol of hospitality that functionally serves as a small handle to lift the object to transport its delicacies. Such a portable dessert server could be carried by a host without the assistance of servants, further forwarding the goal of increased privacy in small group conversations.[18] The Georgian silver *epergne* was widely influential in western and southern Europe during the eighteenth century, demonstrating that such luxury objects in the Chinoiserie and other Rococo modes owed much of their popularity to their promotion of small group conversation and the augmented informality, both diplomatic and social, which characterized the century's middle decades. Chinoiserie, in

[18] I am grateful to James Rothwell, Senior Curator and Adviser on Silver of the National Trust, for sharing his expertise on eighteenth-century silver and for clarifying several issues related to Pitts's, *epergne* and to Settecento Piedmontese and English production, see Rothwell in this volume, p. 194, note 62. I also thank Elizabeth Williams, former curator of decorative arts at the Nelson-Atkins Museum of Art in Kansas City, for allowing me to examine the *epergne* and for answering my numerous questions related to its various functions.

sum, was a highly sophisticated international aesthetic perfectly suited as up-to-date decoration for progressive spaces of enlightened exchange.

The kingdom of Piedmont-Sardinia in the early eighteenth century was one of Europe's two newest monarchies, the other being the Kingdom of Prussia-Brandenburg ruled by the Hohenzollern family. The Savoyard dynasty acknowledged its secondary military and diplomatic status, at least until the post-Napoleonic era, and was well versed in contemporary *realpolitik*. The Savoyards employed cultural diplomacy, marriage alliances and extremely cautious military adventures with remarkable dexterity in order to maintain their independence and even to expand their territories. Both Victor Amadeus II and Charles Emmanuel III had considerable luck in picking the winning side in the ongoing dynastic wars of the Settecento. To the aristocratic and dynastic elites of the Ancien Régime, engaging and negotiating the complex diplomatic networks that dominated Europe was essential to a progressive monarchy, and it was expected that kingship would be performed in appropriate settings. Coupled with rapidly changing social habits and the growing preference for small, exquisitely apportioned spaces in which to communicate, mid-Settecento modernity meant rejecting the bombastic pomp and colossal scale of the baroque and embracing the intimacy and naturalness of *le goût moderne*. Chinoiserie was a major, but certainly not the exclusive, decorative mode with which to trumpet the Savoyards' new royal status to the older European monarchies. Chinoiserie's ubiquity in regal and aristocratic palaces, townhouses and villas in Turin and its environs is eloquent testimony to the dynasty's belief that the style was not only pleasing and exotic, but also capable of allying it convincingly to the visual culture of Old Regime Europe.

CRISTINA MOSSETTI

Throughout the eighteenth century the Savoy court relied on its special envoys to Britain not only for diplomacy, but also in a royal quest to identify and purchase fashionable furnishings, fabrics, glassware, porcelain and clothing to export to Piedmont. Relevant archival documents testify to the broad discretionary powers that the Savoy representatives enjoyed at the royal court in London. New information regarding the availability and concerning the quality of a variety of objects that the Savoy court wished to acquire, along with information the Savoy representatives provided regarding the details of prices of these objects and also regarding the procedures for exchange, deposits and securities (relying also on the mediation of merchants and bankers), can now be analysed.[1]

In the later half of the eighteenth century, for example, Giuseppe Roberto Solaro, Marquis of Breglio, Savoy Minister Extraordinary to Vienna, was supplied with goods from the British market for the refurbishment of his Castle at Govone from 1741–50; Prince Luigi Vittorio of Savoy Carignano acquired 'i daini e i dindoni' ('deer and turkeys') for his estate at Racconigi Castle in 1753 and 1758, as well as Chinese wallpapers for the Castle in 1756; 'Chinese papers' (Chinese wallpapers) were purchased for the Savoy court for the Moncalieri Apartments in 1771 via the merchant Fayotti; and

---

[1] Calapà and Cereia (2005) have conducted further studies following an investigation which started with an exhibition on oriental porcelains (see Griseri and Romano 1986) in the context of research on the Cabinets 'alla China' of Villa della Regina. More data is available in the appendix to the Allemandi inventory of the Royal Palace and in the Accounts of the general treasury of the Royal Family in the database of the Royal Palace, a project backed by the Compagnia di San Paolo, edited by Pierre Rosenberg and Michela Di Macco. See this data for the reimbursements to merchants, bankers and envoys for clothing, porcelains and glassware from 1712–13. Payments are also documented for chandeliers (*lustri*) (1726–7); for the perfecting 'dell' orologgiere Boucherij', subsequently sent to Paris, and reimbursed by the Gentleman of the Bedchamber (Aiutante di Camera) of the Prince of Carignano (1741); 'acceria' of 36 'ventagline' ('trestles' of 36 'little fans') for the queen and for the mounting of other fans (1741); 'salini d'argento d'Inghilterra' ('English silver salt cellars') (1778); bottle carriers 'of English silver plate' (1787). 'Four large sealed cases containing the English glass … conserved for use and model' were in the Fabbrica della Chiusa della Reale Società dei Cristalli e dei Vetri; see: Pettenati 1987: 232.

furnishings for his Castle of Guarene, were acquired in London in 1774, by Traiano Giuseppe Roero di Guarene.[2]

As Savoy Special Envoy first to Dresden and then later to the British court (1749–55), Count Carlo Francesco Baldassarre Perrone di San Martino was renowned for his expertise in the fields of diplomacy and commerce, with copious correspondence from the Count on all these subjects still surviving. He was a trusted source of cultural information to the Savoy court because of his cosmopolitan taste and especially for his contacts that facilitated acquiring gifts and furnishings 'alla China'.[3] From London, Perrone also supervised the furnishing and decoration of his family residence at Ivrea. There he arranged his diverse collections in the niches of the great gallery. Among the 'curiosités ... de la Nature et de l'art', were displayed 'various beautiful rarities of the East and West Indies', Roman artifacts, some placed in the Greek Tempietto, along with pieces from China and Japan.[4] The inventories cite '34 oriental personages' and the 'collection of paintings depicting the cultivation of tea, the cultivation of rice, and the manufacture of silk'. These were most likely works on paper showing Chinese manufacturing processes that recall the same wallpapers used for furnishings throughout Europe, and that had been on view in Piedmont also from an earlier date because of Solaro, Count of Govone, then Marquis of Breglio's previous purchases of similar wallpapers first in Vienna and then later in London.[5]

Baldassarre Perrone's British sojourn was a determining factor for the modifications he made later to his Piedmontese estate. He commissioned the Piedmontese architect Giovanni Battista Borra, whose taste he highly

---

[2] On Govone, see: Brovia 1997: 28; on Racconigi, see: Gabrielli 1972: 52–5, 303–5; Ghisotti 2005a. For the Chinese papers, see: Caterina 2005; 2011. I particularly wish to thank Lucia Caterina, together with Laura D'Agostino and Elena Ragusa, for their suggestions for this paper.

[3] On Perrone, see: Dagna 1968: 19–37; Fragiacomo 2000; Zoller 2013; Calapà and Cereia 2005: 445. The discretion with which Perrone verified gifts on which the court provided precise 'dessein' is notable. He was adviser for the purchase of jewels (preferably from Paris) and for cups in porcelain that he returned because they were not 'assez belles ni d'assez bon gout' ('not pretty enough nor of good taste'), for gifts of 'fish from the Indies' and for the name of a merchant for 'une pièce de Pekin blanc peint à la Chine dans un genre nouveau et extremement joli' ('a piece of white Pekin painted à la Chine in a very charming and new genre'), in the context of the quest for fabrics, then entrusted also to his brother-in-law Lascaris. On the 'pechini', see: D'Agostino 2005; 2008.

[4] Fragiacomo 2000: 319–46.

[5] The 'personages' are probably the same as the 30 panels now at the Museo Garda at Ivrea; see: Ghisotti 2005f: 557; Merlotti and di Netro 2005: 440–1. On the purchase by Solaro (by 1741) and subsequent mounting, see: Caterina 2000. Besides those used at Riva di Chieri at the end of the 1700s, there are two series of papers depicting the Chinese manufacturing processes, today mounted in boiseries at Riggisberg, Fondazione Abegg and in Turin, Museo Accorsi-Ometto: there is no information on where these papers were originally installed, but they were both purchased by the Turin antique dealer Accorsi; see: Caterina 2005: 72.

esteemed, for the refurbishment of the garden of his Ivrea property, comprising the botanical garden and an 'enclos à la chinoisse'.[6] When Borra returned to Piedmont from Britain in 1756, because of the various architectural experiences he had gained while abroad, he personified the ideal designer, as was noted by Olga Zoller,[7] to 'launch in Piedmont the idea of an English park embellished with antique-style monuments'. Indeed, the success of Borra's work for British clients, including Richard Grenville, 1st Lord Temple and Edward Howard, 9th Duke of Norfolk, directly led the architect to the notice of the Prince of Carignano, as well as to other commissions from Piedmontese nobles.[8] Gioachino Bonaventura Argentero, Marquis of Bersezio, was among those who sought Borra's expertise and Borra was commissioned for work for Argentero's palace on the island of Santa Elisabetta in Turin, where Count Perrone resided and which he later purchased.[9]

A wide circle of representatives from the Savoy court stationed in European capitals and attentive to international trends appreciated the taste for exotic furnishings described as 'alla China'.[10] Similar to the British clients who had commissioned work from Borra because of his talents as an 'architect-decorator', the Piedmontese particularly appreciated the architect's decorative knowledge, which he had acquired on an expedition to the Levant that he had undertaken with an Anglo-Irish group.[11] However, while in Britain, Borra also realized decorative commissions described by Zoller as 'an inventive late Baroque style that was rarely to be found in England', stemming from his previous Piedmontese training.[12] As Giuseppe Dardanello has observed, the architect followed a 'dual track ... satisfying the increasing fashion for applying to architecture austere and unadorned elements derived from the archaeological models, surreptitiously introducing into the interiors a decorative sensitivity for a classicism of clearly

[6] See Olga Zoller's chapter in this volume for Borra in Britain.
[7] Zoller 2013: 108–10.
[8] See Zoller in this volume; see also: Dardanello 2013a.
[9] On the Marquis of Bersezio's palace, his museum of mineralogy and his scientific library, see: Vitullo 1959: 31–52; Dagna 1968: 38, 45.
[10] On the vogue for taste 'alla China' which developed among the 'international nobility', see: Merlotti and Ricardi di Netro 2005.
[11] Zoller 2001: 271; 2013; Rowan 2013b. Borra sent Carlo Francesco II Valperga di Masino the French translation of Robert Wood's volume on Paylmyra in 1753; see: Ballaira and Ghisotti 1994: 125, and later probably suggested decorative motifs from Palmira for his castle in Masino.
[12] Zoller 2001: 273–4. On the use of motifs taken from the figures designed by Borra for Wood's volumes (1753 and 1757), see: Dardanello 2001; Zoller 2001: 259ff; Rowan 2013b: 115–18; Zoller 2013: 99; Dardanello 2013b.

Baroque inspiration derived directly from Juvarra'.[13] This aesthetic was indeed the antithesis of English Palladianism.

At Racconigi Castle, Borra made manifest his style in a way that was 'diametrically opposed to the proliferating rococo that triumphed in the Turinese palaces': it turned out to be a 'masterpiece of eclecticism'.[14] An example of this is the Sala d'Ercole, where the Pozzi brothers contributed to the exotic design of the intertwining coffering of the vault, and where the plasterer, Giuseppe Bolina, modelled the splendid decorative stucco elements in the Sala di Diana with an 'unrepeatable unicum in the mixing of models, techniques, and styles orchestrated by the architect and by the plasterer' (Figs 17.1 and 17.2).[15]

The decoration of the rooms containing Chinese wallpapers in the east wing of Racconigi Castle may now tentatively be attributed to Borra. He was the inventor of a unique decorative style that united novel references to international taste with elements which were balanced by an arrangement of the overall ornamental design, which he came to adopt through an awareness of Filippo Juvarra's interiors. In the Sala d'Ercole and the Sala di Diana he avoided the local fashion where every 'rococo indulgence triumphed at that time in the Piedmontese context' with 'unbridled and irreverent fantasies'.[16] In the east wing of Racconigi Castle, freely elaborated motifs from the notes Borra took during his travels in the Middle East are set alongside a repertoire of traditional furnishings. By controlling the decorative elements and carvings, these motifs contribute to characterizing a new proposal for exoticism.

Various facts already known support the attributing to Borra of this design work at Racconigi. The 1873 guide to the castle points out that, prior to 1834, all the most important rooms of the two 'piani nobili' (main floors) were adorned with cloth-backed painted wallpapers like the wall covering still preserved in the Apartment of the Court Grandees, 'that come from China thanks to prince Ludovico in the years 1756'. Based on now untraceable documentation, Noemi Gabrielli was able to establish that these wallpaper purchases had taken place in London.[17]

Of the five rooms that still retain their Chinese wallpapers, three in particular testify to a broader eighteenth-century decorative project, even though these rooms are today presented in an arrangement traditionally

---

[13]   Dardanello 2007b: 252.
[14]   Dardanello 2007b: 252; Zoller 2013: 106.
[15]   Dardanello 2013b: 120–32.
[16]   Dardanello 2007b: 252.
[17]   Casale 1873: 37–8; Gabrielli 1971: 52–5, 303–4; Ghisotti 2005b: 502.

Figure 17.1 Giovanni Battista Borra, Giuseppe Bolina, Giovanni Pietro and Pietro Antonio Pozzo, 'Salone d'Ercole', detail showing the north wall, c. 1756–60, Castello di Racconigi, Photograph: Giuseppe Dardanello.

Figure 17.2 Giovanni Battista Borra and Giuseppe Bolina, 'Sala di Diana', c. 1756-60, Castello di Racconigi, Photograph: Giuseppe Dardanello.

dated to Tsar Nicolas II's visit to the Castle in 1909.[18] Oriented in succession facing onto the internal courtyard, the Sala del Trucco (or Pool table room, now called the Cafè Room) (Fig. 17.3), the Sala di Compagnia (today Salone or drawing-room) (Fig. 17.4) and the Sala d'Angolo (or Corner Room, today Salotto or small drawing-room) (Fig. 17.5) reveal similar arrangements. Nothing more is known presently about the original designations and purposes of the two rooms facing onto the opposite side, rooms which the Tsar used, which are adorned with wallpapers depicting scenes of Chinese life, and the study, featuring wallpaper showing flowers and birds.[19] The decoration of the first three rooms is articulated by wainscoting; by walls

[18] The current names and decorations of the vaults refer to this period. For a historical and technical examination conducted during research on Villa della Regina, see: Ghisotti *et al.* 2005a: 502–19.

[19] It is difficult to decipher the decorative elements remaining because of the evident, but not clear, overlapping of parts that have been protected, recovered, altered and compromised. An important note of warning is the presence of the same decorative motifs of the 'corner room' on the wainscoting and recesses of the adjacent antechamber, which has no Chinese papers and which is part of the nineteenth-century expansion visible on the surviving plans. I wish to thank Roberto Medico for his suggestions on these aspects. On the two rooms, the result of the division of a larger space, see: Ghisotti *et al.* 2005a: 516–19.

Figure 17.3 Attributed to Giovanni Battista Borra, 'Sala del Trucco', west wall showing the project for the 'alla china' setting, c. 1756–60, Castello di Racconigi, Ministero dei Beni e delle Attività Culturali e del Turismo-Polo Museale Regionale del Piemonte, Photograph: Ernani Orcorte.

featuring wallpapers showing scenes of Chinese life, framed as though they were tapestries, by mirrors above the fireplaces, wall tables and over-doors: it is only possible to identify their furnishings because of their description in the documents as 'alla orientale'.[20]

A variety of decorative motifs make up the wooden frames that contain the oriental papers on the walls, the over-doors and the windows. These motifs consist of different colour combinations, predominantly green, grey, pink and ivory – the same colours that are found in the paper panels of the wainscoting; the motifs painted on the wood and the plaster on the door

[20] Billiard tables and card tables are documented, as well as 'cadreghe e cadregoni di canna', 'cadregoni' ('chairs and large cane chairs', 'large chairs' and sofas in taffetas 'alla China', chandeliers (one remains in the corner room), and girandole (candelabra sconces) in iron painted with flowers (still conserved in all the rooms alongside the mirrors), see: Ghisotti 2005b: 504, 508.

Figure 17.4 Attributed to Giovanni Battista Borra, 'Sala di Compagnia', south wall showing the project for the 'alla china' setting, c. 1756–60, Castello di Racconigi, Ministero dei Beni e delle Attività Culturali e del Turismo-Polo Museale Regionale del Piemonte, Photograph: Ernani Orcorte.

panels, the obliquely cut window and door recesses, on the under-windows, and on the carvings of the consoles.[21]

The layout of this series of rooms at Racconigi is innovative for Piedmontese interior decoration for several reasons: oriental papers with scenes of Chinese life are used as wallpaper for numerous rooms, together with the distinctive framing arrangement characterized by a combination of unusual decorative motifs. It is worth noting that the royal court had recently refurbished apartments for the dukes of Savoy following Benedetto Alfieri's designs in the Royal Palace (1749) and in the Palace of Venaria (1753–5), including decorating the small private rooms 'alla China', and favouring boiseries with wooden panels in oriental lacquer and 'Chinese-style gilding'.[22]

---

[21] The decorations of the vault are also related to these colour schemes.

[22] In the Royal Palace, the Duchess's Gabinetto della Toeletta on the second floor was achieved using Chinese lacquers and integrations 'alla China' by the specialist Pietro Massa, and at

Figure 17.5 Attributed to Giovanni Battista Borra, 'Sala d'Angolo', west wall detail, showing the project for the 'alla china' setting, c. 1756–60, Castello di Racconigi, Ministero dei Beni e delle Attività Culturali e del Turismo-Polo Museale Regionale del Piemonte, Photograph: Ernani Orcorte.

According to archival documentation and the evidence of what is still extant today, oriental wallpaper was chosen for the reception rooms, card rooms and cabinets of several apartments for the refurbishment of

the Venaria the overall refurbishment was planned using boiseries with 'vieux lacques' (old lacquers). Oriental lacquers and their imitations were also used by the court for the Cabinets of the Royal Palace (1789) and Moncalieri (1788); see: Cornaglia 1996; Ghisotti 2005a: 406; Ghisotti 2005g: 474; Ghisotti 2005e: 490–3; Cornaglia 2012b: 58.

Racconigi Castle. Therefore, this decorative scheme can be assumed to have been included in what has been defined as Borra's 'eclectic programme'. In alignment with his patrons' tastes, Borra exploited, in an original way, those aesthetic cues provided by the contemporaneous European and British debate on architecture, decoration and its models, in which William Chambers' *Designs of Chinese Buildings* played a leading part.

Chambers' volume did not intend to 'promote a taste so much inferior to the antique' as 'generally speaking, Chinese architecture does not suit European purposes'. Instead the author declared, 'yet in extensive parks and gardens where a great variety of scenes are required, or in immense palaces, containing numerous apartments, I do not see the impropriety of furnishing some of the inferior ones in Chinese taste'.[23] This statement stands as an indicator of the London cultural climate that Borra knew well, especially in view of the fact that Chambers' book appeared a year after Borra's return to Piedmont, and that one of the dedicatees of the volume was the previously mentioned Lord Temple – an important patron of Borra, who employed him at his country seat of Stowe. Soon after designing the classical additions to the garden at Stowe, Borra redesigned Count Perrone's garden at Ivrea, realized 'after the English manner' by adding the 'Grecian Rotunda' to a 'Hermitage, a Grotto, a large Chinese Pagod'.[24]

It is also of interest to signal in this context, the identification of a 'China room or closet' adjacent to the 'State Dressing Room' on the ground-floor plans for Norfolk House in London, where Borra had just introduced his new style as interior designer for Edward Howard. Presently, however, it is not possible from the known documentation to establish any secure links between the purchase of wallpapers in London in 1756 for Racconigi, the architect, the commissioning patron and the British context.[25] Nonetheless, the sharing of a 'passion for Indian papers' that became popular in England via the consolidated tradition of the use of wallpapers, indicates that Borra had adopted Chambers' affirmation that: 'Variety is always delightful, and novelty, attended with nothing inconsistent or disagreeable, sometimes takes places of beauty.'[26]

---

[23] Chambers 1968; Harris 1968: 2. Harris points out that Chambers was aware that a repertoire of Chinese architecture might have compromised his reputation as an architect before he published his treatise on the architectural orders.

[24] Zoller 2013: 108.

[25] The plan is in: Fitz-Gerald 1973: 9; Zoller 2001: 273–7; Dardanello 2013b: 130–1. For Racconigi, the expenses paid out between 1750 and 1753 can be documented for the 'grand'albere piantate attorno al parterra all'inglese' ('the great trees planted around the English parterre'); see: Defabiani 1990: 382.

[26] Saunders 2002: 63–7; Chambers 1968.

The highly fashionable and modern 'Indian papers' were available in large quantities. Cheaper than lacquers, they could be used to complement painted taffetas and chintz, and in Britain they were generally used to cover the entire wall surface, with specially designed paper borders. They were also in great demand in Italy, France and Germany, and were often purchased at very high prices, an example being those acquired by Maria Teresa of Austria for the Castle of Haltburg.[27]

From the 1720s onwards, nobles from Piedmont holding diplomatic posts in the European capitals had also obtained oriental 'alla China' furnishing and 'Indian papers'.[28] 'Indian papers' had been purchased in Vienna early on to decorate two rooms of Govone Castle, and also other interiors for the Marquis Solaro di Breglio, whose brother had a 'teinture de papier de la Chine monté sur toile' ('paper tapestry of China mounted on canvas') in his dining room in Paris.[29] In Turin, Chinese papers are recorded in a dining room of the palace of the Marquis Carron di San Tommaso and in the palace of Count Antonio Maurizio Turinetti di Pertengo. Indeed, Turinetti possessed papers of all types, besides panels and fabrics 'alla China'.[30]

The Count had commissioned Borra's services for refurbishing his palace (as did Count Carlo Emanuele Saluzzo di Garessio, whose wife Teresa, the cultured sister of the Marquis of San Tommaso, had ordered a 'bed from the Indies'). For his Turin residence, Ercole Turinetti di Priero also commissioned Borra to design a room with Chinese papers in a modern style, with narrow frames surrounding plate-glass mirrors. These furnishings can be recognized in an old photograph showing the palace interiors.[31]

At Racconigi, 'Indian papers' were preferred to fabrics and lacquers. Innovative in concept, the decorative motifs were unique, contributing to the successful channelling of Borra's composite cultural training into a unified project. For the decorative motifs for the Chinese rooms, it appears Borra was inspired from his personal experience of an 'orient' whose classical elements he had directly experienced in the Levant, reworking these

[27] See: Saunders 2002: 63–73; Caterina 2000: 42, 47; Caterina 2005: 73; Caterina 2011.

[28] On the purchase of the oriental furnishings and the taste 'alla China' at the end of the 1600s, see: Ghisotti 2005a: 409–16; Merlotti and Ricardi di Netro 2005: 435–43; Caterina 2005: 61–78.

[29] On Govone, see: Brovia 1997: 27–9. On the Marquis Solaro di Breglio's brother, see: Merlotti and Ricardi di Netro 2005: 437.

[30] About the furnishings of Antonio Maurizio Turinetti di Pertengo in 1739, see: Ghisotti 2005e: 574. On the Cabinet with Chinese papers in Palazzo Carron (subsequently Lascaris), see: Ghisotti 2005f: 557.

[31] On the works attributed to Borra by the Derossi Guide of 1781, see: Zoller 1996b; Zoller 2001; Caterino 2013a: 178 (including discussion of questions regarding this attribution). On Count Garessio, see: Merlotti and Ricardi di Netro 2005: 436, 439. On Palazzo Turinetti di Priero, destroyed by bombing in World War II, see: Ghisotti 2005a: 411.

elements so that they could be set alongside the actual papers imported from the Far East. Basing himself on the configuration of the architectural orders, these decorative elements are proposed in various ways, using different techniques on doors, wainscots and under the windows, and they are freely integrated with others that were liberally drawn from Chinese wallpapers, suggesting the contemporaneous presence of imported wallpapers in the castle. The exotic figurative repertoire also included carved and painted frames that were combined in diverse ways to frame the wallpapers, delimiting panels and aperatures, in order to give each room its own specific character. The rooms may originally have been distinguished from one another by different colour schemes.

At Racconigi, however, the decorative 'Chinese' typologies illustrated in Chambers' contemporaneous *Designs of Chinese Buildings* were not utilized.[32] Furthermore, any reference by Borra to Thomas Chippendale's recent *Gentleman and Cabinet-Maker's Director* would appear minimal, as the combinations of rocaille motifs, exotic pavilions and various Chinese-style 'graticci' (trellises) in that publication – a publication that illustrates the typically English tradition of a 'rococo that mixes Gothic and Chinoiserie' – did not suit the refurbishment of Racconigi.[33] Rather, Borra took inspiration from Juvarra's design example at the Gabinetto Cinese (Chinese Cabinet) in the Royal Palace, where, in 1733, Juvarra had designed an arrangement of carved, gilded frames with floral motifs, seashells and festoons containing oriental and 'alla china' (japanned) panels. In this scheme, mirrors featured as an integral part of the design in order that light could become a determining element alongside the reflective surfaces of the Chinese and imitation-Chinese lacquers. Juvarra repeated this design solution for the 'alla China' cabinets at the Villa della Regina (some japanned, some decorated with 'oriental' iconography), and subsequently this decoration was updated in the Royal Palace by Benedetto Alfieri with newer decorative motifs, all the while maintaining the rigorous framework of the boiserie that Juvarra had installed previously in the Chinese Cabinet.[34]

However, this type of installation could not be used for papers acquired in rolls, that were to be placed high up, and set in narrative succession side-by-side, decorated with uninterrupted landscape scenes showing an

[32] Chambers (1968) made available typologies taken from sketches done in Canton and in India to rein in extravagances and inventions because 'at least the knowledge is curious and on particular occasions may likewise be useful to make Chinese compositions'.

[33] See: Roland Michel 1999: 517 (with regard to drawings by John Linnell); Chippendale 1966.

[34] Caterina, Ghisotti and Mossetti 2005. On the Cabinets of Villa della Regina, see: Mossetti 2005; Rolando Perino 2005; Rolando Perino 2008.

evocative, far-away reality. These imported papers were intended to be displayed as a continuous wall covering for an entire wall surface, which was the traditional British manner for wallpaper. What distinguished the Piedmontese style were the separate framed divisions between wainscot, over-doors and mirrors. Imitation wallpapers with 'oriental' scenes (drawn from actual imported papers, but based on a re-elaboration of oriental designs from the repertoire of models by J.-A. Fraisse) were displayed inside decoratively moulded frames, arranged symmetrically and variously decorated with motifs of leaves and floral festoons.[35] The iconographic lack of homogeneity of these furnishings is recomposed into a unified whole by the insertion of the 'alla Chinese' papers in over-doors and fire screens, and also on the mirrors. In this instance, Borra may have drawn on his experience of Alfieri's design for the octagonal room of Palazzo Isnardi di Caraglio – a much celebrated and novel approach to interior decorations with its exuberant rocaille component in the Juvarra tradition.[36] The same observations can be made regarding the console tables (with varying supports, shelves and a centrally sited shell, an integral part of the decorative project). The inspiration for the striking fireplace designs may derive from models of Juvarra and of Bernardo Vittone (1704–70).[37]

The paper wainscoting at Racconigi was inspired by various decorative sources. In the Sala di Compagnia and Sala d'Angolo the exotic motif of the Pronaos of the Funerary Temple at Palmyra is revisited, simplified and set diagonally, while in the Sala del Trucco the motif is a decorative detail taken from Chinese papers.[38] The motif featuring on the wainscoting (on fabric-backed paper), on the doors and on the under-windows (painted directly onto the wood surfaces) of the two rooms, differs only in its colour scheme, which plays on the various nuances of ochre and green, relating to the different backgrounds of the floral motifs. In the Sala del Trucco the same spirit of revisitation dominates. Trellis-like motifs were proposed in

---

[35] On these papers, which reflect the style of the Rebaudengo workshop, in the light of the iconographic motifs used at Rivoli, see: Caterina and Mossetti 2005a; 2005b; Ghisotti *et al.* 2005a; Caterina and Mossetti 2006.

[36] On Palazzo Isnardi di Caraglio the sources indicate Borra's work, which has been disputed by critics, see: Bellini 1978: 211; Zoller 1996a: 183–8; Zoller 2001; Caterino 2013a: 178.

[37] Dardanello 2007a: 241–5; 2008.

[38] The motif utilized for the papers of the wainscoting at Racconigi is composed of a succession of double circumferences with central floral motifs linked to each other, alternating with a flower that has greater prominence; see: Wood 1753; Zoller 2001: 257; Dardanello 2013b. Moreover, the 'fidelity' of the reliefs and their re-proposal in British decorations was at the centre of a debate instigated by Adam; on which, see: Rowan 2013a: 45–6; Dardanello 2013a. Dardanello (2013b: 132) also identifies another page (JLHRS, Wood 17 carta 28) recording the variants immediately recognized by M.-J. Peyre; on which, see: Zoller 2001: 261.

various solutions by the (above all British) repertoires for furnishings that were widely used for ancient-style decorations. Instead, the motif in question here is actually an 'exotic' prompt. Of the diverse trellis-like motifs that separate spaces and landscapes in the Chinese papers, this motif has been taken from the small green gate present in one of the panels on the East wall of the Tsaren gate. Embellished in the centre with a small flower, the same motif reappears on the papers fitted for the Marquis Solaro di Breglio at Govone at the same date (Fig. 17.6).[39]

As in the Magnocavalli Palace at Moncalvo where in 1760 Borra proposed the Palmyrian decorative module he had utilized for the Sala di Diana at Racconigi, the solution of the trellis-like motif would serve to enrich his repertoire for the decoration of interiors for other clients.[40] Differently orientated, this motif was entrusted to the painter Giuseppe Gallo Barelli to decorate the Sala della Pace (the Room of Peace, designed by Borra in 1768) in the Palazzo Salmatoris in Cherasco.[41]

The three Chinese rooms of Racconigi are characterized by a succession of uniformly painted frames, in relief, that alternate with frames of differing heights and motifs. In the Sala di Compagnia, the dominant motif is composed of the alternation and succession of two types of floral motifs, one of which is taken from a study of the decorative elements of Sardis (Fig. 17.7). This motif frames the papers, both of the wainscoting and of the walls, and adorns the console tables, door and window frames, as well as the painted bands under the windows.[42] The result is a continuous undulating decoration, an abstraction and reinterpretation of the motifs recorded several times by Borra at Palmyra, Sardis, Aphrodisias and Laodicea.[43] This is

[39] The motif, in shades of grey and green, is composed of a succession of interwoven overlapping square outlines that create a sort of grid with a small flower in the centre. On this, see: Ghisotti *et al.* 2005a: 517. On Govone and the Chinese Cabinet in Moncalieri, see: Merlotti and Ricardi di Netro 2005: 442; Cornaglia 2012b: 58–9; Cornaglia 2012b: 58–9. Cornaglia, Ghisotti, Merlotti and Mossetti presented papers on these subjects at a workshop organized by Andrea Merlotti on the subject of *L'esotismo ritrovato. Il Gabinetto cinese della Duchessa d'Aosta dal Castello di Moncalieri al Palazzo vescovile di Mondovì* (Moncalieri 15 marzo 2013).

[40] Dardanello 2013b: 132.

[41] Zoller 1996a: 215–17, ill. 84; Caterino 2013a: 179–80.

[42] The inspirations for Racconigi are recorded in one of the notebooks at the University of London (JLHRS Wood donation 15 39r) which I consulted courtesy of Paul Jackson, who I wish to thank. On the notebooks, see: Rowan 2013a; Zoller 2013. On the identification of the subject of the London folio, see: Guglielmetto Mugion and Caterino 2013: 38.

[43] On the notebooks and the London drawings, and the drawings conserved at the Paul Mellon Collection studied by Olga Zoller and Giuseppe Dardanello, see: Zoller: 2001: 267; Dardanello 2013c: 83, 85, 92; Zoller 2013.

Figure 17.6 Vault showing a detail of the Chinese wallpaper, Anti-chamber, Castello di Govone, Ministero dei Beni e delle Attività Culturali e del Turismo–Soprintendenza Belle Arti e Paesaggio per le Province di Alessandria, Asti, Biella, Novara, Verbano Cusio Ossola e Vercelli, Photograph: Ernani Orcorte.

bordered by a foliate bead and dart design similar to examples by Juvarra at the Royal Palace, drawn from antique models.

In addition to the plant motifs that appear in varying proportions on the door and window frames at Racconigi, in the Sala d'Angolo the characteristic design is a succession of ivory-coloured, concatenating circles on a pink background. This had already been used for one of the frames at the centre of the vault in the Sala d'Ercole, and it seems to have been taken, virtually unaltered, from the entablature of the Temple of Bacchus at Baalbek.[44]

Borra also used the notes he took in the Levant, and not only those appearing in the two publications on Palmyra and Baalbek, for the frames of the mirrors, doors, and windows in the Sala del Trucco. He adopted the

---

[44] See the section in the drawing, London, RIBA Library Drawing Collection VOS 142 preparatory for figure XXXVI in Wood (1757) in Dardanello 2013c: 96.

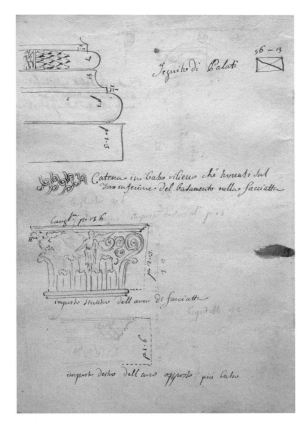

Figure 17.7 Giovanni Battista Borra, 'Sardes', Study of Architectural Details, pencil and brown ink, Joint Library of the Hellenic and Roman Societies, London, reproduced by kind permission of the Joint Library of the Hellenic and Roman Societies.

'bas-relief chain' observed in the order of the theatre at Palati (Fig. 17.8), combined with a Greek fret in ochre on a green background that is the dominant motif of this room. This is paired with a sort of relief decoration, a 'baccellatura', that is partly sculpted and partly painted.[45]

Specialized technical analysis of the Chinese rooms at Racconigi will provide new information. For example, the thick layers of discoloured paints must be examined, and the widespread presence of 'spolveri' (underlying designs) identifiable on the papers in the Sala d'Angolo and on the wooden doors in the Sala di Compagnia, must be thoroughly studied to understand the means

---

[45] The drawing, London, JLHRS, Wood donation 15, 39 v is reproduced by Dardanello (2013c: 79), which matches the reproduction of the preparatory drawing for the Palati theatre conserved in the Paul Mellon Collection. On Borra's unpublished work, see: Zoller 2013: 101–4.

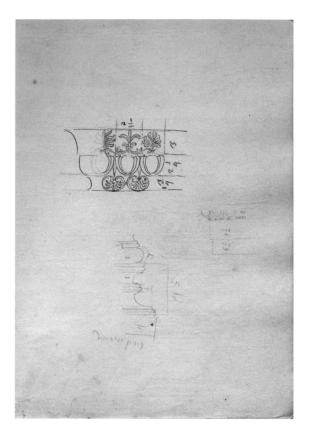

Figure 17.8 Giovanni Battista Borra, *Details of the Palati Theatre*, pencil and brown ink, Joint Library of the Hellenic and Roman Societies, London, reproduced by kind permission of the Joint Library of the Hellenic and Roman Societies.

of production of this typology of decorative paper decoration, taking into account that the activity of transferring the models, by the painters, woodcarvers and printers, can be documented presently only for fabrics 'alla Chinese'.[46] Furthermore, new studies must identify the individual responsibilities for paintings and carvings in what appears to have been a close-knit team, at work with a specific repertoire of ornamental decorations skilfully intermixed with well-established models, in part reutilized subsequently in different contexts.[47]

The exotic decoration of the 'Chinese' rooms of Racconigi Castle was, however, not exclusive for its time, as these designs co-existed with an

[46] Manchinu and Traversi 2005: 258.
[47] Aside from the previous observations, this would seem to be indicated by one of the lost ceilings by the painters Pozzo on the second floor of Villa della Regina; see: Manchinu and Traversi 2005: 255.

established tradition of 'alla China' furnishings. Alongside the rooms with papers, the nineteenth-century inventories describe a bedroom with an alcove and a fabric-covered ceiling painted in oils 'a la chinoise' by the 'célèbre Peter Massa, peintre de la cour' ('the well-known Peter Massa painter of the Court'). It may be possible to identify this room as the 'sala alla Cina' for which payment was made to the gilder Rorato for 'the paint of the frame for the ceiling' in 1760.[48] Indeed, between 1759 and 1760 Massa, with Bartolomeo Brambilla, was paid for 'pictures and paintings' in Turin and Racconigi. Moreover, the date '1759' appears on a canvas 'alla China' initialled 'PM', that has recently reappeared on the antiques market. This canvas, together with a further three panels already known from a photograph of the Baroque exhibition of 1937, and attributed to Massa at that time on the basis of style, provides evidence that the canvas may herald originally from Racconigi, especially considering the 'exotic tale in landscape' it features, inspired more by the oriental papers than by the lacquers (see Fig. 16.6).[49]

Between 1771 and 1778 the Gallery and the Royal Apartments of Moncalieri and Agliè were papered using papers purchased, in part, in Britain. During the same years that Poggio Imperiale in Florence was being re-fitted with Indian chintz, silks and Chinese papers acquired in Brussels, Traiano Giuseppe Roero di Guarene purchased 'Histories on paper' in London. As in many other noble Piedmontese residences, these papers were applied in several rooms, covering the entire wall, with low wainscots decorated 'alla Chinese'.[50]

In 1790, more papers were bought for the upper floors and for the Chiablese Palace of the Villa della Regina, only known by photographs and not well documented. By 1792, the royal court no longer acquired decorative papers.[51]

A decorative novelty 'alla China' was the interior design undertaken at Riva di Chieri for the Countess Faustina Grosso from 1786–90, using papers depicting Chinese manufacturing processes on the walls, and with the vault and wainscoting decorated with red trellis motifs inspired by examples from Thomas Chippendale's publication.[52] During these same

[48] Ghisotti 2005b: 502.

[49] Ghisotti 2005a: 412. The four panels described above were exhibited in 2009 in Florence and Milan by the Pelham Gallery (see *Masterpieces of Italian Decorative Arts*, no date) with indications of their origins from the Medici del Vascello, after passing through the hands of the antique-dealer Accorsi.

[50] Caterina, Ghisotti and Mossetti 2005. On Florence, see: Branca 2011a; Branca 2011b; Caterina 2011. For the Italian situation, see: Morena 2009b.

[51] Caterina 2005; Manchinu and Traversi 2005: 254–6.

[52] On Palazzo Grosso see: Ghisotti *et al.* 2005b: 578–81; Caterina 2008a.

Figure 17.9 Carlo Randoni, the 'Chinese Room', showing a detail of the east wall decoration, c. 1792–4, Rivoli Castle. Vault painted by Francesco Rebaudengo in 1794; the carvings by Giuseppe Gianotti, Giovanni Antonio Gritella and Giovanni Battista Fumari, Ministero dei Beni e delle Attività Culturali e del Turismo–Soprintendenza per il Comune e la Provincia di Torino, Photograph: Ernani Orcorte.

years Carlo Randoni and Giuseppe Battista Piacenza renovated the ducal apartments in Turin, in Moncalieri and at the Venaria, in concordance with the British 'good taste' of Robert Adam.[53] In the vault of the Chinese Cabinet at Moncalieri, featuring 'Chinoiserie' iconography, designed in 1788 by Randoni and Piacenza with Chinese and imitation lacquers (like those of the Royal Palace of the same period), the perimeter motif additionally makes reference to the work of William Chambers.[54] Shortly afterwards, for the royal Duchess's Sala d'Udienza (Audience Chamber) at Rivoli, Randoni made a new proposal 'alla Chinese' (Fig. 17.9). This successful co-mingling

[53] Cornaglia 2012b: 76–8; Colle 2012. And as documented for Valperga di Masino, see: Ballaira and Ghisotti 1994: 120–5; Levi Momigliano 2009.
[54] Chambers 1968: VII; Ghisotti *et al.* 2005b: 484–8, 498–9; Cornaglia 2012b: 58.

Figure 17.10 William Chambers, *Design of Chinese Buildings, Furniture, Dresses, Machines, and Utensils*, plate IX, London 1757, Biblioteca Storica, Castello di Masino, reproduced by kind permission of the FAI – Fondo Ambiente Italiano, Photograph: Paola Rosetta.

of decorative styles was undertaken in conjunction with iconographic motifs carried out by the Rebaudengo workshop. These motifs can be identified on the vault via their referencing of Fraisse's repertoire, as well as on over-doors and mirrors at Racconigi,[55] whereas in the wainscoting and upper band of the walls, the decorative modules reveal an indebtedness to two figures from the 'Designs of Chinese Buildings' by William Chambers. Chambers' publication, at that time still representative of the most widespread repertoire for decoration, was reprinted in 1791 (Fig. 17.10).[56]

---

[55] Caterina and Mossetti 2005b; Manchinu and Traversi 2005: 259–63. Cornaglia 2012b: 78.

[56] Chambers 1968: IX fig. 2 and VII. The furnishings of the room 'alla Chinese' of the castle of Pollenzo, now transferred to the Palazzo Madama, Turin, were dubiously attributed to a British source; see: Pettenati 2004.

18 | The English Garden in Piedmont in the Late Eighteenth Century: Variations on the Picturesque, the Anglo-Chinese and the Landscape Garden

PAOLO CORNAGLIA

> Si je me mets à parler des maisons de France, je ne finirai pas; tout y paraît beau. On est étonné, on est ravi; mais ce ravissement passe bien vite. Elles perdent à l'examen. On a tout vu d'abord; on s'y ennuie. Elles se ressemblent toutes. De malheureuses règles mal entendues, ont produit une patte d'oie, un parterre, des bosquets à la droite, pareils aux bosquets de la gauche. Des arbres épuisés, des charmilles languissantes, des chemins labourés, où l'on ne peut pas se promener, une verdure malsaine, du foin au lieu de gazon. (Charles Joseph de Ligne, 1786).[1]

The Pre-Picturesque English Garden: Venaria Reale

While visiting Italy in the early 1730s the draftsman and engraver Friedrich Bernhard Werner documented the complex of Venaria Reale in three landscape views, two of which depict the gardens.[2] The immense facade of Juvarra's *Citroniera*, clearly conceived as a backdrop for the park at the end of the long Allea Reale, makes a scenographic appearance in a context that can be best described as 'hyper-architectonic', notwithstanding the dominant presence in it of vegetable matter: this is the so-called English Garden. Enclosed within the Portico Inglese, a porticoed structure of elms and hornbeams trained into *berceau* shapes using wooden supports, are two large parterres whose complex design is only partly visible due to the

---

[1] De Ligne 1922 (1786): 164. 'If I were to start talking about French houses, I would never end: everything about them seems so beautiful. One is left astonished, enchanted. But this enchantment does not last long. On closer inspection, they lose their charm. To start with, one has seen it all before; one is bored. They all look alike. Inappropriate rules, poorly interpreted, have produced a network of paths, parterre, groves on the left that are identical to those on the right. Tired trees, languishing arbours, tilled paths on which it is impossible to walk, unhealthy vegetation, hay instead of grass' (Charles Joseph de Ligne, 1786).

[2] Peyrot and Roccia 1994; Cornaglia 1994: 99–102.

angle of view. However, another testimonial of 1724 records the nature and shape of these parterres:

trasferitisi nel detto Giardino all'Inglese … trovasi il medesimo Giardino scompartito in due grandi pezze framezzate dalla continuazione della grande allea … principiante dalla facciata delle dette scuderie e citroniera nuove, detta allea ornata per l'estensione del medemo Giardino all'inglese con due linee d'iffi in numero di quarantadue … ed ognuna di dette pezze avere il centro in forma ovale ne due fianchi, e due teste un Rondeau in cadun luogo e nelli quattro angoli una pezza fatta a disegno, tutto quanto gazonato, ognuno de quali rondeau vedesi havere nel mezzo una pianta di Malva alta fatta a bolla, con cespuglio al piede in forma di cassa … quali tutte pezze gazonate, che formano il disegno di caduna di dette due pezze grandi sono circondate da plata banda bordata da due parti di martello ed ornata dentro con fiori denominati colchico, papaveri, oculi Christi … duecento ottanta otto piante tra rose, siringhe bianche, lillà di Persia, rose di Giudea, tutte fatte a bolla e numero trecentoventiquattro piante d'iffi.[3]

Furthermore, a late eighteenth-century drawing,[4] which coincides with Werner's view, reveals the details of the 'English' parterre, probably executed by Carlo Randoni during the period when the design was simplified, as is apparent from Falchetti and Perratone's large plan of 1796.[5] No aspect of what was described, drawn or surveyed directly relates to the actual appearance of the English garden of the period. In practice, it was one of several kinds of parterre recommended by contemporary publications as part of the still vigorous *jardin à la française*. Antoine Joseph Dezallier d'Argenville, in his work *La Théorie et la pratique du jardinage*, first published in 1709 and subsequently reprinted on numerous occasions, proposed,[6]

---

[3] *Testimoniale di Stato de' Reali Giardini di questo luogo, del dipartimento tenuto da Gasparo Bogino*, 6 April 1724, AST, II Archiviazione, cap.18, par. 303. 'Once inside the said English Garden … the said Garden is found to be divided into two large sections, separated by the extension of the large avenue … starting from the facade of the said stables and the new *citroniera*, and the said avenue being edged for the length of the said English Garden by two rows of box, numbering forty-two in all … and each of these sections has an oval centre on either side, and a roundel at each end, and in the four corners a grassed area with a design, and each of the roundels has a tall mallow plant in the middle, clipped into a ball, with a box-shaped bush at its foot … all the grassed sections, which form the design of each of the two said large sections, are surrounded by a flower-bed edged on both sides with box And embellished internally with flowers called *colchicum*, poppies, *oculus christi* … two hundred and eighty-eight plants, including roses, white lilac, Persian lilies, Damask roses, all clipped into balls and three hundred and twenty-four box plants.'

[4] Cornaglia 1994: 103.

[5] [Giacinto Falchetti and Ludovico Perratone], *Piano Regolare in misura del Parco alto e basso sulle fini della Venaria*, 1826 (but 1796–8), AST, Corte, *Genio Civile, Versamento 1935–36*, m. 13, n. 40.

[6] D'Argenville 1747 (2003): 99–105.

among others, the *parterre de broderie*, the *parterre d'orangerie*, the *parterre de pièces coupées pour les fleurs* and even a *parterre à l'angloise*:

c'est-à-dire tout de gazon, comparti en plusieurs desseins, et entouré d'une plate-bande de fleurs, coupée en différens endroits, et garnie d'ifs et d'arbrisseaux. Ce dessein, quoique formé de gazon, ne laisse pas d'être assez riche.[7]

Compared to the *broderie* parterre, this was a simplified form whose essence, based on the sometimes complex relationship between sand, gravel and lawn, reflected the greater simplicity of the contemporary English garden. However, the difference between a *parterre à l'angloise* and a *parterre de broderie* was in some cases very slight, as can be seen in Charles d'Aviler's treatise.[8]

Charles Joseph de Ligne, Privileged Observer of the Advent of the Picturesque in Continental Europe

As previously mentioned, by the late eighteenth century the English parterre no longer sufficed to evoke a greater proximity to the countryside in the vast open spaces of French gardens. Prince De Ligne, a careful observer of all garden-related novelties, actively promoted the new fashion from across the Channel and his *Coup d'oeil sur Beloeil*[9] contains a perceptive and sometimes derogatory account of the formal gardens of Europe, which had by then enjoyed more than a century of success. His judgements are cutting:

J'aime cent fois mieux la partie sauvage de Marly que celle qui est bien peignée. Il y faudrait un peu plus de vue ... l'herbe dans un jardin français, n'est pas contre sa dignité ... Je ne parle pas de ces ifs, de ces pyramides de buis, de ces colonnes faites à coups de ciseaux.[10]

In a further remark the Prince then added a fatal blow to the creator, the prime mover of this dominance of geometric form over nature: 'Le Nôtre was certainly neither a painter nor in love.'[11] The object of De Ligne's censure was the lack of sentiment in the gardens of Absolutism. This intolerance of

---

[7] D'Argenville 1747 (2003): 94. 'That is say, entirely covered with grass, divided into various patterns and surrounded by a flower-bed, intersected at several points and ornamented with box and shrubs. Although composed solely of grass, this design is no less rich on this account.'
[8] D'Aviler 1710: 190–200.
[9] De Ligne 1922 (1786).
[10] De Ligne 1922 (1786): 162, 170, 173.
[11] De Ligne 1922 (1786): 130.

the product of a system whose rules were suffocating freedom, and a system that would coincidentally lead to an outburst of extreme violence in France, spread across continental Europe, conveyed by printed materials, letter exchanges, garden designers[12] and, above all, individuals like Prince De Ligne. Indeed, the latter went as far as to claim that: 'It is easy enough to describe, but I challenge the Italians to make an English garden. The warmth of the soil and the heat of the sun deprive them of those enchanting meadows so restful to the eyes.'[13]

An English Villa in Racconigi

The traditional genealogy for the advent of the Picturesque in Piedmont locates the first experiments at Racconigi.[14] In fact, this genealogy needs to be both strengthened and revised. Racconigi was indeed the place where an English garden was developed before it made its first real appearance. Prince Luigi Vittorio di Carignano decided to renew the castle in the mid-eighteenth century, after he had inherited it with all the trappings of the *Grand Siècle* transplanted to Italy: a *château massé* designed by Guarino Guarini, clearly along the lines of Salomon de Brosse's at Blérancourt,[15] complete with ship's keel roofs and belvederes, and a huge French-style garden to match the building, that had been designed by André Le Notre in 1670. The prince wanted to modernize the whole complex and, as his architect, he appointed Giovanni Battista Borra, originally from Cuneo but whose main appeal was that of having recently worked for the English aristocracy, both in London (Norfolk House, 1755) and in the counties (he designed the gardens and interiors for Stowe House, 1752–5), and having travelled with Robert Wood on a long trip to Baalbeck and Palmyra.[16] Between 1756 and 1758, Borra renovated the facade of the castle facing the town that had remained incomplete since Guarini's time. Borra had to include Guarini's central structure in the overall design, added to provide a source of overhead light to the otherwise unlit central salon. If this extraneous volume is removed from the engraving showing the facade before

---

[12] The work by Thomas Whately, *Observations on Modern Gardening*, 1770, was translated into French almost immediately with the title *L'art de former les jardins modernes* (Paris 1772).

[13] De Ligne 1922 (1786): 71.

[14] Defabiani 1990.

[15] Cornaglia 2007: 147.

[16] Zoller 2001. Borra drew the plates published in two works by Wood (1753; 1757): see Zoller in this volume for Borra's British commissions.

later extensions,[17] the form of an English country house clearly emerges, transplanted into the fields around Cuneo. The central pronaos, the lateral wings and parapet vases recall a model subsequently published in *Vitruvius Scoticus*[18] in 1812, but that had already been built in 1738–48 by William Adam, father of the more famous brothers, at Duff House in Banffshire.[19]

The Picturesque in Piedmont. The Official Sites, Real or on Paper: Racconigi, Riva di Chieri

Plans for the garden to match this 'English villa' were implemented not by Prince Luigi, who had commissioned Borra's facade, but by his widow, Giuseppina of Lorraine Armagnac. In the literature, which is relatively abundant on this subject, the garden dates from 1787. Leaving aside the personality of Giuseppina, a very refined patron who has already been scrutinized by historians,[20] what interests us here is to define the parameters of the project and place it in the context of Italy at the time. The man behind these innovations in the park at Racconigi, Giacomo Pregliasco,[21] was a designer of coaches, town plans and, quite appropriately, stage sets and costumes. A few years earlier, in Paris, Carmontelle, talking of his Folie de Chartres, had stressed the spirit of these new perspectives by stating: 'Si l'on peut faire d'un jardin un pays d'illusion, pourquoi s'y refuser? On ne s'amuse que d'illusions … Transposons, dans nos jardins, les changements de scène des opéras'.[22] The space allocated to the various scenes, to the sentiments they aroused, and to the variety of possible settings in a single garden – among others, the Parc Monceau included a Dutch landscape, an Italian vineyard, a ruined castle, a rustic farm, Turkish tents, an Arab minaret, entire or ruined Graeco-Roman temples, a wood with tombs complete with Egyptian monuments, a *naumachia* with an island and obelisk, a Chinese garden with a *jeu de bague*, a riding school and a pagoda and a Tartar tent – can also be found at Racconigi, but limited to the large central areas of the park in order to preserve the formal layout of the whole.

---

[17] Anon., *Veduta del fronte sud del castello di Racconigi*, 1820, engraving, private collection. Published in: Defabiani 1990: 393.
[18] Adam 1812.
[19] Rykwert 1984: 22–5.
[20] Calderini 1993.
[21] Cornaglia 2009c.
[22] Louis Carrogis, *Le Jardin de Monceau*, 1779, in: Le Dantec 1996: 224. 'If a garden can be turned into an illusory landscape, why do without? Illusions alone are entertaining … Let us transpose the changing backdrops of our operas into our gardens.'

This principle of co-existence would also be applied at Caserta, where after 1785 John Andrew Graefer's English Garden would be installed alongside the late, monumental French-style garden, conceived by Luigi Vanvitelli but completed by his son, *in articulo mortis* for that particular fashion, and would again be seen in 1778 at Monza where it was used by Giuseppe Piermarini. The layout of the archducal villa of Monza, commissioned by Maria Theresa for her son Ferdinand, included a large formal plan and a specific area planned in keeping with the new sensitivity, to include a small lake and temple. The same combination, in an exact copy of Racconigi, would later be used inside the Habsburg domains in the early nineteenth century, for the Palatine Elector of Hungary's suburban garden at Nador Kert (now demolished): there the formal overall layout contained the Picturesque inside two large central areas, with winding paths, small reliefs, woods, areas for swings and irregular-shaped ponds.[23] In Le Nôtre's park the two central sections contained, according to the list attached to a plan dating from the Napoleonic era (Fig. 18.1), an 'auberge anglais, maison du paysan, maison suisse, le hangard, église gothique, maisonnette, temple de Merlin, grotte, la guérite, bergère (château vieux), maison rurale, la glacière et l'Hermitage'.[24] The sources used by Pregliasco at Racconigi seem quite clear: in 1763 William Chambers had published his book on Kew Gardens, and ten years later his *Dissertation on Oriental Gardening*.[25] Pregliasco's designs, which are in a private collection, part of which was published in 1971 and again in 2007,[26] show us the exotic-British references for his poetics: mosques and minarets and Chinese structures. Traces can even be found in the main source for the diffusion of the new taste across continental Europe, namely Le Rouge's 21 notebooks, published between 1775 and 1789 and dedicated to the Anglo-Chinese Garden:[27] the project for *Bains et Belveder à la Chinoise*[28] shows clear links to the Chinese Pavilion and the Philosopher's House at Bonnelles, in plate 12, notebook 12, published in 1784.[29] Alongside such exotic themes there were also hermitages,

[23] MOL, T14, no. 129 (after the transformation), n. 130 (before the transformation). Drawing no. 129 is published and dated as post 1799 in: Fatsar 2008: 85.

[24] AST, Sezioni Riunite, *Carte topografiche e disegni, Azienda Savoia Carignano, Tipi, Racconigi, Parco*, n. 83. 'An English inn, a peasant's house, a Swiss chalet, the shed, a Gothic church, cottage, Merlin's temple, grotto, sentry box, *bergère* (old castle), farmhouse, glacier and the Hermitage.'

[25] Chambers 1763; 1772.

[26] Gabrielli 1971; Macera 2007: vol. III.

[27] Le Rouge 2004.

[28] Gabrielli 1971: 252.

[29] Le Rouge 2004: 33.

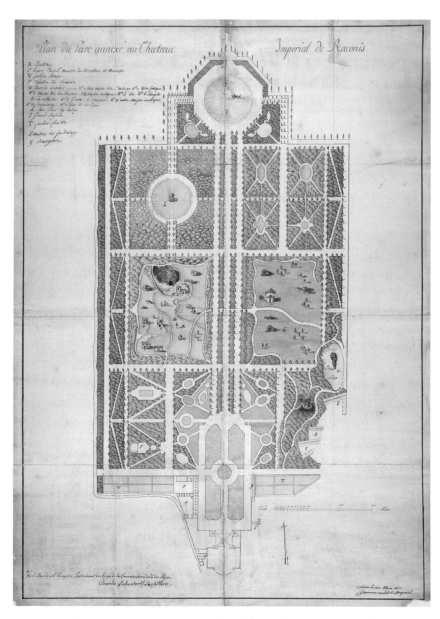

Figure 18.1 Giuseppe Battista Piacenza, *Plan of the Park at Racconigi Castle*, pencil, pen and ink, watercolour, 1812, Turin, Archivio di Stato di Torino, Archivio Savoia Carignano, disegno no. 83. Note Giacomo Pregliasco's interventions of 1787 in the centre of the drawing.

Gothic churches, and above all rustic buildings, filtered by the French experiences of Jean François Leroy at Chantilly (1772–5) and Hubert Robert and Richard Mique at the Petit Trianon (1779–85).

A possible German influence for these sources can be found in the designs by Leopoldo Pollack (1751–1806),[30] a pupil of Giuseppe Piermarini, for the garden belonging to Countess Faustina Mazzetti at Riva di Chieri, the second official staging-post in the spread of the Picturesque through Piedmont.[31] In Milan Pollack also worked on Villa Belgioioso (1790), where his design for the small garden was preferred to Haverfield's, a pupil of Capability Brown. Featuring a lake, with an island and temple, winding paths and large green parterre linking the villa to the lake, the design was appreciated and subsequently published by Ercole Silva in 1801,[32] in the volume entitled *Dell'arte dei giardini inglesi*, which Silva himself acknowledged as owing a debt to the recent treatise by Christian Caj Lorenz Hirschfeld: *Theorie der Gartenkunst* (Leipzig, 1779–85). Pollack then went on to design the new gardens at Palazzo Grosso di Riva, near Chieri (Turin), for the Contessa Faustina Mazzetti between 1796 and 1797. The building started as an exemplary late Baroque 'palace', built by Mario Ludovico Quarini, but after 1786 its interiors underwent a series of decorative renovations commissioned by the countess. The Torricelli brothers, who later also worked for the court at Castello di Rivoli, introduced pictorial themes influenced by Chinese designs and the new vogue for archaeology, whose sources can be traced to *Pitture antiche di Ercolano* (Naples 1755–71) and *Picturae Etruscorum in vasculis* (printed by G.B. Passeri, Rome 1767–75). As on other occasions, the project blended more formal elements with new picturesque details.

An initial drawing (1796) depicts the relatively small area to the side of the palace and clearly shows the artificial nature of the landscape: the winding paths, lawns and woods are intersected by straight avenues, which provided sight lines as well as highlighting scenically positioned objects. This was also the case of a later project for Villa Pesenti at Sombreno (1798). The drawing shows the 'theatre' as being embellished by pedestals, vases and boundary stones, as well as by small temples dedicated to Janus and Concord. The 'scenic' nature of the architecture is highlighted by the pantheon-like structure of the larger temple: standing against the perimeter wall, its geometry is cut diagonally by the edge of the garden and only part of the rotunda was actually built. Two water channels, which accentuate the vistas, link the two small temples on either side of the palace, containing steps down into the garden.

The bulk of the project (1797) relates to the larger part of the garden at the rear of the palace and to the parterres on the terrace. The formal part

---

[30] Agliardi and Cornaglia 2009.
[31] Dalmasso 1980.
[32] Silva 1801.

of this composition lies along the midline of the palace: a long avenue consisting of lawn edged with *berceaux*, linked to the terrace by a semicircular structure. Above this structural element is a formal *potager*, below which we find – in a tripartite design – a picturesque garden with fragments of 'countryside'. In the centre is an area similar to that designed in 1796, featuring open spaces, woods, winding paths and a small lake. On one side is a triangular area, again formally laid out with radial avenues, and on the other side there is a water channel in addition to a vineyard, planted in rows that follow the contours of a semicircular hill rising to the same height as the main terrace with the vineyard worker's house at the top. This same formula was used by Pollack at Villa Pesenti and – in geometrical terms alone – by Giacomo Pregliasco in his enlarged design for the Giardini Nazionali on the urban plan for Turin submitted for the 1802 competition.[33] Many of the decorative elements used by Pollack (pedestals, temples, wooden bridges, for example) are taken from the vocabulary of the 'English garden' found in a collection that was widely circulated in central Europe and published at this time: Johann Gottfried Grohmann's *Ideenmagazin für Liebhaber von Gärten, Englischen Anlagen und für Besitzer von Landgütern* (Leipzig 1796–7).[34] The French occupation of 1798 prevented the countess from building what would have been the most 'European' of Piedmont's new picturesque gardens.

Different Approaches: Filippo Castelli, Gugliemo Gullini, John Wallace

An overview of other names and other places offers a different view of how new garden ideas penetrated Piedmont. The (undated and again unbuilt) projects drawn up by Filippo Castelli (1738–1818) for the Solaro counts at Castello di Macello[35] (Figs 18.2–18.4) offer a good starting point. As in the case of Riva di Chieri, the project blends updated elements with permanent formal features, but uses an approach similar to Charles Bridgemann's work in England, for example at Stowe House, where pre-existing elements of the French garden persist but become 'disjointed', creating a sort of 'explosion' of the formal garden. A trident is superimposed on a diagonal cross,

---

[33] Comoli 1983: 98.
[34] The volumes were extraordinarily successful and were published in other languages, including French (*Recueil d'idées nouvelles pour la décoration des Jardins*, 1799). See also: Grohmann 1796–7; 1835–42.
[35] Cornaglia 2009a.

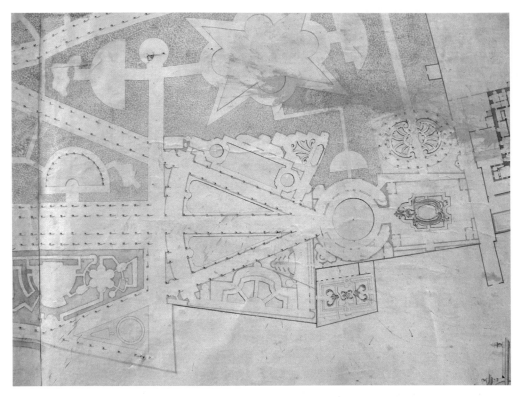

Figure 18.2 Filippo Castelli, *Design for the garden at Castello di Macello*, detail, pencil, pen and ink, watercolour, undated but late eighteenth century, Turin, Archivio di Stato di Torino, Archivio Berroni, cart. 1, no. 19.

but the composition is offset from the building. Throughout the garden there is evidence of a wide range of formal variations in the wooded areas, partly linked to masonic symbols. These comprise a succession of theatres of greenery, exuberantly Rococo parterres and *salles de bosquets* in various shapes, including the sun and moon, fortress plans, triangles, sunbursts and an unmistakable trowel. Snaking through this grid of recognizable shapes is a network of winding paths, a pointer to new ways of feeling. The exquisite purity of Castelli's project is confirmed by two further elements: the watercourse that runs down the side of the garden, and a sort of racecourse that forms part of the general layout, although designed separately. At the start, the watercourse is framed architecturally by a porticoed exedra with a rustic backdrop, but at the point where it meets a small hill there is a rustic fountain, not unlike the 'dovecot' present in Pollack's designs for the small garden at Riva, and also not dissimilar to certain solutions proposed by Grohmann. The area of the racecourse, which may have been influenced by descriptions of Pliny's villas[36] elaborated by Robert Castell in 1728, is defined by a tiered structure embellished by topiary arches and a real building at the end. The whole area is laid to lawn. It is one of the most elegant aspects of the project, again not unlike the formal part of Pollack's design at Riva, in line with the palace, and it shows the extreme sophistication of Filippo Castelli's work as a garden designer. Moreover, Robert Castell's reconstructions presented the blend of formal areas and those characterized by winding paths, diagonal and radial layouts, and small temples, typical of this late eighteenth-century design. Giuseppe Vincenzo Solaro del Borgo (c. 1760–1815), joint owner of Castello di Macello, married Luisa Asinari di San Marzano in 1781, and through this marriage also became the owner of Palazzo Isnardi di Caraglio, the most refined aristocratic palace in Turin, where Filippo Castelli had also worked. As Andrea Merlotti has pointed out,[37] in 1778 Solaro entered the masonic lodge of St Jean de la Mysterieuse in Turin and in 1780 he travelled to Holland to study law at Leiden University. It might be reasonable – also in view of the later reference to the Villa family of Villastellone having commissioned the Anglo-Chinese garden at their country seat – to suggest a link between those nobles who were both Freemasons and the introduction of this new fashion in Piedmont.

Another garden destined to remain on paper, but that was a clear sign of this modernizing process, is the one designed by the gardener Gugliemo Gullini for the Villa family at Villastellone in 1784. The villa was built by Filippo Juvarra in 1732 on the site of an existing medieval castle, and numerous designs for the addition of a formal garden are preserved in the family archive. Gullini's project,[38] to which there are no other references except for this drawing (Figs 18.5 and 18.6),[39] is laid out as an authentic *jardin anglo-chinois* and it draws on many of the solutions outlined in the collection of the same name published between 1775 and 1789. The hermitage, placed at the end of a long *berceau*, is an element frequently introduced into this type of garden, as was also seen at Racconigi, and it is included, together with grottoes, mosques, Moorish, classic or Gothic temples, for example, in *cahier* IV, published by Le Rouge in 1776.

The engravings in the *cahiers* reveal numerous elements that – irrespective of their chronological correspondence to the project in question – highlight Gullini's sphere of reference. Clear links can be identified with the layout

---

[36] Castell 1728 (dedicated to Lord Burlington).
[37] I would like to thank Andrea Merlotti for this information concerning the link between the Solaro family and Freemasonry.
[38] Cornaglia 2009b.
[39] AST, Sezioni Riunite, *Archivio Broglia, Disegni*, n. 5.

Figure 18.3 Filippo Castelli, *Design for the garden at Castello di Macello*, detail of the parterres, pencil, pen and ink, watercolour, undated but late eighteenth century, Turin, Archivio di Stato di Torino, Archivio Berroni, cart. 1, no. 19.

of the Folie Saint James, Paris, built in 1777–80 (*cahier* XX, 1788), with the solutions put forward by Carmontelle for the Hôtel Molé, Paris, particularly in the transition between plain parterres and areas with complex, serpentine pathways (*cahier* IX, 1781), with Gentil's architectural design (datable to around 1785) for the garden at the Pavilion Welgelegen, Haarlem (*cahier* XX, 1788), or with the models proposed by M. Thiemé *jardinier décorateur* (*cahier* II, 1775), particularly those for the *berceaux* structures covered by climbing plants, as in Gullini's 'Chinese garden' in the centre of this design.

Links can also be found between the rose garden and the flower garden designed by Gullini at Villastellone and the *Idée d'un Jardin Chinois* for Monsieur d'Aguesseau by C.J. Chaumier, present in *cahier* VI, 1778. In many areas of Gullini's garden, the structure, planting or names typically identify it as part of the trend spreading across continental Europe: the Temple of Isis, the hall of cypresses, the Chinese Garden itself, centred on a Chinese House of which no drawings of the facade or sections survive, but

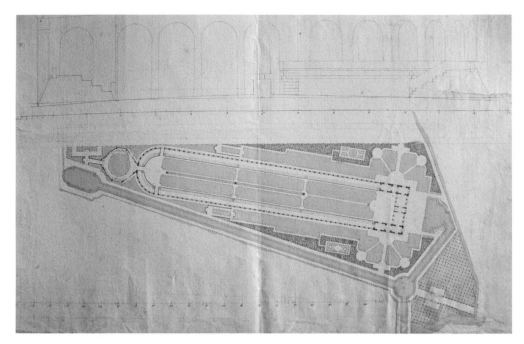

Figure 18.4 Filippo Castelli, *Design for the garden at Castello di Macello*, detail of the racecourse, pencil, pen and ink, watercolour, undated but late eighteenth century, Turin, Archivio di Stato di Torino, Archivio Berroni, cart. 1, no. 19.

whose name is symptomatic, if not of a form (the Chinese House designed by Mario Ludovico Quarini in 1782 for the court garden at Moncalieri is in fact a complex but traditional belvedere pavilion in *treillage*),[40] then at least of a cultural context shared with the northern European designers. On the contrary, an unsigned project[41] has survived for a temple, with a tetrastyle Doric pronaos, created by transforming the late Baroque chapel on the edge of the park and adding a new facade that provided changing perspectives.

While Gullini's garden was never built, the large landscaped park into which a classic temple of this kind would have fitted perfectly had already been created by 1804. Conceived in the style of Capability Brown, as an intensification and enhancement of the 'gran campagna' which, even in Juvarra's day, formed the view from the rear façade, and is datable to the two decades between 1784 (the date of Gullini's unbuilt project) and 1804 (the date of the Napoleonic topographical map on which it appears),[42] it

---

[40] Cornaglia 2009d.
[41] AST, Sezioni Riunite, *Archivio Broglia, Disegni*, n. 8.
[42] Sappa, Fornace, Rossati, *Plan géométrique de la Commune de Villastellon*, 1804 (AST, Corte, Carte Topografiche e Disegni, *Carte Topografiche per A e B, Villastellone*, n. 1).

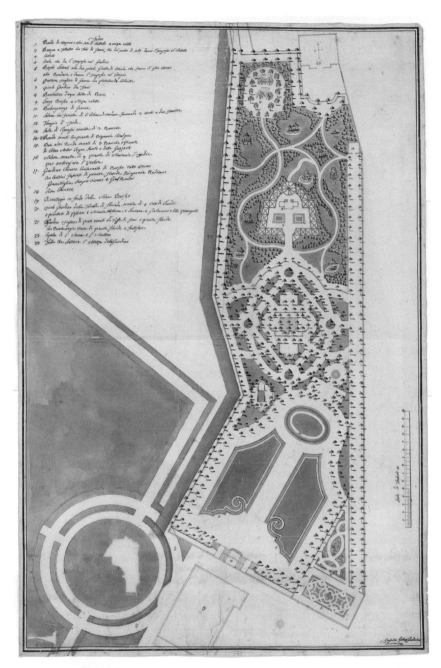

Figure 18.5 Guglielmo Gullini, *Design for the Anglo-Chinese Garden at Castello De Villa in Villastellone*, pencil, pen and ink, watercolour, dated 16 September 1784, Turin, Archivio di Stato di Torino, Archivio Broglia, Disegni, no. 5.

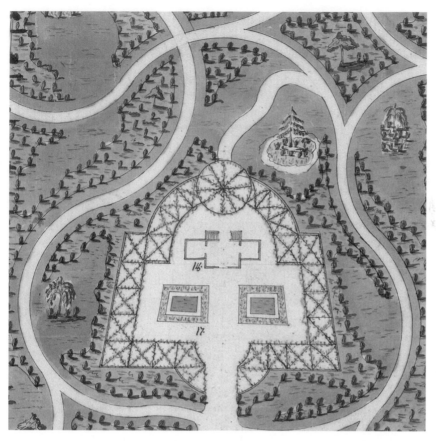

Figure 18.6 Guglielmo Gullini, *Design for the Anglo-Chinese garden at Castello De Villa in Villastellone*, detail of the Chinese House, pencil, pen and ink, watercolour, dated 16 September 1784, Turin, Archivio di Stato di Torino, Archivio Broglia, Disegni, no. 5.

has been attributed – without supporting documentation – to the gardener, John Wallace. The same John Wallace is also thought to have designed an avenue built in 1839 in the park at Castello di Masino, in the Canavese, and the park at the Castello di Montalto Dora, that, according to Maria Adriana Giusti, dates from the same period.[43] In the person of John Wallace we therefore have the tangible presence of a Scottish gardener active in Piedmont, a fact that shifts the spread of the Picturesque away from the influence of publications and contacts and highlights the role of direct intervention. John Wallace is thought to have belonged to a dynasty of Scottish gardeners who were active at Murthly Castle, some of whom emigrated to the United

---

[43] Giusti 2015.

States and are mentioned by John Claudius Loudon in 1828.[44] The following hypothetical family tree of the Wallace family is based on information provided by Grace Ellis (Scottish Garden Society):[45] John Wallace (1709–80), father of Robert, John and William, was the third generation of his family to be gardener at Murthly Castle (Perthshire, Scotland). After his death, he was succeeded by his son, Robert (1761–1829). When the latter also died, the second brother, John (1769–1839), then took over during the rebuilding works on the Castle and in its garden. The son of the third brother, William, who was also called John (1815–56), emigrated to the United States, while yet another John, Robert's son, might be the gardener who moved to Piedmont in the late eighteenth or early nineteenth century. While the dating of the works at Villastellone lead us to hypothesize that this might be John Wallace, Robert's son, the interval between the latter and those at Masino and at Montalto Dora suggest the presence of more than one generation of Wallaces in Piedmont, something that might be explained by the family's Jacobite sympathies. The grandfather John Wallace fought as a Jacobite at Culloden in 1746: Charles Emmanuel IV and Victor Emmanuel I were the heirs of the Stuarts in the early nineteenth century, creating a link with the Kingdom of Sardinia that only became operative after 1814.

The Landscaped Garden: the Empire of Xavier Kurten

The delicate progress of the Picturesque, poised between unrealized formal heritages, isolated realized episodes, and the appeal of wild nature and the setting, did not extend beyond the First Restoration. The peaceful coexistence between the area redesigned by Pregliasco and the French garden at Racconigi was short-lived: the rising star was Xavier Kurten (fl. 1811–40), responsible for introducing a new vogue into Piedmontese gardens in the first half of the nineteenth century (Salina 2009). Kurten, who was born at Brühl (Cologne), followed in the steps of his older brother, who in 1807 had published a treatise entitled *Essai sur les jardins* in Paris. Under Napoleon he was active at the Palazzo Reale and at Villa della Regina in Turin,[46] while

[44] Loudon 1828: III, 227.

[45] My sincere thanks to Grace Ellis for the research she carried out and the contacts with Murthly Castle. I would also like to thank Peter Ranson (Historic Scotland, District Architect) for his kind help.

[46] Kurten (as Antoine Kurtin) became gardener at the Palazzo Imperiale, Turin, in 1813, after working initially at the Vigna (Paolo Cornaglia, *Il Palazzo Reale di Torino. Sintesi degli interventi nei periodi 1805–1820, 1802–1847*, November 1999, unpublished text deposited with Compagnia di San Paolo, Turin).

the Restoration saw him involved in reconverting the larger gardens at residences belonging to the Savoy and their nobility. Successive victims to the new vogue for landscape and to Kurten's designs were the formal gardens of Govone (1819), followed by André Le Nôtre's entire complex at Racconigi (1820, the year when Kurten became director), and Michel Bernard's at Agliè (from 1829 onwards). Kurten also worked at Pollenzo (1838) and was appointed designer at the Giardini Reali in 1831. He followed a vision that was more closely linked to Capability Brown's rural landscape: his most grandiose project was that at Racconigi, where he created Piedmont's largest landscape park. The formal layout had already been erased in 1821,[47] following the destruction of Pregliasco's picturesque *fabriques* (indeed the latter's project for the renewal of the park, submitted in 1818, was not even taken into consideration given that its language was no longer in tune with the wishes of the new patron, Carlo Alberto).[48] A few features were preserved, however, including the Gothic church, the peasant's house, Merlin's cave with the ruined Doric temple above and the swan lake. The large lake at the bottom of the avenue became a pond whose edges were planted with willows, linked to the complex system of waterways. The straight avenues were transformed into curving paths, while clumps of trees appeared in the open spaces. The works by Pelagio Palagi, the artist responsible for the decorations at the royal palaces, completed the reconversion process in the 1830s by introducing dramatic buildings, such as the Neogothic *Margaria* and the adjoining glasshouses by Carlo Sada. Further interventions, including the three emphatic sightlines traversing the park, starting from the large meadow that replaced the parterre, were implemented by Giuseppe Roda in 1880 (Macera and Naretto 2009). The era of the picturesque, and its initial equilibrium with the earlier formal style, had now truly passed. More than a century separates Roda's interventions from the first signs of this fashion from across the Channel. Elsewhere, the time was now ripe for a return to the formal landscapes of the Grand Siècle, as is shown by the formal garden that developed again in France after 1875, and the consequent activity of Henri and Achille Duchêne not only at Vaux-le Vicomte but also – for the latter at least – at Blenheim, England.

---

[47] Benedetto Brunati, *Piano regolare della Derivazione e successivo andamento della bealera di Racconigi*, 1821, AST, Sezioni Riunite, Camerale, Piemonte, art. 663, n. 127.

[48] During the same period Pregliasco also designed and constructed – using well-tested methods – the park at the nearby Villa Berroni (1819). See: Cornaglia 2008.

PART VI

Turin in Britain: Cultural Exchange in Grand Tour Europe

ALASTAIR LAING

On 13 August 1754, Ivory Talbot of Lacock Abbey – whose employment of Victor Alexander Sederbach to make the bizarre terracotta figures that adorn the Gothic Hall shows what an interesting taste in sculpture he had – wrote to the architect of that, Sanderson Miller, to say: 'When at Bath fail not to see a piece of sculpture of Endymion on Mount Patmos, the performance of Mr. Plura, a statuary' (Fig. 19.1).[1]

The drawing-room marble group in question, of *Selene* – or, as she is more commonly known, *Diana – and Endymion*, signed and dated by the Torinese sculptor Giuseppe Antonio Plura ('Jos: Plura Taurinensis Fecit Bathoniae 1752'), is now, appropriately, one of the key works of art in the recently transformed Holburne Museum of Art in Bath. This was a coming home, since, despite Plura's showing it both in Bath and in London, where he later took a studio in Oxford Row, near Poland Street, it was not sold, but was left on the hands of his English widow. It was then inherited by their last surviving child, Mary, Mrs Thomas Bartrum, who died in 1831, and whose great-nephew(?), John Bartrum, wrote in his *Reminiscences of an Old Bath Boy*, around 1900: 'I know that I had for years, in my house in 41 Gay Street, a lovely marble group made by him [Plura] of Adonis awakened by Venus, Cupid remonstrating. I much regretted its removal and could not trace its final destination. Its outline is deeply impressed on my memory.'[2]

When it next surfaced, it was in Italy, in the collection of the solicitor-turned-art-historian, John Fleming, who published it in a detailed article on Plura in the November 1956 issue of *The Connoisseur*. At that point, he and his lifelong companion, Hugh Honour, were not yet living in the delightful Villa Marchio, near Lucca, but at Lerici. They took it with them to Asolo, and then to the Villa Marchio, where it stood in the Entrance Hall; but, following a burglary around 1994 of other items, they became nervous that it was too valuable and vulnerable to keep and sold it to the leading

---

[1] This paper is dedicated to the memory of John Fleming, who first assembled most of the information set out here (Fleming 1956: 175–81). Warwick County Archives, CR.125.B, letter 405; quoted by Fleming (1956: 180, n. 35) and by Roscoe (2009: 1004, *s.v.*).

[2] Bartrum c. 1900: 42.

Figure 19.1 Giuseppe Antonio Plura, *Selene*, marble, signed and dated, 'Jos: Plura Taurinensis Fecit Bathoniae 1752', Holburne Museum of Art, Bath.

French dealer in sculpture of the day, Alain Moatti, who in turn sold it to the foremost London dealer, Daniel Katz. It was bought from him, for a figure (£395,000) much greater than John Fleming and Hugh Honour had been paid for it, by the Holburne Museum in 1996.[3]

It is a beautiful piece, on an unusually small scale for a complex marble group (it measures 1 foot 8.5 inches – or 52 cm – high), and may have been a showpiece carved by the sculptor to demonstrate his virtuosity as an artist.[4] As Fleming hinted, though strikingly close to a marble of the same subject by Agostino Cornacchini in The Hermitage, it has something about it – not least an affinity with Michel-Ange Slodtz's marble of the same subject of

---

[3] Bishop 1999: 38–9; Holburne 2011: 68–9.

[4] It should be noted, however, that the marble presents natural imperfections in the area across the chest of the figure of *Selene* – perhaps the true reason that the piece remained with the sculptor, as it may well have been declined by a patron on account of this flaw.

1740 (private collection, Geneva) – that suggests that Plura, like his fellow Piedmontese, Francesco Ladatte, may have completed his training in Paris.

Who was this Giuseppe Antonio – or Joseph, as he later styled himself – Plura? Where did he come from? And what became of him? Well, he may have proclaimed himself as Turinese, and he was doubtless born and trained there, but his origins, like those of so many sculptors and stuccadors in Italy, lay in the Ticino, in what is now the Italian-speaking canton of Switzerland. His father, about whom we have much more information than we have about him, Carlo Giuseppe Plura, born in Lugano in 1663, later dying near Turin in Borgo San Dalmazzo in 1737, was called an 'intagliatore luganese d'anni 40' ('40-year-old carver from Lugano') when we first have a record of him, in the Turin census of 1705.[5]

Baudi di Vesme found a number of documents regarding sculpture by Carlo Giuseppe, almost always for wooden crucifixes. There are only a few records of sculpture in any other medium by him: a large *Resurrection* group in papier maché in the Basilica Mauriziana in Turin has variously been attributed to him or to the young Francesco Ladatte, while his last recorded work was a statue of *St Anne*, for an altar in the chapel of Saint Andrew in the Confraternità di San Giovanni, Savigliano, in Piedmont, but neither the confraternity building nor the statue survives.

Documents that link Carlo Giuseppe with Britain are the royal accounts of Victor Amadeus II, Duke of Savoy, and King of Sardinia since 1720, that include a payment of 384 *libre* for 14 January 1722: 'Allo scultore Carlo Giuseppe Plura, per prezzo di due piedi di tavola intagliati con figurine, fatti in servizio di Sua Maestà per due tavole di pietra, da mandarsi in Inghilterra, in regalo alla Principessa di Galles' ('To the sculptor, Carlo Giuseppe Plura, for two carved supports with figures, commissioned by his Majesty, for two marble tables, to be sent to England, in donation to the Princess of Wales'). If these tables with marble tops, and with figural supports carved by Carlo Giuseppe Plura, and gilded by Sebastiano Barberis, survive, they have not been identified, according to the Surveyor of the Queen's Furniture and Director of the Royal Collections, Jonathan Marsden. And it can only have been a coincidence that his son Giuseppe Antonio later showed in his studio in Oxford Row, along with the group of *Diana and Endymion*, two tables, with *diaspro* and *antico* tops respectively.

---

[5] Carlo Giuseppe Plura, son of Domenico Plura, was born in Lugano on 3 January 1663. On 30 May 1713, he married Anna Vittoria Bonarda in Turin. He died on 13 April 1737. For these and succeeding details about Carlo Giuseppe Plura, see: Baudi di Vesme 1968: III, 840–4; Gualano 1997; 2000; 2011. I am indebted to Giuseppe Dardanello for providing me with bibliographical sources.

Additional documents, however, almost surely demonstrate that Carlo Giuseppe personally travelled to Britain, to work for prestigious British patrons *in situ*. These consist of a series of payments that were made to a 'Mr. Plewra' and a 'Mr. Bargotee' for work at Castle Howard between June 1710 and August 1712, generally identified with the work related to the stucco chimneypiece and facing *scagliola* niche in the Great Hall of the castle.[6] As Mr Bargotee can certainly be identified as Giovanni Battista Bagutti, the celebrated stuccoist, born at Rovio, near Lugano, in 1681, it is feasible that the great familial networks that made the Ticinese and Comaschi so ubiquitous as stuccadores, painters and sculptors all over Europe, also brought Carlo Giuseppe Plura into the orbit of Bagutti and to Britain to work at Castle Howard.

But the most tempting reason to identify the 'Mr. Plewra' at Castle Howard with Carlo Giuseppe Plura and with Turinese connections, is the stucco there that is often forgotten, because it was lost in the fire of 1940, but which must surely help to account for the large payments made to Bagutti and Plura over the long period between 1710 and 1712: that in the High Saloon (Fig. 19.2).[7] This is of quite different character to what the partnership of Giuseppe Artari and Bagutti were to do subsequently. Does it not – particularly the ornament above the far door – have something of the Piedmontese Baroque about it? It is certainly possible that this could represent Bagutti's and Plura's distinctive vocabulary and style, so that I am much inclined to see it as the product of their collaboration.

If it is highly probable, therefore, that Carlo Giuseppe Plura travelled to Yorkshire to work for a period from 1710 to 1712 as stuccadore and sculptor, he was the first of three generations of Plura family sculptors with close ties to England, a transposition of familial talent which we will see finally came full circle with his grandson in the cultural ambit of the grand tour between Turin and Britain.

Carlo Giuseppe is recorded as having left four sons (Michele Felice, Giuseppe Antonio, Michel Angelo and Giovanni Battista) when he died in an accident in Turin in 1737.[8] In July of that year his widow and sons were paid – as he had been since at least 1730 – 'per la manutenzione a di lui carico delle macchine et apparati soliti farsi la settimana santa in San Giovanni' ('for the maintenance of the machines and decorations for

---

[6] See: Beard 1981: 244, 276 (citing payments to Bagutti and Plura in the Building Books in the Castle Howard Archives), colour plate 4. See also: Saumarez-Smith 1990: 109.

[7] See: Lees-Milne 1970: 148–65 and esp. figs 244–7, 252–4; Saumarez-Smith 1990: 29–31.

[8] See note 5 above.

Figure 19.2 Giovanni Battista Bagutti and Carlo Giuseppe Plura, stucco decorations, the High Saloon, Castle Howard (destroyed by fire in 1914), Country Life archives, © Country Life.

the customary Holy Week celebrations for the church of San Giovanni, which are his responsibility'). These payments continued to their dwindling number right up to 1798, when Michel Angelo was the sole survivor of the brothers. Already, by 1755, only he and Giuseppe Antonio remained.

Giuseppe Antonio was trained as a sculptor in marble by Simone Martinez in Turin between 1740 and 1745.[9] This allows the possibility that between then and 1749, when he may have arrived in England, he had – as Fleming suggested – further training in Paris. We do not know exactly when, or under what circumstances, he did come to England, but the clue seems to reside in the 'contemporary letters in private possession' that were known to Rupert Gunnis,[10] whose evidence is supported by the published family tradition cited by Fleming, that it was actually he who carved the statue of *Beau Nash*, now in the Pump Room in Bath, whose author is generally given as Prince Hoare.

The first that we know of this statue is George Vertue's note, made in January 1750, that:

as soon as a young statuary came to England from Italy, where he had been to make his studies, about 7 or 8 years, it was advertised in the News papers that Prince Hoare, statuary, being at Bath, some of the Citizens there had proposed by Subscription to erect a statue of Marble to the memory of Rich[d] Nash Esq., who had for forty years past so much encouraged the Interest and wellfare of that place. – This project was much encouraged by his Brother Hoare, an ingenious and well-esteemed painter of Portraits, principally in Crayons, who had great Success in his way and much esteemed for his Skill and his conduct. This young statuary, his Brother, was educated under Mr. Scheemaker, and in early dayes – growing a tall handsom agreeable person, and somewhat skill'd in musick-bids fair for a great man.[11]

Others did not think so highly of Prince Hoare, however. A little earlier, Horace Mann, with whom he stayed in Florence, considered him able but lazy, writing to Horace Walpole that he was 'very clever in copying, but I have seen nothing original of his doing. Had he application equal to his skill, I believe he would make a great figure, at least in England, where sculpture is not at any great pitch.'[12] In May 1751 Prince Hoare married an heiress, which will have removed commercial pressures on him; and in 1752 his brother William moved to London. He may well have accompanied him, since Bath and Somerset commissions tail off after that date. The statue of Beau Nash was finished in that year. Was it just chance that Giuseppe Antonio Plura was conveniently available in Bath to carve it? Or might he actually have been picked up by Prince Hoare, and brought to England as his practitioner?

[9] Dardanello 2005: 212.
[10] Gunnis 1968: 309.
[11] Vertue 1968: 152.
[12] *The Yale Edition of Horace* Walpole's Correspondence 1960: 86, letter of 26 August 1749.

Plura certainly married in Bath (but John Fleming's implication that he had done so as early as 1749 rested on a misreading of a later document), and found employment there on his own soon after carving the statue of *Beau Nash*. He modelled – probably in 1752 – a bust of *Gratiana Rodd, Mrs. Sharington Davenport* (a relation by marriage of Ivory Talbot of Lacock Abbey), and finished the carving of it the next year. The marble of this, signed *J.ᵖʰPlura Bath 1753* – a year after the group of *Diana and Endymion* – is on loan from the Davenport Family Trust to Lacock Abbey, the seat of Sharington Davenport's Talbot cousins, whilst the plaster model is on loan from it to No.1, Royal Crescent, Bath. By May 1753 he had carved, and in the same year was paid 25 guineas for the City Arms for the pediment of King Edward's School. This was designed and built between 1752 and 1754 by Thomas Jelly for the City Council, with Plura's father-in-law, John Ford, as master-mason. In 1755, he received 41 guineas for five busts of *Worthies* over the dies of the parapet (which were taken down and removed to storage in 1978).[13]

The two monuments by Plura listed by Ingrid Roscoe in her superb redoing of Gunnis, the *Biographical Dictionary of Sculptors in Britain* – to William Bowles in the church of All Saints, Newchurch, Isle of Wight; and to the Reverend William Alsop in the church of Saint James's, West Littleton, Gloucestershire – are to men who died in 1748 and 1750 respectively; but there is no need to suppose that the monuments to them were put up promptly. That to William Bowles is described in David Wharton's revised edition of Nikolaus Pevsner as a 'Cartouche with scrolled Rococo surround'.[14] The one to the Reverend William Alsop, Rector of Langridge and Vicar of Stanton Drew – both in Somerset – is a purely architectural tablet of coloured marbles, that could equally well have been made by Plura's master-mason father-in-law, but it is signed *Joseph Plura of Bath fecit*.

Giuseppe Antonio – or, as we can see he now called himself, Joseph – Plura, despite his marriage to Ford's daughter Mary, which produced a

---

[13] See: Ison 1980: 90 and plate opp. 88; Roscoe 2009: 1004 (note 2).

[14] Wharton and Pevsner 2006: 170. There is an anomaly here, however. Roscoe (2009: 1004) lists this memorial as by Joseph Plura, giving Rupert Gunnis's unpublished papers as her source, but neither David Wharton (who gives Bowles's year of death as 1749 rather than 1748, but that is probably the New Style rather than Old Style calendar), nor any other guide that mentions the church, names Plura as the author of it. William Bowles, M. P. died in 1748, but nothing in his life or death links him with the Isle of Wight or Bath. The Wikipedia entry on All Saints, Newchurch calls William Bowles 'author', but there is no book by him in the British Library or in The National Union Catalogue, and nothing links him with Bath. It seems possible either that there is a confusion in Rupert Gunnis's notes, and that the memorial by Plura is elsewhere, or that his notes have been misinterpreted.

daughter (born in 1751) and two sons (born in 1753 and 1755), evidently failed to find enough patronage in Bath, because by 1755 he had moved to London and taken the studio in Oxford Row. I had originally intended to write that he must have fared no better in the capital, since, in April of that year the Piedmontese Ambassador to the Court of Saint James's, Perrone, wrote to the Royal minister in Turin, Ossorio, to say that: 'There is here a Piedmontese called Plura, who works extremely well in marble and who desires to enter the service of the King.'[15] But, thanks to the generosity of Olga Zoller, I have been made aware of a reference to his work for an exalted client in London. Tessa Murdoch, in her article in *Apollo* entitled 'A French carver at Norfolk House; the mysterious Mr Cuenot', cites a reference to him in the Arundel Castle archives, given to her by Greg Sullivan.[16] The Carpenter and Joyner's bill of William Edwards for work at Norfolk House (the Music Room of which, rescued when the house was demolished in 1938, has been partially recreated in the Victoria and Albert Museum) includes, under 27 October 1755: 'To cutting away and making good to the chimneypiece put up by Mr. Plura.' Was this chimney-piece moved within the house? Was it the somewhat hybrid chimney-piece in the Music Room? Or – more plausibly – the one in the Great Drawing Room, which has (not 'had', for it was rediscovered in 1983)[17] great affinity with, for instance, such Piedmontese examples as one in the Palazzo Carignano in Turin?[18] Whichever the case, Ossorio replied to Perrone, indicating that the Royal Household would have work for him. But, in the following March, the new Sardinian Ambassador, de Viry, wrote to Ossorio to say that Plura had died of a malign fever, just when he was on the point of returning to Turin. This was followed by a letter in November 1756, explaining that Plura's Protestant English widow, who knew neither French nor Italian, did not want to go to Piedmont herself, nor could she bear to be separated from her children, by allowing them to go there. She promised, however, to leave them free to do so, once they had reached the age of discretion.

There were three children: the eldest, Mary, born in 1751, who was to marry Thomas Bartrum; Joseph, born in 1753, who is the one that concerns us here (called hereafter, Joseph the Younger); and John, born in 1755,

---

[15] 'Il y a ici un piémontois appellé Plura, qui travaille extrêmement bien en marbre et qui souhaite fort d'entrer au service du Roi'; see: Baudi di Vesme 1968: III, 843 (for this and the subsequent correspondence).

[16] See: Murdoch 2006: 54–63, esp. pp. 56 and 57 n. 6.

[17] See 'Rare Rococo fireplace found in garage', By Our Saleroom Correspondent, *The Times*, 18 February 1983, p. 14.

[18] See: Fitz-Gerald 1973: esp. pp. 13 and 33, and colour frontispiece and pls 1, 8, 9, 10 and 32.

who was to stay in Bath and become an auctioneer, and to marry Frances (Fanny) Delaval, the illegitimate daughter of Sir Francis Blake Delaval of Seaton Delaval and Betty Roach. We hear nothing more of Joseph the Younger, until he entered the Royal Academy Schools in 1773, when he was twenty. It seems more likely that it was not then, but later, that he worked for Joseph Nollekens as – according to J.T. Smith – he was 'among his best workmen',[19] for in May 1777 he was already leaving for Italy, with letters from the author and friend of Samuel Johnson, Giuseppe Baretti (who was himself from Turin), who described him as the son of one who had been a great friend, and of a 'donna di garbo' ('a well-mannered woman').[20] Before going to Italy – perhaps with Baretti's help – Joseph the Younger did a wax relief bust of him, which in 1902 belonged to the *cavaliere* Antonio Abate, and which was inscribed on the back by the sitter: '1777. Mio ritratto fatto da G.e Plura inglese oriondo Piemontese, piccolo figlio del famosissimo Scultore' ('1771. My portrait done by G.e Plura, Englishman, originally Piedmontese, younger son of the famous Sculptor').[21]

When in Italy, Plura the Younger befriended Thomas Jones, who – not having mentioned him previously – wrote in his diary under 1778: 'September – Friday 11th – After passing the Afternoon with some of our Friends – Plura the Sculptor and myself set off by the *Procaccio* for Naples at about half past nine o'clock.' Plura was evidently well provided with funds, since the 3½ day journey, with beds and one meal a day, cost them 7 *Sechins*, or 3½ guineas. Once in Naples, they took 'two small Apartments at 4 Carlines a day', boarding in a house on the Molo kept by a Swiss with an English wife, 'drinking Punch, Dorchester beer, and living much in the English manner'. Plura stayed until 10 November, making a number of excursions with Jones, before returning to Rome in the company of the future architect, John Henderson, another friend of Jones, who himself remained behind.[22]

In 1779 Plura the Younger made a bust of the later Sir John Coxe Hippisley 1st Bt of Ston Easton[23] and it was evidently the latter who on 24 September brought to Plura's studio George Augustus, Lord Herbert – later

---

[19] See: Smith 1920: I, 97, calling him 'Plara'. Contrary to Roscoe (2009: 1004), Plura the Younger was probably one of Nollekens's assistants only after his return from Italy. Between 1773 and going to Rome to continue his studies in 1777 he would have been attending the Royal Academy Schools. At that early period Nollekens's chief assistants were Giuseppe Angelini and Nathaniel Smith.

[20] *Opere* vol. IV: 251, 258, cited by Fleming 1956: 181, n 41; and in Baudi di Vesme 1968: III, 843–4.

[21] Baudi di Vesme 1968: III, 844.

[22] Oppé 1951: 75, 77, 78, 80, 81.

[23] I am grateful to Jonathan Yarker, for telling me that this sculpture still belongs to a descendant.

11th Earl of Pembroke – to whom he was acting as *cicerone*. Lord Herbert wrote in his diary, with some disappointment: 'In the evening went to see his [Hippisley's] Bust not yet finished, by a young English artist, viz: Plura, but could not see it to advantage as he was then placing the cast upon it.'[24]

It must have been around the same time that he made another lost 'Busto', of the then celebrated Jesuit priest, antiquary, and *cicerone*, the abbé Grant, though that was not shown at the Royal Academy until two years after the latter's death in 1784. For in November 1779 Hippisley wrote to Lord Herbert to say: 'Should you receive this at Florence, pray tell Sir Horace [Mann] and Lord [Cowper] how <u>like</u> Grant's bust is, and that Grant means to send them a Cast in a few weeks.'[25] Interestingly, when Plura exhibited this, he gave his address as that of the Huguenot carver and frame-maker, Dufour, in Little Titchfield Street. He exhibited one other bust at the Academy, that of an unnamed 'Nobleman' in 1782: might that have been of the 11th Earl of Pembroke, of which the Earl did not take delivery (since no bust of him by Plura appears to be at Wilton House today)?

In the same year, from the address of 11 Broad Street, Soho, he exhibited two 'Portraits of Gentlemen; models in wax'. These were presumably reliefs, like the lost one of Baretti, and like his undated *Self-Portrait*, which is on loan to the Victoria and Albert Museum, originally from Mrs Mary Bate; and one of a certain *Mr. Smith, of Bath*, signed and dated 1783, that belonged to T. Sainsbury in Bournemouth in 1973.[26]

These, sadly, are all that we either have, or know of, by Joseph Plura the Younger. It is particularly regrettable that no other free-standing sculpture by his father has been identified either; it is hard to believe that the *Diana and Endymion* was a one-off. But the one attempt to attribute such a thing to him – John Fleming's attribution to him of the late Sir Brinsley Ford's *The Virgin Caressing the Christ Child* – has not met with acceptance.[27] If this chapter serves any useful purpose, it will be if it stimulates someone to renew the search, and to come up with a more convincing attribution.

---

[24] Charles 1939: 274. See also: Fleming 1956: 181.
[25] Charles 1939: 269. See also: Fleming 1956: 181.
[26] Pyke 1973: 112.
[27] See: Fleming 1956: 181, fig. 8; Ford and Penny 1998: II, 103, 277, cat. no. RBF604; I: fig. 72, colour plate 9.

'A memorable era in the instrumental music of this kingdom': Piedmontese Musicians in London in the Latter Half of the Eighteenth Century

ANNARITA COLTURATO

Comparing Turin and London from a musical point of view, and particularly during the latter half of the eighteenth century, might seem a mere exercise of style. The Savoy capital was a city with only a tenth of the population of that of Britain, and completely different social, cultural and economic conditions, where the music scene revolved primarily around three institutions: the Cappella Metropolitana (Metropolitan Chapel), affiliated to the Cathedral; the Regia Cappella (Royal Chapel); and the Teatro Regio (Royal Theatre), which, not without differences from the organizational and financial stand-points, depended upon the Court.

Securely documented since the tenth century, by the second half of the eighteenth century the Cappella Metropolitana consisted of a master, half a dozen 'choristi' (clergymen who sang the plainchant during liturgical offices, including the Liturgy of the Hours), from three to twelve 'musici' (salaried laymen who performed the polyphonic vocal music during processions, the offices of mass, vespers and compline) and a number of instrumentalists.[1]

The Regia Cappella, founded in Chambéry at the beginning of the fifteenth century, and reorganized after the Savoy rulers established themselves in Turin after 1563, comprised a far more numerous ensemble than the Cappella Metropolitana, and featured musicians of greater stature. Eventually the Regia Cappella gained an international reputation that considerably enhanced the prestige of the Savoy court, especially during the eighteenth century. The 'meilleure symphonie de l'Europe' ('the best

The author wishes to thank Jennifer Cooke and Andrew Jonathan Hunt for their kindness and help.
[1] On the Cappella Metropolitana, see: Cordero di Pamparato 1915; Borghezio 1924; Bouquet 1968; Bouquet-Boyer 1989; Bouquet-Boyer 2001.

orchestra in Europe')[2] included some of the foremost European musicians of the time, such as the violinists Giovanni Battista Somis and Gaetano Pugnani; in the woodwind section – occasionally replenished by instrumentalists from the Scuderia (Écurie) – such virtuosos as the Besozzi brothers; as well as such celebrated singers as Luigi Marchesi.[3] Many of the instrumentalists able to surprise the audience for their ability and harmony ('the performers know their business so well that there is no want of a person to beat time, as in the opera and Concert Spirituel at Paris', recorded Charles Burney in the journal of his Italian tour)[4] also joined the court theatre orchestra, which since 26 December 1740 had been housed in a purpose-built structure designed by Benedetto Alfieri, an ideal setting to stage the premieres of world-famous opera composers and the virtuoso performances of revered singers.[5]

The Teatro Regio, a privileged location intended for the *repraesentatio maiestatis*, opened its doors only during the carnival season, for Savoy dynastic events and diplomatic visits of foreign kings and princes. Throughout the other months of the year, the Teatro Carignano became the musical focus for the Turin public: they attended tragedies by Alfieri and Corneille, comedies by Molière and Marivaux, *opere buffe* by Paisiello and Cimarosa, *opéras-comiques* by Grétry and Philidor, performances of travelling artists, or of those who were free on Friday nights because of the ban on staging operas, puppet shows and rope jumpers.[6] A thriving music scene that included concerts organized in aristocratic houses; nonetheless, by the latter half of the eighteenth century even the rich variety of musically centred entertainments in Turin could not be compared to what London offered, as that city had become the European capital of concerts and musical performances.

While British religious and court music institutions might no longer have featured musicians such as John Blow, Henry Purcell or Georg Friedrich Haendel, and even though they may have been duller than many European royal counterparts in this respect, on the other hand, the King's Theatre in London offered the British public Italian operas and ballets with star

[2] Rousseau 1782 (1959), II: 45–87: esp. p. 72.
[3] For the Regia Cappella, see: Bouquet 1968; Bouquet-Boyer 1987; Moffa 1990; Bouquet-Boyer 2000. For more on music and ceremonial at the Savoy court, see: Colturato 2010b.
[4] Burney 1771 (1959): 55–6.
[5] On the Teatro Regio, see: Basso 1976; Bouquet 1976; Viale Ferrero 1980; Tamburini 1983; Bouquet *et al.* 1988; Basso 1991.
[6] On Turin theatres in the eighteenth century, see: Tamburini 1966. On the Carignano Theatre in the eighteenth century, see: Avanzini 1984–5; Bassi 1988–9.

singers and dancers, and Covent Garden and Drury Lane offered performances of English music theatre.[7] Most significantly, the tradition of public
concerts that had originated at the end of the seventeenth century along
with the creation of various musical societies now fed a 'rage for music' that
promoted concerts as main events in social and cultural life on a par with
opera. Dozens of musical activities, strikingly different from one another in
nature, repertoire and the audiences' social profile, and thousands of concerts, where concert-goers could choose from masterpieces from a more or
less distant past, for example, events at the Academy of Ancient Music or at
the Madrigal Society, and the latest creations by the best known composers
of the day, such as the series directed by Johann Christian Bach and Carl
Friedrich Abel or Johann Peter Salomon, are well documented. Such diversity was unparalleled at this time in Europe, and this rich musical scene was
further enlivened by entertainments set up in outdoor pleasure gardens,
with musical performances held in charitable institutions and with concerts
presented in private residences.[8]

In no other European country was music so enthusiastically appreciated as by the British public, and yet, simultaneously, so meagrely catered
for by local composers' work.[9] Those who profited from the opportunities
offered by such unprecedented dynamic social and economic circumstances, from a music industry free from restrictions, from hundreds of
musical societies and concerts, from aristocratic patronage and from one
of the most thriving publishing industries, were mainly foreign artists.
Indeed, these foreign artists were the protagonists of, and often, simultaneously, the victims of what musicologists have defined as a migration
or a true *diaspora* of Italian musicians in the eighteenth century:[10] a phenomenon that in the case of violinists – the most likely instrumentalists
to be recruited into orchestras – registered striking numbers, and that
concerned some of the main exponents of the so-called Piedmontese
school of violin playing, whose recognized master was Giovanni Battista
Somis.

'The arrival of Giardini in London [in 1751] forms a memorable era
in the instrumental music of this kingdom', wrote Burney in his *General*

---

[7] For a broad, though somewhat outdated, bibliography on these institutions, see the entry
London in: Sadie 2001: XV, 91–166.

[8] For an overview of concert events in London and Britain, see: McVeigh 1993; Caldwell 1999;
Wyn Jones 2000; Wollenberg and McVeigh 2004.

[9] 'There is positively no Nation in Europe, where Music is so generally patronized and so little
professed, as in our own'; see *The Oracle*, 14 February 1792 (quoted in: McVeigh 1993: 228).

[10] Dahlhaus 1985; Finscher 1993; Strohm 2001.

History of Music.[11] Felice Giardini introduced the British public, until then accustomed to 'the tranquil enjoyment of the productions of [Arcangelo] Corelli, [Francesco] Geminiani, and [Georg Friedrich] Handel',[12] to the pre-classical Italian instrumental music that would soon rival the Austrian and German tradition, represented by Joseph Haydn. At the time of his first London public appearance, Giardini was 35 years old. Born in Turin, he had studied singing, harpsichord and composition in Milan, and then violin with Somis in his hometown, which he later left. An atypical proponent of the Piedmontese school of violin playing, Giardini was immortalized in an engraving entitled *Professori celebri di suono* (*Famous Professors of Violin Music*) near Geminiani and Francesco Maria Veracini, violinists who made their mark on the British musical scene during the first half of the eighteenth century, rather than being portrayed together with other well-known Somis students, such as Carlo Chiabrano and Gaetano Pugnani, or with later followers of Somis's school, such as Giovanni Battista Viotti (see Fig. 20.1).

For at least two decades, London presented Giardini with a series of golden opportunities. As one of the most prolific contemporaneous composers, within six years after his arrival he debuted *Rosmira* (30 April 1757) at the King's Theatre, followed by two further operas, some pasticcio operas and several songs, duets, catches and glees.[13] For some time, Giardini's oratorio *Ruth* was performed at Lock Hospital as a counterpart to Haendel's *Messiah* performed at the Foundling Hospital,[14] and this, it must be noted, was significant in a nation where works composed a few years before were revered, and where Haendel was considered a legend.[15] But it was mainly in instrumental works that Giardini's fresh expressive style was the perfect response to those who stigmatized empty virtuosity and welcomed formal symmetries, homophonic textures, simple harmonic schemes, periodic phrase structure and melodic elegance: the ideal setting for Giardini, representative of the 'modern school', a composer who seemed to remind listeners, in brilliant passages just as much as in the expressive ones, that after all his music should be considered a pleasant and refined form of entertainment (we might add a 'galant' one too, resorting to the label usually

[11] Burney 1776–89: IV, 460.
[12] Burney 1776–89: IV, 673.
[13] Giardini composed *Enea e Lavinia* (5 May 1764) and *Il re pastore* (7 March 1765); on pasticcio operas and vocal pieces for operas by other authors, see: Price *et al.* 1995.
[14] McVeigh 1988.
[15] Burney 1785: V. For an example of the contemporaneous interest in ancient music, see: *Cathedral Music*, ed. by W. Boyce (1760–73).

Figure 20.1 Luigi Scotti, *Professori celebri di Suono (Famous Professors of Violin Music)*, Firenze, Studio Rainaldi, c. 1805, Musei Civici Monza.

For Giardini, London was a modern musical *eldorado*: clubs, Masonic lodges and other social gatherings featured music prominently; theatres and concert societies craved talented composers and instrumentalists; aristocratic families lured virtuosos for private academies and lessons; music publishers raced against Parisian and Dutch colleagues to print the latest musical compositions; newspapers were eager to crown new celebrities and spur artistic rivalries.

applied to the style of this period, marked not only by a combination of music-technical features, but mostly by the fact of being appreciated by *galant hommes*).[16] This did not stop him from leaving his mark in contemporary music, however: in 1751, Giardini wrote one of the earliest examples of keyboard sonatas with violin or flute accompaniment (op. 3), where the keyboard was no longer relegated to executing the *continuo*, as in most violin sonatas (violin solos, in England), but it became a melodic and *concertante* instrument; in his trios, quartets and quintets for different instrument combinations, he explored all viable solutions once the *continuo* had gradually disappeared, and he experimented with a variety of scoring and new timbric and textural possibilities.

Similar to his contemporaries, who supported their precarious musical careers with more or less lucrative outside activities, Giardini worked on several occasions as a manager and an impresario at the King's Theatre, leading, reforming and revitalizing the orchestra.[17] The *Ten Commandments* he drew up in 1763 for his agent, engaged in an expedition to recruit singers and dancers, was nonetheless enough to protect him from such consequences that would make him risk going to gaol.[18] As a promoter and manager, Giardini organized some of the most important concert series of his time. As a performer, he took part in many concerts where 'the brilliancy and fullness of his tone, the sweetness, spirit, and variety of his expression, his amazing rapidity of execution, and exuberance of fancy, joined with the most perfect ease and gracefulness in the performance', insured his reputation as an unrivalled soloist.[19] Moreover, he sold musical scores and musical instruments, and because of his thriving career as a music teacher he was able to circulate in royal family circles and in the most exclusive British milieus. In a culture where knowing how to play an instrument or singing a glee was considered a fundamental social prerequisite, he was music master for the Dukes of Gloucester and Cumberland, for the Prince of Wales, and indeed, one need only peruse the names of those to whom his compositions were dedicated, including the Dukes of Devonshire and Dorset and the Duchess of Marlborough, or consider the names of the artists who painted his likeness, such as Reynolds and Gainsborough, to demonstrate his contacts with the cosmopolitan British élite.

---

[16] Dahlhaus 1978: 501–2. For the term 'galant' in musicology, see: Heartz 2003; Gjerdingen 2007.

[17] Burney 1776–89: IV, 464.

[18] Price *et al.* 1992. On Giardini's ventures as a leader of the orchestra and an impresario, see: Price *et al.* 1995; Woodfield 2001; Burden 2013.

[19] Avison 1752: 103.

As Giuseppe Baretti, the contemporary diarist of Italo-British affairs previsaged, however, *eldorado* was fiercely competitive. In order to make a living in a city like London, even in a best-case scenario, musicians 'trotta-vano' – used to 'trot' from theatres to concert halls to their pupils' houses – and in the worst-case scenarios, were arrested as debtors and forced to return home to Italy as poor as when they had first arrived.[20] In 1772, the violinist Wilhelm Cramer arrived in London to lead the concerts organized by Johann Christian Bach and Carl Friedrich Abel, eventually becoming Giardini's main rival. A decade later, in 1781, Johann Peter Salomon arrived in the capital, and by the 1790s, Salomon organized a series of concerts that crowned the British music public's new idol, Haydn. Giardini's star, polemically absent from the most colossal musical event of the time – the performances in commemoration of the Haendel centenary in 1784 – began to wane, revealing how fragile the cultural terrain was for musical careers, which had been constructed on a combination of personal enter-prise and aristocratic patronage, and how unstable the fortunes that were constructed from a daily recipe of talent and pragmatism, a pragmatism that, for instance, during the June 1780 Gordon Riots impelled the com-poser not only to remove his name-plate from his front door, as many other Italians did, but also to daub 'No Popery' on it.[21] Years of frustrated ambi-tions and travel followed, until the itinerant, impoverished Giardini died in Moscow at the age of 80.[22]

Despite Giardini's tragic demise, the European fame and reputation of the Piedmontese violin school survived, marked – as the 'Allgemeine musikalische Zeitung' noted in 1811 – particularly by a large, strong, full tone, by the combination of this with a powerful, penetrating, singing *legato cantabile*, by contrasts of light and shade obtained with the greatest diversity of bowing, and represented in London by two other musicians who studied under Somis: Carlo Chiabrano, and, particularly, by Gaetano Pugnani.[23]

Born in Turin in 1723, Chiabrano, a nephew of Somis, had been a mem-ber of the Regia Cappella and Teatro Regio orchestras. Like many of his colleagues, he sought international success at the Concert Spirituel in Paris, where he performed in 1751, subsequently moving to London. Charles

---

[20] Baretti 1768: I, 149–50.

[21] Price *et al.* 1995: 248. During the Riots the Sardinian Chapel in London was destroyed; on the chapel, whose musical activity (including the involvement of Piedmontese artists) is still to be examined, see Paolo Cozzo's chapter in this book.

[22] For a profile on Giardini, see: McVeigh 1983; 1989. On Italian violinists in London, see: McVeigh 1993; Sadie 1993; McVeigh 2001.

[23] 'Allgemeine musikalische Zeitung', 3 July 1811, col. 452. For the Piedmontese school, see: Basso 1985.

Collé wrote of him: 'Ce Chiabran … est un oiseau de passage … Il est de
la musique du roi de Sardaigne, qui lui à donné un congé pour voyager
et se perfectionner' ('Chiabran … is a passing bird … He belongs to the
Savoy Royal Chapel, and the king granted him a leave to travel and improve
his skills').[24] Indeed, between 1752 and 1754, Chiabrano competed with
Giardini for London's musical limelight, but after that date, his career is
difficult to trace.[25]

Few biographies of the period better illustrate this transitional age, in
terms of social reputation and career possibilities for musicians, than those
of Giardini and Pugnani. It is true that 'the composer of galant music, rather
than being a struggling artist alone against the world, was more like a pros-
perous civil servant' and that he 'necessarily worked in the here and now';[26]
yet, life of those for whom the here and now consisted of the – often anything
but stimulating – requirements of serving the court may yield a less unfortunate outcome from the potentially just as thrilling risky life of those who had
resigned from court service or had not considered it in the first place.

Born in Turin in 1731, Gaetano Pugnani was a court musician. An exceptionally talented violinist, he joined the Teatro Regio and the Regia Cappella
orchestras at a very young age. When he was eighteen, he was sent to Rome
to study, and upon his return to the Savoy capital in 1750, he initiated his
ascent through the court's musical hierarchy: leader of the Teatro Regio
orchestra, he was subsequently appointed 'primo violino della Cappella e
Camera' ('first violin of the Chapel and Chamber') in 1770, 'primo virtuoso della Camera di Sua Maestà, e direttore generale della musica instro-
mentale' ('first virtuoso of the Royal Chamber, and director of instrumental
music'), in 1776, and 'direttore della musica militare' ('director of military
music') in 1786. Pugnani not only rose rapidly through the ranks of musical life at court, it should be noted here, that moreover, the most glorious
period of Savoy music ended with his death – and with the arrival of the
French army – in 1798.[27]

Although Pugnani was a Savoy courtier, he was not immune to temp-
tations, also because his performances abroad (at the Concert Spirituel,
where he debuted in 1754, and at the courts where he performed during

[24] See: Collé 1805–7 quoted in: La Laurencie 1922–4: II, 334; also see Bouquet-Boyer 1987: 102–
3; Bouquet-Boyer 1988: XV.

[25] For Carlo and further Chiabrano family members who played a part in the musical life of
London, see: Bouquet-Boyer 1987; Bouquet-Boyer 1988; Price *et al.* 1995; Milhous *et al.* 2000;
McVeigh 2001.

[26] Gjerdingen 2007: 6.

[27] On Pugnani, see: Zschinsky-Troxler 1939; Müry 1941; Lister 2009; Colturato 2012.

the tour that he undertook from 1780 to 1781 accompanied by his pupil Giovanni Battista Viotti) and the compositions published by the foremost European publishers were successful. In 1767, Pugnani's reputation facilitated his taking up the position of leader of the King's Theatre orchestra in London, where he had travelled as Savoy court musician, introduced by a letter of recommendation from the First Secretary of Foreign Affairs, who pleaded with the Savoy ambassador in London to keep an eye on the musician, as it was suspected that he had an independent spirit: 'une certaine tournure d'esprit qui le rend susceptible de prendre aisément des engagements' ('A certain way of thinking which makes him prone to easily take on commitments'),[28] a suspicion later borne out by facts, as Pugnani remained two years in London, rather than one, as initially agreed.

Pugnani's protracted stay allowed him to debut as opera composer at the King's Theatre with *Nanetta e Lubino* (8 April 1769), as well as to participate fully in the London concert scene, although he seems to have been less well received critically as a musician than Giardini. In describing one of his performances at the Regia Cappella 1770, Burney stated that there was no need to digress about Pugnani, 'his talents being too well known in England'.[29] But Samuel Sharp, who had heard him in Turin in 1766, wrote: 'It is said, that Pugnani draws out a louder tone from the upper part of the fiddle, than Giardini does; and this, it must be granted, is his forte; but, with submission to Italian ears, mine were a little shocked in several parts of his solo. I wished he had been a little more sweet, though he had been less forte; and, from this example of so excellent a performer, it may be suspected that a very short string will not admit of a sweet tone beyond such a degree of loudness. His taste and elegance I thought by no means comparable to Giardini's.'[30] More nervous than elegant, more eloquent than charming: a judgement of Pugnani confirmed by his contemporaries' testimonies (Robbio di San Raffaele remembered his moving, yet stern performances, the 'suono limpido pieno pronunziato' of his instrument, equipped with 'corde grossissime'; Arteaga commented on his noble style and his vigorous sound, subsequently mitigated by his disciples 'con una certa dolcezza e soavità'),[31] and by his compositions, more and more

---

[28] Torino, Archivio di Stato, *Materie politiche per rapporto all'estero, Lettere Ministri, Gran Bretagna*, m. 73 (Turin, 5 September 1767). On 16 October, the ambassador announced that the composer had arrived a few days earlier.

[29] Burney 1771 (1959): 59.

[30] Sharp 1766 (1767²): 277–8.

[31] See: Robbio di San Raffaele 1778: 7, 22; 'full, clear, pronounced tone'; 'very thick strings'. Arteaga 1783–8: II, 89, 'with a certain sweetness and gentleness'.

inclined over the years to abandon gallantry and pleasantness for a deeper expression, giving in to passionate, restless emotions.[32]

Giuseppe Baretti – whom Pugnani visited several times in 1769 while the writer was imprisoned – wrote in a letter to his brother that an opinion fostered by such critical circumstances would not have deterred Pugnani from returning to England.[33] And indeed, between 1772 and 1773, the violinist returned to London: on this occasion a flurry of correspondence was again exchanged between ministers and ambassadors,[34] and on 30 March 1773, Pugnani's *Apollo e Issea* was staged at the King's Theatre.[35] Notwithstanding the consensus of appreciation he received from the London public and from many European courts, Pugnani, son of a royal employee, could not be dissuaded from abandoning the security and prestige of royal service. With some qualms about the choice he had made, when he was well over sixty, he admitted in a letter to Viotti, dated 16 October 1793, that he had approached a 'certain Salomon' passing through Turin in vain, and that he had also approached Luigi Borghi (another student of his working in England)[36] about publishing concerts, symphonies and the melodrama *Werther* in London. But over there – Borghi told him – the audience only had ears for Haydn, and the situation prevented him from going across France to show English people how wrong they had been in forgetting about him.[37]

If Giardini was no court musician, and Pugnani did not have the courage to stop being one, Giovanni Battista Viotti, born in 1755 in a village near Vercelli, was a different model of composer. After training at the Savoy court, where he was a violinist/violist in the orchestra of the Teatro Regio from 1773 to 1779, and at the Regia Cappella from 1775 to 1786, he took his chances in the European capitals. He first spent a period in Paris (1782–92),

---

[32] For example, see: Rangoni 1790: 59–63.

[33] See: Baretti 1857: 299–300 (London, 7 November 1769).

[34] Torino, Archivio di Stato, *Materie politiche per rapporto all'estero, Lettere Ministri, Gran Bretagna*, m. 78 (letter from the Savoy Ministry of Foreign Affairs, Turin, 19 September 1772, and letter from the ambassador, London, 20 October).

[35] Pugnani's *Apollo e Issea* was performed as *Issea* in Turin in 1771 for the occasion of Marie Joséphine of Savoy's wedding to the future Louis XVIII, and again at the Palácio de Queluz, in 1772; see: Colturato 2012: 33–53.

[36] On Borghi, see: Price *et al.* 1995; Milhous *et al.* 2000; McVeigh 2001.

[37] This letter is in the New York Public Library; for the transcription, see: Yim 2004, 271–3. Gertrud Elisabeth Mara Schmeling, who sang in *Demetrio a Rodi*, written by Pugnani in 1789 for the Duke of Aosta's wedding to Maria Theresa of Hapsburg, had often sung the composer's arias in operas and concerts (see *The London Magazine*, 1784, 498; Price *et al.* 1995: 358; McVeigh 2006: 117), and Pugnani's instrumental compositions were still performed and published.

then, given the political situation there, in London (1792–8), later going back and forth between the two cities, accused variously of being either a Bourbonist or a Jacobin, undertaking several musical successes, ambitious projects, prestigious tasks, withdrawals from public life and ill-advised business ventures.

In this sense, 1781 marked a turning point in his life. At the end of the aforesaid two-year-long European tour with Pugnani, during which he had already had the chance to shine as a performer and a virtuoso, Viotti was indeed granted permission to travel to the French capital, where his talent, his connections with the court, and his affiliation to Freemasonry[38] earned him an income as well as fame. The first two years he spent in Paris, he was the most esteemed violinist at the Concert Spirituel and one of the composers most sought after by publishers. From 1788 to 1792 he was the soul of the newly created Théâtre de Monsieur (from the title of the count of Provence, the future King Louis XVIII, patron of this enterprise, for whose wedding Pugnani had composed the previously mentioned *Issea*).[39]

However, being a free agent was a difficult choice and one that Viotti took as the result of circumstances. He was officially released from the Regia Cappella orchestra in 1786, and in his autobiographical Précis there is no mention of either this episode or of Pugnani's name:[40] six years later he left Turin on the European tour, and three years later he suddenly withdrew from public concerts to join the service of the Queen of France, under conditions that still remain unclear.

When, in the summer of 1792, Viotti arrived as a fugitive in London – without the pension Marie Antoinette had promised him, but with Salomon's substantial employment – Haydn had just left the English capital and, contrary to all expectations, did not return until almost two years later. Preceded by his reputation as an outstanding virtuoso ('the first violin in the world', as a concert review described him),[41] Viotti 'electrified'

---

[38] In 1783, Viotti joined the Lodge of 'Saint-Jean d'Écosse du Contrat Social' and in 1786 the Lodge of 'Olympique de la Parfaite Estime'. The majority of the musicians discussed in this paper were affiliated to Freemasonry: Giardini – as well as Abel, Bach, Borghi, Cramer – joined the Lodge of the Nine Muses (1778), Pugnani joined the Lodge of 'Saint Jean de la Mystérieuse' (1768). On this subject, see: Basso 1994; McVeigh 2000. For Freemasonry and the British in Turin, see Andrea Merlotti in this volume.

[39] On the Théâtre de Monsieur, see: Di Profio 2003.

[40] *Précis de la vie de J. B. Viotti depuis son entrée dans le monde jusqu'au 6 mars 1798*, the London Royal College of Music, transcribed in: Giazotto 1956: 229–31. There are many studies on Viotti: for his biography, see: Lister 2009; Yim 2004; also Pougin 1888; Giazotto 1956; White 1957; White 1985; Sala 2006.

[41] *The Morning Post*, 1 January 1793 (quoted in: Landon 1976–80: III, 213).

Londoners;[42] but sometimes the English seemed to him 'des buches, des ignorans' ('logs, ignoramuses') who boasted of a non-existent sensibility.[43] Once more, the musician tried to take advantage of all the occasions offered him to build a career and make a decent living. Concerts aside, Viotti was the acting manager at the King's Theatre (1794–5), an impresario, a leader of the orchestra and a performer at the Opera Concerts (1795–8), and a member of the most exclusive circles. The Duke of Cambridge wrote him letters full of praise; the Prince of Wales welcomed him into his entourage; he frequented the Chinnery household (the family with which he became affiliated shortly after his arrival in London, sharing their lives, losses and misadventures from 1796 onwards), where he kept company with important artists and poets.

Applauded as a performer and as a composer, Viotti gave the impression of being able to mediate between 'ancient' music, feeding the myth of Corelli and Haendel, and 'modern' as represented by Giardini, Bach and Muzio Clementi.[44] About one of his concerts, it was written that 'In style it was neither perfectly ancient nor modern, though it partook of the beauties of both;[45] and testimonials proclaimed Viotti the foremost interpreter of an aesthetic sensitivity that combined naturalness and pathos, expressiveness and harmonic refinement: *The Oracle* wrote in 1793, 'He has a soul capable of magnifying Simplicity into the Wonderful', while a year later *The Sun* wrote, 'Viotti displayed all his fine taste and astonishing execution in a violin concerto, which, though deeply scientific, was no less pleasing.'[46]

The pinnacle of Viotti's instrumental work, his London concertos, moderated the audacity and drama of those published in his Parisian period: the orchestra grew larger, the texture richer, the interaction between the orchestra and the soloist deeper, and the virtuosity less explosive. The quest for expressiveness, that had always been emphasized as one of the most remarkable aspects of his performances, became even more fine-tuned, and almost pre-Romantic frissons pervaded the most likeable melodies.

---

[42] *The Morning Post*, 8 February 1793 (quoted in: Lister 2009: 179).

[43] Letter to Margaret Chinnery of 18 April 1794, Sydney (Powerhouse Museum), transcribed in: Yim 2006: 412–14.

[44] Clementi was a prominent exponent of the group of musicians to whom we owe the affirmation of the piano, that was to become the bard of new expression. In Piedmont, a territory with a great violin-making tradition, the piano only became popular a half century later, see: Colturato 2007. On the piano in London in the latter eighteenth century, see: Temperley 1988; Salwey and McVeigh 1997; Salwey 2001.

[45] *The Morning Chronicle*, 19 February 1794 (quoted in McVeigh 1993, 227).

[46] *The Oracle*, 20 February 1793 (quoted in: McVeigh 1993: 148); *The Sun*, 11 February 1794 (quoted in: Yim 2004: 63).

In 1820 the *Allgemeine musikalische* Zeitung defined him as 'Europe's first and most classical violinist', despite his music's sometimes less rigorous structure and its rich inventiveness often unmatched by an appropriate thematic-motif development.[47]

As previously stated, in 1798 Viotti, accused of being a Jacobin, was forced to leave England. He returned there a few months later, and – once again – travelled back and forth between London and Paris (or wistfully wandered, if one were to detect an autobiographical allusion in the 1804 'canzonetta' *Vo triste tacito*). He resisted retiring definitively from public life, and in 1813 he took part in the founding of the Philharmonic Society, directed the Paris Opéra (1819–21), and finally experienced the *Méthode de violon* by his former disciples, or self-perceived disciples such as Pierre Rode, Pierre Baillot and Rodolphe Kreutzer, imbued with his teachings, adopted in the Conservatory of the French capital.

The paths of the principal Piedmontese musicians who travelled to Britain have been traced in this paper, starting in 1751 – when Giardini arrived in England – the same year that Bach's *The Art of Fugue* was published, and the first volume of the *Encyclopédie* appeared. Viotti died in London in 1824, the year that Bedřich Smetana and Anton Bruckner were born. A little more than five years later, François-Antoine Habeneck, who published the fragment of a method for violin by Viotti in his own *Méthode théorique et pratique de violon*, conducted Hector Berlioz' *Symphonie fantastique* in Paris. The Piedmontese school continued to flourish, particularly on French soil, but its last descendants in Turin did not attain a similar success to their predecessors. Ultimately, for Turin it was the end of a season that, despite Savoy's occupying centre stage during the Italian Unification, from a musical point of view could never again be equalled.

We shall conclude with returning to the eighteenth century, when, as highlighted by diplomats and by travellers' accounts,[48] Turin prided itself on its festive musical events, including operas and celebratory works that marked pivotal moments in political and social occasions, especially those organized at the Savoy court for royal weddings and for the receptions of illustrious personages. In the second half of the eighteenth century, such festive performances were held for Emperor Joseph II (1769), Grand Duke Paul Petrovič (1782), Archduke Ferdinand of Hapsburg (1783), Gustav III of

---

[47] Quoted in: White 1992: 348.

[48] See for example, Andrew Moore and Karin Wolfe on British travellers in Turin and their accounts of musical performances in this volume; Dutens 1806a: I, 155–6 (on a concert of Caterina Gabrielli, Pugnani and the two Besozzis, probably 1760–2); Lady Mary Coke 1888–96: IV, 305–7 (1774; quoted in: Lister 2009: 23, 414–15).

Sweden (1784), Ferdinand of Naples (1785);[49] perhaps the same happened in 1764, when – in view of the Duke of York's visit to Piedmont[50] – the magistrate and librettist Jacopo Durandi wrote the 'drammatico componimento' *Cesare in Bretagna*.[51]

Whether music was ever composed for *Cesare in Bretagna*, and whether the piece was ever performed, remains conjectural. Previous research conducted by Francesco Blanchetti[52] and further research carried out for this chapter have not uncovered any evidence for a musical score, nor for the performance of this work.[53] However, it is known that during the Duke's first visit to Turin (12 February to 7 March 1764) he participated in balls and entertainments, and attended the Teatro Regio every night, where, from 4 February until 6 March, Galuppi's *Sofonisba* was performed by the acclaimed soprano Giovanni Manzuoli. Incidentally, it is interesting to note here that Manzuoli was cast the following season at the King's Theatre in London, where his benefit performance was in Giardini's *Il re pastore*, and that together with the composer, and the adapter of Metastasio's text, he signed a dedication to the Duke, published in the libretto.[54] The Duke's second sojourn in Turin (11 July to 26 July) was also filled with entertainments and attendance at balls, but again, no evidence for a performance of *Cesare in Bretagna* has been uncovered. In any case, it should be noted that only four of eighteen works that Durandi authored (such as *Armida*, set to music by Antonio Sacchini and titled *Rinaldo*, that went on stage at King's Theatre in 1780) are known to have been performed.

Nevertheless, further research is warranted, as the references in the text to British colonial expansion,[55] to the King of England's title as Elector of

---

49 See: Colturato 2010a; Blanchetti 2011; Merlotti 2011; Colturato 2012.
50 See De Gregory 1817: 13.
51 Durandi 1766: IV, 219–36.
52 Blanchetti 1991.
53 For the celebrations for the Duke of York, see Torino, Biblioteca Reale, Storia Patria 726, II: 108–36, 167–79, and Misc. 102/8; Torino, Archivio di Stato, *Materie politiche per rapporto all'estero, Lettere Ministri, Gran Bretagna*, m. 69–70.
54 On Manzuoli's work in this period, see: Burney 1776–89: IV, 484–5, 487; Terry 1929; Bouquet 1976; Gibson 1990; Price *et al.* 1992; Woodfield 1995 (p. 191 for the reference to the Duke's admiration for the singer); Butler 2001; Burrows-Dunhill 2002, particularly 426–7, 430–2, 434, 441–3; Butler 2002.
55 To the Britons, who 'following the sun's great course, / something never attempted before, / will be feared and famed in the East / and, as they sail the Ocean, will discover / unknown stars and unknown lands and seas' ('… seguendo il gran cammin del sole / non mai tentato ancora, / saran temuti in Oriente, e chiari, / e scopriran per l'Oceano allora / ignote stelle, e terre ignote, e mari').

Hanover,[56] and in praise of George III,[57] indicate that it is likely that the piece was performed for the Duke; and the ties that existed between Turin and London[58] are highlighted in the final aria of the libretto, in which Durandi, perhaps prompted by this commission from Charles Emmanuel III, celebrates the British sovereign, writing: 'The promised Hero, / well worthy of that age, will come / to avenge himself / and extend his Kingdom. // He will make war cease / if he speaks in gentle tones, and / if in the future the earth should quake, / he will make the sea tremble too.'[59]

[56] 'Then we too will / play a part and have a say / in the great councils of the Roman Empire' ('Allor noi pure avremo, / avrem parte, e pensiero / ne' gran consigli del Romano Impero').

[57] 'At last, in violent / and bloody times, when Germany, / and every land in Europe, / seethes with a serious conflagration of war, / Britain will have a great and provident Prince, / … / and lasting peace will return / to his Kingdom' ('… Ne' duri alfine, / e sanguinosi giorni, in cui Germania, / e di Europa ogni terra / in grave incendio fremerà di guerra: / Britannia un Prence avrà provido, e grande / … / stabile nel suo Regno / la pace tornerà. …').

[58] A 'vast city, of grave yet pleasant aspect, / in whose bosom the fine arts will flourish', according to a prophecy of the Britons' general ('cittade immensa in grave aspetto, e ameno / cui cresceranno le bell'arti in seno').

[59] 'Verrà l'Eroe promesso / di quell'età ben degno, / a vendicar sestesso, / suo Regno a dilatar. // Farà cessar la guerra, / se dolce parla, e insieme / farà tremar, se freme / quindi la terra, e 'l mar'.

21 | The British Baretti: Didactics and Criticism

CRISTINA BRACCHI

Giuseppe Baretti's *An Account of the Manners and Customs of Italy; with Observations on the Mistakes of some Travellers with Regard to that Country*, published in London in 1768, is an exhaustive narrative of Italian traditions and habits. It is also a source of information about relations between eighteenth-century British and Italian culture. The primary goal of the publication was to illustrate the customs of Italy and its population, but the author also wanted to analyse British texts recounting trips to Italy, most of which contained stereotypes and quaint, popular descriptions, which only partially represented Italian culture: 'In the following work I censure with great freedom the accounts given of Italy by several English and several foreign writers of travels.'[1]

Mediation pervades Baretti's descriptions. By adeptly using the English language, certain specific topics and a number of locations dear to the British to lessen the cultural gap between the two cultures, he was able to explicitly criticize the conceptual and methodological shortcomings and imprecise statements found in British writings about Italy. His account of journeys made between Venice, central Italy and Naples explores themes of literature and travel as well as issues such as the political structure and social fabric of the Italian states, religion, civic duties, the death penalty, the development of commerce, regional traditions and common habits. As a text, the *Account* belongs to two literary genres and, together with its function as a cultural mediator between Britain and Italy,[2] it allows for a focus on Baretti's main concerns: didacticism and criticism. The former is apparent in the linguistic, lexicographic and translational aspect of the work, the latter is present in its literary, historical and cultural side, which is narrated with irony and a polemical tone.

Baretti's principal interest was in literature. This decision was pivotal to his choice of 'criteria for the selection of exceptional figures', which are obtained through the multilingual intertextuality that pervades his work. There are three main motives underlying Baretti's prose, which hark back to

---

[1] Baretti 1768: *Dedication*, IV.
[2] Bracchi 1999.

his other writings on travel: first, to provide a precise portrait of his country to the British; second, to renew prestigious cultural and civil ties between Italy and Britain; and third, to respond to the personal suffering he felt due to his immigrant status. Moreover, Baretti harboured no compulsions about translating his work from English into Italian. While it is true that in the first half of the eighteenth century Italians who read and communicated in English were few and far between (amongst them Rolli, Conti, Maffei and Algarotti), it is also the case that, from the mid-seventeenth century, interest in English had started to intensify, in line with the growing prestige of Britain in Europe, a shift that led more people to study the English language. The usefulness of understanding the works of Locke, Newton and Addison was not lost on the Italians. Nor was the joy of reading Milton, Swift, Pope, Samuel Richardson, Thomas Gray, Laurence Sterne and, of course, Shakespeare. The English language also represented a tool by which people could take part in lively business talks occurring between the two countries, and offered a translation opportunity for the publishing and book industry. Finally, even the lexicographic tools that Baretti contributes suggest an openness to English, which was seen as more of a 'civil' than an 'artistic' language, and as one suited to the expression of philosophical and scientific reasoning that could stand up to the French rationalism of the *philosophes*. All these associations contributed to the interest in Britain that swept seventeenth-century Italy.[3]

There were two opposing schools of thought regarding linguistic debate in Italy: the purists and the Europhiles. There were also outliers who preferred to act rather than talk, of which Baretti was one: his writings prepared Italy to accept the writer's freedom to compose in any language, regardless of origin (a concept based on the dynamic nature of language proposed by Melchiorre Cesarotti in his essay of 1785, 'On the philosophy of language'). Baretti also used other European languages, including in his daily life, and advocated the necessity of natural and spontaneous thought. In fact, he believed that obeisance to fourteenth-century traditions and language halted the vitality and development of language itself. His decision to write predominantly in English caused him to become quicker, more neutral, clearer and more concise. And even when he used Italian, despite retaining his own personal style, his language was devoid of the typical archaic expressions he criticized,[4] thus adopting Descartes' approach even

---

[3] Vitale 1984: 11–36; Graziano 1984: 373–94.

[4] On the linguistic choices of Baretti, including the use of regional words from Piedmont and the choice to drop them, see: Dionisotti 1988: 15.

in philology. Hence the ornamental function of language was replaced by its functional one, a quality that would become cemented, theoretically and philosophically, with Cesarotti's essay.

Baretti's activity in this area was constant. In 1772 he wrote *Remarks on the Italian Language and Writers*; in 1753, *The Italian Library Containing an Account of the Lives and Works of the Most Valuable Authors of Italy*; and in 1757, *An Introduction to the Most Useful European Languages, Consisting of Select Passages from the Most Celebrated English, French, Italian and Spanish Authors* – a compilation of didactic writings meant for students, which found their way into the hands of many readers. These were supplemented in 1753 by *A Dissertation upon Italian Poetry, in which are Interspersed some Remarks on Mr. Voltaire's 'Essay on the Epic Poets'*, in which he defended Italian language and literature in reply to Voltaire's criticism (an act which was met with approval in anti-French conservative circles), followed by the *Account* in 1768, which is of particular interest on account of its variety of topics. In 1760 Baretti produced *A Dictionary of the English and Italian Languages*, and in 1762 *A Grammar of the Italian Language*, written in English and directed at a broad audience, in which he propagates, interprets and defends Italian culture. The general trend of reading works in English translation was not undermined by the fact that extraordinary works were written in Italian by Machiavelli, Ariosto and Tasso. But although a desire to learn Italian grew during the course of the eighteenth century, especially among young aristocratic men and women, it was not reflected in a desire to read and purchase books written in Italian,[5] despite the fact that having an Italian tutor – a tradition with roots in the Grand Tour – strengthened the fervour of British scholars to study Italian, some of whom revealed a genuine interest in the language and culture of Italy. Moreover, Baretti's explanations on the different translation solutions he proposed all outline a shift in the definition of translation.

The year 1768 falls between two periods of Baretti's life when he had misgivings regarding translation, which were expressed around 1760 when he translated Samuel Johnson's *History of Rasselas* into French (although this was never published) and in his musings in the preface of *A Dictionary of the English and Italian Languages*, where he seems to have lost faith in Italian as a language fit for translation. In 1777, with *Discours sur Shakespeare et sur Monsieur de Voltaire*, his misgivings spread to translation in general: he realized it was impossible to transfer an idea accurately between two

---

[5] On the Italian book industry, see: Verri and Verri 1980: 299.

languages.[6] Two years later, addressing the reader of *Introduction to the Carmen Seculare* by Orazio, he confirmed this scepticism, stating, 'I will only add that in the translation opposite the text I have done my best to convey the sense of it to those who are not acquainted with the Latin tongue'.[7] The aim of the translation in this case was to explain the text to a reader with no knowledge of Latin, not to create a system of equivalences that would provide the closest possible meaning.

This is a typical Baretti characteristic: to speak his mind on conservative positions, as can be seen in the *Quarrel of the Ancients and the Moderns*, which also involves translation and debates the relationship between the 'letter' and 'true meaning' of the text. In this translation, it is clear how ancient languages were considered above reproach in comparison with modern languages, which are seen as inferior and unable to express the richness, nobility, finesse and true meaning of a word. Competing with the original text, however, is not an issue; rather, Baretti takes on the role of the seventeenth-century interpreter, analysing an ancient text and adapting it to the taste of his contemporaries. This position differs greatly from his comments in the *Prefazione Al Signor Don Remigio Fuentes* of 1747–8, which aim to elevate the themes of Corneille's tragedies and reveal a change of tone.[8] In attempting to produce a faithful translation, he tries not to be too literal or to allow the translator, that is himself, to come across too strongly. The first draft of the translation is seen only as a first step in the goal of preparing a final version that goes beyond the mere structure and simplistic meaning of words, to focus on their 'philological' aspect.[9]

However, Baretti's artistic aspiration was impaired by his academic predisposition, which underscored his activity as a lexicographer. The lexical and grammatical correspondences between English and Italian, which are at the heart of his 1760 *Dictionary* and 1762 *Grammars*, are seen as the foundation of language as a practical, rather than an artistic, tool. The same applies to *Easy Phraseology for the Use of Young Ladies, who Intend to Learn the Colloquial Part of the Italian Language* (1775), an Italian phraseology compendium with translations compiled for a young student.[10] Here translation is treated as both skill and teaching method rather than as artistic

[6] Mattioda 1993: 61–75. On the use of French for the translation of Johnson's tale, see: Carbonara 1970.

[7] Baretti 1994: 63.

[8] Baretti 1933: 33–65.

[9] For the eighteenth-century translation, see: Mounin 1965: 20–1, 45–51. For a summary of the translation theory of Italian authors in the eighteenth and nineteenth centuries, see: Alcini, 1991. For the theory and practice of translation by Cesarotti, see: Mari, 1994: 161–234.

[10] Iamartino 1994: 383–419.

endeavour. In *Discours sur Shakespeare et sur Monsieur de Voltaire* Baretti's reflection compensates for the didacticism of his linguistic lexicography, but in not trying to produce the perfect translation, he limits it to one that is useful only for teaching purposes.

Baretti wrote the *Account* at the height of his personal struggle with these conflictual ideas surrounding translation, which would inform his decision not to translate the text into Italian and to leave the critical and didactic aspect of his work in English. He therefore shied away from the transformational process that occurs in translating from a source to a target language.[11] His dismay in attempting to reconcile his own opposing impulses is evident, though he overcomes this discomfort when he translates the *Lettere familiari* from Italian into English.[12]

The Critical Style

The *Account* is a reply to Samuel Sharp's work, *Letters from Italy, describing the Customs and Manners of that Country, in the Years 1765, and 1766. To which is Annexed, An Admonition to Gentlemen who Pass the Alps, in their Tour through Italy*, published by R. Cave in London in 1766. Baretti wrote to James Boswell of his imminent publication:

I am likewise printing an account of Italy in two small volumes, and am handling pretty roughly some of your British travellers and their Italian Itineraries. The impertinence of these people has of late exceeded all bounds, and I will endeavour to put a stop to it for the future, by vindicating my Country, and proving that they are but silly liars when they say, that there is nothing in Italy but ignorance and folly, vice and poverty.[13]

The vociferous debate over Baretti's work led Sharp to write a reply of his own defending his position, *A View of the Customs, Manners, Drama, etc. of Italy*. On 18 August, Baretti wrote that he would shortly respond to Sharp's 'quibbling defense' with a work that would be published within fifteen days, and this duly appeared, entitled: *An Appendix Added, in Answer to Samuel Sharp*. On 12 August 12 1769, Baretti reminded his friend Vincenzo Bujovich that his book, *Sui costumi e modi dell'Italia*, had gone through three editions, two in London and one in Dublin.[14]

---

[11] Steiner 1975; 1992: 23–77.

[12] By 1770 Baretti had written another work in English, *A Journey from London to Genoa, through England, Portugal, Spain and France*; see: Anglani 1997: 187–275.

[13] See: Baretti 1976; letter to James Boswell, 7 November 1767: p. 72.

[14] For the publishing history, translations and the overall analysis of the work, see: Bracchi 1998.

Baretti judged his own work as 'the best of the best parts of the *Frusta*', a periodical (the *Frusta letteraria*) he founded in 1763.[15] He believed he had invented a new, original manner of text, based on the tried and tested genre of writing that featured in his periodical. He was also aware of having tempered the aggressive nature of debate and of having honed Aristarco's (Baretti chose as his pen-name Aristarco Scannabue) critical skills, improving his wording both conceptually and formally, and directing them in the articulate and finished form of a book. This result was achieved because of the articles Baretti wrote between 1763 and 1765. Nineteenth-century scholars have isolated three aspects of Baretti's *Account*. These definitions have the aim of analysing the content of the texts, while the descriptive nature of the book highlights its didactic aspect. A similar though different quality is what could be called, in the strictest sense, its preparatory aspect, which turns the *Account* into a compendium of useful information on the nature and character of the Italians – a well-reasoned guide to aid a trip to Italy. It is precisely the wealth of useful information that ensures the *Account* is defined as a 'travel book', a fashionable genre at the time, according to Franco Fido, who compares the work to the likes of the *Journey* for including lively reports on the subjects' daily lives. However, Fido also considers it a supplement and a palinode of the *Frusta letteraria*.[16] This last aspect, in line with the polemical and critical aspects of the *Account*, becomes even more obvious in the choice of the title: *Account* instead of *Essay*, which allowed the author greater subjectivity in his criticism.

The question of wanting to change a critical approach is at the heart of Baretti's work. A similar shift occurs in his research on the authors of Italian literary traditions: he abandons the authoritative, critical approach,[17] which might support the strengthening of his critical self, and instead adopts a more neutral stance to help build a new interpretation. More of a writing style, than a writing genre, results from this approach. Baretti believed that one should not attempt to understand a text by forcing it into a genre, which can then be interpreted in terms of its overarching characteristics, as per the epistemological principle based on Kant: there can be no data without a category. Rather, the key to understanding the text is the critical word, which supports the *Account* in its free fluctuation from a teaching manual to travel book, from apologia to tourist guide. Hence the *Account* does not

---

[15] Baretti 1936: I, 369. Aristarco Scannabue was the pen-name, but also alter-ego fictional character invented by Baretti, an unstoppable mercenary dedicated to literature.

[16] See: Marshall 1934: 79; Jonard 1963: 318–19; Fido 1967: 614; Fido 1989: 130.

[17] Crotti 1992.

fulfil a particular genre but uses a critical approach and style aimed at communicating with its audience.

The range of material found in the *Account* is fundamental and explains the connection between writing and travelling. Variety livens up the more descriptive and polemical pages, bringing them closer to the descriptive style of the *Frusta letteraria*, which brought about the comparison with travelling. It is also this variety that makes the *Account* a 'travelling' diary, as the notion of a journey itself is conspicuous by its absence: only a sketch of an itinerary follows the locations Baretti and Sharp visited. The *Account* is therefore a memoir of sorts, a 'textual journey' (using Corti's metaphor), which is experienced all at once. This sense of a 'here and now' influences the two essential functions of the *Account*: narration and criticism. The former is achieved through a pedagogical approach that follows the liberal methods of Locke and Comenius, as well as through an objective teaching method, as seen in the works of the Moravian pedagogue Jan Amos Komensky (1592–1670) in the middle of the seventeenth century. A marked spiritual and religious vein pervades Comenius, yet he avails himself of Galileo and Descartes to support his methodology: the necessity of using one's own senses to verify the evidence, assisting the knowledge found in books with direct experience of the world; what we see mediates our learning. This happens to Baretti during his journeys, where observing equates to knowing, and he welcomes Locke's thoughts on practical knowledge aiding the acquisition of the tools and skills that shape an individual – the gentleman of public life – which was the true purpose of the Grand Tour. While I have not found any documentary proof that Baretti knew the works of Comenius, it is certain that he knew those of Locke. In chapter seventeen of the *Account* we find references to the latter's *Some Thoughts Concerning Education* of 1693,[18] which takes the view that education is based on social class and that this allows the subject to judge and criticize the opinions, traditions and superstitions of the world to which he belongs.

Baretti was searching for a way to make an impact on public opinion. For example, we find him making the Italian lifestyle more 'dramatic' than it actually is, recounting a tale about prejudice that promises catharsis and repentance. The tale is both subjective and objective in its view of the Italian world and British judgement. The plot, for want of a better word, focuses on Italian national traits and character, while the style of narration is based on that of an epic poem. The hero lives outside the pages of the book narrating the text, while Baretti himself becomes the knight battling prejudice,

[18] Baretti 1768: chapter XVII, 298–9.

ignorance and lack of critical spirit. The *Account* is therefore a journey, a drama and an epic, but it is all the while a piece of controversial writing.

Indeed, Sharp sees the figure of Aristarco Scannabue as closer to Baretti, reminding us that both the arrogant mercenary and the incorrigible censor came from the pen of the same author, who wanted to bring Italian people and settings back to life. London magazines applauded Sharp's criticism, admiring the cunning with which the surgeon, temporary champion of the literati, mounted his attack on the *Frusta*. The Scottish intellectual community based in London, which included Smollet, was described by Baretti as a lobby organized by small societies of authors, which in publications such as the *Monthly Review* and the *Critical Review*, discredited whoever did not belong to their circle.[19] Moreover, Baretti's view of London did not include Johnson,[20] and in the nineteenth edition of the *Frusta* he lambasted the city for its noise, dirt and population of beggars, as well as for its community of Scottish journalists, who took every opportunity to express their ancient rivalry with the English (who, instead, embraced Italian traditions and habits).[21] The city, it seems, had temporarily withdrawn its favour from Baretti, offended by the views expressed in the *Account*. Accustomed to the style of the *Spectator*, London did not appreciate Baretti's pungent style (which lacked Addison's *esprit)* and the fact that he made no attempt to please the public.

Baretti found it difficult to explain the difference in his critical approach towards literary topics in the *Account* and the *Frusta*, and he chastized Sharp for being ignorant and prejudiced towards Italians, a sentiment that intensified during the trip itself: 'He was ignorant of the Italian language; was not of high rank, and was afflicted with bodily disorders.'[22] Consequently, Baretti believed that Sharp had no interest in learning more about his country and its culture, and that Sharp's melancholic disposition distorted his perception of reality (*Account*, chapter II). All this contributes to what Baretti defined as 'Mr. Sharp's odd method in accounting.' However, Sharp realized that Aristarco was his strongest argument against Baretti and, to support this, he translated a number of Baretti's/Aristarco's thoughts from the *Frusta*. When strung one after another, with no explanation or context,

---

[19]   Baretti 1932: I, n. IX, 245–8.
[20]   He praised the *Account*, using a statement from Boswell's biography of Johnson, contained in the pages relating to 1768; Boswell 1791: I, 434. On the reserved welcome given to the *Account* by Johnson's circle, see: Collison-Morley 1909: 185–8.
[21]   The English are treated benignly, except in their attitude to Voltaire; see: Piccioni 1946: 138–40.
[22]   Baretti 1768: cap. I, 4.

these thoughts give the impression of contradicting that idea of Italian culture and literature contained in the *Account*. Sharp's quotation of the words of Aristarco are unequivocable:

In Piedmont and Lombardy I do not know of any one author who writes good prose. [...] Authors from Rome and Naples all write badly (n. XIII, p. 343);
I've started hoping that our universal tendency of composing sonnets and ballads, amorous stanzas and eclogues, of free verse and verses ending with a proparoxytone word, will not last for long [...] as for more than half a century it has wreaked untold havoc in our country on logic, good taste and common sense (n. XXI, p. 163);
    However (as I angrily told myself more than once), is our noble country a sewer, that all kinds of men have the right to leave their brain's excrements here? Is it not possible to find a way, if not to rid it of such trashy literature, to at least save it from the diarrhoea of these coarse and trouserless rakes? (n. XXI, p. 142).[23]

Baretti relied on individual poets to bring new life to Italian literature, and to shake off the decadence and uniformity of Arcadian poetry: Metastasio and, even though he did not like him, Goldoni. In the *Account*, Baretti took this view to an extreme point, failing to recognize the reforming role of the literary academies.[24] Condemning Arcadia led to a refusal to recognize the academy as an institution tasked with bringing about new and long-lasting poetry. Baretti was wary of collaboration, preferring individuality, and in his attitude can be detected the notion of the 'self-made man' of preindustrial society, a concept shaped in Britain during the second half of the eighteenth century.

A 'Nation of Nations'

The *Account* was published between two works of literary criticism, *Frusta letteraria* and the *Discours sur Shakespeare et sur Monsieur de Voltaire*, revealing a union between the British empiricist aesthetic and the subjective interpretation of what the author considered 'beautiful'. In Baretti's own words, the essential was: 'Do not simply write, write well, and meaningful content.'[25] For admission to a circle of exceptional people, Baretti also considered of utmost importance style, creativity and a skill to appeal to a wide, but not necessarily well-read, audience. He took for granted the superiority of the epic genre when contemplating the authors of the past,

---

[23] Baretti 1932: II, n. XXI, 142.
[24] Denina 1796.
[25] Baretti 1932: I, 7.

and of drama for contemporary and modern authors. He identified style in Metastasio, cunning in Goldoni, creativity in Carlo Gozzi and Ariosto, epic magnificence in Tasso and promising poetry in Parini. This circle of exceptional people became his model of Italy as a 'nation of nations', a concept which he explained, albeit from a biased point of view, to the British. Indeed, Baretti's excellent critical skills remained pervaded by the notion of required education and teaching, by the classical concepts of *emendare e perficere*, taken up once again by the learning of the eighteenth century. His critical spirit also evinces a taste for reformation, irony, and a preference for Johnson's conservative view rather than for the reformation of the European Enlightenment. The change of perspective in the late eighteenth century – a shift from thinking to acting – is still latent in Baretti's writing, which is why in the Italy described for the benefit of the British there is no discussion of the Italian Enlightenment, nor mention of its main characters: Antonio Genovesi, Cesare Beccaria, the Verri brothers, the Café. Similarly, the periodicals are all omitted when observing the judicial system, prisons, the economy or the constitutions of the different states of the peninsula. Baretti's contradictory personality – his modern spirit together with his love of tradition – is an obstacle when trying to define how far he shared the ideas of the Enlightenment.[26]

Many eighteenth-century writers considered Italy's multicultural scene. Two years before the publication of the *Account*, the imaginary traveller of *Lettere inglesi* by Saverio Bettinelli ponders:

I was amused by changing nations and traditions and finding novelties, which is one of the benefits of travelling at every step. However, I was bored by never knowing where Italy was, and where to find ... Italian theatre? What is Italian poetry and Italian oratory? You could show me one thousand of them, yet never one. Therefore, I say there is no Italian literature, nor Italian taste. We have Roman, Neapolitan, Sicilian tastes, no different from the Porta del Popolo or Porta Pia in Rome itself.[27]

Instead, in the *Account* Baretti tries to define a common talent and nature among the different Italian populations, while simultaneously admitting that this is impossible:

a large nation, or rather a cluster of little nations, which differ among themselves not only in manners and in customs, but in government and in laws, and even in dress and in language.[28]

---

[26] See: Jonard 1990: 1; Anglani 1977; Bracchi 1995: CXII, vol. CLXXII, fasc. 557, 116–29.
[27] Bettinelli 1977: 71–2, 90.
[28] Baretti 1768: cap. I, 14.

However, in the 1818 Italian translation of the *Account*, by Girolamo Pozzuoli, entitled *Gl'Italiani o sia relazione degli usi e costumi d'Italia*, the traditions and characters of Italy live on in the Romantic appeal to the concept of nation, population and ancient memory, although the concepts of identity and independence, normally shaped by the Romantic movement through notions of patriotism, are still missing. The *Account* embodies the essence of 'Italian' in its oscillation between the solitary and authoritative figure of Foscolo, and the more public figure of the bi-weekly newspaper, the *Conciliatore*, published from 1818. But there is one aspect that explains why Bareti's book survived despite it being destined for the antiquarian bookshop as soon as it was written: the fact that the *Account* was created with the precise aim of influencing British public opinion.[29] Throughout Europe, in the years following the French revolution and Napoleon's reign, society was increasingly affected by public attitudes and, in speaking to that audience, the *Account* acquired a modern rationale. Moreover, when translated as *Gl'Italian*i, it revealed its sympathy with liberalism, one of the political and ideological ideas that was most submissive to public opinion,[30] and was central to the formation of Europe from 1815. The *Account* is therefore balanced between liberalism and nationalism, only becoming 'contemporary' 50 years after its publication, and confirms the author's role as a mediator in civil society, albeit in a diachronic dimension.

Early nineteenth-century scholars focused on the critical aspect of Baretti's writing.[31] Liberal opinion, especially that prevailing in Lombardy, recognized modern criticism and the will to reform contemporary literary culture, a culture that was carefully analysed by the Romantics. This modern criticism already can be found in the pages of the *Frusta letteraria*, *Discours* and Baretti's writings in English. Pietro Borsier introduced the *Account* to the readership of the *Conciliatore* on 20 September, 1818, in a review of *Costumi e usi d'Italia*, presenting it as a defence and promulgation of Italian literature and society:

It is appropriate that one of our writers, leaving rhetorical embellishments to the side, defended his compatriots, examining with maturity, governments, laws, public bodies, religion, traditions, education and national literature and their influence on the state of Italy, and on the character of its inhabitants.[32]

---

[29] On English public opinion see: Habermas 1962; Caracciolo and Colombo 1979.
[30] Caracciolo 1989: 100.
[31] See: Di Benedetto 1993: 75–99.
[32] Borsieri 1948: 97.

Gl'Italiani was read during a time of cultural and political reflection, when its audience was intrigued by the literary embodiment of a 'nation' but open to more concrete militant and political interventions. Culture already embodied a national conscience, which pervaded some social groups: the desire to be a 'civil nation', to assert a sense of uniqueness and identity and to aspire to some sort of unity. Comparisons with Britain were still being made, however: the topics contained in Foscolo's works of 1817– 24 – *Lettere dall'Inghilterra* and *La letteratura periodica italiana* – are reminiscent of those of Baretti. For Leopardi, on the other hand, in his *Discorso sopra lo stato presente dei costumi degl'Italiani* of 1824, the *Account* was a missed opportunity due to the overzealous writing of its author.[33]

The *Account* was born from a will to showcase national traits, but increasingly there was a desire to explore real issues of identity and to reveal the deeper factors driving the move towards nationhood. One therefore finds both a growing interest in the connection between literary and political experience (Leopardi), and a call to action. If, after the Vienna Congress of 1814–15, *Gl'Italiani* represented a first step by liberal intellectuals towards shaping a national identity, as a precursor to unity and independence, then around the middle of the nineteenth century the *Account* slowly came to be seen as an answer to British relations with Italy rather than as a solution to overcoming the ideological point of view set out in the pages of the *Conciliatore*. For the pragmatism of the Enlightenment, the *Account* appeared too descriptive, despite sharing its critical and didactic ambitions.

---

[33] Leopardi 1992: 123.

FRANCESCA FEDI

In the field of Italian Studies it is a well-known fact that for Count Vittorio Alfieri (1749–1803) Britain represented a sort of myth, a paradigm of the best form of society and government in the Europe of his time. While contemporary scholarship continues to examine Alfieri's ties with the English-speaking world, the most wide-ranging contribution on the subject remains John Lindon's 1995 monograph. The product of a painstaking perusal of Alfieri's *opera omnia*, the papers assembled in Lindon's volume highlight a variety of crucial data, which will be referenced point by point, as a premise to this chapter.

a) As early as his adolescence, Alfieri showed a predilection for Britain, demonstrating a deep-seated desire to emulate the liberty he witnessed that characterized the customs and behaviour of the British cadets at the Turin Royal Academy (the 'Accademia Reale').[1] His own intense individualism emerged and matured by means of the yardstick these fellow cadets from the 'far north' represented. The Englishmen were unfettered by the constraints of the customs and rules to which Alfieri had to submit as an aristocrat of the House of Savoy.

b) For Alfieri, British culture, and indeed the English language itself (which he never gained complete mastery of), represented a robust alternative to French 'imperialism', as well as a means of distancing himself from the unease he felt when confronting the legacy of 'Italianess', a categorization that he felt was weak and yet foreign.[2]

---

[1] Bianchi 2003a; 2003b.

[2] Alfieri recalled his attempts to appear foreign by 'stammering barbarously' in English during his first journey through Italy: 'Having lived for more than two years alongside Englishmen; having heard their power and wealth lauded by all; having been a witness to their great political influence: then did I have to see Italy laid low; the Italians divided, weak, dispirited and in servitude; and greatly was I ashamed to be, or even to seem, Italian, and wanted no truck with them, either in thought or action' ('Avendo per più di due anni vissuto con Inglesi; sentendo per tutto magnificare la loro potenza e ricchezza; vedendone la grande influenza politica: e per l'altra parte vedendo l'Italia tutta esser morta; gl'Italiani, divisi, deboli, avviliti e servi; io grandemente mi vergognava d'essere, e di parere Italiano, e nulla delle cose loro non voleva né praticar, né sapere'); see Alfieri 1951: I, 67.

c) Alfieri's admiration for the British way of life, British culture and British institutions can not be explained as mere 'anglomania'.[3] Rather, this admiration was the result of a cogent evaluation, an evaluation that encompassed a critical stance towards both the line taken by the British government in some of the more difficult phases of international politics (including the first dispute over the Falkland Islands and the Anglo-American conflict), as well as the problematical figure of George III. There is an evident link between Alfieri's firm condemnation of Jacobin, republican France and his reassessment of the English myth, which, in his literary output subsequent to 1790, Alfieri exploited in an anti-republican vein.[4]

Without revisiting those issues, thoroughly examined by Lindon, it is intended here to review particular questions through the lens of Alfieri's distinctive relationship with Britain in order to build on existing knowledge regarding his cultural biography, as well as to gain insight into several of his literary choices.

Alfieri's Career Prospects

The most obvious places to search for information about Alfieri's affinity for Britain ('a country both fortunate and free')[5] are his autobiography and his literary output. It cannot be overstated that the *Vita* was written on the principle that 'less is more' ('per via di levare'): but by this method the author left numerous unanswered questions in his text, many of which concern precisely his relationship with Britain and with the English.[6] It is significant that Alfieri's reticence in this regard characterizes the period of the crucial years he spent at the Turin Royal Academy, and that the same reticence continued to make itself felt in his account of his first Italian Grand Tour.[7] Alfieri was granted permission to undertake this journey only because of the security afforded by his chosen company: two former academy attendees ('one Flemish, the other Dutch') and above all 'an English Catholic tutor, … a very mature individual, and quite the thing'.[8] Recently,

---

[3] On Italian 'anglomania', see: Graf 1911, a contribution that gained widespread recognition but which now, in light of some recent critical developments, requires updating.

[4] Lindon 1995: 57.

[5] Alfieri 1951: I, 86. 'quel fortunato e libero paese'.

[6] The option of a narrative style free of 'chatter' and 'verbosity' ('chiacchiere' and 'lungaggini') is first outlined in: Alfieri 1951: I, 6–7.

[7] Bianchi 2003b: 102.

[8] Alfieri 1951: I, 61–2. 'Un ajo inglese cattolico, … uomo più che maturo, e di ottimo grido'.

Angelo Fabrizi has uncovered the identity of the three anonymous travellers, demonstrating that the tutor was not John Turbervillle Needham, as previously believed,[9] but may instead be identified with a certain Mr Bulstrode. The few sources known about him point to a military and diplomatic tradition within his family, who were linked to the Stuarts. This Jacobite background had aroused the suspicions of the spy Philipp von Stosch and attracted the attention of the British resident in Florence, Horace Mann, when in 1740 the tutor accompanied other aristocratic pupils (among whom was George Talbot, Lord Shrewsbury) on the classic legs of the Italian Grand Tour.[10]

In the *Vita*, Alfieri recalls primarily Bulstrode's extraordinary capacity to maintain a stiff upper lip, as well as his annoying capacity to 'shilly-shally' around whatever city they were visiting. But there are valid reasons that indicate Bulstrode's slow progress along such well-travelled routes was intentional; in this manner the guide could make the most of a more or less official network of contacts, supported by the typical eighteenth-century intermingling of pursuits such as antique collecting, the Masonic *reseaux* and the interweavings of international diplomacy.[11] Because of Bulstrode, at any rate, Alfieri came into contact with a variety of scholars and diplomats, and several of these exerted a significant influence on him.

A case in point is Giuseppe Lascaris di Castellar, special emissary to Naples for the King of Sardinia. Not only did Lascaris di Castellar present the young Count Alfieri at court – as was his duty – and introduce him to many 'salons', but he also actively supported Alfieri's quest for independence, encouraging him to gain a foothold on the 'diplomatic ladder'.[12] However inexperienced and uncultivated (according to his autobiography) Alfieri may have been, he must have seemed an ideal candidate for this career: he was a nobleman, he was probably already initiated as a Mason,[13] and he had just returned from a Grand Tour that was more formative than even he may have wanted to admit, principally because of Bulstrode's direction. Alfieri's anglophilia must have constituted an additional accomplishment in the eyes of Lascaris di Castellar, as, after the Paris Treaty, the Savoy Ambassador had been one of the strongest supporters of an intensification of the ties between Turin and London,[14] and the outcome of the Seven Years

---

[9] Fabrizi 2008.

[10] See: Ingamells 1997: 858; with references above all to Walpole (1954).

[11] Fedi 2004; 2006. On the importance of the Massonic element in the cultural links between England and Savoy, see also Merlotti's chapter in this volume.

[12] Alfieri 1951: I.

[13] For a recent contribution on Alfieri's Masonic links, see: Tocchini 2013.

[14] Stumpo 1978.

War had reconfirmed to him the idea that the focal point for Savoy foreign policy must indeed be Britain. Alfieri's admiration for Britain surely gave rise to a special feeling of benevolence in the accomplished minister, and Lascaris di Castellar was assured that a new ally could be created for his own policies within the following generation of Piedmontese diplomats.

From the *Vita* we know that the prospect of such a career ('of all the types of servitude, the least servile') 'delighted' Alfieri, and prompted him, if not to study, at least to attempt to maintain a line of conduct that was 'moderate and decent in everything'.[15] In portraying himself, Alfieri gives no hint of a personal interest in the world of diplomacy, yet his autobiography is filled with references to this ambit, especially up to the section entitled *Giovinezza* ('Youth'), which coincides with the years 1766–75.[16] Not only were Piedmontese 'ministers' always the first recipients of any visits that Alfieri sparingly paid in the various places he stopped off at on his tour of Italy; some of these offical figures, akin to Lascaris di Castellar, even established a rapport with him that was more cordial and fruitful than might be expected, given the rigid customs and formal stance of the Savoy government.[17]

Britain as a 'New Rome' and Machiavelli's Legacy

While not the subject of this chapter, the network of relationships that Alfieri established between the spring of 1767 and January of 1768, above all during his extended stays in Venice, Marseilles and Paris, must be noted, as these diplomatic connections facilitated his first stay in England. Indeed, Alfieri's choice of travelling companion from Paris to London (a Piedmontese 'gentleman', who was 'remarkably handsome', yet also uncultivated and a slave to high society) cannot be explained other than as a tribute to his new diplomatic friendship, as his young mate was the Marquis of Rivarolo, a cousin of the Sardinian Minister in Paris and a 'nephew of the Prince of Masserano, who was at that time the Spanish ambassador to London'.[18]

As was the case with the Count of Rivera (a bibliophile diplomat who, when he met Alfieri in Rome, tried to draw the young Count's attention to his own passion for Virgil, albeit prematurely), the Prince of Masserano was

---

[15] Alfieri 1951: I, 72.

[16] There is a short, but valuable catalogue of diplomats mentioned in the *Vita* and in Alfieri's *Epistolario*; see: Ricuperati 2003: 12–13.

[17] On the duties and customs of Piedmontese diplomats, see: Bianchi 2012b.

[18] Alfieri 1951: I, 85.

also mentioned in the *Vita* in especially fond terms, as 'a capital old chap' of Piedmontese origin, motivated by 'paternal benevolence'.[19] Alfieri does not go into detail about the nature of the advice and the suggestions with which the Savoy Spanish Ambassador had facilitated his entry into society in the British capital. It is not possible, therefore, to establish whether, and to what extent, Alfieri's growing enthusiasm for Britain, a country and a culture that he was now experiencing first hand, was based on the opinions of a mentor such as Masserano. None the less, it was during his first sojourn there that Alfieri's attitude about Britain's primacy began to take form. For him Britain represented a model of liberty not only because of its customs and the behaviour of the English, but, above all, because of its 'equitable government'.

So that, despite not having yet studied their constitution in depth (the source of such prosperity), I still managed sufficiently to observe and evaluate its divine effects.[20]

The characteristic reserve Alfieri maintained throughout the *Vita* does not allow for a clear timeline for when he began an 'in-depth study' of the English constitution. What is known is that, during the subsequent stage of Alfieri's European tour, the Portuguese Minister to Holland, José da Cuhna, presented the young Count with Machiavelli's complete works, destined to occupy a pre-eminent place in his library and spurring his desire to tackle the crucial theme of anti-despotism.[21] Da Cuhna introduced Alfieri to a 'republican' Machiavelli, in line with the critical interpretation of the legendary humanist handed down in the British tradition from writers such as Bacon, Milton, Harrington and Bolingbroke.[22] These figures favoured an interpretation of Machiavelli's inclination towards the political system adopted in ancient Rome, based upon a so-called 'mixed government', that in turn provided the basis for an apologia of modern English constitutionalism.

This initial introduction to Machiavelli's writings left its mark on Alfieri. When later, in the 1770s, he found himself closely studying Machiavelli's text, the republican interpretation fell on fertile terrain. The immediate outcome of that study, in addition to the conception of *La Congiura de' Pazzi*, were the two books constituting *Della Tirannide*. In these writings Machiavelli became a cornerstone (along with the Montesquieu of *L'Esprit*

---

[19] Alfieri 1951: I, 86. Vittorio Filippo Amedeo Ferrero Fieschi di Masserano (1713–77) was born in Madrid, where his Piedmontese father settled after serving in the Spanish army. See: Bianchi 2015a.

[20] See: Alfieri 1951: I, 87 ('Onde, benché io allora non ne studiassi profondamente la costituzione, madre di tanta prosperità, ne seppi però abbastanza osservare e valutare gli effetti divini').

[21] For a recent analysis of the theme of Alfieri's Machiavellianism, see Fedi 2014.

[22] For the copious bibliography on this subject, see, in the first instance: Pocock 1975; Burtt 1992.

des Lois) for Alfieri's ideological choice of admiration for Britain. Alfieri was by then prepared, also on a theoretical level, to defend the idea that the true heir to ancient Rome was the 'English Republic' (not that of Cromwell, but rather the nation that emerged from the Glorious Revolution): the only country in the world guided by a non-tyrannical king (since he was bound by laws), and therefore the home of true liberty.[23]

Political Crisis and Private Scandal: Alfieri's Second Sojourn in Britain

At the time he wrote the volumes that make up the treatise *Della Tirannide*, however, Alfieri had, in part, reconsidered his judgement of Britain, above all in light of the contemporaneous political policies pursued by George III, whom the Whig opposition accused of attempting to do away with the executive, thus undermining constitutional principles dating back to 1688.[24] When faced with the British reaction to the Spanish attempt to take over the Falkland Islands, Alfieri had expressed, as early as January 1771, a certain uneasiness and even doubt that he might have been 'taken in' (*trompé*) in celebrating British primacy in Europe. But his words of condemnation for the parliament, comparing it to the period of the senate under Tiberius – 'vendu, et corrompu' – need to be evaluated in the context of an overall political analysis addressed to a friend and 'brother' (fellow mason), a French diplomat in service at Catherine the Great's court.[25] This was Honoré-Auguste Sabatier de Cabre, previously a Secretary at the embassy in Turin (in the 1760s), where he had guided the 'Saint-Jean de la Mystérieuse' Masonic lodge.[26] Alfieri had met him (or met him again) the previous year in Russia, on the last leg of a journey through northern central Europe. Alfieri recorded his trip as memorable for the discovery of a wild, 'sublime' sort of nature, but disappointing on the other hand, and a source of contempt because of the 'servitude' imposed on the populace by the 'disgraceful rulers' in Berlin and, especially, in St Petersburg.[27]

---

[23] For the passage in which Alfieri inaugurates the use of the syntagma 'English Republic', during a digression on the distinctive characteristics of the British nobility, see the treatise *Della Tirannide*, Alfieri 1951–67: I, 61.

[24] See: Lindon 1995: 18 (and *passim*, including bibliographical references).

[25] Alfieri 1963–89: I, 10–13.

[26] See also: Tocchini 2013.

[27] Alfieri 1951: I, 104.

Writing from London, Alfieri started off with a merciless comparison between Sabatier de Cabre's condition, 'gémissant dans le centre de la méfiance et de la tyrannie', and his own happiness in finding himself safe 'au sein de la liberté même'.[28] Despite being weighed down by the threat of 'prochaine decadence', therefore, England had not yet lost its hold on his imagination as a 'réfuge à l'oppression, et a la tyrannie militaire'.[29] It is significant that Alfieri revealed his concerns regarding the weakness of Britain in the 'affaire de Falkland' to the French ambassador, as France was the very power that Spain had called on during those dramatic circumstances to drum up support against the British. Apparently, Alfieri wished to convey to Sabatier de Cabre not so much the disavowal of his anglophilia, as a testimony of the grave political crisis presently under way, and, if anything, he wished to show his approval of the political line taken by the opposition under William Pitt, praised for the 'éloquence et fermeté' of his parliamentary interventions.[30] Above all, this letter provides us with a picture of a young man who was fully at ease in the role of 'diplomat in training': a keen observer, self-assured, capable of irony alongside the allusive (or coded) style of language suited to confidential and diplomatic correspondence.[31]

Nonetheless, this phase of his diplomatic training remains nebulous in Alfieri's biography, paling into insignificance compared with the notorious scandal that characterized his second sojourn in Britain. In the spring of 1771, Alfieri entered into a liaison with the charming (married) daughter of George Pitt, Penelope.[32] Penelope's husband, Viscount Ligonier, an army officer, discovered the liaison, challenging his rival to a duel. Ligonier was satisfied with inflicting a slight injury to Alfieri, but he immediately sought a divorce from Penelope. In the aftermath of the scandal, it was thought that the adulterers would embark on a marriage of reparation with George Pitt's blessing. But in an unexpected turn of events, and before Alfieri could discover the facts in the newspapers, Penelope confessed to him that she had previously been unfaithful to her husband with a manservant.

This 'horrible deception', as Alfieri decried the episode, was not the worst consequence he suffered, as he had also been served with a legal summons using his full name.[33] The outcry surrounding the affair was such that

---

[28]   Alfieri 1963–89: I, 10.

[29]   Alfieri 1963–89: I, 11.

[30]   Alfieri 1963–89: I, 11.

[31]   See Santato 2003: 248; who points out 'clear Masonic references' in the letter.

[32]   George Pitt (1721–1803), ambassador to Turin from 1761 to 1768, is described by Alfieri as a 'person very well known *to him* for several years'. See Alfieri 1951: I, 119.

[33]   Vincent 1957. *Disinganno orribile* is the title of the chapter in the *Vita* where this episode is narrated at length.

Alfieri's diplomatic career prospects were ruined forever. Despite the prom-ise of support from the Marquis Caracciolo (the Neapolitan Ambassador to London, who was also very influential in Turin, where he had been Ambassador from 1754 to 1764), the highest ranks of diplomacy would now be permanently off-limits to the young Count.

'Lo Spione Italiano' (The Italian Spy)

On behalf of the true and long-lasting nature of Alfieri's friendship with Caracciolo, a suspicion arises of Alfieri having managed to mantain, despite the London scandal, at least an unofficial role as an observer of international politics and as a recipient of classified information. The strongest support for this hypothesis came from the dissemination in 1782 of a periodical, the self-styled *Lo spione italiano, o sia Corrispondenza segreta e famigliare fra il march. Di Licciocara e il conte Rifiela, tutti e due viaggiatori incogniti per le diverse Corti dell'Europa* (*The Italian Spy or the Secret and Intimate Correspondence between the Marchese Di Licciocara and the Count Rifiela, both Incognito Travellers in Diverse European Courts*). This publication represented a controversial editorial operation, which not even Pier Carlo Masini's painstaking studies have managed to fully explain.[34] However, the anagram-pseudonyms of the two correspondents clearly point to Caracciolo and Alfieri, who were long-standing friends and Masonic 'brothers' engaged in a dialogue on the topical issues of religious freedom and the balance of power in Europe. *Lo spione* may be interpreted as an attempt to implicate and discredit the reputations of Caracciolo and Alfieri by attributing 'dan-gerous' observations to them. However, it is more likely that the publication (edited by the Sienese Catani) was instead a 'serious' political experiment motivated by a desire to uphold the widespread instances of jurisdiction-alism in Europe at the time of Pius VI's crucial journey to Vienna, through the far-reaching Masonic network.[35]

The periodical was cancelled after the third issue: such censorship indi-cates how adroitly the two correspondents acted, as they kept their silence and remained discreet about the whole business. In any case, Caracciolo had already arrived in Palermo as viceroy and was engaged in the arduous task of instituting a plan of reform to sidestep the privileges of the barons; it was in his interest to ensure that a further front of attack did not open up.

---

[34] Masini 1997.
[35] Masini 1997: 11.

Alfieri, on the other hand, was experiencing wider difficulties, having just made his debut in the literary world, where he was well known 'on the social scene'.[36] Additionally, only a few months previously, he had completed the complex process of renouncing his rights as a feudal Lord of Savoy. Finally, and most importantly, he had entered into a long-term relationship with Princess Louise Maximilienne Caroline Emmanuele of Stolberg-Gedern, known as the Countess of Albany, wife of Charles Edward Stuart, the Jacobite claimant to the English and Scottish thrones.

The 'Countess of Albany' and her Husband

The account of Alfieri's 'worthy love', which blossomed in the autumn of 1777, represents one of the most substantial narrative strands in the *Vita*. The Countess was celebrated for the role she assumed as a 'spur, and comfort and example for every good work', becoming a decisive factor in Alfieri's literary maturation.[37] However, Alfieri fictionalized the autobiographical elements to veil the actual circumstances of their union: this is why, for instance, we do not know the identity of the 'acquaintance' that introduced Alfieri to Louise Stolberg, who had previously been judged too 'dangerous' to be presented due to her 'abundance of qualities' and her fame as an unhappy bride.[38] For the purposes of our research, it would be decisive if we could establish exactly whether this meeting with the Countess was really the outcome of a rare act of obeisance to social niceties on the part of the melancholy traveller, or whether it had been promoted by British individuals linked to Horace Mann's circle. These British intermediaries include Frederick Augustus Hervey, for whom Alfieri put in a good word with Candido Pistoi on 9 November 1777, during the weeks – or perhaps during the very days – when Alfieri made his first appearance at the Countess's salon.[39]

Such mediation, deriving from Alfieri's association with diplomatic circles, strengthens the hypothesis also regarding Alfieri's unofficial involvement in anti-Stuart policies, whose strategically placed stronghold was

---

[36]   Masini 1997: 16.

[37]   Alfieri 1951: I, 206–9.

[38]   Alfieri 1951: I, 208.

[39]   Alfieri 1963–89: I, 33. On the singular figure of Hervey ('a tireless traveller and esteemed scientist', as well as an important mediator 'between Anglo-Saxon and continental culture', see: Tongiorgi 2003: 38); moreover, Fothergill's monograph is still vital, and has recently been re-edited (Fothergill 2010). It should be noted that Hervey and Alfieri both figure in a list of those affiliated with the Neapolitan lodge 'La Vittoria' (1782).

Florence. In Florence Charles Edward, by then innocuous because of his advanced age and physical frailty, was still under the surveillance of British agents, and especially in the year 1777, when a rumour had spread among masons of Strict Observance that he might indeed be the mysterious Grand Master in incognito, 'the restorer of the purity of the ancient orders'.[40] It is highly likely that Alfieri was encouraged by some friend or 'brother' from the British Masonic circle to frequent the Countess of Albany's residence, and that he acted under instructions to be an observer, gaining access by playing up his credentials as a Piedmontese nobleman and based on the long-standing ties that existed between the Savoys and Stuarts.

The risks of triggering a diplomatic incident were serious, however. Alfieri, already an unwilling 'vassal' to the Savoy court, would have known of the trial under way in Turin that winter (1777–8), against his former companion from the Royal Academy, Luigi Garretti di Ferrere. Garretti di Ferrere faced an extremely harsh sentence on the charge of *lèse-majesté* because of his criticism of the actions undertaken by the Piedmontese Prime Minister's government.[41] Andrea Merlotti has noted that Garretti's fate influenced Alfieri's decision to 'de-Piedmontify' himself during those weeks;[42] indeed, it is plausible that it was precisely his relationship with the Countess of Albany, and the possible repercussions of a scandal in Turin, that gave him most cause for concern at this juncture. More than the risk of an accusation of adultery, he was running the risk of being accused of plotting against the Pretender, to whom – at least officially – he owed the consideration accorded to a foreign king, an accusation for which Alfieri would have had to answer directly to Victor Amadeus III.

Alfieri's mounting sense of unease, while not revealed in his autobiography, appears instead in a note, dated 3 March 1778, addressed to his manservant, Elia, to whom two other letters, that were to be delivered immediately to Turin, were entrusted. In the first letter Alfieri announced his decision to give up his patrimony to his sister Giulia and to relinquish feudal rights in her favour. In the second letter (which has been lost), addressed to Count Agostino Tana, Alfieri charged Tana with burning 'all the papers that you will find both in the writing desk and the writing table'.[43] These destroyed

---

[40] Pasta 2006: 451.

[41] There is an account of this in: Bianchi 2002: 251–61.

[42] Merlotti 2003c: 156.

[43] Alfieri 1963–89: I, 36. 'tutte le carte che troverete tanto nella scrivania quanto nella tavola da scrivere'. For an explanation for the distinction between 'desk' and 'writing table', see *Esquisse du jugement universel* (Alfieri 2004: 63–4), where a *Table à écrire*, alluding to the divinity in its triangular shape, occupies the centre of a room in which the meetings of a pseudo-Masonic society were held.

papers surely would have illuminated questions of Alfieri's links with the British in Tuscany, and above all would have shed light on his ties to the Florentine anti-Stuart circle.

Maria Stuarda: Tragedy of the Stuart Dynasty

It is precisely in the context of this personally and politically crucial moment, that Alfieri's *Maria Stuarda*, a tragedy dedicated to a historical figure who occupied 'a prominent position among European literary figures', must be considered.[44] The inspiration for the play dates to the summer of 1778, as Alfieri revealed the topic had been suggested to him at that time 'with a certain solicitude ... by a person to whom I can refuse nothing'.[45] Nevertheless, perhaps because the work did not display that 'violent impulse' that the author was fond of claiming as the principal quality underpinning his inspiration, Alfieri remained dissatisfied with the tragedy and particularly discontented by the weakness of the central figure of Mary Stuart. But apart from the aesthetic qualities of the text, it is interesting for us to evaluate the choice of the central episode in the drama. Alfieri did not opt for the traditional clash between Mary and Elizabeth, and the consequent beheading of the Scottish queen, but rather for the accidents surrounding the death of Mary's second husband, Henry Darnley, betrayed and killed by the power-mad Lord Botthwell.

If the Countess of Albany persuaded Alfieri to write *Maria Stuarda* in order to 'clear' the reputation of the tragic figure of Mary 'of having deliberately murdered her husband', her objective was not achieved.[46] Queen Mary, both suspicious and irresolute, is not credible in her role in the play as a victim of court intrigue: indeed, her husband criticizes her for her unwillingness to share power with him, as well as the relationships that she has with too many 'ministers, or friends, or advisors, or slaves'. One of these characters, whose horrible death in March 1566 is referenced during the opening scene of the play, was a Piedmontese subject, Davide Rizzio. A talented musician who had arrived in Scotland as a member of the retinue of the Savoy ambassador, he had enjoyed immediate success in his career at the Stuart court, thus triggering the suspicion and stirring up the hatred of Darnley, and of the Protestant barons who, fearing he

---

[44] Nozzoli 2003: 583.
[45] Alfieri 1978: 110.
[46] This appears in the dedication of the play to the Countess (1782), which remained unpublished; see also: Nozzoli 2003: 587.

might be a papist spy, had him ruthlessly murdered while he stood along-side the Queen, who was at that time expecting the heir to the throne. The episode was notorious. As a Piedmontese, Alfieri would have been aware of the gruesome event, and moreover, there are several pages devoted to Rizzio's murder in David Hume's *History of England*, one of the most sig-nificant hypotexts in Alfierian tragedy.[47] In Hume's account, furthermore, the gruesome murder takes on a strategic importance as it opens up the way for the definitive clash between Mary and her husband, destined shortly to fall victim to the 'implacable' revenge of the queen.

The characters of the sovereigns in *Maria Stuarda* lack depth, and the dramatic death of Rizzio is relegated to the background, although it main-tains its value as the source of the offences Maria and Arrigo give to each other. In the final act, moreover, Rizzio's memory recalls in the horrifying prophecy pronounced by Lamorre, the most difficult character to pin down from a historical point of view and 'absolutely superfluous' to the action, but capable of rendering it 'much livelier, and quite extraordinary':[48]

whereby whoever is listening is swayed by the different opinions, so bloodthirsty and fearsome, which were prevalent at that time in Scotland, and were the same that led the unhappy Maria to death by beheading. Lamorre's prophetically poetic part in the fifth act may in some way compensate for a great deal of the previous and subsequent defects in the tragedy.[49]

The sense behind this sibylline judgement may in fact be grasped through an analysis of the vision that overwhelms Maria and opens her eyes to the real objectives of her advisor. In a trance, Lamorre – in a grisly sequence of images – sees the succession of events that will tragically strike the Stuarts: these range from Arrigo's imminent murder at Maria's wedding to the trai-tor Botuello, to the immolation of the Queen and to the death of Charles I, right up to the fall of the dynasty ('as damaging to itself as to others'), to the flight of their descendants, and to the vain attempts by the Pretenders to reconquer the throne. This tragic cycle is rounded off by a reference to

[47] It is currently thought that Alfieri came across the *History* in a French translation by Prévost (London 1760). But a new English edition of Hume's work had appeared posthumously in 1778, and it is certainly possible that Alfieri was aware of it, also because of his association with the British circle in Florence. Regarding Alfieri's reception of Hume's work (and, in general, models for the figure of Mary Stuart), see: Nozzoli 2003: 591–5. See further: Hume 1983–5: IV, 80.

[48] Alfieri 1978: 111.

[49] '… ove chi ascolta si voglia pure prestare alle diverse opinioni, che in que' tempi regnavano nella Scozia, cosi sanguinosamente feroci, e che furon poi quelle che trassero la infelice Maria a morir sovra un palco. La parte profeticamente poetica di Lamorre nel quint'atto, potrebbe forse in qualche modo scusare molti degli antecedenti e susseguenti difetti della tragedia.'

the by-now grotesque figure of Charles Edward, who has found 'shelter' in the midst of 'Italian baseness', which gives an audacious stamp to the work, covering both the role the Stuarts played in British history, and the outcome of the only regicide (up to that moment) in modern European history. Indeed, a reflection of such pertinence might well have functioned as the crucial turning-point of the play; but Alfieri decided otherwise, leaving the text 'defective'.

Surely a vast quantity of historical material needed to be included for the story and developing it fully would have required a cycle of plays (along the lines of the Medicean cycle), rather than just one tragedy. As is recorded in the *Vita*, Alfieri had previously written a first draft of a work dedicated to *Charles Premier* in French: but the Count's alleged 'freezing up' of inspiration later led to the abandonment of this project. The writing of *Maria Stuarda* had to take into account a fresh perspective influenced by the overlapping of autobiographical and historical circumstances. In the principal scene comprising Lamorre's prophecy, Alfieri's attempt to address the longstanding problem of Stuartism is acknowledged: this may have been due, in part, to the Countess of Albany, but was surely due equally to the audience of Alfieri's informed friends who were highly interested also in what the future held politically for Great Britain, as the conflict gradually worsened between the American colonies and the motherland.

'Libertas Britannica' and 'Libertas Americana'

As has been described, *Maria Stuarda* was difficult for Alfieri to write. It coincided with the last phase of the Anglo-American conflict and was finished in Rome in 1782, a few months before Alfieri (following upon a happy and productive two-year period) had to abandon the city when his liaison with the Countess of Albany was uncovered. The inevitable period of separation from his companion was the motive behind a new series of journeys, that once again brought him to England. In the *Vita*, Alfieri writes that this third sojourn in England led, for the umpteenth time, to the purchase of horses, a 'raving passion' of his. But yet again it may now be assumed that this journey, scarcely documented even in the *Epistolario*, had taken place for other, more complex, reasons.

Among the objectives of Alfieri's third British tour was the promotion of the first edition of the tragedies, which had just been published in Siena. For reasons of political delicacy, both the anti-Medicean cycle and *Maria Stuarda* were not included. Having celebrated – in the five odes to *America*

Libera – first the Colonists' victory and then the Independence sanctioned by peace in Paris in 1783, Alfieri wished to personally re-evaluate these latest changes to the British social and political scene.[50] If this hypothesis put forward above is true, and if Alfieri-Rifiela was behind the *Lo spione* episode also, then it is easy to imagine how he might have taken on the role of observer in London once again, between December 1783 and April 1784, particularly considering his documented relationship with Filippo Mazzei, who in turn was associated with Caracciolo in his official capacity as a member of the 'Masonic International', that sided with the Insurgents against their 'English brothers' (English fellow masons).[51]

Anglophilia and Anti-French Sentiment

Finally, it was Alfieri's fourth sojourn in Britain, officially a 'diplomatic' mission, but with a primarily private scope, that was the only trip he was to enjoy there in the company of the Duchess of Albany. The journey had been undertaken because of pecuniary interests of the Duchess, specifically for her to seek a royal annuity in Britain. Even though she had been separated since 1784, and a widow since 1788, she had continued to receive a pension assigned to her by the French crown following her marriage to the Pretender. But the course taken by revolutionary events had threatened its continuance: for this reason Alfieri and his companion planned to leave Paris, where they had been living since 1786, in order to move to England and seek a royal annuity. The failure of this venture led the lovers back to Paris, described by Alfieiri as a 'cloaca massima', from whence they departed definitively in August 1792, escaping with the help of the Venetian ambassador only a few hours before Louis XVI's arrest. For Alfieri, the complete and permanent rejection of anything relating to France from that time onwards also brought about a return to his earlier interests in the ideal of English liberty. Having wavered on this question, because of episodes of parliamentary corruption, mercantile fanaticism and the attempt to suppress the Insurgents, he now enthusiastically embraced the myth of his youth once again, especially when viewed in contrast to the contemporary 'French tyranny' he had witnessed.

---

[50] The first four odes were written in December 1781, the last in June 1783, in celebration of the end of the conflict; see: Alfieri 1951–67: II, 75–100.

[51] For the relationship between Alfieri and Mazzei and the support given to the Insurgents, see: Fedi 2007: 108–9.

Unresolved issues linked to the well-known narrative arc of Alfieri's anglophilia linger, however, which have only been touched upon in this article. One of these, and perhaps the most significant, concerns Alfieri's ideal 'English library', that is, the *corpus* of works that left the most lasting mark on his culture. An initial catalogue may be compiled from the treatise *Del principe e delle lettere* of great English and Scottish 'masters', worthy in their inspiring conception of liberty of a place alongside the classics: Milton, Locke, Robertson and Hume.[52] But what still requires more study would be Alfieri's undertaking to translate Pope's *The Windsor Forest*, a masterpiece dear also to his Turin friends at the 'Accademia Sanpaolina', and especially intriguing from the point of view of its political ramifications.[53]

It has been the intention in this chapter to confirm the importance of the historic-political component in Alfieri's English myth, which was originally espoused from a sense of Alfieri's imagining himself a kindred spirit to the British, but which was then cultivated over his lifetime through study and through an attempt to acquire a detached and objective view of Italian anomalies. Alfieri's anglophilia may be understood as a continuation of that introduced by Giuseppe Baretti, and as a critical paradigm later embraced by Foscolo and many other admirers of Alfieri, reconciled to Britain following the conclusion of the Napoleonic interlude.

---

[52] Lindon 1995: 25; Nozzoli 2003: 590.
[53] See Fedi 2015 for a recent survey on this issue.

Appendix I British Diplomats and Visitors in Turin in the Eighteenth Century

CHRISTOPHER STORRS

Ancaster, Duchess of[1]
Annandale, Marquis of[2]
Astley, Lady[3]
Berkeley, Mr[4]
Bertie, Lady Charlotte[5]
Bowman, Mr[6]
Braithwaite, Mr[7]
Brand, Mr[8]
Buchan, Mr[9]
Buckingham, Duke and Duchess of[10]
Carlisle, Earl of[11]
Cavendish, Lord Charles (Nice)[12]
Chesterfield, Lord[13]
Conway, Lord[14]
Coke, Mr (son of Lord Lovett)[15]

This list is by no means exhaustive in terms of the period covered or the social range of visitors since it largely comprises those referred to in the despatches of successive British diplomats between c. 1720 and 1789. Names are given as in the letters cited. Inevitably, this was a very socially select group of travellers and visitors. Nevertheless, despite these qualifications, the list might usefully be set alongside and compared with that of Ingamells (1997). Some of those listed here were attending the Turin Academy and thus also appear on the list in Appendix III.

[1] Trevor to Carmarthen, 1 April 1786, London, Kew, National Archives, Foreign Office (FO) 67/5.
[2] Villettes to Newcastle, 4 June 1737, London, Kew, National Archives, State Papers (SP) 92/41.
[3] Trevor to Carmarthen, 22 May 1784, FO 67/3.
[4] Villettes to Newcastle, 4 September 1737, SP 92/41.
[5] Trevor to Carmarthen, 1 April 1786, FO 67/5.
[6] Villettes to Newcastle, 31 August 1737, SP 92/41.
[7] Trevor to Carmarthen, 2 June 1786, FO 67/5.
[8] Villettes to Newcastle, 4 September 1737, SP 92/41.
[9] Villettes to Newcastle, 4 September 1737, SP 92/41.
[10] Allen to Newcastle, 25 November and 2 December 1730, SP 92/33.
[11] Potter to Shelburne, 27 February 1768, SP 92/73.
[12] Allen to Newcastle, 27 October 1731, SP 92/33.
[13] Trevor to Carmarthen, 2 February 1785, FO 67/4.
[14] Villettes to Newcastle, 31 August 1737, SP 92/41.
[15] Villettes to Newcastle, 7 February 1739, SP 92/42.

Cornbury, Lord (1730)[16]

Cowper, Lord[17]

Cumberland, Duchess of[18]

Dashwood, Sir Francis[19]

Drummond, Mr (brother of Lord Perth)[20]

Dussaux, Mr[21]

Euston, Lord[22]

[A] Fiennes Cliunton, later Earl of Lincoln and Duke of Newcastle

Forbes, Mr[23]

Forster, Capt[24]

Fotheringay, Mr, a Scotch gentleman[25]

Fox, Mr[26]

Fox Lane, Mr[27]

Gloucester, Duke of[28]

Graham, James, 4th Marquis and 1st Duke of Montrose[29]

Gray, Mr[30]

Grenville, Lord[31]

Hamilton, Duke of[32]

Hampden, Lord[33]

Harrington, Lord, his two sons[34]

Hillsborough, Lord[35]

---

[16] Allen to Newcastle, 7 October 1730, SP 92/33.

[17] Trevor to Carmarthen, 19 April 1786, FO 67/5.

[18] Trevor to Carmarthen, 2 June 1786, FO 67/5.

[19] Allen to Newcastle, 29 December 1731, SP 92/33; Villettes to Newcastle, 30 November 1740, SP 92/33.

[20] Villettes to Newcastle, 28 January 1739, SP 92/42.

[21] Villettes to Newcastle, 31 August 1737, SP 92/41.

[22] Essex to Newcastle, 10 November 1734, SP 92/; Villettes to Couraud, 19 November 1735, Villettes to Newcastle, 26 February 1736, Turin, SP 92/40.

[23] Villettes to Newcastle, 4 September 1737, SP 92/41.

[24] Villettes to Newcastle, 4 June 1737, SP 92/41.

[25] Villettes to Newcastle, 24 April 1737, SP 92/41.

[26] Sherdley to Shelburne, 8 November 1766, SP 92/72.

[27] Trevor to Carmarthen, 7 December 1785, FO 67/4.

[28] Trevor to Carmarthen, 8 November 1786 and 2 June 1787, FO 67/5, 6.

[29] Cf. his account of his visit (1698) in National Archives of Scotland GD220/6/1748.

[30] Villettes to Newcastle, 7 November 1739, SP 92/42.

[31] Sherdley to Shelburne, 8 November 1766, SP 92/72.

[32] Allen to Newcastle, 1 January 1729, SP 92/33.

[33] Trevor to Carmarthen, 7 August 1784, FO 67/3.

[34] Villettes to Newcastle, 4 September 1737, SP 92/41.

[35] Sherdley to Conway, 28 May 1766, SP 92/72.

Holland, Lord and Lady[36]

Howard, Mr (son of Howard of Corby) (Catholic in Sardinian service)[37]

Kingston, Duke of[38]

Lovelace, Lord[39]

Luttrell, Lady Elizabeth[40]

Middlesex, Lord[41]

Milner, Mr, son of sir William Milner of Yorkshire[42]

Montagu, later Earl of Sandwich

Nassau, Count (nephew of Lord Grantham)[43]

Norfolk, Duke of[44]

Northampton, Lord[45]

Osborne, Sir Davies[46]

Payne, Mr[47]

Pitt, George[48]

Ponsonby, Mr[49]

Portland, Duke of[50]

Ratcliff(e), Mr[51]

Sabine, son of Gen.[52]

Sherrard Manners, Lord[53]

Stuart, Col.[54]

Stewart, Archibald, of Fintarloch[55]

Sunbury, Lord[56]

[36] Sherdley to Shelburne, 8 November 1766 and 6 May 1767, SP 92/72.
[37] Trevor to Carmarthen, 30 July 1786, FO 67/5.
[38] Allen to Newcastle, 27 October 1731, SP 92/33.
[39] Allen to Newcastle, 22 December 1731, SP 92/33.
[40] Trevor to Carmarthen, 2 June 1786, FO 67/5.
[41] Allen to Newcastle, 27 October 1731, SP92/33; Essex to Newcastle, 31 July 1736, SP 92/40.
[42] Newcastle to Villettes, 14 December 1744, SP 36/64/3 f. 63.
[43] Allen to Newcastle, 16 February 1732, Turin, SP 92/33.
[44] Allen to Newcastle, 3 February 1731, SP 92/33.
[45] Pitt to Egremont, 11 June 1763, SP 92/70.
[46] Villettes to Newcastle, 31 August 1737, SP 92/41.
[47] Sherdley to Shelburne, 8 November 1766, SP 92/72.
[48] Trevor to Carmarthen, 2 February 1785, FO 67/4.
[49] Essex to Newcastle, 31 July 1736, SP 92/40.
[50] Allen to Newcastle, 15 December 1731, SP 92/33.
[51] Essex to Newcastle, 21 July 1736, SP 92/40.
[52] Villettes to Newcastle, 4 September 1737, SP 92/41.
[53] Villettes to Newcastle, 2 November 1737, SP 92/41.
[54] Mountstuart to Hillsborough, 16 February 1782, Add Mss 36802.
[55] Villettes to Newcastle, 11 September 1739, SP 92/42.
[56] Villettes to Newcastle, 31 August 1737, SP 92/41.

Vernon, Messrs.[57]
Walpole, Edward[58]
Walpole, Horace[59]
Warren, Mr[60]
Wentworth, Lady[61]
Wilkes, John[62]

[57] Villettes to Newcastle, 13 October 1736, SP 92/40.
[58] Allen to Newcastle, 27 January 1731.
[59] Villettes to Newcastle, 7 November 1739, SP 92/42.
[60] Villettes to Newcastle, 24 April 1737, SP 92/41.
[61] Sherdley to Conway, 28 May 1766, SP 92/72.
[62] Dutens to Halifax, 9 January 1765, SP 92/71.

Appendix II   Sabaudian Diplomats in London in the Eighteenth Century

ANDREA MERLOTTI

1713–16	Eleazar Wilcardel de Fleury, Marquis de Triviè (Trivero, †1732)[1]
1716–19	Count Jean François Bertrand de la Perouse (†1751)[2]
1719–25	Ercole Tommaso Roero, Marquis of Cortanze (1661–1747)[3]
1725–29	Victor-Amédée Seyssel d'Aix, Marquis de Sommariva (1679–1754)[4]
1729–49	*cavalier* (chevalier) Giuseppe Ossorio Alarçon (1697–1763)[5]
1749–55	Count Carlo Baldassarre Perrone di San Martino (1718–1802)[6]
1755–63	Count François-Joseph de Viry (1707–66)[7]
1763–5	Marquis Filippo Francesco Ferrero della Marmora (1719–89)[8]
1765–9	Count François-Justin de Viry, Baron de la Perrière (1737–1813)[9]
1769–74	Count Giuseppe Filippo Ponte di Scarnafigi (1730–88)[10]
1774–84	Victor-Amédée Sallier de La Tour, Marquis de Cordon[11]

See Archivio di Stato di Torino, Corte, Lettere ministri, Gran Bretagna.

[1] From Savoy. Envoy extraordinary to Charles III of Habsburg, King of Spain, in Barcelona (1707–11); Envoy extraordinary to London (1713); from 1720 in Poland.

[2] From Savoy. Provisional Secretary of war (1713) and Auditor General of war (1723) in Turin.

[3] From Piedmont. Governor of Alessandria (1707), Envoy to Vienna (1707–8), Viceroy of Sardinia (1727–30), Governor of Alessandria (1727–34) and of the citadel of Turin (1734–47), General of artillery (1731).

[4] From Savoy. General (1725), Capitain of the Royal Bodyguards (1729), Governor of the citadel of Turin (1731), Governor of the Milan Castle (1734), Lieutenant General of infantry (1734), *Gran mastro* of artillery (1736).

[5] From Sicily. Envoy to Netherlands (1723) and to London (1729); Sabaudian representative to the Peace of Aquisgrana (1748); Ambassador to Madrid (1749), Secretary of State to the Foreign Office in Turin (1750–63).

[6] From Piedmont. Attendee at the Turin Royal Academy (1732–3), cavalry Officer then General (1780), Envoy to Dresden (1745–9) and to London (1749–55), Secretary of State to the Foreign Office in Turin (1777–89).

[7] From Savoy. Envoy to Bern (1738–41), Envoy extraordinary to Netherlands (1750–5) and to London (1755–63), Secretary of State to the Foreign Office in Turin (1763–6).

[8] From Piedmont. Attendee at the Turin Royal Academy (1731–4); officer in the Regiment *Dragoni di Genevese*; Envoy to Netherlands (1760–3), Plenipotentiary to London (1763–5), Ambassador to Paris (1765–73); Viceroy of Sardinia (1773–7), General lieutenant of cavalry (1780).

[9] From Savoy. Envoy extraordinary to Netherlands (1764–5) and to London (1765–9), Ambassador to Madrid (1769–73) and to Paris (1773–7). Senator under Napoleon I (1804).

[10] From Piedmont. Plenipotentiary to Lisbon (1765–9), Envoy extraordinary to London (1769–74) and to Wien (1774–7), Ambassador to Paris (1777–88).

[11] From Savoy. Ambassador in Netherlands (1768–74), Envoy extraordinary to London (1774–84), Ambassador to Paris (1788–90).

1784–7   Count Giuseppe Spirito Nomis di Pollone (1749–1823)[12]
1787–1813   Filippo San Martino di San Germano, Count of Front (1748–1813)[13]

---

[12] From Piedmont. Attendee at the Turin Royal Academy (1765–9); cavalry Officer in the Regiment *Piemonte Reale*, Plenipotentiary to Berlin (1779), Envoy extraordinary to London (1784) and to Lisbon (1789), Ambassador to Madrid (1796).

[13] From Piedmont. Ambassador to Lisbon (1785), Envoy extraordinary to London (1787).

Appendix III   British Attendees at the Turin Royal Academy

PAOLA BIANCHI

Primo Appartamento (First Apartment)

Anderson[1]	1756
Archer	1748–9
Archer	1756
Henry Bellings, 8th Baron of Arundel[2]	1758–9
Atthembs	1748
Axender	1745
Balmain	1766–7
Richard Barry, 6th Earl of Barrymore[3]	1764
Barret	1769–70
Pierre Bathurst	1747–8
Bellin	1779–81
Berkeley[4]	1737

This appendix lists the British attendees (students and their tutors) at the Turin Royal Academy, systematized by 'apartments', as documented in the Treasury archives of the Turin Royal Academy. The spelling used throughout replicates that of the handwritten registries kept in the Archivio di Stato di Torino, Camerale, art. 216, *Conti Accademia Reale de' studi* (1731–98), 2 mz. (1731–60; 1761–98, excluding the year 1773). Doubts remain concerning the spelling of certain surnames; these, however, are probably not of British origin. Of the total attendees enrolled and paying a fee (except for those who were admitted without being charged, especially the Court page boys), British attendees account for 9.8% of the total, almost all of whom were residents in the first 'apartment'.

[1] Archer's travelling companion.

[2] 1740–1808. The eldest son of the 7th Baron of Arundel, he attended the Jesuit college of Saint Omer, in the north of France, from 1753 to 1758. He inherited his father's title in 1756. His journey around Italy extended to Genoa, Florence (1759), Rome (1760) and Parma. His tutor was the Jesuit, Charles Booth, with whom he continued his Grand Tour in Genoa and Florence. Described by Walpole as 'a devout Catholic Lord' (*Correspondence* XXI, p. 309), during his educational travels in Italy, he acquired a number of paintings of sacred themes. His agent in Rome (1759) for that purpose was father John Thorpe, who also acted as mediator for Batoni. Clark 1985: 341; Ingamells 1997: 29–30.

[3] 1745–73. The eldest son of the 5th Earl of Barrymore, he had succeeded his father in 1751. By that time he had been educated at the public schools of Eton and Westminster. He had a brilliant military career and became Captain of the 9th Regiment of the Dragoons of the British army (1767). He arrived in Turin with Captain Dobson. In Turin he met Gibbon in late April and from July to August, John Holroyd. On Holroyd's travel journal, see: Black 1984: 159; Ingamells 1997: 58.

[4] Norborne Berkley (*c.* 1717–70), Frederick Augustus's uncle. He was accompanied by his tutor, George Barclay. Ingamells 1997: 81.

Frederick Augustus Berkeley[5]	1762–4
Bernam [Bernham][6]	1784–6
Bodhenam [Bodenham]	1777–9
milord Bolingbrok [Bolingbroke]	1752
Charles Thomas Boothby Skrymsher[7]	1759
Charles Booth[8]	1759
Bouquet[9]	1749–50
Brograve	1750–1
Charles Cornwallis Brome[10]	1759
Browne	1775–6
Browne[11]	1775
Bulstrode[12]	1765–6
Thomas Charles Bunbury[13]	1759–60

[5] 1745–1810. 5th Earl of Berkeley. He succeeded his father in 1755. He chose a military career and rose to the rank of Colonel in 1779. After leaving Turin, he continued his Grand Tour in Naples, Rome, Florence and Genoa. He had been introduced into Turin's aristocratic *milieu* by his grandfather, Norborne Berkley. His tutor was Richard Phelps, Secretary of the British legation in Turin. In 1764, he met Gibbon in Turin. Ingamells 1997: 81; Black 1999: 39.

[6] Tutor of d'Arvillars.

[7] Horace Walpole's third cousin, he did not pursue a public career. He continued his Italian tour in Florence, where he was painted by Thomas Patch. He was in Turin for only a brief time, but, according to Louis Dutens (*Mémoires*), he was admitted into the circle of the famous *salonnière* Madame de Saint Gilles. Ingamells 1997: 104.

[8] 1707–97. A Jesuit, he attended the college of Saint-Omer (1715–24), in France, where he took holy orders in 1731. He lived in Loreto between 1742 and 1746, and he later became Governor of Arundel. In 1761–2 he was appointed Rector of the English College in Rome, from which he was expelled in 1766 after openly siding with the Jacobite pretender to the throne of England on a visit to Rome. Ingamells 1997: 104.

[9] Philip Stanhope (1732–68), natural son of Philip Stanhope, 4th Earl of Chesterfield, and Elizabeth du Bouchet. Bianchi 2003a.

[10] 1738–1805. A Viscount and the eldest son of the 1st Earl of Cornwallis, he was educated at Eton and Cambridge. He became an officer in the British Army, taught in the 1st Infantry Regiment (1756), later became Captain of the 8th Infantry Regiment (1761) and finally, General (1793). He also sat in Parliament (1760–2) and succeeded his father as 2nd Earl (1762). He was Envoy Extraordinary to Prussia (1785) and Governor-General of India (1786–93). He travelled with a Prussian tutor, Captain De Roguin. He remained in Turin, possibly until the summer, and then he travelled to the German Courts, where he joined the troops to fight the war as aide-de-camp of Lord Granby. Ingamells 1997: 132.

[11] Brother of the preceding, Charles Cornwallis Brome.

[12] He accompanied Count Coloma, who was at the Turin Royal Academy in the same years. Former tutor of George Talbot Shrewsbury (1719–87), who had undertaken his Grand Tour of Italy in Florence and Rome (1739–40), through Count Coloma he entered pro-Jacobite Catholic circles in Albano. Bulstrode would later also accompany George Talbot's younger brothers. Ingamells 1997: 858. For Bulstrode, see: Fabrizi 2008: 229.

[13] 1740–1821. The eldest son of Sir William Bunbury of Barton, he was educated at Westminster and Saint Catherine Hall in Cambridge (1757). He succeeded his father in 1764 as 4th Baronet of Barton. He was a Member of Parliament from 1761 to 1784, and again from 1790 to 1812. He continued his Grand Tour to Rome, to Florence, to Venice, and then returned again to Florence and to Venice. He arrived in Turin together with the Viscount of Torrington. In

Burton	1748–9
Barton (Burton?)	1752
Caldwell[14]	1757–8
Cambelt [Cambell?][15]	1789–90
milord George Cavendisch [Cavendish]	1749–50
milord Federik Cavendisch[16]	1749–50
Chamberlangue [Chamberlain][17]	1770
Chaplin	1748
milord Charlemont[18]	1747–8
Chatwyn	1750
Child	1768–9
Clements[19]	1752
Codre	1748
Codrington	1741
Coke	1738–9
Coke[20]	1772
Conjers [Conyers]	1738
Conyers	1768–9
milord Coote	1743–4
Cope	1737

Florence he was portrayed by Patch (1760–1). In Venice he met Thomas Robinson and Jacob Houblon. Ingamells 1997: 154–5.

[14] Probably related to Sir James Caldwell (1720–c. 1784), who had been in Turin from 1747 to 1749, he joined the Austrian army in the years of the war of succession. James Caldwell served under the King of Sardinia to negotiate with General Thomas Wenthworth. In 1749, Maria Theresa made him Earl of Milan. Ingamells 1997: 173–4.

[15] He was tutor ('governatore') of Ferningham.

[16] For the two Cavendishes, see the letter of Rochford in the British Library, Manuscripts, Eg. 3419, f. 196. The preceptor of the two Cavendishes was Robert Lowth (1710–87), later Bishop of London, who does not appear in the Treasury's list. For Lowth, see: Black 1999: 39.

[17] Lincoln's travelling companion.

[18] James Caulfeild, 4th Viscount and 1st Earl of Charlemont. After returning to Britain, he expressed his appreciation of the Turin Royal Academy when he wrote to Lord Bruce: 'Have you any thoughts of the Academy at Turin? If it remains on the footing on which it stood in my time, it is certainly the most desirable Academy in Europe, from its being so intimately connected with the court and so immediately under the inspection of the king himself.' Wynne 1996: 149; Black 1999: 129.

[19] Probably Robert Clements, first son of Nathaniel Clements (1705–77). Robert was a Member of Parliament from 1765 until 1768. He was made a Peer in 1783 and later was created 1st Earl of Leitrim (1795). An art enthusiast and collector, he lived in Rome for some time with other Irish travellers and was part of Batoni's circle. Clark 1985: 257–8.

[20] Thomas William Coke (1754–1842), 1st Earl of Leicester (second creation) whom Batoni portrayed in 1773–4 (Clark 1985: 332–3). After leaving Eton in 1771, he undertook a three year Grand Tour until 1774, visiting Turin, Naples, Florence and Rome. He took possession of his father's estate in Norfolk and Derbyshire in 1776, and he served in Parliament from 1777 to 1782. On the previous journey of another Coke (Thomas), who was at the Turin Royal Academy in about 1715, see: Trease 1967: 136–45, and, in this volume, Andrew Moore.

Couts [Coutts]	1758–9
captain Crawford[21]	1764
Dancom	1747
Davidson	1744–5
Dawkins	1743
Charles Dillon[22]	1764–5
Dobson[23]	1764
Francis Stuart Doune[24]	1759–60
milord D[o]uglas[25]	1748
D[o]uglas[26]	1775–6
Felloucs [Fellowes?]	1749–50
Ferningham	1789–90
milord Fingal [Fingall]	1750–2
Forbes	1737
Freeman[27]	1745
Freeman	1766

[21] In 1764 he met the English traveller, John Holroyd, in Turin, but in 1765 he was in Geneva with other British travellers. Ingamells 1997: 252.

[22] 1745–1813. Son of the 11th Viscount of Dillon, he was a member of the Royal Society (1767) and a Member of Parliament (1770–4). He travelled with John Needham, his tutor. Together with Thomas Gascoigne, unbeknownst to Needham, he organized an escapade to Paris. In 1765, he was in Geneva. Ingamells 1997: 301–2.

[23] Captain, travel companion of Lord Barrymore.

[24] 1737–1810. The eldest son of the 8th Earl of Moray, he was at the Turin Royal Academy from the autumn 1759 to the following spring. He continued his journey in Venice, Florence (where, like other fellow British travellers who were at the Turin Royal Academy, he was portrayed by Thomas Patch), Capua and Rome. Ingamells 1997: 308–9.

[25] Possibly the Scotsman Sholto Douglas, 15th Earl of Morton, Grand Master of the Lodge of Scotland (1755–7), later Grand Master of the Lodge of England (1757–61).

[26] Douglas Douglas-Hamilton, 8th Duke of Hamilton (1756–99), son of a peer of Scotland, James Hamilton, 6th Duke of Hamilton. He spent four years (1772–6) in Continental Europe with his 'tutor, preceptor, friend and physician', John Moore. He succeeded his older brother as 8th Duke in 1769. Originally hired to treat the 6th Duke, after his death, Moore accompanied the 8th Duke to Paris, Geneva, Vienna, Rome, Naples and, on his way back, to Rome, Florence, Bologna, Turin and Genoa (Ingamells 1997). Pompeo Batoni painted Douglas Hamilton's portrait in 1755. He entered the House of Lords (1782) as 5th Duke of Brandon, a peer of Scotland whose title was also recognized in England pursuant to the agreements contained in the Act of Union (1707). In 1786 he was created Knight of the Thistle. In 1793 another Douglas arrived in Turin accompanied by 'Mr. Ballard' as his tutor (British Library, Manuscripts, Add. 59025, letter from the Secretary of State Grenville, Whitehall, London, 29 July 1793, to the British Envoy to Turin, John Trevor, and letter from Trevor, Turin, 20 December 1793, to Grenville).

[27] Sambroocke Freeman (1721–82). Second son of John Cooke, who had taken the surname Freeman. He was educated at Oxford University College (1739), leaving a journal of his travels containing notes and architectural sketches. He travelled to Padua and to Venice (1744), then attended the Royal Academy in Turin for ten months. His Grand Tour continued in Switzerland, whereupon he returned to Italy. Ingamells 1997: 382–3.

Freeman[28]	1777–8
Gage	1738–9
Garlies[29]	1756–7
Thomas Gascoine[30]	1764
Gell	1745
milord Anthony Preston Gormanston[31]	1760–1
Grameston	1767
Andrew Gray[32]	1764–5
de Grey	1770–1
Grimston[33]	1770–1
Hailes[34]	1776–7

[28] Strickland Freeman (1753–1821). Adopted by George Strickland, he was the son of John Freeman of Aston. He was educated at Oxford before leaving for a Grand Tour that took him to Genoa, Livorno (Leghorn), Rome, Naples and Paestum (1779), which he visited together with John Soane and Sir George Strickland, his soon-to-be adoptive father. Ingamells 1997: 383.

[29] Probably John Stewart, Lord of Garlies and 7th Earl of Galloway. In Bristol's letter to William Pitt, dated Turin, 26 January 1757, he wrote: 'His Sardinian Majesty, who never fails any opportunity of distinguishing the king's subjects, has within these few days given lord Garlies, son to the earl of Galloway, a proof of his attention to the British nation: the young gentlemen at the Academy have always danc'd at court according to their seniority, but the king of Sardinia gave orders that lord Garlies, who has been at Turin only two months, shou'd have precedence of the other academists, and dance with the duchess of Savoy and the other princesses' (National Archives, State Papers, Sardinia 92/65).

[30] 1745–1810; 8th Baronet of Parlington, third son of 6th Baronet, Edward Gascoigne was born in Cambrai, where his Catholic family had retreated two years earlier. He succeeded his elder brother in 1762. Gascoigne, a Catholic (until 1780), followed a military career and became a Captain (1788) and later a Colonel (1794); he was also a Member of Parliament (1780–4, 1795–6). He was also educated in Paris, where he became friends with Henry and Martha Swinburne. His Grand Tour continued in Rome and Florence (1765). He went on another tour of Continental Europe with the Swinburnes in 1775–9: they travelled to France, Spain and Italy, where they met artists and art collectors. A portrait of Gascoigne was painted in 1779 by Batoni. Friedman 1976: 17–23; Black 1984: 159; Clark 1985: 349; Ingamells 1997: 393–5.

[31] 1736–86. Eldest son (and, as such, the 11th Viscount) of the 10th Viscount Gormansthon. He succeeded his father in 1757. He travelled with the antiques dealer, Needham. His continued his tour to Venice, Milan and Rome. Ingamells 1997: 412.

[32] 1742–67. Eldest son of the 11th Baron Gray. Before travelling to Piedmont he had been educated at Eton. In Turin he met James Boswell, who described him as a 'good, brisk, little fellow' (Boswell 1955: 25, 30, 41). Ingamells 1997: 424–6.

[33] James Bucknall Grimston, later 3rd Viscount of Grimston (1747–1809). Originally from Gorhambury, in Hertfordshire, he succeeded his father in 1773 as 3rd Viscount of Grimston (Ireland) and Baron of Dunboyne (Ireland). In 1790, he was created Baron of Verulam (England). Educated at Eton (1761–6) and Cambridge (1766–9), he was a Member of Parliament (1773–84, 1784–90) and an independent supporter of the Pitt government. He rebuilt the new Gorhambury House in Palladian style. He was a fellow of the Royal Society and the Society of Arts. He took his Grand Tour in 1770–2 with Thomas de Grey, son of Lord Walsingham (see *supra*). He was in Rome from November 1771 to January 1772. Clark 1985: 321.

[34] Travelling companion to Vilmot.

Hale	1774
Hapbton [Hampton]	1748
Harpur [Harper]	1758–9
Harwey [Hervey][35]	1751–2
Hay	1749
Hawker	1747–8
Head	1778–9
Henry[36]	1753–4
Henry	1761
Jacob Houblon[37]	1758–9
Howard[38]	1750–1

[35] Possibly Frederick Augustus Hervey, 4th Earl of Bristol and Bishop of Derry (1730–1803). Between 1765 and 1803 he visited Italy repeatedly, acquiring many artworks in Rome that he planned to exhibit in a vast collection open to a public of men 'who can not afford to travel into Italy'. His art collection was seized in Rome by the French in 1798. Extremely wealthy, the owner of estates in Ireland and England, he was the brother of George Hervey (1721–75), who later became Lord Lieutenant of Ireland. Frederick was appointed first Bishop of Cloyne (1766) and later Bishop of Derry (1767), Ireland's wealthiest diocese. He succeeded his brother Augustus (1724–79) as Earl of Bristol in 1779. After his death, Hervey's art collections were sold at auction; for the catalogue, see: Figgis 1993.

[36] Possibly the Irishman Joseph Henry of Straffan, from Kildare County, son of the Dublin banker, Hugh Henry, and of Anne Leeson. In 1751 he was in Rome with his uncle, Joseph Leeson, 1st Earl of Milltown, and with his cousin (who had been at the Turin Royal Academy during 1748–9). In Rome he was portrayed by Batoni. Clark 1985: 250.

[37] 1736–83. Eldest son of Jacob Houblon of Hallingsbury, in Essex. He attended Saint John College in Cambridge (1754). Between 1759 and 1760 he travelled to several Italian cities: Rome, Naples, Siena, Florence, Lucca, Livorno, and then Naples, Rome and Siena again, and later Florence, Venice and Padua. He travelled with the Reverend Jonathan Lipyeatt, his tutor. In Turin he met the Duke of Savoy (the future Victor Amadeus III) and the Minister Ossorio and, after being presented by Lord Charlemont, he gained access to the exclusive salon of the Marquise of Saint Gilles. He remained in Turin for only six months, but he spoke enthusiastically to his father about his stay: 'We live very well, are well lodged and have good masters. Our dancing master is reckoned one of the best in Europe.' After returning from his tour of Italy, he visited Turin again in 1761, where he participated in the festivities for the carnival. Ingamells 1997: 525. His friend and mentor James Caulfeild (1728–99), 4th Viscount and later 1st Earl of Charlemont, who had been at the Turin Royal Academy from 1747 to 1748 (resident in the first apartment), was heir to an English noble family then living in Ireland, and was an indefatigable traveller, art enthusiast and collector, perhaps best known for commissioning the construction of one of the most significant neoclassical buildings in the history of architecture, the Casino at Marino, a few miles outside Dublin. O'Connor 1999; Black 1999: 129.

[38] The Irish Ralph Howard, later 1st Viscount of Wicklow, of whom a portrait was painted in Rome by Batoni in 1752, today in the J.B. Speed Museum of Louisville, Kentucky. Clark 1985: 255. Eldest son of the Reverend Robert Howard, Bishop of Elphin, whose possessions were inherited by his son in 1740, Ralph attended Trinity College in Dublin in 1743. High Sheriff of Wicklow in 1749 and of Carlow in 1754, he was a Member of Parliament from 1761 to 1768. In 1770 he was appointed to the Irish Privy Council. He was raised to the Irish peerage as Baron Clonmore of Clonmore Castle, county of Carlow. In 1785 he was elevated as Viscount of Wicklow. Details of his Grand Tour can be found in the family archives, partly studied by the art historian Sir Brinsley Ford. In Turin, he was accompanied by a tutor, 'Mr.

Edward Howard[39]	1763
Hurt	1774
Hutchinson[40]	1761–2
Irwin	1749
milord Kenmark	1741–2
Ker	1743
John Ker[41]	1760–1
milord Kilmaurs o Kilmours o Kilmorre[42]	1766–7
Langdale[43]	1763
Law[44]	1756–7
Leeson[45]	1748–9

Benson' (not listed in the Treasury registries). He continued his Grand Tour to Florence, Rome (1752) and Venice, returning to Ireland via Milan and Paris (1752). In Italy he commissioned artworks not only from Batoni, but also from various English artists who were studying in Florence and Rome at the time. His agent in Rome was James Russel, who became one of the foremost *ciceroni* in Italy for foreign visitors. Howard is well known as the patron of Joshua Reynolds and Richard Wilson. Wynne 1996: 151.

[39] 1744–67. Second son of Philip Howard of Buckenham, in Norfolk. After Turin he went to Florence and Rome, together with Langdale. His portrait was painted in Rome by Batoni. Ingamells 1997: 526–31.

[40] Tutor of Massereene. Son of the Bishop of Killala, in Ireland. Ingamells 1997: 647–8.

[41] John Ker, 3rd duke of Roxburghe (1740–1804). A remarkable book collector, John Ker was born in London; he was the eldest son of Robert Ker. In 1755 he succeeded his father as Duke. Originally from Switzerland, he was a friend and travelling companion to Casanova and to the Marquis of Priè. Casanova wrote that in Turin Ker had fallen in love with Madame Martin. A friend of George III, in 1801 he was appointed a Knight of the Garter. He was also a friend of the great Scottish novelist, Walter Scott, who described him as a man with a keen intellectual curiosity. His vast library, which was split up after his collection was sold on the market in 1812, was formerly conserved in his house in Saint James's Square, London. *DNB* XXXI: 51–2; Ingamells 1997: 826–7.

[42] On 23 May 1776 in Turin, the Minister of Internal Affairs wrote to the Marquis Solaro di Govone, Governor of Cuneo, about the arrest in Limone of 'milord Kilmorre' and 'captain Bredan', two English gentlemen who were students at the Turin Royal Academy, who were taken into custody because they were suspected of 'fabbricazione di falsa moneta' (producing counterfeit money) and were later released by the governor of Nice because the accusation was unsubstantiated. Solaro was required to apologize officially to the two. The letters from the Minister are in Archivio di Stato di Torino, Corte, Materie economiche, Piemonte giuridico, reg. 32; those from the Governor are in Archivio di Stato di Torino, Corte, Lettere di particolari, S, mz. 75.

[43] Companion to Howard. Ingamells 1997: 526.

[44] Travelling companion to Oliver.

[45] From Ireland. Joseph Leeson (1730–1801), later Earl of Milltown. He was in Rome in 1750. A year later he commissioned a portrait from Batoni as had his father had before him (1744). He was the son of Joseph Leeson (1701–83), 1st Earl of Milltown, in Parliament from 1743 to 1756, great art collector for the house that he had built in Russborough, Wicklow County, designed by the Palladian architect Richard Castle. Heir to his family's considerable wealth, he became Viscount of Russborough in 1760. Three years later he was admitted to the Privy Council, and later he was created Earl of Milltown. During his Grand Tour (in 1750 the first Earl had accompanied his son to Rome) the father and son had collected a great deal of artwork to enrich the collection of their London house. In 1902 the collection was transferred

Leighton	1768–9
milord Leinster[46]	1741
Leygh	1747
milord Lincoln[47]	1739–40
milord Lincoln	1770
Lipyeatt[48]	1758–9
Clotworthy Skeffington[49]	1761–2
milord Midelton [Middleton][50]	1749–50
Milner [Miller?]	1745
Mitchell[51]	1758–61

to the National Gallery of Dublin. Leeson Senior was introduced to the world of art collecting in Rome via other Irish travellers, including Lord Charlemont (at the Turin Royal Academy from 1747–8). Clark 1985: 233–4.

[46] James Fitzgerald, 1st Duke of Leinster (1722–73). His son William Robert Fitzgerald, 2nd Duke of Leinster (1748/9–1804), Marquis of Kildare, resided in Turin from October 1767 to September 1768, but not at the Turin Royal Academy. His father insisted that he travel to Vienna. Wynne 1996: 150, 152–3.

[47] Henry Fiennes Clinton, 9th Earl of Lincoln (1720–94), nephew of the Duke of Newcastle, Secretary of State in London, in charge of diplomatic relations for the King of Sardinia. Clinton left London accompanied by the Reverend Joseph Spence (1699–1768), an Oxford professor, who was also his tutor on his Grand Tour. In Turin he fell ill and it appears that, in September 1740, he was forced to leave Piedmont on this account. Spence wrote *memorandum* for him (*Paper copy'd from Mr. J. Spence's Wrote at Turin Relating to the Affairs of the Kingdom,* National Archives, 30/29/3/1, fols 14–19), which can be described as an exercise in which he offered a historical-institutional description of the State of Savoy; see: Black 1989 (where this document is published in full).

[48] Tutor of Jacob Houblon.

[49] 2nd Earl of of Massereene (1742–1805). Irish, eldest son of the 1st Earl of Massereene, in 1758 he entered Corpus Christi College, Cambridge. After Turin he travelled to Florence, Naples, Rome, Bologna and Venice. In Paris he was jailed for debts (1770–9). A bizarre character and a ballet enthusiast, he was portrayed by the Secretary of the English legation to Turin, Phelps, as a young man 'famous for breaking thro' all the rules of the Academy'. The National Archives, State Papers, 105, reg. 314, f. 162 (12 May 1762). Ingamells 1997: 647–8.

[50] Henry Willoughby, later 5th Baron of Middleton. Son of Thomas Willoughby (Member of Parliament), Henry arrived in Rome to pose for a portrait by Batoni by 1754. He succeeded his cousin, Thomas Willoughby, as 5th Lord Middleton (1781). Clark 1985: 259–60.

[51] After two years at the Turin Royal Academy, he asked the historian and versatile writer, Carlo Denina (1731–1812) for Italian lessons (*Vita di Denina*, ms. in Biblioteca Nazionale di Torino, R.IV.103, c. 3). Denina described him as an Irish gentleman who 'mostrava di non esser soddisfatto de' maestri ordinari, che gli facean lezione' ('appeared not satisfied with the teachings of his regular masters'). It is unclear what kind of relationship existed between him and Andrew Mitchell (1708–71), who had travelled to Italy in 1731–5, and who had stayed in Turin as well; but this Mitchell fathered, according to the *DNB*, only one daughter, not a son. Andrew Mitchell was the son of a wealthy English pastor who had been Moderator of the Church of Scotland five times. He attended the University of Leiden in 1730–1, and then he left on his Grand Tour. Undersecretary of State in Scotland (1742–6), Ambassador to Brussels (1752–5), in 1756, Andrew was appointed English Envoy to Berlin, where he remained until his death. He was also a member of the English Parliament (1747–54, 1755–71). In Paris, in the salon of Madame Tencin, he met the greatest *philosophes*, including Montesquieu. His travel journals are conserved at the British Library in London, Manuscripts, Add.58313–58320. See

Modifford Heywod [Modyford?]	1751
Mongomery [Montgomery]	1765
Riccardo [Richard] Moore[52]	1733
Stefano [Stephen] Moore	1733
Moor [Moore?][53]	1772–4
Alexander Moray[54]	1759–61
John Mytton[55]	1759
John Turberville Needham[56]	1760–1

also Black 1984: 145. A letter from the Savoy Ambassador to London, de Viry, dated 22 April 1756, in Archivio di Stato di Torino, Corte, Lettere ministri, Gran Bretagna, mz. 60, reports that he had left for Berlin: 'monsieur Mitchell, désigné charge d'affaires de S.M. Britannique à la cour de Berlin, etoît parti pour sa destination' ('lord Mitchell, chargé d'affaires of H.R.M. of Britain at the Berlin Court, has departed for his destination'). Another letter written by de Viry, dated 14 March 1758, states that: 'L'on dit que Mr. Yorcke [sic] partira dans peu pour la cour de Prusse. Les uns prétendent qu'il va exécuter une commission particulière, et des autres veulent que ce soit pour y résider à la place de Mr. Mitchell, qui, suivant ces derniers, en sera rappellé' ('It is rumored that Mr. Yorcke will be departing shortly for the Court of Prussia. Some maintain that he has been called to perform a special mission, others that he will replace Mr. Mitchell who, according to the latter, will be recalled', *ibidem*, mz. 63).

[52] Brother of the following. They were sons of the Irish Colonel Stephen Moore (1689–1750), owner of an estate in County Tipperary. Wynne 1996: 149.

[53] Probably John Moore (1729–1802), tutor, preceptor and friend of the 8th Duke of Hamilton (1756–99), at the Turin Royal Academy in 1775–6. However, it is not clear why Moore appears in the Treasury's register two years before his pupil. A doctor and a man of letters, Moore was in Holland in 1747. He had studied in Paris and in London. He published some of the writings of his patient Tobias Smollett. He was the author of a *View of Society and Manners in Italy* (1779–81, 3 vols). His son John (1761–1809), who would choose a military career, also travelled with him in Italy. Hibbert 1987: 20; Wilton and Bignamini 1997: 59; Ingamells 1997: 674.

[54] Probably the eldest son (1743–84) of James Moray, a landowner from Abercairny. Ingamells 1997: 673–4. He was admitted to the first apartment of the Turin Royal Academy, where he studied French, music, equitation and dancing. He left Turin and moved to Nice for reasons of health, and he continued his journey through Italy with stops in Genoa, Pisa, Rome and Naples, as reported by the British Envoy in Turin James Stuart Mackenzie in 1759 (although he was of a very young age). A portrait of James Moray is in: Clark 1985: fig. 239; a book that also contains a portrait of James Francis Edward Moray (1762), identified as James's eldest son.

[55] A friend of Thomas Robinson and Thomas Wynn. Ingamells 1997: 817.

[56] 1713–81. A Catholic clergyman, and a man of science with a keen interest in naturalistic studies, he heralded originally from London and was admitted to the Royal Society in 1747. He was in Turin 1760–2 and 1764–5. He was appointed to supervise both Lord Gormansthon and Charles Dillon. Additionally a scholar of archaeology, Needham believed that the writing on a famous bust that was part of the Savoy collection in Turin was Egyptian and that this showed similarities to the Chinese language. He became friends with the Turin-based chemist and artilleryman, Giuseppe Angelo Saluzzo, but was criticized by Voltaire and Gibbon (who none the less remained his friend) for his theories. Together with Lord Gormansthon, after leaving Turin, he moved to Milan. Ferrone 1988: 98–9; Ingamells 1997: 699. For his stay in Turin, see the correspondence to and from Needham in the British Library, Manuscripts, Add. 21416, fols 3–5, 16; Add. 28540, fols 73, 77–82. See also Wortley Montagu 1763 (one letter is in the library of the British School at Rome).

John Turberville Needham[57]	1764–5
Oliver	1756–7
Orton[58]	1778–9
T[h]omas Panton	1754–5
milord Parker	1746–7
Filips [Philips][59]	1738
Phipps	1738
Playdel [Pleydell-Bouverie?]	1777–8
Potter[60]	1767–9
Powlett	1749
Quim [Quin][61]	1774–5
Ramsay	1754–5
Rice	1744–5
Thomas Robinson[62]	1758–9
John Rushout[63]	1758–9

[57] The previous one, in 1764–5, Dillon's tutor.

[58] Travelling companion to Smith.

[59] Gage's tutor. Perhaps Erasmus Philips (Black 1999: 182).

[60] 'Quando sir Pitt era ministro inglese a Torino, lui assente, ed assente pure lo spiritoso suo segretario Dutens, venne incaricato degli affari della legazione sir Potter che da più di un anno risiedeva in Torino come accademista. Ciò prima del 22 marzo 1769, giorno in cui fu presentato al re sir Lynch, nuovo inviato d'Inghilterra' ('When Sir Pitt was English Minister in Turin, in his absence, and in the absence also of his witty secretary Dutens, Sir Potter was charged of the affairs of the legation, who had resided in Turin for more than a year as an "accademista". This was before 22 March 1769, the day when Sir Lynch was presented to the king as the new English Envoy') (Saint-Croix 1876: 312). This was Thomas Potter, who took the place of the British Representative between 1768 and 1769. Horn 1934: I, 126; Wynne 1996: 154–5.

[61] This may be the Irishman Valentine Richard Quin, 1st Earl of Dunraven (1752–1824), in Parliament 1799–1800, after being created Baronet (1781). Admitted to the peerage in 1800 as Baron Adare of Adare, he received the title of Viscount of Mount-Earl in 1816 and lastly Viscount Adare and Earl of Dunraven and Mont-Earl in 1822. Batoni painted a portrait of him (1773). Little is known of his grand tour. Clark 1985: 329.

[62] 1738–86. Eldest son of the British diplomat Sir Thomas Robinson, 1st Baron of Grantham, he had been educated at Westminster and Cambridge (1755). He entered Parliament (1761–70), and was Ambassador in Madrid (1771–9). From Turin, his Grand Tour continued to Genoa, Milan, Florence, Naples, Rome, Parma, returning again to Florence, Genoa and Venice. He arrived back in Britain in 1762. He wrote to his sister from Turin in 1759, criticizing the quality of Italian dramaturgy. In Rome he met the painters Mengs and Batoni, and wrote about them to his father, commenting on their works. He was portrayed in Florence by Patch. In Venice he met regularly with Lady Mary Wortley Montagu. Black 1983: 54; Ingamells 1997: 816–17; Black 1999: 283.

[63] 1738–1800. Only son of the homonymous Sir John Rushout (1684–1775), in England he had attended Eton and Oxford (1756). Ingamells 1997: 829–30. On 24 January 1756 his father had written to the Duke of Newcastle, from Bloomsbury Square, London: 'Sir James Rushout my father was by King William appointed ambassador at Constantinople to negotiate the peace of Carlowitz … I have had the honour of having been a commissioner of the Treasury, then the treasurer of the Navy and ever since of the Privy Council. … I have only one son, about 17 years of age, now at Eton under the care of Dr. Barnard' (British Library, Manuscripts, Add.

milord Sandouich [Sandwich][64]	1736–7
Seabright	1744–5
milord Shrewsbury[65]	1738–9
Sikes	1784–5
Smith	1756–7
Smith	1778–9
Smythe[66]	1760–1
Spencer	1752
milord Stafort [Stafford]	1738–9
Stanhope[67]	1733
Guillaume Stanhope[68]	1737
Thomas Stanhope	1737
Staples[69]	1772
Stuart [o Stewart]	1758
Stuart	1759
Stuart[70]	1766–7
milord Sussex	1748

32862, fol. 218). And Newcastle wrote to John Rushout Senior, from home, on 28 February 1762, in a tone of a certain intimacy: 'As an old friend and servant, you will allow me to wish that you, your son and my good friend, Mr. Middleton, would be at the house tomorrow upon the report of the militia bill' (*ibidem*, Add. 32935). Rushout's voyage in Italy included many cities after Turin: Milan, Lodi, Piacenza, Parma, Modena, Bologna, Florence, Siena, Perugia, Cortona, Arezzo, Pisa, Lucca, Livorno, Rome, Capua and Naples. In Florence (1760) he was among many British gentlemen portrayed by the painter Thomas Patch. Like his father before him, he sat in Parliament (1761–96). His family, originally from France and engaged in commerce, had moved to England under Charles I. His father, 4th Baronet of Milnst-Maylards (1711), had inherited the family title, but not the Maylard's estate in Essex, that was passed down to another branch of the family. He was Lord Commissioner of the Treasury in the Carteret government and a Member of Parliament (1713–68) and of the Privy Council (1744). *DNB* XLIX: 418.

[64] The famous John Montagu, 4th Earl of Sandwich (1718–92). Bianchi 2003a.

[65] George Talbot Shrewsbury (1719–87) accompanied by Sir Bulstrode. On his Grand Tour of Italy he travelled to Florence and Rome in 1739–40, and with his travel companion he became familiar with the Catholic pro-Jacobite *milieus* in Albano. Bulstrode would also accompany George Talbot's younger brothers. Ingamells 1997: 858.

[66] Travelling companion of Rouxbourgh. Ingamells 1997: 871.

[67] Philip Stanhope, 2nd Earl of Stanhope. Black 1999: 39.

[68] William Stanhope (1719–79), Earl of Harrington, son of the 1st Earl of Harrington (1690? – 1756). His father, in the 1740s, during the War of the Austrian Succession, was Secretary of the Northern Department. *DNB* LIV: 44.

[69] The family relationship with John Staples (1734–1820), Member of Parliament and of the Privy Council of Ireland, is unclear. Clark 1985: 329. Ingamells 1997: 890.

[70] John Stuart Lord Mountstuart (1744–1814), after 4th Earl and 1st Marquis of di Bute. During his Grand Tour of Italy he was in Rome and in Tuscany. In 1765 Boswell wrote from Lucca that he had met Lord Mountstuart with a Scottish Colonel and with Mallet, a professor from Geneva, as his tutors. Boswell painted a lively, intellectual portrait of the young man: a pragmatic gentleman with a joy for life and little interest in didactic routine, but sharp-minded and curious. Boswell 1955: 8–9; and in particular: Bianchi 2012b.

Talbot[71]	1769–70
Thompson	1766
Thompson[72]	1766
Tilson	1745
George Byng[73]	1759–60
Tristal	1739
Turner	1750
Waller	1747–8
Walpole	1744–5
Wentworth	1748–9
Villowghby [Willoughby]	1746–7
Wilson[74]	1772
Thomas Wynn Newborough, I baron of Glynnllivon[75]	1759
Yonge	1752

Secondo Appartamento (Second Apartment)

Smith	1775–6
Smith (written also: Smithe)	1784–8

[71] Possibly John Chetwynd Talbot, 1st Earl Talbot (1750–93). He has been identified as the subject of a portrait by Batoni (Clark 1985: 300). Educated at Eton and Oxford (1766), he sat in Parliament (1777–82) and was appointed Lord Commissioner of Trade in 1781. He was in Rome in September 1773, but little else is known of his Grand Tour.

[72] Two brothers.

[73] 4th Viscount of Torrington (1740–1812). He arrived in Turin with Thomas Charles Bunbury. He was educated at Westminster and Cambridge (1757). Later he became Minister Plenipotentiary in Brussels (1783–92). Ingamells 1997: 155, 945.

[74] Daniel Wilson (1746–1828). Only son of Edward Wilson, member of Parliament, died in 1764. His presence in Rome is attested to in 1773. Clark 1985: 326–7.

[75] 1736–1807. Eldest son of Sir John Wynn, he was educated at Cambridge (1754). His Grand Tour continued to Genoa, Milan, Florence, Naples, Rome, and back again to Florence, Bologna, Venice and Verona. He returned to Italy years later, staying in Florence from 1782 to 1791, where he married his second wife Maria Stella Petronilla Chiappini. He also sat in Parliament (1761–80, 1796–1807). Ingamells 1997: 702–3.

KARIN WOLFE

Archivio di Stato di Firenze, Carte Galilei, pezzo 21, inserto 1

Appendix IV.1

fols 33r–34r
Molesworth to Galilei
Turin Jan: the 15.te 1721 NS

Sir

You understand English so well that I need no other language to acquaint you with my Arrival here, and that I should be very well pleas'd if my return into this Climate and our near Neighbourhood could be of any Use to you. I was very glad to hear that you had at last obtain'd a tolerable Settlement and a Creditable Post at home, which may be perhaps a little precarious, but will serve to entertain you till something happen's that shall transplant you into our Country. I am persuaded that if ever you can return with an Increase of reputation join'd to that you have allready acquir'd there, it will not be in the power of Malice to obstruct your makeing a good fortune. For this purpose two things are necessary: One, that you should procure your self to be the undertaker of some good building at home, the fame of which may reach England: the other, that in case [33v] you find no probability of being so employ'd, you should get leave (if possible) to take another little journey to Rome where certainly a stay of three months would be of great Use and reputation: and as well there, as on your way, take occasion to visit and examine all the renown'd Theaters (for example that at Fano) for when I left London there was great talk of building a New one for the Opera. I suppose the fall of the S. Sea has put a Stop to that and many other great projects for raising Palaces and Villas: but I don't doubt but in a Year or two when the Nation recovers it's fright, there will be Employment enough for an Able Architect.

Pray give my affectionate Services in a very particular manner to Sig.ri Senator Pandolfini, Giann. Lorenzo de' Pucci and his Son, Abbate Salvini, Benedetto Bresciani and all others whom you know me to be a sincere [34r] freind to: And when you write give me an exact account of their health: let me know whether the good Old Governour lives (I mean the Senator's Kinsman) and what other news you think agreeable.

I trouble you with th'enclos'd which I desire you would carry your self to the Portico when you make a visit to your sister there: for besides that I would h[lacuna] a letter go safe after the loss of many.

I believe you will give me a good acco[lacuna] of the Ladys there particularly of her whom it is directed to. I am Sir with great Sincerity

Your Affectionate humble Ser.t J. Molesworth

Appendix IV.2

fols 35r–36r
Molesworth to Galilei
Turin April the 16.th 1721 N.S.

Sir

I have receiv'd your's of the 27.th past, and am glad that your being employ'd on various designs takes up your time: those occupations are every way usefull and I hope profitable to you.

I had a letter from Sig.r Abbate Salvini about Montauti who has finish'd my statues: he des[ired] that I would send him some Money which is indeed a reasonable request, and yet at this juncture of time it will be very hard for me to comply with it. The villainuos management of the South-Sea Directors has brought such a confusion upon us and so destroy'd Credit, that it is with all the difficulty imaginable we procur […] the necessary Cash for present subsistence: All the Bankers of Turin can scarce furnish 300.th of the best Bills of Exchange as I have occasion [35v] to know by experience since my arrival here: And really at home things are come to that dismal pass that three parts of our Nobility are ruin'd; trade is quite dead, credit sunk, our rents all deficient, and the Bankers all broke; so that if it were not for the Vigorous proceedings of Parliament to restore our former flourishing condition, I should despair of seeing our Nation make that figure in Europe that it did but few months ago.

I try'd however by the means of an English Merchant here to procure some money at Leghorne to be from thence remitted to Florence as I should order it, but the Answer he receiv'd was that it was harder to advance 5.th now than 500.th six months ago, and that we must wait till affairs were a little settl'd.

In the mean time I have desir'd Abbate Salvini to get the Statues valu'd, in which matter I have begg'd the Assistance of Sig.r Sen.r Pandolfini and Sig.r Gio: Lor: Pucci, it must be remember'd that I furnish'd the money for buying the marble which together with what other Summs Montauti had from me, or M.r Gould since my [36r]departure, should be accounted for and what remains due for his workmanship I will take care to let him have as Opportunity serves.

I should be glad that you would impartially view these Statues and let me know your private Opinion of the performance and what you think the workmanship may deserve: it shall be a secret, but may serve me for a rule to go by in bespeaking several other things before I leave Italy.

Pray give my services sincerely to all our worthy [lacuna] I have sent a table pendulum clock to Leghorne [lacuna].

I designed it for one of those Gentlemen, but would not [lacuna] you say any thing of it till I accompany it with a letter. I fear it has suffer'd by the damp of the Sea, but I have Order'd it to be carefully clean'd and regulated at Leghorne if there be a good Clock [lacuna] there: if not I shall desire it may be directed to you and must trouble you to see it well adjusted and keep it till further orders. I am Sir with true Affection.

> Your faithfull humble servant
> J molesworth

Appendix IV.3

fols 37r–38r
Molesworth to Galilei
Turin June the 4.th N.S. 1721

Sir,

I here send enclos'd a Note for the table pendulum clock I mention'd to you, which you may desire any freind of yours at Leghorne to call for and send carefully to Florence it must have the pendulum ty'd up, for which there is a knack on purpose, and a good wooden Case line'd to preserve it safe. It was made by a very good workman and will certainly go well unless the rust it contracted at Sea may have injur'd the great exactness of the several pinns and sockets: but I hope not. I am inform'd it has been allready clean'd, so that you will have no more trouble with it than to let it stand upon one of your tables and observe how it goes: if you find any irregularity, you will get the best and honestest watch-maker you have to regulate it. In a post or two I will send you directions how you must dispose of it.

I have been considering, in relation to your future wellfare in our Country, that one may venture to lay down as a Maxim that no man ever made a fortune by exceling in his profession unless in those which are of absolute necessity to Mankind [37v] for those which conduce only to the pleasure of the Rich as Architecture etc. whoever would thrive by them, must look one way and row t'other as our Seamen's proverb is: I mean that they must acquire a competent Skill in some other Art, under the Covert of which they may introduce their own. Thus you Saw that D.r Garth by being a good Poet. D.r Wellwood by excelling in History, carry'd on their business in Physic; as S.r John Vanbrook commenc'd Architect[ure] by writeing Comedies. This being granted, I should think that you have now leisure and an excellent Opportunity to put this rule in practise. You may chuse out of several Elegancys which Italy is fam'd for, one besides your own, to excell in; and a little

Study would easily make you Master of any, especially those that have some relation to what you allready possess.

I will mention the knowledge of <u>Medals</u>; the Skill of conducting water and contriving <u>Fountains</u>; <u>Painting</u>, especially Landskape or <u>Pictoresc Architecture</u> with Ruines, Caverns etc; <u>Scenical Architecture</u> with th'invention of Machines etc in Bibiena's stile: <u>Criticism in Pictures</u>, drawings, Basso rilievos etc with the distinction of the hands of the Several Masters; [38r] the <u>disposition of Gardens</u>, Grottos, Labyrinths etc., to which purpose you might take the Sketch of any remarkable pieces you could observe at Florence, Rome, France or elswhere in your travels. These or indeed any more important operations in Geometry would be in [lacuna] your pursuit; and would serve to recommen'd you to the Great Men while you should dissemble your Skill in Architecture till their good opinion of you in other Matters should open their Eyes.

I have dwelt long upon this Subject and been even tedious in explaining it because I am really convinc'd that such a comendable artifice would much conduce to your gaining access to the Genius of our Nation which is yet in the dark as to Building: but if ever it recover from the dreadfull Abyss it is now plung'd in, I believe we shall be less wanton and consequently more Apt to hear good Advice as well in matters of taste, as of prudence

My humble services constantly attend our friends and I am ever

Sir

Your affec.d humble serv.t J. Molesworth;

All'Ill.mo Sig.r Sig.r mio Pros. Osserva.mo

Al Sig. Alessandro Galilei

Primo Ingegniere ed Architetto

Di S.A.R. in Firenze

Appendix IV.4

fol. 48r–v (without date, but 1721)
Galilei to Molesworth
Eccellenza ho ricevuto onore

Dal Gentilissimo e graditis.mo foglio di V.E.delli 21 del corrente dal quale ho inteso quanto ella si sia degnato d'impormi circa alle statue dl Montauti. Anche p. eseguire i suoi pregiatis.mi comandi mi sono portato dal med.o Montauti, e gli hò comunicato il desiderio che V.E. tiene V.E. di sapere a quanto ascenda il prezzo delle statue, e siccome ancora quanto egli abbia ricevuto p. acconto dal med.mo, egli mi ha pregato a ringraziare V.E. della memoria che tiene di lui e del buon genio che ha di favorirlo, e mi ha detto che di prezzare le med.me statue Egli non si è resoluto fidare di se stesso ma le ha fatte vedere a vari Professori i q.li gli e l'anno stimate scudi cinquecento, ma che egli con tuttociò si rimette in tutto e p. tutto il prezzo delle med.me nella Bontà di V.E. dicendo, che è Padrone di soddisfarlo in quella maniera che più li piacerà. E ciò credo che il sud.o prezzo niente ecceda il valore delle med.me statue p. esservi di moltissimo lavoro, e p. avervi il d.o montauti usato molta diligenza nel terminarle quantunque esse siano le sue prime opere, et in oltre il Ganimede e si può dire che sia un gruppo, e non una sola statua. V.E. che è buon. mo giudice in questo particolare conoscerà tutto questo meglio di me. Quanto a quello che lui abbia fino adesso ricevuto da M.r Gould egli mi ha detto, che non ha memoria nessuna salvo che alcune lettere, ma p. saperlo esattam.te egli ha scritto a M.r Gould che gliene mandi una nota, e poi V.E. lo potrà ancora ritrarre dalle ricecvute che avrà appressio di se; e che quanto a quello che lei gli diede dà p. sé quando era qua p comprare il marmo furono solam.te nove ruspi? Cioè venti talleri di questa moneta conforme potrà riscontrare dalla ri\cevuta, e che tal appunto fù il valore del marmo il q.le mi hà detto che si costuma [48v] il non considerarlo nel prezzo della fattura, poiché è solito, che sempre il P.ne delle Statue è tenuto a dare il marmo allo scultore ma che p. lei è padrone di servirsi come comanda intendendo egli di non volere disgustare in conto alcuno non so mancato di portare i suoi saluti a tutti questi sig.ri suoi amici, ui quali gli rendono infiniti. E si sono rallegrati a quell segno maggiore d'intende re che ella sia p. onorare questa città con la sua venuta, poiché tutti desiderano estremam.te di poterla rivedere et io benché il più intimo ma più obbligato di tutti i suoi servitori hò goduto in fino all'anima di sentire sì lieta nuova per avere la sorte di potermi inchinare a quel [sic] al Più Caro Padrone che io abbia nel mondo la di cui memoria porterò sempre impresso nel mio cuore finché avrò vita.

La prego as considerarmi il suo Stimatis.mo

Appendix IV.5

fols 153r–v, 154r–v
Molesworth to Galilei
Turin Oct the 11.th 1724 N.S.

Dear Sir

I do not write to you often because I scruple putting you to the trouble and expense of empty letters, the present State of the world affording little matter worth communicateing. You have heard, no doubt, of my journey to Savoy and that it did me considerable Service in regard to my health. I wish it may enable me to pass through this Winter without new Accidents, for in that case I might flatter my self with hopes of an entire recovery. Our vast heats are now succeeded by sharp Cold but without rain or snow; I am the more sensible of them because the hot Baths have open'd my pores; but I intend not to stir out of my house all this Winter, except in the mornings, and by those precautions join'd with others in Dyet, good hours etc

I hope to avoid the inconveniences of this Climate [153v]

In order to bear this retirement with more patience I am prepareing all the amusements I can think of, and among the rest intend to apply to Architecture.

I propose to get over the Mechanical part of it by my own Study, that when we meet I may be in a better capacity of learning from you the refinement and *buon gusto*. I do this with a View to your Service, for whoever undertakes to recommend, must be known to understand something himself.

I don't know whether you ever saw the pictures done by my Orders at Florence. I took a good deal of pains to instruct the Painter Rhedi in several little Criticisms which I find he has not carefully Observ'd, since the Pictures are rather done according to his first thought than according to what was afterwards settl'd between us. I could specify many particulars, but I wonder chiefly at the Errors in design: that is what I Thought him incapable of: they are however Evident in the figure of [154r] Brutus where he has quite miss'd the true <u>torso</u> or turn of the body and that right arm has no shoulder, while the left arm from the Elbow upwards seems a little too short.

It is pity, for the rest of the picture is fine especially as to the colouring. In two pictures w.ch are intended to match or be Companions, the figures ought to be of the same size; whereas those of the Cincinnatus are a large degree bigger than those in the Brutus. A Nobleman of the first quality here ask'd me whether I knew any Painter at Florence famous for <u>Fresco</u>. I told him there was one Gabbiani but he was old and Slow: upon w.ch he desir'd me to enquire whether there were any younger, but excellent in that Art, who would care to be employ'd in painting some Cieling pieces of rooms here. I therefore desire you, if you know any such, to inform me by the first Opportunity; the person that wants him being one it imports me to oblige, and the Commission being likely to prove [154v] advantageous to any deserveing man who has an Ambition to gain a reputation out of his own Country.

I am Sir with unalterable sincerity
Your most Affecitionate humble Sevant
J[hon] Molesworth

Appendix IV.6

fols 163r–v, 164r
Molesworth to Galilei
Turin Jan: the 3rd 1725. N. S.

Sir

Since the arrival of the Court in town, I have spoken about the Painter and was answer'd that as Don Filippo the King's Architect was to pass through Florence soon in his return from Venice and Rome, he should be desir'd to view some of that Painters works where they are finish'd in their Several Situations at the Palaces you mention, and upon his report this Nobleman would take his resolutions. I took an opportunity of mentioning him to the King himself who has some rooms to finish at Rivoli; so that I am of Opinion it would be for his service to send me a Couple of Sketches in Oil to Show. He may chuse the subjects and the dimensions provided they be such as will admit of [163v] Noble designs. My thought is that two Storys of the Roman History, both relateing to the Great Camillus, might be express'd with vast dignity. One is, the Gauls Masters of Rome with their King (Brennus, if I be not mistaken) at the head of them, expressing their surprise and reverence at the Sight of the Roman Senate and Chief Magistrates Seated in their Curule Chairs with great gravity waiting their Fate: the Other, is the Arrival of Camillus just as the Gaul was weighing his Sword etc.

He must read Livius and imprint both Storys perfectly in his Mind wth all their Circumstances in order to make a Choice of those that will best adorn pictures. These pieces need not be extremely finish'd; but will please most if they be touch'd Masterly wth great fire and invention: I am sure the Arguments are [164r] very proper to inspire a good Genius.

It is now extremely Cold, notwithstanding wch I hold up to admiration, tho' the great fatigue of Eight Audiences on the New Year was a severe tryal of my Constitution. This subject put's me in mind of wishing you and your family all health and happiness on the same occasion; And I desire you to make proper Complements for me to all my worthy freinds whom I need not name because you know them. They will be so good as to excuse my not doing it myself by a letter to each, because writing much is prejudicial to my health, and I have already too much of that sort of business on my hands. I dare say they are all thoroughly persuaded of my sincerity, and that will attone for the want of punctuality.

I am Sir, Your most Affectionate and humble Servant

J. Molesworth."

Appendix IV.7

fols 174r–175r
Molesworth to Galilei
Turin, May the 2d 1725 N.S.

Don Philippo has brought me the prints of your Catafalco which are very pretty and well engraven; I give you many thanks, but you are too liberal of them in sending so many. He appear's very well satisfy'd with the Painters performances, and tell's me has settl'd the Conditions on which he is to come hither. Perhaps his Recommendation may suffise to establish that Artists reputation here: however I would have him continue those Sketches I gave him the Subjects of; for a Sample of a Man's Capacity has ever a more forcible effect that any fame by Hearsay: and after they have been sufficiently consider'd; if the King does not seize them I intend to take them my self: the sooner they are sent the better.

I am sorry to hear you have so many just reasons of Complaint, and entirely agree [174v] with you that the Climate you now live in is absolutely to be chang'd. As to this place, I do no see it will be praticable to procure you the Post Don Philippo fill's. I find he is very uncertain of Employment at Rome, and probably will not quit but upon very advantageous and sure terms. I hope the other project of seeing England again is much more likely to succeed, and I have Allready begun to take measures for it, but it will require some time to bring them to bear. My return to that Country will contribute most effectually to the fixing our design on a right bottom; and if it cannot be brought to pass at first with all the forms of a ceremonious Introduction, we must be content to gain a footing, and leave the rest to Fortune.

The Great Duke has been reported dead these two or three days past: but I look on this piece of news as a Turin invention: it is very hard, I find, to know the true State of his health since [175r] he is invisible even to his Ministers. Whatever you learn on that subject will be very acceptable to me, as being at this juncture highly important. I am afraid our Resident who live's in the Country will be the last to know what passes at the Palace: yet, one ought naturally to believe he keep's some body in town to have a watchful Eye on an Event that so much concern's us.

I am Sir

Your most affectionate humble Servant

J. Molesworth

Appendix IV.8

fols 189r–190v
Molesworth to Galilei
London Jan the 13th 1725/6 O.S.

Dear Sir

The enclosed recommend's itself to your Care. I have been for these six week past exceeding ill, almost in the same condition as a Pisa, and am even now very low but free from my distemper and pretty easy. The unheard of ill weather we have had this Summer, my long and tiresome journeys by sea and land, together with some dangerous Colds I got on these occasions, have in all probability brought this misfortune upon me. However I mend apace and hope to escape this bout; but cannot think of a journey to Italy till Spring, if then. When I was in Ireland, I did not forget the inclination you have express'd to me of returning to these Dominions; and imagineing it might be easier to introduce you at first into that Kingdome in order to your comeing afterwards hither, I propos'd that a Number of Virtuosi, ten for example, would subscribe ten guineas apiece to make you up 100 per annum for three years [189v] till you could get into tolerable business, and I offer'd to subscribe 20. gu. my self: the town was then very empty, but I left my commission with a Gentleman who promis'd to propose it upon the meeting of that Parliament: I do not yet know what success he has had.

Since I took the resolution to write to you, I have receiv'd yours of Dec.br y 28 th NS. by which I see you continue in the desire of removeing hither. I really have not the Credit to procure you any stable settlement here, and you know what is the invincible objection against it; but I am not without hopes that next Spring may afford me an opportunity of employing you here in building and I will heartily endeavour it. But that you may not lye under any disappointment in your expectations, I must fairly give you warning that you must at first take up with what little we can procure by any means to support you till better times, I would [190v] willingly have the whole merit my self of serveing you in this point, but my father has left a great debt and a number of Sons upon me, so that I am (at present) less rich for being master of an Estate, till these encumbrances are clear'd off, w.ch I am endeavouring.

I must give you one piece of necessary advice w.ch is in the mean time to take the first possible opportunity of engageing some of our travellers to carry you with them into Lombardy, particularly to Venice and Vicenza: for here the reigning taste is Palladio's style of building, and a man is a Heretick that should talk of Michael Angelo or any other modern Architect. You must diligently Copy all the noted fabricks of Palladio, for those very draughts would introduce you here, and without them you may despair of success.

You shall in some little time hear further from me if I have any prospect of serveing you, in the mean while I am ever.

Dear Sir your affect.t humble serv.t
Molesworth

Bibliography

Adam, R. (1764) *Ruins of the Palace of the Emperor Diocletian at Spalatro in Dalmatia by Robert Adam F.R.S F.S.A. Architect to the King and to the Queen*, [London]: printed for the author.

Adam, W. (1812) *Vitruvius Scoticus*. Mineola, NY, Dover Publications.

Agliardi, G. and Cornaglia, P. (2009) Pollack Leopoldo. In V. Cazzato (ed.), *Atlante del giardino italiano 1750–1940. Dizionario biografico di architetti, giardinieri, botanici, committenti, letterati e altri protagonisti* I: 271–327. Rome, Istituto Poligrafico e Zecca dello Stato.

Alcini, L. (1991) Tradurre 'ut interpres'. Tradurre 'ut orator': il fenomeno traduttivo tra storia della lingua e della letteratura. *Gli Annali* 17: 59–100.

Alfieri, V. (1951–67) *Scritti politici e morali*, ed. P. Cazzani, 3 vols. Asti, Casa d'Alfieri.

Alfieri, V. (1951) *Vita scritta da esso*, ed. L. Fassò. Asti, Casa d'Alfieri.

Alfieri, V. (1963–89) *Epistolario*, ed. L. Caretti. 3 vols. Asti, Casa d'Alfieri.

Alfieri, V. (1978) *Parere sulle tragedie e altre prose critiche*, ed. M. Pagliai. Asti, Casa d'Alfieri.

Alfieri, V. (1981) *Vita*, ed. G. Dossena. Turin, Einaudi.

Alfieri, V. (1987) *Vita*, ed. A. Dolfi. Milan, A. Mondadori.

Alfieri, V. (1993) *Tragedie*, eds S. Romagnoli and L. Toschi, 2 vols. Turin, Einaudi.

Alfieri, V. (2004) *Esquisse du jugement Universel*, ed. G. Santato. Florence, Olschki.

Allegra, L. (1990) L'Ospizio dei catecumeni di Torino. *Bollettino Storico Bibliografico Subalpino* 88 (2): 513–73.

Anderson, J. (1756) *The Constitutions of the Ancient and Honourable Fraternity of Free and Accepted Masons*. London, Scott.

Androsov, S.O. (2011) Architektor Nikola Miketti i drugie katoliki v Peterburge (1721–1723 gg.). *Trudy Gosudarstvennogo Ėrmitaža* 58: 34–43.

Angelicoussis, E. (2001) *The Holkham Collection of Classical Sculptures*. Mainz am Rhine, Philipp von Zabern.

Angiolieri Alticozzi, V. (1746) *Relazione della compagnia de' liberi muratori estratta da varie memorie e indirizzata all'abate Carlo Antonio Giuliani da cavalier V.A.A. patrizio cortonese, guardia del corpo di S.M.I.* Naples, Salzano e Castaldo.

Angiolini, F. (2006) Medici e Savoia. Contese per la precedenza e rivalità di rango in età moderna. In P. Bianchi and L.C. Gentile (eds), *L'affermarsi della corte sabauda. Dinastia, poteri, élites in Piemonte e Savoia fra tardo medioevo e prima età moderna*: 435–79. Turin, Zamorani.

Anglani, B. (1997) *Il mestiere della metafora. Giuseppe Baretti intellettuale e scrittore.* Modena, Mucchi.

Aprile, A., Rizzo, A. and Dardanello, G. (2007) Alfieri, Borra, Birago e Dellala: architetti e cantieri per ornati e rilievi di Giuseppe Bolina. In G. Dardanello (ed.), *Arte in Piemonte*, 21. *Disegnare l'ornato. Interni piemontesi di Sei e Settecento*: 241–64. Turin, Fondazione Cassa di Risparmio.

Arciszewska, B. (2005) 'Despairing of success': Giacomo Leoni and Alessandro Galilei in eighteenth century London. *Rocznik Historii Sztuki* 30: 135–45.

Arisi, F. (1986) *Gian Paolo Panini e i fasti della Roma del '700* (second edition). Rome, Ugo Bozzi.

Arnold, R. (1959) *Northern Lights: the Story of Lord Derwentwater.* London, Constable.

Arteaga, S. (1783–8) *Le rivoluzioni del teatro musicale italiano dalla sua origine fino al presente*, 3 vols. Bologna, Trenti.

Aschbach Ettinger, A. (1984) *Oglethorpe. A Brief Biography.* Macon, Mercer University Press.

Associazione Casalese Arte e Storia/Associazione Idea Valcerrina/Città di Casale Monferrato/Città di Moncalvo (2005) *Francesco Ottavio Magnocavalli (1707–1788). Architettura, letteratura e cultura europea nell'opera di un casalese. Atti del congresso internazionale, Casale Monferrato, 11–12 October 2002, Moncalvo, 13 October 2002.* San Salvatore Monferrato, Tipografia Barberis.

Avanzini, R. (1984–5) *Le stagioni d'opera buffa al Teatro Carignano di Torino dal 1753 al 1797.* University of Bologna, dissertation.

Avison, C. (1752) *An Essay on Musical Expression.* London, C. Davis.

Ayres, P. (1992) Burlington's Library at Chiswick. *Studies in Bibliography* 35: 113–27.

Ayres, P. (1997) *Classical Culture and the Idea of Rome in Eighteenth-century England.* Cambridge, Cambridge University Press.

Babelon, J.-P. (1993) (ed.) *Versailles et les tables royales en Europe.* Paris, Réunion des Musées Nationaux.

Bagliani, F., Cornaglia, P., Maderna, M. and Mighetto, P. (2000) *Architettura, governo e burocrazia in una capitale barocca: la zona di comando di Torino e il piano di Filippo Juvarra del 1730.* Turin, Celid.

Baine, R.M. and Williams, M.E. (1989) James Oglethorpe in Europe. Recent findings in his military life. In P. Spalding and H.H. Jackson (eds), *Oglethorpe in Perspective: Georgia's Founder after Two Hundred Years*: 112–21. Tuscaloosa, University of Alabama.

Balani, D. (1987) *Il vicario tra città e stato. L'ordine pubblico e l'annona nella Torino del Settecento.* Turin, Deputazione Subalpina di Storia Patria.

Balani, D. (1995) La demografia di Torino nel Settecento: primi risultati di una ricerca. In U. Levra and N. Tranfaglia (eds), *Dal Piemonte all'Italia. Studi in onore di Narciso Nada nel suo settantesimo compleanno*: 13–46. Turin, Comitato di Torino per la Storia del Risorgimento Italiano.

Balani, D. (1996) *Toghe di Stato. La facoltà giuridica dell'Università di Torino e le professioni nel Piemonte del Settecento*. Turin, Deputazione Subalpina di Storia Patria.

Bald, R. (1950) Sir William Chambers and the Chinese garden. *Journal of the History of Ideas* 11: 287–320.

Ballaira, E. and Ghisotti, S. (1994) Il Castello di Masino negli inventari storici. *Bollettino della Società Piemontese di Archeologia e Belle Arti*, nuova serie 46: 109–34.

Ballaira, E., Ghisotti, S. and Griseri, A. (2012) (eds) *La barca sublime (Mostra, Reggia di Venaria, Scuderie Juvarriane, 16 nov.–31 dic. 2012)*. Cinisello Balsamo (Milan), Silvana.

Barberis, W. (1988) *Le armi del Principe. La tradizione militare sabauda*.Turin, Einaudi.

Barberis, W. (2007) (ed.) *I Savoia. I secoli d'oro di una dinastia europea*. Turin, Einaudi.

Barbero, A. (2002) *Il Ducato di Savoia: amministrazione e corte di uno stato franco-italiano, 1416–1536*. Rome/Bari, Laterza.

Baretti, G. (1768) *An Account of the Manners and Customs of Italy; with Observations on the Mistakes of Some Travellers, with Regard to That Country*, 2 vols. London, T. Davies, L. Davis and C. Rymers.

Baretti, G. (1768) *An Appendix Added, in Answer to Samuel Sharp*. London, T. Davies.

Baretti, G. (1857) *Lettere famigliari*. Turin, Società Editrice Italiana di M. Guigoni.

Baretti, G. (1932) *La Frusta letteraria*, ed. L. Piccioni. Bari, Laterza.

Baretti, G. (1933) Prefazioni alle tragedie di Pier Cornelio tradotte in versi italiani. In G. Baretti, *Prefazioni e polemiche*, ed. L. Piccioni: 30–65. Bari, Laterza.

Baretti, G. (1936) *Epistolario*, ed. L. Piccioni. Bari, Laterza.

Baretti, G. (1976) *Lettere sparse*, ed. F. Fido. Turin, Centro Studi Piemontesi.

Baretti, G. (1994) *The Introduction to the Carmen Seculare of Horace. Set to Music by Mr. Philidor*, ed. R. Caira Lumetti. Rome, CISU.

Bargoni, A. (1963) Argenti. In V. Viale (ed.), *Mostra del Barocco piemontese* III: *Argenti*: 1–32 plus plates 1–71. Turin, Pozzo-Salviati-Gros Monti.

Barnard, T. and Clark J. (1995) (eds) *Lord Burlington. Architecture, Art and Life*. London, Hambledon Press.

Barr, E. (1980) *George Wickes 1698–1761 Royal Goldsmith*. London, Studio Vista/ Christie's.

Bartrum, J. (*c.* 1900) *The Personal Reminiscences of an old Bath Boy*. Bath (?).

Bassi, P. (1988–9) *Storia del Teatro Carignano di Torino. Dalle origini al 1799*. University of Turin, dissertation.

Basso, A. (1976–88) (ed.) *Storia del Teatro Regio di Torino*, 5 vols. Turin, Cassa di Risparmio di Torino.

Basso, A. (1976) *Il teatro della città dal 1788 al 1936 (Storia del Teatro Regio di Torino*, ed. A. Basso, II). Turin, Cassa di Risparmio di Torino.

Basso, A. (1985) Osservazioni sulla scuola strumentale piemontese del Settecento. *Studi Musicali* 14 (1): 135–56.

Basso, A. (1991) (ed.) *L'arcano incanto. Il Teatro Regio di Torino 1740–1990*. Milan, Electa.

Basso, A. (1994) *L'invenzione della gioia. Musica e massoneria nell'età dei Lumi*. Milan, Garzanti.

Battistoni, M. (2009) *Franchigie, dazi, transiti e territori negli stati sabaudi del secolo XVIII*. Alessandria, Edizioni dell'Orso.

Baudi di Vesme, A. (1968) *L'arte in Piemonte dal XVI al XVIII secolo II*. Turin, Società Piemontese di Archeologia e Belle Arti.

Baudi di Vesme, A. (1986) *L'arte in Piemonte dal XVI al XVIII secolo III*. Turin, Società Piemontese di Archeologia e Belle Arti.

Bazzoni, A. (1871) I matrimoni Spagnuoli. *Archivio Storico Italiano* 64: 4–32; 65: 193–212.

Beard, G. (1981) *Craftsmen and Interior Decoration in England, 1660-1820*. Edinburgh, Holmes and Meier.

Beaurepaire, P.-Y. (2003) *L'espace des francs-maçons: une sociabilité européenne au XVIIIᵉ*. Rennes, Presse Universitaire de Rennes.

Béchu, P. and Taillard, C. (2004) *Les Hôtels de Soubise et de Rohan-Strasbourg: marchés de construction et décor*. Paris, Somogy Éditions d'Art.

Bell, G.M. (1990a) *A Handlist of British Diplomatic Representatives, 1509-1688*. Woodbridge/Rochester, NY, Boydell and Brewer.

Bell, G.M. (1990b) *A Handlist of British Diplomatic Representatives 1509-1688*. London, Royal Historical Society.

Bellabarba M. and Merlotti A. (2014) (eds) *Stato sabaudo e Sacro Romano Impero*. Bologna, Il Mulino.

Bellesi, S. (2012) Antonio Montauti. In *Dizionario biografico degli italiani* 76: 1–5. Rome, Istituto della Enciclopedia Italiana.

Bellini, A. (1978) *Benedetto Alfieri*. Milan, Electa.

Bély, L. (2013) La naissance d'una nouvelle monarchie: la Savoie et la paix d'Utrecht (1713). In L. Perrillat (ed.), *Couronne Royale. Colloque international autour du 300° anniversaire de l'accession de la Maison de Savoie au trone royal de Sicile, Annecy, 12 et 13 avril 2013*: 41–53. Annecy-Chambéry, Académie Salésienne et le Laboratoire LLS.

Bergadani, R. (1926) *Carlo Emanuele I*. Turin, Paravia.

Bernardi, A., Marchiando Pacchiola, M., Merlo, G. and Pazé, P. (2001) *Il Settecento religioso nel pinerolese*. Pinerolo, Museo Diocesano.

Bertana, C.E. (1983) Il ritratto di uno Stuart alla corte dei Savoia. *Studi Piemontesi* 12: 423–8.

Bertana, C.E. (1991) Un ritratto di Elisabetta Stuart di Marcus Gheeraerts nelle collezioni sabaude. *Studi Piemontesi* 20: 387–90.

Bertini, F. (1989) La massoneria in Toscana dall'età dei Lumi alla Restaurazione. In Z. Ciuffoletti (ed.), *Le origini della massoneria in Toscana (1730–1890)*: 43–164. Livorno, Bastogi.

Bettinelli, S. (1977) Lettere sopra vari argomenti di letteratura scritte da un Inglese ad un Veneziano. In S. Bettinelli, *Lettere virgiliane e lettere inglesi*, ed. E. Bonora. Turin, Einaudi.

Bevington, M. (1994) *Stowe. The Garden and the Park*. Sheffield, Juma Printing and Publishing.

Bianchi, A. (1936) *Maria e Caterina di Savoia (1594–1656, 1595–1640)*. Turin, Paravia.

Bianchi, P. (1992) L'Università di Torino e il governo provvisorio repubblicano (9 dicembre 1798–26 maggio 1799). *Annali della Fondazione Luigi Einaudi* 26: 241–66.

Bianchi, P. (1993) L'Università di Torino dopo la chiusura, nella crisi dell'antico regime (1792–1798). Lo sfaldamento e la sopravvivenza dell'organizzazione didattica. *Annali della Fondazione Luigi Einaudi* 27: 353–93.

Bianchi, P. (1995) Fra università e carriere pubbliche. Strategie nella nomina dei rettori dell'ateneo torinese (1721–1782). *Annali della Fondazione Luigi Einaudi* 29: 308–9.

Bianchi, P. (1998) Università e riforme: la relazione dell'Università di Padova di Francesco Filippo Picono (1712). *Quaderni per la Storia dell'Università di Padova* 31: 165–203.

Bianchi, P. (2001) La guerra franco-piemontese e le Valli valdesi (1792–1799). In G.P. Romagnani (ed.), *La Bibbia, la coccarda e il tricolore. I Valdesi fra due emancipazioni (1798–1848)*: 73–117. Turin, Claudiana.

Bianchi, P. (2002) *Onore e mestiere. Le riforme militari nel Piemonte del Settecento*. Turin, Zamorani.

Bianchi, P. (2003a) In cerca del moderno. Studenti e viaggiatori inglesi a Torino nel Settecento. *Rivista Storica italiana* 115: 1021–51.

Bianchi, P. (2003b) 'Quel fortunato e libero paese'. L'Accademia Reale e i primi contatti del giovane Alfieri con il mondo inglese. In M. Cerruti, M. Corsi and B. Danna (eds), *Alfieri e il suo tempo*: 89–112. Florence, Olschki.

Bianchi, P. (2005a) Militari, banchieri, studenti. Presenze protestanti nella Torino del Settecento. In P. Cozzo, F. De Pieri and A. Merlotti (eds), *Valdesi e protestanti a Torino (XVIII–XX secolo). Convegno per i 150 anni del Tempio valdese (1853–2003)*: 39–63. Turin, Zamorani.

Bianchi, P. (2005b) 'Politica e polizia' in una realtà d'antico regime: le sfide contro vecchi e nuovi disordini nello Stato sabaudo fra Sei e Settecento. *Bollettino Storico Bibliografico Subalpino* 103 (fasc. I): 473–504.

Bianchi, P. (2007a) La corte dei Savoia: disciplinamento del servizio e delle fedeltà. In W. Barberis (ed.), *I Savoia. I secoli d'oro di una dinastia europea*: 135–74. Turin, Einaudi.

Bianchi, P. (2007b) Huguenots in the army of Savoy-Piedmont: Protestant soldiers and civilians in the Savoyard state in the seventeenth and eighteenth century. In M. Glozier and D. Onnekink (eds), *War, Religion and Service. Huguenot soldiering 1685–1713*: 213–28. Aldershot, Ashgate.

Bianchi, P. (2008) Al servizio degli alemanni. Militari piemontesi nell'Impero e negli stati tedeschi fra Sei e Settecento. In P. Bianchi, D. Maffi and E. Stumpo (eds), *Italiani al servizio straniero in età moderna*: 55–72. Milan, Angeli.

Bianchi, P. (2010a) Una palestra di arti cavalleresche e di politica. Presenze austro-tedesche all'Accademia Reale di Torino nel Settecento. In M. Bellabarba and

J.P. Niederkorn (eds), *Le corti come luogo di comunicazione. Gli Asburgo e l'Italia (secoli XVI–XIX). Höfe als Orte der Kommunikation. Die Habsburger und Italien (16. Bis 19. Jh.)*: 135–53. Bologna/Berlin, il Mulino/Dunker and Humblot.

Bianchi, P. (2010b) Politica matrimoniale e rituali fra Cinquecento e Settecento. In P. Bianchi and A. Merlotti (eds), *Le strategie dell'apparenza. Cerimoniali, politica e società alla corte dei Savoia in età moderna*: 39–72. Turin, Zamorani.

Bianchi, P. (2012a) *Sotto diverse bandiere. L'internazionale militare nello Stato sabaudo d'antico regime*. Milan, Franco Angeli.

Bianchi, P. (2012b) Nella specola dell'ambasciatore. Torino agli occhi di John Stuart, Lord Mountstuart e Marchese di Bute (1779–1783). In E. Piccoli and F. De Pieri (eds), *Architettura e città negli Stati sabaudi. Studi in onore di Franco Rosso*: 135–60. Macerata, Quodlibet.

Bianchi, P. (2014) Conservazione e modernità: il binomio corte-città attraverso il prisma dell'Accademia Reale di Torino. In M. Formica, A. Merlotti and A.M. Rao (eds), *La città nel Settecento. Saperi e forme di rappresentazione*: 107–23. Rome, Edizioni di Storia e Letteratura.

Bianchi, P. (2015a) I Ferrero Fieschi di Masserano nella Spagna del Settecento. *Rivista Storica Italiana* 127 (fasc. 1): 248–73.

Bianchi, P. (2015b) Perrone, Carlo Baldassarre. In *Dizionario biografico degli italiani*, 82: 448–53. Rome, Istituto della Enciclopedia Italiana.

Bianchi, P. and Gentile, L.C. (2006) (eds) *L'affermarsi della corte sabauda. Dinaste, poteri, élites in Piemonte e Savoia fra tardo medioevo e prima età moderna*. Turin, Zamorani.

Bianchi, P. and Merlotti, A. (2013) Uno spazio politico d'antico regime. La Compagnia di San Paolo fra corte, Stato e Consiglio di città (XVII–XIX sec.). In W. Barberis (ed.) *La Compagnia di San Paolo I*: 252–315. Turin, Einaudi.

Bianchi, P. and Merlotti, A. (2017) *Storia degli Stati sabaudi*. Brescia, Morcelliana.

Binaghi, R. (1999) Architetti e ingegneri nel Piemonte sabaudo tra formazione universitaria ed attività professionale. In G.P. Brizzi and A. Romano (eds), *Studenti e dottori nelle università italiane (origini–XX secolo). Atti del convegno di studi, Bologna 25–27 novembre 1999*: 263–89. Bologna, Clueb.

Binaghi, R. (2003) Architetti e ingegneri tra mestiere e arte. In D. Balani and D. Carpanetto (eds), *Professioni non togate nel Piemonte d'antico regime*: 143–241. Turin, il Segnalibro.

Binaghi, R. (2010) Il Palazzo dell'Università di Torino: da Garove a Garolli. In P. Cornaglia (ed.), *Michelangelo Garove: 1648–1713. Un architetto per Vittorio Amedeo II*: 183–204. Rome, Campisano.

Binaghi R. (2012) La matematica nella formazione degli ingegneri e degli architetti civili nel Piemonte di antico regime. In A. Ferraresi and M. Visioli (eds), *Formare alle professioni. Architetti, ingegneri, artisti (sec. XV–XIX)*: 107–28. Milan, FrancoAngeli.

Bindoff, S.T., Malcom Smith, E.F. and Webster, C.K. (1934) *British Diplomatic Representatives (1789–1852)*. London, Royal Historical Society.

Bishop, P. (1999) *Holburne Museum of Art: Souvenir Guidebook*. Bath, Holburne of Menstrie Museum.

Black, J. (1983) The development of Anglo-Sardinian relations in the first half of the eighteenth century. *Studi Piemontesi* 12 (1): 48–60.

Black, J. (1984) The Grand Tour and Savoy-Piedmont in the eighteenth century. *Studi Piemontesi* 13 (1): 140–64.

Black, J. (1989) An analysis of Savoy-Piedmont in 1740. *Studi Piemontesi* 18 (1): 229–32.

Black, J. (1999) *The British Abroad, The Grand Tour in the Eighteenth Century*. London, Sandpiper.

Black, J. (2001) *British Diplomats and Diplomacy, 1688–1800*. Exeter, University of Exeter Press.

Black, J. (2003) *Italy and the Grand Tour*. New Haven, CT/London, Yale University Press.

Blanchetti, F. (1991) Le vicende letterarie e teatrali di un magistrato piemontese del Settecento: i drammi per musica di Jacopo Durandi. In A. Basso (ed.), *Miscellanea di studi* 3: 7–35. Turin, Centro Studi Piemontesi/Fondo 'Carlo Felice Bona'.

Blanchetti, F. (2011) Francesco Bianchi e Angelo Tarchi autori di feste teatrali per il Teatro Regio di Torino (1782 e 1784). In A. Colturato and A. Merlotti (eds), *La festa teatrale nel Settecento. Dalla corte di Vienna alle corti d'Italia. Proceedings of the International conference (Reggia di Venaria, 13–14 November 2009)*: 217–35. Lucca, Libreria Musicale Italiana.

Bonino, M. and Moraglio, M. (2006) *Inventare gli spostamenti: storia e immagini dell'autostrada Torino–Savona*. Turin, Allemandi.

Borghezio, G. (1924) La fondazione del Collegio nuovo 'Puerorum Innocentium' del Duomo di Torino. *Note d'Archivio per la Storia Musicale* 1: 200–66.

Borra, G.B. (1734) *Corso d'architettura civile sopra li cinque ordini di Giacomo Barozzio da Vignola disegnato da Giambattista Borra di Dogliani sotto la direzzione del Signor Architetto & Accademico di Roma Bernardo Vitone in Torino 1734 (Raccolta di disegni inediti, varia 738)*. Turin, Biblioteca Reale di Torino.

Borra, G.B. (1748) *Trattato della cognizione pratica delle resistenze geometricamente dimostrato dall'architetto Giambatista Borra ad uso d'ogni sorta d'edifizj, coll' aggiunta delle armature di varie maniere di coperti, volte, ed altre cose di tal genere*. Turin.

Borra, G.B. (1749) *Vedute principali di Torino disegnate in prospettiva, ed intagliate in rame dall'architetto Giambatista Borra. Parte prima*. Turin.

Borsieri, P. (1948) *Il Conciliatore*, I (1818), ed. V. Branca. Florence, Le Monnier.

Boswell, G. (1791) *Life of Samuel Johnson*. London, H. Baldwin. (Translated into Italian as: G. Boswell (1982), *Vita di Samuel Johnson*, trans. A. Prospero. Milan, Garzanti. First edition 1954.)

Boswell, J. (1955) *On the Grand Tour: Italy, Corsica and France. 1765–1766*, eds F. Brady and F.A. Pottle. Melbourne, W. Heinemann.

Bottari, G. (1757) *Raccolta di lettere sulla pittura, scultura ed architettura scritte da' più celebri personaggi che in dette arti fiorirono dal secolo XV al XVII*, 2 vols. Rome, Pagliarini.

Bottari, G. (1822) *Raccolta di lettere sulla pittura, scultura ed architettura*. Rome, G. Silvestri.

Bouquet, M.-T. (1968) *Musique et musiciens à Turin de 1648 à 1775*. Turin, Accademia delle Scienze (then Paris, A. et J. Picard, 1969).

Bouquet, M.-T. (1976) *Il teatro di corte dalle origini al 1788 (Storia del Teatro Regio di Torino*, ed. A. Basso, I). Turin, Cassa di Risparmio di Torino.

Bouquet, M.-T., Gualerzi, V. and Testa, A. (1988) *Cronologie (Storia del Teatro Regio di Torino*, ed. A. Basso, V). Turin, Cassa di Risparmio di Torino.

Bouquet-Boyer, M.-T. (1987) *Turin et les musiciens de la cour, 1619–1775. Vie quotidienne et production artistique*. University of Paris-Sorbonne, Ph.D. thesis.

Bouquet-Boyer, M.-T. (1988) Note biografiche sulla famiglia Chiabrano. In G. Chiabrano, *44 Sonate da camera per due violoncelli obbligati, per violoncello e basso, per violoncello solo o fagotto e basso: Libro I, Sonate 1–15*, ed. A. Pais: v–xviii. Milan, Suvini Zerboni.

Bouquet-Boyer, M.-T. (1989) Contribution à l'étude de la Chapelle musicale de la Cathédrale Saint-Jean-Baptiste de Turin aux XVᵉ et XVIᵉ siecle. In A. Basso (ed.), *Miscellanea di studi* II: 7–39. Turin, Centro Studi Piemontesi/Fondo 'Carlo Felice Bona'.

Bouquet-Boyer, M.-T. (2000) Cenni storici sulla Cappella Regia. In E. Demaria, *Il fondo musicale della Cappella Regia Sabauda*: ix–xxxvi. Lucca, Libreria Musicale Italiana.

Bouquet-Boyer, M.-T. (2001) Cenni storici sulla Cappella Metropolitana di Torino. In E. Demaria, *Il fondo musicale della Cappella dei Cantori del Duomo di Torino*: ix–xl. Lucca, Libreria Musicale Italiana.

Bourdon, E. (2009) Les relations entre voyage, construction du savoir et connaissance des territoires à travers l'œuvre de Giovanni Tomaso Borgonio. *Rives Méditerranéennes* 34: 27–43.

Bowdler, T., Esq. (1815) (ed.) *A Short View of the Life and Character of Lieutenant-General Villettes, Late Lieutenant-Governor and Commander of the Forces in Jamaica. To which are Added Letters Written during a Journey from Calais to Geneva, and St. Bernard, in the year 1814*. Bath, Roichard Cruttwell.

Bracchi, C. (1995) Rassegna barettiana (1989–1993). *Giornale Storico della Letteratura Italiana* 172 (fasc. 557): 116–29.

Bracchi, C. (1998) *Prospettiva di una nazione di nazioni. An Account of the Manners and Customs of Italy di Giuseppe Baretti*. Alessandria, Edizioni dell'Orso.

Bracchi, C. (1999) La civiltà italiana nella prosa inglese di *An Account*. In C. Prosperi (ed.), *Giuseppe Baretti: Rivalta Bormida, le radici familiari, l'opera. Atti del convegno nazionale, Rivalta Bormida, 6 settembre 1997*: 161–7. Alessandria, Edizioni dell'Orso.

Branca, M. (2011a) I parati in carta 'della China' nelle stanze del quartiere dell'ala sinistra del piano nobile. In M. Branca (ed.), *Viaggio nell'esotismo settecentesco alla Villa del Poggio Imperiale a Firenze. Il riallestimento della stanza dei quadri cinesi e i restauri nei quartieri leopoldini al piano nobile*: 31–7. Livorno, Sillabe.

Branca, M. (2011b) Il restauro dei parati tessili orientali di due stanze, nel quartiere dell'ala destra del piano nobile. In M. Branca (ed.), *Viaggio nell'esotismo settecentesco alla Villa del Poggio Imperiale a Firenze. Il riallestimento della stanza dei quadri cinesi e i restauri nei quartieri leopoldini al piano nobile*: 23–9. Livorno, Sillabe.

Brayda, C., Coli, L. and Sesia, D. (1963) (eds) *Ingegneri e architetti dei Sei e Settecento in Piemonte*. Turin, Comune di Torino/Società Ingegneri e Architetti.

Brewer, J. (1989) *The Sinews of Power. War, Money and the English State 1688–1783*. London, Unwin Hyman.

Brilli, A. (2006) *Il viaggio in Italia. Storia di una grande tradizione culturale*. Bologna, Il Mulino.

Brilli, A. (2010) *Il viaggio della capitale. Torino, Firenze e Roma dopo l'Unità d'Italia*. Turin, Utet.

Brindle, S. (2013) Kent and Italy. In S. Weber (ed.), *William Kent. Designing Georgian Britain. Exhibition's catalogue (New York 2013/London 2014)*: 89–109. New Haven, CT/London, Yale University Press.

Brizzi, G.P. (1976a) La pratica del viaggio d'istruzione in Italia nel Sei-Settecento. *Annali dell'Istituto Storico Italo-germanico in Trento* 2: 203–91.

Brizzi, G.P. (1976b) *La formazione della classe dirigente nel Sei-Settecento: i seminaria nobilium nell'Italia centro-settentrionale*. Bologna, Il Mulino.

Bromley, W. (1705) *Remarks in the Grand Tour of France and Italy. Perform'd by a Person of Quality, in the year 1691*. London, Printed for John Nutt, near Stationers Hall.

Brotton, J. (2006) Buying the Renaissance: Prince Charles's art purchases in Madrid, 1623. In A. Samson (ed.), *The Spanish Match: Prince Charles's Journey to Madrid, 1623*: 9–26. Farnham/Burlington, VT, Ashgate.

Brovia, S. (1997) L'architettura fra modelli, progetti e cantieri. In L. Moro (ed.), *Il Castello di Govone. L'architettura*: 25–43. Turin, Celid.

Brown, J. and Elliott, J. H. (2002) (eds) *The Sale of the Century. Artistic Relations between Spain and Great Britain, 1604–1655*. New Haven, CT/London, Yale University Press.

Bulman, L.C. (2003) Moral education on the Grand Tour: Thomas Coke and his contemporaries in Rome and Florence. *Apollo* 157.2003, 493: 27–34.

Burden, M. (2013) *Regina Mingotti: Diva and Impresario at the King's Theatre*, London/Burlington, VT, Ashgate.

Burney, C. (1771) *The Present State of Music in France and Italy, or the Journal of a Tour through Those Countries, Undertaken to Collect Materials for a General*

History of Music. London, Becket. (Second edition, corrected, London, Becket & Co., 1773. Scholes, P.A. (ed.), London, Oxford University Press, 1959).

Burney, C. (1776–89) *A General History of Music. From the Earliest Ages to the Present Period*, 4 vols. London, The Author.

Burney, C. (1785) *An Account of the Musical Performances in Westminster Abbey, and the Pantheon... in Commemoration of Handel.* London, Payne and Robinson.

Burrows, D. and Dunhill, R. (2002) *Music and Theatre in Handel's World. The Family Papers of James Harris, 1732–1780.* Oxford, Oxford University Press.

Burton, E.H. (1909) *The Life and Times of Bishop Challoner, 1691–1781*, II. London, Longmans, Green and Co.

Burton, J.H. (ed.) (1849) *Letters of Eminent Persons Addressed to David Hume.* Edinburgh, W. Blackwood.

Burtt, S.G. (1992) *Virtue Transformed. Political Argument in England, 1688–1740.* Cambridge, Cambridge University Press.

Busiri Vici, A. (1977) Ritratti a Roma di Domenico Duprà. *L'Urbe* 2 (XI): 1–16.

Butler, M. (2001) *Operatic Reform at Turin's Teatro Regio. Aspects of Production and Stylistic Change in the 1760s.* Lucca, Libreria Musicale Italiana.

Butler, M. (2002) Administration and innovation at Turin's Teatro Regio: producing *Sofonisba* (1764) and *Oreste* (1766). In *Cambridge Opera Journal* 14 (3): 243–62.

Calapà, N. and Cereia, D. (2005) Fondamenta di carta. Gli archivi per lo studio di Villa della Regina: bilancio di una ricerca in corso. In L. Caterina and C. Mossetti (eds), *Villa della Regina*: 444–51. Turin, Umberto Allemandi.

Calderini E. (1993) Il giardino all'inglese nel parco di Racconigi, 'isola felice' di Giuseppina di Lorena Carignano. In *Studi Piemontesi*, vol. XXII, fasc. 1: 81–94.

Caldwell, J. (1999) *The Oxford History of English Music*, II. Oxford, Oxford University Press.

Calendar of Stuart Papers (1902–16), 6 vols. London, Mackie & Co.

Cameron, E. (1993) Medieval heretics as Protestant martyrs. In D. Wood (ed.), *Martyrs and Martyrologies (Studies in Church History 30)*: 185–207. Oxford, Blackwell.

Campbell, C. (1715–25) (ed.) *Vitruvius Britannicus, or the British Architect*, 3 vols (vol. I, 1715; vol. II, 1717, vol. III, 1725). London.

Canavesio, W. (1997) Anni di apprendistato. Giovanni Battista Borra nello studio di Vittone. *Studi Piemontesi* 2: 365–81.

Canella, M. (2005) Riti funebri e sepolture nella comunità valdese di Torino. In P. Cozzo, F. De Pieri and A. Merlotti (eds), *Valdesi e protestanti a Torino (XVIII–XX secolo). Convegno per i 150 anni del Tempio valdese (1853–2003)*: 212–30. Turin, Zamorani.

Caracciolo, A. (1989) *Alle origini della storia contemporanea.* Bologna, Il Mulino.

Caracciolo, A. and Colombo, R.M. (1979) (ed.) *Nascita dell'opinione pubblica in Inghilterra (Quaderni Storici* 14 (fasc. III)).

Caraffa, C. (2006) *Gaetano Chiaveri (1689–1770), architetto romano della Hofkirche di Dresda (Studi della Bibliotheca Hertziana 1).* Cinisello Balsamo/Milan, Silvana Editoriale.

Carbonara, R. (1970) *Giuseppe Baretti e la sua traduzione del 'Rasselas' di Samuel Johnson*. Turin, Giappichelli.

Cardoza, A. and Symcox, G. (2006) *A History of Turin*. Turin, Einaudi.

Carey, B. (2012) 'The worse than Negro barbarity of the populace': Ignatius Sancho witnesses the Gordon Riots. In I. Haywood and J. Seed (eds), *The Gordon Riots. Politics, Culture and Insurrection in Late Eighteenth-century Britain*: 144–61. Cambridge, Cambridge University Press.

Carpanetto, D. (1998) *Scienza e arte del guarire. Cultura, formazione universitaria e professioni mediche a Torino tra Sei e Settecento*. Turin, Deputazione Subalpina di Storia Patria.

Carpanetto, D. (2009) *Divisi dalla fede. Frontiere religiose, modelli politici, identità storiche nelle relazioni tra Torino e Ginevra (XVII–XVIII secolo)*. Turin, Utet.

Carré, J. (1994) *Lord Burlington (1694–1753): le connaisseur, le mécène, l'architecte*, 2 vols. Clermont-Ferrand, Adosa.

Carutti, D. (1875–1880) *Storia della diplomazia della corte di Savoia (1494–1773)*, 4 vols. Turin, Bocca.

Casale, G. (1873) *Guida del Reale Castello e parco di Racconigi*. Savigliano, Racca e Bressa.

Cassetti, M. (2005) *Vicende storiche e architettoniche di Palazzo San Martino Provana di Parella già de Rossillon di Bernezzo in Torino*. Vercelli, Gallo Arti Grafiche.

Castell, R. (1728) *Villas of the Ancients illustrated*. London.

Castello, L.C. (1991) *Palazzo Graneri: Dal 1858 sede del Circolo degli artisti di Torino*. Turin, D. Piazza.

Castronovo, V. (1977) Carlo Emanuele I di Savoia. *Dizionario biografico degli italiani* 20: 326–40. Rome, Istituto della Enciclopedia Italiana.

Catarinella, A. and Salsotto, I. (1998) L'università e i collegi. In G. Ricuperati (ed.), *Storia di Torino*, III. *Dalla dominazione francese alla ricomposizione dello Stato (1536–1630)*: 523–67. Turin, Einaudi.

Catarinella, A. and Salsotto, I. (2002) L'Università degli Studi in Piemonte tra il 1630 e il 1684. In G. Ricuperati (ed.), *Storia di Torino*, IV. *La città fra crisi e ripresa (1630–1730)*: 546–56. Turin, Einaudi.

Caterina, L. (2000) Le stanze cinesi del castello dei Solaro a Govone: lettura storico-artistica. In L. Moro (ed.), *Il Castello di Govone. Gli Appartamenti*: 41–59. Turin, Celid.

Caterina, L. (2005) L'Oriente in Piemonte. In L. Caterina and C. Mossetti (eds), *Villa della Regina. Il riflesso dell'Oriente nel Piemonte del Settecento*: 53–78. Turin, Umberto Allemandi.

Caterina, L. (2008a) La sala cinese. In F. Dalmasso (ed.), *Palazzo Grosso a Riva presso Chieri. Le camere delle meraviglie e il giardino pittoresco di Faustina Mazzetti*: 89–101 Turin, EdiTO.

Caterina, L. (2008b) Le porcellane cinesi a Villa della Regina. In C. Mossetti and P. Traversi (eds), *Juvarra a Villa della Regina: le storie di Enea di Corrado Giaquinto*: 127–32. Turin, Editris Duemila.

Caterina, L. (2011) Le stanze cinesi nella Villa del Poggio Imperiale. In M. Branca (ed.), *Viaggio nell'esotismo settecentesco alla Villa del Poggio Imperiale a Firenze. Il riallestimento della stanza dei quadri cinesi e i restauri nei quartieri leopoldini al piano nobile*: 11–15. Livorno, Sillabe.

Caterina, L. and Mossetti, C. (2005a) I Gabinetti di Villa della Regina. Modelli e confronti. In L. Caterina and C. Mossetti (eds), *Villa della Regina. Il riflesso dell'Oriente nel Piemonte del Settecento*: 123–52. Turin, Umberto Allemandi.

Caterina, L. and Mossetti, C. (2005b) (eds) *Villa della Regina. Il riflesso dell'Oriente nel Piemonte del Settecento*. Turin, Umberto Allemandi.

Caterina, L. and Mossetti, C. (2006), Modelli orientali per le botteghe piemontesi del Settecento. Oriental models for eighteenth century workshops in the Piedmont. *DecArt* 6: 46–59.

Caterina, L. and Mossetti, C. (2007) Il gusto dell'esotico in Piemonte. Riflessioni in corso. In P. Amalfitano and L. Innocenti (eds) *L'Oriente. Storia di una figura nelle arti occidentali (1700–2000)*: I, 241–56. Naples/Rome, Associazione Sigismondo Malatesta.

Caterina, L. and Mossetti, C. (2008) (eds) Stupinigi, Palazzina di Caccia: sala da gioco, già camera longa appartamento di levanter, piano terreno. In *Villa della Regina*: 530–3. Turin/London/Venice /New York, Umberto Allemandi.

Caterina, L. Ghisotti, S. and Mossetti, C. (2005) (eds) Repertorio dei luoghi 'alla China' in Piemonte nel Settecento. In L. Caterina and C. Mossetti (eds), *Villa della Regina. Il riflesso dell'Oriente nel Piemonte del Settecento*: 453–627. Turin, Umberto Allemandi.

Caterino, R. (2013a) Giovanni Battista Borra (1713–1770). Percorso biografico. In G. Dardanello (ed.), *Giovanni Battista Borra da Palmira a Racconigi*: 177–82. Turin, Editris.

Caterino, R. (2013b) Giovanni Battista Borra e la Parrochiale di Trinità. In G. Dardanello (ed.), *Giovanni Battita Borra da Palmira a Racconigi*: 135–44. Turin, Editris.

Cazzaniga, G.M. (ed.) *Storia d'Italia. Annali 21. La Massoneria*: 447–83. Turin, Einaudi.

Cesarotti, M. (1785) *Saggio sulla filosofia delle lingue*. Padua, Stamperia Penada.

Chambers, W. (1763) *Plans, Elevations, Sections, and Perspective Views of the Gardens and Buildings at Kew in Surry the Seat of Her Royal Highness the Princess Dowager of Wales*. London, John Haberkorn for the Author.

Chambers, W. (1772) *Dissertation on Oriental Gardening*, London.

Chambers, W. (1968) *Designs of Chinese Buildings, Furniture, Dresses, Machines, and Utensils* (reprint of the 1757 publication). New York, B. Blom.

Chambers, W. (2012) *A Treatise on the Decorative Part of Civil Architecture: with Illustrations, Notes and an Examination of Grecian architecture, Edited by J. Gwilt* (1759). Cambridge, Cambridge University Press.

Chandler, R., Revett, N. and Pars, W. (1769) (eds) *Ionian Antiquities, Published With Permission of The Society of Dilettanti*. London, T. Spilsbury and T. Haskell.

Chaney, E. (1998) *The Evolution of the Grand Tour. Anglo-Italian Cultural Relations since the Renaissance*. London, Routledge.

Chaney, E. (2000) *The Evolution of the Grand Tour: Anglo-Italian Cultural Relations since the Renaissance*. London, Taylor and Francis.

Chaney, E. (2006) *Inigo Jones's 'Roman Sketchbook'*, 2 vols. London, Roxburghe Club.

Chaney, E. and Wilks, T. (2013) *The Jacobean Grand Tour. Early Stuart Travellers in Europe*. London/New York, I.B. Tauris.

Chaney, E. and Wilks, T. (2014) (eds) *The Jacobean Grand Tour: Early Stuart Travellers in Europe*. London/New York, I.B. Tauris.

Charles, S. [Lord Herbert] (1939) *Henry, Elizabeth and George (1734–81): Letters and Diaries of Henry Tenth Earl of Pembroke and his Circle*. London.

Chauvard, J.-F., Cozzo, P., Merlotti, A. and Visceglia, M.A. (2015) *Casa Savoia e curia romana*. Rome, École Française de Rome.

Chevallier, P. (1964) *Le ducs sous l'acacia ou les premiers pas de la franc-maçonnerie française. 1725–1743*. Paris, Librairie Philosophique Vrin.

Chiavia, C. (2003) Luoghi d'interesse valdese a Torino. In G. Platone (ed.), *I valdesi a Torino. Nascita e storia di una comunità protestante*. Turin, Claudiana.

Chicco, G. (1995) *La seta in Piemonte, 1650–1800: un sistema industriale d'ancien régime*. Milan, Franco Angeli.

Chicco, G. (2002) La politica economica statale e i 'banchieri-negozianti' nel Settecento. In G. Ricuperati (ed.), *Storia di Torino*, V. *Dalla città razionale alla crisi dello Stato d'Antico Regime (1730–1798)*: 155–84. Turin, Einaudi.

Chippendale, T. (1966) *The Gentleman and Cabinet-Maker's Director* (reprint of the 1754 publication). Mineola, NY, Dover Publications Inc.

Churchill, A. (1745) *A Collection of Voyages and Travels*. London.

Cicognara, F.L. (1821) *Catalogo ragionato dei libri d'arte e d'antichità posseduti dal Conte Cicognara*, 2 vols. Pisa, Niccolò Capurro.

Claretta, G. (1872) *Il principe Emanuele Filiberto di Savoia alla corte di Spagna. Studi storici sul Regno di Carlo Emanuele I*. Turin, Civelli.

Claretta, G. (1873) *Sulle avventure di Luca Assarino e Gerolamo Brusoni chiamati alla corte di Savoia nel secolo XVII ed eletti istoriografi ducali*. Turin, Stamperia Reale.

Claretta, G. (1878) *Sui principali storici piemontesi e particolarmente sugli storio-grafi della Real Casa di Savoia. Memorie storiche, letterarie e biografiche*. Turin/Rome/Milan/Florence, Paravia.

Claretta, G. (1887) Sui primordi dell'Accademia Militare di Torino. Nota storico-diplomatica. *Il Filotecnico* 2 (fasc. V–VI): 135–42.

Claretta, G. (1892) *La regina Cristina di Svezia in Italia*. Turin, Roux & C.

Clark, A.M. (1985) Introduction. In E.P. Bowron (ed.), *Pompeo Batoni: a Complete Catalogue of his Works*. Oxford, Phaidon.

Clark, J. (1989a) The mysterious Mr Buck: patronage and politics 1688–1745. *Apollo* 129.327: 317–22.

Clark, J. (1989b) For kings and senates fit. *The Georgian Group Report and Journal* (August): 55–63.

Clarke, G. (1973) The gardens of Stowe. *Apollo* May–June 97: 558–71.

Clarke de Dromantin, P. (2005) *Les réfugiés jacobites dans la France du XVIIIe siècle: l'exode de toute une noblesse pour cause de religions*. Bordeaux, Presse Universitaire de Bordeaux.

Clifford, H. (2004) *Silver in London, the Parker and Wakelin Partnership 1760–1776*. New Haven, CT/London, Yale University Press.

Cogswell, T. (1989) *The Blessed Revolution: English Politics and the Coming of War, 1621–1624*. Cambridge, Cambridge University Press.

Coke, M. (1889–96) *The Letters and Journals of Lady Mary Coke*, ed. J.A. Home, 4 vols. Edinburgh, David Douglas.

Collé, C. (1805–7) *Journal historique ou mémoires critiques et littéraires sur les ouvrages dramatiques et sur les événements les plus mémorables, depuis 1748 jusqu'en 1751 [–1772] inclusivement*. Paris, Imprimerie Bibliographique.

Colle, E. (2012) Prefazione. In P. Cornaglia (ed.), *Giuseppe Battista Piacenza e Carlo Randoni. I reali Palazzi fra Torino e Genova (1773–1831)*: 9–11. Turin, Celid.

Collison-Morley, L. (1909) *Giuseppe Baretti with an Account of his Literary Friendships and Feuds in Italy and in England in the Days of Dr. Johnson*. London, John Murray.

Colturato, A. (2007) Un'industria 'troppo imperfetta': la fabbricazione dei piano-forti a Torino nell'Ottocento. *Fonti Musicali Italiane* 12: 167–214.

Colturato, A. (2010a) Un espectáculo para el Archiduque: la Dora festeggiante y l'accorta cameriera de Martín y Soler. Con referencias a otras de sus obras representadas en Turín antes del fin del siglo XVIII. In D. Link and L.J. Waisman (eds), *Los siete mundos de Vicente Martín y Soler. Proceedings of the International Conference (Valencia, 14–18 November 2006)*: 205–38. Valencia, Institut Valencià de la Música/Generalitat Valenciana.

Colturato, A. (2010b) Musica e cerimoniale nel Settecento. In P. Bianchi and A. Merlotti (eds), *Le strategie dell'apparenza. Cerimoniali, politica e società alla corte dei Savoia in età moderna*: 167–99. Turin, Zamorani.

Colturato, A. (2012) *Mettere in scena la regalità. Le feste teatrali di Gaetano Pugnani al Regio di Torino*. Lucca, Libreria Musicale Italiana.

Colvin, H. (1995) *A Bibliographical Dictionary of British Architects 1600–1840* (third edition). New Haven, CT/ London, Yale University Press.

Comoli, V. (1983) *Torino*. Roma-Bari, Laterza.

Connor, T.P. (1998) The fruits of the Grand Tour – Edward Wright and Lord Parker in Italy, 1720–22. *Apollo* July: 23–30.

Connor, T.P. (2005) *The Macclesfield Sculpture: the Fruits of Lord Parker's Grand Tour 1720–22. Sale Catalogue, 1 December 2005*. London, Christie's.

Cont, A. (2013) Educare alla e attraverso l'amicizia: precettori e governatori nella società nobiliare italiana del Seicento. *Annali di Storia dell'Educazione e delle Istituzioni Scolastiche* 20: 83–103.

Conti, F. (2003) *Storia della massoneria italiana. Dal Risorgimento al Fascismo*. Bologna, Il Mulino.

Contini, A. and Volpini, P. (2007) (eds) *Istruzioni agli ambasciatori e inviati medicei in Spagna e nell'Italia spagnola (1536–1648)*, 2 vols. Rome, Direzione Generale per gli Archivi.

Cordero di Pamparato, S. (1915) *La cappella musicale del Duomo di Torino*. Turin, STEN.

Cornaglia, P. (1994) *Giardini di marmo ritrovati. La geografia del gusto in un secolo di cantiere a Venaria Reale (1699–1798)*. Torino, Lindau.

Cornaglia, P. (1996) 'Alla China': i Gabinetti cinesi di Venaria Reale nel Castello di Moncalieri. In F. Pernice (ed.), *Il Castello di Moncalieri. Gli appartamenti reali*: 60–73. Turin, Celid.

Cornaglia, P. (2008) L'illusione e la natura. Parchi e giardini in Piemonte tra XVIII e XIX secolo. In G. Dardanello and R. Tamborrino (eds), *Guarini, Juvarra e Antonelli. Segni e simboli per Torino*, catalogo della mostra (Torino, Palazzo Bricherasio, 28 June–14 September): 190–3. Cinisello Balsamo, Silvana Editoriale.

Cornaglia, P. (2009a) Castelli, Filippo. In V. Cazzato (ed.), *Atlante del giardino italiano 1750–1940. Dizionario biografico di architetti, giardinieri, botanici, committenti, letterati e altri protagonisti* I: 36–9. Rome, Istituto Poligrafico e Zecca dello Stato.

Cornaglia, P. (2009b) Gullini Guglielmo. In V. Cazzato (ed.), *Atlante del giardino italiano 1750–1940. In Dizionario biografico di architetti, giardinieri, botanici, committenti, letterati e altri protagonisti* I: 58–9. Rome, Istituto Poligrafico e Zecca dello Stato.

Cornaglia, P. (2009c) Pregliasco Giacomo. In V. Cazzato (ed.), *Atlante del giardino italiano 1750–1940. Dizionario biografico di architetti, giardinieri, botanici, committenti, letterati e altri protagonisti* I: 99–103. Rome, Istituto Poligrafico e Zecca dello Stato.

Cornaglia, P. (2009d) Quarini Mario Ludovico. In V. Cazzato (ed.), *Atlante del giardino italiano 1750–1940. Dizionario biografico di architetti, giardinieri, botanici, committenti, letterati e altri protagonisti* I: 105–7. Rome, Istituto Poligrafico e Zecca dello Stato.

Cornaglia, P. (2010) (ed.) *Michelangelo Garove: 1648–1713. Un architetto per Vittorio Amedeo II, Atti del convegno, Torino 2009*. Rome, Campisano.

Cornaglia, P. (2012a) (ed.) *Benedetto Alfieri: 1699–1767, architetto di Carlo Emanuele III. Atti del convegno internazionale, Reggia di Venaria, Torino, 14–16 ottobre 2010* (*Architettura e potere* 2). Rome, Campisano Editore.

Cornaglia, P. (2012b) *Giuseppe Battista Piacenza e Carlo Randoni. I reali palazzi fra Torino e Genova (1773–1831)* Turin, Celid.

Corp, E. (1998) (ed.) *Lord Burlington: the Man and his Politics* (*Studies in British History* 48). Lewiston, NY/Lampeter, Edwin Mellen Press.

Corp, E. (2003) (ed.) *The Stuart Court in Rome. The Legacy of Exile*. Aldershot, Ashgate.

Corp, E. (2004a) *A Court in Exile: the Stuarts in France, 1689–1718*. Cambridge, Cambridge University Press.

Corp, E. (2004b) La Franc-Maçonnerie jacobite et la bulle papale *In Eminenti* d'avril 1738. *La Regle d'Abraham* 18: 13–44.

Corp, E. (2009) *The Jacobites at Urbino: an Exiled Court in Transition*. Basingstoke /New York, Palgrave Macmillan.

Corp, E. (2011a) *The Stuarts in Italy 1719–1766: a Court in Permanent Exile*. Cambridge, Cambridge University Press.

Corp, E. (2011b) The Stuart Court and the patronage of portrait-painters in Rome 1717–1757. In D.R. Marshall, S. Russell and K. Wolfe (eds), *Roma Britannica: Art Patronage and Cultural Exchange in Eighteenth-century Rome*: 39–53. London, British School at Rome.

Corp, E. (2013) *I giacobiti a Urbino: la corte in esilio di Giacomo III re d'Inghilterra*. Bologna, Il Mulino.

Correspondance des directeurs (1881–1914) *Correspondance des directeurs de l'Académie de France à Rome avec les surintendants des bâtiments*, 18 vols, ed. A. De Montaiglon. Paris, Charavay.

Courtney, W.P. (1900) Wood, Robert. In *Dictionary of National Biography* 62: 373–5. New York/London, MacMillan Company/Smith Elder & Co.

Cousins, W.F. Jr (1982) *The Ideal Port and the 'Concorsi Clementini' of 1728, 1732 and 1738 at the Accademia di San Luca in Rome*. Pennsylvania State University, PhD thesis.

Cozzo, P. (2006) *La geografia celeste dei Duchi di Savoia, religione, devozione e sacralità in uno stato di età moderna (secoli XVI–XVII)*. Bologna, Il Mulino.

Cozzo, P., De Pieri, F. and Merlotti, A. (2005) (eds) *Valdesi e protestanti a Torino. XVIII–XX secolo*. Turin, Zamorani.

Craig, M.J. (1948) *The Volunteer Earl*. London, Cresset Press.

Crespo Solana, A. and Schmidt-Voges, I. (in press) (eds) *New Worlds? Transformations in the Culture of International Relations c. 1713*. Aldershot, Ashgate.

Crinò, A.M. (1957) *Fatti e figure del Seicento anglo-toscano. Documenti inediti sui rapporti letterari, diplomatici, culturali fra Toscana e Inghilterra*. Florence, Olschki.

Croft, P. (1999) Can a bureaucrat be a favourite? Robert Cecil and the strategies of power. In J.H. Elliott and L.W.B. Brockliss (eds), *The World of the Favourite*: 81–95. New Haven, CT/London, Yale University Press.

Crotti, I. (1992) *Il viaggio e la forma. Giuseppe Baretti e l'orizzonte dei generi letterari*. Modena, Mucchi.

Curti, G. (1897) *Carlo Emanuele I secondo i più recenti studi*. Milan, *Tip. Bernardoni*.

Cusmano, S.C. (1998) Note sull'attività romana di Alessandro Galilei: alcuni progetti poco conosciuti. *Palladio* n.s. 11 (21): 87–102.

D'Agliano, A. (2008) (ed.) *Ricordi dell'antico: sculture, porcellane e arredi all'epoca del Grand Tour*. Rome, Musei Capitolini.

D'Agostino, L. (2005) Echi d'Oriente nelle tappezzerie della villa. I documenti d'archivio e le rare sopravvivenze. In L. Caterina and C. Mossetti (eds), *Villa della Regina. Il riflesso dell'Oriente nel Piemonte del Settecento*: 229–39. Turin, Umberto Allemandi.

D'Agostino, L. (2008) Le tappezzerie nelle stanze del Re tra storia e suggestioni. In C. Mossetti and P. Traversi (eds), *Juvarra a Villa della Regina. Le storie di Enea di Corrado Giaquinto*: 21–5. Turin, Editris.

D'Argenville, A.J. (1747) *La théorie et la pratique du jardinage*. Paris, P.J. Mariette. New edition (2003): Arles, Actes Sud /ENSP.

D'Aviler, C. (1710) *Cours d'Architecture*. Paris, Mariette.

Dagna, P. (1968) Un diplomatico ed economista del settecento: Carlo Baldassarre Perrone di San Martino (1718–1802). In P. Dagna *et al.*, *Figure e gruppi della classe dirigente piemontese nel Risorgimento*: 9–46. Turin, Istituto per la Storia del Risorgimento.

Dahlhaus, C. (1978) Storia europea della musica nell'età del classicismo viennese. *Nuova Rivista Musicale Italiana* 12 (4): 499–516.

Dahlhaus, C. (1985) Die italienische Instrumentalmusik als Emigrantenkultur. In C. Dahlhaus (ed.), *Neues Handbuch der Musikwissenschaft*, V (C. Dahlhaus *et al.* (eds), *Die Musik des 18. Jahrhunderts*): 210–16. Laaber, Laaber Verlag.

Dalmasso, F. (1980), La contessa Faustina Mazzetti a Riva presso Chieri. In E. Castelnuovo and M. Rosci (eds), *Cultura figurativa e architettonica negli Stati del Re di Sardegna / 1773–1861*, I: 170–3. Turin, Regione Piemonte.

Dangeau, P. de Courcillon de (1860) *Journal de marquis de Dangeau*. Paris, Didot Freres.

Dardanello, G. (1993a) Il Collegio dei Nobili e la piazza del principe di Carignano (1675–1684). In G. Romano (ed.), *Torino 1675–1699. Strategie e conflitti del Barocco*: 175–252. Turin, Cassa di Risparmio di Torino.

Dardanello, G. (1993b) La scena urbana. In G. Romano (ed.), *Torino 1675–1699. Strategie e conflitti del Barocco*: 15–120. Turin, Editris.

Dardanello, G. (2001) Filippo Juvarra: 'chi poco vede niente pensa'. In G. Dardanello (ed.), *Sperimentare l'architettura. Guarini, Juvarra, Alfieri, Borra e Vittone*: 97–176. Turin, Editris.

Dardanello, G. (2005) Simone Martinez e lo Studio di scultura a Torino. In G. Dardanello (ed.), *Sculture nel Piemonte del Settecento. 'Di differente e ben intesa bizzarria'*: 199–235. Torino, Fondazione CRT.

Dardanello, G. (2007a) Notizie di alcuni palazzi più riguardevoli di Torino. In G. Dardanello (ed.), *Disegnare l'ornato. Interni piemontesi di Sei e Settecento*: 241–5. Turin, Editris.

Dardanello, G. (2007b) Il variare nel gusto del disegno di ornato. In G. Dardanello (ed.), *Disegnare l'ornato. Interni piemontesi di Sei e Settecento*: 252–9. Turin, Editris.

Dardanello, G. (2008a) A gara, sui modelli di ornato di Sei e Settecento. In G. Dardanello and R. Tamborrino (eds), *Guarini, Juvarra e Antonelli. Segni e simboli per Torino*: 195–201. Cinisello Balsamo, Silvana Editoriale.

Dardanello, G. (2008b) Due disegni di Juvarra per la 'rimodernazione' di Villa della Regina. In C. Mossetti and P. Traversi (eds), *Juvarra a Villa della Regina: le storie di Enea di Corrado Giaquinto*: 59–70. Turin, Editris Duemila.

Dardanello, G. (2011) (ed.) *Beaumont e la scuola del disegno. Pittori e scultori in Piemonte alla metà del Settecento*. Cuneo, Nerosubianco.

Dardanello, G. (2013a) (ed.) *Giovanni Battista Borra da Palmira a Racconigi*. Turin, Editris.

Dardanello, G. (2013b) Da Palmira a Racconigi. Classicismi ellenistici alla prova della tradizione. In G. Dardanello (ed.), *Giovanni Battista Borra da Palmira a Racconigi*: 119–32. Turin, Editris.

Dardanello, G. (2013c) Topografo e vedutista. I disegni di Borra nel Levante. In G. Dardanello (ed.), *Giovanni Battista Borra da Palmira a Racconigi*: 65–96. Turin, Editris.

Davico, R. (1986) Banchi e 'famiglie' israelite e protestanti nel XVIII secolo in Piemonte. In *Mercati e consumi, organizzazione e qualificazione del commercio in Italia dal XII al XX secolo*: 109–33. Bologna, Analisi.

Davies, G. (1959) *The Early Stuarts 1603–1660*. Oxford, Clarendon.

Daynes, G.W. (1924) The Duke of Lorraine and English Freemasonry in 1731. *Ars Quatuor Coronatorum* 37: 107–43.

De Bernardin, S. (1983) I riformatori dello studio: indirizzi di politica culturale nell'Università di Padova. In *Storia della cultura veneta*, 4/1: 65–72. Vicenza, Neri Pozza.

De Blasi, S. (2012) (ed.) *Il Bucintoro dei Savoia (Atti del convegno internazionale di studi, Venaria Reale, 22–23 marzo 2012)*. Turin, Editris.

de Carvalho, A. (1958) Domenico Duprà: royal portrait painter to various European courts. *Connoisseur Year Book*: 78–85.

De Gregory, G. (1817) *Vita di Jacopo Durandi*. Turin, Pomba.

De Jesus, F. (1869) *El hecho de los tratados del matrimonio pretendido per el Principe de Gales con la Serenissima Infante de Espana*. London, Cadmen.

De Ligne, C.J. (1922) *Coup d'oeil sur Beloeil et sur une grande partie des jardins de l'Europe*. Paris, Bossard (original publication: Paris, 1786).

De Sainte-Maure, C. (1725) *A New Journey through Greece, Aegypt, Palestine, Italy, Swisserland, Alsatia, and the Netherlands Written by a French Officer, who Travelled those Countries in the Years, 1721 … 1723; Now First Done into English*. London, J. Batley.

Defabiani, V. (1990) Racconigi. Castello. In C. Roggero Bardelli, M.G. Vinardi and V. Defabiani (eds), *Ville Sabaude*: 368–409. Milan, Rusconi.

Defoe, D. (1748) *A Tour Thro' the Whole Island of Great Britain*, 4 vols (fourth edition). London.

Del Negro, P. (2003) L'istituzione di un principe collettivo: la formazione del patriziato veneziano quale classe politica nel Settecento. In *L'institution du prince au XVIIIe siècle*: 95–102. Ferney-Voltaire, Centre International d'Étude du XVIIIe Siècle.

Delaforce, A. (2002) *Art and Patronage in Eighteenth Century Portugal*. Cambridge, Cambridge University Press.

Dell'Oro, G. (2007) *Il regio economato. Il controllo statale sul clero nella Lombardia asburgica e nei domini sabaudi*. Milan, Franco Angeli.

Delpiano, P. (1997) *Il trono e la cattedra. Istruzione e formazione dell'élite nel Piemonte del Settecento*. Turin, Deputazione Subalpina di Storia Patria.

Denbigh, C. (1915) *Royalist Father and Royalist Son. Being the Memoirs of the First and Second Earls of Denbigh, 1600–1675*. London.

Denina, C. (1796) *Considérations d'un italien sur l'Italie ou mémoires sur l'état actuel des lettres et des arts en Italie et le caractere de ses habitants. Précédés d'une lettre sur le tour de l'Allemagne, la Suisse, et la Savie*. Berlin, Pitra.

Desgodetz, A. (1682) *Les edifices antiques de Rome, dessinés et mesurés très exactement par Antoine Desgodetz architecte*. Paris, Jean Baptiste Coignard.

Di Benedetto, A. (1993) *Varia fortuna di Giuseppe Baretti nell'Ottocento*. In A. Martorelli (ed.), *Giuseppe Baretti letterato e viaggiatore. Atti del convegno (Napoli, 15 dicembre 1989)*: 75–99. Naples, Valentino Editore.

Di Profio, A. (2003) *La révolution des bouffons. L'opéra italien au Théâtre de Monsieur 1789–1792*. Paris, CNRS Éditions.

Di Tocco, V. (1926) *Ideali d'indipendenza in Italia durante la preponderanza spagnola*. Messina, Principato.

Dionisotti, C. (1988) Piemontesi e spiemontizzati. In *Appunti sui moderni: Foscolo, Leopardi, Manzoni e altri*. Bologna, Il Mulino.

DNB (1895 following) *Dictionary of National Biography*. London, Smith, Elder & Co.

Downes, K. (1959) *Nicholas Hawksmoor*. London, Zwemmer.

Downes, K. (1982) *The Architecture of Christopher Wren*. London, Granada.

Duboin, F.A. (1818–69) *Raccolta per ordine di materie delle leggi cioè editti, patenti, manifesti ecc. … emanate negli Stati di terraferma sino l'8 dicembre 1798 dai sovrani della Real Casa di Savoia, compilata dall'avvocato Felice Amato Duboin*, 24 vols. Turin, Baricco e Arnaldi.

Dubost, J.-F. (2000) Les étrangers à Paris au siècle des lumières. In D. Roche (ed.), *La ville promise*: 221–88. Paris, Fayard.

Durandi, J. (1766) *Opere drammatiche*, 4 vols. Turin, Davico.

Dutens, L. (1806a) *Mémoires d'un voyageur qui se repose; contenant des anecdotes historiques, politiques et littéraires, relatives à plusieurs des principaux personnages du siècle*, 3 vols. Paris, Bossange, Masson et Besson.

Dutens, L. (1806b) *Memoirs of a Traveller, Now in Retirement, Written by himself Interspersed with Historical, Literary and Political Anecdotes*, 5 vols. London, Richard Phillips.

El Kenz, D. and Gantet, C. (2003) *Guerre et paix de religion en Europe XVI–XVII siècles*. Paris, Collin.

Elliott, J.H. (1983) A question of reputation: Spanish foreign policy. *Seventeenth Century. Journal of Modern History* 55: 475–83.

Erba, A. (1979) *La chiesa sabauda tra Cinque e Seicento. Ortodossia tridentina, gallicanesimo savoiardo e assolutismo ducale (1580–1630)*. Rome, Herder.

Erskine, D. (1953) (ed.) *Augustus Hervey's Journal*. London, William Kimber.

Erskine, D. (2002) (ed.) *Augustus Hervey's Journal. The Adventures Afloat and Ashore of a Naval Casanova*. London, Chatham Publishing.

Eustace, J.C. (1815) *A Classical Tour through Italy. MDCCCI* (third edition), 4 vols. London, Mawman.

Evenden, E. and Freedman, T.S. (2011) *Religion and the Book in Early Modern England: the Making of John Foxe's Book of Martyrs*. Cambridge, Cambridge University Press.

Evinson, D. (1998), *Catholic Churches of London*. Sheffield, Sheffield Academic Press.

Fabrizi, A. (2008) Alfieri 1766. *Seicento e Settecento. Rivista di Letteratura Italiana* 3: 211–31.

Facey, J. (1987) John Foxe and the defence of the English Church. In P. Lake and M. Dowling (eds), *Protestantism and the National Church in Sixteenth Century England*. London/New York/Sydney, Croom Helm.

Farrell, J.K.A. (1967) *The Church of St. Anselm and St. Cecilia: a Short History*. London, Burleigh Press.

Fatsar, K. (2008), *Magyarországi Barokk Kertművészet*. Budapest, Helikon.

Fedi, F. (2004) Diplomazia, collezionismo e massoneria nel tardo Settecento (il caso Denon). In F. Fedi, *Artifici di numi. Favole antiche e utopie moderne fra Illuminismo ed età napoleonica*: 113–35. Rome, Bulzoni.

Fedi, F. (2006) Comunicazione letteraria e 'generi massonici' nel Settecento italiano. In G.M. Cazzaniga (ed.), *Storia d'Italia. Annali 21. La Massoneria*: 50–89. Turin, Einaudi.

Fedi, F. (2007) Fra Corinto e il Nuovo Mondo: il paradigma di Timoleone nel dramma di Alfieri. In F. Fedi, *Un programma per Melpomene. Il concorso parmigiano di poesia drammatica e la scrittura tragica in Italia*: 91–112. Milan, Unicopli.

Fedi, F. (2014) Alfieri, Vittorio. In G. Sasso (ed.), *Enciclopedia Machiavelliana*, I: 39–42. Roma, Istituto della Enciclopedia Italiana.

Fedi, F. (2015) Una foresta tra storia e politica: osservazioni su Alfieri traduttore di Pope. In L. Bani and M. Sirtori (eds), *Lo sguardo tra prosa e lirica nella letteratura italiana, Studi in onore di Matilde Dillon Wanke*: 117–29. Bergamo, Lubrina.

Fénelon, F. Salignac de La Mothe (1999) *Fénelon, Correspondance*, XVII, *Les dernières années, 1712–1715*, eds J. Orcibal, J. Le Brun and I. Noye. Geneva, Droz.

Ferrer Benimeli, J.A. (1985) La prima loggia a Firenze. In M. Moramarco (ed.), *250 anni di Massoneria in Italia*: 15–48. Livorno, Bastogi.

Ferrer Benimeli, J.A. (2010) La présence de la Franc-Maçonnerie stuardiste à Madrid et à Rome. *Politica hermetica* 24: 68.

Ferrone, V. (1988) *La Nuova Atlantide e i Lumi. Scienza e politica nel Piemonte di Vittorio Amedeo III*. Turin, Meynier.

Ferrone, V. (1991) La massoneria settecentesca in Piemonte e nel Regno di Sardegna. In Z. Ciuffoletti (ed.), *La massoneria e le forme di sociabilità nell'Europa del Settecento* (*Il Vieusseux*, IV, 11): 103–30. Florence, Gabinetto Scientifico Letterario il Vieusseux.

Ferrone, V. (1998) The Accademia delle scienze: cultural sociability and men of letters in Turin of the Enlightenment under Vittorio Amedeo III. *Journal of Modern History* 70: 519–60.

Ferrone, V. and Tocchini, G. (2006) La massoneria nel Regno di Sardegna. In G.M. Cazzaniga (ed.), *Storia d'Italia. Annali,* 21, *La Massoneria*: 333–54. Turin, Einaudi.

Fido, F. (1967) *Introduzione a Baretti, G. Opere.* Milan, Rizzoli.

Fido, F. (1989) In Inghilterra: reportage e letteratura comparata. In F. Fido, *Le muse perdute e ritrovate. Il divenire dei generi letterari fra Sette e Ottocento.* Florence, Vallecchi.

Figgis, N. (1993) The Roman property of Frederick Augustus Hervey, 4th Earl of Bristol and Bishop of Derry (1730–1803). *The Walpole Society Journal*: 77–104.

Fina, G. (1997) *Maestri argentieri ed argenterie alla corte di Carlo Emanuele III e Vittorio Amedeo III 1730–1796.* Turin, Tipografia Intergraph.

Fina, G. and Mana, L. (2012) *Argenti Sabaudi del XVIII secolo.* Milan, Silvana Editoriale.

Finscher, L. (1993) Italienische Komponisten und italienische Instrumentalmusik in der Fremde: Bemerkungen zur ‚italienischen Instrumentalmusik als Emigrantenkultur' im 18. Jahrhundert. In *Luigi Boccherini e la musica strumentale dei maestri italiani in Europa tra Sette e Ottocento. Proceedings of the international conference (Siena, 29–31 July 1993) = Chigiana* 43, n.s. 23: 353–62.

Firminger, W.K. (1937) Freemasonry in Savoy. Studies in continental XVIIIth century Freemasonry and Freemasonry so called. *Ars Quatuor Coronatorum* 46: 325.

Firpo, L. (1965–84) (ed.) *Relazioni di ambasciatori veneti al Senato, tratte dalle migliori edizioni disponibili e ordinate cronologicamente,* 14 vols. Turin, Bottega d'Erasmo.

Fischer von Erlach, J.B. (1721) *Entwurff einer Historischen Architektur, in Abbildung Unterschiedener Berühmten Gebäude, des Alterthums, und Fremder Völker.* Vienna.

Fitz-Gerald, D. (1973) *The Norfolk House Music Room.* London, HMSO.

Fleming, J. (1956) The Pluras of Turin and Bath. *The Connoisseur* November 1956: 175–81.

Foa, S. (1930) *Vittorio Amedeo I (1587–1637).* Turin, Paravia.

Ford, B. and Penny, N. (1998) *The Ford Collection* – II. *The Sixtieth Volume of The Walpole Society.* London, Walpole Society.

Formica, M., Merlotti, A. and Rao, A.M. (2014) (eds) *La città nel Settecento. Saperi e forme di rappresentazione.* Rome, Edizioni di Storia e Letteratura.

Fortgesetzte Neue Genealogisch-historische (1769) *Fortgesetzte Neue Genealogisch-historische Nachrichten von den Vornehmsten.* Leipzig, Heinsius.

Fossier, F. (1997) *Les dessins du fonds Robert de Cotte de la Bibliotheque Nationale de France. Architecture et décor.* Paris, Bibliothèque Nationale de France.

Fothergill. B. (2010) *The Mitred Earl. Frederick Hervey, Earl of Bristol and Bishop of Derry. An Eighteenth Century Eccentric.* London, Faber and Faber.

Foussard, D. and Barbier, G. (1988) (eds) *Baroque Niçois et Monégasque.* Paris, Picard.

Fragiacomo, G. (2000) Un esempio settecentesco di collezionismo in canavese: il caso del conte Baldassarre Perrone di San Martino. In B. Signorelli and P. Uscello (eds), *Archeologia e arte in canavese. Atti del Convegno della Società Piemontese di Archeologia e Belle Arti 11–12 settembre 1998*: 313–49. Turin, Celid.

Francovich, C. (1974) *Storia della Massoneria in Italia dalle origini alla Rivoluzione francese*. Florence, La Nuova Italia.

Fratini, M. (2004) (ed.) *L'annessione sabauda del marchesato di Saluzzo, tra dissidenza religiosa e ortodossia cattolica, secc. XVI–XVIII*. Turin, Claudiana.

Friedman, T.F. (1976) Sir Thomas Gascoigne and his friends in Italy. *Leeds Art Calendar* 78: 16–23.

Friedmann, T. (1988) Lord Harrold in Italy 1715–16: four frustrated commissions to Leoni, Juvarra, Chiari and Soldani. *The Burlington Magazine* 130.1028: 836–45.

Futter, C. (2008) Grugliasco, regione Gerbido Villa Vacchetta, già il Palazzo: Gabinetto Cinese. In L. Caterina and C. Mossetti (eds), *Villa della Regina. Il riflesso dell'Oriente nel Piemonte del Settecento*: 567–73. Turin/London/Venice/New York, Allemandi.

Futter, C. and Twilley, J. (2010) Chinoiserie in northern Italy: japanned decoration in a rare eighteenth-century Piedmontese 'Gabinetto' in the Nelson-Atkins Museum of Art. *Furniture History* 66: 137–55.

Gabrielli, N. (1971) *Racconigi*. Turin, Istituto Bancario San Paolo di Torino.

Gady, A. (2010a) 'Bâti entérement dans le gôut françois?' Jules Hardouin-Mansart et l'architecture française en Europ. In P. Cornaglia (ed.), *Michelangelo Garove: 1648–1713. Un architetto per Vittorio Amedeo II*: 25–37. Rome, Campisano.

Gady, A. (2010b) (ed.) *Jules Hardouin-Mansart: 1646–1708*. Paris, Éditions de la Maison des Sciences de l'Homme.

Gal, S. (2012) *Charles-Emmanuel de Savoie. La politique du précipice*. Paris, Payot et Rivages.

Gallet, M. (1995) *Les architectes parisiens du XVIIIᵉ siècle. Dictionnaire biographique et critique*. Paris, Mengès.

Garms, J. (1969) Die Architekturthemen des Concorso Clementino der Accademia di San Luca von 1732. *Wiener Jahrbuch für Kunstgeschichte* 22: 194–200.

Gaspari, G.M. (1995) Stendhal e il mito dell''école de Milan'. *Studi Settecenteschi* 15: 331–64.

Geraghty, A. (2007) *The Architectural Drawings of Sir Christopher Wren at All Souls College, Oxford: a Complete Catalogue*. Aldershot, Lund Humphries.

Ghisotti, S. (2005a) Fonti per la ricerca sulla cineseria in Piemonte nel Settecento: tempi, luoghi, artisti e committenti. In L. Caterina and C. Mossetti (eds), *Villa della Regina. Il riflesso dell'Oriente nel Piemonte del Settecento*: 403–22. Turin, Umberto Allemandi.

Ghisotti, S. (2005b) Racconigi, Castello. In L. Caterina and C. Mossetti (eds), *Villa della Regina. Il riflesso dell'Oriente nel Piemonte del Settecento*: 502–5, 508, 512, 516. Turin, Umberto Allemandi.

Ghisotti, S. (2005c) Venaria Reale, Castello. In Caterina, L. and Mossetti, C. (eds), *Villa della Regina. Il rifl esso dell'Oriente nel Piemonte del Settecento*: 490–93. Turin, Umberto Allemandi.

Ghisotti, S. (2005d) Torino, Palazzo Lascaris. In L. Caterina and C. Mossetti (eds), *Villa della Regina. Il riflesso dell'Oriente nel Piemonte del Settecento*: 517. Turin, Umberto Allemandi.

Ghisotti, S. (2005e) Chieri, Villa Moglia. In L. Caterina and C. Mossetti (eds), *Villa della Regina. Il riflesso dell'Oriente nel Piemonte del Settecento*: 574. Turin, Umberto Allemandi.

Ghisotti, S. (2005f) Ivrea, Palazzo Perrone poi Giusiana. In L. Caterina and C. Mossetti (eds), *Villa della Regina. Il riflesso dell'Oriente nel Piemonte del Settecento*: 626. Turin, Umberto Allemandi.

Ghisotti, S. (2005g) Torino, Palazzo Reale. Gabinetto cinese già Gabinetto di toeletta. Appartamento della duchessa di Savoia. In L. Caterina and C. Mossetti (eds), *Villa della Regina. Il riflesso dell'Oriente nel Piemonte del Settecento*: 474–6. Turin, Umberto Allemandi.

Ghisotti, S. (2005h) Govone, Castello. In L. Caterina and C. Mossetti (eds), *Villa della Regina. Il riflesso dell'Oriente nel Piemonte del Settecento*: 592–3. Turin, Umberto Allemandi.

Ghisotti, S., Manchinu, P. and Traversi, P. (2005a) Racconigi, Castello. In L. Caterina and C. Mossetti (eds), *Villa della Regina. Il riflesso dell'Oriente nel Piemonte del Settecento*: 502–19. Turin, Umberto Allemandi.

Ghisotti, S., Manchinu, P. and Traversi, P. (2005b) Riva di Chieri, Palazzo Grosso Torino, Palazzo Reale. Gabinetto cinese già Gabinetto di toeletta. Appartamento della duchessa di Savoia. Moncalieri, Castello Gabinetto Cinese. In L. Caterina and C. Mossetti (eds), *Villa della Regina. Il riflesso dell'Oriente nel Piemonte del Settecento*: 484–88, 498–501, 578–81. Turin, Umberto Allemandi.

Gialluca, B. (2014) (ed.) *Seduzione etrusca. Dai segreti di Holkham Hall alle meraviglie del British Museum*. Milan, Skira.

Giarrizzo, G. (1994) *Massoneria e Illuminismo nell'Europa del Settecento*. Venice, Marsilio.

Giazotto, R. (1956) *Giovan Battista Viotti*. Milan, Curci.

Gibson, E. (1987) The Royal Academy of Music (1719–28) and its directors. In S. Sadie and A. Hicks (eds), *Handel Tercentenary Collection*. Rochester, NY, University of Rochester Press.

Gibson, E. (1990) Italian Opera in London, 1750–1775: management and finances. *Early Music* 18 (1): 47–59.

Gilardi, L.M. (1998) Padre Carlo Maurizio Vota e il suo epistolario con la Real Casa di Savoia. In *La Compagnia di Gesù nella Provincia di Torino dagli anni di Emanuele Filiberto a quelli di Carlo Alberto*: 113–32. Turin, Società Piemontese di Archeologia e Belle Arti [Celid].

Gilman, T. (2013) *The Theatre Career of Thomas Arne*. Plymouth, University of Delaware Press.

Girgenti, A. (1994) Vittorio Amedeo II e la cessione della Sardegna: trattative diplomatiche e scelte politiche. *Studi Storici* 35 (3): 677–704.

Giusti, M.A. (2015) Giardini e parchi del Canavese. Montalto Dora, San Giorgio. In P. Cornaglia and M.A. Giusti (eds), *Il risveglio del giardino. Dall'hortus al paesaggio, studi, esperienze, confronti*: 114–36. Lucca, Maria Pacini Fazzi Editore.

Giusto, R.M. (2010) *Alessandro Galilei: Il trattato di architettura*. Rome, Argos.

Gjerdingen, R.O. (2007) *Music in the Galant Style*. Oxford, Oxford University Press.

Goodwin, G. (2004/2008) (ed.) Hervey, George William, second earl of Bristol (1721–1775). Rev. R.D.E. Eagles. In H.C.G. Matthew and B. Harrison (eds), *Oxford Dictionary of National Biography*. Oxford, Oxford University Press (2004). Online edition, edited L. Goldman, 2008.

Graf, A. (1911) *L'anglomania e l'influsso inglese in Italia nel secolo XVIII*. Turin, Loescher.

Grant, K. (2011) Planting 'Italian Gusto' in a 'Gothick Country': the influence of Filippo Juvarra on William Kent. In D.R. Marshall, S. Russell and K.E. Wolfe (eds), *Roma Britannica. Art Patronage and Cultural Exchange in Eighteenth-century Rome*: 225–39. London, British School at Rome.

Graziano, A. (1984) Uso e diffusione dell'inglese. In L. Formigari (ed.), *Teorie e pratiche linguistiche nell'Italia del Settecento*: 373–94. Bologna, Il Mulino.

Greig, J.Y.T. (1932) *The Letters of David Hume*. Oxford, Oxford University Press.

Gribaudi, P. (1904–5) Questioni di precedenza fra le corti italiane nel secolo XVI. Contributo alla storia della diplomazia italiana. *Rivista di Scienze Storiche* 1: 164–77, 278–5, 347–56; 2: 29–38, 126–41.

Griseri, A. (2004) Torino 1731: il palcoscenico sul fiume e le sue quinte. In D. Lenzi (ed.), *Arti a confronti. Studi in onore di Anna Maria Matteucci*: 269–75. Bologna, Editrice Compositori.

Griseri, A. and Romano, G. (1986) (eds) *Porcellane e Argenti del Palazzo Reale di Torino*. Milan, Fabbri Editori.

Griseri, A. and Romano, G. (1989) (eds) *Filippo Juvarra a Torino. Nuovi progetti per la città*. Turin, Cassa di Risparmio di Torino.

Gritella, G. (1992) *Juvarra. L'architettura*, 2 vols. Modena, Panini.

Griva, L. (1995) La peota di Carlo Emanuele III di Savoia (1730). Nuovi documenti. *Studi Piemontesi* 10–11: 411–17.

Grohmann, J.G. (1796–7) *Ideenmagazin für Liebhaber von Gärten, Englischen Anlagen und für Besitzer von Landgütern*. Leipzig, F.G. Baumgärtner.

Grohmann, J.G. (1805) *Recueil de dessins d'une execution peu dispendieuse*. Venice, Remondini.

Grohmann, J.G. (1835–42) *Ideen-Magazin für Architekten, Künstler und Handwerker*. Leipzig, Baumgartner.

Gualano, F. (1997) Carlo Giuseppe Plura, scultore in legno nel Piemonte Sabaudo. *Studi Piemontesi* 26 (2): 277–99.

Gualano, F. (2000) Un 'quartetto' rococò nella chiesa torinese di San Filippo Neri. *Bollettino della Società Piemontese di Archeologia e Belle Arti* 49: 147–54.

Gualano, F. (2011) Il 'signor Plura, scultore rarissimo'. Un Luganese alla corte sabauda. In G. Mollisi (ed.), *Svizzeri a Torino nella storia, nell'arte, nella cultura, nell'economia dal Cinquecento ad oggi*. Lugano, Edizioni Ticino Management: 376–97.

Guasti, C. (1857) Di un trattato di nozze tra la casa di Savoia e i reali d'Inghilterra. *Giornale Storico degli Archivi Toscani* 1: 55–71, 175–282.

Guglielmetto Mugion, D. and Caterino, R. (2013) I luoghi disegnati nel viaggio nel Levante. In G. Dardanello (ed.), *Giovanni Battista Borra da Palmira a Racconigi*: 38–40. Turin, Editris.

Gunnis, R. (1968) *Dictionary of British Sculptors 1660–1851*. London, Abbey Library.

Habermas, J. (1962) *Strukturwandel der Oeffentlichkeit*. Neuwied, H.Luchterhand Verlag. Italian translation: Illuminati, A., Masini, F. and Perretta, W. (1988) *Storia e critica dell'opinione pubblica*. Bari, Laterza; first edition 1971.

Hager, H. (1970) *Filippo Juvarra e il concorso di modelli del 1715 bandito da Clemente XI per la nuova sacrestia di S. Pietro*. Rome, De Luca.

Halsband, R. (1973) *Lord Hervey, Eighteenth-century Courtier*. Oxford, University Press.

Handover, P.M. (1965) *A History of The London Gazette: 1665–1965*. London, HMSO.

Hans, N. (1958) The Masonic Lodge in Florence in the eighteenth century. *ARS Quatuor Coronatorum (Transactions of the Quatuor Coronati Lodge)* 71: 109–12.

Harris, J. (1968) Introduction. In *A Treatise on the Decorative Part of Civil Architecture London, Smeeton 1791*. New York/London, Blom.

Harris, E. and Savage, N. (1990) *British Architectural Books and Writers 1556–1785*. Cambridge, Cambridge University Press.

Harting, J.H. (2012) *History of the Sardinian Chapel, Lincoln's Inn Fields (1905)*. London, Nabu Press.

Haskell, F. and Penny, N. (1981) (eds) *Taste and the Antique. The Lure of Classical Sculpture, 1500–1900*. New Haven, CT/London, Yale University Press.

Hatfield, J.A. (1981) *The Relationship Between Late Baroque Architecture and Scenography 1703–1778: the Italian Influence of Ferdinando and Giuseppe Bibiena, Filippo Juvarra, and Giovanni Battista Piranesi*. Wayne State University, PhD thesis.

Hayden, J.M. (1973) Continuity in the France of Henry IV and Louis XIII. French foreign policy, 1598–1615. *Journal of Modern History* 45: 1–23.

Hazard, P. (1968) *La crisi della coscienza europea*. Milan, Il Saggiatore.

Heartz, D. (2003) *Music in European Capitals. The Galant Style 1720–1780*. New York/London, W.W. Norton & Company.

Hervey, Rev. S.A.H. (1894) (ed.) *The Diary of John Hervey, first Earl of Bristol. With Extracts from his Book of Expenses, 1688 to 1742*. Wells, Ernest Jackson.

Hewlings, R. (1985) James Leoni c. 1685–1746. An Anglicized Venetian. In R. Brown (ed.), *The Architectural Outsiders*: 21–43. London, Waterstone.

Hewlings, R. (1994) *Chiswick House and Gardens, Greater London*. London, English Heritage.

HHA: Holkham Hall Archives, Holkham Hall, Wells-next-to-the-Sea, Norfolk, UK.

Hibbard, C. (1983) *Charles I and the Popish Plot*. Chapel Hill, University of North Carolina Press.

Hibbert, C. (1987) *The Grand Tour*. London, Thames Methuen.

Hirst, D. (1999) *England in Conflict 1603–1660, Kingdom, Community, Commonwealth*. London, Arnold.

Historical Manuscripts Commission (1902–23) *The Stuart Papers at Windsor Castle*, 7 volumes. London, HM Stationery Office.

Historical Manuscripts Commission (1911) *Report on the Manuscripts of the Earl of Denbigh Preserved at Newnham Paddox, Warwickshire*, V, Part I. Hereford, HMSO.

Historical Manuscripts Commission (1913) *Report on MSS. in Various Collections*, VIII. London. (The Manuscripts of The Hon Frederick Lindley Wood; M.L.S. Clements Esq.; S. Philip Unwin, Esq.).

Holburne (2011) *The Holburne Museum*. London, Scala Publishers.

Horn, D.B (1932), *British Diplomatic Representatives, 1689–1789 (Camden Series)*. London, Royal Historical Society.

Hughan, W.J. (1910) *The Jacobite Lodge in Rome (1735–37)*. Leicester, Lodge of Research.

Hughes, C.E. (1901) Dawkins, James. In S. Lee (ed.), *Dictionary of National Biography*, Supplement II: 119–20. London, Smith, Elder & Co.

Hume, D. (1983–5) *The History of England from the Invasion of Julius Caesar to the Revolution in 1688. Based on the Edition of 1778, with the Author's Last Corrections and Improvements*, 6 vols. Indianapolis, IN, Liberty Fund.

Hyde Minor, H. (2010) *The Culture of Architecture in Enlightenment Rome*. University Park, PA, Pennsylvania State University Press.

Iamartino, G. (1994) Baretti maestro d'italiano in Inghilterra e l'easy phraseology.' In R.S. Crivelli and L. Sampietro (eds), *Il 'passaggiere' italiano. Saggi sulle letterature di lingua inglese in onore di Sergio Rossi*: 383–419. Rome, Bulzoni.

Ilchester, Earl of (1950) *Lord Hervey and his Friends 1726–38*. London, John Murray.

Ingamells, J. (1997) (ed.) *A Dictionary of British and Irish Travellers in Italy. 1701–1800, Compiled from the Brinsley Ford Archive*. New Haven, CT/London, Yale University Press.

Ison, W. (1980) *The Georgian Buildings of Bath from 1700 to 1830*. Bath, Kingsmead Press.

Jacobsen, H. (2014) *Luxury and Power. The Material World of the Stuart Diplomat, 1660–1714*. Oxford, Oxford University Press.

James, C.W. (1929) *Chief Justice Coke His Family and Descendants at Holkham*. London, Country Life.

Jestaz, B. (2008) *Jules Hardouin-Mansart*. Paris, Picard.

Johns, C. (2016) *China and the Church: Chinoiserie in Global Context*. Berkeley, University of California Press.

Jonard, N. (1963) *Giuseppe Baretti (1719–1789). L'homme et l'oeuvre*. Clermont-Ferrand, G. de Bussac.

Jonard, N. (1990) G. Baretti e gli illuministi francesi. In M. Cerruti and P. Trivero (eds), *Giuseppe Baretti: un piemontese in Europa. Atti del convegno di studi (Torino, 21–22 settembre 1990)*: 1–20. Alessandria, Edizioni dell'Orso.

Jones, K. and Garibaldi, C. (2006) Crespin or Sprimont? A question revisited. *Silver Studies* 21: 24–38.

Jori, I. (1942) *Genealogia sabauda*. Bologna, Zanichelli.

Kamen, H. (1969) *The War of Succession in Spain, 1700–15*. London, Weidenfeld and Nicolson.

Kamen, H. (2001) *Philip V of Spain: the King Who Reigned Twice*. New Haven, CT/London, Yale University Press.

Kieven, E. (1973) Alessandro Galilei in England. *Country Life* 3944: 210–12.

Kieven, E. (1975) The Gascoigne Monument by Alessandro Galilei. *Leeds Art Calendar* 77: 13–23.

Kieven, E. (2008a) An Italian architect in London: the case of Alessandro Galilei (1691–1737). *Architectural History* 51: 1–31.

Kieven, E. (2008b) Models of perfection: John Talman and Roman baroque architecture. In C.M. Sicca (ed.), *John Talman. An Early Eighteenth-century Connoisseur* (*Studies in British Art* 19): 189–209. New Haven, CT/London, Yale University Press.

Kieven, E. and Ruggero, C. (2014) (eds) *Filippo Juvarra (1678–1736), architetto dei Savoia, architetto in Europa. Atti del Convegno internazionale (Torino, 2011)*, 2 vols. Rome, Campisano.

Kishlansky, M. (1996) *A Monarchy Transformed. Britain 1603–1714*. London, Penguin.

Kneas Hill, P. (1977) *The Oglethorpe Ladies and the Jacobite Conspiracies*. Atlanta, GA, Cherokee Publishing Company.

Koller, A. (2008) (ed.) *Die Außenbeziehungen der Römischen Kurie unter Paul V. Borghese (1605–1621)*. Tübingen, Niemeyer.

La Laurencie, L. de (1922–4) *L'école française de violon de Lully à Viotti. Études d'histoire et d'esthétique*, 3 vols. Paris, Librairie Delagrave.

Landon, H.C.R. (1976–80) *Haydn: Chronicle and Works*, 5 vols. London, Thames and Hudson (Bloomington, Indiana University Press, 1980).

Larminie, V. (2006) The Jacobean diplomatic fraternity and the Protestant cause: Sir Isaac Wake and the view from Savoy. *The English Historical Review* 121: 1300–26.

Lart, C.E. (1912) *The Parochial Registers of Saint-Germain-en-Laye: Jacobite Extracts*, II. London, Saint Catherine Press.

Le Bihan, A. (1967) Aux origines de la Franc-Maçonnerie française. *Annales. Économies, Sociétés, Civilisations* 22 (2): 396–411.

Le Dantec, J.P. (1996) *Jardins et paysages*. Paris, Larousse.

Le Rouge, G.L. (2004), *Les jardins anglo-chinois* (par Véronique Royet). Paris, Bibliothèque Nationale de France.

Lees-Milne, J. (1962) Richard Boyle 3rd earl of Burlington 1694–1753. In J. Lees-Milne, *The Earls of Creation. Five Great Patrons of Eighteenth-century Art*: 83–169. London, Richard Clay.

Lees-Milne, J. (1970) *English Country Houses: Baroque 1685–1715*. Feltham, Antique Collectors Club.

Lees-Milne, J. (1986) *Earls of Creation, Five Great Patrons of Eighteenth-century Art*. London, Century Hutchinson.

Leoni, G. (1715) *The Architecture of A. Palladio, in Four Books*. London.

Leopardi, G. (1989, 1992) *Discorso sopra lo stato presente dei costumi degl'Italiani*, ed. A. Placanica. Venice, Marsilio.

Les Français à Saint-Petersbourg (2003) *Les Français à Saint-Petersbourg*. Paris, Palacé Édition.

Levi Momigliano, L. (2009) Da Casale a Aix-en-Provence: calchi in gesso, stucchi e modelli: confronti suggeriti da Giovanni Romano in visita a Masino. In G. Agosti, G. Dardanello, G. Galante Garrone and A. Quazza (eds), *Per Giovanni Romano. Scritti di amici*: 106–7. Savigliano, L'Artistica.

Levi, G. (1967) La seta e l'economia piemontese del Settecento. A proposito di un saggio inedito di Dalmazzo Francesco Vasco. *Rivista Storica Italiana*: 803–00.

Levy Peck, L. (1990) *Court Patronage and Corruption in Early Stuart England*. London, Routledge.

Lewis, L. (1961) *Connoisseurs and Secret Agents in Eighteenth-century Rome*. London, Chatto and Windus.

Lewis, W.S. (1937–83) (ed.) *Horace Walpole's Correspondence*, 48 vols. New Haven, CT, Yale University Press.

Lewis, W.S. (1955) *The Yale Edition of Horace Walpole's Correspondence*, XXI. New Haven, CT, Yale University Press.

Lewis, W.S. (1974) *The Yale Edition of Horace Walpole's Correspondence*, XXXVIII. New Haven, CT, Yale University Press.

Lindon, J. (1995) *L'Inghilterra di Vittorio Alfieri e altri studi alfieriani*. Modena, Mucchi.

Lister, W. (2009) *Amico. The Life of Giovanni Battista Viotti*. Oxford, Oxford University Press.

Lomax, J. (1992) *British Silver at Temple Newsam and Lotherton Hall*. Leeds, Leeds Art Collections Fund/ W.S. Maney and Son.

Lords (1771) *Journal of the House of Lords*, XI *(1660–66)*. London.

Lorenzo, C.C. (1991) *Palazzo Graneri: dal 1858 sede del Circolo degli artisti di Torino*. Turin, D. Piazza.

Loudon, J.C. (1828) *The Gardener's Magazine* 3: 227.

McCarthy, M. (2001) (ed.) *Lord Charlemont and his Circle. Essays in Honour of Michael Wynne* (*UCD Studies in the History of Art* 1). Dublin, Four Courts Press.

McCarthy, M. (2007) Drawings of Rome and Tivoli in 1750 by Giovanni Battista Borra. In J.V. Luce, C. Morris and C. Souyoudzoglou-Haywood (eds), *The Lure of Greece. Irish Involvement in Greek Culture, Literature, History and Politics, A Selection of Papers Presented at a Conference Organised by the Irish Institute of Hellenic Studies at Athens, and Held in the National University of Ireland, Galway, 19–21 September 2003*: 89–99. Dublin, Hinds Publishers.

McDonnell, H. (1996) *The Wild Geese of the Antrim MacDonnells*. Sallins, Irish Academic Press.

Macera, M. (2007) (ed.) *Un giardino per Josephine. Paesaggi di una principessa del Settecento*. Racconigi, Le Terre dei Savoia Edizioni.

Macera, M. and Naretto, M. (2009) Roda Giuseppe Pietro, Roda Marcellino. In V. Cazzato (ed), *Atlante del giardino italiano 1750–1940. Dizionario biografico di architetti, giardinieri, botanici, committenti, letterati e altri protagonisti* I: 115–21. Rome, Istituto Poligrafico e Zecca dello Stato.

McKay, D. and Scott, H.M. (1983) *The Rise of the Great Powers 1648–1815*. Harlow, Longman.

McParland, E. (1994) Sir Thomas Hewett and the new junta for architecture. In G. Worsley (ed.), *The Role of the Amateur Architect*: 21–6. London, Georgian Group.

McParland, E. (1995) Edward Lovett Pearce and the new junta for architecture. In T. Barnard and J. Clark (eds), *Lord Burlington. Architecture, Art and Life*: 151–65. London, Bloomsbury Academic.

McParland, E. (2001) *Public Architecture in Ireland, 1680–1760*. New Haven, CT, Yale University Press.

McVeigh, S. (1983) Felice Giardini: a violinist in late eighteenth-century London. *Music and Letters* 64 (3–4): 162–72.

McVeigh, S. (1988) Music and lock hospital in the 18th century. *The Musical Times* 129 (1743): 235–40.

McVeigh, S. (1989) *The Violinist in London's Concert Life 1750–1784. Felice Giardini and his Contemporaries*. New York, Garland.

McVeigh, S. (1993) *Concert Life in London from Mozart to Haydn*. Cambridge, Cambridge University Press.

McVeigh, S. (2000) Freemasonry and musical life in London in the late eighteenth century. In D. Wyn Jones (ed.), *Music in Eighteenth-century Britain*: 72–100. Aldershot, Ashgate.

McVeigh, S. (2001) Italian violinists in eighteenth-century London. In R. Strohm (ed.), *The Eighteenth-century Diaspora of Italian Music and Musicians*: 139–76. Brepols, Turnhout.

McVeigh, S. (2006) Viotti and London violinists during the 1790s: a calendar of performances. In M. Sala (ed.), *Giovanni Battista Viotti. A Composer between the Two Revolutions*: 87–119. Bologna, Ut Orpheus.

Maczak, A. (2002) *Viaggi e viagiatori nell'Europa moderna*, translated by R. Panzone and A. Litwornia). Rome/Bari, Laterza. (Original edition, 1978; Warszawa, Panstwowy Instytut Wydawniczy.)

Maffei, S. (1738) Elogio del Signor Abate Filippo Ivara architetto. In S. Maffei, *Osservazioni letterarie che possono servir di continuazione al Giornale de' letterati d'Italia*, III: 193–204. Verona.

Manchinu, P. and Traversi, P. (2005) Tracce per le sale 'alla China' tardosettecentesche a Villa della Regina e confronti con gli allestimenti per i duchi del Chiablese e d'Aosta nelle residenze sabaude. In L. Caterina and C. Mossetti (eds), *Villa della Regina. Il riflesso dell'Oriente nel Piemonte del Settecento*: 253–66. Turin, Umberto Allemandi.

Manfredi, T. (1995) La biblioteca di architettura e i rami incisi dell'eredità Juvarra. In V. Comoli Mandracci and A. Griseri (eds), *Filippo Juvarra: architetto delle capitali. Da Torino a Madrid, 1714–1736*: 286–97. Turin, Fabbri.

Manfredi, T. (2001) Juvarra e Roma (1714–1732): la diplomazia dell'architettura. In G. Dardanello (ed.), *Sperimentare l'architettura: Guarini, Juvarra, Alfieri, Borra, Vittone*: 177–96. Turin, CRT Editris.

Manfredi, T. (2010) *Filippo Juvarra. Gli anni giovanili*. Rome, Argos.

Manfredi, T. (2011) Roma Communis Patria: Filippo Juvarra and the British. In D.R. Marshall, S. Russell and K.E. Wolfe (eds), *Roma Britannica. Art Patronage and Cultural Exchange in Eighteenth-century Rome*: 207–23. London, British School at Rome.

Manfredi, T. (2012a) 'Iter in Britanniam'. Juvarra a Londra (first part). *Palladio* n.s. 25 (49): 39–56.

Manfredi, T. (2012b) 'Iter in Britanniam'. Juvarra a Londra (second part). *Palladio* n.s. 25 (50): 41–62.

Manfredi T. (2013) 'Libri d'uomini eccellenti'. Filippo Juvarra, Filippo Vasconi e lo studio d'architettura civile. In A. Antinori, *Studio d'architettura civile. Gli atlanti di architettura moderna e la diffusione dei modelli romani nell'Europa del Settecento*: 95–113. Rome, Edizioni Quasar.

Manfredi, T. (2014) 'Il giro per l'Inghilterra, e la Francia'. Il Grand Tour architettonico di Filippo Juvarra. In E. Kieven and C. Ruggero (eds), *Filippo Juvarra 1678–1736, architetto dei Savoia, architetto in Europa*, vol. 2: 229–53. Rome, Campisano Editore.

Manners, E. (2007) Some continental influences on English porcelain. *English Ceramics Circle Transactions* 19 (3): 429–70.

Mannucci, E. (2012) *Casa Savoia: ascesa e declino della più antica dinastia europea*. Milan, Dalai Editore.

Mansord, C.A. (1824) *Du droit d'aubaine et des étrangers en Savoie*. Chambéry, Routin, Bottero et Alessio.

Marabottini, A. (1981) (ed.) Vita del cavaliere don Filippo Juvarra. Abate di Selve e Primo Architetto di S.M. di Sardegna. In L. Pascoli, *Vite de' pittori, scultori ed architetti viventi: dai manoscritti 1383 e 1743 della Biblioteca Comunale Augusta di Perugia*: 255–350. Treviso, Canova.

Marconcini, F. (1965) I trattati di Bruzolo. *Segusium* 2: 74–143.

Marconi, P., Cipriani A. and Valeriani, E. (1974) (eds) *I disegni di architettura dell'Archivio Storico dell'Accademia di San Luca*, 2 vols. Rome, De Luca.

Marder, T.A. (1980) The Porto di Ripetta in Rome. *Journal of the Society of Architectural Historians* 39 (1): 28–56.

Mari, M. (1994) Le tre Iliadi di Melchiorre Cesarotti. In *Momenti della traduzione fra Settecento e Ottocento*: 161–234. Milan, Istituto Propaganda Libraria. (Published also in *Giornale Storico della Letteratura Italiana* 167 (1990): 1–75.)

Marinello, G. (2012) La committenza di Vittorio Amedeo II. Aspetti economici, giuridici e costruttivi. In S. De Blasi (ed.), *Il Bucintoro dei Savoia (Atti del convegno internazionale di studi, Venaria Reale, 22–23 marzo 2012)*: 75–86. Turin, Editris.

Marraccini, C. (1748–50) *Apologia per l'Ordine de' Frati Minori*, 3 vols. Lucca, Benedini.

Marshall, D.R. (2003) Piranesi, Juvarra, and the Triumphal Bridge Tradition. *The Art Bulletin* 85: 321–52.

Marshall, D.R., Russell, S. and Wolfe, K. (2011) (eds) *Roma Britannica. Art Patronage and Cultural Exchange in Eighteenth-century Rome*. London, British School at Rome.

Marshall, J. (2006) *John Locke, Toleration and Early Enlightenment Culture*. Cambridge, Cambridge University Press.

Marshall, R. (1934) *Italy in English Literature. 1755–1815. Origins of the Romantic Interest in Italy*. New York, Columbia University Press.

Martelli, F and Galasso, C. (2007) (eds) *Istruzioni agli ambasciatori e inviati medicei in Spagna e nell'Italia spagnola (1536–1648)*, 2 vols. Rome, Direzione Generale per gli Archivi.

Maruzzi, P. (1922) Sulle logge muratorie d'Alessandria durante il periodo napoleonico. *Rivista di Storia, Arte e Archeologia della Provincia di Alessandria* 5 (21), 21–2 (serie III): 71–6.

Maruzzi, P. (1928–9) Notizie e documenti sui liberi muratori in Torino nel secolo XVIII. *Bollettino Storico-Bibliografico Subalpino* 30: 115–213, 397–514; 31: 33–100.

Maruzzi, P. (1990) *La stretta osservanza templare e il regime rettificato in Italia nel secolo XVIII*. San Giovanni in Persiceto, Atanór.

Masini, P.C. (1997) *Alfieri*. Pisa, Biblioteca Franco Serantini.

Masoero, M., Mamino, S. and Rosso, C. (1999) (eds) *Politica e cultura nell'età di Carlo Emanuele I. Torino, Parigi, Madrid. Convegno internazionale di studi (Torino, 21–24 febbraio 1995)*. Florence, Olschki.

Masterpieces of Italian Decorative Arts. Capolavori di Arti decorative Italiane (no date). Paris/London, Galleria Pelham/ Pelham's Gallery.

Mattioda, E. (1993) Baretti e il problema della traduzione. In M. Cerruti and P. Trivero (eds), *Giuseppe Baretti: un piemontese in Europa. Atti del convegno di studi (Torino, 21–22 settembre 1990)*: 61–75. Alessandria, Edizioni dell'Orso.

Maylender, M. (1926–30) *Storia delle accademie d'Italia*. Bologna, Cappelli.

Mazza, E. (2012) *La peste in fondo al pozzo. L'anatomia astrusa di David Hume*. Milan/Udine, Mimesis.

Mazza, E. and Piccoli, E. (2011a) Disguised in scarlet. Hume and Turin in 1748. *I Castelli di Yale* 11: 71–108.

Mazza, E. and Piccoli, E. (2011b) 'La grande variété de gout'. David Hume à Paris. In D. Rabreau and C. Henry, *Le public et la politique des arts au siècle des lumières*: 121–43. Bordeaux, William Blake & Co.

Mazza Boccazzi, B. (1976) La vicenda dei 'tombeaux des princes': matrici, storia e fortuna della serie Swiny tra Bologna e Venezia. *Saggi e Memorie di Storia dell'Arte* 10: 79–102.

Mears, N., Raffe, A., Taylor, S. and Williamson, P. (2013) (eds) *National Prayers: Special Worship since the Reformation. Volume I: Special Prayers, Fasts and Thanksgivings in the British Isles, 1553–1688*. Woodbridge, Boydell Press.

Medvedkova, O. (2003) (1) Les architectes et les artistes français à Saint-Pétersbourg: présences et indirectes. (2) Le plan général de Saint-Pétersbourg de Le Blond: vision utopique ou projet moderne? In *Les Français à Saint-Pétersbourg*. St Petersburg, Palace Édition.

Medvedkova, O. (2007) *Jean-Baptiste Alexandre Leblond: architecte 1679–1719; de Paris à Saint-Péterbourg*. Paris, Baudry.

Merlin, P. (1991) *Tra guerre e tornei, la corte sabauda nell'età di Carlo Emanuele I*. Turin, Sei.

Merlin, P. (2010) *Nelle stanze del re. Vita e politica nelle corti europee tra XV e XVIII secolo*. Rome, Salerno.

Merlin, P., Rosso, C., Symcox, G. and Ricuperati, G. (1994) *Il Piemonte Sabaudo. Stato e territori in età moderna*. Turin, Utet.

Merlotti, A. (1998) Giovanni Battista Gabaleone. *Dizionario biografico degli italiani* 50: 817–19.

Merlotti, A. (2001a) (ed.) *Giochi di palla nel Piemonte medievale e moderno*. Rocca de' Baldi, Centro Studi Storico-etnografici Museo Storico-etnografico A. Doro.

Merlotti, A. (2001b) Da fortezza militare a fortezza religiosa? Spunti per una storia civile di Pinerolo nel Settecento sabaudo. In A. Bernardi and G.G. Merlo (eds), *Il Settecento religioso nel Pinerolese*: 73–136. Pinerolo, Diocesi di Pinerolo.

Merlotti, A. (2003a) (ed.) *Nobiltà e stato in Piemonte. I Ferrero d'Ormea. Atti del convegno (Torino–Mondovì, 3–5 ottobre 2001)*. Turin, Zamorani.

Merlotti, A. (2003b) Il caso Dunand: vitalità e insidie della sociabiltà nella Torino di Alfieri (1772–1777). In M. Cerruti, M. Corsi and B. Danna (eds), *Alfieri e il suo tempo*: 131–77. Florence, Olschki.

Merlotti, A. (2003c) 'Compagni de' giovanili errori'. Gli amici di Alfieri fra Accademia Reale e Societé des Sansguignons (1772–1778). In R. Maggio Serra, F. Mazzocca, C. Sisi and C. Spantigati (eds), *Vittorio Alfieri aristocratico ribelle*: 154–6. Milan, Electa.

Merlotti, A. (2004) Salotti in una città cosmopolita. Gentildonne e conversazioni nella Torino del secondo Settecento. In M.L. Betri and E. Brambilla (eds),

Salotti e ruolo femminile in Italia tra fine Seicento e primo Novecento: 125–52. Venice, Marsilio.

Merlotti, A. (2006) Disciplinamento e contrattazione. Dinastia, nobiltà e corte nel Piemonte sabaudo da Carlo II alla guerra civile. In P. Bianchi and L.C. Gentile (eds), *L'affermarsi della corte sabauda. Dinastie, poteri, élites in Piemonte e Savoia fra tardo medioevo e prima età moderna*: 227–84. Turin, Zamorani.

Merlotti, A. (2009) Politique dynastique et alliance matrimoniales de la Maison de Savoie au XVII siècle. *XVIIe Siècle* 243: 239–55.

Merlotti, A. (2011) 'Il y a ici quelque étiquette?'. Cerimonie e sociabilità per la visita di Giuseppe II a Torino nel 1769. In A. Colturato and A. Merlotti (eds), *La festa teatrale nel Settecento. Dalla corte di Vienna alle corti d'Italia. Proceedings of the international conference (Reggia di Venaria, 13–14 November 2009)*: 155–71. Lucca, Libreria Musicale Italiana.

Merlotti, A. (2012) I regi elemosinieri alla corte dei Savoia, re di Sardegna (secc. XVIII–XIX). In J. Martínez Millán, M. Riveiro Rodríguez and G. Versteegen (eds), *La corte en Europa: política y religión (siglos XVI–XVIII)*, II: 1025–57. Madrid, Polifemo.

Merlotti, A. (2013a) La courte enfance de la duchesse de Bourgogne (1685–1696). In F. Preyat (ed.), *Marie Adélaide de Savoie. Duchesse de Bourgogne enfant terribile de Versailles. Actes de colloque international Bruxelles, 17–18 octobre 2013 (Études sur le XVIIIe siècle)*: 29–46. Brussels, Édition de l'Université de Bruxelles.

Merlotti, A. (2013b) Ossorio Alarcon Giuseppe Antonio. In *Dizionario biografico degli italiani*, 79: 786–8. Rome, Istituto della Enciclopedia Italiana.

Merlotti, A. (2014) Corte e città in una capitale dell'assolutismo. L'immagine di Torino nella letteratura del Settecento. In M. Formica, A. Merlotti and A.M. Rao (eds), *La città nel Settecento. Saperi e forme di rappresentazione*: 247–67. Rome, Edizioni di Storia e Letteratura.

Merlotti, A. and Ricardi di Netro, T. (2005) Una dichiarazione di status? Ipotesi sul gusto 'alla China' nell'aristocrazia piemontese del Settecento. In L. Caterina and C. Mossetti (eds), *Villa della Regina. Il riflesso dell'Oriente nel Piemonte del Settecento*: 435–43. Turin, Umberto Allemandi.

Middleton, R. (1998a) Robert Wood (1717–1770), *The Ruins of Palmyra, Otherwise Tedmor in the Desart*. In *The Mark J. Millard Architectural Collection, II. British Books. Seventeenth through Nineteenth Centuries*: 344–8. Washington/New York, National Gallery of Art/George Braziller.

Middleton, R. (1998b) Robert Wood (1717–1770), *Les Ruines de Balbec, Autrement Dite Heliopolis dans la Coelosyrie*. In *The Mark J. Millard Architectural Collection, II. British Books. Seventeenth through Nineteenth Centuries*: 349–51, Washington/New York, National Gallery of Art/George Braziller.

Mignot, C. (2010) Mansart et l'agence des Bâtiments du roi Jules Hardouin-Mansart. In A. Gady (ed.), *Julies Hardouin-Mansart: 1646–1708*: 45–58. Paris, Éditions de la Maison des Sciences de l'Homme.

Milhous, J., Dideriksen, G. and Hume, R.D. (2000) *Italian Opera in Late Eighteenth-century London, II. The Pantheon Opera and its Aftermath, 1789–1795*. Oxford, Clarendon Press.

Miller, S. (1978) Portugal and Rome c.1748–1830: an aspect of the Catholic Enlightenment. *Miscellanea Historiae Pontificiae, Pontificia Universitas Gregoriana* 44: 28–106.

Moffa, R. (1990) *Storia della Regia Cappella di Torino dal 1775 al 1870*. Turin, Centro Studi Piemontesi/Fondo 'Carlo Felice Bona'/Associazione Piemontese per la Ricerca delle Fonti Musicali.

Mola, A.A. (1976) *Storia della massoneria italiana dall'Unità alla Repubblica*. Milan, Bompiani.

Molesworth, W. (2010) *John Molesworth (1679–1726) as a Patron of Art: Complacence, Connoisseurship and Commission*. Trinity College Dublin, M.Litt. dissertation.

Molle, P. (2014) *La chiesa italiana di Londra: la storia dei primi Pallottini in Inghilterra*. Todi, Fondazione Migrantes.

Monbeig Goguel, C. (1994) Tommaso Redi: un dessinateur à l'époque du Grand Tour. *Antichità Viva. Rassegna d'Arte* 33 (2–3): 82–92.

Monod, P. (1633) *Trattato del titolo regio dovuto alla Serenissima Casa di Savoia*. Turin, Eredi G.D. Taurino.

Montagu, J. (1975) Antonio Montauti's 'Return of the Prodigal Son'. *Bulletin of the Detroit Institute of Arts* 54 (1): 14–23.

Moore, A. (2014) Becoming a perfect virtuoso and a great lover of pictures: Thomas Coke on his Grand Tour 1712–1718. In B. Gialluca (ed.), *Seduzione etrusca. Dai segreti di Holkham Hall alle meraviglie del British Museum*. Milan, Skira.

Moreland, S. (1658) *History of the Evangelical Churches in the Valleys of Piedmont*. London.

Morena, F. (2009a) *Chinoiserie: the Evolution of the Oriental Style in Italy from the 14th to the 19th Century* (translation E. Leckey). Florence, Centro Di.

Morena, F. (2009b) *Cineseria. Evoluzioni del gusto per l'Oriente in Italia dal XIV al XIX secolo*. Florence, Centro Di.

Mörschel, T. (2002) *Buona Amicitia? Die Römisch-Savoyischen Beziehungen unter Paul V (1605–1621). Studien zur Frühneuzeitlichen Mikropolitik in Italien*, Mainz, von Zabern.

Mossetti, C. (2005) I Gabinetti di Villa della Regina. Modelli e confronti. In L. Caterina and C. Mossetti (eds), *Villa della Regina. Il riflesso dell'Oriente nel Piemonte del Settecento*:123–52. Turin, Umberto Allemandi.

Mounin, G. (1965) *Traductions et traducteurs* (Italian translation by S. Morganti (1991) *Teoria e storia della traduzione*. Turin, Einaudi.

Muir, T.E. (2008) *Roman Catholic Church Music in England, 1791–1914: a Handmaid of the Liturgy?* Aldershot, Ashgate.

Murdoch, T. (2006) A French carver at Norfolk House: the mysterious Mr Cuenot. *Apollo* June 2006: 54–63.

Müry, A. (1941) *Die Instrumentalwerke Gaetano Pugnanis. Ein Beitrag zur Erforschung der Frühklassischen Instrumentalmusik in Italien*. Basel, G. Krebs.

Myers, M.L. (1975) (ed.) *Architectural and Ornament Drawings. (Exhibition The Metropolitan Museum of Art 1974)*. New York, Metropolitan Museum of Art.

N.N. (1904) *The Microcosm of London or London in Miniature*, I. London, Methuen & Co.

Nagiski, E. (2009) *Sculpture and Enlightenment*. Los Angeles, Getty Publications.

Neue Genealogisch-historische (1756) *Neue Genealogisch-historische Nachrichten von den Vornehmsten*: LXXIII. Leipzig, Heinsius.

Neuman, R. (1994) *Robert De Cotte and the Perfection of Architecture in Eighteenth-century France*. Chicago, University of Chicago Press.

Newman, A. (1958) The political patronage of Frederick Lewis, Prince of Wales. *The Historical Journal* 1: 68–75.

Nicolas, J. (1978) *La Savoie au XVIIIe: noblesse et bourgeoisie*. Paris, Maloine.

Nobili Vitelleschi, A.A. (1905) *The Romance of Savoy, Victor Amadeus II and his Stuart Bride*. London, Hutchinson & Co.

Nozzoli, A. (2003) Intorno all'Alfieri 'inglese': Maria Stuarda. In E. Ghidetti and R. Turchi (eds), *Alfieri tragico* (*La Rassegna della Letteratura Italiana* 107 (2): 583–7.

O'Connor, C. (1999) *The Pleasing Hours. James Caulfeild, First Earl of Charlemont 1728–99. Traveller, Connoisseur and Patron of the Arts in Ireland*. Wilton, Collins Press.

Oberli, M. (1999) *'Magnificentia principis'. Das Mäzenatentum des Prinzen und Kardinals Maurizio von Savoyen (1593–1657)*. Weimar, Verlag und Datenbank für Geisteswiss.

Oechslin, W. (1972) Bildungsgut und Antikenrezeption im frühen Settecento in Rom. In *Studien zum Römischen Aufenthalt Bernardo Antonio Vittones*. Zurich, Atlantis Verlag.

Oman, C. (1966) The plate of the chapel of the Sardinian embassy. *The Burlington Magazine* 108 (763): 500–3.

Oppé, A. (1951) Memoirs of Thomas Jones. *The Thirty-Second Volume of The Walpole Society 1946–1948*: 75, 77, 78, 80 and 81.

Oresko, R. (1991) The Glorious Revolution of 1688–89 and the House of Savoy. In J. Israel (ed.), *The Anglo-Dutch Moment*: 365–88. Cambridge, Cambridge University Press.

Oresko, R. (1997) The House of Savoy in search of a royal crown in the seventeenth century. In R. Oresko, G.C. Gibbs and H.M. Scott (eds), *Royal and Republican Sovereignty in Early Modern Europe*: 272–350. Cambridge, Cambridge University Press.

Oresko, R. (1999) The Duchy of Savoy and the Kingdom of Sardinia: the Sabaudian Court 1563–c.1750. In J. Adamson (ed.), *The Princely Courts of Europe: Ritual, Politics and Culture under the Ancien Régime 1500–1750*: 231–53. London, Weidenfeld and Nicolson.

Oresko, R. (2004) Maria Giovanna Battista of Savoy-Nemours (1644–1724): daughter, consort and regent of Savoy. In C. Campbell-Orr (ed.), *Queenship in Europe, 1660–1815*: 16–55. Cambridge, Cambridge University Press.

Oresko, R., Gibbs, G.C. and Scott, H. (1997) (eds) *Royal and Republican Sovereignty in Early Modern Europe. Essay in Memory of Ragnhild Hatton*. Cambridge, Cambridge University Press.

Orrell, J. (1977) The Agent of Savoy at 'Somerset Masque'. *Review of English Studies* 28: 301–4.

Osborne, T. (2002) *Dynasty and Diplomacy in the Court of Savoy. Political Culture and the Thirty Years' War*. Cambridge, Cambridge University Press.

Osborne, T. (2007a) The surrogate war between the Savoys and the Medici. Sovereignty and precedence in early modern Italy. *International History Review* 29: 1–21.

Osborne, T. (2007b) Van Dyck, Alessandro Scaglia and the Caroline court: friendship, collecting and diplomacy in the early seventeenth century. *The Seventeenth Century* 22: 24–41.

Osborne, T. (2013) The house of Savoy and the theatre of the world. Performances of sovereignty in early modern Rome. In M. Vester (ed.), *Sabaudian Studies. Political Culture, Dynasty and Territory 1400–1700*: 167–90. Kirksville, Truman State University Press.

Osborne, T. (2014) Language and sovereignty: titles of address and the royal edict of 1632. In S.A. Stacey (ed.), *Political, Religious and Social Conflict in the Duchy of Savoy 1400–1700*: 15–34. Bern, Peter Lang.

Oxford Dictionary of National Biography. Oxford, Oxford University Press.

Palmer F.M. (2006) *Vincent Novello(1781–1861): Music for the Masses*. Aldershot, Ashgate.

Palmucci, L. (2003) Palazzi, castelli, arredi e giardini: l'opulenza non mediocre' dei Ferrero d'Ormea nel Settecento. In A. Merlotti (ed.), *Nobiltà e stato in Piemonte. I Ferrero d'Ormea*: 457–73. Turin, Zamorani.

Panicucci, E. (1996) La questione del titolo granducale. Il carteggio diplomatico tra Firenze e Madrid. In *Toscana e Spagna nel secolo XVI. Miscellanea di studi storici*: 7–58. Pisa, ETS.

Paoli, M.P. (2005) Anton Maria Salvini (1653–1729): il ritratto di un 'letterato' nella Firenze di fine Seicento. In J. Boutier, B. Marin and A. Romano (eds), *Naples, Rome, Florence. Une histoire comparée des milieux intellectuels italiens (XVIIe–XVIIIe siècles)*: 501–44. Rome, École Française de Rome.

Parker, M. St J. (2004a) Wood, Robert (1716–1771). In *Oxford Dictionary of National Biography*. Oxford, Oxford University Press. Online edition.

Parker, M. St J. (2004b) Dawkins, James (1722–1757). In *Oxford Dictionary of National Biography*. Oxford, Oxford University Press. Online edition.

Pascal, A. (1924) Valdesi a Torino sulla fine del secolo XVII (1686–1690). *Bollettino Storico Bibliografico Subalpino* 26 (3–4): 186–210.

Pascal, A. (1937) Notizie e documenti sulla colonia protestante di Torino nella prima metà del secolo XVIII. *Bollettino della Società di Studi Valdesi* 67: 11–62.

Pascoli, L. (1981) *Vite de' pittori, scultori ed architetti viventi: dai manoscritti 1383 e 1743 della Biblioteca comunale Augusta di Perugia.* Treviso, Canova.

Passamonti, E. (1934–5) Relazioni anglo-sabaude dal 1603 al 1625. *Bollettino Storico-bibliografico Subalpino* 36: 264–317, 488–543; 37: 94–124.

Pasta, R. (2006) Fermenti culturali e circoli massonici nella Toscana del Settecento. In G.M. Cazzaniga (ed.), *La massoneria*: 447–83. Turin, Einaudi.

Pastor, L. von (1899–1953), *The History of the Popes from the Close of the Middle Ages Drawn from the Secret Archives of the Vatican and Other Original Sources*, 40 vols. London, Kegan Paul, Trench, Turner and Co.

Pennini, A. (2012) Le missioni del conte di Cartignano (1611–1612). Un progetto di matrimonio inglese per il principe di Piemonte. *Bollettino Storico Bibliografico Subalpino* 110: 141–73.

Pennini, A. (in press) Le prospettive internazionali di Carlo Emanuele alla luce del suo 'testamento politico'. In A. Raviola (ed.) *Les Etats de Savoie entre France et Espagne. Atti del convegno internazionale (Vallée d'Aoste 24–26 mai 2011)*. Rome, Carocci.

Perrillat, L. (2013) (eds) *Couronne royale. Colloque international autour du 300° anniversaire de l'accession de la Maison de Savoie au trone royal de Sicile, Annecy, 12 et 13 avril 2013.* Annecy-Chambéry, Académie salésienne et le Laboratoire LLS.

Pérpechon, F. (1895) Les nécrologes de Chambéry. *Mémoires et Documents Publiés par la Société Savoisienne d'Histoire et d'Archeologie* 34: 351–421.

Petrucci, F. (2010) *Pittura di ritratto a Roma: il Settecento, I–II.* Rome, Andreina and Valneo Budai.

Pettenati, S. (1987) Forniture per la corte: vetri, specchi, cristali, porcellane, carrozze. In S. Pinto (ed.), *Arte di corte a Torino da Carlo Emanuele III a Carlo Felice*: 215–48. Turin, Cassa di Risparmio di Torino.

Pettenati, S. (2004) Mobilità degli arredi del Castello. In G. Carità (ed.), *Pollenzo. Una città romana per una 'real villeggiatura' romantica*: 243–75. Savigliano, Editrice Artistica Piemontese.

Peyrot, A. and Roccia, R. (1994) (eds) *Torino nei disegni di Friedrich Bernhard Werner, viaggiatore e vedutista del Settecento.* Turin, Archivio Storico della Città di Torino.

Pezzolo, L. (2003) Ricchezza, miseria e nobiltà. Note sull'economia nobiliare nell'Italia moderna. In A. Merlotti (ed.), *Nobiltà e stato in Piemonte. I Ferrero d'Ormea*: 403–14. Turin, Zamorani.

Piccioni, L. (1946) Giuseppe Baretti e la stampa periodica inglese dei suoi tempi. *Giornale Storico della Letteratura Italiana* 62 (3): 131–45.

Piccoli, E. (2012) Il Portico all'antica di Alfieri a Ginevra. In P. Cornaglia, E. Kieven and C. Roggero (eds), *Benedetto Alfieri 1699–1767, architetto di Carlo Emanuele III*: 357–73. Rome, Palmisano.

Piccoli, E. and De Pieri, F. (2012) (eds) *Architettura e città negli Stati sabaudi. Studi in onore di Franco Rosso.* Macerata, Quodlibet.

Pinto, J. (1992) Nicola Michetti and eighteenth-century architecture in St Petersburg. In H.A. Millon and S. Scott Munshower (eds), *An Architectural Progress in the Renaissance and Baroque*: 526–65. University Park, PA, Pennsylvania State University Press.

Pinto, J. (2000) Architettura da esportare. In G. Curcio and E. Kieven, *Storia dell'architettura italiana. Il Settecento*: 110–33. Milan, Electa.

Pinto, J. (2012) *Speaking Ruins. Piranesi, Architects and Antiquity in Eighteenth-century Rome (Jerome Lectures Twenty-Fourth Series)*. Ann Arbor, University of Michigan Press.

Pinto, S. (1987) (ed.) *Arte di Corte a Torino da Carlo Emanuele III a Carlo Felice*. Turin, Cassa di Risparmio di Torino.

Placella, V. (1973) *Alfieri comico*. Bergamo, Minerva Italica.

Platone, G. (2003) (ed.) *I valdesi a Torino. Nascita e storia di una comunità protestante*. Turin, Claudiana.

Pocock, J.G.A. (1975) *The Machiavellian Moment. Florentine Political Thought and the Atlantic Republican Tradition*. Princeton, NJ/London, Princeton University Press.

Pollak, M. (1991) *Turin, 1564–1680: Urban Design, Military Culture and the Creation of the Absolutist Capital*. Chicago, University of Chicago Press.

Pommer, R. (1967) *Eighteenth-century Architecture in Piedmont. The Open Structures of Juvarra, Alfieri, and Vittone*. New York/London, University Press.

Pompei, A. (1735) *Li Cinque Ordini dell'Architettura Civile di M. Sanmicheli*. Verona.

Ponza, G. (1684) *La science de l'homme de qualité … pour l'usage de messieurs les academistes de l'Academie Royale de Savoye*. Turin, Gianelli.

Pougin, A. (1888) *Viotti et l'école moderne de violon*. Paris, Schott.

Pound, R. (2009) The master mason slain: the Hiramic legend in the Red Velvet Room at Chiswick. *English Heritage Historical Review* 4: 154–63.

Powell, W.S. (1977) *John Pory, 1572–1636: the Life and Letters of a Man of Many Parts*. Chapel Hill, University of North Carolina Press.

Price, C., Milhous, J. and Hume, R.D. (1992) *The Impresario's Ten Commandments. Continental Recruitment for Italian Opera in London 1763–64*. London, Royal Musical Association.

Price, C., Milhous, J. and Hume, R.D. (1995) *Italian Opera in Late Eighteenth-century London, I. The King's Theatre, Haymarket, 1778–1791*. Oxford, Clarendon Press.

Priuli, F. (2006) *Con quest'ordine disordinato. Relazione dell'ambasceria in Savoia (1603)*. Rome/Padua, Antenore.

Procès-verbaux (1911) – (1911–26) *Procès-verbaux de l'Académie Royale d'architecture, 1671–1793*, 9 vols. Paris.

Protopapa, I. (2003) La paggeria: una scuola per la giovane nobiltà. In S. Bertelli and R. Pasta (eds), *Vivere a Pitti. Una reggia dai medici ai Savoia*: 27–44. Florence, Olschki.

Pursell, B.C. (2003) *The Winter King. Frederick V of the Palatinate and the Coming of the Thirty Years' War*. Aldershot, Ashgate.

Pyke, E.J. (1973) *A Biographical Dictionary of Wax Modellers*. Oxford, Clarendon Press.

Pyne, W.H. and Combe, W. (1904) The Roman Catholic Chapel. Lincoln's Inn Fields. In *The Microcosm of London or London in Miniature*, I: 114–18. London, Methuen & Co.

Quazza, R. (1930b) *Margherita di Savoia. Duchessa di Mantova e vice-regina del Portogallo*. Turin, Paravia.

Quazza, R. (1930a) Una vertenza fra principi italiani del Seicento. *Rivista Storica Italiana* 47: 233–54, 369–87.

Raggi, G. (2014) Juvarra a Lisbona: due progetti per un teatro regio e una complessa questione musicale. In E. Kieven and C. Ruggero (eds), *Filippo Juvarra (1678–1736), architetto dei Savoia, architetto in Europea. Atti del convegno internazionale (Torino, 2011)*: 209–228. Rome, Campisano.

Rangoni, G.B. (1790) *Saggio sul gusto della musica col carattere de' tre celebri sonatori di violino i signori Nardini, Lolli, e Pugnani*. Livorno, Tommaso Masi e Comp.

Raulich, I. (1896) *Storia di Carlo Emanuele I duca di Savoia con documenti degli archivi italiani e stranieri*, 2 vols. Milan, Hoepli.

Raviola, B.A. (2005) Prima del viceregno: Ercole Tommaso Roero di Cortanze patrizio di Asti, militare e diplomatico. In P. Merlin (ed.), *Governare un regno. Viceré, apparati burocratici società nella Sardegna del Settecento*: 83–104. Rome, Carocci.

Raviola, B.A. (2007) *Lo spazio sabaudo. Intersezioni, frontiere e confini in età moderna*. Milan, Franco Angeli.

Reineri, M.T. (2006) *Anna Maria d'Orléans: regina di Sardegna, duchessa di Savoia*. Turin, Centro Studi Piemontesi.

Reynolds, S. (2014) Thomas Hobart, 'a Governor of sound judgement and admirable addresse'. In B. Gialluca (ed.), *Seduzione etrusca. Dai segreti di Holkham Hall alle meraviglie del British Museum*. Milan, Skira.

Rice, G. (1989) Lord Rochford at Turin, 1749–55: a pivotal phase in Anglo-Italian relations in the eighteenth century. In J. Black (ed.), *Knights Errant and True Englishmen. British Foreign Policy 1600–1800*: 92–113. Edinburgh, John Donald.

Ricotti, E. (1861–69) *Storia della monarchia Piemontese*, 6 vols. Florence, Barbera.

Ricuperati, G. (2003) Vittorio Alfieri, società e stato sabaudo: fra appartenenza e distanza. In M. Cerruti, M. Corsi and B. Danna (eds), *Alfieri e il suo tempo, Atti del convegno internazionale (Torino–Asti 2001)*: 3–45. Florence, Olschki.

Ricuperati, R. (1968) Bernardo Andrea Lama professore e storiografo nel Piemonte di Vittorio Amedeo II. *Bollettino Storico Bibliografico Subalpino* 66: 12–101.

Riley, W.E. and Gomme, L. (1912) (eds) *Survey of London*, 3. *The Parish of St. Giles-in-the-Fields: Lincoln's Inn Fields*, part I (general editorship of L. Gomme and P. Norman). London, London County Council.

Rinaudo, C. (1891) *Carlo Emanuele I, duca di Savoia*. Turin, F.lli Bocca.

Ringot, B. and Sarmant, T. (2010) La surintendance des bâtiments du roi sous Jules Hardouin-Mansart. In A. Gady (ed.), *Jules Hardouin-Mansart: 1646–1708*: 59–68. Paris, Éditions de la Maison des Sciences de l'Homme.

Robbio di San Raffaele, B. (1778) *Lettere due sopra l'arte del suono*. Vicenza, Antonio Veronese.

Roccia, R. (2000) (ed.) *Theatrum Sabaudiae. Teatro degli stati del duca di Savoia*, 2 vols. Turin, Archivio Storico della Città di Torino.

Roche, D. (2002) Voyages, mobilités, lumières. *Revue de Synthèse* 123:17–35.

Rodger, N.A.M. (1993) *The Insatiable Earl: a Life of John Montagu, Fourth Earl of Sandwich, 1718–1792*. London, HarperCollins.

Roggero, M. (1981) *Scuola e riforme nello stato sabaudo. L'istruzione secondaria dalla Ratio studiorum alle Costituzioni del 1772*. Turin, Deputazione Subalpina di Storia Patria.

Roggero, M. (1987) *Il sapere e la virtù. Stato, università e professioni nel Piemonte tra Sette e Ottocento*. Turin, Deputazione Subalpina di Storia Patria.

Roland Michel, M. (1999) John Linnell. In H. Millon (ed.), *I Trionfi del Barocco. Architettura in Europa 1600–1750*: 517. Cinisello Balsamo, Bompiani.

Rolando Perino, G. (2005) Il rilievo degli arredi di Villa della Regina. In L. Caterina and C. Mossetti (eds), *Villa della Regina. Il riflesso dell'Oriente nel Piemonte del Settecento*: 153–64. Turin, Umberto Allemandi.

Rolando Perino, G. (2008) Le boiseries della Villa al Quirinale attraverso il rilievo. In C. Mossetti and P. Traversi (eds), *Juvarra a Villa della Regina. Le storie di Enea di Corrado Giaquinto*: 95–102. Turin, Editris.

Romagnani, G.P. (2000) I mestieri del denaro fra norma e trasgressione. Negozianti, banchieri e 'ginevrini' nella Torino del Settecento. In M. Meriggi and A. Pastore (eds), *Le regole dei mestieri e delle professioni. Secoli XV–XIX*: 152–75. Milan, Franco Angeli.

Romagnani, G.P. (2002) Presenze protestanti a Torino tra Sei e Settecento. In G. Ricuperati (ed.), *Storia di Torino, V. Dalla città razionale alla crisi dello Stato d'Antico Regime (1730–1798)*: 423–51. Turin, Einaudi.

Romagnani, G.P. (2007) Maffei, Scipione. In *Dizionario biografico degli italiani* 67: 256–63. Rome, Istituto della Enciclopedia italiana.

Romano, G. (1995) (ed.) *Le collezioni di Carlo Emanuele I di Savoia*. Turin, Fondazione CRT.

Roscoe, I. (2009) *A Biographical Dictionary of Sculptors in Britain 1660–1851*. New Haven, CT/London, Yale University Press.

Rosoman, T.S. (1985) The decoration and use of the principal apartments at Chiswick House, 1727–70. *The Burlington Magazine* 127 (991): 663–77.

Rossa, W. (2014) L'anello mancante: Juvarra, sogno e realtà di un'urbanistica delle capitali nella Lisbona settecentesca. In E. Kieven and C. Ruggero (eds), *Filippo Juvarra (1678–1736), architetto dei Savoia, architetto in Europa. Atti del convegno internationale (Torino, 2011)*: 183–96. Rome, Campisano.

Rosso, C. (1992) *Una burocrazia di Antico regime. I segretari di stato dei duchi di Savoia 1559–1637*. Turin, Deputazione Subalpina di Storia Patria.

Rostain, A. (1940) Valdesi e 'religionari' in Piemonte durante le guerre della Lega di Augusta. Note e documenti desunti dall'epistolario dei nunzi di Savoia (1690–1694). *Bollettino della Società di Studi Valdesi* 59 (73): 29–30.

Rotta, S. (1990) L'accademia fisico-matematica ciampiniana: un'iniziativa di Cristina? In *Cristina di Svezia. Scienza ed alchimia nella Roma barocca*: 99–174. Bari, Dedalo.

Rousseau, J.-J. (1782) Les confessions. *Oeuvres complètes*, eds B. Gagnebin and M. Raymond, I. Paris, Gallimard, 1959, 1–656.

Rowan, A. (2013a) Al servizio degli inglesi nel Levante: 'Borra took several views of these noble ruins'. In G. Dardanello (ed.), *Giovanni Battista Borra da Palmira a Racconigi*: 41–6. Turin, Editris.

Rowan, A. (2013b) Giovanni Battista Borra a Stowe: novità antiche nello sviluppo del parco inglese. In G. Dardanello (ed.), *Giovanni Battista Borra da Palmira a Racconigi*: 111–18. Turin, Editris.

Ruggero, C. (2008) (ed.) *La forma del pensiero*. Rome, Campisano.

Ruggero, C. (2010) 'piacciate […] dare al presente mio tenuissimo Dono un luogo nel suo clementissimo gradimento'. Filippo Juvarras, disegni di prospettiva ideale' als Gabe für die königliche Kunstsammlung in Dresden (1732). *Jahrbuch der Staatlichen Kunstsammlungen Dresden* 36: 72–81.

Ruggero, C. (2014) 'Disegni di prospettiva ideale': un album di Filippo Juvarra per la corte di Dresda (1732). In E. Kieven and C. Ruggero (eds), *Filippo Juvarra 1678–1736, architetto in Europa (Architettura e potere, lo Stato sabaudo e la costruzione dell'immagine in una corte europea 3,2)*: 256–72. Rome, Campisano.

Rykwert, J. (1984) *Adam. Nascita di uno stile*. Milan, Electa.

Sadie, S. (1993) Italians and Italian instrumental music in eighteenth-century London. In *Luigi Boccherini e la musica strumentale dei maestri italiani in Europa tra Sette e Ottocento. Proceedings of the International Conference (Siena, 29–31 July 1993)* (Chigiana 43, n.s. 23): 297–309.

Sadie, S. (2001) (ed.) *The New Grove Dictionary of Music and Musicians*, 29 vols. London, Macmillan.

Saint-Croix (1876) *Relazione del Piemonte del segretario francese Sainte-Croix annotata da A.Manno*. Turin, Paravia.

Sala, M. (2006) (ed.) *Giovanni Battista Viotti. A Composer between the Two Revolutions*. Bologna, Ut Orpheus.

Salina, A. (2009), Kurten Antonius Xaverius. In V. Cazzato (ed.), *Atlante del giardino italiano 1750–1940. Dizionario biografico di architetti, giardinieri, botanici, committenti, letterati e altri protagonisti* I: 59–62. Rome, Istituto Poligrafico e Zecca dello Stato.

Salwey, N. (2001) *The Piano in London Concert Life, 1750–1800*. University of Oxford, PhD thesis.

Salwey, N. and McVeigh, S. (1997) The piano and harpsichord in London's concert life, 1750–1800. A calendar of advertised performance. In *A Handbook for Studies in 18th-Century English Music* VIII: 27–72. Oxford, Burden and Cholij.

Sancho, J.L. (2014) El Proyecto de Filippo Juvarra para el Palacio Real de Madrid. In E. Kieven and C. Ruggero (eds), *Filippo Juvarra 1678–1736, architetto in Europa (Architettura e potere, lo Stato sabaudo e la costruzione dell'immagine in una corte europea 3,2)*: 273–88. Rome, Campisano.

Sansone, S. (2014) Il progetto per Buenos Aires e l'architettura di Filippo Juvarra per Dom João V di Portogallo. In E. Kieven and C. Ruggero (eds), *Filippo Juvarra 1678–1736, architetto in Europa (Architettura e potere, lo Stato sabaudo e la costruzione dell'immagine in una corte european 3,2)*: 197–208. Rome, Campisano.

Santarem, M.F. de B. (Visconde de) (1842–60) *Quadro elementar das relações politicas e diplomaticas de Portugal com as diversas potenticas do mundo V*. Lisbon, Typographia da Academia Real das Sciencias.

Santato, G. (2003) Alfieri e Caluso. In M. Cerruti, M. Corsi and B. Danna (eds), *Alfieri e il suo tempo, Atti del Convegno Internazionale (Torino–Asti 2001)*: 243–74. Florence, Olschki.

Saumarez-Smith, C. (1990) *The Building of Castle Howard*. London, University of Chicago Press.

Saunders, G. (2002) *Wallpaper in Interior Decoration*. London, V&A Publications.

Schmidt, L., Keller, C. and Feversham, P. (2005) (eds) *Holkham*. Munich, Prestel Verlag.

Schuchard, M.K. (2011) *Emanuel Swedenborg, Secret Agent on Earth and in Heaven: Jacobites, Jews and Freemasons in Early Modern Sweden*. Leiden, Brill.

Sclopis, F. (1853) *Delle relazioni politiche tra la dinastia di Savoia ed il governo britannico (1240–1815)*. Turin, Stamperia Reale.

Scott, H.M. (1989) 'The true principles of the revolution': the Duke of Newcastle and the idea of the old system. In J. Black (ed.), *Knights Errant and True Englishmen. British Foreign Policy 1600–1800*: 55–91. Edinburgh, John Donald.

Scott, J. (1754) *The Pocket Companion and History of Free-masons, Containing their Origine, Progress and Present State*. London, Scott and Baldwin.

Scott, K. (1995) *The Rococo Interior: Decoration and Social Spaces in Early Eighteenth-Century France*. New Haven, CT, Yale University Press.

Scott, K. (2003) Playing games with otherness: Watteau's Chinese cabinet at the Château de la Muette. *Journal of the Warburg and Courtauld Institutes* 66: 189–248.

Scott Munshower, S. (1995) *Filippo Juvarra's Spatial Concepts and Italian Stage Design: the Consummation of a Renaissance Discovery*. Pennsylvania State University, PhD thesis.

Seeley, B. (1750) *Views of the Temples and other Ornamental Buildings in the Gardens at Stowe*. London, Printed for B. Seeley.

Sereno, P. (2009) Aspetti della viabilità di una capitale d'Antico regime. In P. Sereno (ed.), *Torino. Reti e trasporti. Strade, veicoli e uomini dall'Antico regime all'età contemporanea*: 3–26. Turin, Comune di Torino.

Shaftesbury (1790) Miscellany III. Miscellaneous reflections on the preceding treatises, and other critical subjects, chapter 1. In *Characteristics of Men, Manners, Opinions, Times, with a Collection of Letters, Antony Earl of Shaftesbury* III. Basil, J.J. Tourneisen and J.L. Legrand.

Shakeshaft, P. (1986) 'To much bewiched with thoes intysing things': the letters of James, Third Marquis of Hamilton and Basil, Viscount Feilding, concerning collecting in Venice 1635–1639. *The Burlington Magazine* 128: 114–34.

Sharp, S. (1766) *Letters from Italy, Describing the Customs and Manners of that Country, in the Years 1765, and 1766. To which is Annexed, An Admonition to Gentlemen who pass the Alps, in their Tour through Italy*. London, R. Cave. (Second edition 1767.)

Sharp, S. (1768) *A View of the Customs, Manners, Drama, &c. of Italy, as they are Described in The Frusta Letteraria; and in The Account of Italy in English, Written by Mr. Baretti; compared with The Letters from Italy, Written by Mr. Sharp*. London, W. Nicoll.

Sicca, C. (1986) On William Kent's Roman Sources. *Architectural History* 29: 134–67.

Sicca, C. (1987) *Lord Burlington (1694–1753), Architect and Collector of Architectural Drawings*. University of Leicester, PhD thesis.

Sicca, C. (2008) (ed.) *John Talman. An Early-eighteenth-century Connoisseur* (*Studies in British Art* 19). New Haven, CT/London, Yale University Press.

Sicca, C. (2011) Sculture per l'Europa: modalità della contrattazione nelle opere durante il Seicento. *Ricerche di Storia dell'Arte* 101: 53–63.

Silva, E. (1801, anno IX) *Dell'arte dei giardini inglesi*, Milan, Stamperia e Fonderia al genio Tipografico. (Reprinted in 1985; Bologna, Arnaldo Forni.)

Silvestrini, M.T. (1997) *La politica della religione. Il governo ecclesiastico nello Stato sabaudo del XVIII secolo*. Florence, Olschki.

Silvestrini, M.T. (2002) La Chiesa, la città e il potere politico. In G. Ricuperati (ed.), *Storia di Torino*, IV. *La città fra crisi e ripresa (1630–1730)*: 1129–88. Turin, Einaudi.

Simon, J. (1994) Frame studies II: Allan Ramsay and picture frames. *The Burlington Magazine* 136 (1096): 452.

Simoncini G. (1994) (ed.) *Sopra i porti di mare*, 4 vols. Florence, Olschki.

Siri, V. (1677–9) *Memorie recondite dall'anno 1601 fino al 1640*, 8 vols. Paris, Ronco.

Skinner, C. (1958) Some Scottish portraits by Domenico Duprà. *The Scottish Art Review* 6: 4.

Smith, J.T. (1920 reprint) *Nollekens and his Times* I, ed. W. Whitten. London.

Smith, L.P. (1907a) (ed.) *The Lives and Letters of Sir Henry Wotton*, 2 vols. Oxford, Clarendon Press.

Smith, L.P. (1907b) *Life and Letter of Sir Henry Wotton*, 2 vols. Oxford, Clarendon Press.

Smuts, R.M. (2008) Religion, European politics and Henrietta Maria's circle, 1625–41. In E. Griffey (ed.), *Henrietta Maria. Piety, Politics and Patronage*: 13–38. Farnham/Burlington, VT, Ashgate.

Sodini, C. (2001) *L'Ercole tirreno. Guerra e dinastia medicea nella prima metà del Seicento*. Florence, Olschki.

Sommervogel, C. (1890–1909) *Bibliothèque de la Compagnie de Jésus*, 10 vols. Brussels/Paris, Picard.

Soriga, R. (1919) Settecento massonizzante e massonismo napoleonico nel primo Risorgimento italiano. *Bollettino della Società Pavese di Storia Patria* 19 (1–4): 23–86.

Spagnoletti, A. (2003) *Le dinastie Italiane nella prima età moderna*. Bologna, Il Mulino.

Spagnoletti, A (2009) La tregua di Anversa e la pace di Asti. Ovvero come la Spagna perse la propria reputazione. *Dimensioni e Problemi della Ricerca Storica* 2: 163–86.

Stanford, W.B. and Finopoulos, E.J. (1984) *The Travels of Lord Charlemont in Greece and Turkey 1749*. London, Trigraph.

Steiner, G. (1975, 1992) *After Babel. Aspects of Language and Translation*. New York/ London, Oxford University Press. Italian translation: Bianchi, R. and Béguin, C. (1995; first edition 1994) *Dopo Babele. Aspetti del linguaggio e della traduzione*. Milan, Garzanti.

Stendhal (1973) *Voyages en Italie, textes établis, présentés et annotés par Del Litto*, V. Paris, Gallimard.

Storrs, C. (1999) *War, Diplomacy and the Rise of Savoy, 1690–1720*. Cambridge, Cambridge University Press.

Storrs, C. (2000) Savoyard diplomacy in the eighteenth century (1684–1798). In D. Frigo (ed.), *Politics and Diplomacy in Early Modern Italy*: 210–53. Cambridge, Cambridge University Press.

Storrs, C. (2003) Ormea as Foreign Minister 1732–45: the Savoyard State between England and Spain. In A. Merlotti (ed.), *Nobiltà e stato in Piemonte. I Ferrero d'Ormea. Atti del convegno (Torino–Mondovì, 3–5 ottobre 2001)*: 231–48. Turin, Zamorani.

Storrs, C. (2010) British diplomacy in Switzerland (1689–1789) and eighteenth century diplomatic culture. In E. Pibiri and G. Poisson (eds), *Le diplomate en question (XVe–XVIIIe siecles)*: 181–215. Lausanne, Université de Lausanne.

Storrs, C. (2012) 'Grosse Erwartungen': Britische Subsidienzahlungen an Savoyen im 18. Jahrhundert. In P. Rauscher, A. Serles and T. Winkelbauer (eds), *Das 'Blut des Staatskorpers'. Forschungen zur Finanzgeschichte der Fruhen Neuzeit*, special issue of *Historische Zeitschrift* 56: 87–126.

Stoye, J.W. (1952) *English Travellers Abroad 1604–1667*. London, Jonathan Cape.

Strachey, N. (1998) *Ickworth*. London, National Trust.

Strohm, R. (2001) (ed.) *The Eighteenth-century Diaspora of Italian Music and Musicians*. Brepols, Turnhout.

Strong, R. (1986a) *Henry Prince of Wales and England's Lost Renaissance*. London, Thames and Hudson.

Strong, R. (1986b) England and Italy. The marriage of Henry Prince of Wales. In R. Ollard and P. Tudor-Craig (eds), *For Veronica Wedgwood these Studies in Seventeenth-century History*: 59–97. London, Harper Collins.

Stuart, J. and Revett, N. (1762) (eds) *The Antiquities of Athens Measured and Delineated by James Stuart F.R.S. and F.S.A. and Nicholas Revett Painters and Architects. Volume the First.* London, J. Haberkorn.

Stumpo, E. (1978) Castellar, Giuseppe Vincenzo Francesco Maria Lascaris. In *Dizionario Biografico degli Italiani* 21: 649–52. Rome, Edizioni dell'Enciclopedia Italiana.

Stumpo, E. (1984) Finanze e ragion di Stato nella prima età moderna. Due modelli diversi. Piemonte e Toscana, Savoia e Medici. In A. De Maddalena and H. Kellenbenz (eds), *Finanze e ragion di Stato in Italia e Germania nella prima età moderna*: 181–231. Bologna, Il Mulino.

Sweet, R. (2012) *Cities and the Grand Tour: the British in Italy, c. 1690–1820.* Cambridge, Cambridge University Press.

Symcox, G. (1983a) *Victor Amadeus II. Absolutism in the Savoyard State (1675–1730).* London, Thames and Hudson.

Symcox, G. (1983b) Britain and Victor Amadeus II: or, The use and abuse of Allies. In S.B. Baxter (ed.), *England's Rise to Greatness, 1660–1713*: 151–84. Berkeley, University of California Press.

Symcox, G. (1983c) *Victor Amadeus II: Absolutism in the Savoyard State, 1675–1730.* Berkeley, University of California Press.

Symondson, A. (2003) A place where 18th century Catholic London lives on. *The Catholic Herald* 10 October: 14.

Tafel, R.L. (1877) (ed.) *Documents Concerning the Life and Character of Emanuel Swedenborg, Collected, Translated, and Annotated.* London, Swedenborg Society.

Talucchi, F. (1960–1) *Louis Dutens, un diplomatico inglese nel Piemonte della seconda metà del Settecento.* Università di Torino, dissertation.

Tamburini, L. (1966) *I teatri di Torino. Storia e cronache.* Turin, Edizioni dell'Albero.

Tamburini, L. (1983) Lamburini, L. dalle origini al 1936. In A. Basso (ed.), *Storia del Teatro Regio di Torino*, 5 vols: 1976–88. Turin, Cassa di Risparmio di Torino.

Tassoni, A. (1855) *Le filippiche contra gli Spanguoli precedute da un discorso.* Florence, Felice le Monnier.

Temperley, N. (1988) London and the Piano, 1760–1860. *The Musical Times*, 129 (1744): 289–93.

Terry, C.S. (1929) *John Christian Bach.* London, Oxford University Press.

The Church (2009) *The Church of St Anselm and St Cæcilia: Kingsway, London WC2: a Centenary Celebration 1909–2009.* Church of St Anselm and St Cecilia.

Tocchini, G. (2013) Alfieri, Vittorio. In C. Porset and C. Révauger (eds), *Le monde maçonnique des Lumières (Europe-Amériques). Dictionnaire prosopographique.* Paris, Champion.

Toesca, I. (1952) Alessandro Galilei in Inghilterra. In M. Praz (ed.), *English Miscellany: a Symposium of History, Literature and the Arts* III: 189–220. Rome, Edizioni di Storia e Letteratura (for the British Council).

Tongiorgi, D. (2003) Committenze inglesi nel Settecento veneto: il 'caso Gray' e la traduzione dell'*Elegy* di Cesarotti. In Id. *'Nelle grinfie della storia'. Letteratura e letterati fra Sette e Ottocento*: 25–47. Pisa, ETS.

Toynbee, P. (1903) (ed.) *The Letters of Horace Walpole, Fourth Earl of Orford* (16 vols), III. *1750–1756*. Oxford, Clarenden Press.

Toynbee, P. (1928) (ed.) Horace Walpole's visits to country seats. *The Walpole Society* XVI.

Trease, G. (1967) *The Grand Tour*. London, Heinemann.

Turner, N. and Plazzotta, C. (1994) (eds) *Drawings by Guercino from British Collections with an Appendix Describing the Drawings by Guercino, his School and his Followers in the British Museum*. London, British Museum Press in association with Leonardo-De Luca Editori.

Twigge, R.W. (1913) Jacobite papers at Avignon. *The Scottish Historical Review* 10: 60–75.

Vaes, M. (1942) Il soggiorno di Antonio Van Dyck alla corte di Torino 4 dicembre 1622–febbraio 1623. *Bolletino Storico-bibliografico Subalpino* 43: 227–39.

Vallauri, T. (1844) *Delle società letterarie del Piemonte*. Turin, Favale.

Vaughan, H. (2002) *Nicholas Hawksmoor: Rebuilding Ancient Wonders*. New Haven, CT, Yale University Press.

Venice (1905) *Calendar of State Papers Relating to English Affairs in the Archives in Venice, 12 (1610–13)*. London, H.M. Stationary Office.

Venice (1907) *Calendar of State Papers Relating to English Affairs in the Archives in Venice, 13 (1613–15)*. London, H.M. Stationary Office.

Venturi, F. (1956) Il Piemonte dei primi decenni del Settecento nelle relazioni dei diplomatici inglesi. *Bollettino Storico Bibliografico Subalpino* 54 (2): 227–71.

Venturi, F. (1969) *Settecento Riformatore, Vol. 1. Da Muratori a Beccaria*. Turin, Einaudi.

Venturi, F. (1973) L'Italia fuori d'Italia. In *Storia d'Italia, III. Dal primo Settecento all'Unità*: 987–1481. Turin, Einaudi.

Venzi, F. (2008) *Massoneria e fascismo: dall'intesa cordiale alla distruzione delle logge*. Rome, Castelvecchi.

Vermale, F. (1909) Joseph De Maistre frans-maçon. *Annales Révolutionnaire* 2: 356–76.

Vermale, F. (1912) *La Franc-Maçonnerie savoisienne a l'époque révolutionnaire, d'après des registres secrets*, with a preface by A. Mathiez. Paris, Leroux.

Verri, P. and Verri, A. (1980) *Viaggio a Parigi e Londra, carteggio (1766–1767)*, ed. G. Gaspari. Milan, Adelphi.

Vertue, G. (1968 reprint*)* *Vertue Notebooks, vol. III. The Twenty-Second Volume of the Walpole Society 1933–1934*. London, Walpole Society.

Viale Ferrero, M. (1970) *Filippo Juvarra scenografo e architetto teatrale*. Turin, Pozzo.

Viale Ferrero, M. (1980) La scenografia dalle origini al 1936. In A. Basso (ed.), *Storia del Teatro Regio di Torino*, III. Turin, Cassa di Risparmio di Torino.

Villani, S. (2009) Il matrimonio di una principessa. Le trattative per le nozze di Caterina di Ferdinando Medici con il principe Enrico d'Inghilterra. In M. Aglietti (ed.), *Nobildonne, monache e cavaliere dell'Ordine di Santo*

Stefano. Modelli e strategie femminili nella vita pubblica della Toscana gran-ducale. Convegno internazionale di Studi Pisa 22–23 maggio 2009: 21–234. Pisa, ETS.

Vincent, E.R. (1957) L'amore londinese di Vittorio Alfieri. *La Rassegna della Letteratura Italiana* 1: 31–51.

Viora, M. (1930) *Storia delle leggi sui valdesi di Vittorio Amedeo II.* Bologna, Zanichelli.

Vita (1981) *Vita del cavaliere don Filippo Juvarra. Abate di Selve e primo architetto di S.M. di Sardegna*, ed. A. Marabottini. In L. Pascoli, *Vite de' pittori, scultori ed architetti viventi: dai manoscritti 1383 e 1743 della Biblioteca Comunale Augusta di Perugia*: 255–350. Treviso, Canova.

Vitale, M. (1984) Proposizioni teoriche e indicazioni pratiche nelle discussioni linguistiche del Settecento. In L. Formigari (ed.), *Teorie e pratiche linguistiche nell'Italia del Settecento*: 11–36. Bologna, Il Mulino.

Vitullo, F. (1959) *I Palazzi della 'Provvidenza' Perrone di San Martino e della Cassa di Risparmio*. Turin, Cassa di Risparmio di Torino.

Vivian, F. (1990) (ed.) *Da Raffaello a Canaletto. La collezione del Console Smith (catalogo mostra Venezia 15.09-18.11.1990)*. Milan, Electa.

Vlaardingerbroek, K. (1991) Faustina Bordoni applauds Jan Alensoon: a Dutch music-lover in Italy and France in 1723–4. *Music and Letters* 72 (4): 536–51.

Wain, J. (1991) (ed.) *The Journals of James Boswell 1762–1795*. New Haven, CT/London, Yale University Press.

Walpole, H. (1954) *Horace Walpole's Correspondence with Sir Horace Mann*, I (*16 April 1740-21 July 1742*), eds W.S. Lewis, W.H. Smith and G.L. Lam. New Haven, CT, Yale University Press.

Walpole, H. (1960) *The Yale Edition of Horace Walpole's Correspondence*. New Haven, CT/London.

Watson, F. (1950) A portrait of Farinelli by Bartolomeo Nazari. *The Burlington Magazine* 92: 266–7.

Weber S. (2013) (ed.) *William Kent. Designing Georgian Britain, exhibition's catalogue (New York 2013/London 2014)*. New Haven, CT/London, Yale University Press.

Wharton, D. and Pevsner, N. (2006) (eds) *The Buildings of England: the Isle of Wight*. New Haven, CT/London, Yale University Press.

Whately, T. (1770) *Observations on Modern Gardening*. London, Payne.

Whately, T. (1772) *L'art de former les jardins modernes*. Paris, Jombert.

Whistler, L. (1957) Signor Borra at Stowe. *Country Life* 29 August: 390–3.

White, C. (1957) *Giovanni Battista Viotti and his Violin Concertos*, 2 vols. Princeton University, PhD thesis.

White, C. (1985) *Giovanni Battista Viotti (1755–1824). A Thematic Catalogue of his Works*. Philadelphia, Pendragon Press.

White, C. (1992) *From Vivaldi to Viotti: a History of the Early Classical Violin Concerto*. New York, Gordon and Breach.

White, D.M. (2004) Wood, Robert (1716/17–1771). In *Oxford Dictionary of National Biography*. Oxford, Oxford University Press. Online edition.

Whitelock, B. (1732) *Memorials of English Affairs from the Beginning of the Reign of Charles the First to the Happy Restoration of King Charles the Second*. London.

Wiebenson, D. (1969) *Sources of Greek Revival*. London, A. Zwemmer.

Wilcox, S. and Sánchez-Jáuregui, D. (2012) (eds) *The English Prize: the Capture of the Westmorland; an Episode of the Grand Tour*. Oxford, Ashmolean Museum.

Wilton, A. and Bignamini, I. (1997) (eds) *Grand Tour. Il fascino dell'Italia nel XVIII sec.* Milan, Skira. (First edition: 1996, London, Tate Gallery).

Wilton-Ely, J. (1973) (ed.) *Apollo of the Arts: Lord Burlington and his Circle. Exhibition Art Gallery Nottingham 22.01–17.02.1973*. Nottingham, University of Nottingham.

Wilton-Ely, J. (1984) Lord Burlington and the virtuoso portrait. *Architectural History* 27: 376–81.

Wittkower, R. (1949) Un libro di schizzi di Filippo Juvarra a Chatsworth. *Bollettino della Società Piemontese d'Archeologia e di Belle Arti* 3: 94–118.

Wittkower, R. (1974a) English literature on architecture. In R. Wittkower, *Palladian and English Palladianism*: 93–112. London, Thames and Hudson.

Wittkower, R. (1974b) Lord Burlington and William Kent. In R. Wittkower, *Palladian and English Palladianism*: 113–32. London, Thames and Hudson.

Wittkower, R. (1975) A sketchbook of Filippo Juvarra at Chatsworth. In R. Wittkower, *Studies in the Italian Baroque*: 187–210. London, Thames and Hudson.

Wolfe, K. (2007) Francesco Trevisani and Landscape: *Joseph Sold into Slavery* in the National Gallery of Melbourne. In D. Marshall (ed.), *Art, Site and Spectacle: Studies in Early Modern Visual Art* (*Melbourne Art Journal* 9–10): 44–61.

Wolfe, K. (2011) Acquisitive tourism: Francesco Trevisani's Roman studio and British visitors. In D.S. Marshall, S. Russell and K.E. Wolfe (eds), *Roma Britannica: Art Patronage and Cultural Exchange in Eighteenth-Century Rome*: 83–101. London, British School at Rome.

Wolfe, K. (2014a) Filippo Juvarra, Francesco Trevisani e la memoria della pittura. In E. Gabrielli (ed.), *La Palazzina di Caccia di Stupinigi (I Quaderni di Palazzo Carignano)*: 77–93. Florence, Olschki Editore.

Wolfe, K. (2014b) L'architetto e il pittore: rapporti artistici tra Filippo Juvarra e Francesco Trevisani. In P. Cornaglia, A. Merlotti and C. Roggero (eds), *Filippo Juvarra 1678–1736, architetto dei Savoia, architetto in Europa*, vol. 1: 245–58, 295–303. Rome, Campisano Editore.

Wollenberg, S. and McVeigh, S. (2004) *Concert Life in Eighteenth-century Britain*. Aldershot, Ashgate.

Wood, R. (1753) *The Ruins Of Palmyra, Otherwise Tedmor, In The Desart*. London.

Wood, R. (1757) *The Ruins Of Balbec, Otherwise Heliopolis In Cœlosyria*. London.

Wood, R. (1775) *Essay on the Original Genius and Writings of Homer: with a Comparative View of the Ancient and Present State of the Troade. Illustrated with Engravings. By the Late Robert Wood, Esq; Author of the Description of Palmyra and Balbec*. London, H. Hughes.

Wood, R. (1971) *The Ruins of Palmyra, otherwise Tedmor in the Desert* (1753). Farnborough, Gregg International.

Wood, R. (no date) Manuscripts. *Wood-Donation* 18: 25–6. London, Joint Library of Hellenic and Roman Societies.

Woodfield, I. (1995) New light on the Mozart's London visit: a private concert with Manzuoli. *Music and Letters* 76 (2): 187–208.

Woodfield, I. (2001) *Opera and Drama in Eighteenth-century London. The King's Theatre, Garrick and the Business of Performance*. Cambridge, Cambridge University Press.

Woodhouse J. (2008) Venice's European diaspora: the case of James Leoni (1685–1746). *The Modern Language Review* 103 (4): 33–54.

Woolf, S.J. (1961) English public opinion and the Duchy of Savoy. *English Miscellany, A Symposium of History, Literature and the Arts* 12: 211–58.

Woolfson, J. (1998) *Padua and the Tudors. English Students in Italy, 1485–1603*. Cambridge, James Clarke & Co.

Wortley Montagu, E. (1763) *Observations upon a Supposed Antique Bust at Turin. In Two Letters, Addressed to the Right Honourable the Earl of Macclesfield, President of the Royal Society. By Edward Wortley Montagu, Esq. F.R.S. Read before the Royal Society, November 25, 1762* (second edition). London, T. Becket and P.A. De Hondt.

Wyn Jones, D. (2000) (ed.) *Music in Eighteenth-century Britain*. Aldershot, Ashgate.

Wynne, M. (1994) From Ireland to Turin. A marriage thwarted. *Studi Piemontesi*, 23: 157–9.

Wynne, M. (1995) Some Jacobites in Turin in the eighteenth century. *Studi Piemontesi* 24: 127–30.

Wynne, M. (1996) Some British diplomats, some Grand Tourists and some students from Great Britain and Ireland in Turin in the eighteenth century. *Studi Piemontesi* 25 (1): 145–60.

Yim, D. (2004) *Viotti and the Chinnerys. A Relationship Charted Through Letters*. Aldershot, Ashgate.

Yim, D. (2006) Selected letters from G.B. Viotti to Mrs Margaret Chinnery, 1793–1798, including one to her husband W.B. Chinnery, 1812. In M. Sala (ed.), *Giovanni Battista Viotti. A Composer between the Two Revolutions*: 395–423. Bologna, Ut Orpheus.

Zikos, D. (2005) *The Macclesfield Sculpture: the Fruits of Lord Parker's Grand Tour 1720–22, Sale Catalogue, 1 December 2005*. London, Christie's.

Zoller, O. (1996a) *Der Architekt und der Ingenieur Giovanni Battista Borra (1713–1770)*. Bamberg, Wissenschaftlicher Verlag.

Zoller, O. (1996b) Borra, Giovanni Battista. In J. Turner (ed.), *Dictionary of Art* (34 vols), IV: 422–3. London, Macmillan Publisher.

Zoller, O. (1997) Borra, Giovanni Battista. In J. Banham (ed.), *Encyclopedia of Interior Design,* I: 160–1. London/Chicago, Fitzroy Dearborn Publishers.

Zoller, O. (2001) Giovanni Battista Borra disegnatore e architetto nel Levante e in Inghilterra. In G. Dardanello (ed.), *Sperimentare l'architettura. Guarini, Juvarra, Alfieri, Borra e Alfieri*: 217–24, 257–79. Turin, Fondazione Cassa di Risparmio di Torino.

Zoller, O. (2012) Giovanni Battista Borra and Robert Wood: arguments for the revival of a mid-eighteenth century book project. In L. Mulvin (ed.), *A Culture of Translation: British and Irish Scholarship in the Gennadius Library (1740–1840) (New Griffon 13)*: 71–70. Athens, Gennadius Library, American School of Classical Studies.

Zoller, O. (2013) Giovanni Battista Borra: un nuovo tipo di professionalità come architetto-ingegnere e la sua fortuna nel mondo anglosassone. In G. Dardanello (ed.), *Giovanni Battista Borra da Palmira a Racconigi*: 99–110. Turin, Editris.

Zonta, C. (2000) Studenti stranieri in Italia: gli slesiani nell'età moderna. In G.P. Brizzi and A. Romano (eds), *Studenti e dottori nelle università italiane (origini–XX secolo)*: 31–40. Bologna, CLUEB.

Zschinsky-Troxler, E.M. von (1939) *Gaetano Pugnani (1731-1798). Ein Beitrag zur Stilerfassung Italienischer Vorklassik. Mit Thematischem Verzeichnis.* Berlin, Atlantis-Verlag.

Index